JOHN CONSTANTINE
HELLBLAZER
BLOODY CARNATIONS

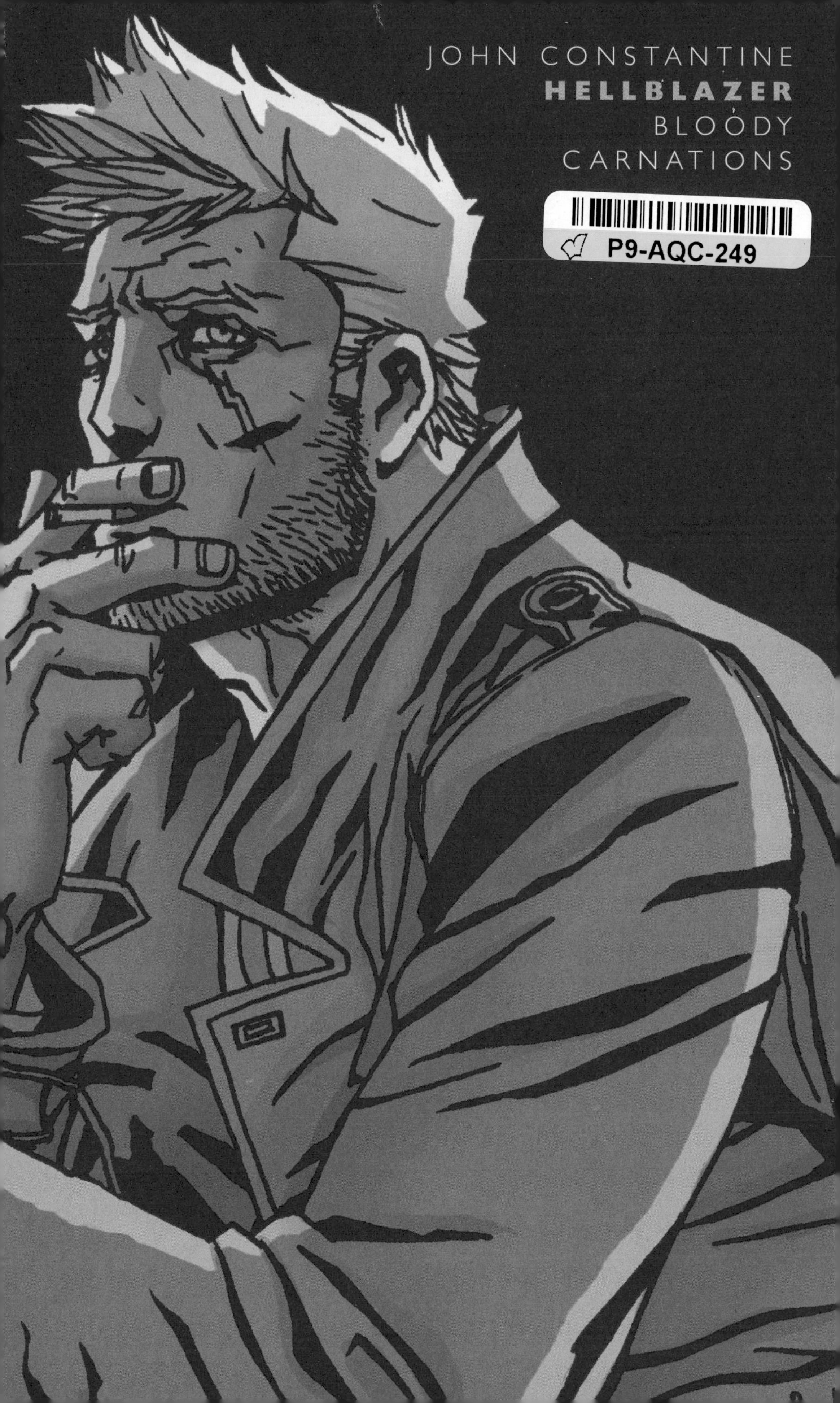

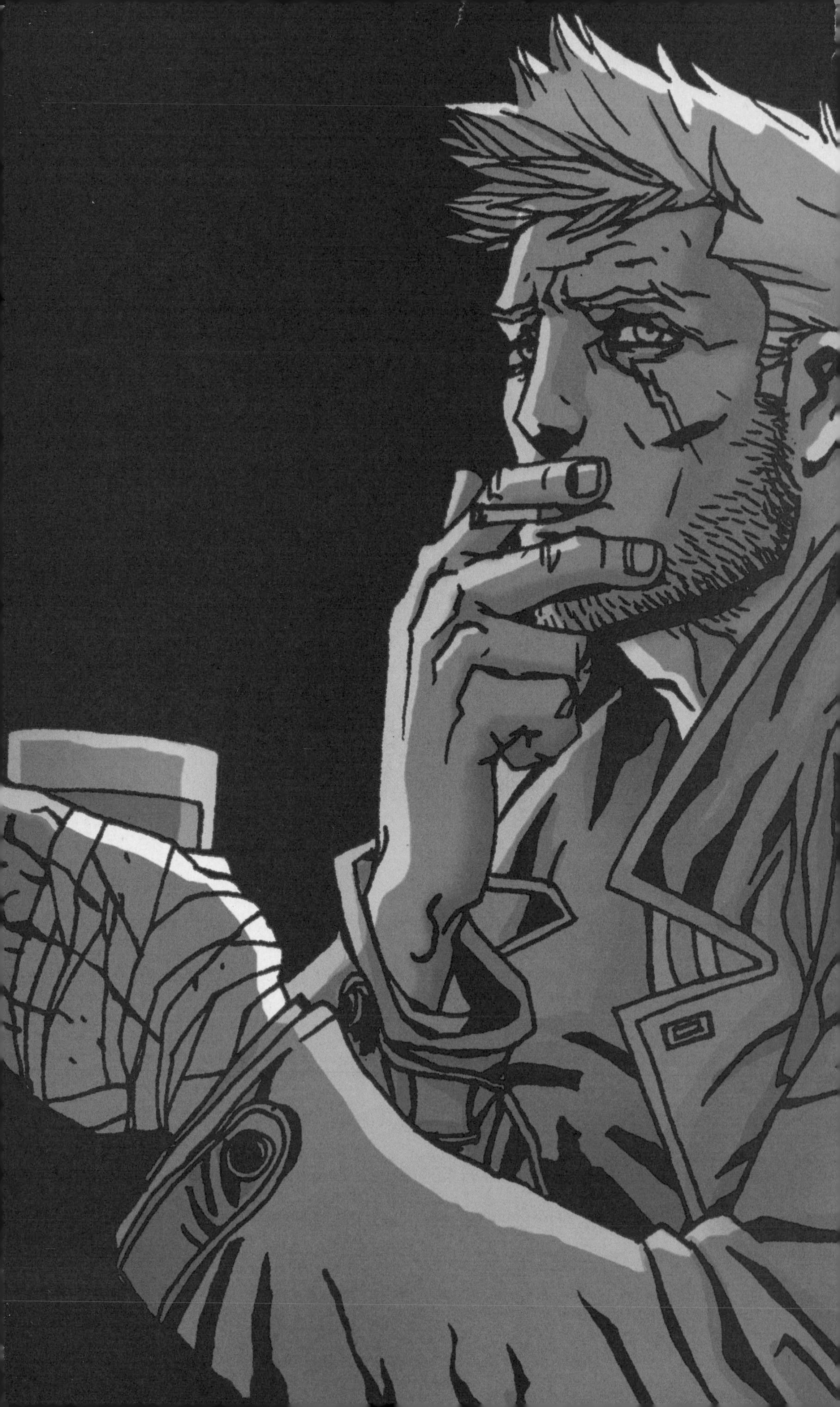

JOHN CONSTANTINE
HELLBLAZER
BLOODY CARNATIONS

Peter Milligan
writer

Giuseppe Camuncoli Stefano Landini
Simon Bisley
Shawn Martinbrough
artists

Trish Mulvihill Brian Buccellato
Lee Loughridge
colorists

Sal Cipriano
letterer

Simon Bisley
cover artist

Robbie Biederman
publication design

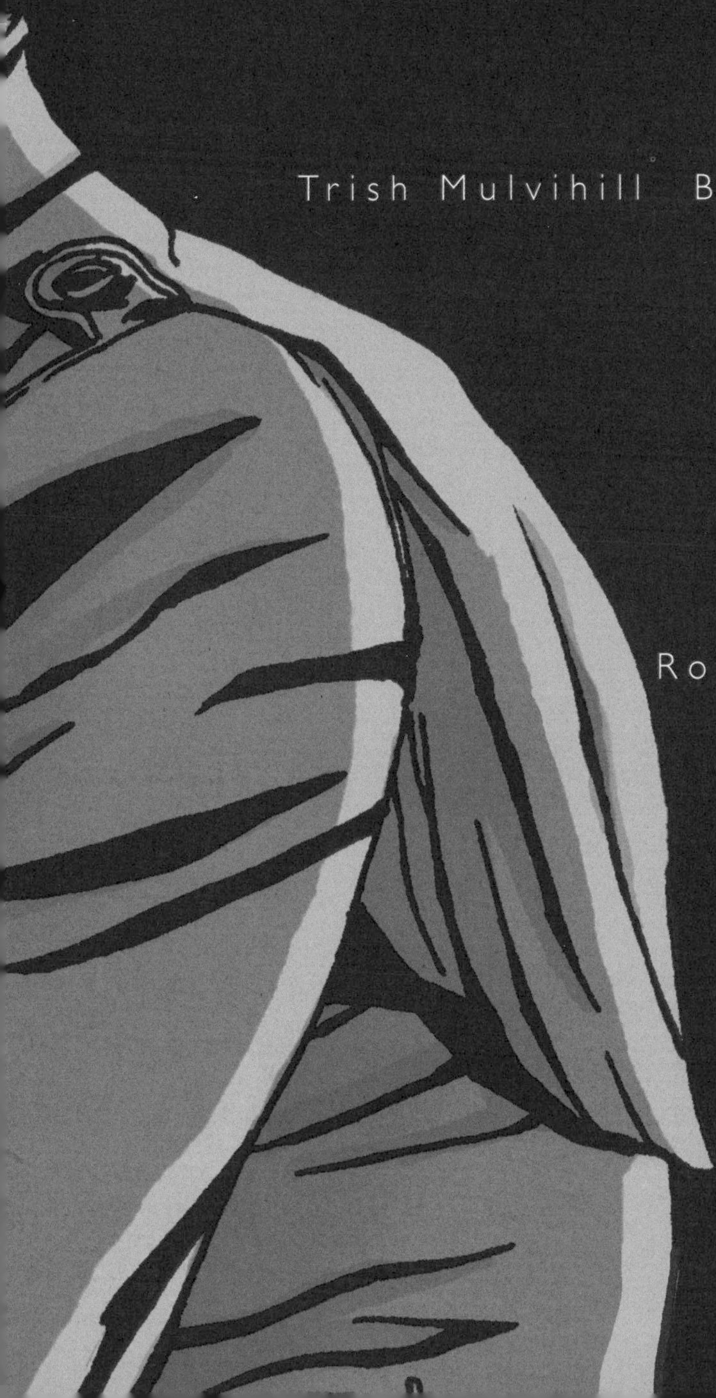

THE

JOHN CONSTANTINE
HELLBLAZER

READER'S GUIDE

ORIGINAL SINS Collecting issues #1-9 and Swamp Thing #76-77
THE DEVIL YOU KNOW Collecting issues #10-13, Annual #1 and The Horrorist 1-2
THE FEAR MACHINE Collecting issues #14-22
THE FAMILY MAN Collecting issues #23-24, 28-33
RARE CUTS Collecting issues #11, 25-26, 35, 56, 84
DANGEROUS HABITS Collecting issues #41-46
BLOODLINES Collecting issues #47-50, 52-55, 59-61
FEAR AND LOATHING Collecting issues #62-67
TAINTED LOVE Collecting issues #68-71, Special #1, Vertigo Jam #1
DAMNATION'S FLAME Collecting issues #72-77
RAKE AT THE GATES OF HELL Collecting issues #78-83
SON OF MAN Collecting issues #129-133
HAUNTED Collecting issues #134-139
SETTING SUN Collecting issues #140-143
HARD TIME Collecting issues #146-150
GOOD INTENTIONS Collecting issues #151-156
FREEZES OVER Collecting issues #157-163
HIGHWATER Collecting issues #164-174
RED SEPULCHRE Collecting issues #175-180
BLACK FLOWERS Collecting issues #181-186
STARING AT THE WALL Collecting issues #187-193
STATIONS OF THE CROSS Collecting issues #194-200
REASONS TO BE CHEERFUL Collecting issues #201-206
THE GIFT Collecting issues #207-215
EMPATHY IS THE ENEMY Collecting issues #216-222
THE RED RIGHT HAND Collecting issues #223-228
JOYRIDE Collecting issues #230-237
THE LAUGHING MAGICIAN Collecting issues #238-242
THE ROOTS OF COINCIDENCE Collecting issues #243-244, 247-249
SCAB Collecting issues #250-255
HOOKED Collecting issues #256-260
INDIA Collecting issues #261-266

Look for these other important **HELLBLAZER** collections:
LADY CONSTANTINE
PAPA MIDNITE
CHAS — THE KNOWLEDGE
ALL HIS ENGINES
PANDEMONIUM
CITY OF DEMONS

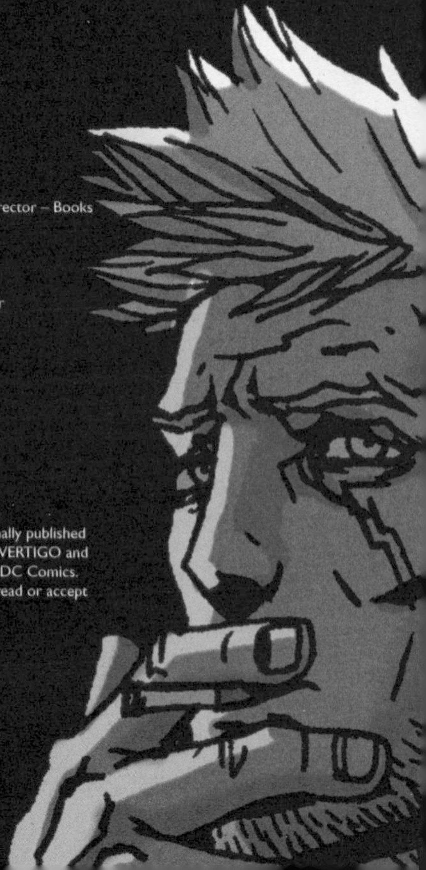

SHELLY BOND Editor – Original Series ANGELA RUFINO Associate Editor – Original Series
GREGORY LOCKARD Assistant Editor – Original Series
IAN SATTLER Director Editorial, Special Projects and Archival Editions ROBBIN BROSTERMAN Design Director – Books

KAREN BERGER Senior VP – Executive Editor, Vertigo
BOB HARRAS VP – Editor in Chief

DIANE NELSON President DAN DIDIO and JIM LEE Co-Publishers GEOFF JOHNS Chief Creative Officer
JOHN ROOD Executive VP – Sales, Marketing and Business Development
AMY GENKINS Senior VP – Business and Legal Affairs NAIRI GARDINER Senior VP – Finance
JEFF BOISON VP – Publishing Operations MARK CHIARELLO VP – Art Direction and Design
JOHN CUNNINGHAM VP – Marketing TERRI CUNNINGHAM VP – Talent Relations and Services
ALISON GILL Senior VP – Manufacturing and Operations DAVID HYDE VP – Publicity
HANK KANALZ Senior VP – Digital JAY KOGAN VP – Business and Legal Affairs, Publishing
JACK MAHAN VP – Business Affairs, Talent NICK NAPOLITANO VP – Manufacturing Administration
RON PERAZZA VP – Online SUE POHJA VP – Book Sales
COURTNEY SIMMONS Senior VP – Publicity BOB WAYNE Senior VP – Sales

JOHN CONSTANTINE, HELLBLAZER: BLOODY CARNATIONS

DC Comics
1700 Broadway, New York, NY 10019. A Warner Bros. Entertainment Company
Printed in the USA. 6/24/11. First Printing. ISBN: 978-1-4012-3152-1

SUSTAINABLE FORESTRY INITIATIVE Certified Fiber Sourcing

Fiber used in this product line meets the sourcing requirements of the SFI program. www.sfiprogram.org SGS-SFICOC-0130

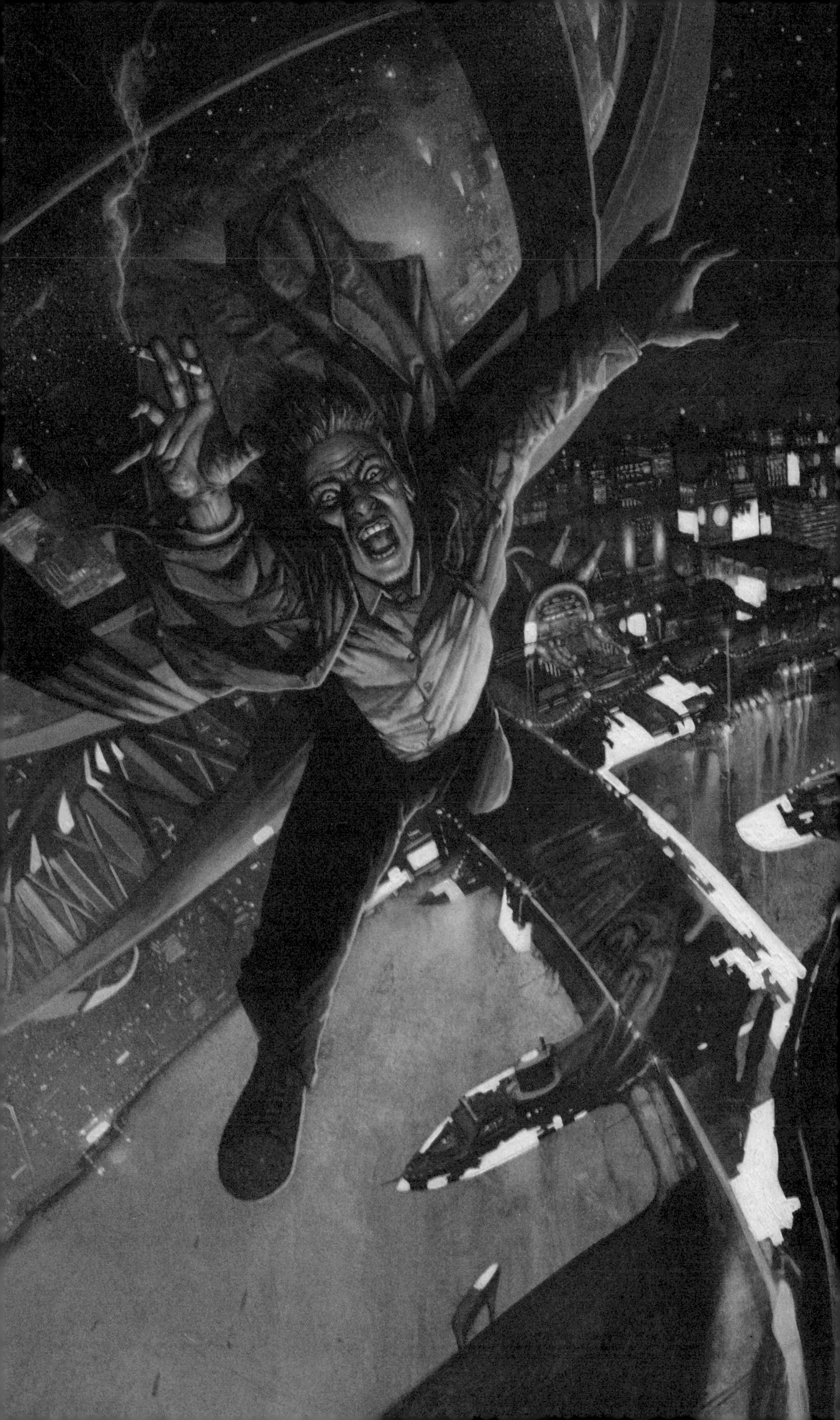

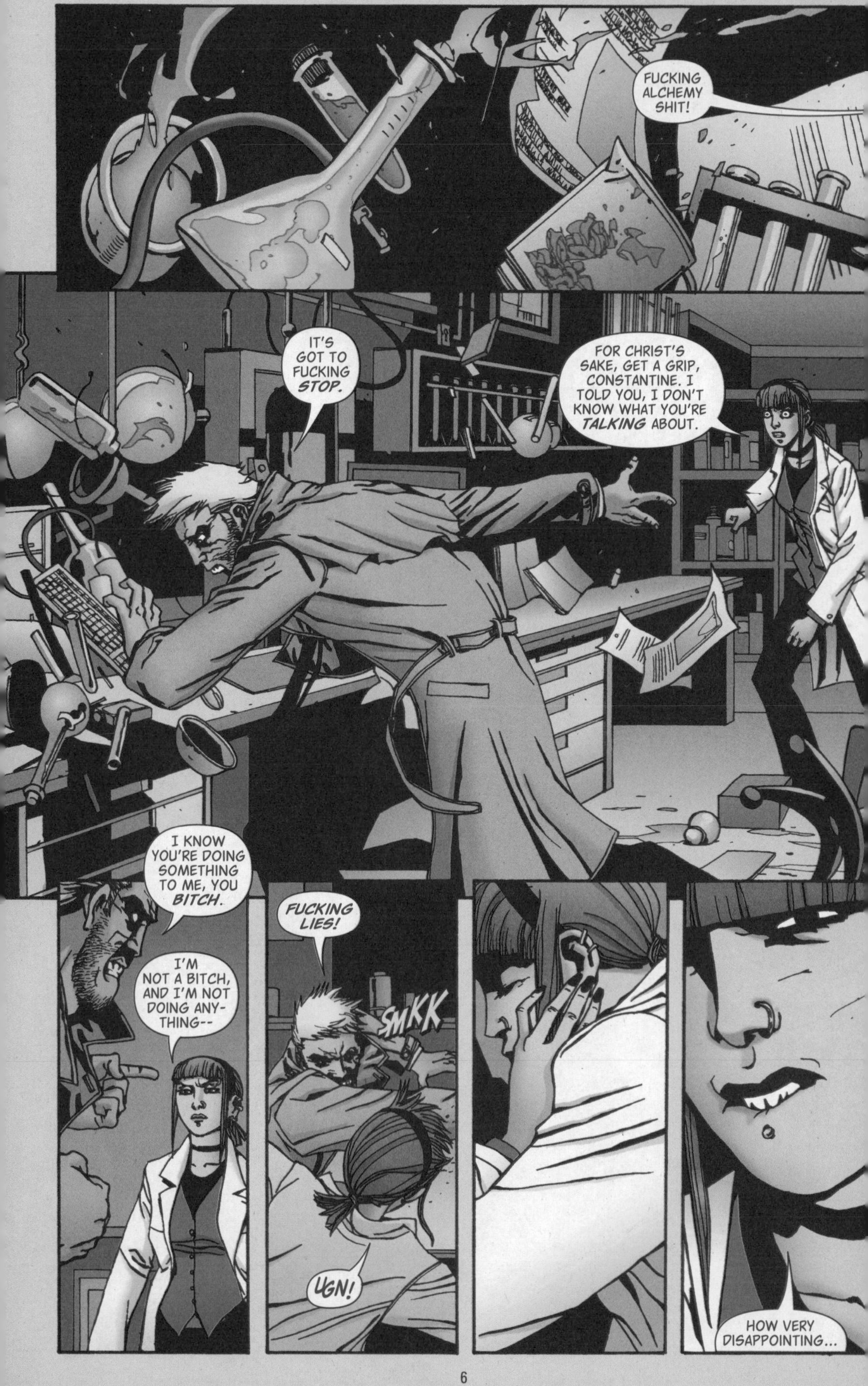
FUCKING ALCHEMY SHIT!
IT'S GOT TO FUCKING *STOP.*
FOR CHRIST'S SAKE, GET A GRIP, CONSTANTINE. I TOLD YOU, I DON'T KNOW WHAT YOU'RE *TALKING* ABOUT.
I KNOW YOU'RE DOING SOMETHING TO ME, YOU *BITCH*.
I'M NOT A BITCH, AND I'M NOT DOING ANY-THING--
FUCKING LIES!
SMKK
UGN!
HOW VERY DISAPPOINTING...

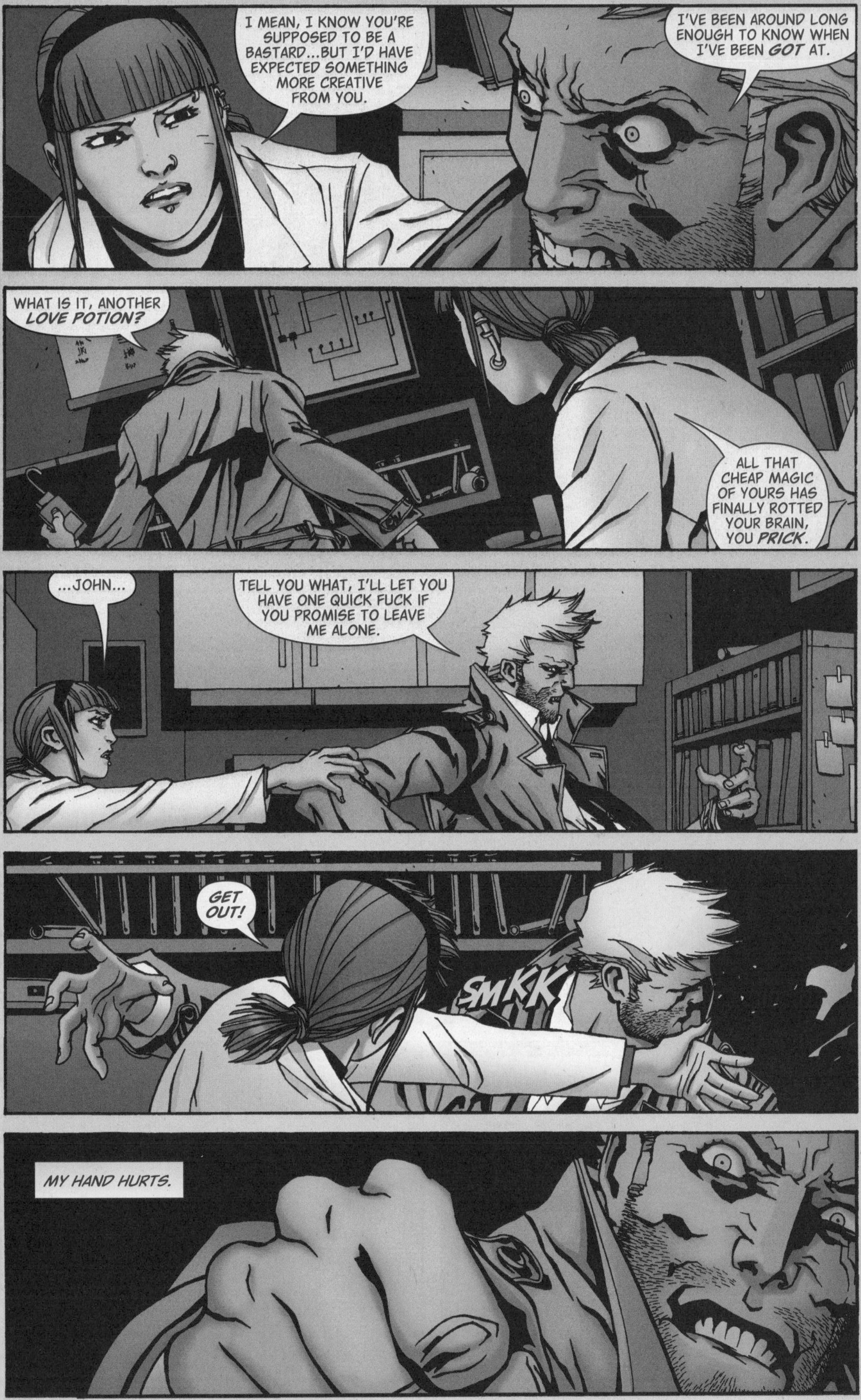
I MEAN, I KNOW YOU'RE SUPPOSED TO BE A BASTARD...BUT I'D HAVE EXPECTED SOMETHING MORE CREATIVE FROM YOU.
I'VE BEEN AROUND LONG ENOUGH TO KNOW WHEN I'VE BEEN GOT AT.
WHAT IS IT, ANOTHER LOVE POTION?
ALL THAT CHEAP MAGIC OF YOURS HAS FINALLY ROTTED YOUR BRAIN, YOU PRICK.
...JOHN...
TELL YOU WHAT, I'LL LET YOU HAVE ONE QUICK FUCK IF YOU PROMISE TO LEAVE ME ALONE.
GET OUT!
SMKK
MY HAND HURTS.

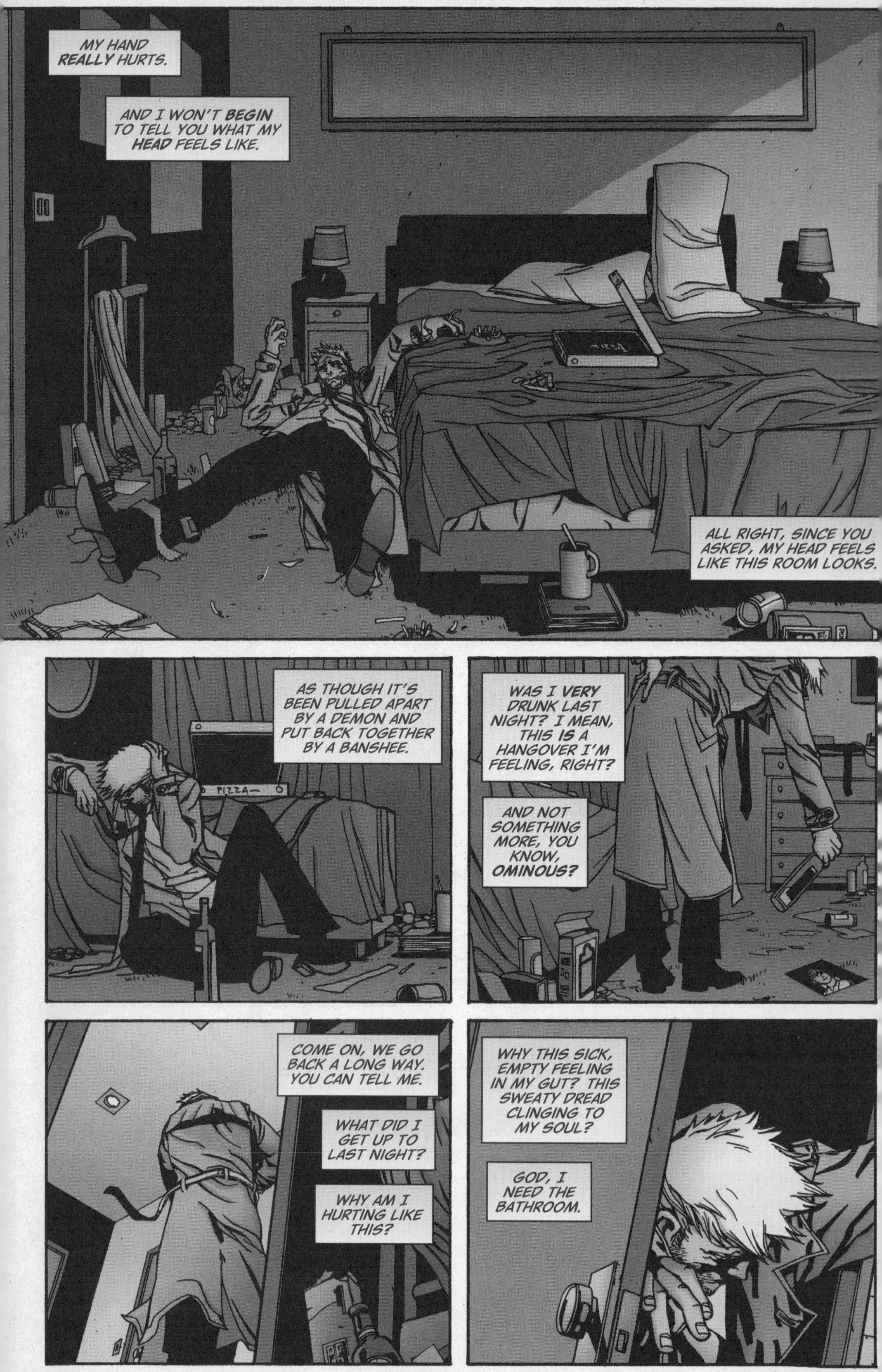

MY HAND REALLY HURTS.
AND I WON'T BEGIN TO TELL YOU WHAT MY HEAD FEELS LIKE.
ALL RIGHT, SINCE YOU ASKED, MY HEAD FEELS LIKE THIS ROOM LOOKS.
AS THOUGH IT'S BEEN PULLED APART BY A DEMON AND PUT BACK TOGETHER BY A BANSHEE.
PIZZA
WAS I VERY DRUNK LAST NIGHT? I MEAN, THIS IS A HANGOVER I'M FEELING, RIGHT?
AND NOT SOMETHING MORE, YOU KNOW, OMINOUS?
COME ON, WE GO BACK A LONG WAY. YOU CAN TELL ME.
WHAT DID I GET UP TO LAST NIGHT?
WHY AM I HURTING LIKE THIS?
WHY THIS SICK, EMPTY FEELING IN MY GUT? THIS SWEATY DREAD CLINGING TO MY SOUL?
GOD, I NEED THE BATHROOM.

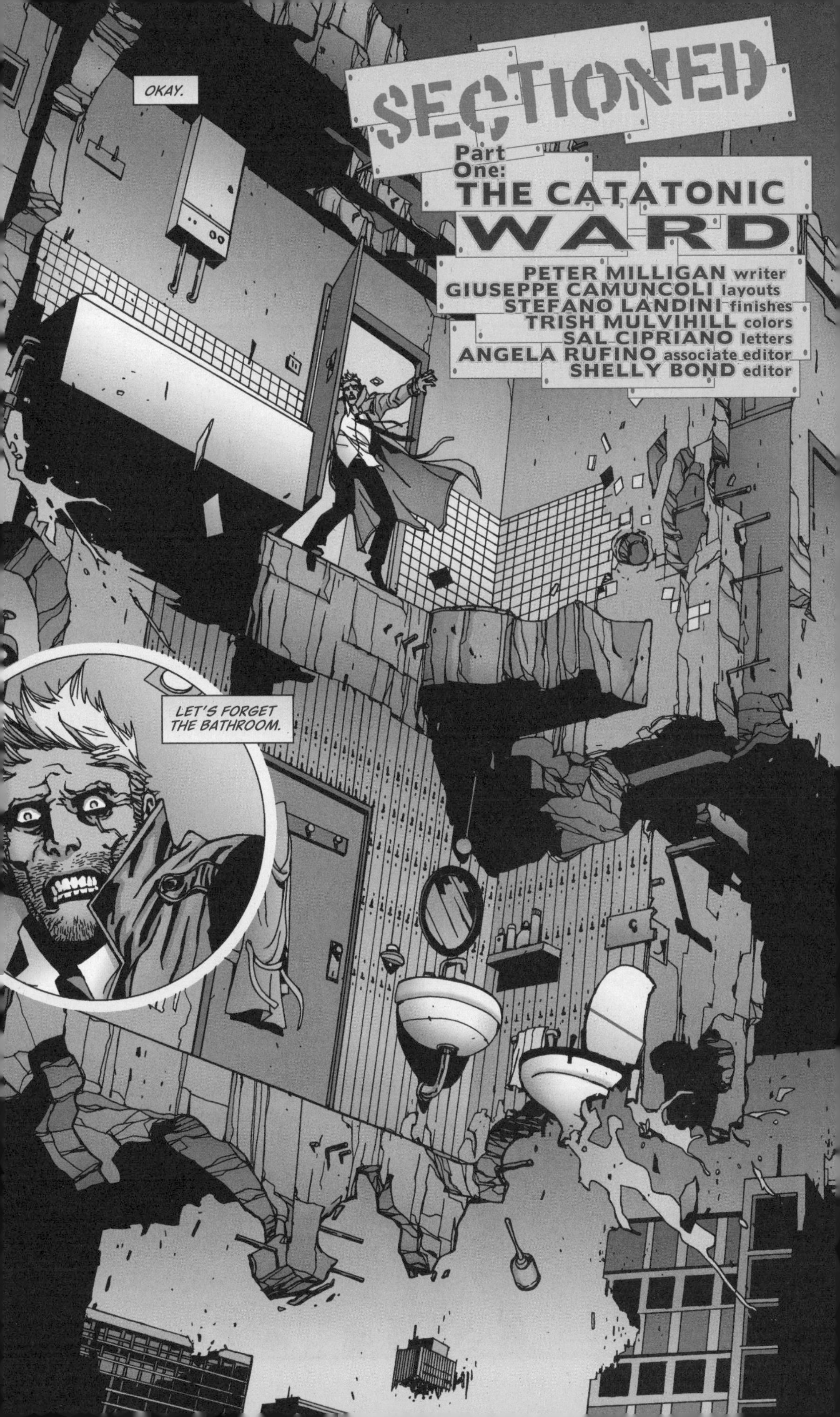
OKAY.
SECTIONED
Part One: THE CATATONIC WARD
PETER MILLIGAN writer
GIUSEPPE CAMUNCOLI layouts
STEFANO LANDINI finishes
TRISH MULVIHILL colors
SAL CIPRIANO letters
ANGELA RUFINO associate editor
SHELLY BOND editor
LET'S FORGET THE BATHROOM.

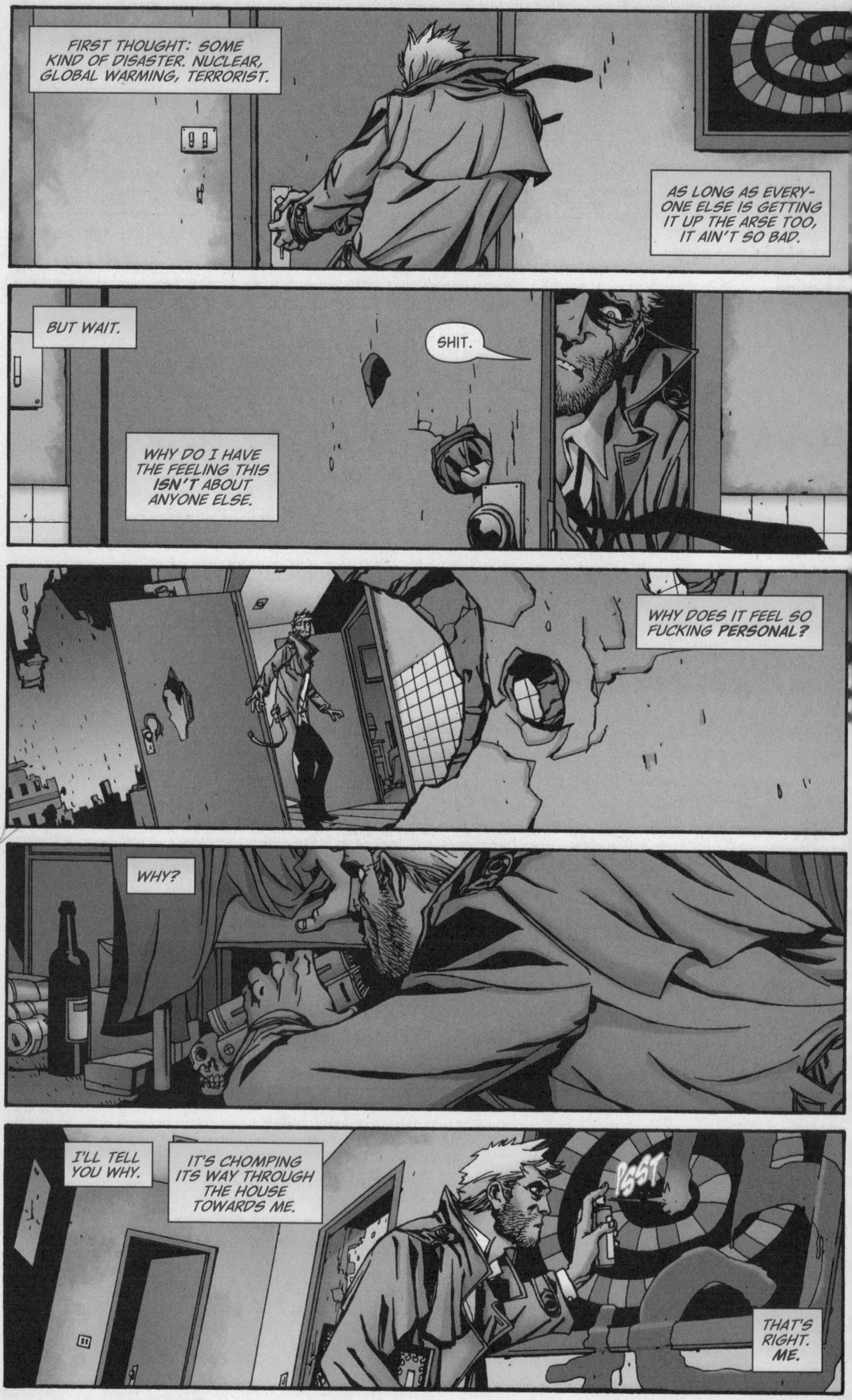
FIRST THOUGHT: SOME KIND OF DISASTER. NUCLEAR, GLOBAL WARMING, TERRORIST.
AS LONG AS EVERY-ONE ELSE IS GETTING IT UP THE ARSE TOO, IT AIN'T SO BAD.
BUT WAIT.
SHIT.
WHY DO I HAVE THE FEELING THIS ISN'T ABOUT ANYONE ELSE.
WHY DOES IT FEEL SO FUCKING PERSONAL?
WHY?
I'LL TELL YOU WHY.
IT'S CHOMPING ITS WAY THROUGH THE HOUSE TOWARDS ME.
PSST
THAT'S RIGHT. ME.

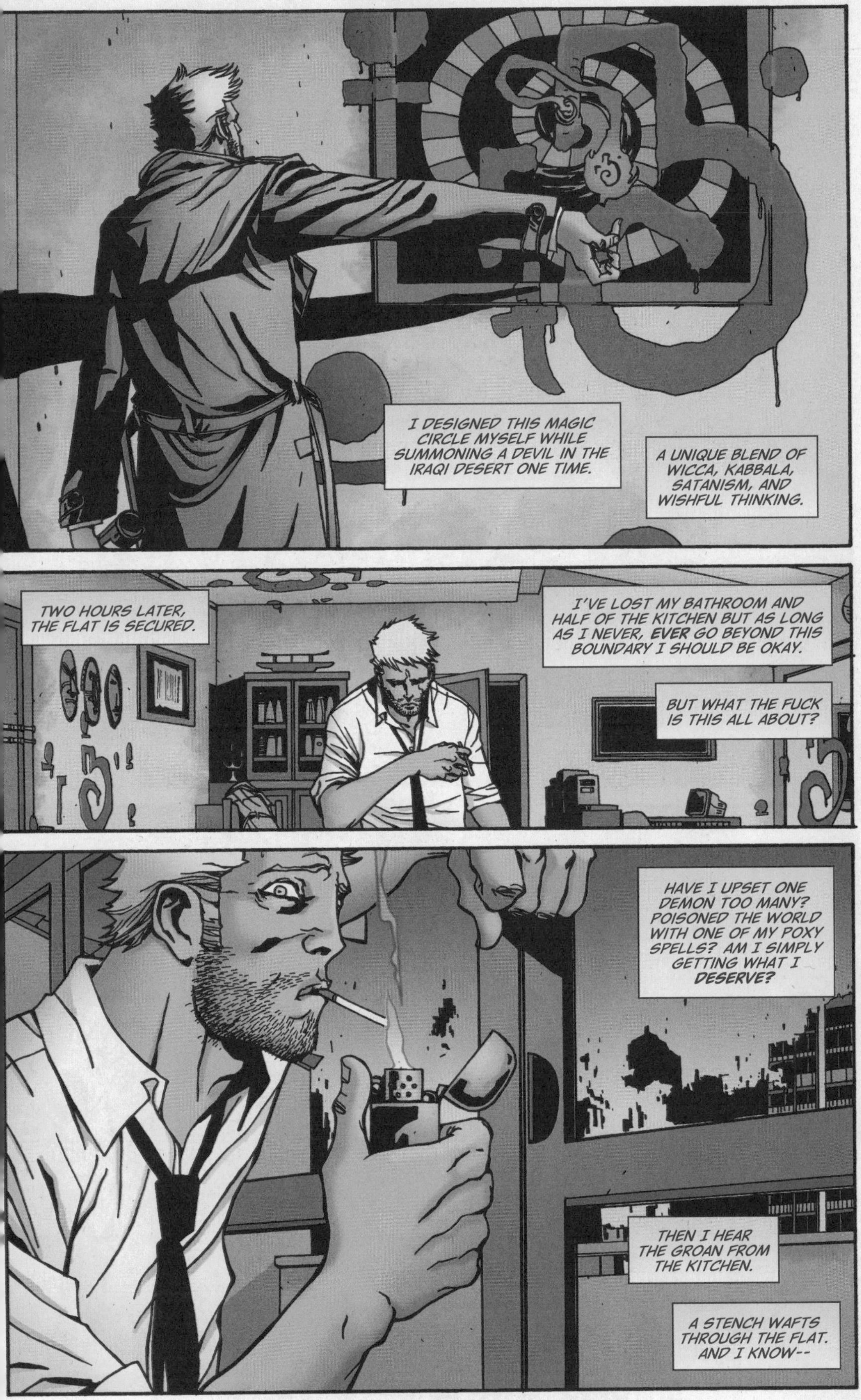
I DESIGNED THIS MAGIC CIRCLE MYSELF WHILE SUMMONING A DEVIL IN THE IRAQI DESERT ONE TIME.
A UNIQUE BLEND OF WICCA, KABBALA, SATANISM, AND WISHFUL THINKING.
TWO HOURS LATER, THE FLAT IS SECURED.
I'VE LOST MY BATHROOM AND HALF OF THE KITCHEN BUT AS LONG AS I NEVER, EVER GO BEYOND THIS BOUNDARY I SHOULD BE OKAY.
BUT WHAT THE FUCK IS THIS ALL ABOUT?
HAVE I UPSET ONE DEMON TOO MANY? POISONED THE WORLD WITH ONE OF MY POXY SPELLS? AM I SIMPLY GETTING WHAT I DESERVE?
THEN I HEAR THE GROAN FROM THE KITCHEN.
A STENCH WAFTS THROUGH THE FLAT. AND I KNOW--

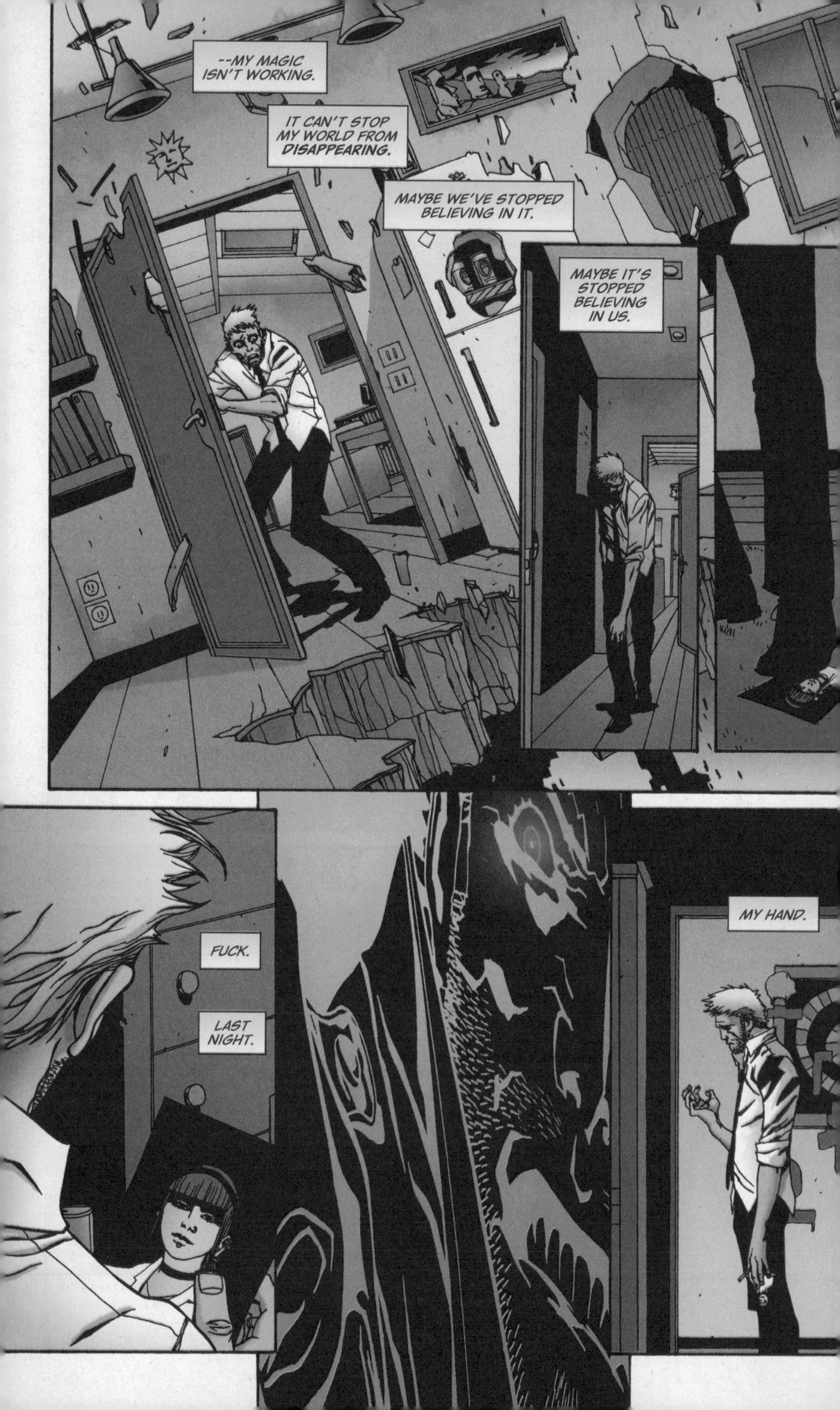
--MY MAGIC ISN'T WORKING.
IT CAN'T STOP MY WORLD FROM DISAPPEARING.
MAYBE WE'VE STOPPED BELIEVING IN IT.
MAYBE IT'S STOPPED BELIEVING IN US.
FUCK.
LAST NIGHT.
MY HAND.

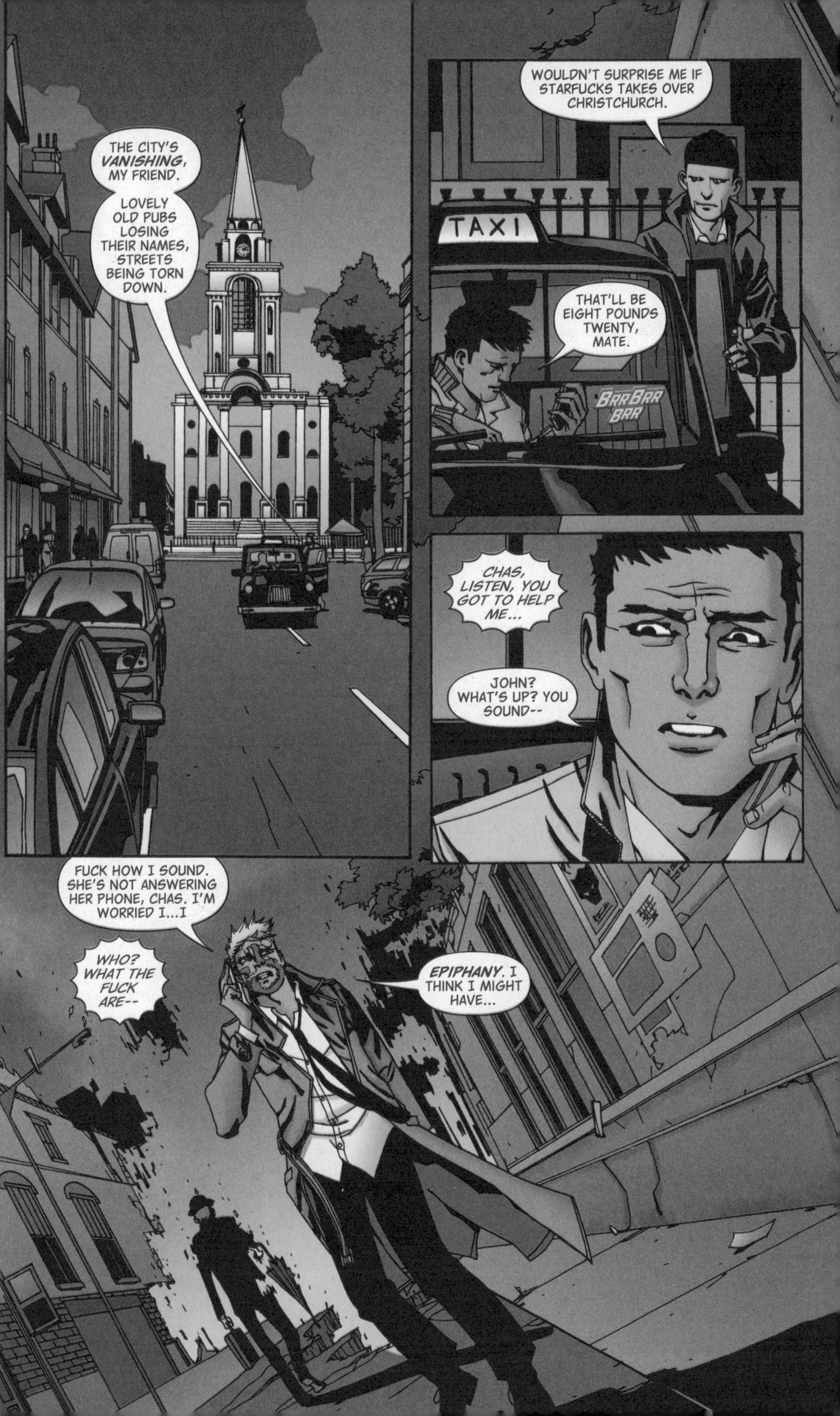
THE CITY'S *VANISHING*, MY FRIEND.
LOVELY OLD PUBS LOSING THEIR NAMES, STREETS BEING TORN DOWN.
WOULDN'T SURPRISE ME IF STARFUCKS TAKES OVER CHRISTCHURCH.
TAXI
THAT'LL BE EIGHT POUNDS TWENTY, MATE.
BRRBRR BRR
CHAS, LISTEN, YOU GOT TO HELP ME...
JOHN? WHAT'S UP? YOU SOUND--
FUCK HOW I SOUND. SHE'S NOT ANSWERING HER PHONE, CHAS. I'M WORRIED I...I
WHO? WHAT THE FUCK ARE--
EPIPHANY. I THINK I MIGHT HAVE...

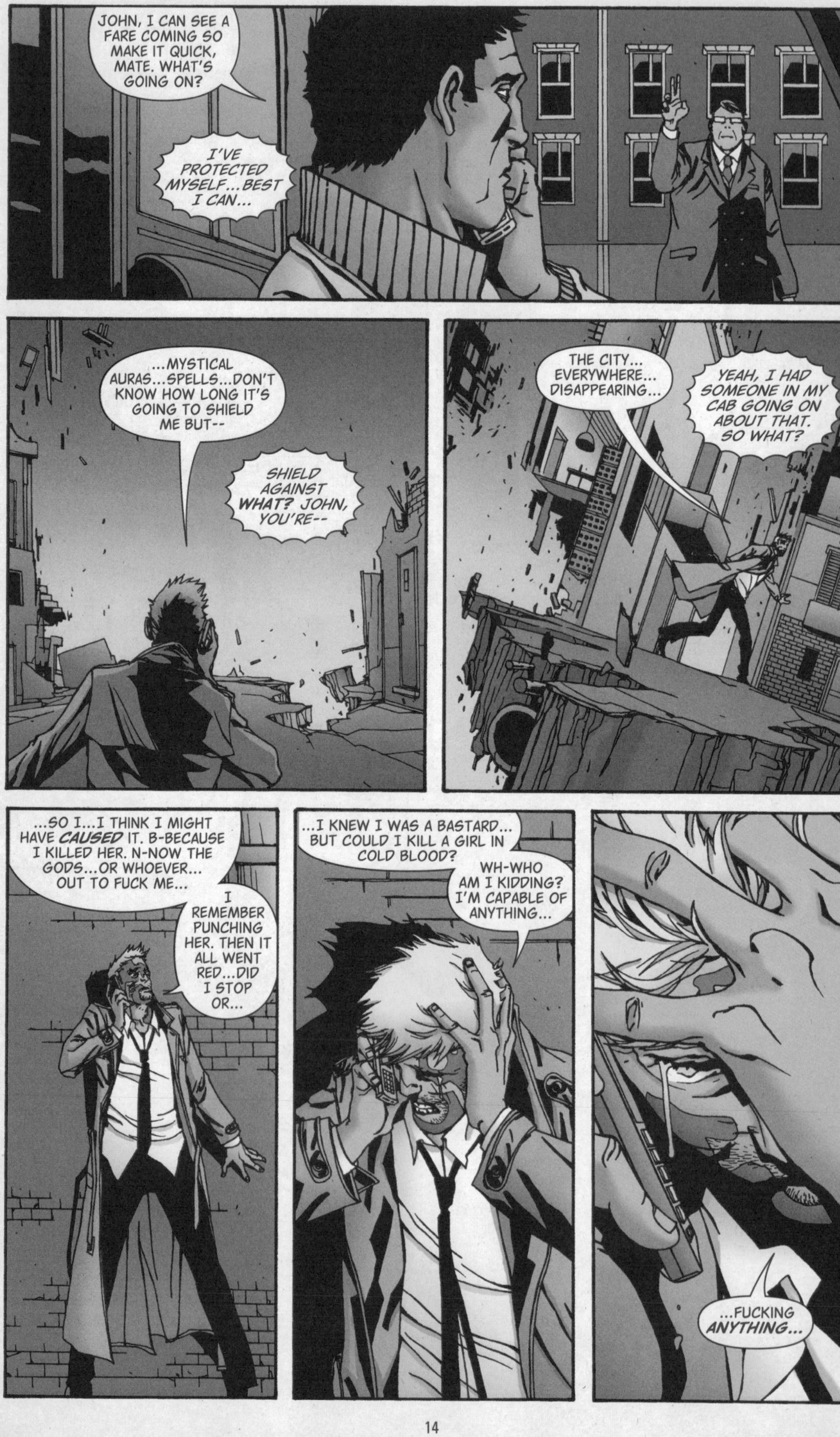
JOHN, I CAN SEE A FARE COMING SO MAKE IT QUICK, MATE. WHAT'S GOING ON?
I'VE PROTECTED MYSELF...BEST I CAN...
...MYSTICAL AURAS...SPELLS...DON'T KNOW HOW LONG IT'S GOING TO SHIELD ME BUT--
SHIELD AGAINST WHAT? JOHN, YOU'RE--
THE CITY... EVERYWHERE... DISAPPEARING...
YEAH, I HAD SOMEONE IN MY CAB GOING ON ABOUT THAT. SO WHAT?
...SO I...I THINK I MIGHT HAVE CAUSED IT. B-BECAUSE I KILLED HER. N-NOW THE GODS...OR WHOEVER... OUT TO FUCK ME...
I REMEMBER PUNCHING HER. THEN IT ALL WENT RED...DID I STOP OR...
...I KNEW I WAS A BASTARD... BUT COULD I KILL A GIRL IN COLD BLOOD?
WH-WHO AM I KIDDING? I'M CAPABLE OF ANYTHING...
...FUCKING ANYTHING...

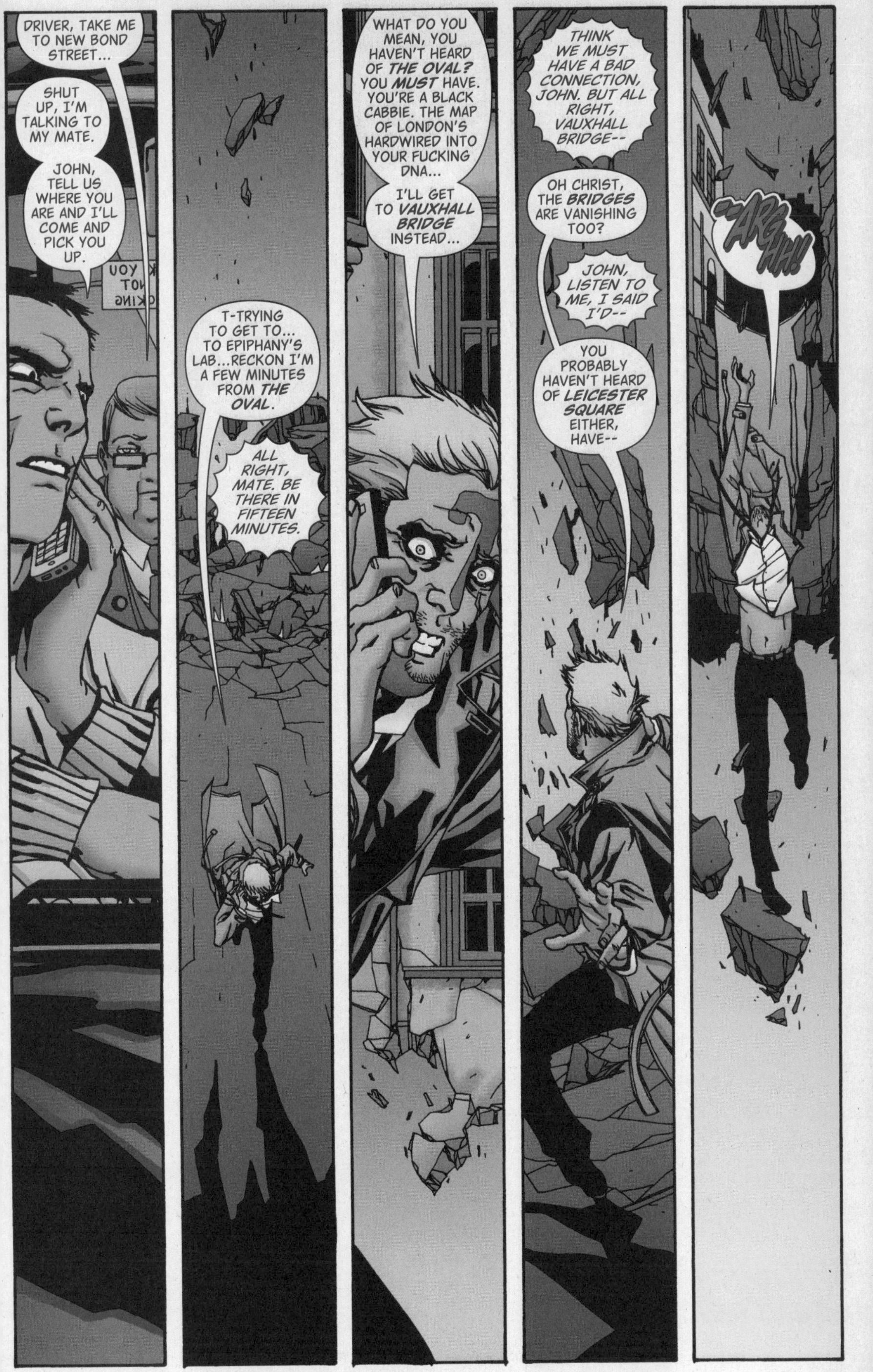
DRIVER, TAKE ME TO NEW BOND STREET...
SHUT UP, I'M TALKING TO MY MATE.
JOHN, TELL US WHERE YOU ARE AND I'LL COME AND PICK YOU UP.
T-TRYING TO GET TO... TO EPIPHANY'S LAB...RECKON I'M A FEW MINUTES FROM THE OVAL.
ALL RIGHT, MATE. BE THERE IN FIFTEEN MINUTES.
WHAT DO YOU MEAN, YOU HAVEN'T HEARD OF THE OVAL? YOU MUST HAVE. YOU'RE A BLACK CABBIE. THE MAP OF LONDON'S HARDWIRED INTO YOUR FUCKING DNA...
I'LL GET TO VAUXHALL BRIDGE INSTEAD...
THINK WE MUST HAVE A BAD CONNECTION, JOHN. BUT ALL RIGHT, VAUXHALL BRIDGE--
OH CHRIST, THE BRIDGES ARE VANISHING TOO?
JOHN, LISTEN TO ME, I SAID I'D--
YOU PROBABLY HAVEN'T HEARD OF LEICESTER SQUARE EITHER, HAVE--
--ARGHH!!

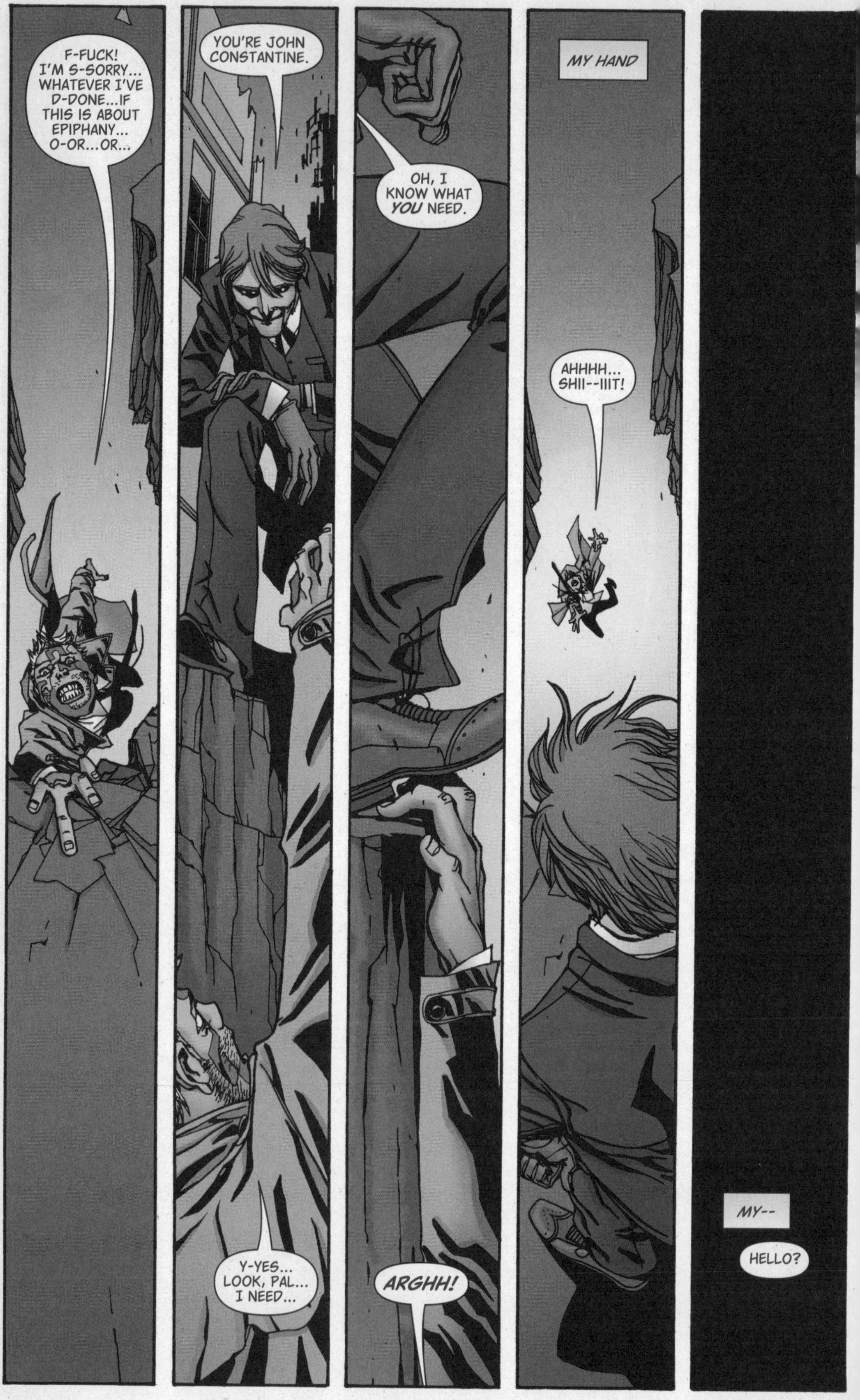
F-FUCK! I'M S-SORRY... WHATEVER I'VE D-DONE...IF THIS IS ABOUT EPIPHANY... O-OR...OR...
YOU'RE JOHN CONSTANTINE.
Y-YES... LOOK, PAL... I NEED...
OH, I KNOW WHAT YOU NEED.
ARGHH!
MY HAND
AHHHH... SHII--IIIT!
MY--
HELLO?

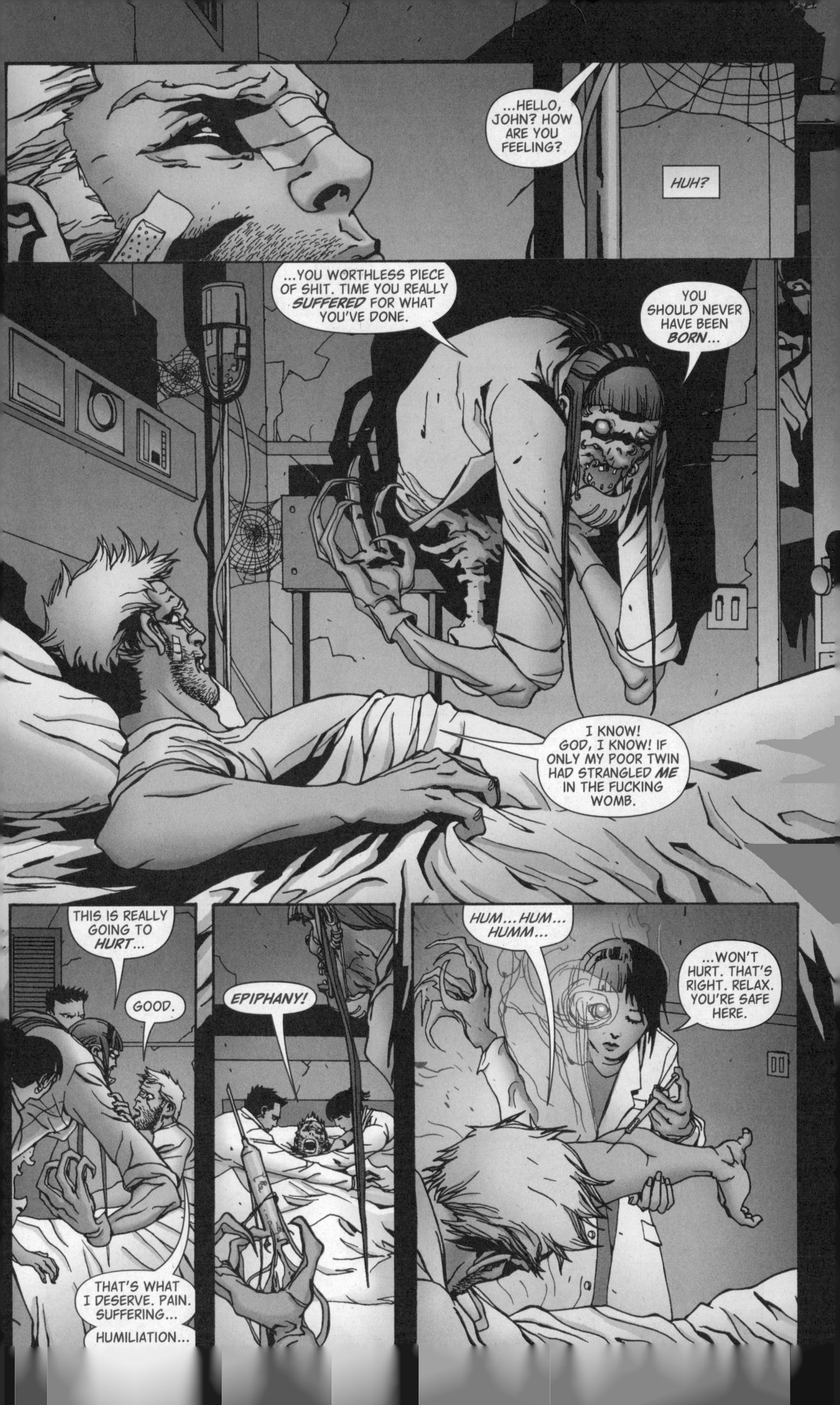

...HELLO, JOHN? HOW ARE YOU FEELING?
HUH?
...YOU WORTHLESS PIECE OF SHIT. TIME YOU REALLY SUFFERED FOR WHAT YOU'VE DONE.
YOU SHOULD NEVER HAVE BEEN BORN...
I KNOW! GOD, I KNOW! IF ONLY MY POOR TWIN HAD STRANGLED ME IN THE FUCKING WOMB.
THIS IS REALLY GOING TO HURT...
GOOD.
THAT'S WHAT I DESERVE. PAIN. SUFFERING...
HUMILIATION...
EPIPHANY!
HUM... HUM... HUMM...
...WON'T HURT. THAT'S RIGHT. RELAX. YOU'RE SAFE HERE.

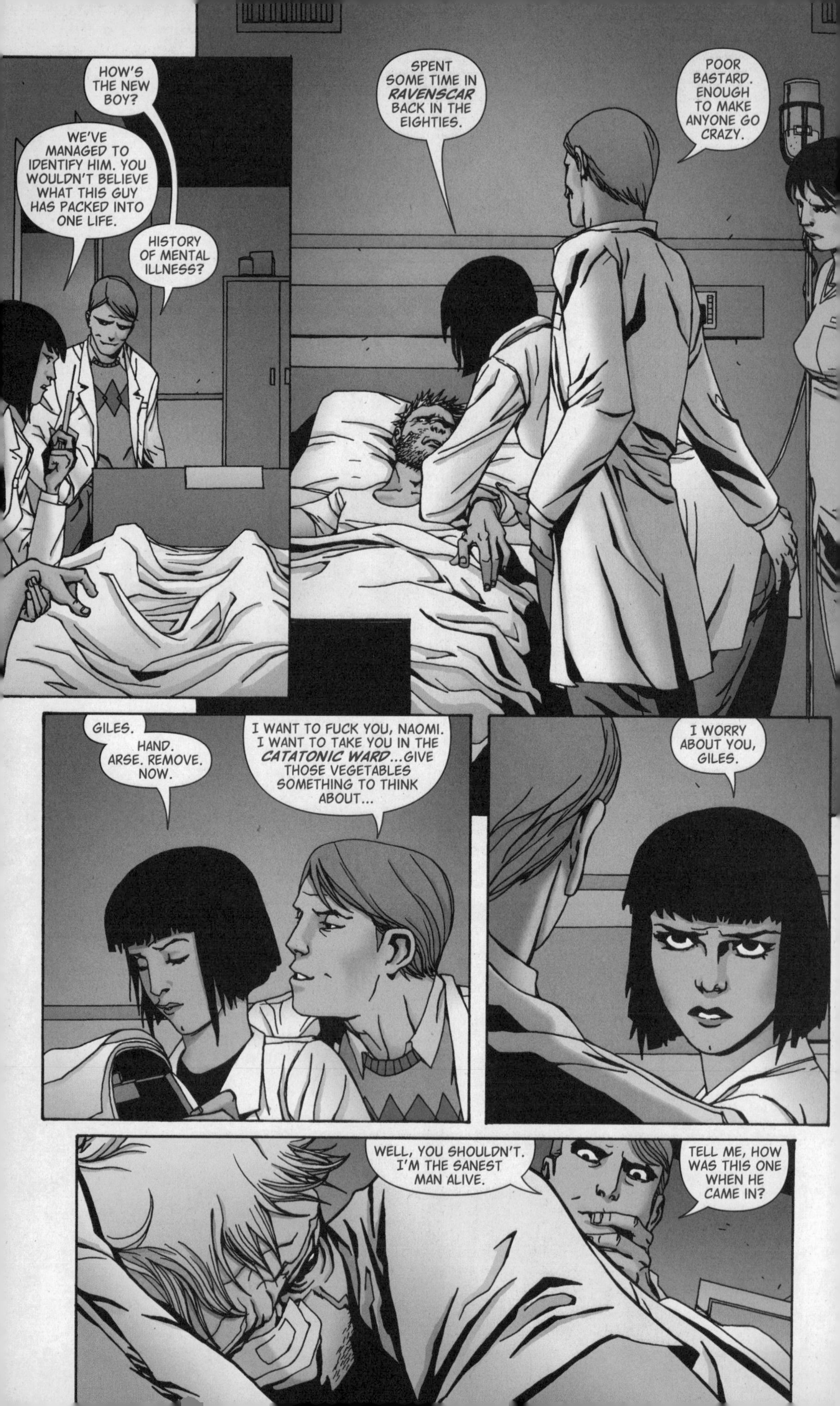
HOW'S THE NEW BOY?
WE'VE MANAGED TO IDENTIFY HIM. YOU WOULDN'T BELIEVE WHAT THIS GUY HAS PACKED INTO ONE LIFE.
HISTORY OF MENTAL ILLNESS?
SPENT SOME TIME IN RAVENSCAR BACK IN THE EIGHTIES.
POOR BASTARD. ENOUGH TO MAKE ANYONE GO CRAZY.
GILES.
HAND. ARSE. REMOVE. NOW.
I WANT TO FUCK YOU, NAOMI. I WANT TO TAKE YOU IN THE CATATONIC WARD...GIVE THOSE VEGETABLES SOMETHING TO THINK ABOUT...
I WORRY ABOUT YOU, GILES.
WELL, YOU SHOULDN'T. I'M THE SANEST MAN ALIVE.
TELL ME, HOW WAS THIS ONE WHEN HE CAME IN?

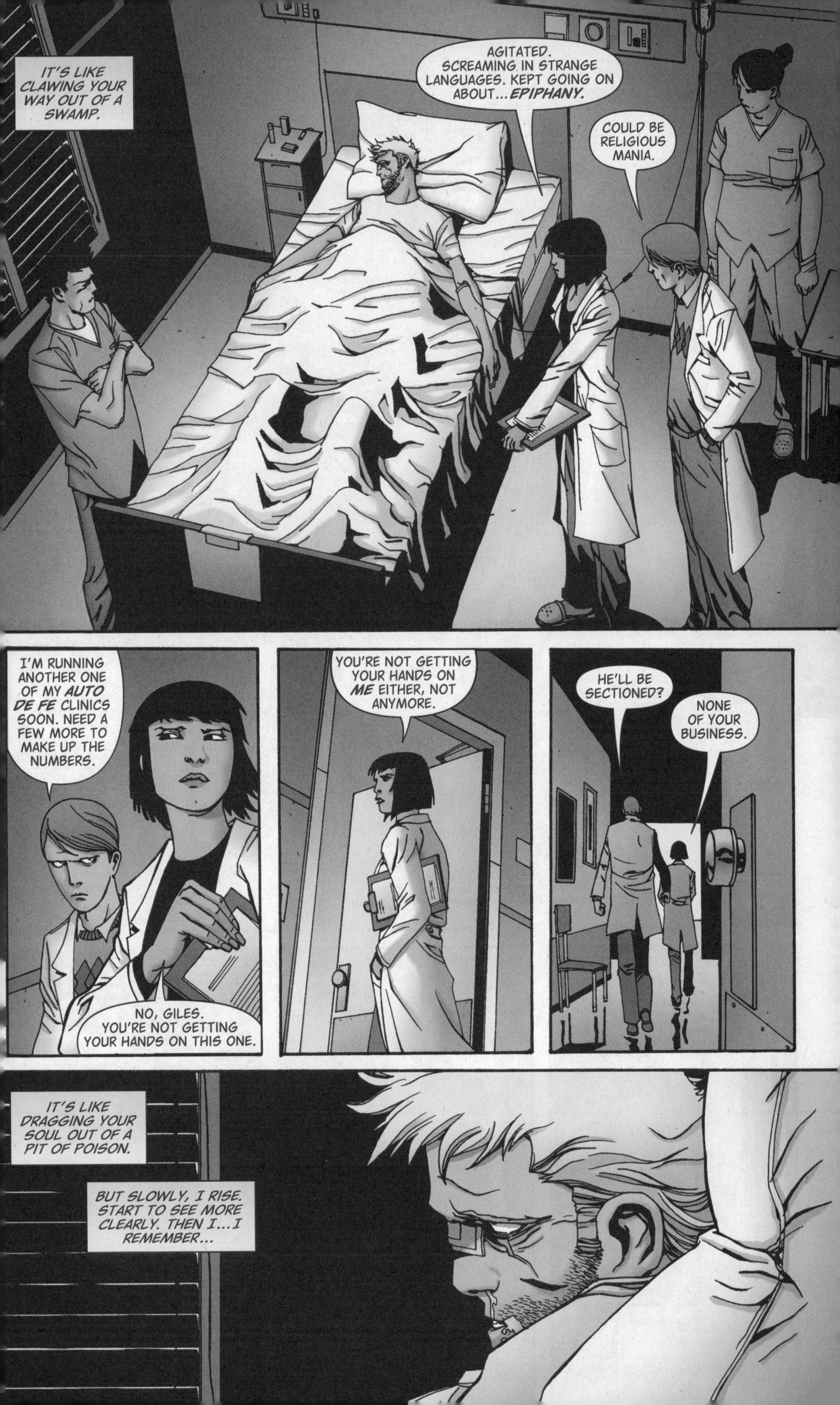
IT'S LIKE CLAWING YOUR WAY OUT OF A SWAMP.
AGITATED. SCREAMING IN STRANGE LANGUAGES. KEPT GOING ON ABOUT... EPIPHANY.
COULD BE RELIGIOUS MANIA.
I'M RUNNING ANOTHER ONE OF MY AUTO DE FE CLINICS SOON. NEED A FEW MORE TO MAKE UP THE NUMBERS.
NO, GILES. YOU'RE NOT GETTING YOUR HANDS ON THIS ONE.
YOU'RE NOT GETTING YOUR HANDS ON ME EITHER, NOT ANYMORE.
HE'LL BE SECTIONED?
NONE OF YOUR BUSINESS.
IT'S LIKE DRAGGING YOUR SOUL OUT OF A PIT OF POISON.
BUT SLOWLY, I RISE. START TO SEE MORE CLEARLY. THEN I... I REMEMBER...

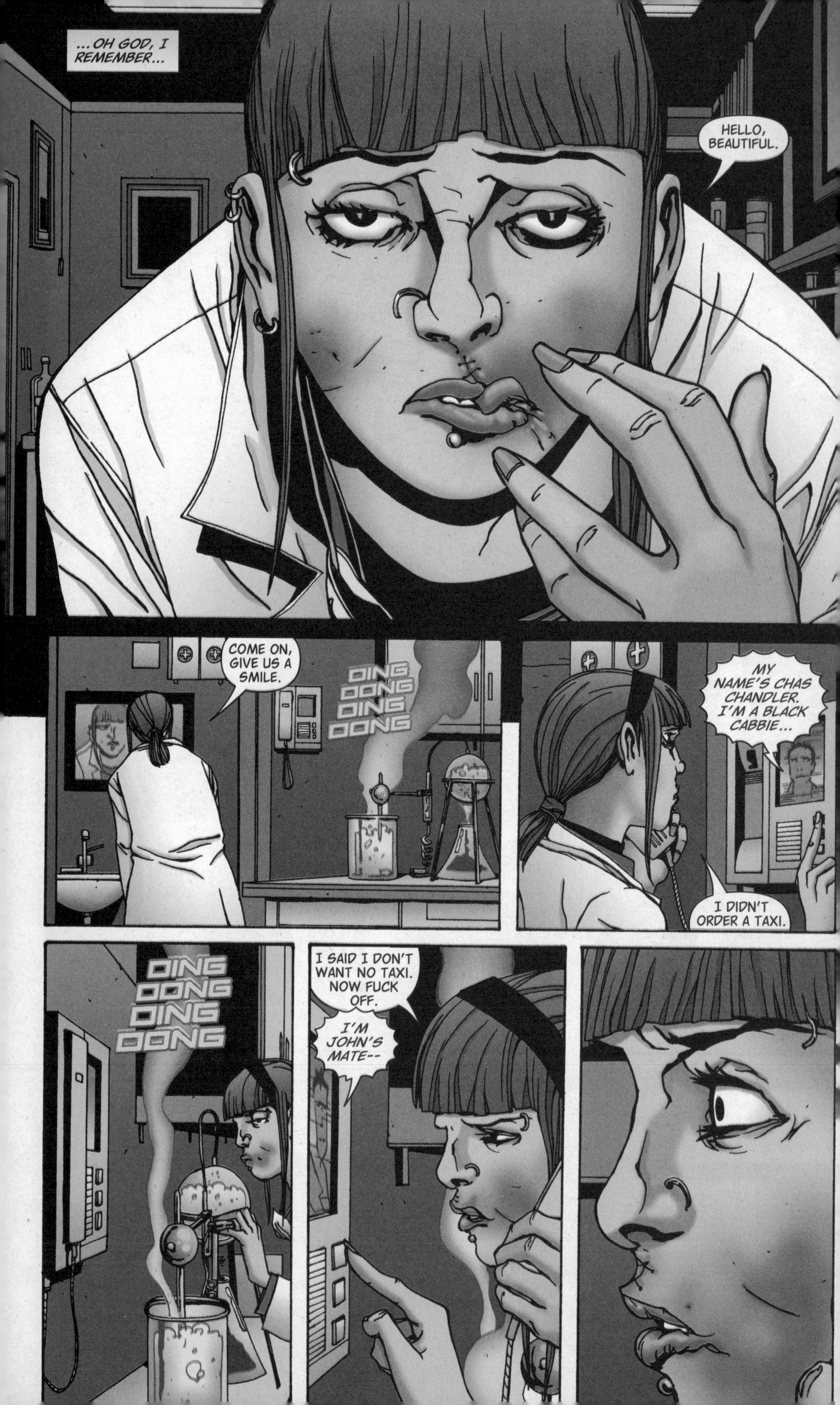
...OH GOD, I REMEMBER...
HELLO, BEAUTIFUL.
COME ON, GIVE US A SMILE.
DING DONG DING DONG
MY NAME'S CHAS CHANDLER. I'M A BLACK CABBIE...
I DIDN'T ORDER A TAXI.
DING DONG DING DONG
I SAID I DON'T WANT NO TAXI. NOW FUCK OFF.
I'M JOHN'S MATE--

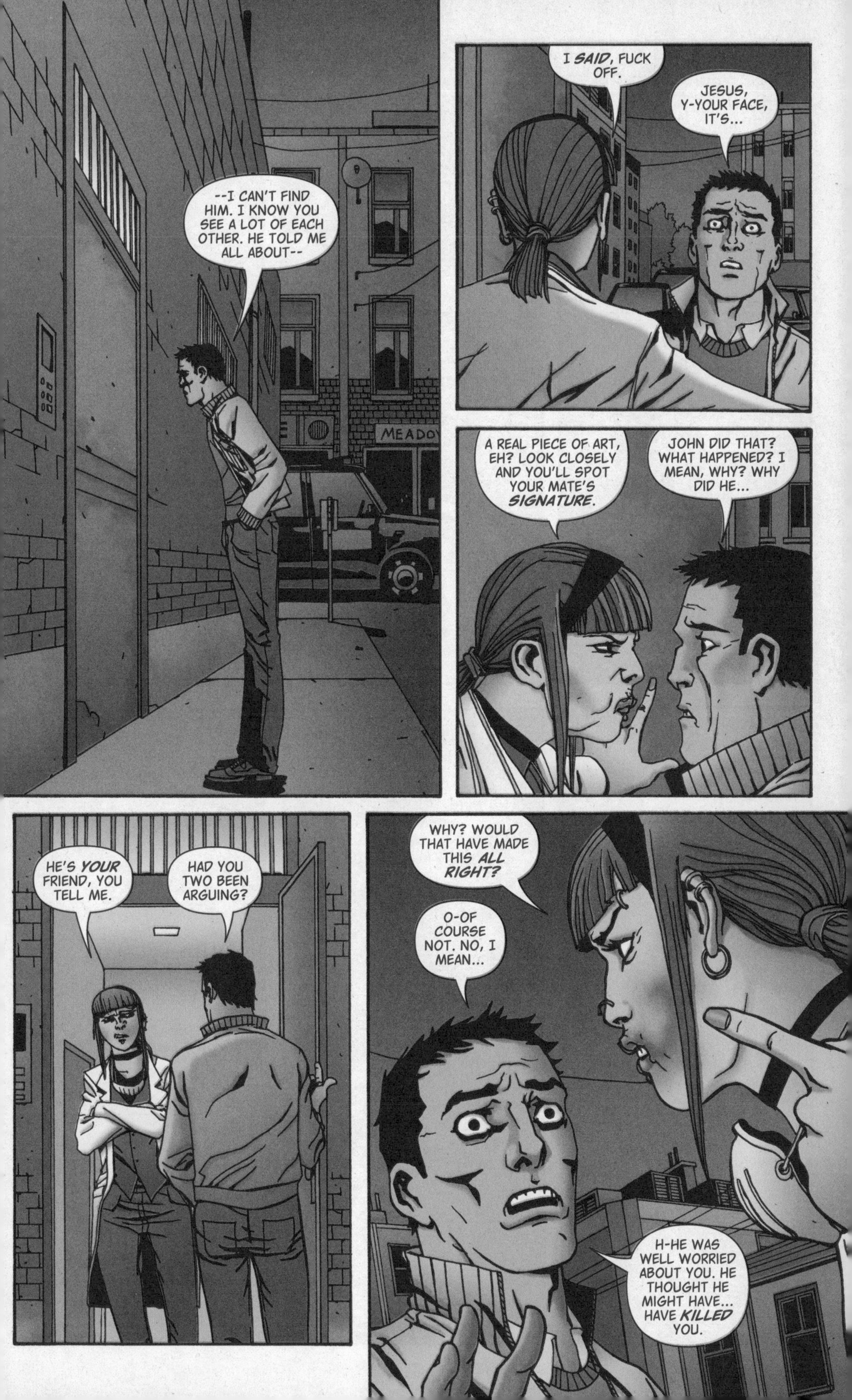
--I CAN'T FIND HIM. I KNOW YOU SEE A LOT OF EACH OTHER. HE TOLD ME ALL ABOUT--
MEADOW
I SAID, FUCK OFF.
JESUS, Y-YOUR FACE, IT'S...
A REAL PIECE OF ART, EH? LOOK CLOSELY AND YOU'LL SPOT YOUR MATE'S SIGNATURE.
JOHN DID THAT? WHAT HAPPENED? I MEAN, WHY? WHY DID HE...
HE'S YOUR FRIEND, YOU TELL ME.
HAD YOU TWO BEEN ARGUING?
WHY? WOULD THAT HAVE MADE THIS ALL RIGHT?
O-OF COURSE NOT. NO, I MEAN...
H-HE WAS WELL WORRIED ABOUT YOU. HE THOUGHT HE MIGHT HAVE... HAVE KILLED YOU.

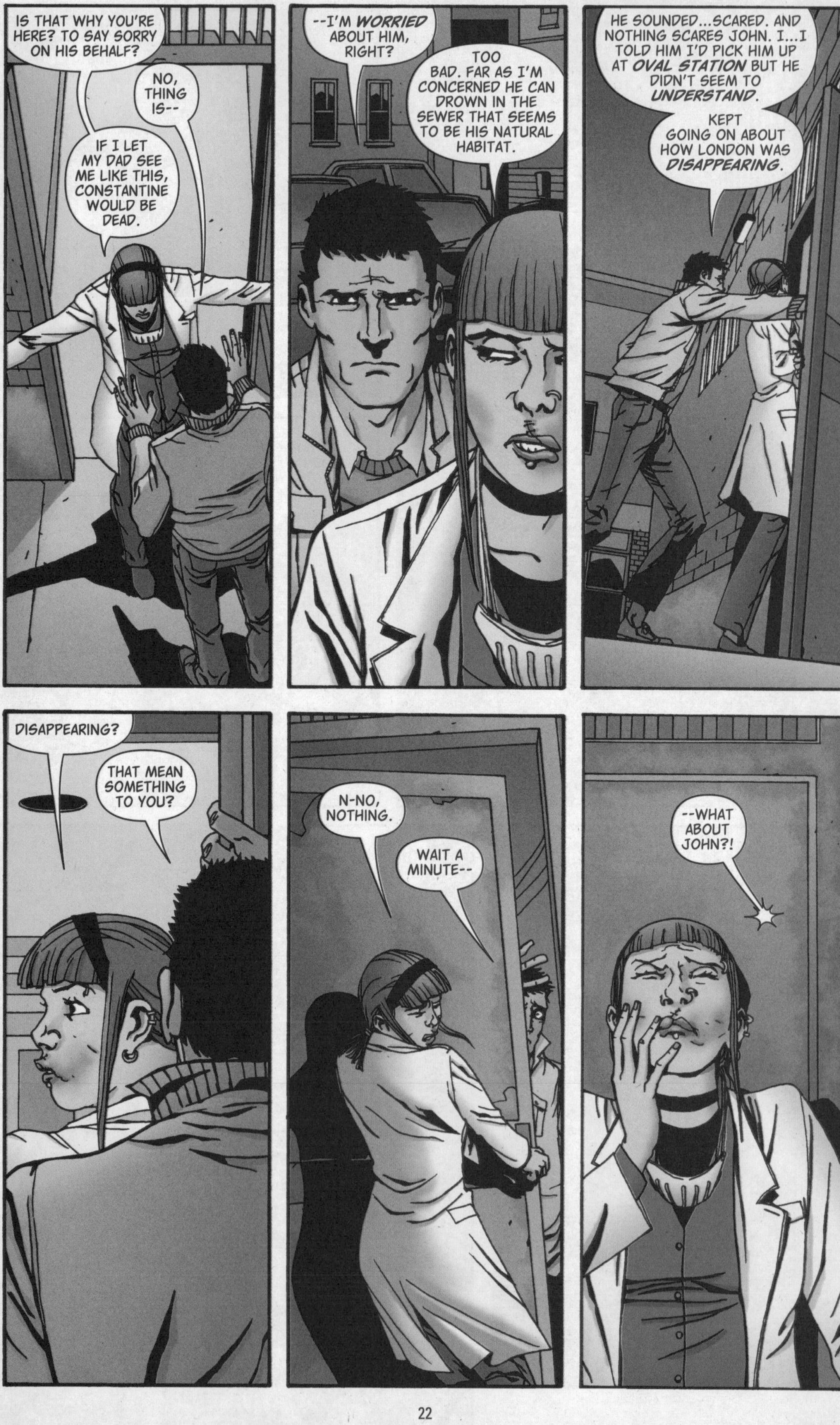
IS THAT WHY YOU'RE HERE? TO SAY SORRY ON HIS BEHALF?
NO, THING IS--
IF I LET MY DAD SEE ME LIKE THIS, CONSTANTINE WOULD BE DEAD.
--I'M WORRIED ABOUT HIM, RIGHT?
TOO BAD. FAR AS I'M CONCERNED HE CAN DROWN IN THE SEWER THAT SEEMS TO BE HIS NATURAL HABITAT.
HE SOUNDED...SCARED. AND NOTHING SCARES JOHN. I...I TOLD HIM I'D PICK HIM UP AT OVAL STATION BUT HE DIDN'T SEEM TO UNDERSTAND.
KEPT GOING ON ABOUT HOW LONDON WAS DISAPPEARING.
DISAPPEARING?
THAT MEAN SOMETHING TO YOU?
N-NO, NOTHING.
WAIT A MINUTE--
--WHAT ABOUT JOHN?!

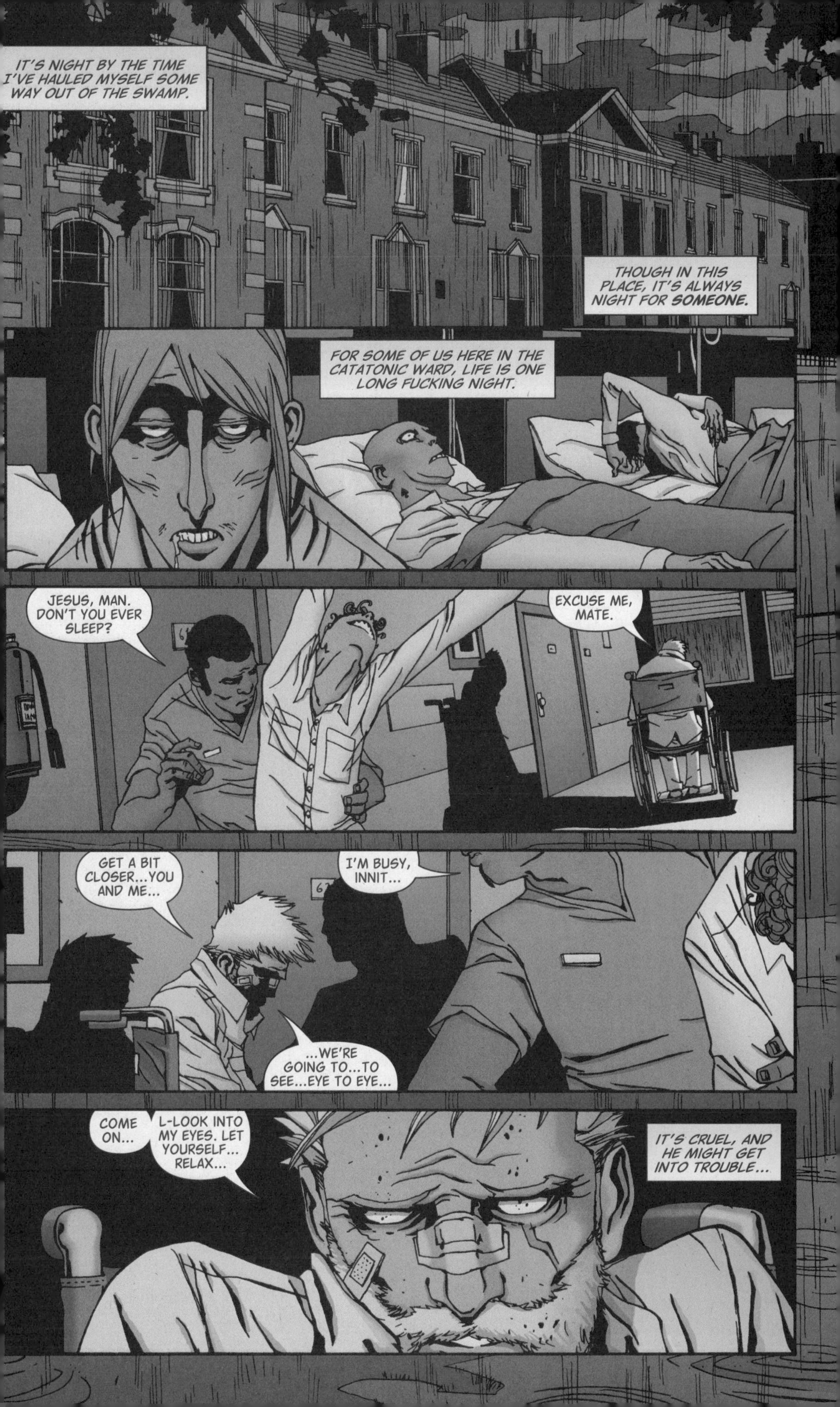
IT'S NIGHT BY THE TIME I'VE HAULED MYSELF SOME WAY OUT OF THE SWAMP.
THOUGH IN THIS PLACE, IT'S ALWAYS NIGHT FOR SOMEONE.
FOR SOME OF US HERE IN THE CATATONIC WARD, LIFE IS ONE LONG FUCKING NIGHT.
JESUS, MAN. DON'T YOU EVER SLEEP?
EXCUSE ME, MATE.
GET A BIT CLOSER...YOU AND ME...
I'M BUSY, INNIT...
...WE'RE GOING TO...TO SEE...EYE TO EYE...
COME ON...
L-LOOK INTO MY EYES. LET YOURSELF... RELAX...
IT'S CRUEL, AND HE MIGHT GET INTO TROUBLE...

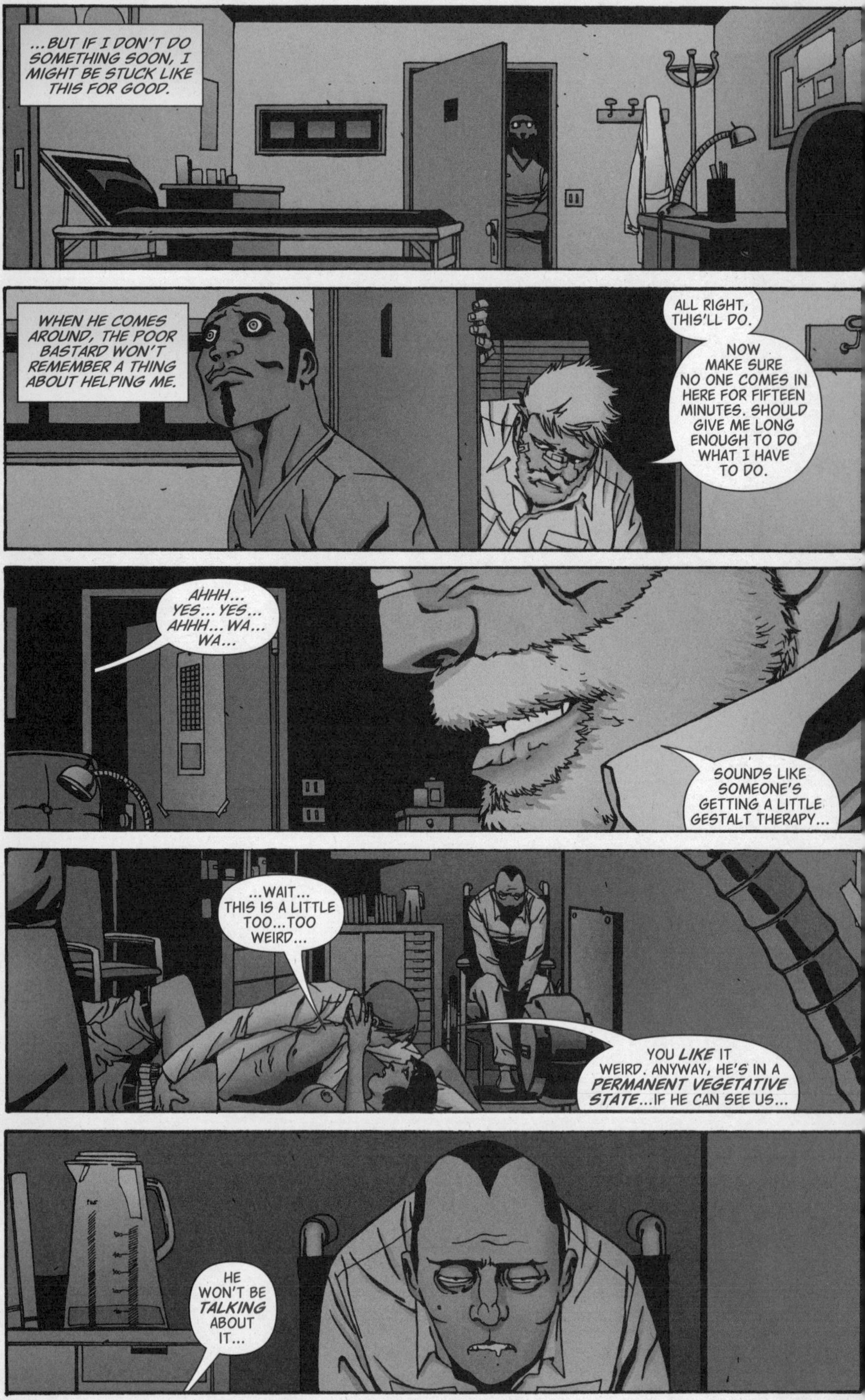
...BUT IF I DON'T DO SOMETHING SOON, I MIGHT BE STUCK LIKE THIS FOR GOOD.
WHEN HE COMES AROUND, THE POOR BASTARD WON'T REMEMBER A THING ABOUT HELPING ME.
ALL RIGHT, THIS'LL DO.
NOW MAKE SURE NO ONE COMES IN HERE FOR FIFTEEN MINUTES. SHOULD GIVE ME LONG ENOUGH TO DO WHAT I HAVE TO DO.
AHHH... YES...YES... AHHH... WA... WA...
SOUNDS LIKE SOMEONE'S GETTING A LITTLE GESTALT THERAPY...
...WAIT... THIS IS A LITTLE TOO...TOO WEIRD...
YOU LIKE IT WEIRD. ANYWAY, HE'S IN A PERMANENT VEGETATIVE STATE...IF HE CAN SEE US...
HE WON'T BE TALKING ABOUT IT...

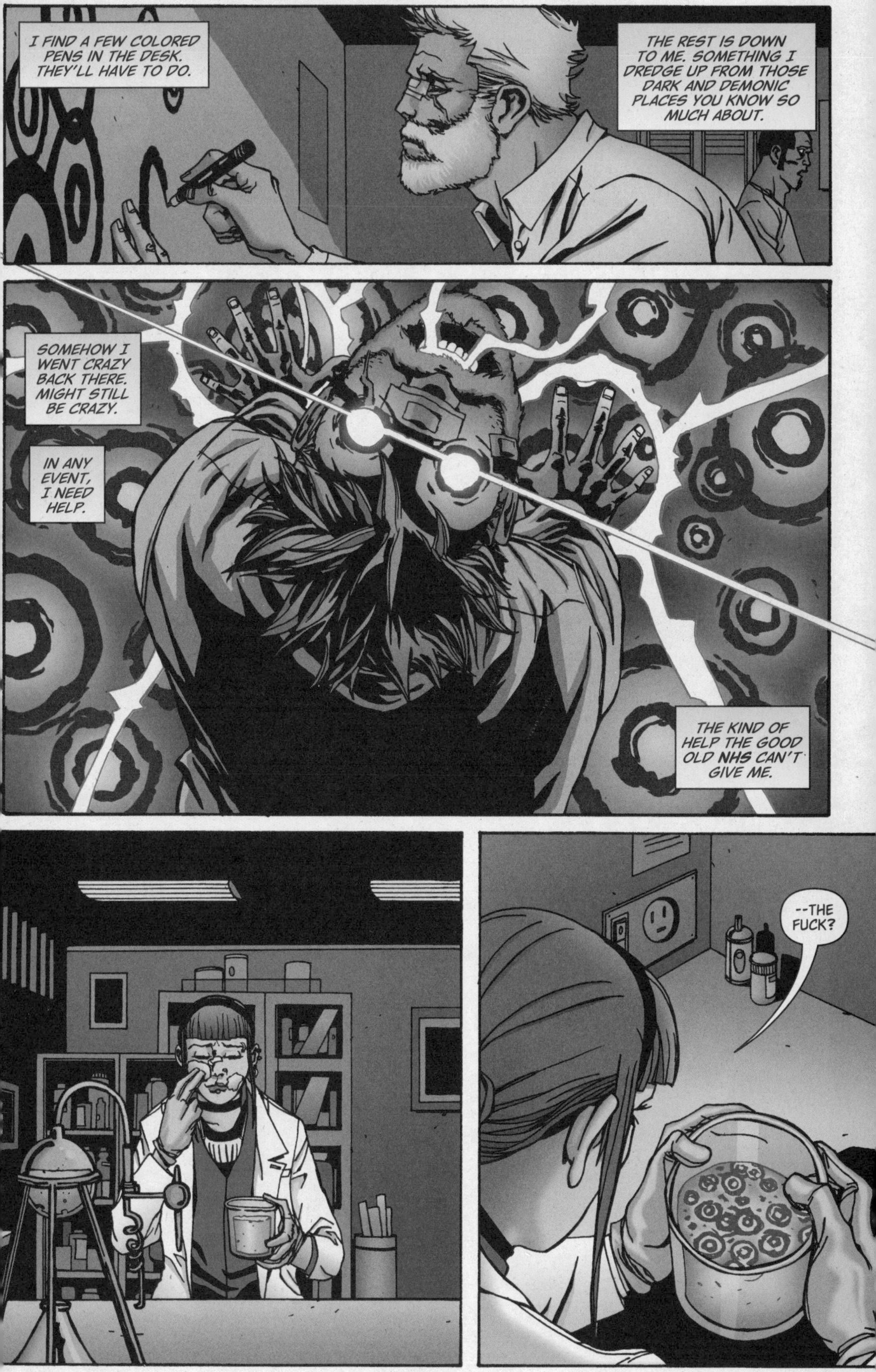
I FIND A FEW COLORED PENS IN THE DESK. THEY'LL HAVE TO DO.
THE REST IS DOWN TO ME. SOMETHING I DREDGE UP FROM THOSE DARK AND DEMONIC PLACES YOU KNOW SO MUCH ABOUT.
SOMEHOW I WENT CRAZY BACK THERE. MIGHT STILL BE CRAZY.
IN ANY EVENT, I NEED HELP.
THE KIND OF HELP THE GOOD OLD NHS CAN'T GIVE ME.
--THE FUCK?

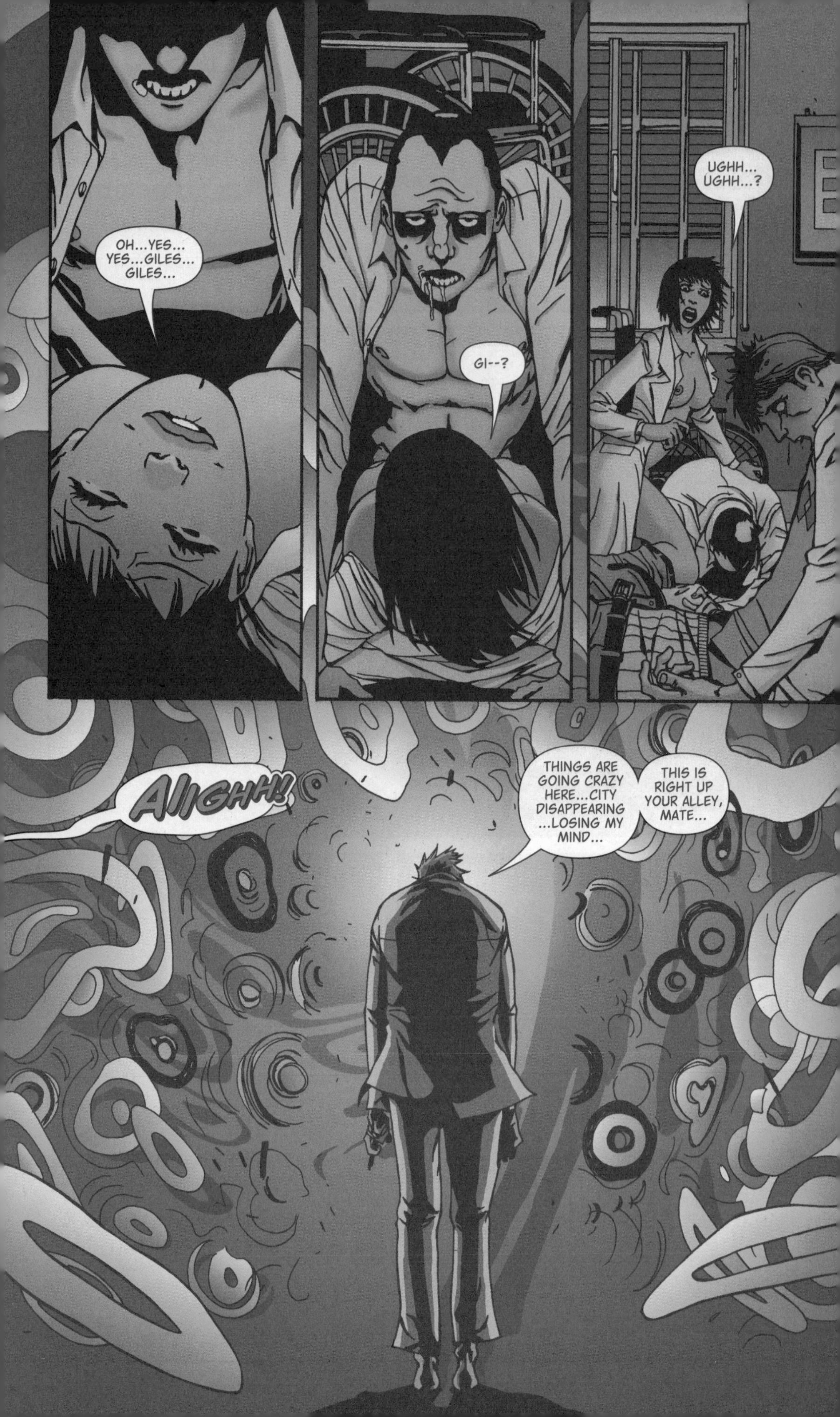
OH...YES...
YES...GILES...
GILES...
GI--?
UGHH...
UGHH...?
AIIGHH!
THINGS ARE GOING CRAZY HERE...CITY DISAPPEARING ...LOSING MY MIND...
THIS IS RIGHT UP YOUR ALLEY, MATE...

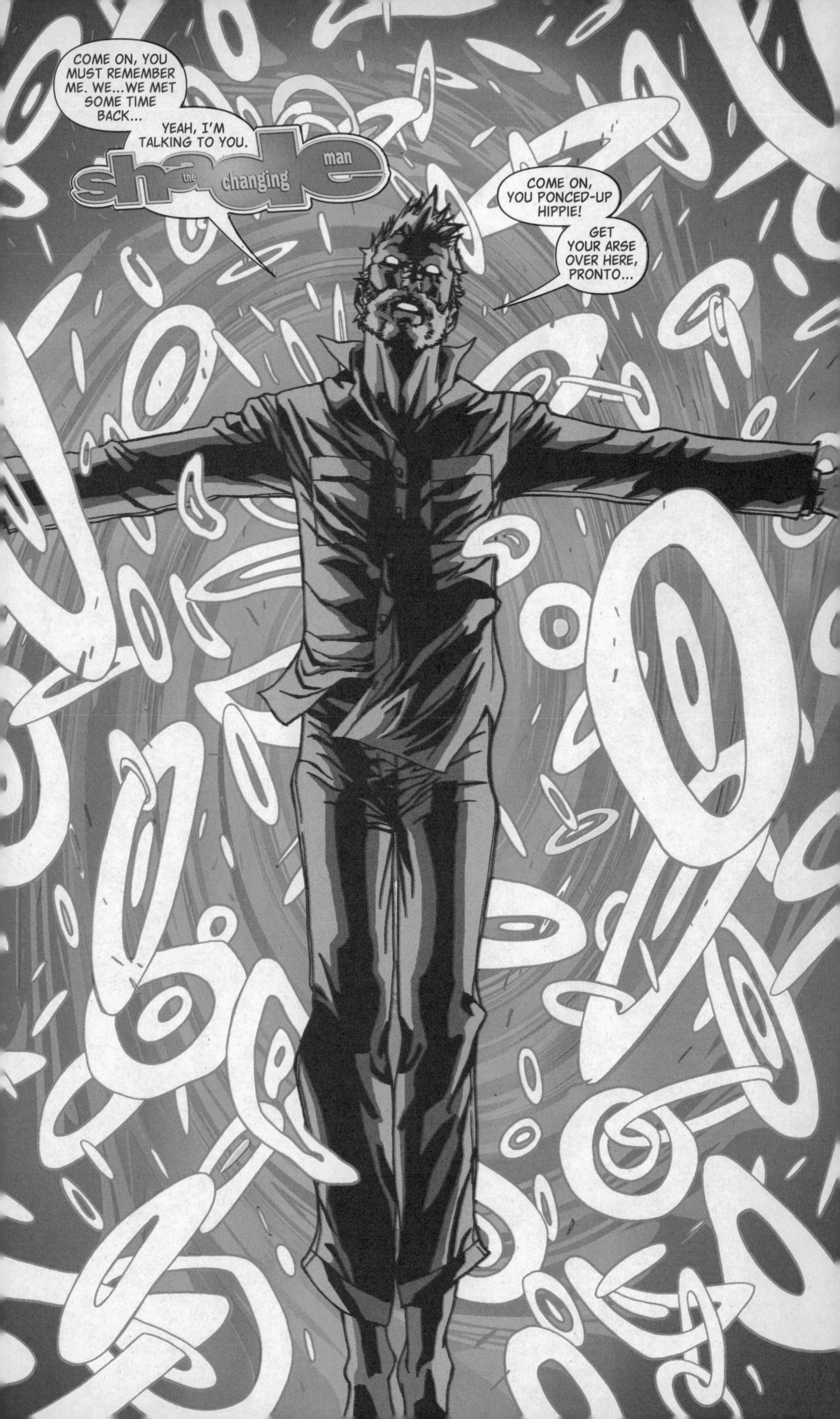
COME ON, YOU MUST REMEMBER ME. WE...WE MET SOME TIME BACK...
YEAH, I'M TALKING TO YOU.
shade the changing man
COME ON, YOU PONCED-UP HIPPIE!
GET YOUR ARSE OVER HERE, PRONTO...

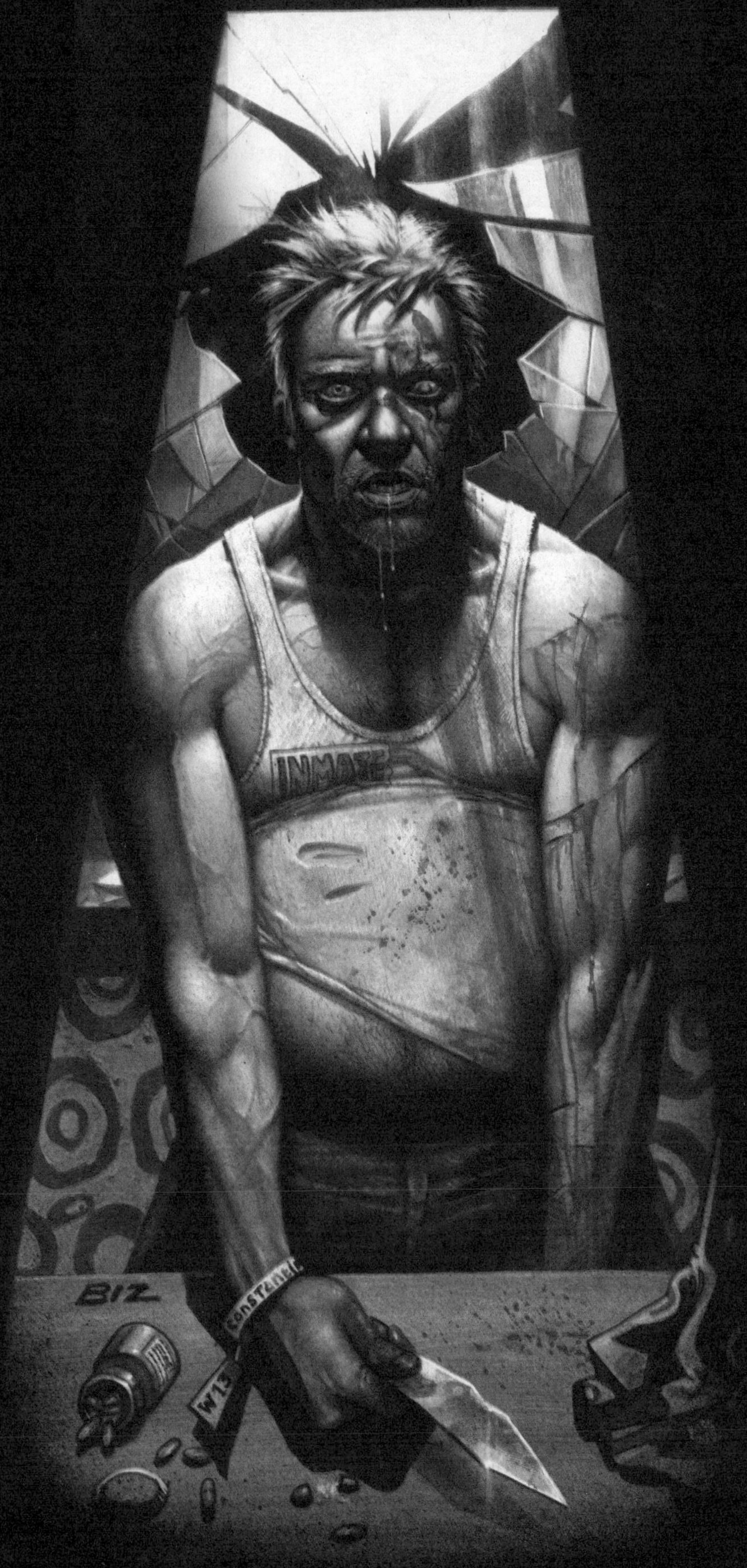
INMATE
BIZ

OH GOD, OH GOD, OH GOD...

DR. GREEN? WHAT'S--

--OH JESUS, JOSEPH, AND MARY.

WHAT HAVE YOU DONE TO DOCTOR MCKAY?

ME? NO, N-NOT ME, IT...IT WAS THE PATIENT.

HE...HE RAPED ME...AND HE...HE KILLED GILES...

THE PATIENT? YOU MEAN *DONALD*?

DONALD HASN'T MOVED A MUSCLE FOR FIFTEEN YEARS, DOCTOR GREEN.

LOOK AT HIM. HE CAN'T EVEN BLINK.

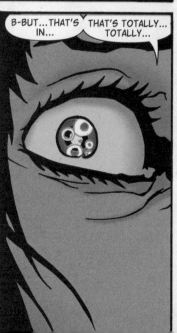

B-BUT...THAT'S IN... THAT'S TOTALLY... TOTALLY...

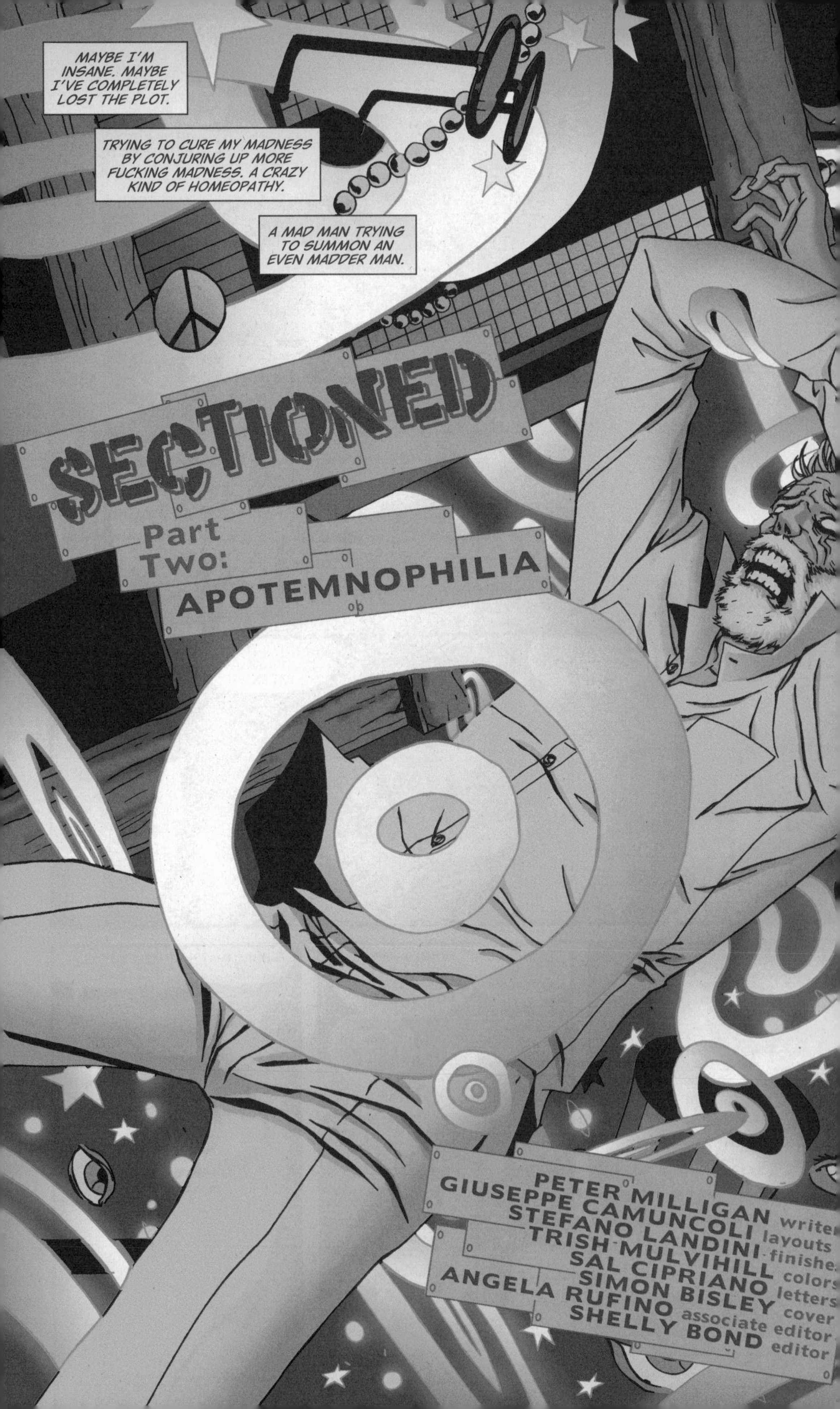

MAYBE I'M INSANE. MAYBE I'VE COMPLETELY LOST THE PLOT.
TRYING TO CURE MY MADNESS BY CONJURING UP MORE FUCKING MADNESS. A CRAZY KIND OF HOMEOPATHY.
A MAD MAN TRYING TO SUMMON AN EVEN MADDER MAN.
SECTIONED
Part Two: APOTEMNOPHILIA
PETER MILLIGAN writer
GIUSEPPE CAMUNCOLI layouts
STEFANO LANDINI finishes
TRISH MULVIHILL colors
SAL CIPRIANO letters
SIMON BISLEY cover
ANGELA RUFINO associate editor
SHELLY BOND editor

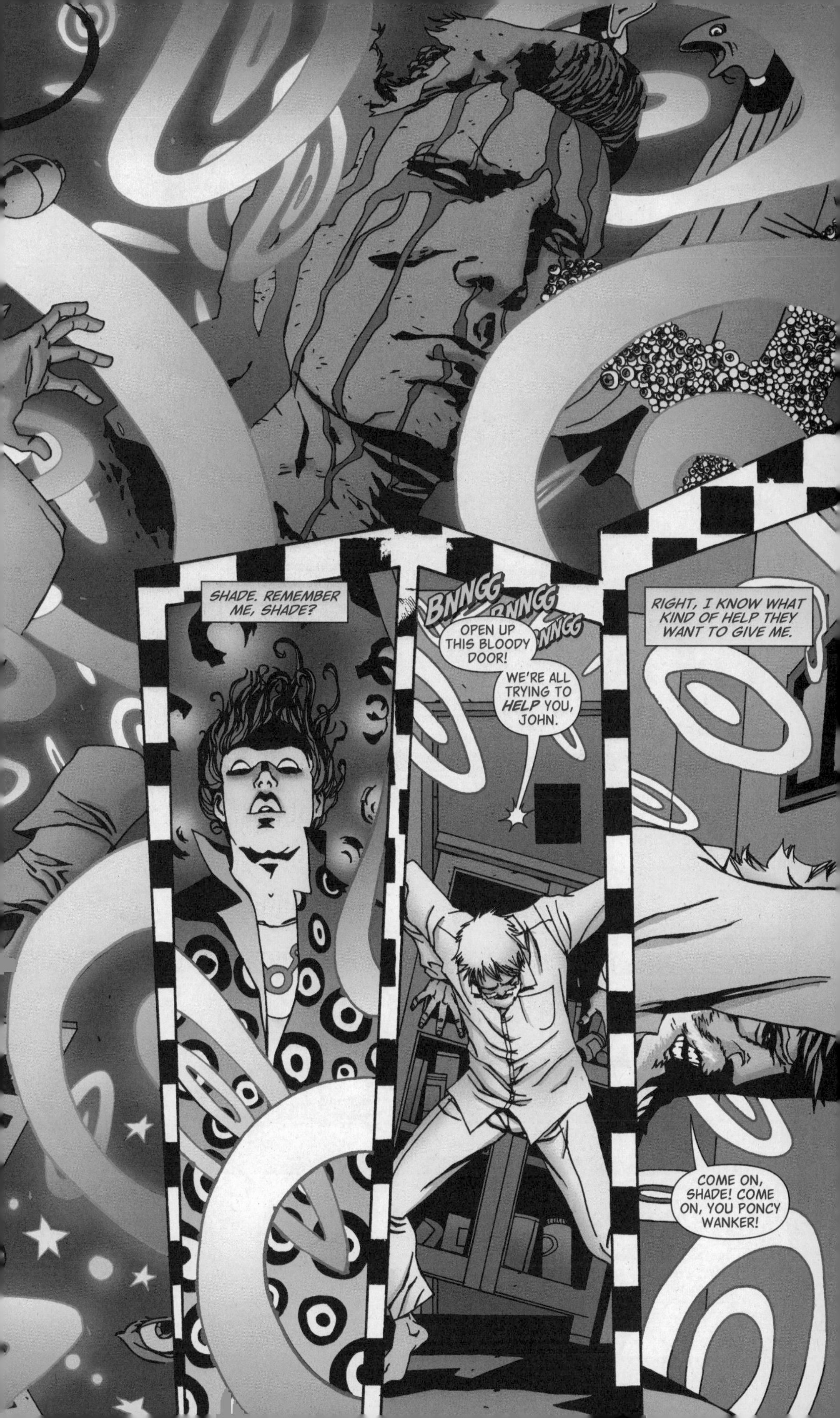
SHADE. REMEMBER ME, SHADE?
BNNGG BNNGG BNNGG
OPEN UP THIS BLOODY DOOR!
WE'RE ALL TRYING TO HELP YOU, JOHN.
RIGHT, I KNOW WHAT KIND OF HELP THEY WANT TO GIVE ME.
COME ON, SHADE! COME ON, YOU PONCY WANKER!

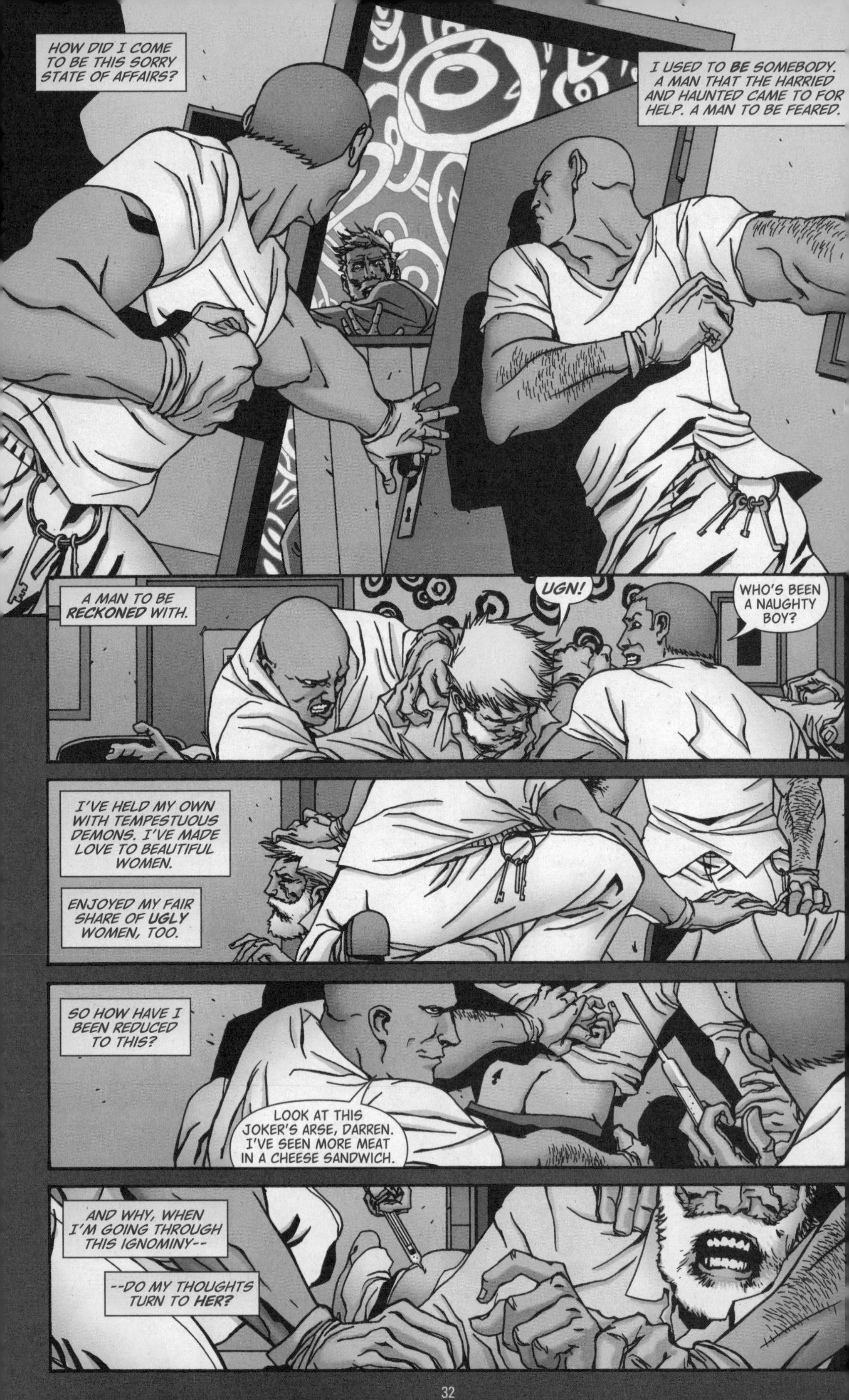
HOW DID I COME TO BE THIS SORRY STATE OF AFFAIRS?
I USED TO BE SOMEBODY. A MAN THAT THE HARRIED AND HAUNTED CAME TO FOR HELP. A MAN TO BE FEARED.
A MAN TO BE RECKONED WITH.
UGN!
WHO'S BEEN A NAUGHTY BOY?
I'VE HELD MY OWN WITH TEMPESTUOUS DEMONS. I'VE MADE LOVE TO BEAUTIFUL WOMEN.
ENJOYED MY FAIR SHARE OF UGLY WOMEN, TOO.
SO HOW HAVE I BEEN REDUCED TO THIS?
LOOK AT THIS JOKER'S ARSE, DARREN. I'VE SEEN MORE MEAT IN A CHEESE SANDWICH.
AND WHY, WHEN I'M GOING THROUGH THIS IGNOMINY--
--DO MY THOUGHTS TURN TO HER?

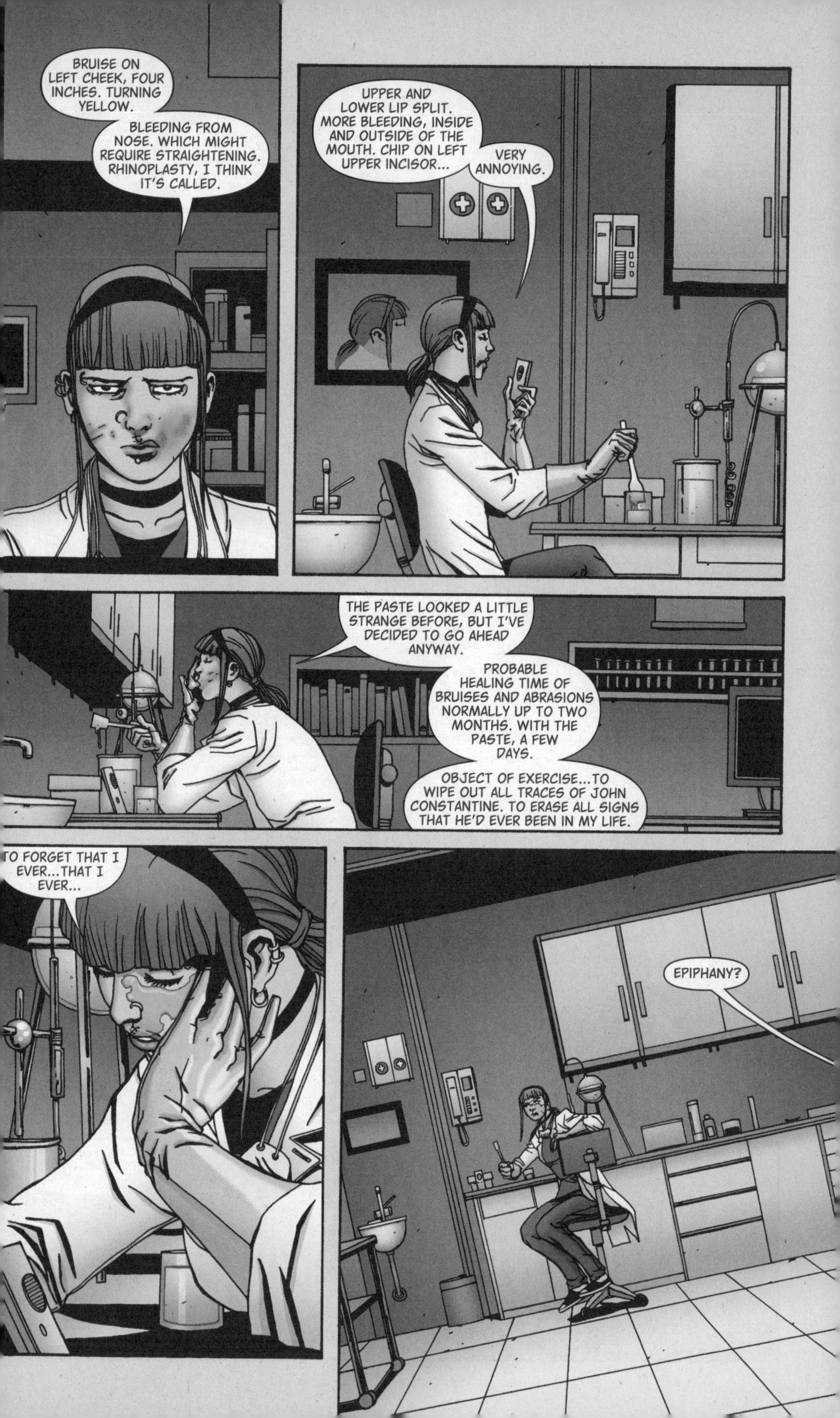
BRUISE ON LEFT CHEEK, FOUR INCHES. TURNING YELLOW.
BLEEDING FROM NOSE. WHICH MIGHT REQUIRE STRAIGHTENING. RHINOPLASTY, I THINK IT'S CALLED.
UPPER AND LOWER LIP SPLIT. MORE BLEEDING, INSIDE AND OUTSIDE OF THE MOUTH. CHIP ON LEFT UPPER INCISOR...
VERY ANNOYING.
THE PASTE LOOKED A LITTLE STRANGE BEFORE, BUT I'VE DECIDED TO GO AHEAD ANYWAY.
PROBABLE HEALING TIME OF BRUISES AND ABRASIONS NORMALLY UP TO TWO MONTHS. WITH THE PASTE, A FEW DAYS.
OBJECT OF EXERCISE...TO WIPE OUT ALL TRACES OF JOHN CONSTANTINE. TO ERASE ALL SIGNS THAT HE'D EVER BEEN IN MY LIFE.
TO FORGET THAT I EVER...THAT I EVER...
EPIPHANY?

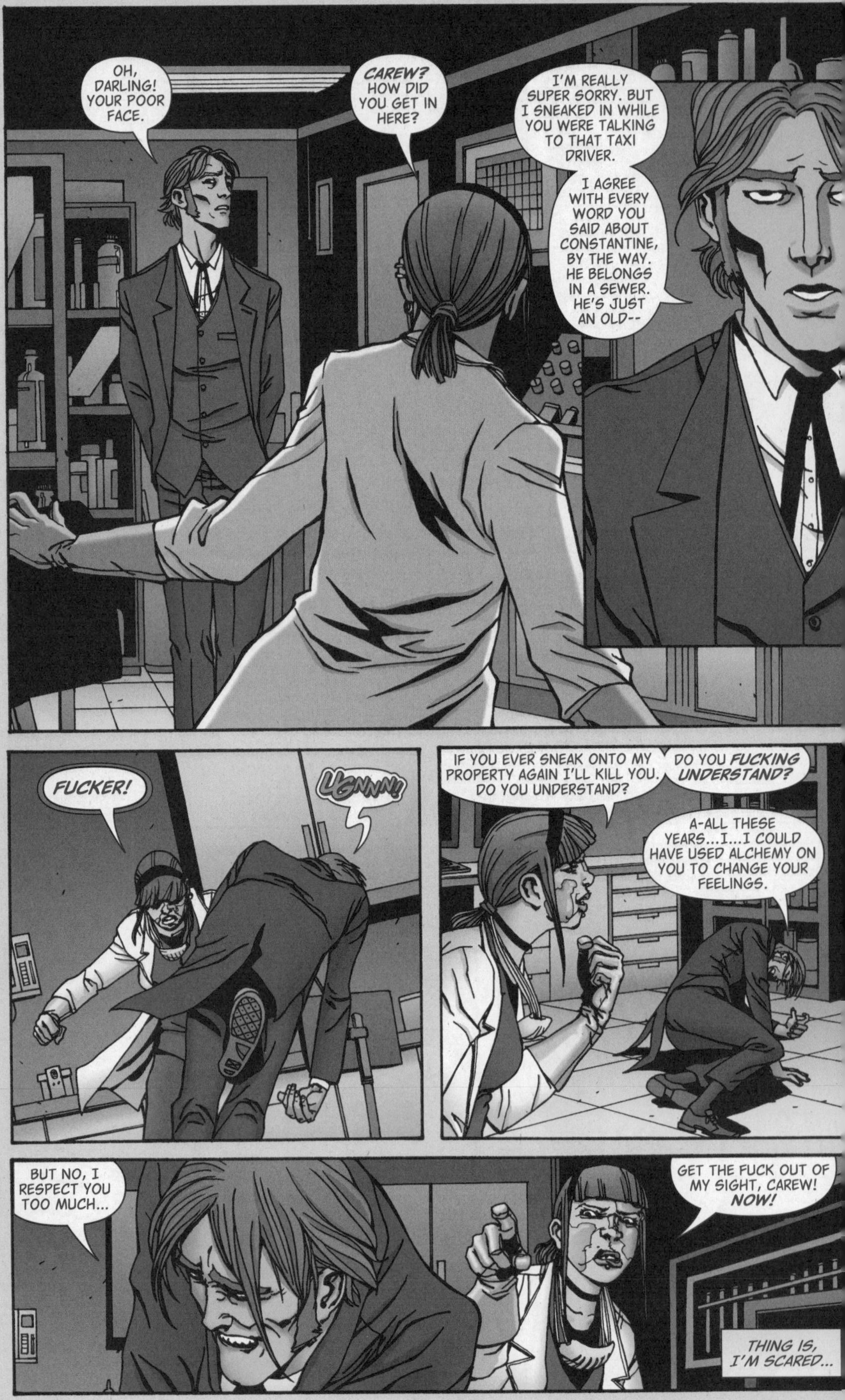
OH, DARLING! YOUR POOR FACE.
CAREW? HOW DID YOU GET IN HERE?
I'M REALLY SUPER SORRY. BUT I SNEAKED IN WHILE YOU WERE TALKING TO THAT TAXI DRIVER.
I AGREE WITH EVERY WORD YOU SAID ABOUT CONSTANTINE, BY THE WAY. HE BELONGS IN A SEWER. HE'S JUST AN OLD--
FUCKER!
UGNNN!!
IF YOU EVER SNEAK ONTO MY PROPERTY AGAIN I'LL KILL YOU. DO YOU UNDERSTAND?
DO YOU FUCKING UNDERSTAND?
A-ALL THESE YEARS...I...I COULD HAVE USED ALCHEMY ON YOU TO CHANGE YOUR FEELINGS.
BUT NO, I RESPECT YOU TOO MUCH...
GET THE FUCK OUT OF MY SIGHT, CAREW! NOW!
THING IS, I'M SCARED...

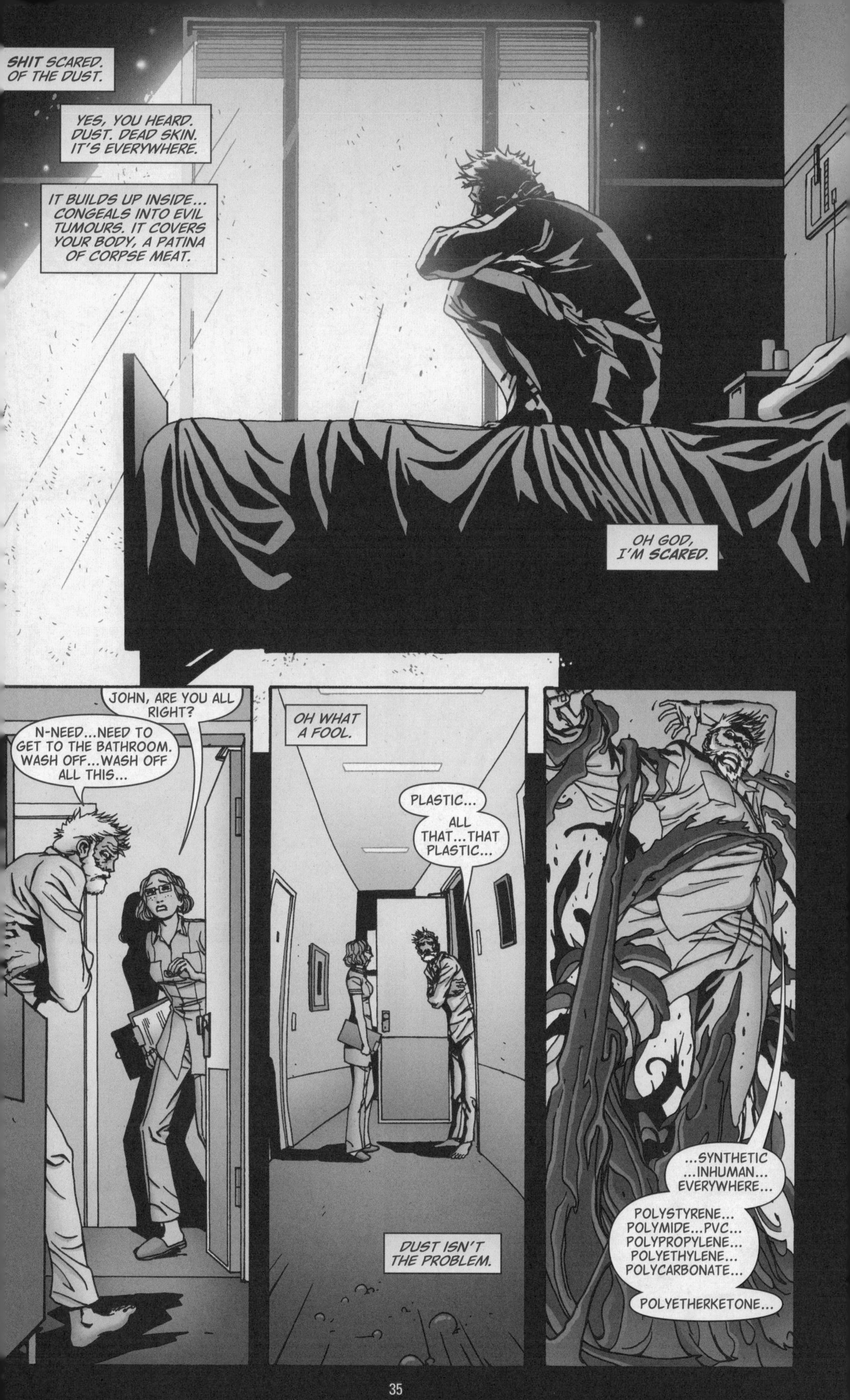
SHIT SCARED. OF THE DUST.
YES, YOU HEARD. DUST. DEAD SKIN. IT'S EVERYWHERE.
IT BUILDS UP INSIDE... CONGEALS INTO EVIL TUMOURS. IT COVERS YOUR BODY, A PATINA OF CORPSE MEAT.
OH GOD, I'M SCARED.
JOHN, ARE YOU ALL RIGHT?
N-NEED...NEED TO GET TO THE BATHROOM. WASH OFF...WASH OFF ALL THIS...
OH WHAT A FOOL.
PLASTIC...
ALL THAT...THAT PLASTIC...
DUST ISN'T THE PROBLEM.
...SYNTHETIC ...INHUMAN... EVERYWHERE...
POLYSTYRENE... POLYMIDE...PVC... POLYPROPYLENE... POLYETHYLENE... POLYCARBONATE...
POLYETHERKETONE...

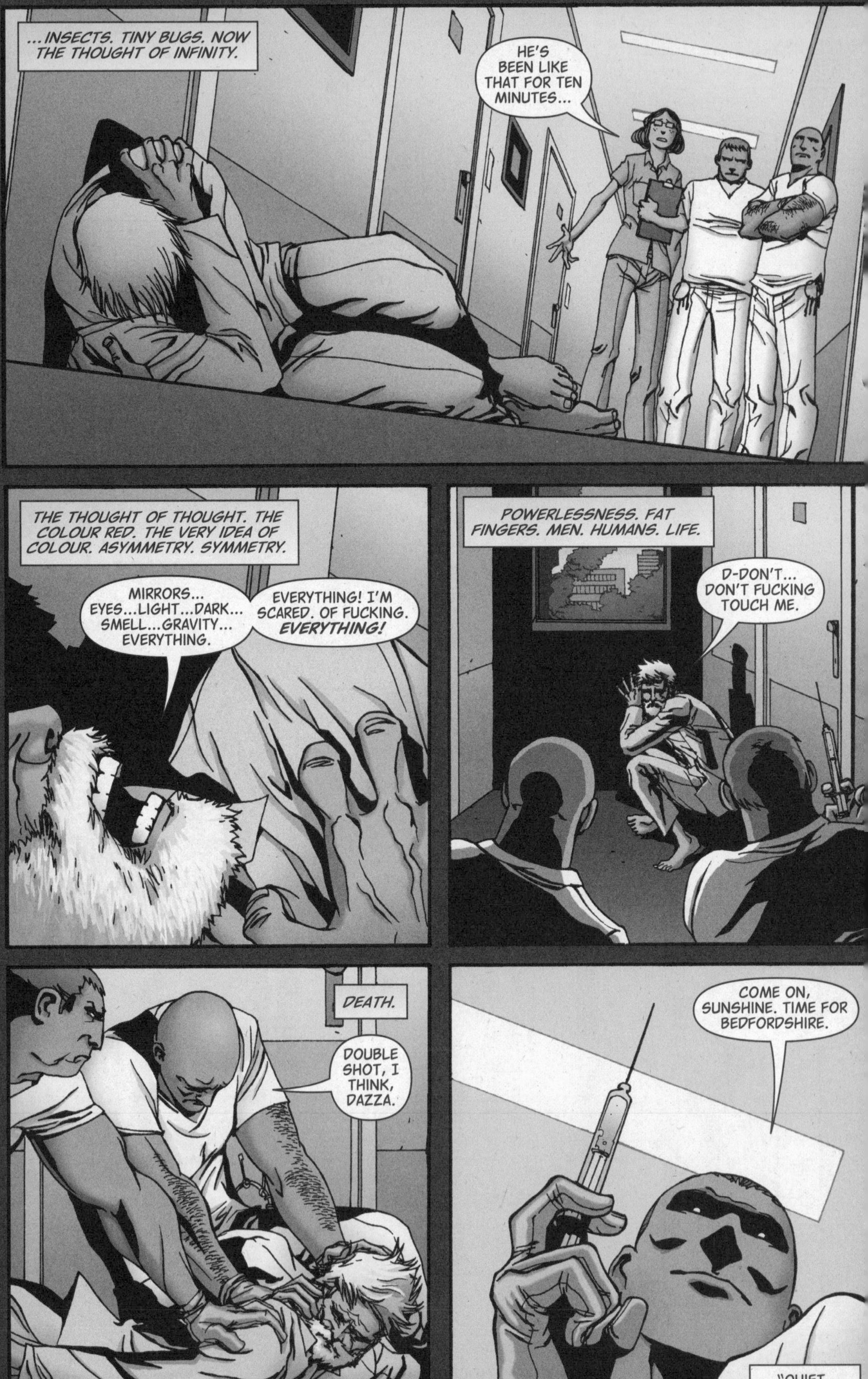
...INSECTS. TINY BUGS. NOW THE THOUGHT OF INFINITY.
HE'S BEEN LIKE THAT FOR TEN MINUTES...
THE THOUGHT OF THOUGHT. THE COLOUR RED. THE VERY IDEA OF COLOUR. ASYMMETRY. SYMMETRY.
MIRRORS... EYES...LIGHT...DARK... SMELL...GRAVITY... EVERYTHING.
EVERYTHING! I'M SCARED. OF FUCKING. EVERYTHING!
POWERLESSNESS. FAT FINGERS. MEN. HUMANS. LIFE.
D-DON'T... DON'T FUCKING TOUCH ME.
DEATH.
DOUBLE SHOT, I THINK, DAZZA.
COME ON, SUNSHINE. TIME FOR BEDFORDSHIRE.
"QUIET, CHILDREN..."

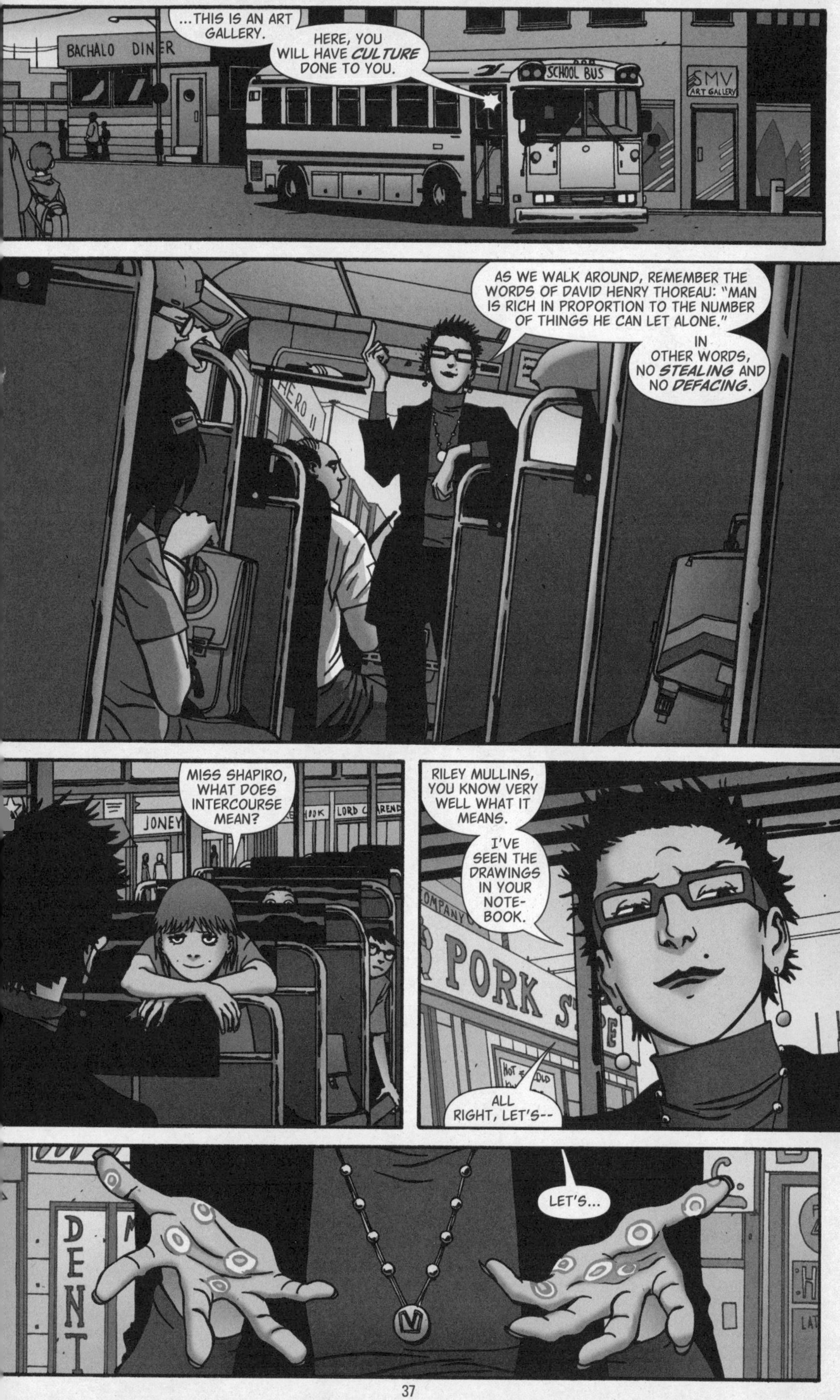

...THIS IS AN ART GALLERY.
HERE, YOU WILL HAVE CULTURE DONE TO YOU.
BACHALO DINER
SCHOOL BUS
SMV ART GALLERY
AS WE WALK AROUND, REMEMBER THE WORDS OF DAVID HENRY THOREAU: "MAN IS RICH IN PROPORTION TO THE NUMBER OF THINGS HE CAN LET ALONE."
IN OTHER WORDS, NO STEALING AND NO DEFACING.
HERO II
MISS SHAPIRO, WHAT DOES INTERCOURSE MEAN?
JONEY
RILEY MULLINS, YOU KNOW VERY WELL WHAT IT MEANS.
I'VE SEEN THE DRAWINGS IN YOUR NOTE-BOOK.
PORK
ALL RIGHT, LET'S--
LET'S...
DENT

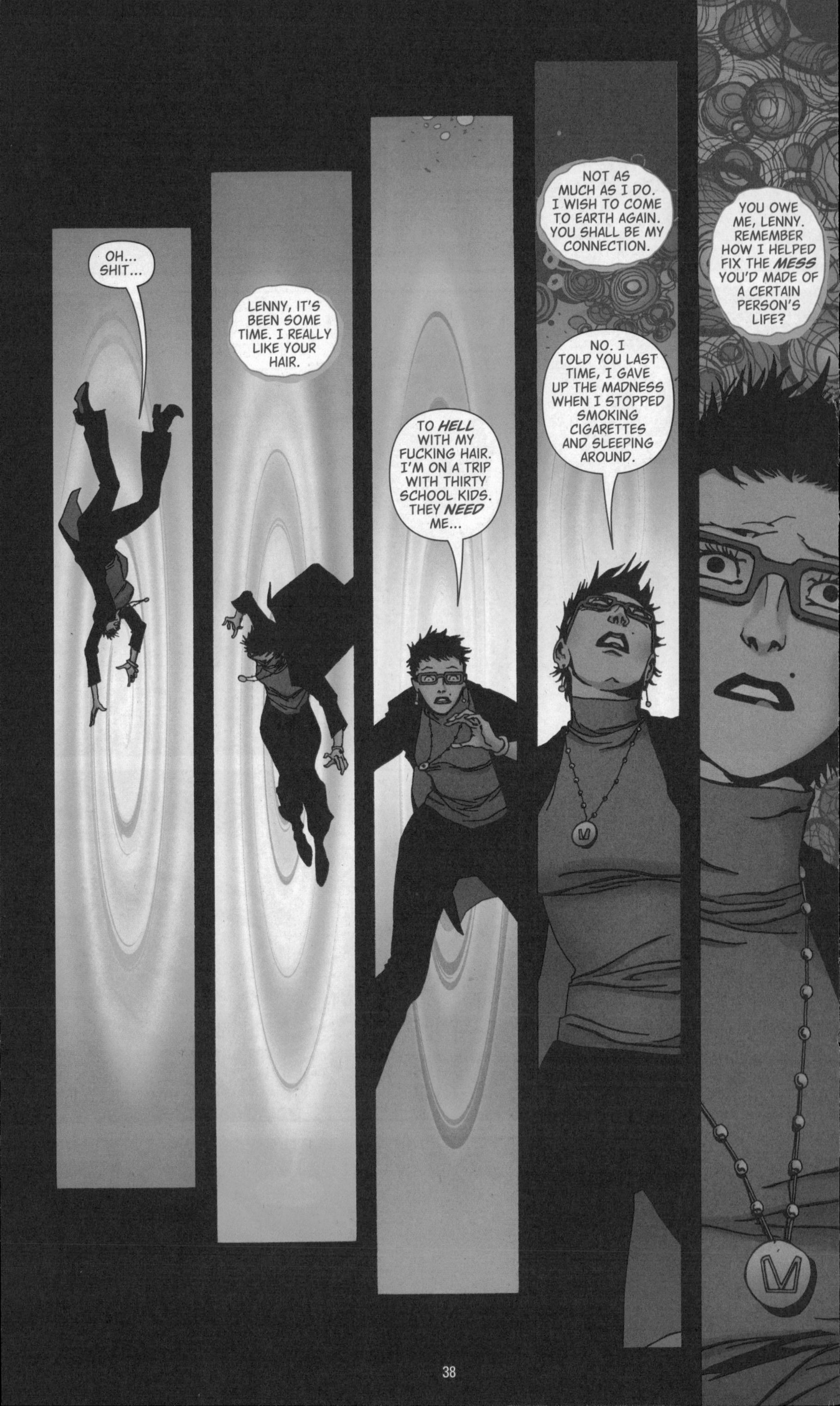
OH... SHIT...
LENNY, IT'S BEEN SOME TIME. I REALLY LIKE YOUR HAIR.
TO HELL WITH MY FUCKING HAIR. I'M ON A TRIP WITH THIRTY SCHOOL KIDS. THEY NEED ME...
NOT AS MUCH AS I DO. I WISH TO COME TO EARTH AGAIN. YOU SHALL BE MY CONNECTION.
NO. I TOLD YOU LAST TIME, I GAVE UP THE MADNESS WHEN I STOPPED SMOKING CIGARETTES AND SLEEPING AROUND.
YOU OWE ME, LENNY. REMEMBER HOW I HELPED FIX THE MESS YOU'D MADE OF A CERTAIN PERSON'S LIFE?

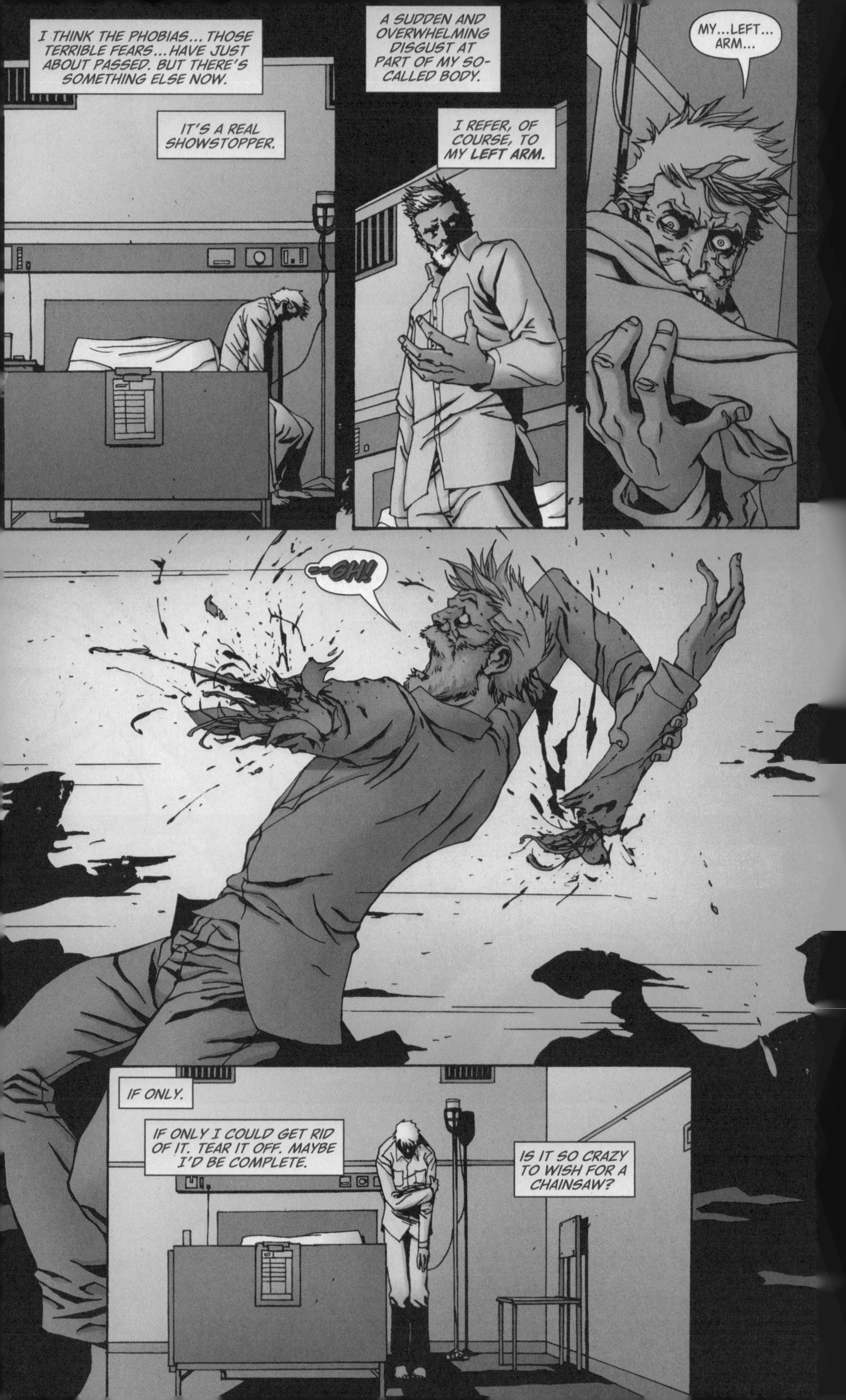

I THINK THE PHOBIAS... THOSE TERRIBLE FEARS... HAVE JUST ABOUT PASSED. BUT THERE'S SOMETHING ELSE NOW.
IT'S A REAL SHOWSTOPPER.
A SUDDEN AND OVERWHELMING DISGUST AT PART OF MY SO-CALLED BODY.
I REFER, OF COURSE, TO MY LEFT ARM.
MY...LEFT... ARM...
--GH!
IF ONLY.
IF ONLY I COULD GET RID OF IT. TEAR IT OFF. MAYBE I'D BE COMPLETE.
IS IT SO CRAZY TO WISH FOR A CHAINSAW?

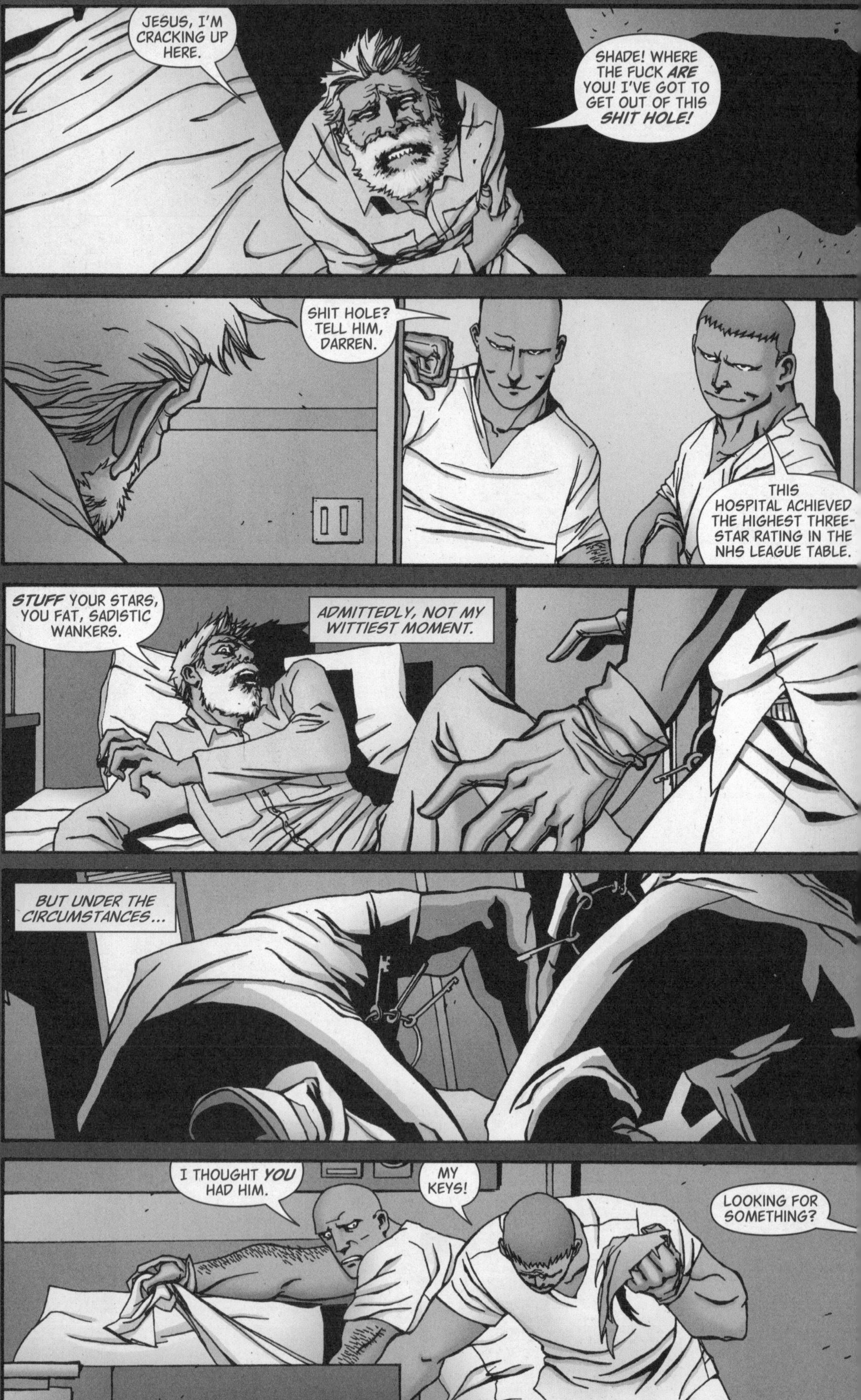
JESUS, I'M CRACKING UP HERE.
SHADE! WHERE THE FUCK ARE YOU! I'VE GOT TO GET OUT OF THIS SHIT HOLE!
SHIT HOLE? TELL HIM, DARREN.
THIS HOSPITAL ACHIEVED THE HIGHEST THREE-STAR RATING IN THE NHS LEAGUE TABLE.
STUFF YOUR STARS, YOU FAT, SADISTIC WANKERS.
ADMITTEDLY, NOT MY WITTIEST MOMENT.
BUT UNDER THE CIRCUMSTANCES...
I THOUGHT YOU HAD HIM.
MY KEYS!
LOOKING FOR SOMETHING?

 YOU WANT TO BE MORE CAREFUL OF THESE, LARD BOY.

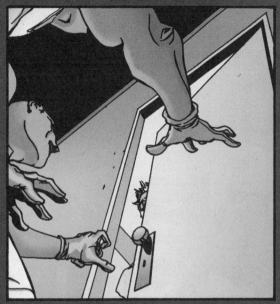

 DUM DE DUM DE DUM--

BNNCG BNNCG BNNCG

UNLOCK THIS FUCKING DOOR, YOU SKINNY PRICK!

 I'D MOVE FASTER WITHOUT THIS ARM ATTACHED TO ME. THIS *ALIEN* THING WEIGHING ME DOWN.

JOHN, MAN...

 DON'T KNOW HOW I'VE LIVED THIS LONG WITH SOMETHING SO ABHORRENT GLUED TO MY SHOULDER.

EXCUSE ME.

--GH!

 HE'S OUT.

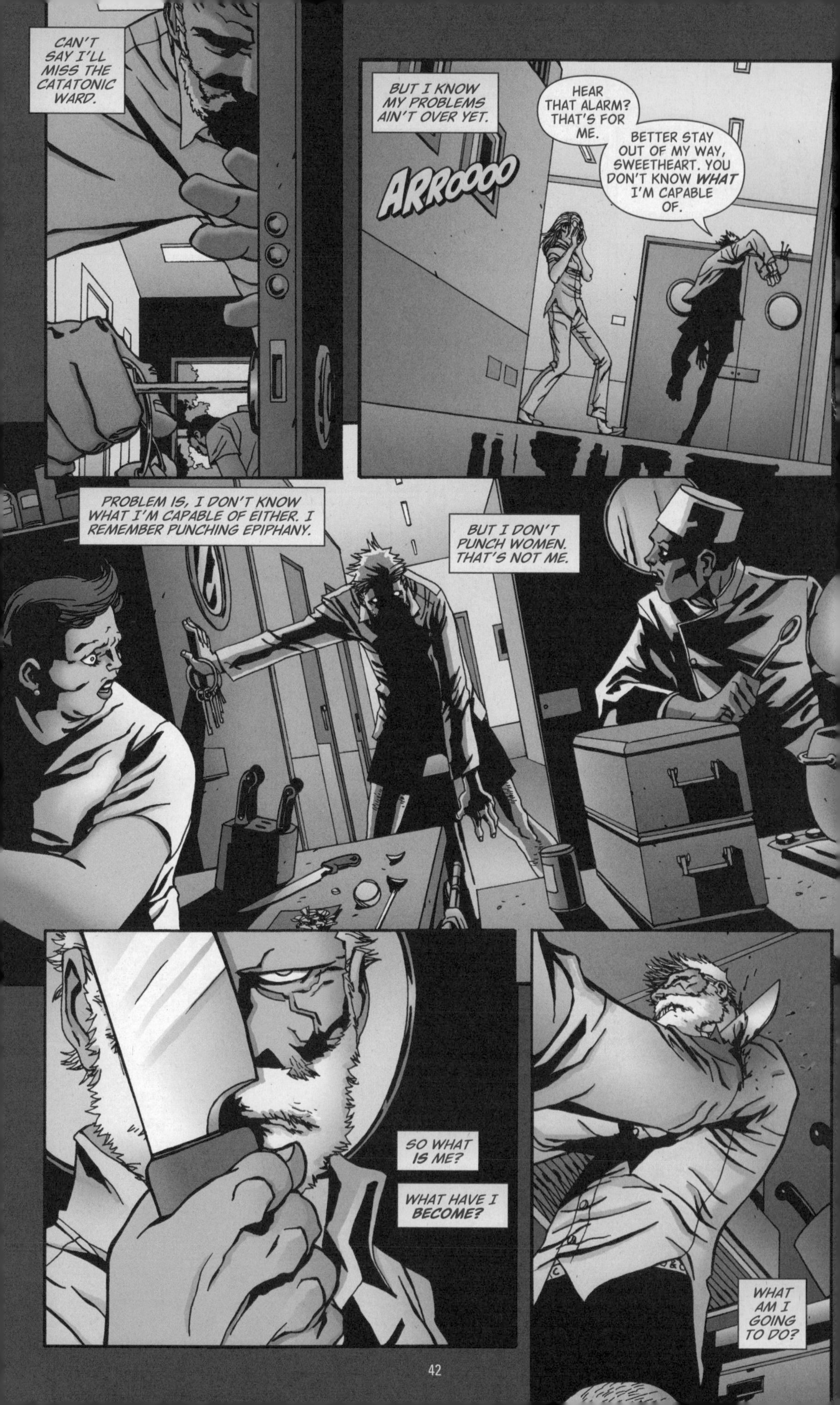
CAN'T SAY I'LL MISS THE CATATONIC WARD.
BUT I KNOW MY PROBLEMS AIN'T OVER YET.
ARROOOO
HEAR THAT ALARM? THAT'S FOR ME.
BETTER STAY OUT OF MY WAY, SWEETHEART. YOU DON'T KNOW WHAT I'M CAPABLE OF.
PROBLEM IS, I DON'T KNOW WHAT I'M CAPABLE OF EITHER. I REMEMBER PUNCHING EPIPHANY.
BUT I DON'T PUNCH WOMEN. THAT'S NOT ME.
SO WHAT IS ME?
WHAT HAVE I BECOME?
WHAT AM I GOING TO DO?

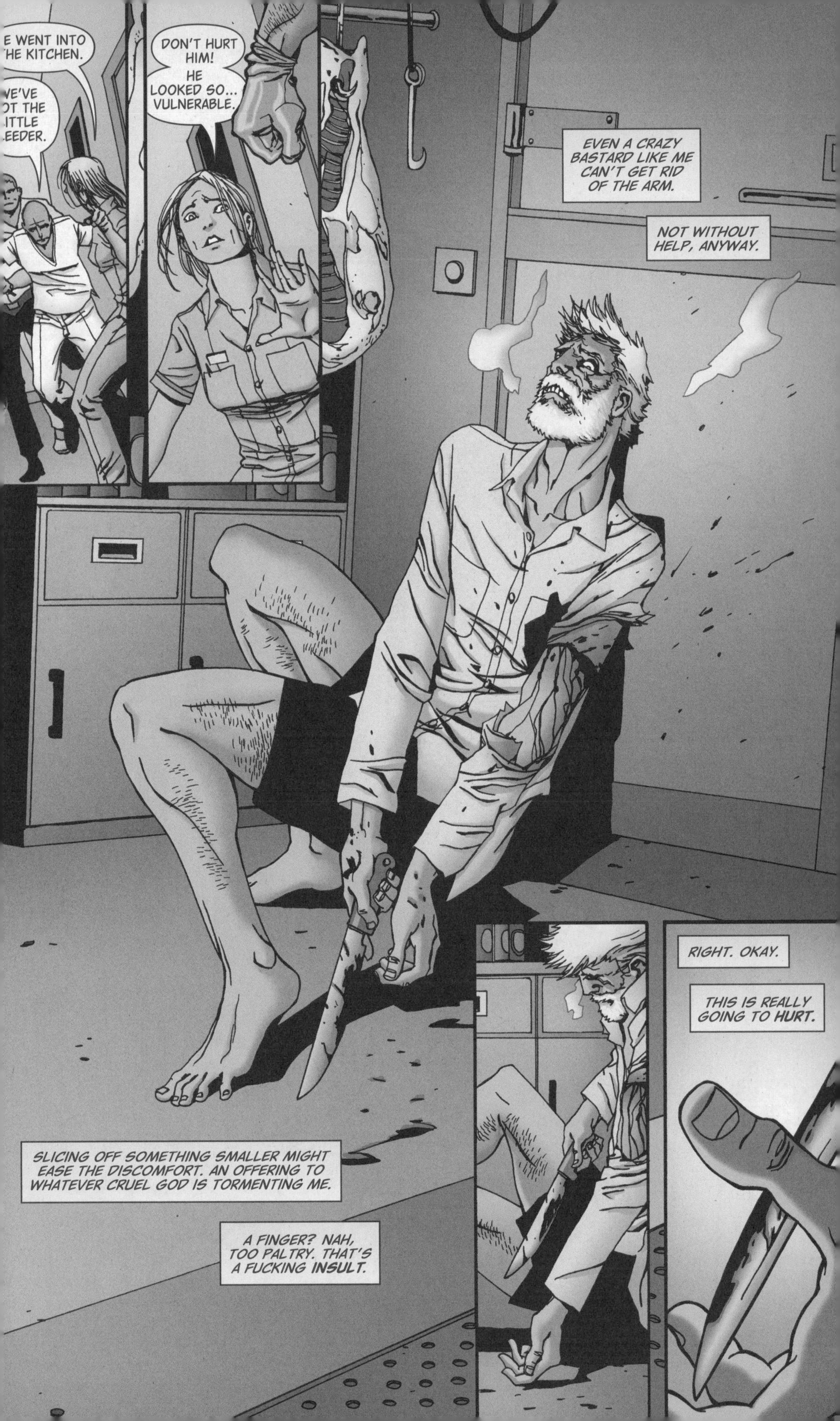
E WENT INTO
THE KITCHEN.
WE'VE
OT THE
ITTLE
EEDER.
DON'T HURT HIM! HE LOOKED SO... VULNERABLE.
EVEN A CRAZY BASTARD LIKE ME CAN'T GET RID OF THE ARM.
NOT WITHOUT HELP, ANYWAY.
SLICING OFF SOMETHING SMALLER MIGHT EASE THE DISCOMFORT. AN OFFERING TO WHATEVER CRUEL GOD IS TORMENTING ME.
A FINGER? NAH, TOO PALTRY. THAT'S A FUCKING INSULT.
RIGHT. OKAY.
THIS IS REALLY GOING TO HURT.

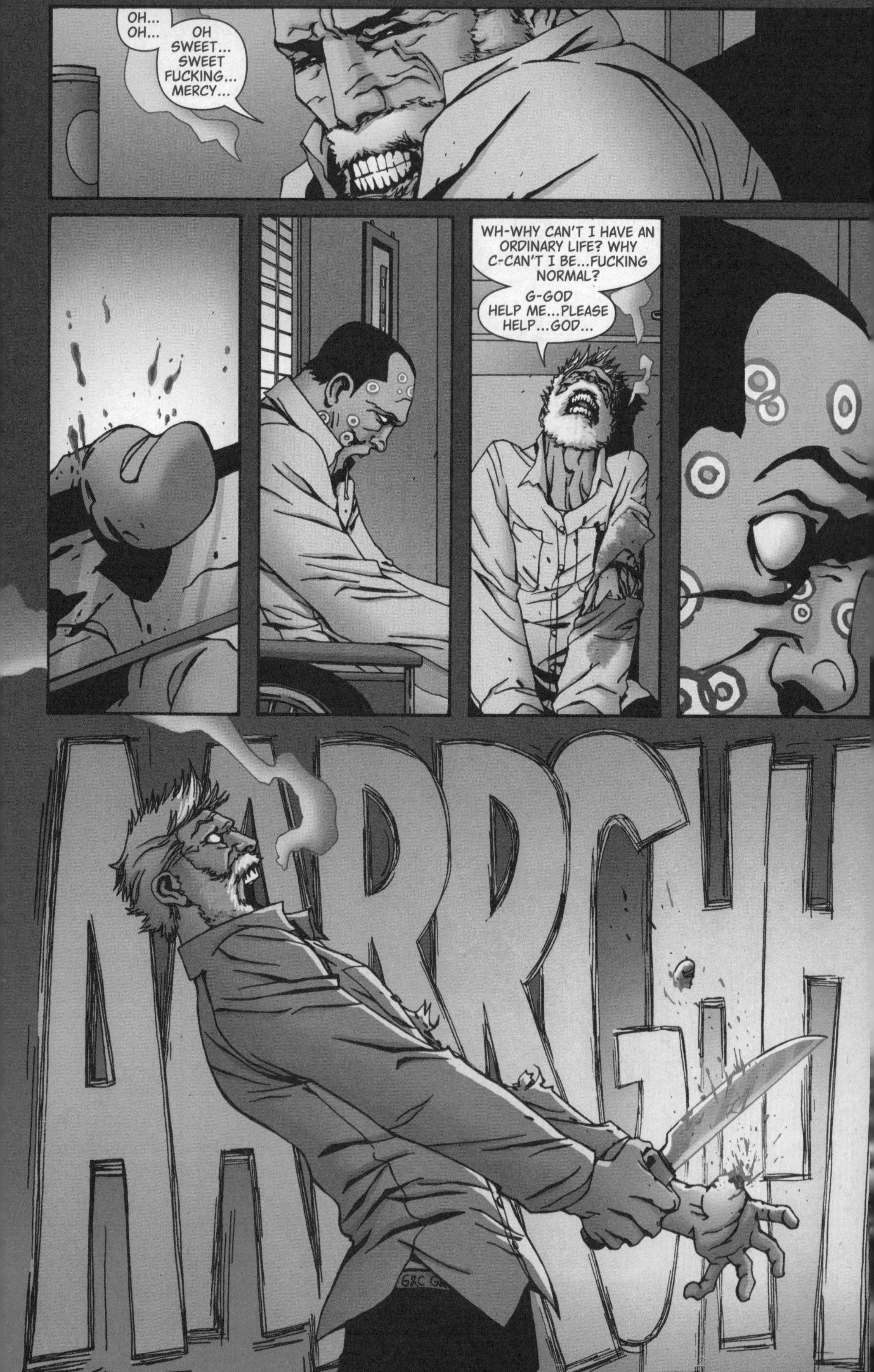
OH... OH...
OH SWEET... SWEET FUCKING... MERCY...
WH-WHY CAN'T I HAVE AN ORDINARY LIFE? WHY C-CAN'T I BE...FUCKING NORMAL?
G-GOD HELP ME...PLEASE HELP...GOD...
AARRGHH

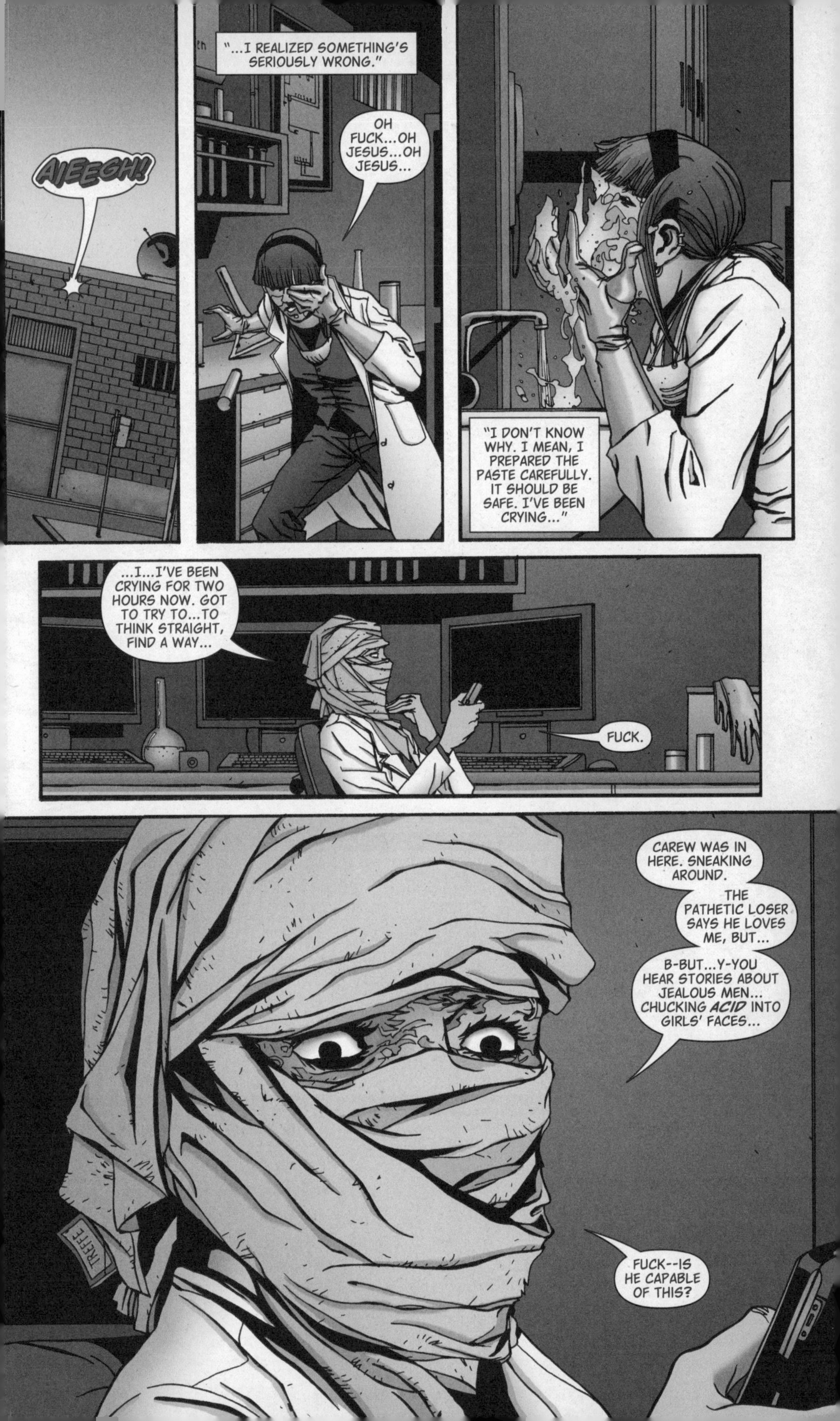
AIEEGH!!
"...I REALIZED SOMETHING'S SERIOUSLY WRONG."
OH FUCK...OH JESUS...OH JESUS...
"I DON'T KNOW WHY. I MEAN, I PREPARED THE PASTE CAREFULLY. IT SHOULD BE SAFE. I'VE BEEN CRYING..."
...I...I'VE BEEN CRYING FOR TWO HOURS NOW. GOT TO TRY TO...TO THINK STRAIGHT, FIND A WAY...
FUCK.
CAREW WAS IN HERE. SNEAKING AROUND.
THE PATHETIC LOSER SAYS HE LOVES ME, BUT...
B-BUT...Y-YOU HEAR STORIES ABOUT JEALOUS MEN... CHUCKING ACID INTO GIRLS' FACES...
FUCK--IS HE CAPABLE OF THIS?

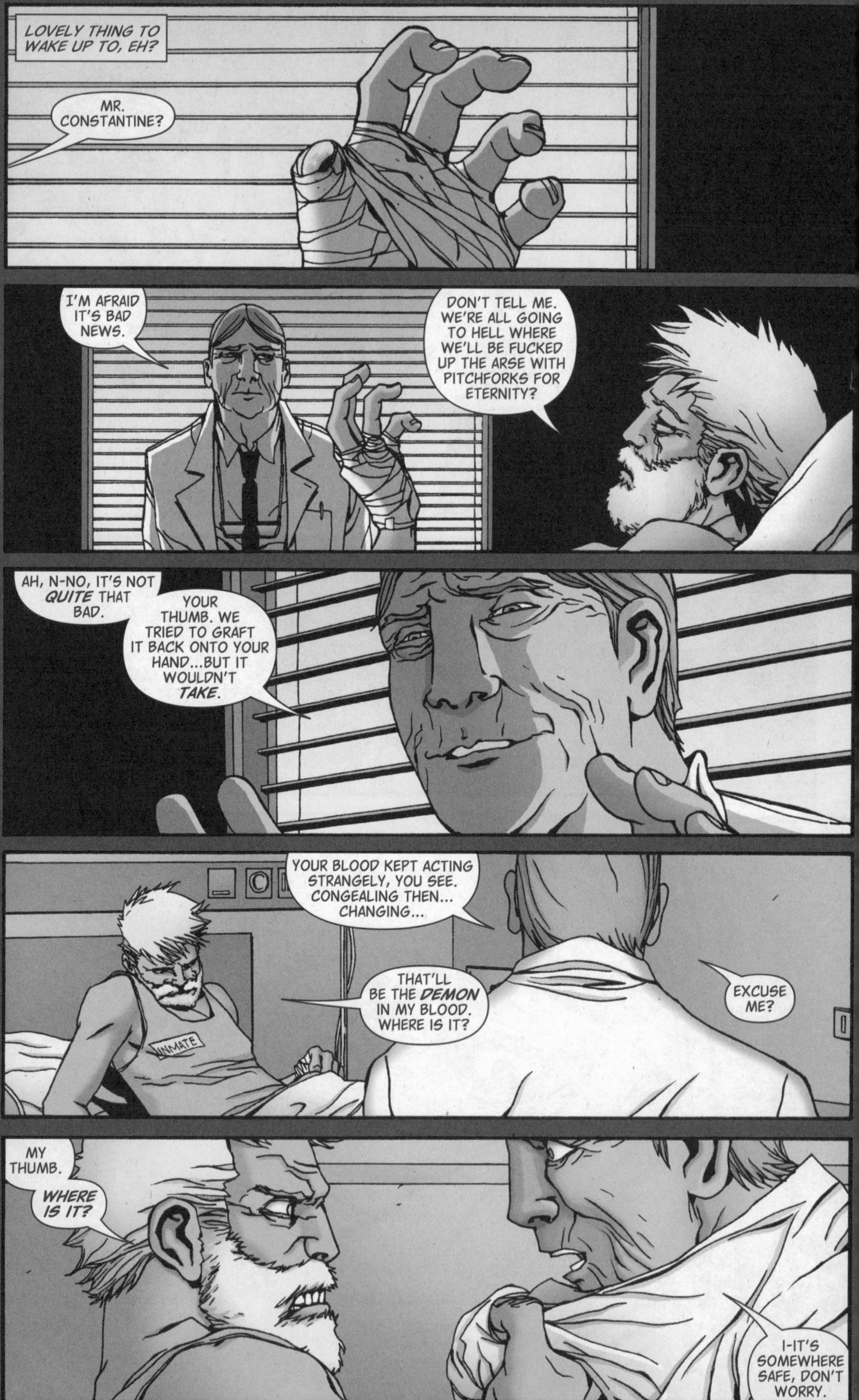
LOVELY THING TO WAKE UP TO, EH?
MR. CONSTANTINE?
I'M AFRAID IT'S BAD NEWS.
DON'T TELL ME. WE'RE ALL GOING TO HELL WHERE WE'LL BE FUCKED UP THE ARSE WITH PITCHFORKS FOR ETERNITY?
AH, N-NO, IT'S NOT QUITE THAT BAD.
YOUR THUMB. WE TRIED TO GRAFT IT BACK ONTO YOUR HAND...BUT IT WOULDN'T TAKE.
YOUR BLOOD KEPT ACTING STRANGELY, YOU SEE. CONGEALING THEN... CHANGING...
THAT'LL BE THE DEMON IN MY BLOOD. WHERE IS IT?
EXCUSE ME?
INMATE
MY THUMB. WHERE IS IT?
I-IT'S SOMEWHERE SAFE, DON'T WORRY.

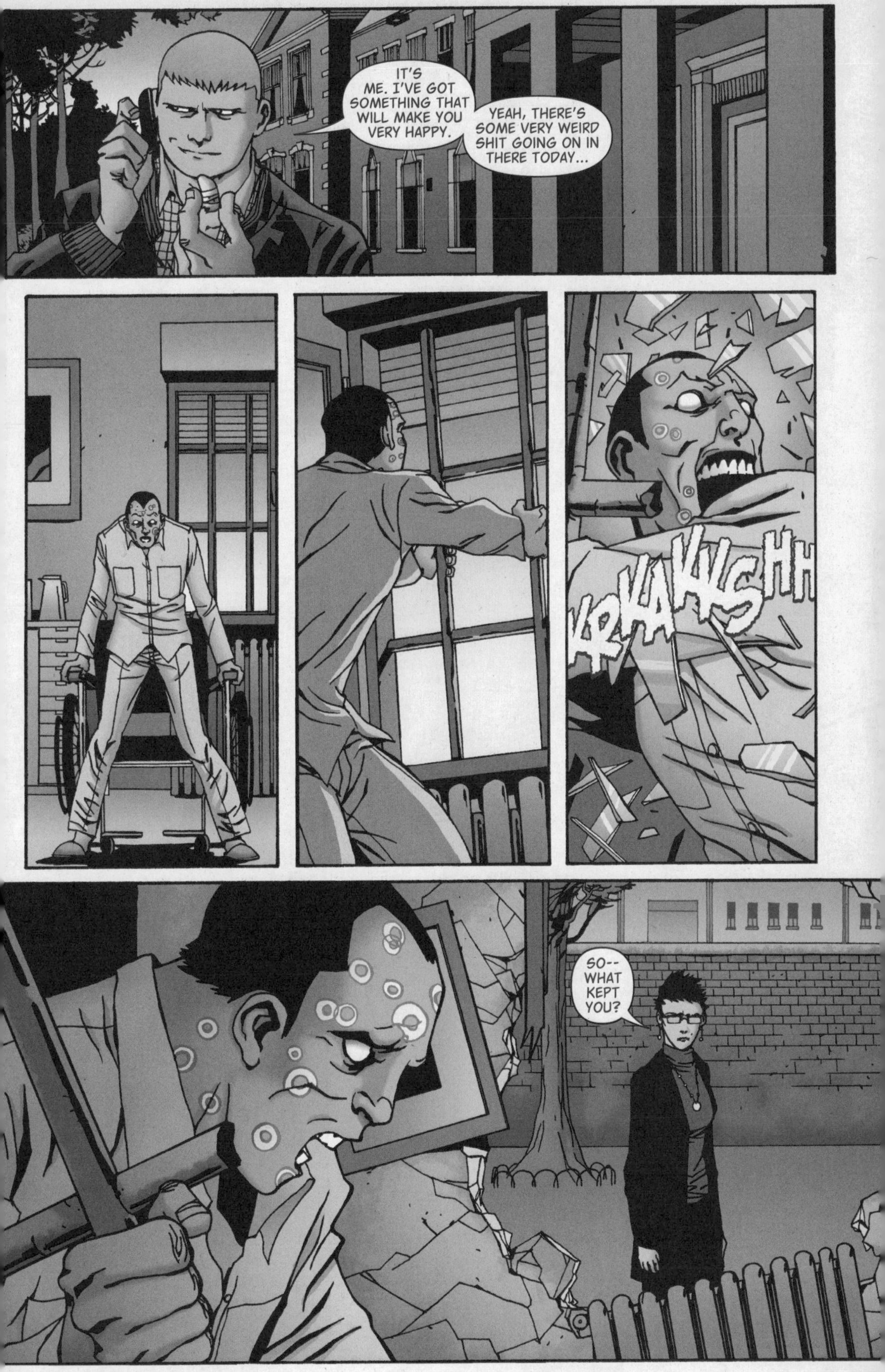
IT'S ME. I'VE GOT SOMETHING THAT WILL MAKE YOU VERY HAPPY.
YEAH, THERE'S SOME VERY WEIRD SHIT GOING ON IN THERE TODAY...
KRAKAKSHH
SO-- WHAT KEPT YOU?

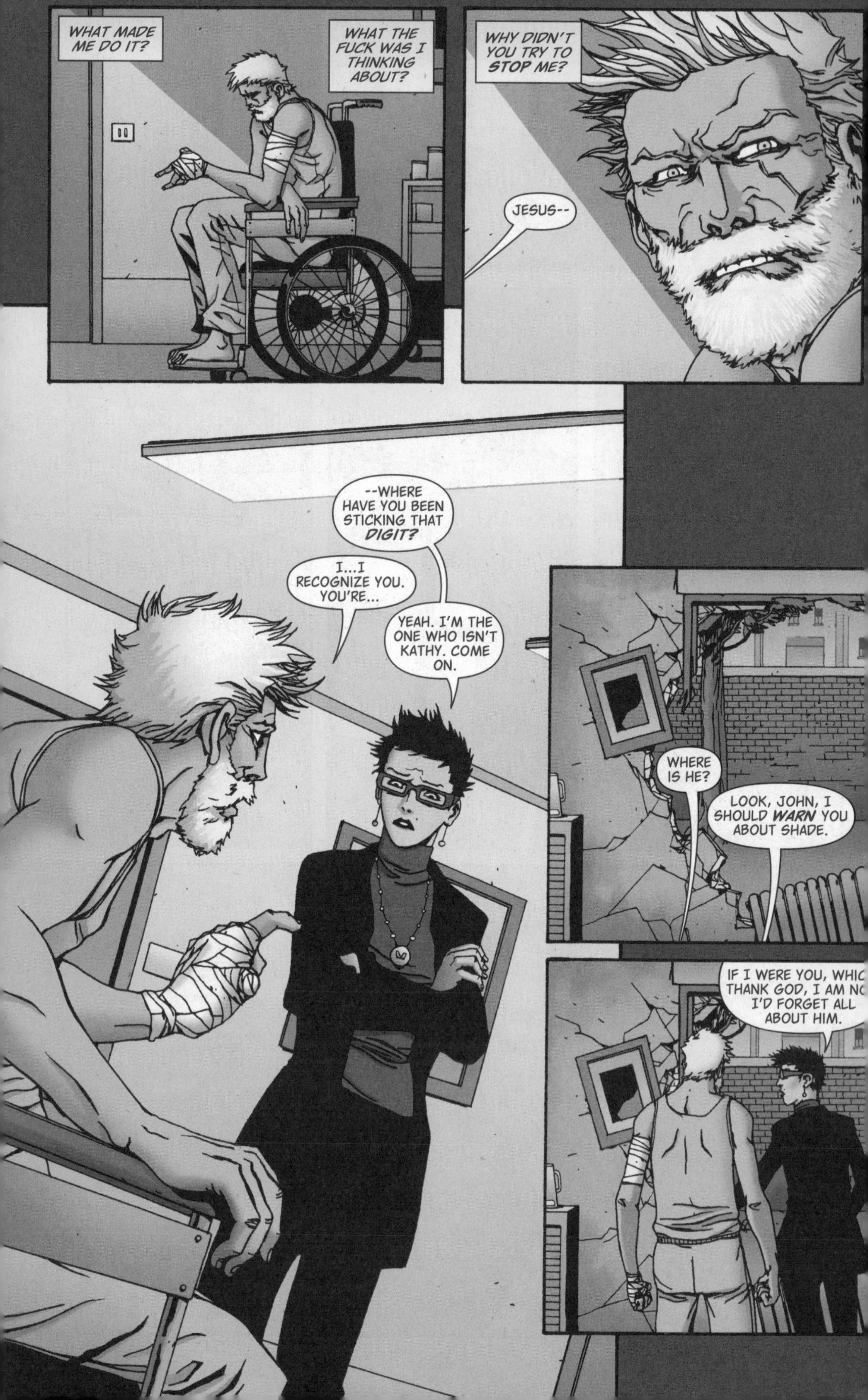
WHAT MADE ME DO IT?
WHAT THE FUCK WAS I THINKING ABOUT?
WHY DIDN'T YOU TRY TO STOP ME?
JESUS--
--WHERE HAVE YOU BEEN STICKING THAT DIGIT?
I...I RECOGNIZE YOU. YOU'RE...
YEAH. I'M THE ONE WHO ISN'T KATHY. COME ON.
WHERE IS HE?
LOOK, JOHN, I SHOULD WARN YOU ABOUT SHADE.
IF I WERE YOU, WHIC
THANK GOD, I AM NO
I'D FORGET ALL ABOUT HIM.

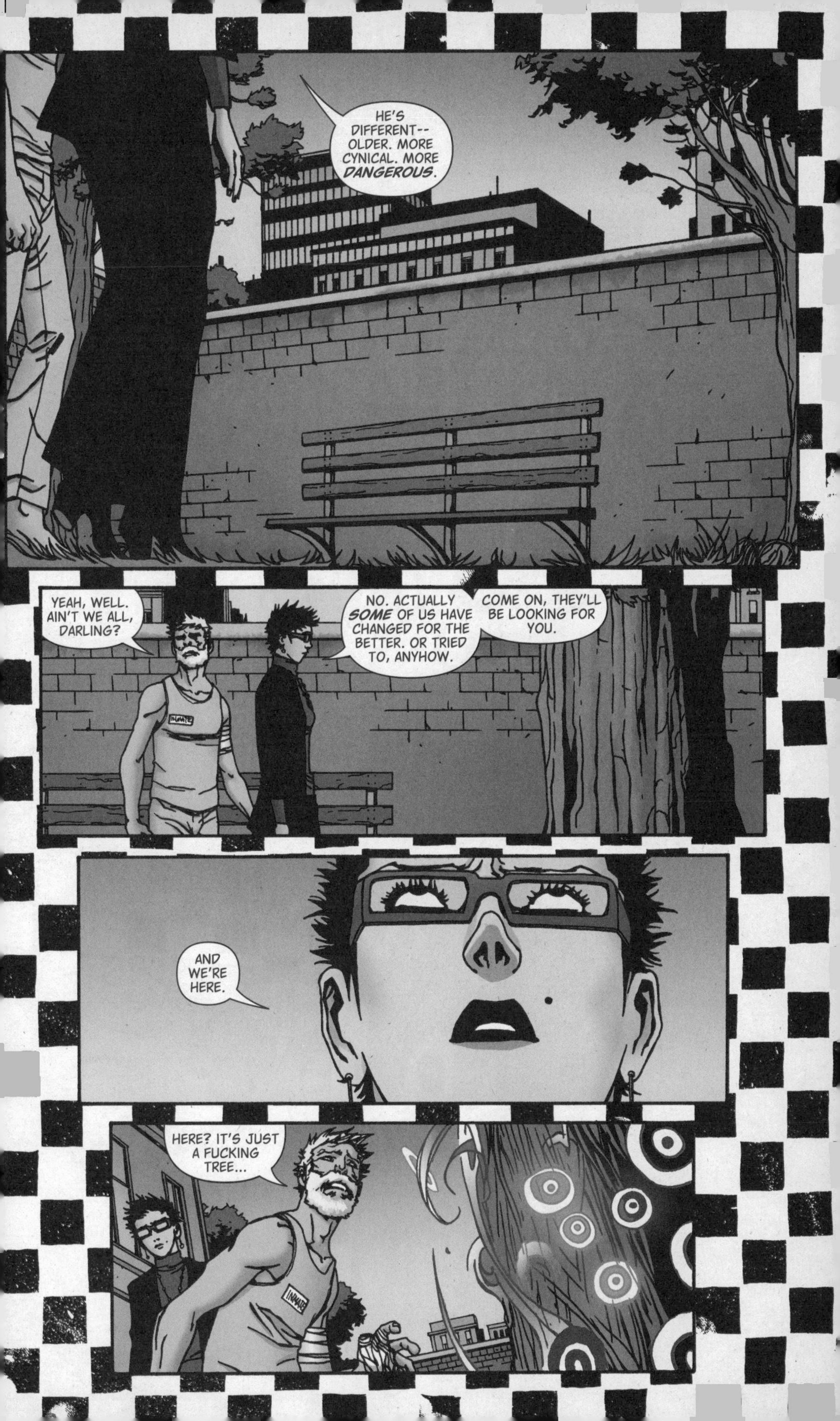
HE'S DIFFERENT-- OLDER. MORE CYNICAL. MORE DANGEROUS.
YEAH, WELL. AIN'T WE ALL, DARLING?
NO. ACTUALLY SOME OF US HAVE CHANGED FOR THE BETTER. OR TRIED TO, ANYHOW.
COME ON, THEY'LL BE LOOKING FOR YOU.
AND WE'RE HERE.
HERE? IT'S JUST A FUCKING TREE...

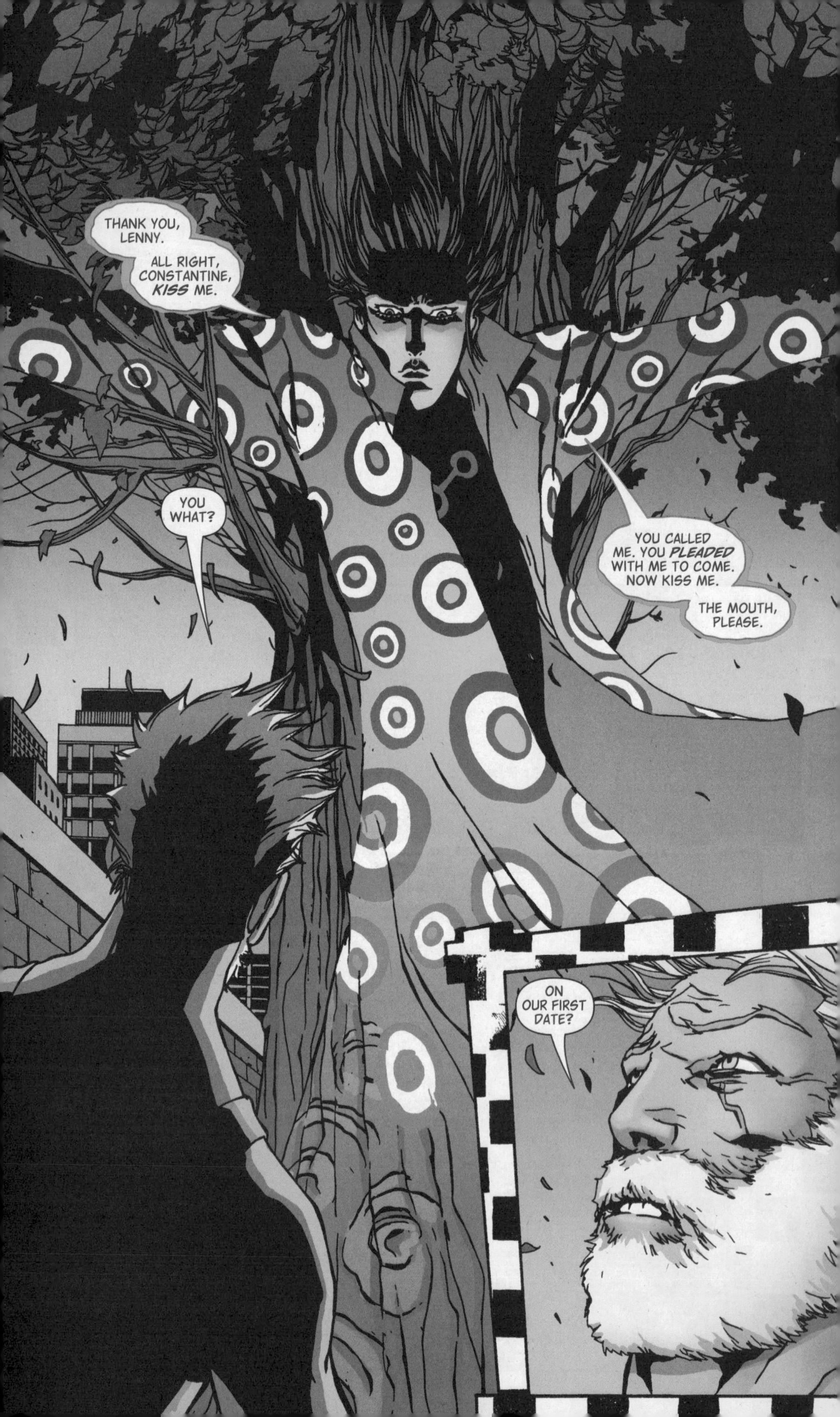
THANK YOU, LENNY.
ALL RIGHT, CONSTANTINE, *KISS* ME.
YOU WHAT?
YOU CALLED ME. YOU *PLEADED* WITH ME TO COME. NOW KISS ME.
THE MOUTH, PLEASE.
ON OUR FIRST DATE?

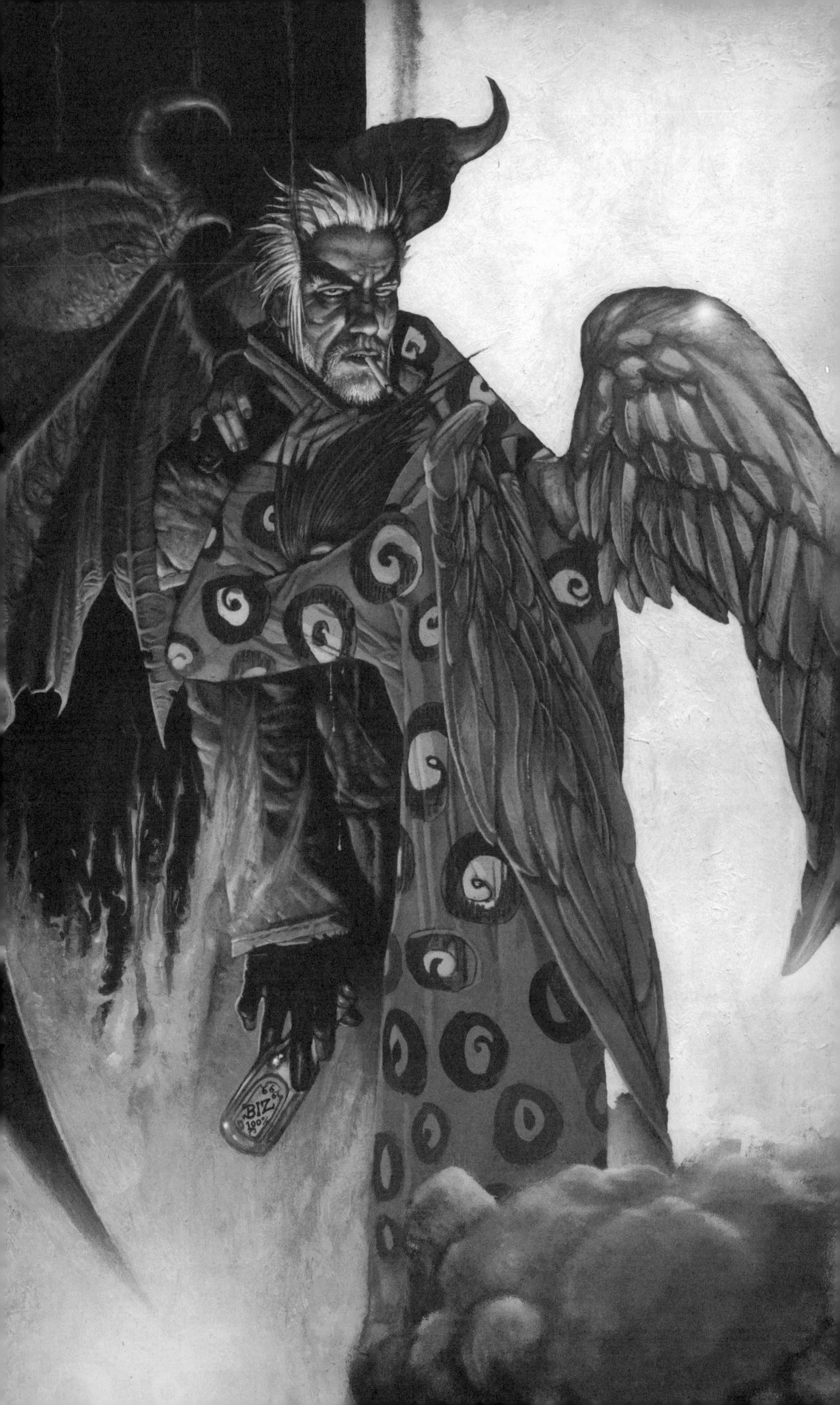
666
BIZ
190%

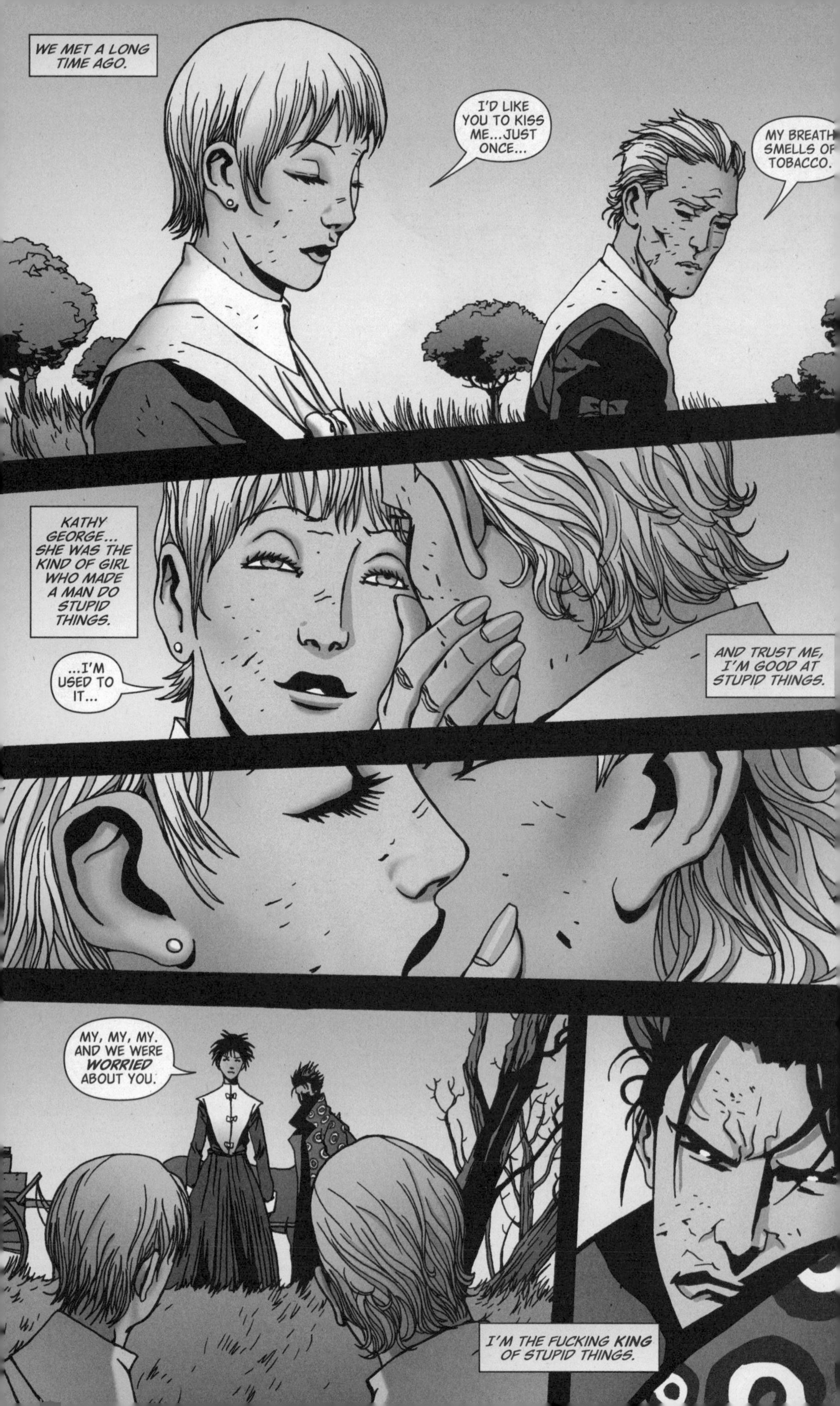
WE MET A LONG TIME AGO.
I'D LIKE YOU TO KISS ME...JUST ONCE...
MY BREATH SMELLS OF TOBACCO.
KATHY GEORGE... SHE WAS THE KIND OF GIRL WHO MADE A MAN DO STUPID THINGS.
...I'M USED TO IT...
AND TRUST ME, I'M GOOD AT STUPID THINGS.
MY, MY, MY. AND WE WERE WORRIED ABOUT YOU.
I'M THE FUCKING KING OF STUPID THINGS.

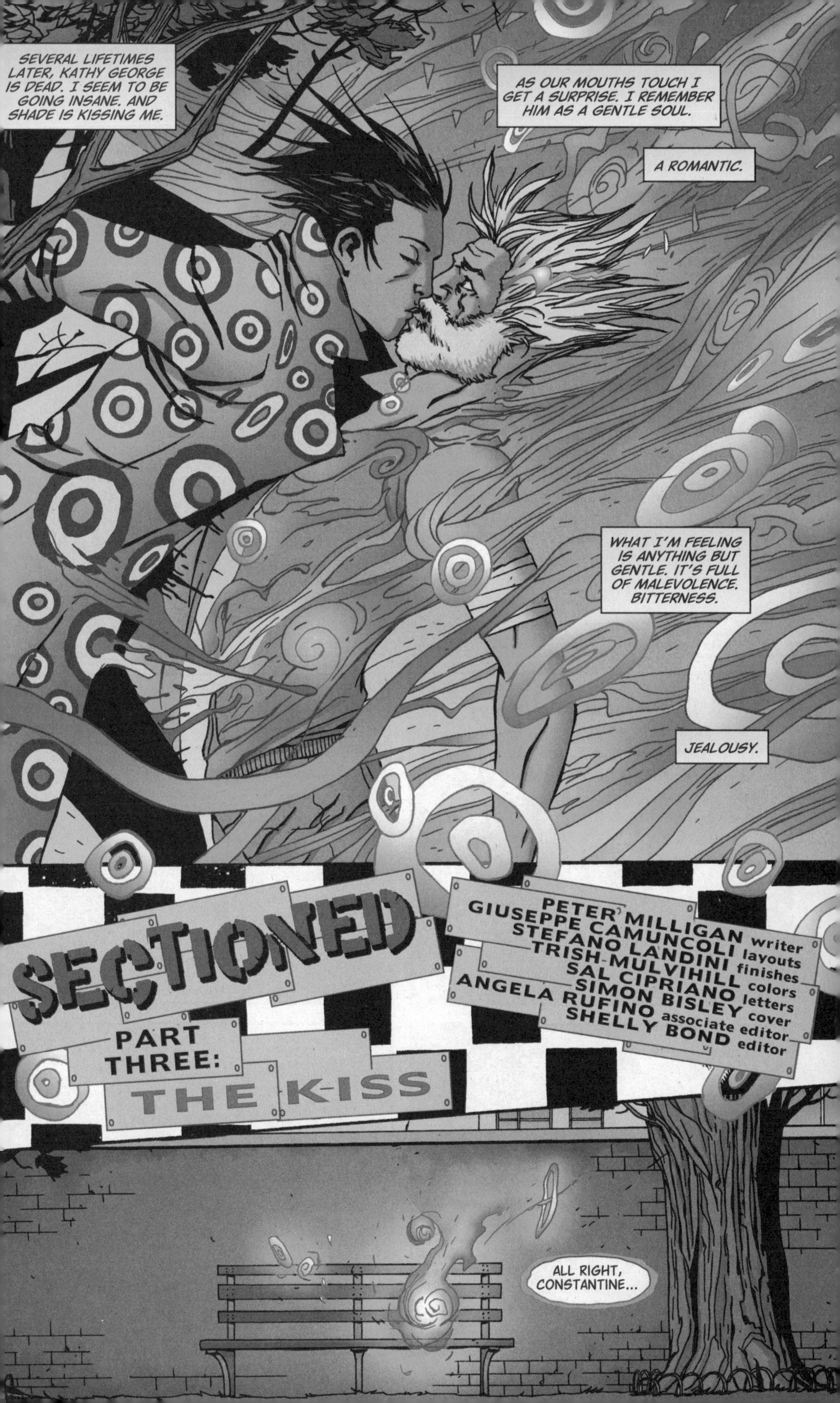
SEVERAL LIFETIMES LATER, KATHY GEORGE IS DEAD. I SEEM TO BE GOING INSANE. AND SHADE IS KISSING ME.
AS OUR MOUTHS TOUCH I GET A SURPRISE. I REMEMBER HIM AS A GENTLE SOUL.
A ROMANTIC.
WHAT I'M FEELING IS ANYTHING BUT GENTLE. IT'S FULL OF MALEVOLENCE. BITTERNESS.
JEALOUSY.
SECTIONED
PART THREE: THE KISS
PETER MILLIGAN writer
GIUSEPPE CAMUNCOLI layouts
STEFANO LANDINI finishes
TRISH MULVIHILL colors
SAL CIPRIANO letters
SIMON BISLEY cover
ANGELA RUFINO associate editor
SHELLY BOND editor
ALL RIGHT, CONSTANTINE...

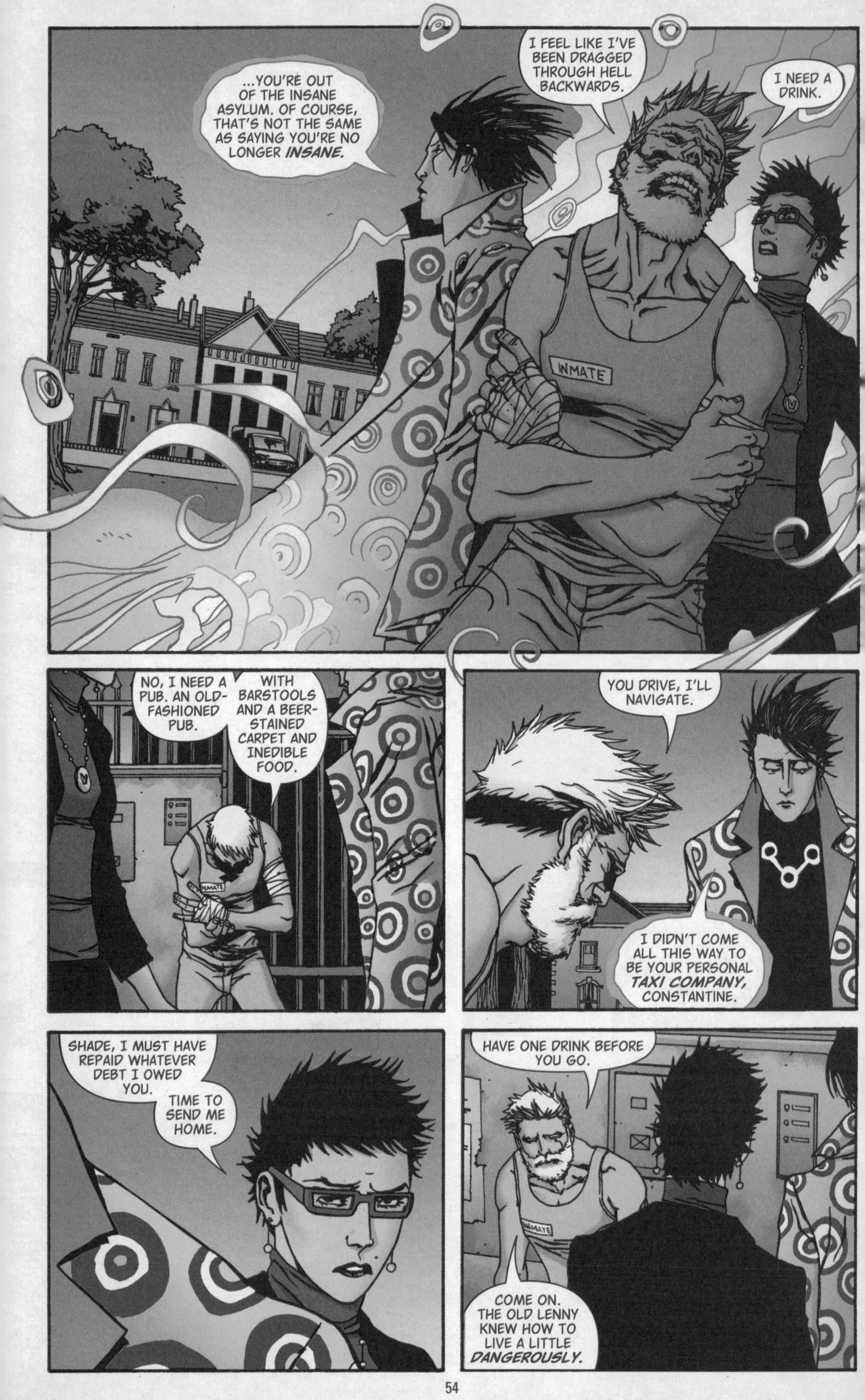
...YOU'RE OUT OF THE INSANE ASYLUM. OF COURSE, THAT'S NOT THE SAME AS SAYING YOU'RE NO LONGER *INSANE.*
I FEEL LIKE I'VE BEEN DRAGGED THROUGH HELL BACKWARDS.
I NEED A DRINK.
INMATE
NO, I NEED A PUB. AN OLD-FASHIONED PUB.
WITH BARSTOOLS AND A BEER-STAINED CARPET AND INEDIBLE FOOD.
YOU DRIVE, I'LL NAVIGATE.
I DIDN'T COME ALL THIS WAY TO BE YOUR PERSONAL *TAXI COMPANY,* CONSTANTINE.
SHADE, I MUST HAVE REPAID WHATEVER DEBT I OWED YOU.
TIME TO SEND ME HOME.
HAVE ONE DRINK BEFORE YOU GO.
COME ON. THE OLD LENNY KNEW HOW TO LIVE A LITTLE *DANGEROUSLY.*

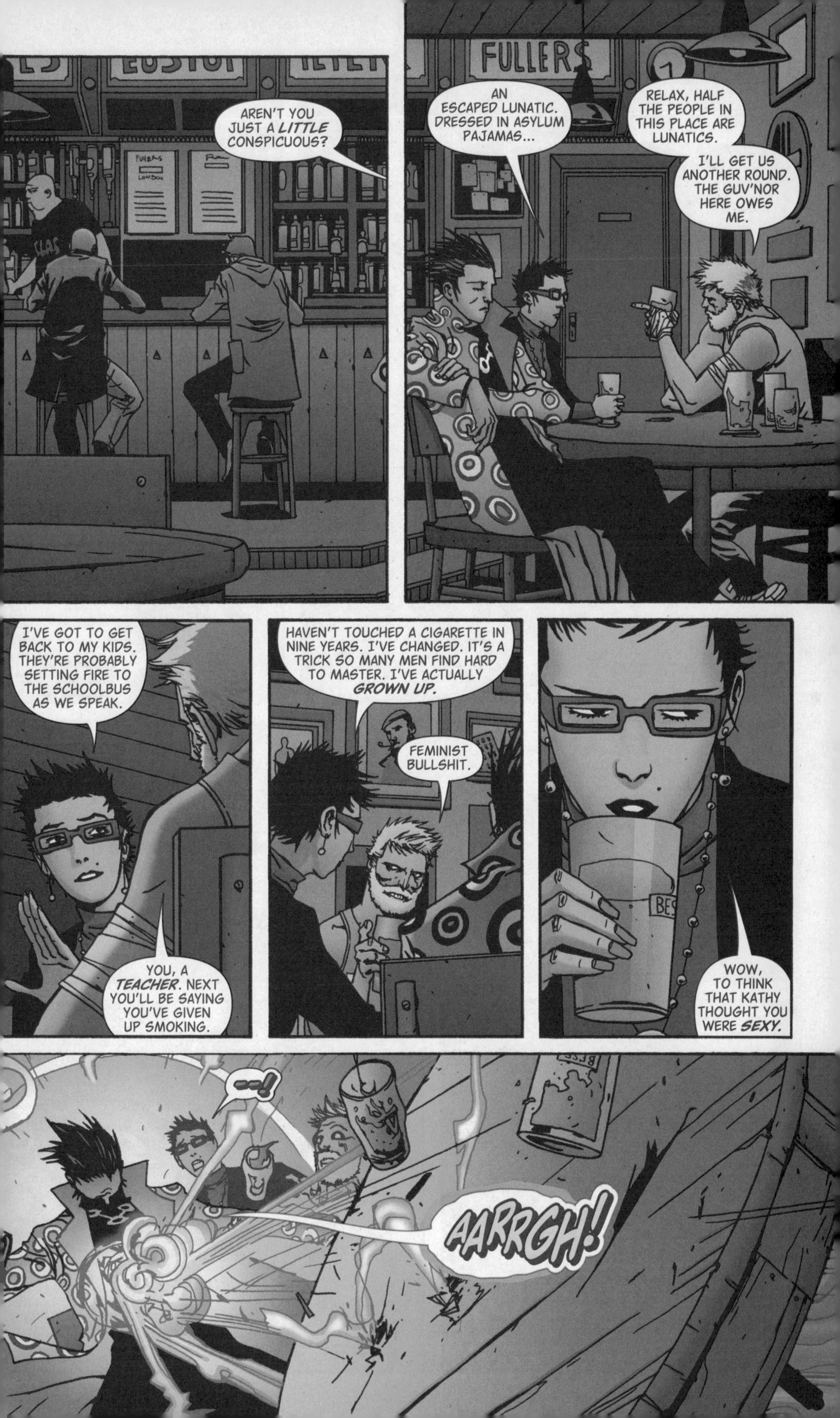
AREN'T YOU JUST A LITTLE CONSPICUOUS?
AN ESCAPED LUNATIC. DRESSED IN ASYLUM PAJAMAS...
RELAX, HALF THE PEOPLE IN THIS PLACE ARE LUNATICS.
I'LL GET US ANOTHER ROUND. THE GUV'NOR HERE OWES ME.
FULLERS
I'VE GOT TO GET BACK TO MY KIDS. THEY'RE PROBABLY SETTING FIRE TO THE SCHOOLBUS AS WE SPEAK.
YOU, A TEACHER. NEXT YOU'LL BE SAYING YOU'VE GIVEN UP SMOKING.
HAVEN'T TOUCHED A CIGARETTE IN NINE YEARS. I'VE CHANGED. IT'S A TRICK SO MANY MEN FIND HARD TO MASTER. I'VE ACTUALLY GROWN UP.
FEMINIST BULLSHIT.
WOW, TO THINK THAT KATHY THOUGHT YOU WERE SEXY.
AARRGH!

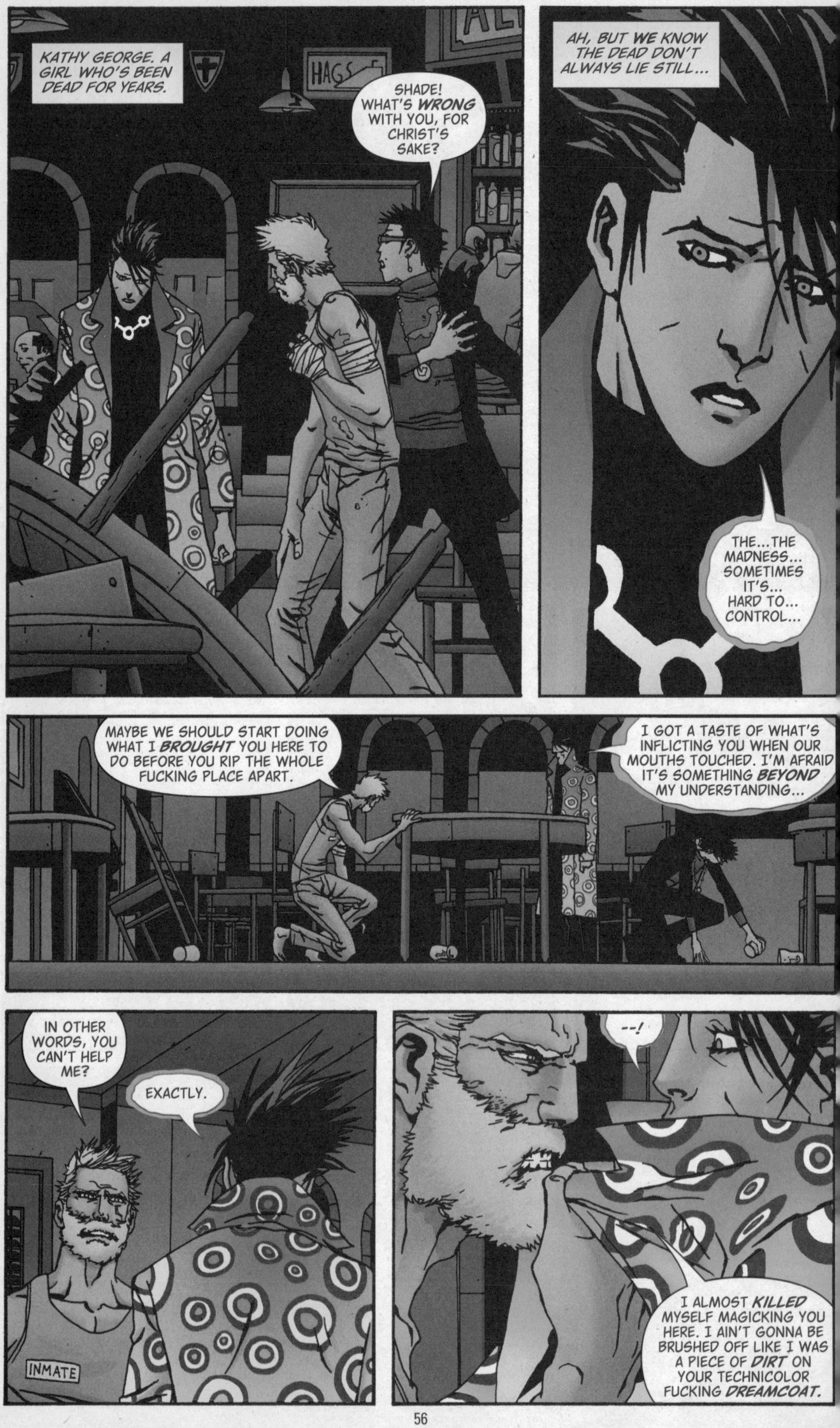

KATHY GEORGE. A GIRL WHO'S BEEN DEAD FOR YEARS.
SHADE! WHAT'S WRONG WITH YOU, FOR CHRIST'S SAKE?
AH, BUT WE KNOW THE DEAD DON'T ALWAYS LIE STILL...
THE...THE MADNESS... SOMETIMES IT'S... HARD TO... CONTROL...
MAYBE WE SHOULD START DOING WHAT I BROUGHT YOU HERE TO DO BEFORE YOU RIP THE WHOLE FUCKING PLACE APART.
I GOT A TASTE OF WHAT'S INFLICTING YOU WHEN OUR MOUTHS TOUCHED. I'M AFRAID IT'S SOMETHING BEYOND MY UNDERSTANDING...
IN OTHER WORDS, YOU CAN'T HELP ME?
EXACTLY.
INMATE
--!
I ALMOST KILLED MYSELF MAGICKING YOU HERE. I AIN'T GONNA BE BRUSHED OFF LIKE I WAS A PIECE OF DIRT ON YOUR TECHNICOLOR FUCKING DREAMCOAT.

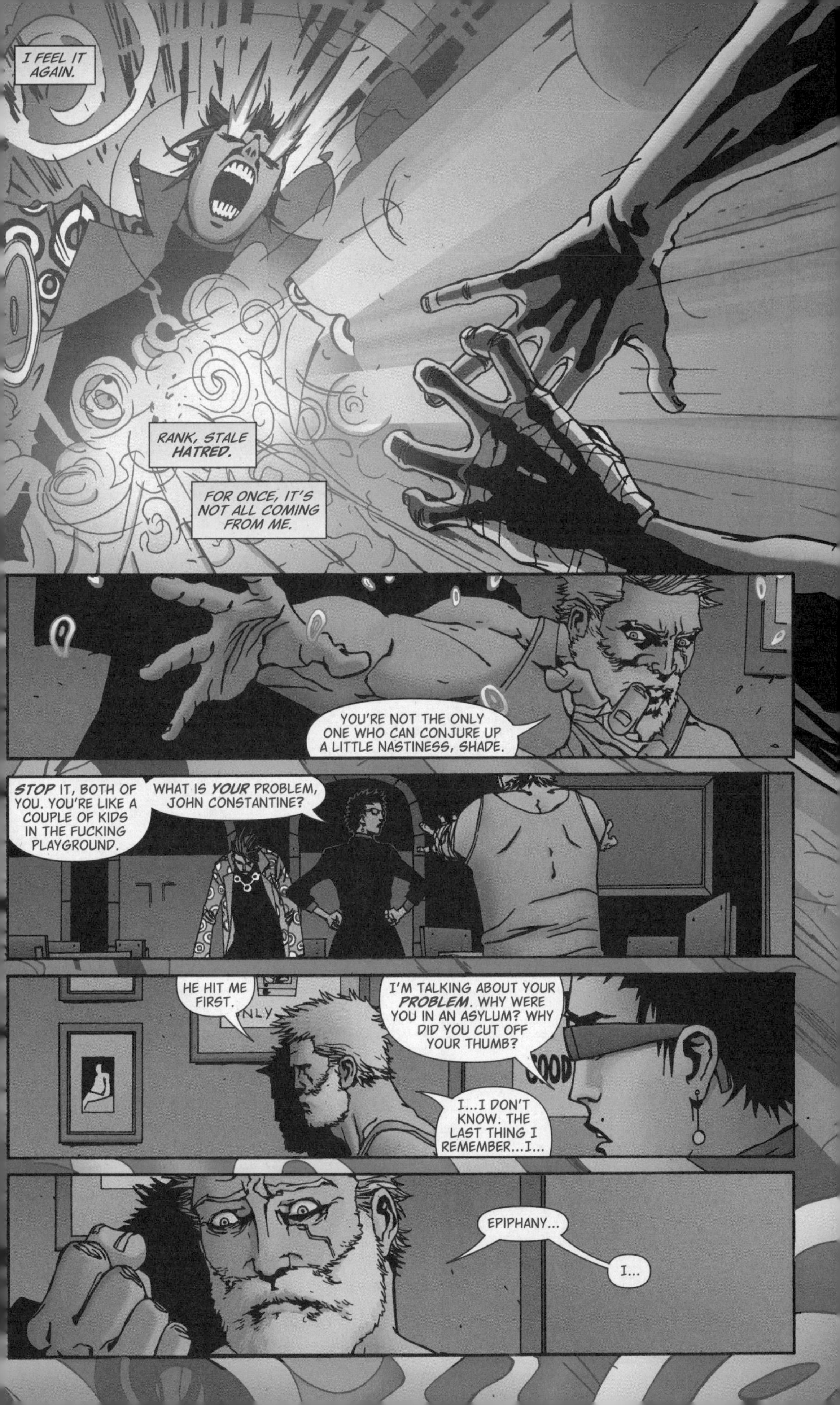
I FEEL IT AGAIN.
RANK, STALE HATRED.
FOR ONCE, IT'S NOT ALL COMING FROM ME.
YOU'RE NOT THE ONLY ONE WHO CAN CONJURE UP A LITTLE NASTINESS, SHADE.
STOP IT, BOTH OF YOU. YOU'RE LIKE A COUPLE OF KIDS IN THE FUCKING PLAYGROUND.
WHAT IS YOUR PROBLEM, JOHN CONSTANTINE?
HE HIT ME FIRST.
I'M TALKING ABOUT YOUR PROBLEM. WHY WERE YOU IN AN ASYLUM? WHY DID YOU CUT OFF YOUR THUMB?
I...I DON'T KNOW. THE LAST THING I REMEMBER...I...
EPIPHANY...
I...

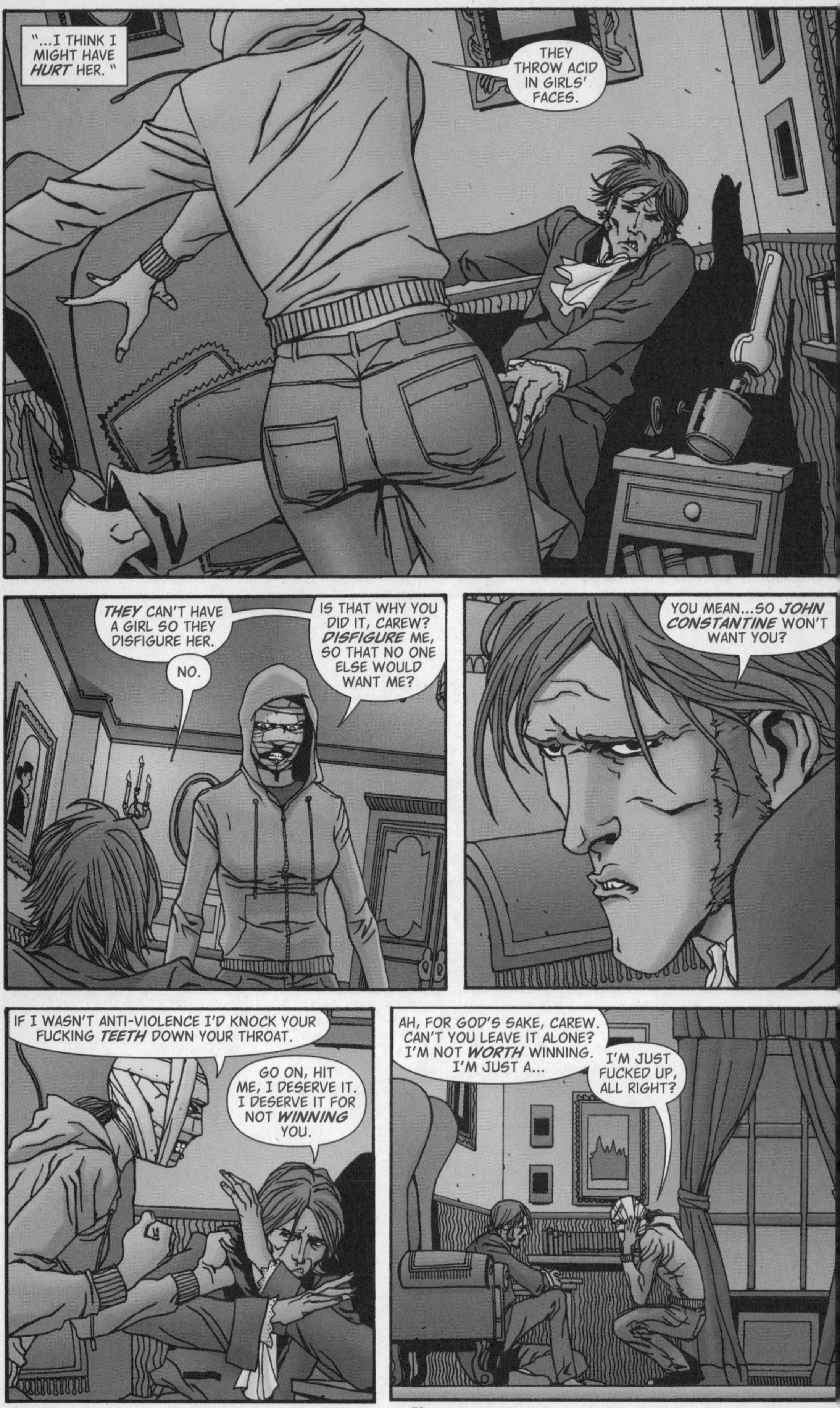
"...I THINK I MIGHT HAVE HURT HER."
THEY THROW ACID IN GIRLS' FACES.
THEY CAN'T HAVE A GIRL SO THEY DISFIGURE HER.
NO.
IS THAT WHY YOU DID IT, CAREW? DISFIGURE ME, SO THAT NO ONE ELSE WOULD WANT ME?
YOU MEAN...SO JOHN CONSTANTINE WON'T WANT YOU?
IF I WASN'T ANTI-VIOLENCE I'D KNOCK YOUR FUCKING TEETH DOWN YOUR THROAT.
GO ON, HIT ME, I DESERVE IT. I DESERVE IT FOR NOT WINNING YOU.
AH, FOR GOD'S SAKE, CAREW. CAN'T YOU LEAVE IT ALONE? I'M NOT WORTH WINNING. I'M JUST A...
I'M JUST FUCKED UP, ALL RIGHT?

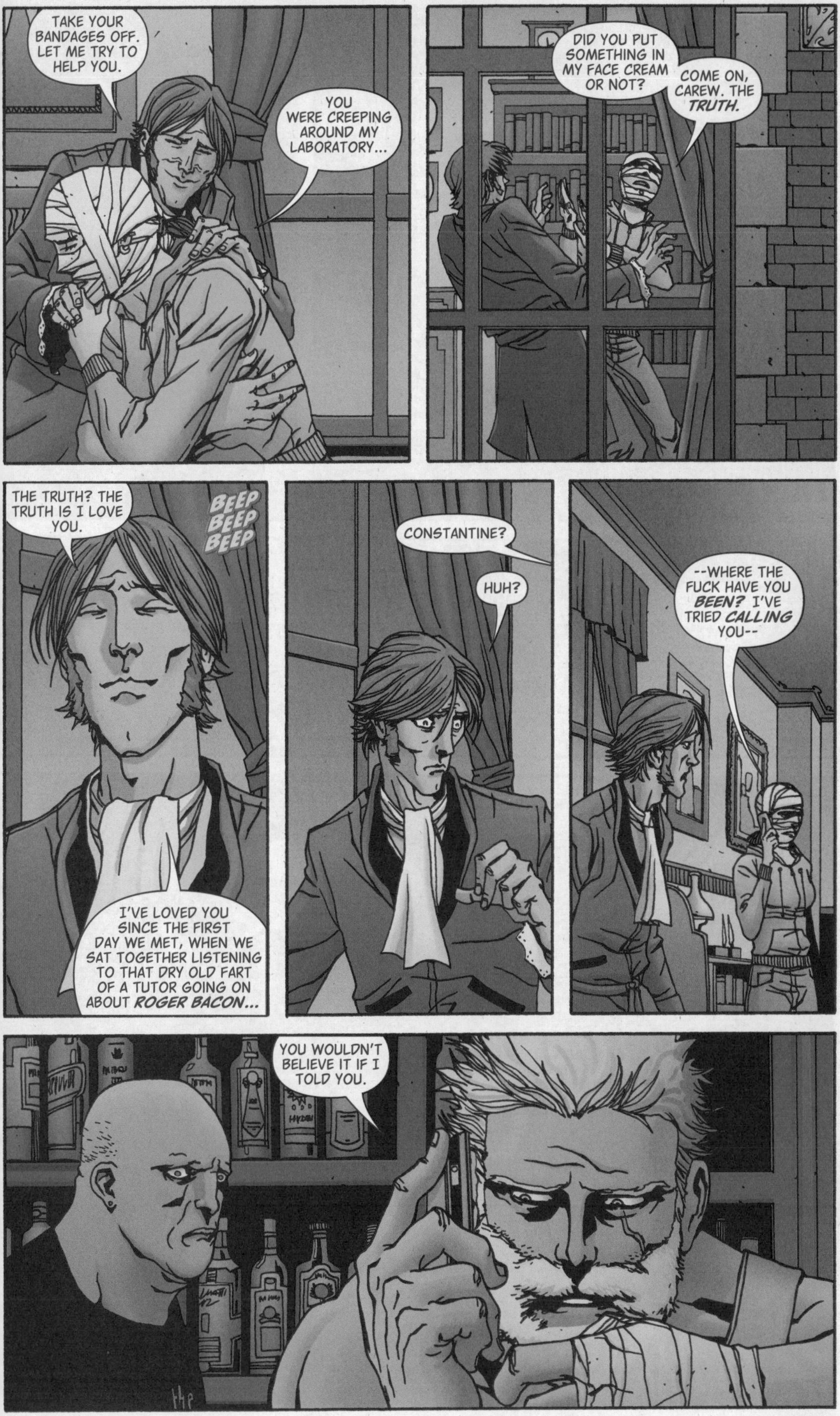
TAKE YOUR BANDAGES OFF. LET ME TRY TO HELP YOU.
YOU WERE CREEPING AROUND MY LABORATORY...
DID YOU PUT SOMETHING IN MY FACE CREAM OR NOT?
COME ON, CAREW. THE *TRUTH.*
THE TRUTH? THE TRUTH IS I LOVE YOU.
BEEP BEEP BEEP
I'VE LOVED YOU SINCE THE FIRST DAY WE MET, WHEN WE SAT TOGETHER LISTENING TO THAT DRY OLD FART OF A TUTOR GOING ON ABOUT *ROGER BACON...*
CONSTANTINE?
HUH?
--WHERE THE FUCK HAVE YOU *BEEN?* I'VE TRIED *CALLING* YOU--
YOU WOULDN'T BELIEVE IT IF I TOLD YOU.

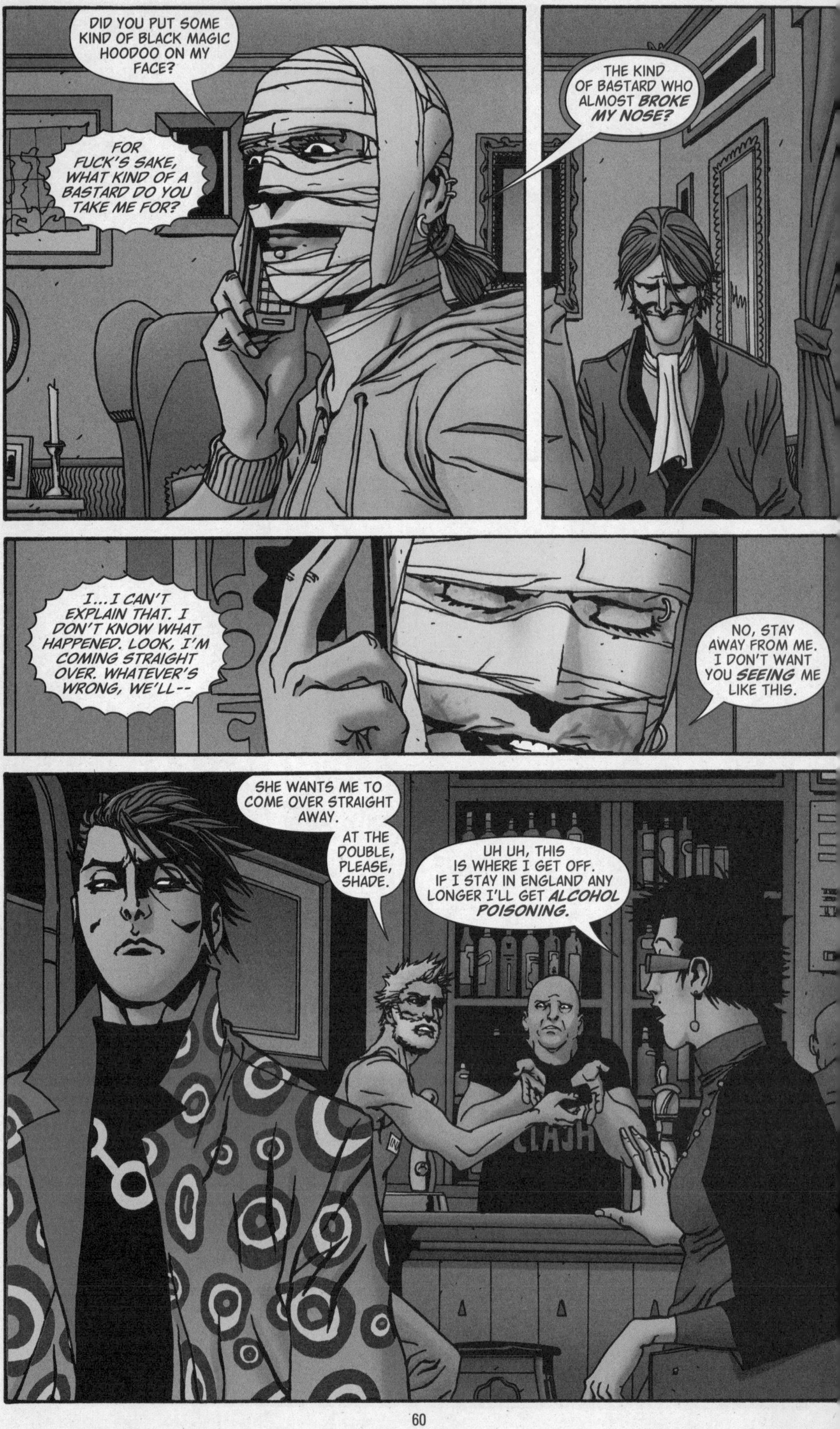
DID YOU PUT SOME KIND OF BLACK MAGIC HOODOO ON MY FACE?
FOR FUCK'S SAKE, WHAT KIND OF A BASTARD DO YOU TAKE ME FOR?
THE KIND OF BASTARD WHO ALMOST BROKE MY NOSE?
I...I CAN'T EXPLAIN THAT. I DON'T KNOW WHAT HAPPENED. LOOK, I'M COMING STRAIGHT OVER. WHATEVER'S WRONG, WE'LL--
NO, STAY AWAY FROM ME. I DON'T WANT YOU SEEING ME LIKE THIS.
SHE WANTS ME TO COME OVER STRAIGHT AWAY.
AT THE DOUBLE, PLEASE, SHADE.
UH UH, THIS IS WHERE I GET OFF. IF I STAY IN ENGLAND ANY LONGER I'LL GET ALCOHOL POISONING.

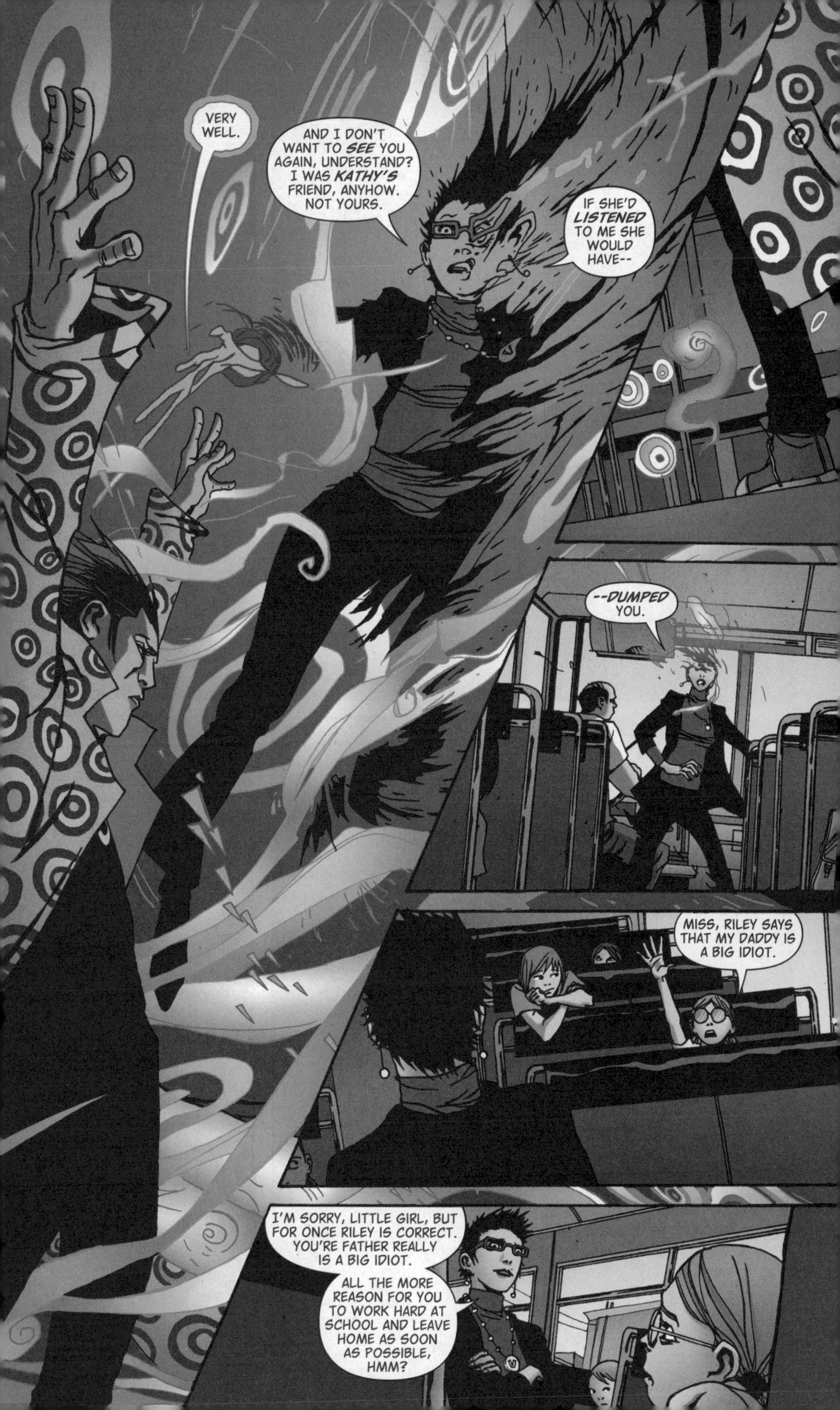
AND I DON'T WANT TO SEE YOU AGAIN, UNDERSTAND? I WAS KATHY'S FRIEND, ANYHOW. NOT YOURS.
VERY WELL.
IF SHE'D LISTENED TO ME SHE WOULD HAVE--
--DUMPED YOU.
MISS, RILEY SAYS THAT MY DADDY IS A BIG IDIOT.
I'M SORRY, LITTLE GIRL, BUT FOR ONCE RILEY IS CORRECT. YOU'RE FATHER REALLY IS A BIG IDIOT.
ALL THE MORE REASON FOR YOU TO WORK HARD AT SCHOOL AND LEAVE HOME AS SOON AS POSSIBLE, HMM?

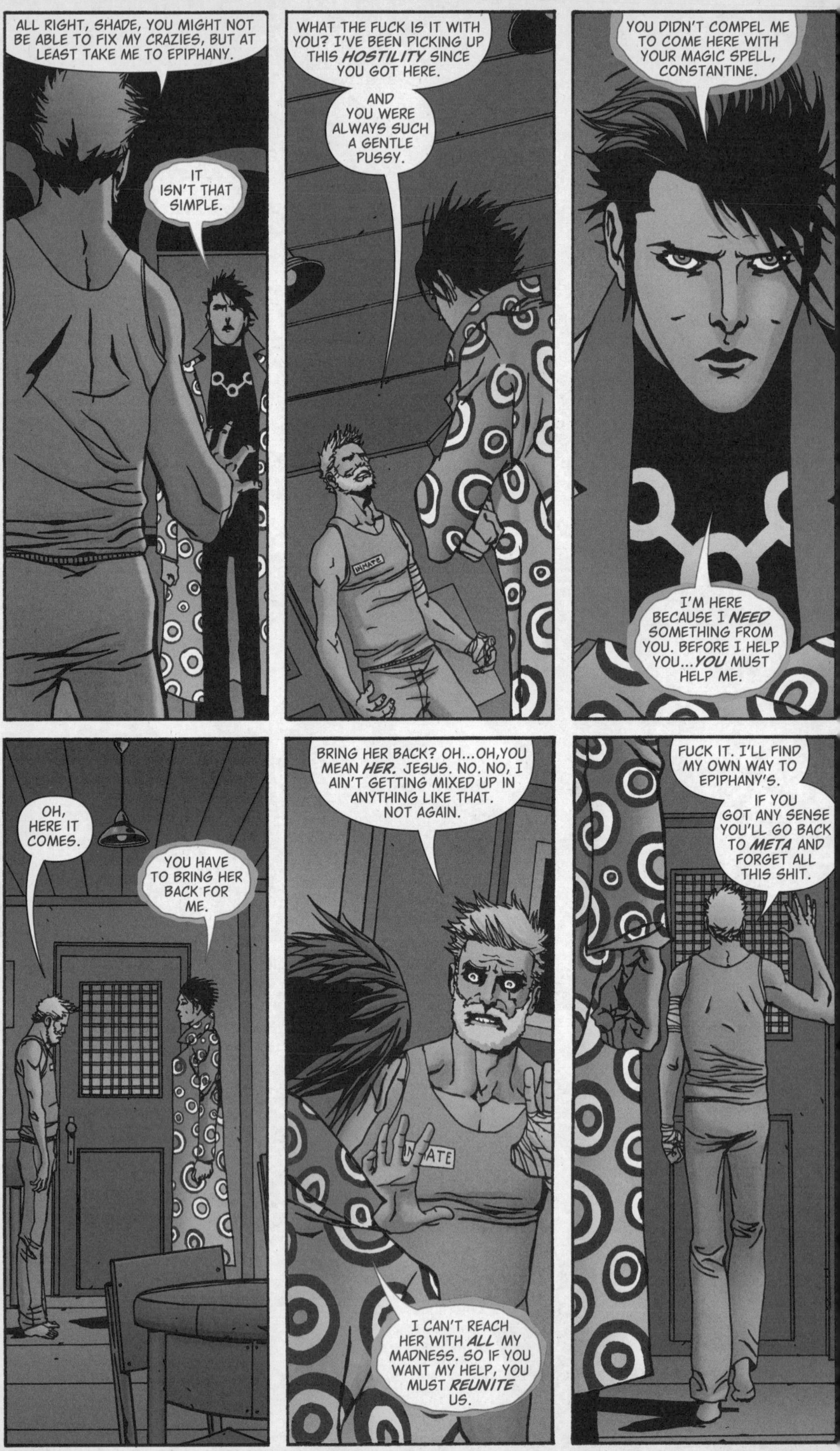
ALL RIGHT, SHADE, YOU MIGHT NOT BE ABLE TO FIX MY CRAZIES, BUT AT LEAST TAKE ME TO EPIPHANY.
IT ISN'T THAT SIMPLE.
WHAT THE FUCK IS IT WITH YOU? I'VE BEEN PICKING UP THIS HOSTILITY SINCE YOU GOT HERE.
AND YOU WERE ALWAYS SUCH A GENTLE PUSSY.
YOU DIDN'T COMPEL ME TO COME HERE WITH YOUR MAGIC SPELL, CONSTANTINE.
I'M HERE BECAUSE I NEED SOMETHING FROM YOU. BEFORE I HELP YOU...YOU MUST HELP ME.
OH, HERE IT COMES.
YOU HAVE TO BRING HER BACK FOR ME.
BRING HER BACK? OH...OH,YOU MEAN HER. JESUS. NO. NO, I AIN'T GETTING MIXED UP IN ANYTHING LIKE THAT. NOT AGAIN.
INMATE
I CAN'T REACH HER WITH ALL MY MADNESS. SO IF YOU WANT MY HELP, YOU MUST REUNITE US.
FUCK IT. I'LL FIND MY OWN WAY TO EPIPHANY'S.
IF YOU GOT ANY SENSE YOU'LL GO BACK TO META AND FORGET ALL THIS SHIT.

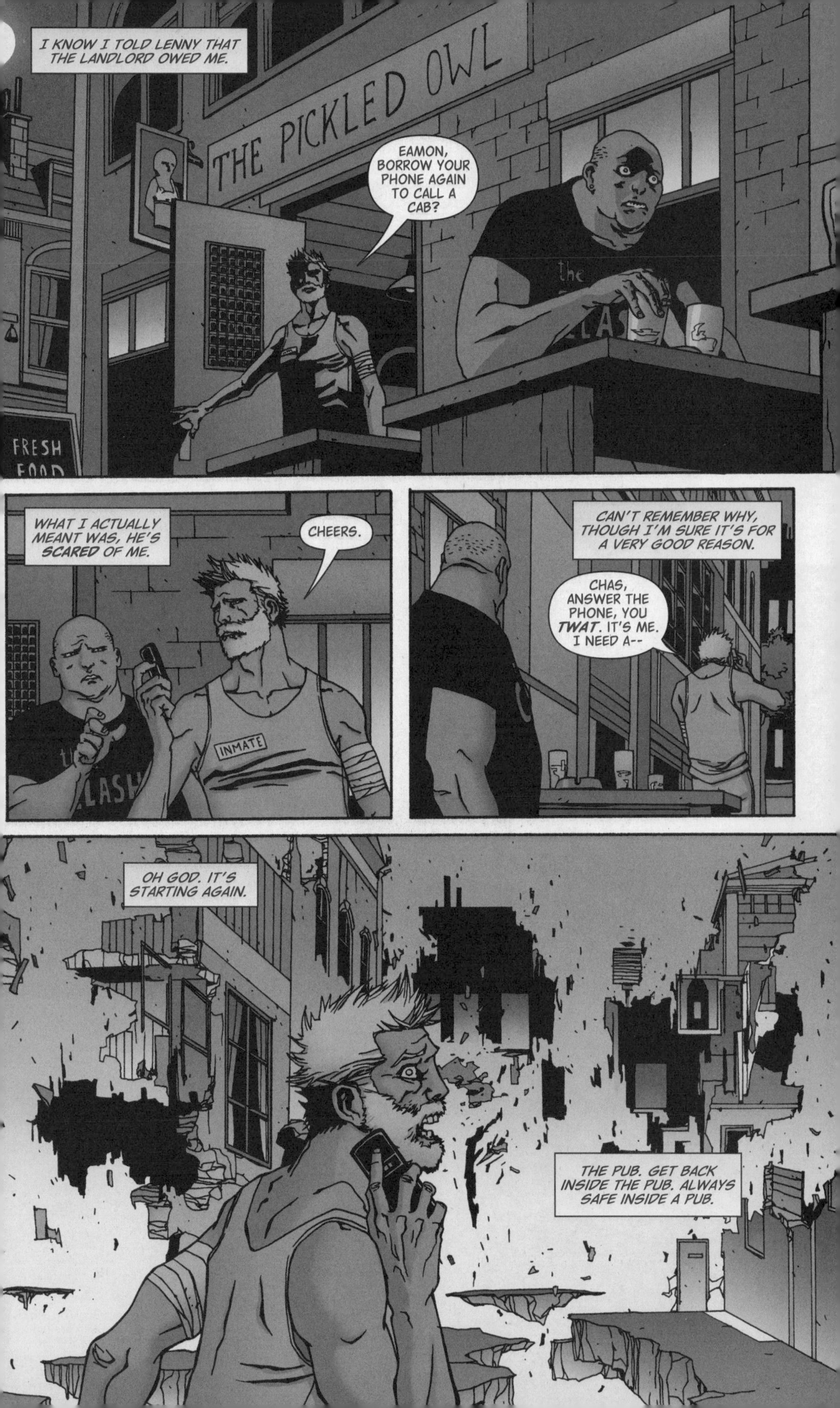
I KNOW I TOLD LENNY THAT THE LANDLORD OWED ME.
THE PICKLED OWL
EAMON, BORROW YOUR PHONE AGAIN TO CALL A CAB?
FRESH FOOD
WHAT I ACTUALLY MEANT WAS, HE'S SCARED OF ME.
CHEERS.
INMATE
CAN'T REMEMBER WHY, THOUGH I'M SURE IT'S FOR A VERY GOOD REASON.
CHAS, ANSWER THE PHONE, YOU TWAT. IT'S ME. I NEED A--
OH GOD. IT'S STARTING AGAIN.
THE PUB. GET BACK INSIDE THE PUB. ALWAYS SAFE INSIDE A PUB.

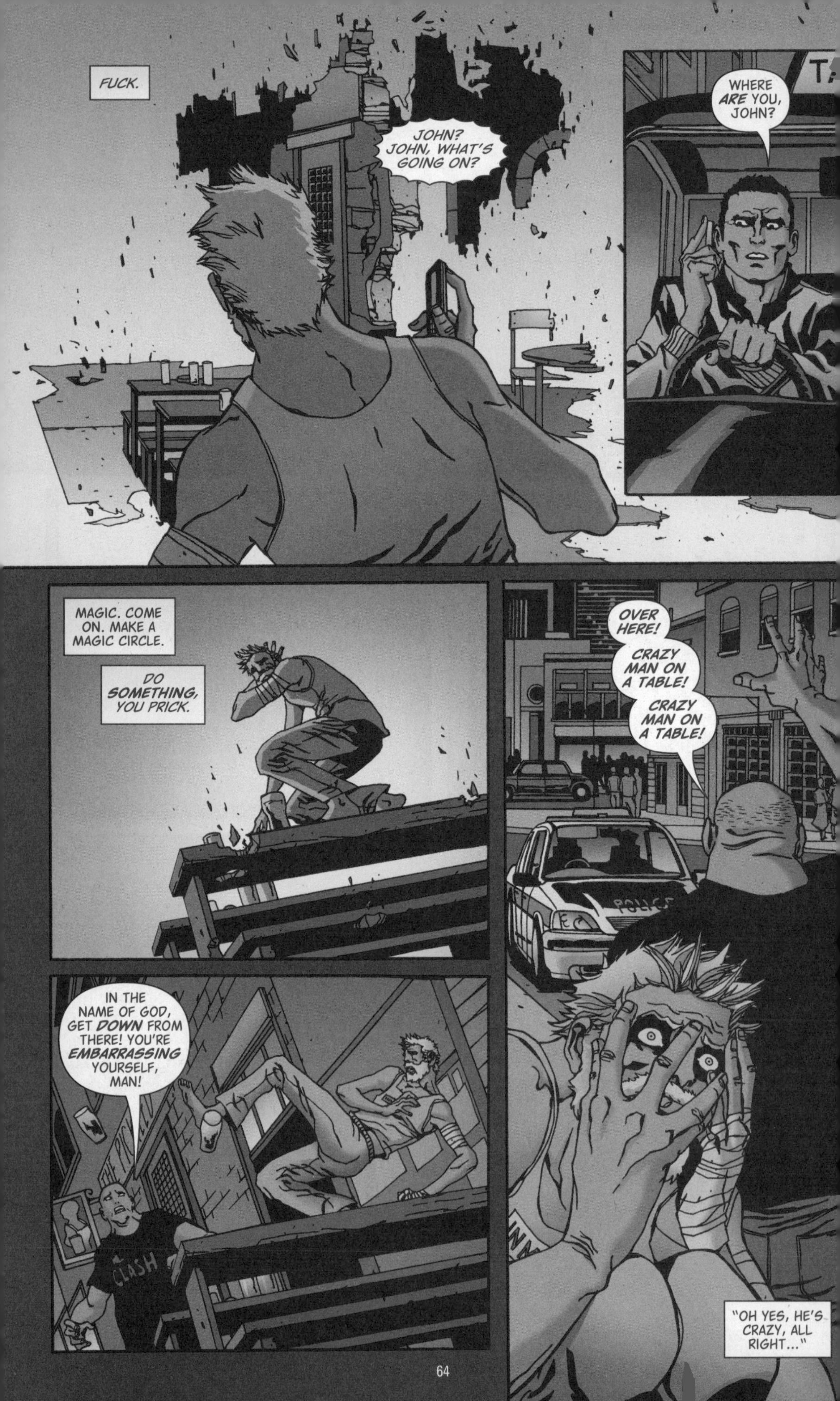
FUCK.
JOHN? JOHN, WHAT'S GOING ON?
WHERE ARE YOU, JOHN?
MAGIC. COME ON. MAKE A MAGIC CIRCLE.
DO SOMETHING, YOU PRICK.
IN THE NAME OF GOD, GET DOWN FROM THERE! YOU'RE EMBARRASSING YOURSELF, MAN!
OVER HERE!
CRAZY MAN ON A TABLE!
CRAZY MAN ON A TABLE!
POLICE
"OH YES, HE'S CRAZY, ALL RIGHT..."

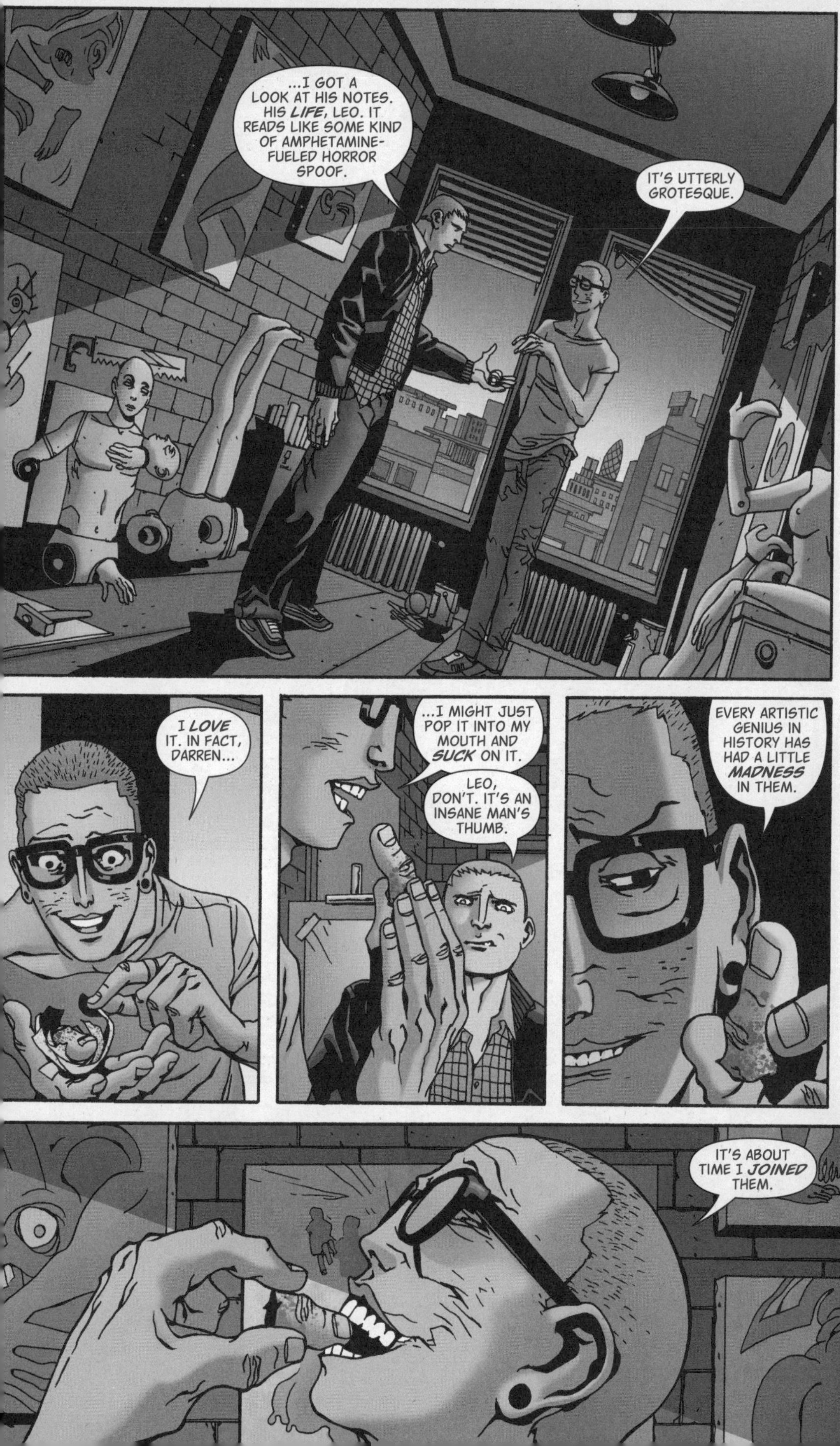
...I GOT A LOOK AT HIS NOTES. HIS LIFE, LEO. IT READS LIKE SOME KIND OF AMPHETAMINE-FUELED HORROR SPOOF.
IT'S UTTERLY GROTESQUE.
I LOVE IT. IN FACT, DARREN...
...I MIGHT JUST POP IT INTO MY MOUTH AND SUCK ON IT.
LEO, DON'T. IT'S AN INSANE MAN'S THUMB.
EVERY ARTISTIC GENIUS IN HISTORY HAS HAD A LITTLE MADNESS IN THEM.
IT'S ABOUT TIME I JOINED THEM.

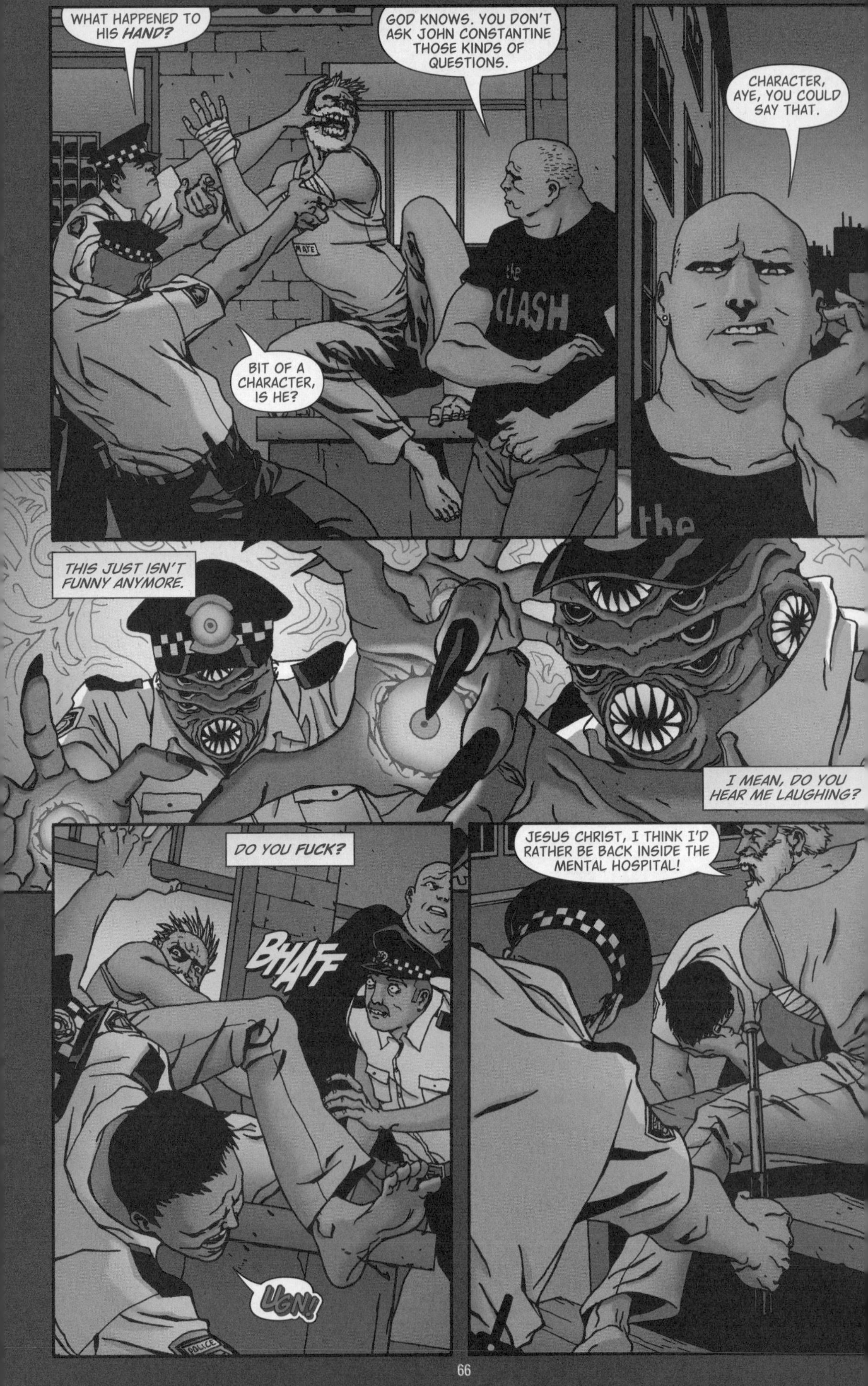
WHAT HAPPENED TO HIS *HAND?*
GOD KNOWS. YOU DON'T ASK JOHN CONSTANTINE THOSE KINDS OF QUESTIONS.
BIT OF A CHARACTER, IS HE?
CHARACTER, AYE, YOU COULD SAY THAT.
THIS JUST ISN'T FUNNY ANYMORE.
I MEAN, DO YOU HEAR ME LAUGHING?
DO YOU FUCK?
BHAFF
UGN!!
JESUS CHRIST, I THINK I'D RATHER BE BACK INSIDE THE MENTAL HOSPITAL!

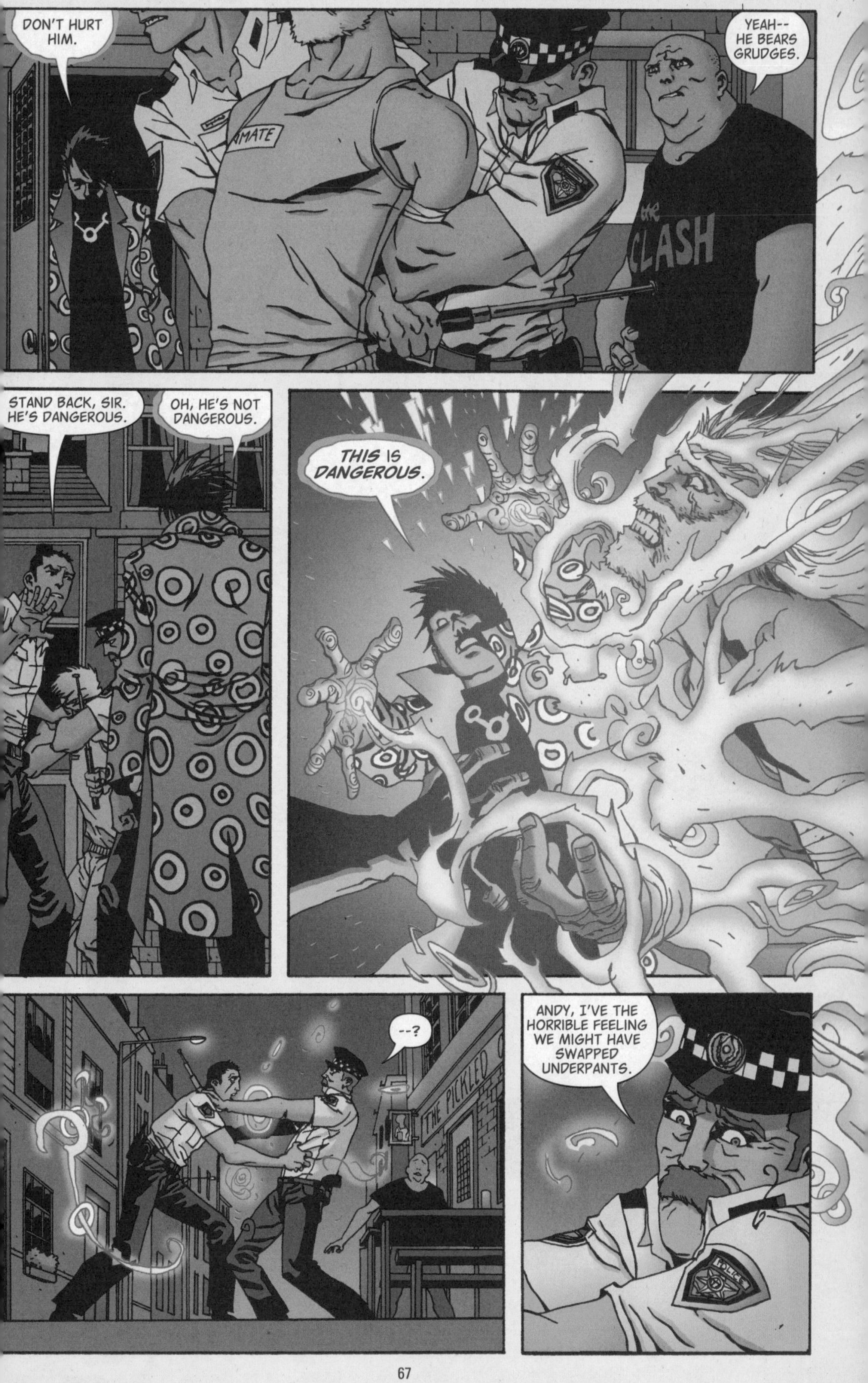
DON'T HURT HIM.
YEAH-- HE BEARS GRUDGES.
INMATE
THE CLASH
STAND BACK, SIR. HE'S DANGEROUS.
OH, HE'S NOT DANGEROUS.
THIS IS DANGEROUS.
--?
THE PICKLED
ANDY, I'VE THE HORRIBLE FEELING WE MIGHT HAVE SWAPPED UNDERPANTS.
POLICE

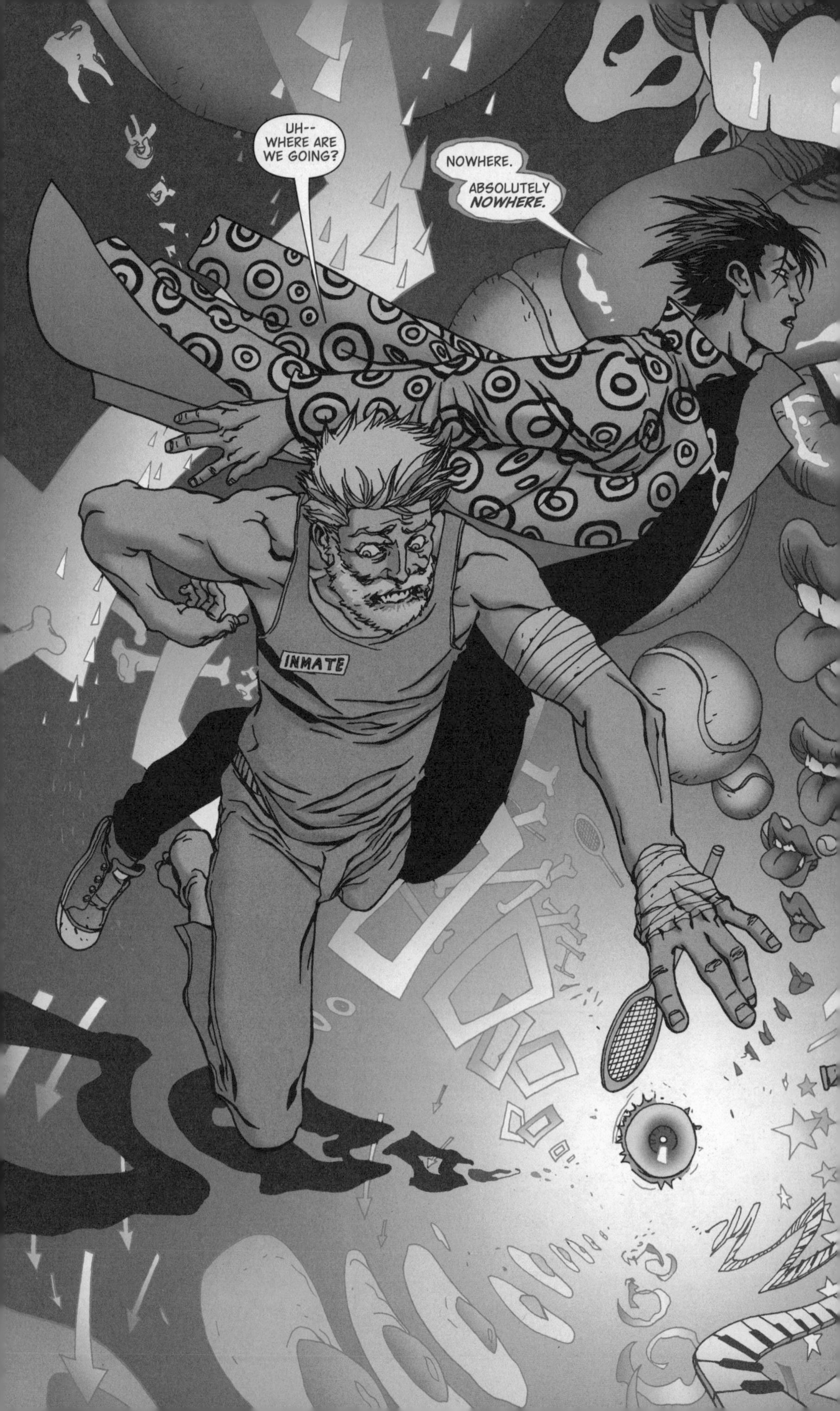
UH-- WHERE ARE WE GOING?
NOWHERE.
ABSOLUTELY *NOWHERE.*
INMATE

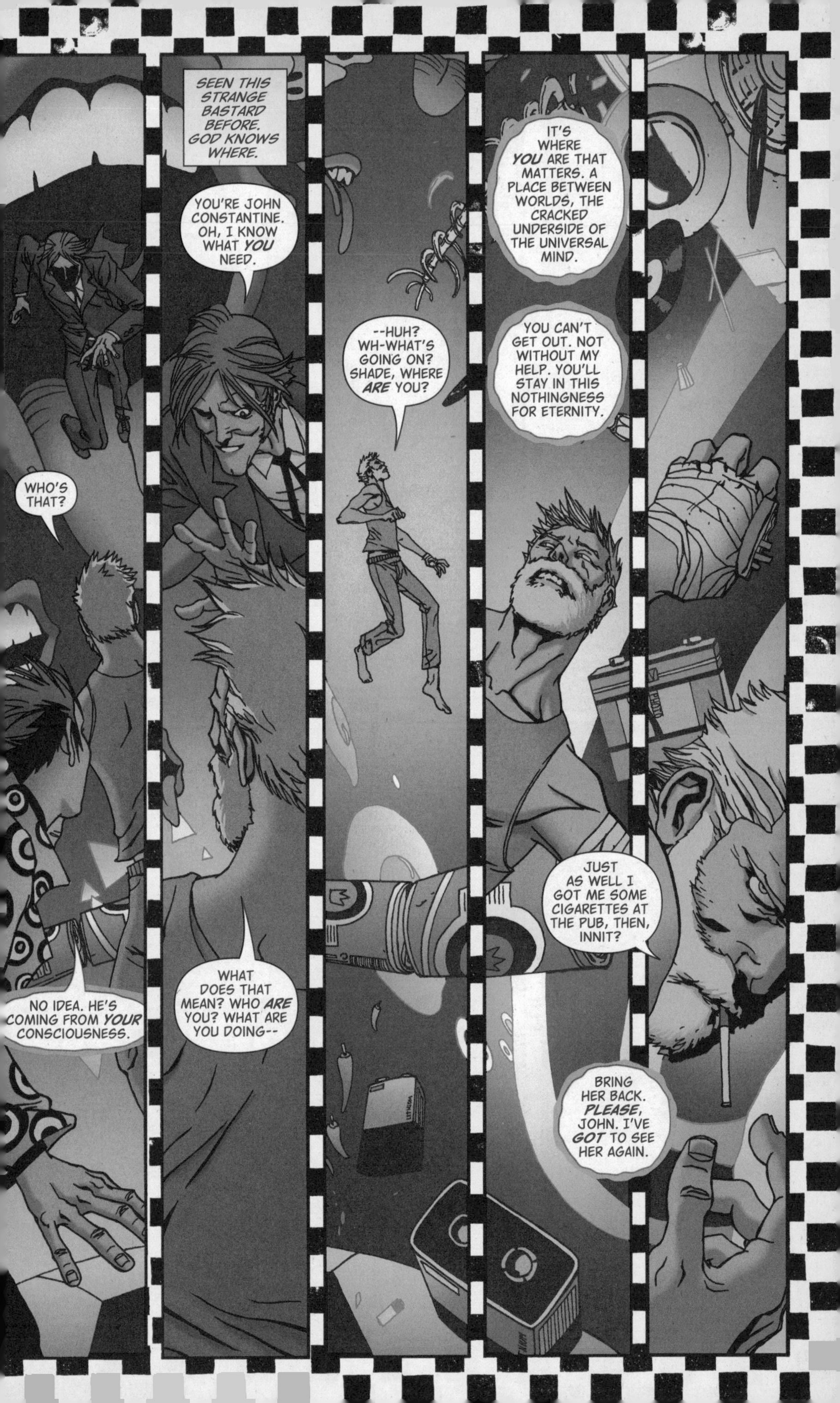
WHO'S THAT?
NO IDEA. HE'S COMING FROM YOUR CONSCIOUSNESS.
SEEN THIS STRANGE BASTARD BEFORE. GOD KNOWS WHERE.
YOU'RE JOHN CONSTANTINE. OH, I KNOW WHAT YOU NEED.
WHAT DOES THAT MEAN? WHO ARE YOU? WHAT ARE YOU DOING--
--HUH? WH-WHAT'S GOING ON? SHADE, WHERE ARE YOU?
IT'S WHERE YOU ARE THAT MATTERS. A PLACE BETWEEN WORLDS, THE CRACKED UNDERSIDE OF THE UNIVERSAL MIND.
YOU CAN'T GET OUT. NOT WITHOUT MY HELP. YOU'LL STAY IN THIS NOTHINGNESS FOR ETERNITY.
JUST AS WELL I GOT ME SOME CIGARETTES AT THE PUB, THEN, INNIT?
BRING HER BACK. PLEASE, JOHN. I'VE GOT TO SEE HER AGAIN.

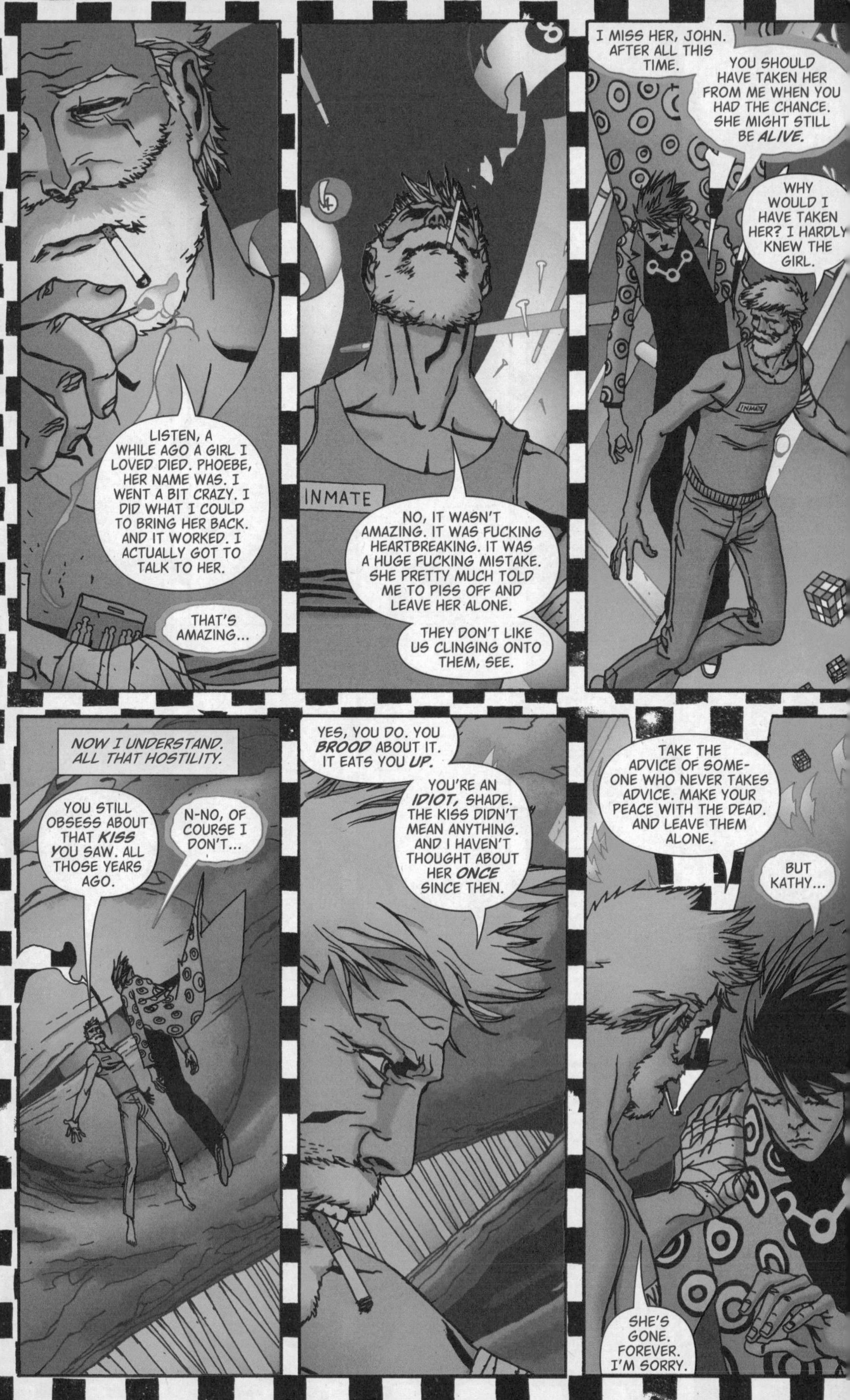
LISTEN, A WHILE AGO A GIRL I LOVED DIED. PHOEBE, HER NAME WAS. I WENT A BIT CRAZY. I DID WHAT I COULD TO BRING HER BACK. AND IT WORKED. I ACTUALLY GOT TO TALK TO HER.
THAT'S AMAZING...
INMATE
NO, IT WASN'T AMAZING. IT WAS FUCKING HEARTBREAKING. IT WAS A HUGE FUCKING MISTAKE. SHE PRETTY MUCH TOLD ME TO PISS OFF AND LEAVE HER ALONE.
THEY DON'T LIKE US CLINGING ONTO THEM, SEE.
I MISS HER, JOHN. AFTER ALL THIS TIME.
YOU SHOULD HAVE TAKEN HER FROM ME WHEN YOU HAD THE CHANCE. SHE MIGHT STILL BE ALIVE.
WHY WOULD I HAVE TAKEN HER? I HARDLY KNEW THE GIRL.
NOW I UNDERSTAND. ALL THAT HOSTILITY.
YOU STILL OBSESS ABOUT THAT KISS YOU SAW. ALL THOSE YEARS AGO.
N-NO, OF COURSE I DON'T...
YES, YOU DO. YOU BROOD ABOUT IT. IT EATS YOU UP.
YOU'RE AN IDIOT, SHADE. THE KISS DIDN'T MEAN ANYTHING. AND I HAVEN'T THOUGHT ABOUT HER ONCE SINCE THEN.
TAKE THE ADVICE OF SOME-ONE WHO NEVER TAKES ADVICE. MAKE YOUR PEACE WITH THE DEAD. AND LEAVE THEM ALONE.
BUT KATHY...
SHE'S GONE. FOREVER. I'M SORRY.

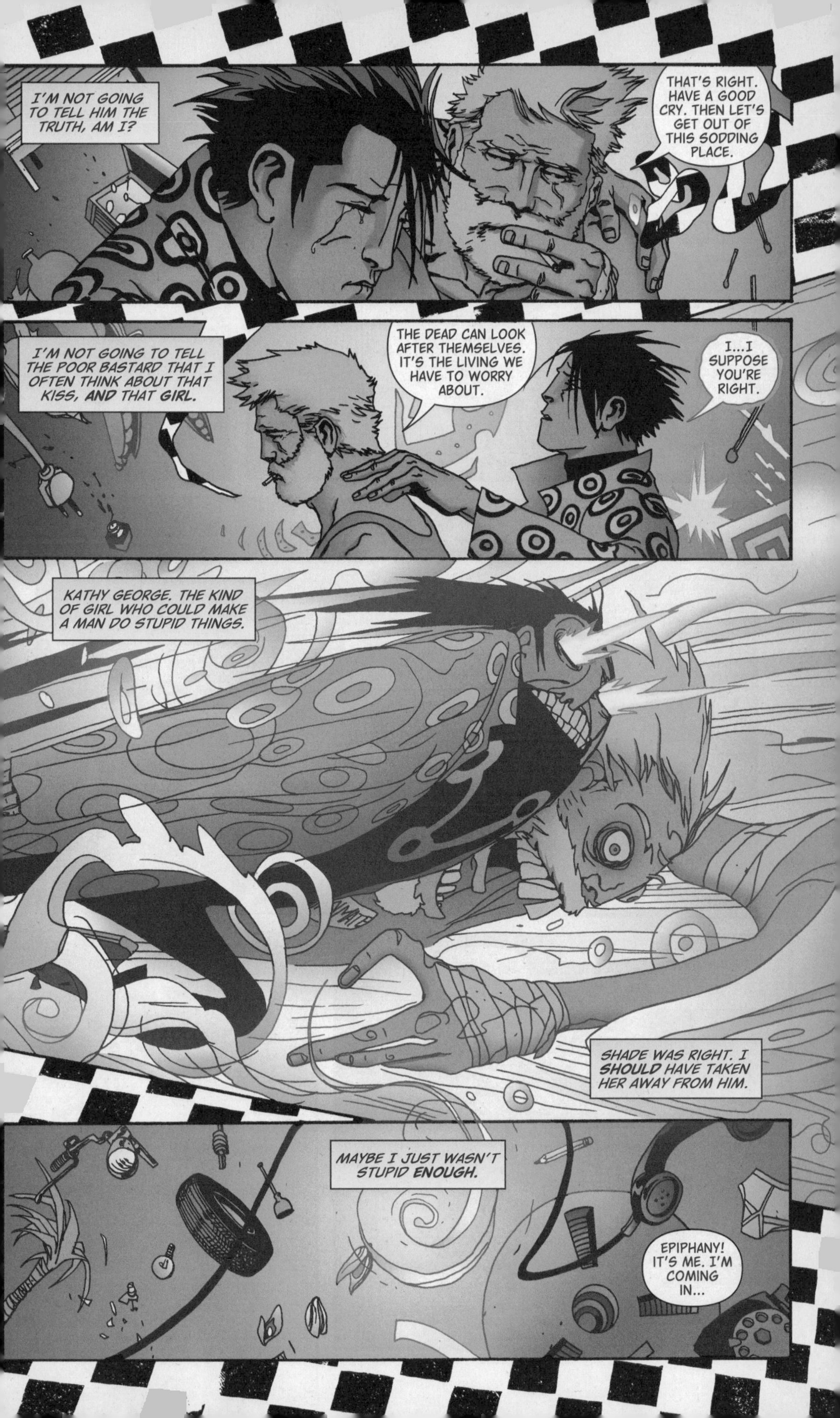

I'M NOT GOING TO TELL HIM THE TRUTH, AM I?
THAT'S RIGHT. HAVE A GOOD CRY. THEN LET'S GET OUT OF THIS SODDING PLACE.
I'M NOT GOING TO TELL THE POOR BASTARD THAT I OFTEN THINK ABOUT THAT KISS, AND THAT GIRL.
THE DEAD CAN LOOK AFTER THEMSELVES. IT'S THE LIVING WE HAVE TO WORRY ABOUT.
I...I SUPPOSE YOU'RE RIGHT.
KATHY GEORGE. THE KIND OF GIRL WHO COULD MAKE A MAN DO STUPID THINGS.
SHADE WAS RIGHT. I SHOULD HAVE TAKEN HER AWAY FROM HIM.
MAYBE I JUST WASN'T STUPID ENOUGH.
EPIPHANY! IT'S ME. I'M COMING IN...

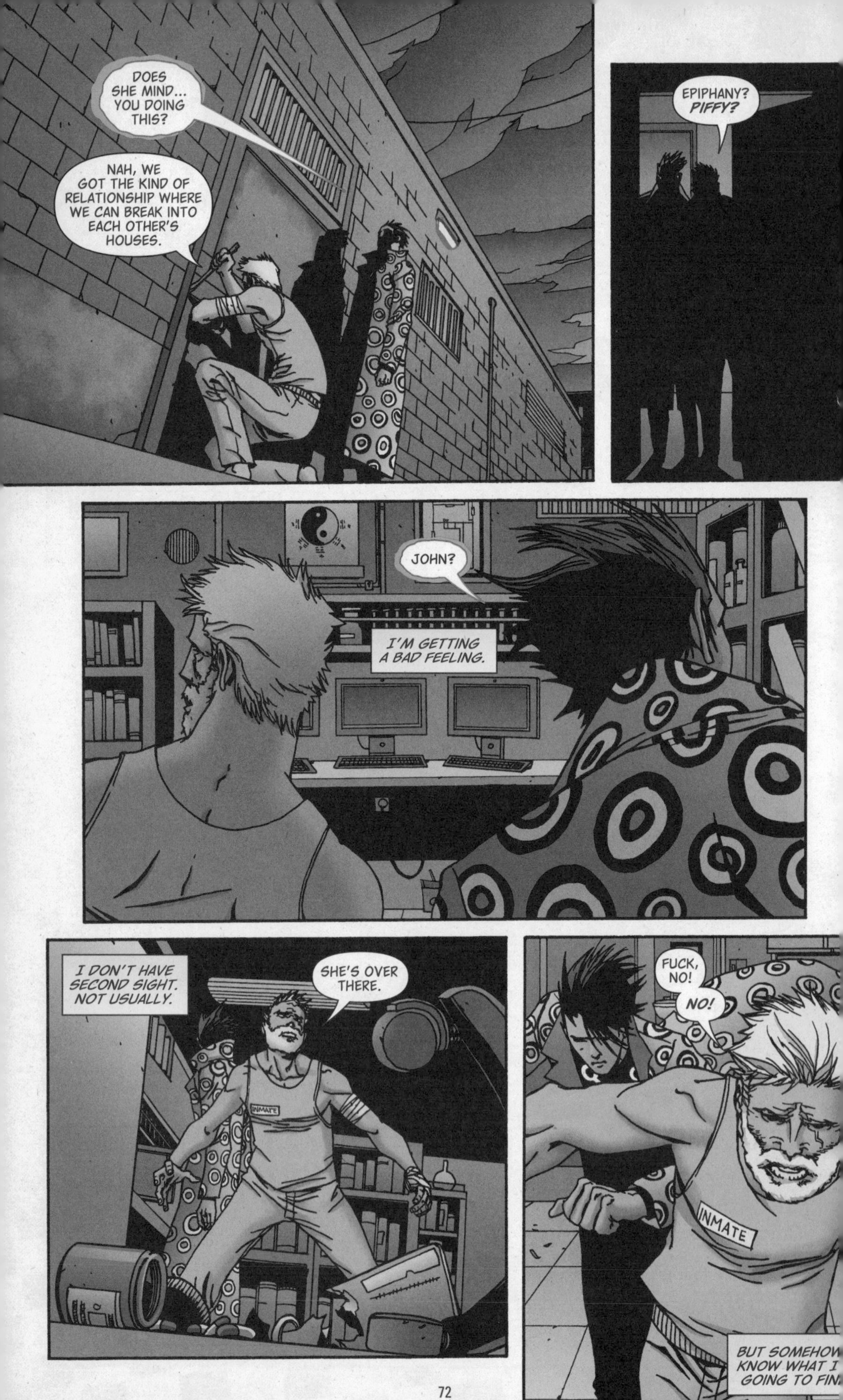

DOES SHE MIND... YOU DOING THIS?
NAH, WE GOT THE KIND OF RELATIONSHIP WHERE WE CAN BREAK INTO EACH OTHER'S HOUSES.
EPIPHANY? *PIFFY?*
JOHN?
I'M GETTING A BAD FEELING.
I DON'T HAVE SECOND SIGHT. NOT USUALLY.
SHE'S OVER THERE.
FUCK, NO!
NO!
INMATE
BUT SOMEHOW KNOW WHAT I GOING TO FIN

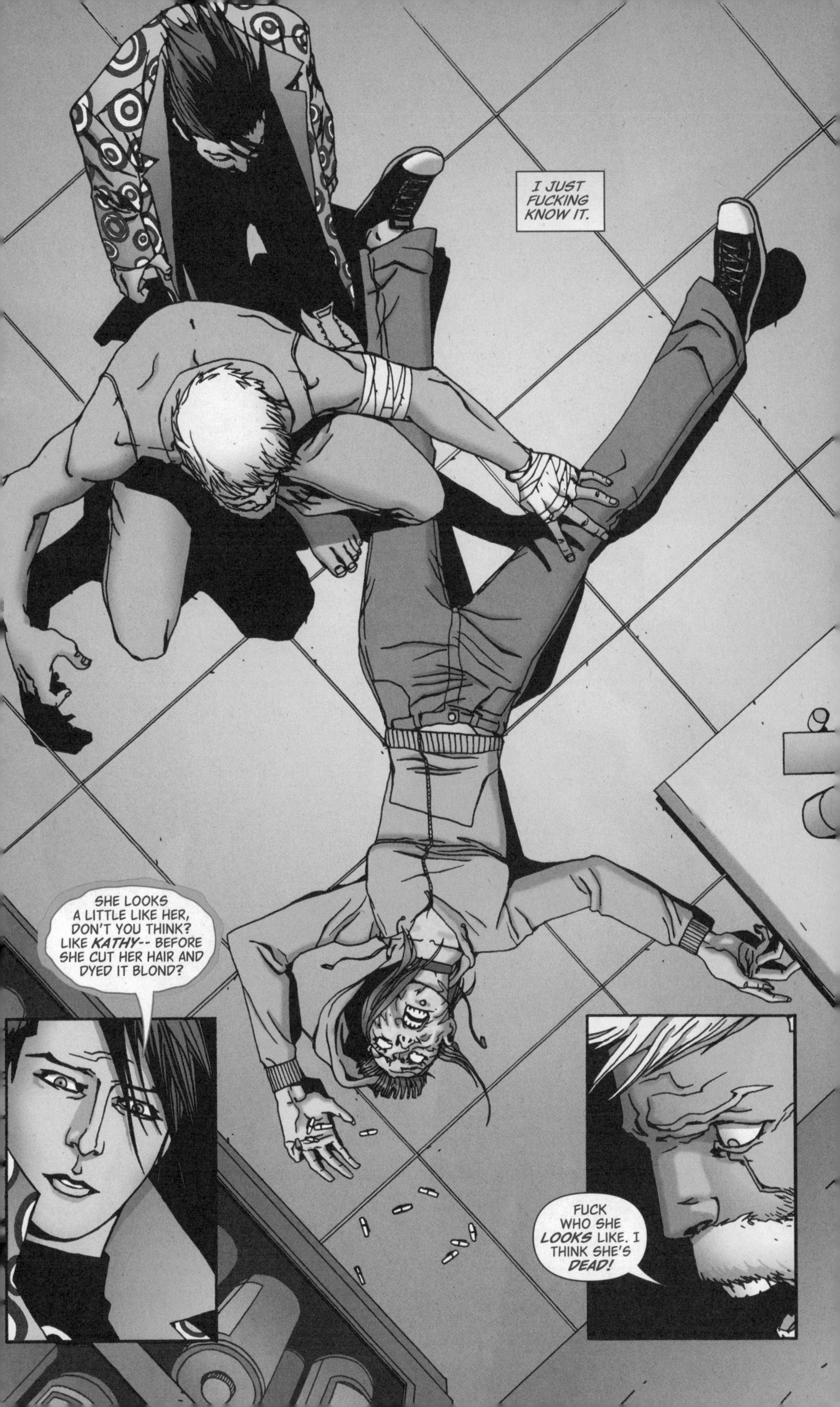
I JUST FUCKING KNOW IT.
SHE LOOKS A LITTLE LIKE HER, DON'T YOU THINK? LIKE *KATHY*-- BEFORE SHE CUT HER HAIR AND DYED IT BLOND?
FUCK WHO SHE *LOOKS* LIKE. I THINK SHE'S *DEAD!*

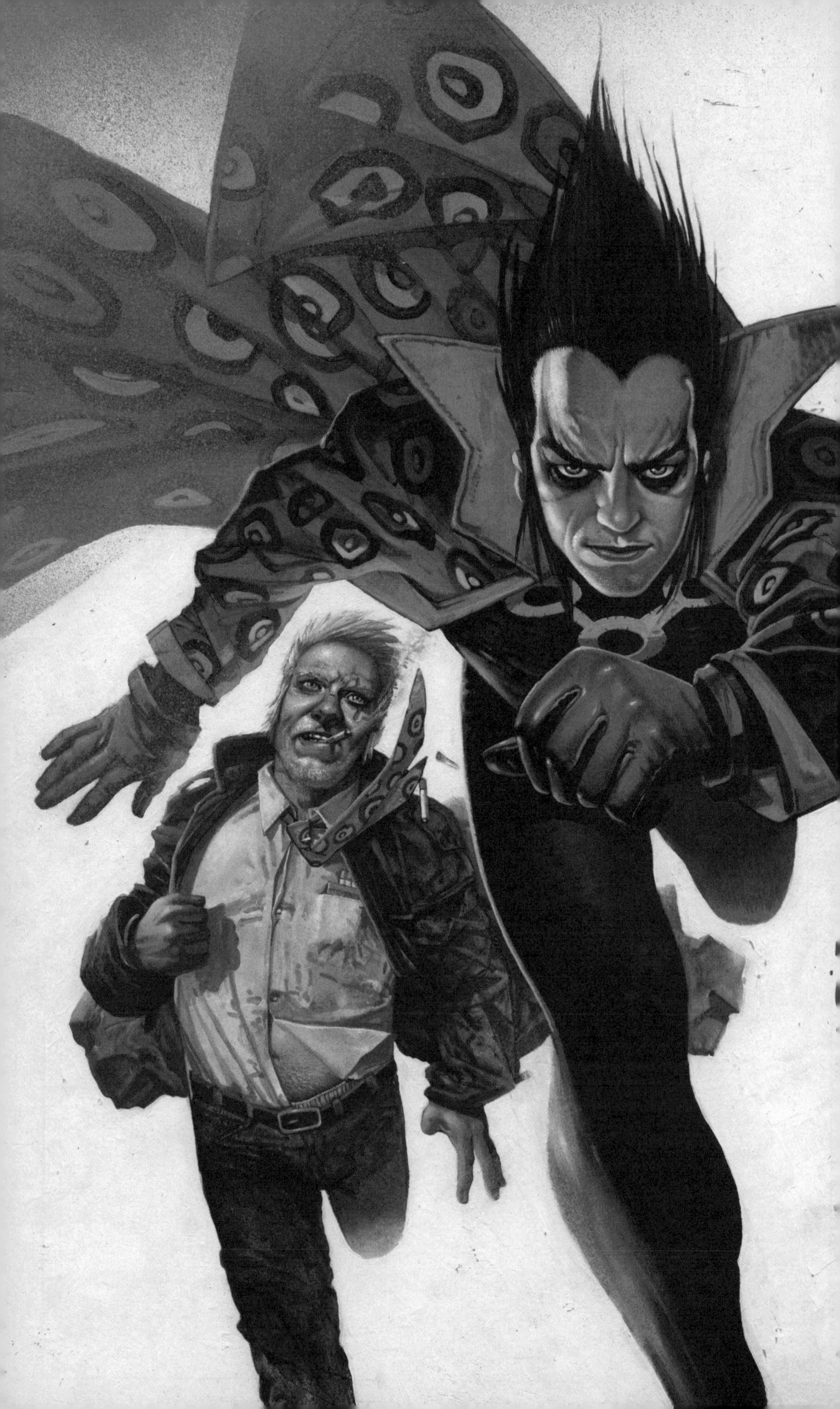

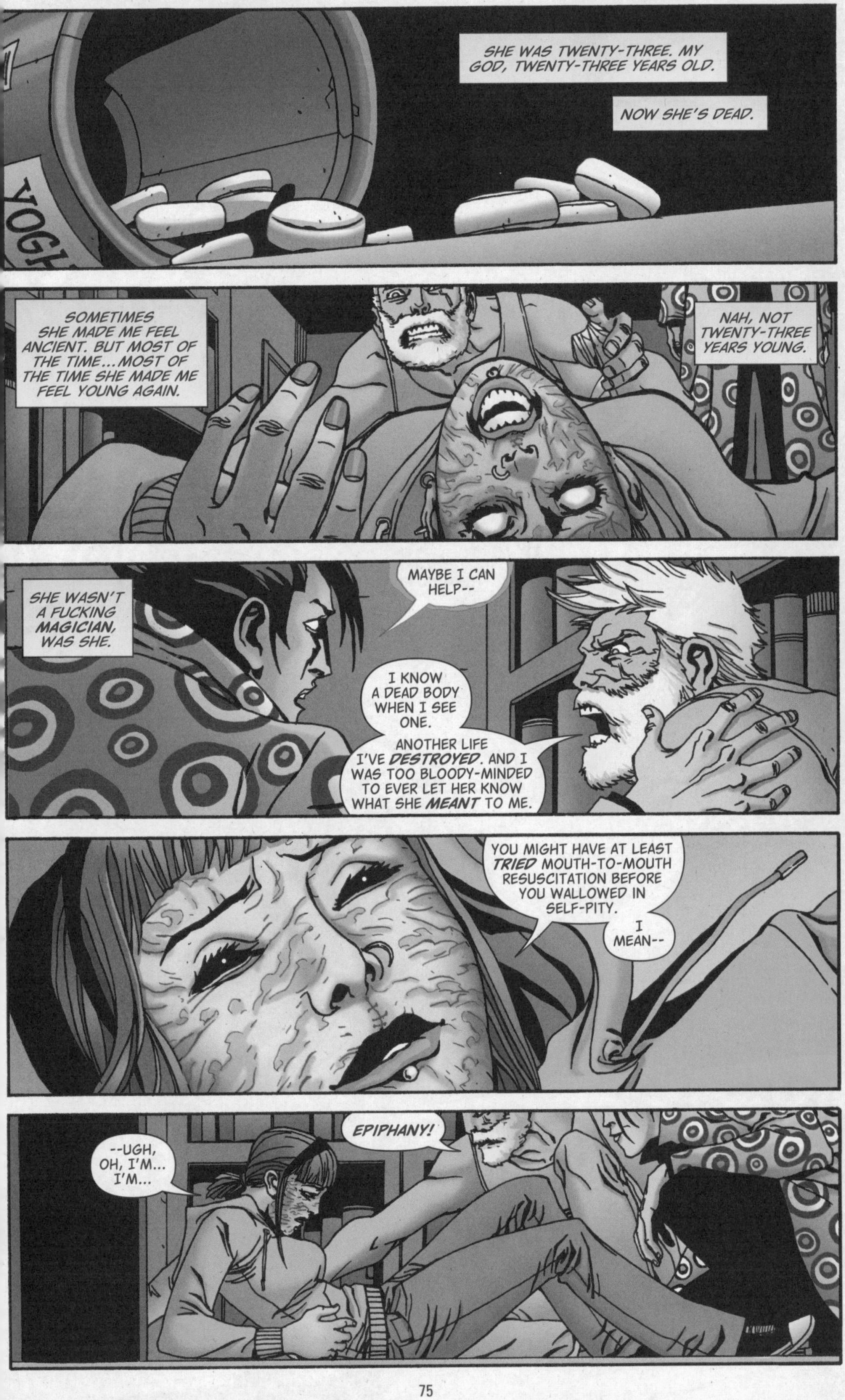
SHE WAS TWENTY-THREE. MY GOD, TWENTY-THREE YEARS OLD.
NOW SHE'S DEAD.
SOMETIMES SHE MADE ME FEEL ANCIENT. BUT MOST OF THE TIME...MOST OF THE TIME SHE MADE ME FEEL YOUNG AGAIN.
NAH, NOT TWENTY-THREE YEARS YOUNG.
SHE WASN'T A FUCKING MAGICIAN, WAS SHE.
MAYBE I CAN HELP--
I KNOW A DEAD BODY WHEN I SEE ONE.
ANOTHER LIFE I'VE DESTROYED. AND I WAS TOO BLOODY-MINDED TO EVER LET HER KNOW WHAT SHE MEANT TO ME.
YOU MIGHT HAVE AT LEAST TRIED MOUTH-TO-MOUTH RESUSCITATION BEFORE YOU WALLOWED IN SELF-PITY.
I MEAN--
EPIPHANY!
--UGH, OH, I'M... I'M...

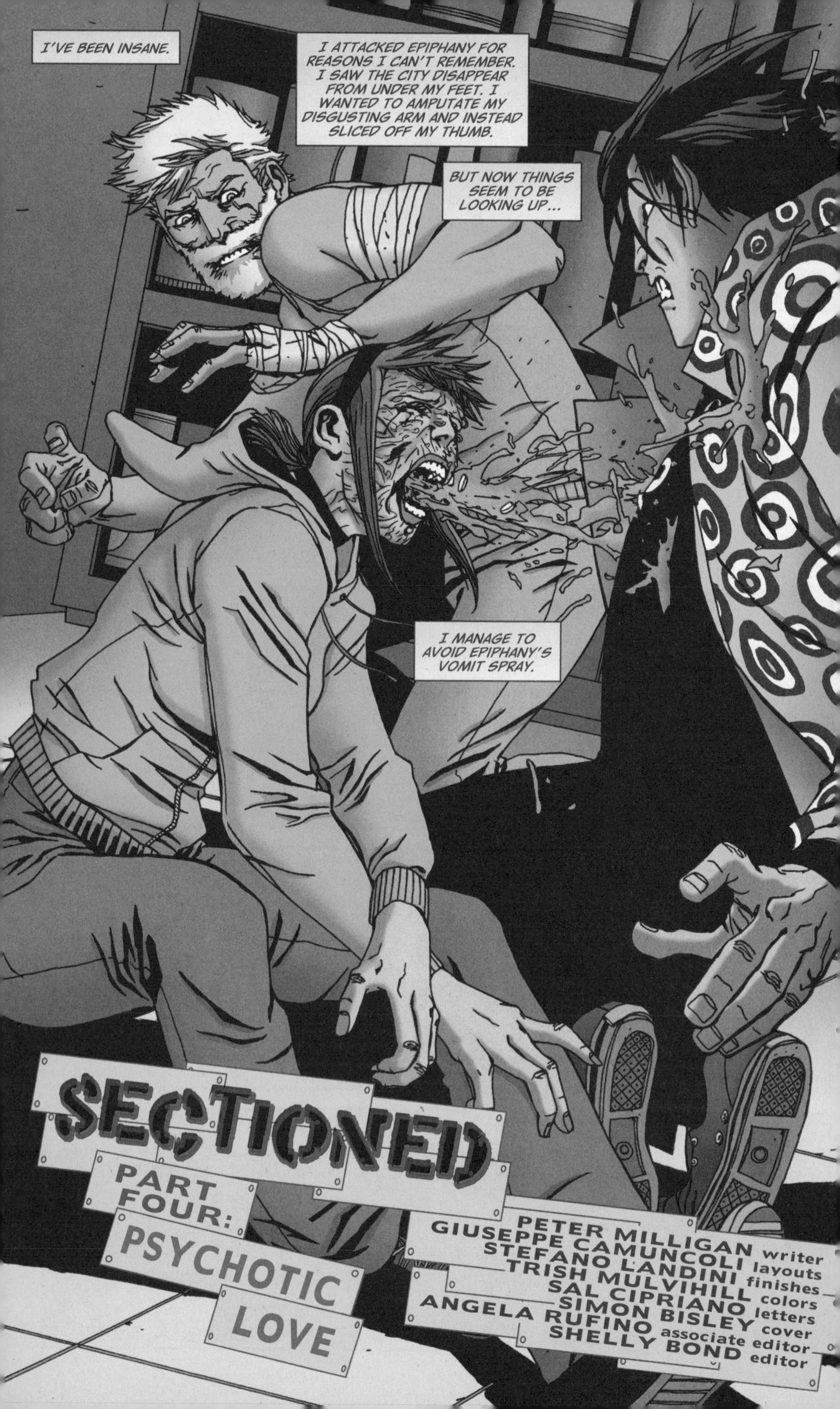
I'VE BEEN INSANE.
I ATTACKED EPIPHANY FOR REASONS I CAN'T REMEMBER. I SAW THE CITY DISAPPEAR FROM UNDER MY FEET. I WANTED TO AMPUTATE MY DISGUSTING ARM AND INSTEAD SLICED OFF MY THUMB.
BUT NOW THINGS SEEM TO BE LOOKING UP...
I MANAGE TO AVOID EPIPHANY'S VOMIT SPRAY.
SECTIONED
PART FOUR:
PSYCHOTIC LOVE
PETER MILLIGAN writer
GIUSEPPE CAMUNCOLI layouts
STEFANO LANDINI finishes
TRISH MULVIHILL colors
SAL CIPRIANO letters
SIMON BISLEY cover
ANGELA RUFINO associate editor
SHELLY BOND editor

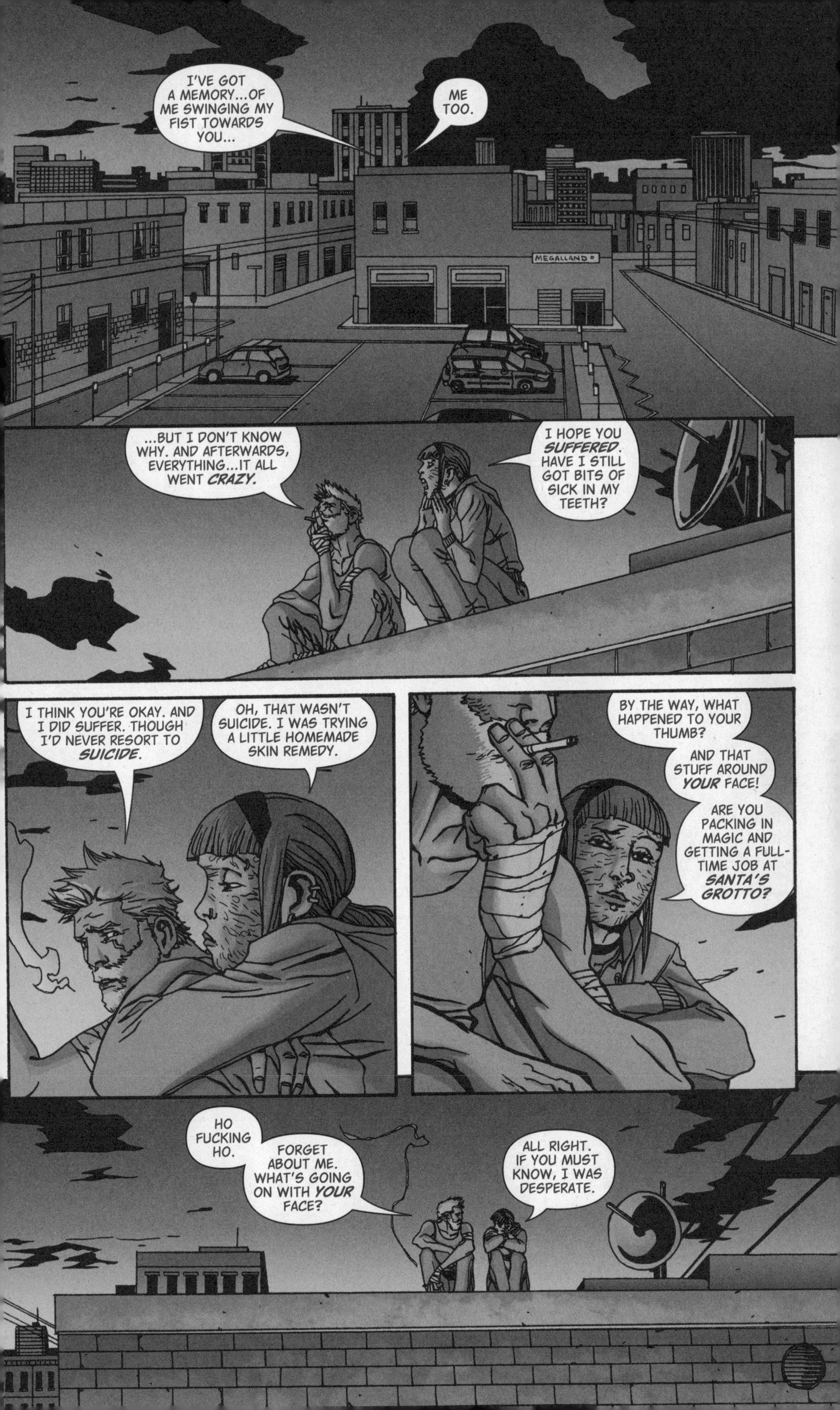
I'VE GOT A MEMORY...OF ME SWINGING MY FIST TOWARDS YOU...
ME TOO.
MEGALLAND
...BUT I DON'T KNOW WHY. AND AFTERWARDS, EVERYTHING...IT ALL WENT CRAZY.
I HOPE YOU SUFFERED. HAVE I STILL GOT BITS OF SICK IN MY TEETH?
I THINK YOU'RE OKAY. AND I DID SUFFER. THOUGH I'D NEVER RESORT TO SUICIDE.
OH, THAT WASN'T SUICIDE. I WAS TRYING A LITTLE HOMEMADE SKIN REMEDY.
BY THE WAY, WHAT HAPPENED TO YOUR THUMB?
AND THAT STUFF AROUND YOUR FACE!
ARE YOU PACKING IN MAGIC AND GETTING A FULL-TIME JOB AT SANTA'S GROTTO?
HO FUCKING HO.
FORGET ABOUT ME. WHAT'S GOING ON WITH YOUR FACE?
ALL RIGHT. IF YOU MUST KNOW, I WAS DESPERATE.

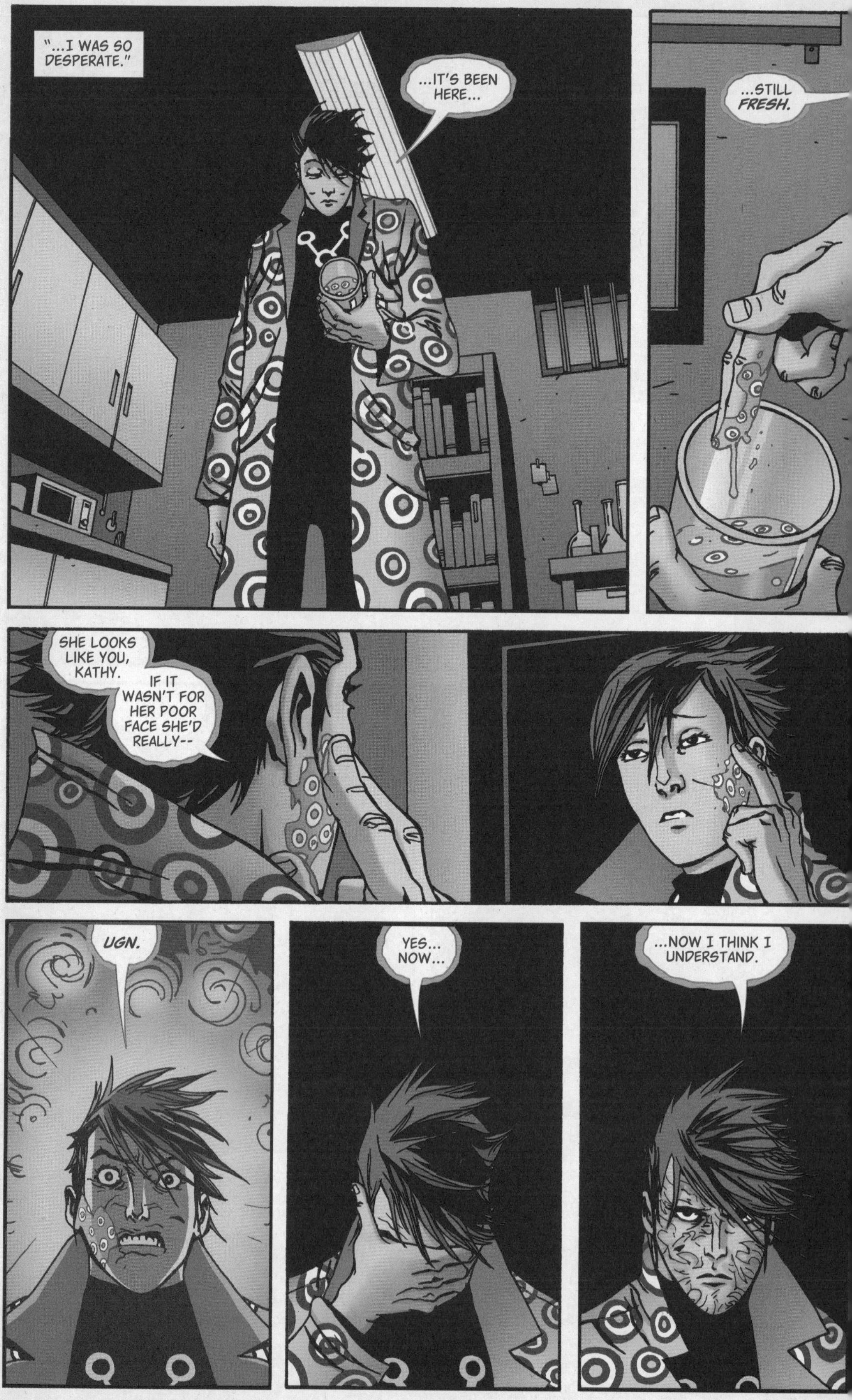
"...I WAS SO DESPERATE."
...IT'S BEEN HERE...
...STILL FRESH.
SHE LOOKS LIKE YOU, KATHY.
IF IT WASN'T FOR HER POOR FACE SHE'D REALLY--
UGN.
YES... NOW...
...NOW I THINK I UNDERSTAND.

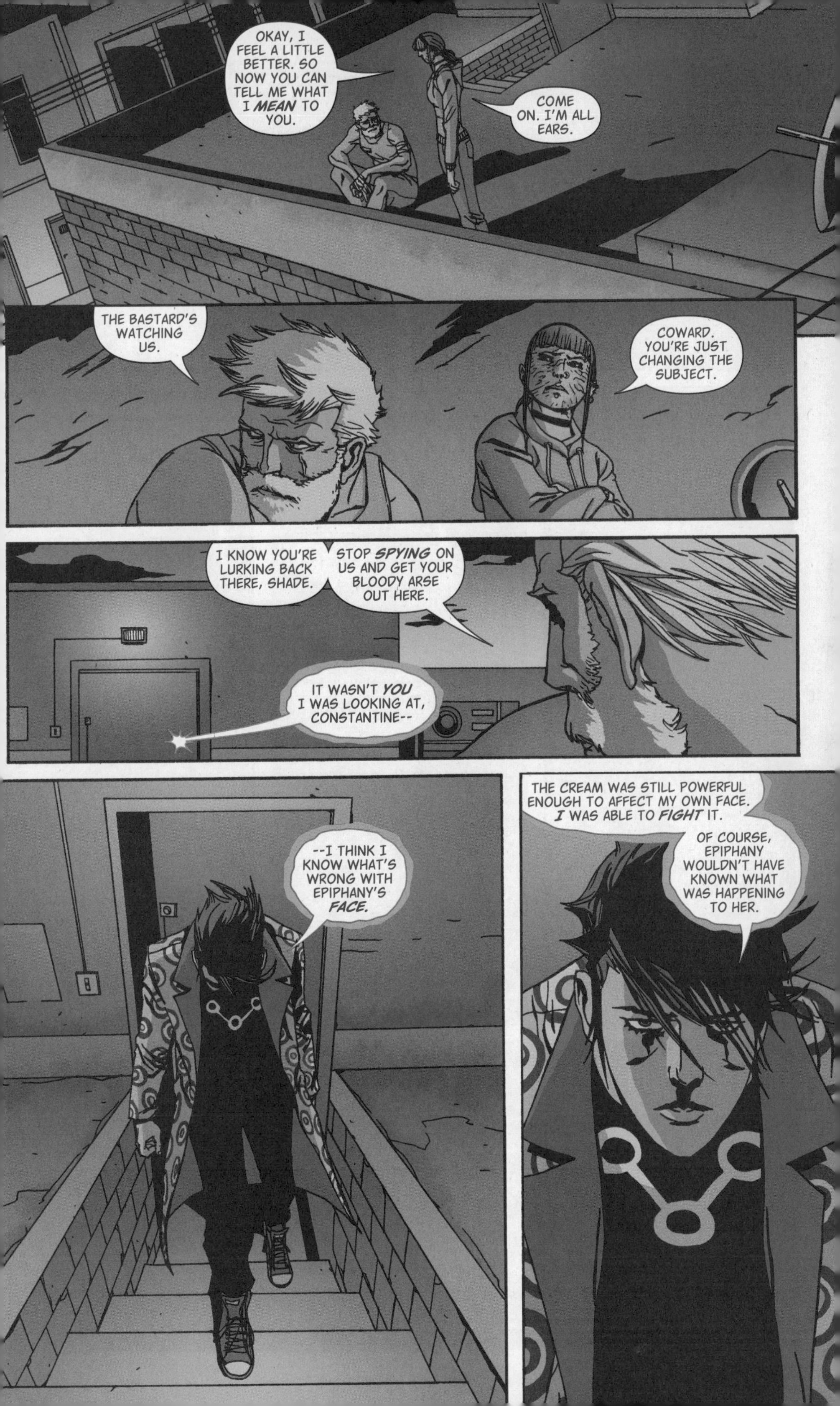
OKAY, I FEEL A LITTLE BETTER. SO NOW YOU CAN TELL ME WHAT I MEAN TO YOU.
COME ON. I'M ALL EARS.
THE BASTARD'S WATCHING US.
COWARD. YOU'RE JUST CHANGING THE SUBJECT.
I KNOW YOU'RE LURKING BACK THERE, SHADE.
STOP SPYING ON US AND GET YOUR BLOODY ARSE OUT HERE.
IT WASN'T YOU I WAS LOOKING AT, CONSTANTINE--
--I THINK I KNOW WHAT'S WRONG WITH EPIPHANY'S FACE.
THE CREAM WAS STILL POWERFUL ENOUGH TO AFFECT MY OWN FACE. I WAS ABLE TO FIGHT IT.
OF COURSE, EPIPHANY WOULDN'T HAVE KNOWN WHAT WAS HAPPENING TO HER.

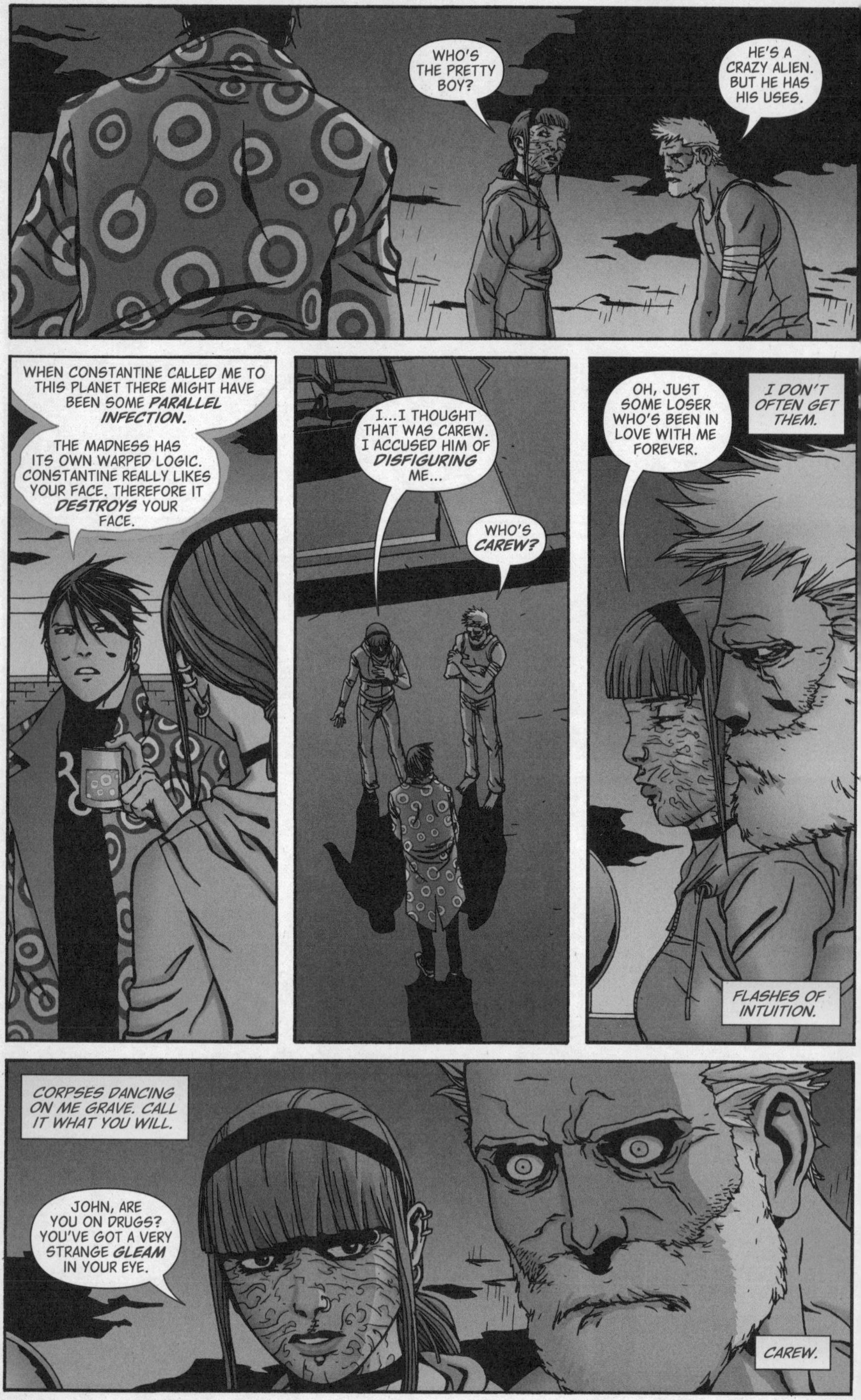
WHO'S THE PRETTY BOY?
HE'S A CRAZY ALIEN. BUT HE HAS HIS USES.
WHEN CONSTANTINE CALLED ME TO THIS PLANET THERE MIGHT HAVE BEEN SOME PARALLEL INFECTION.
THE MADNESS HAS ITS OWN WARPED LOGIC. CONSTANTINE REALLY LIKES YOUR FACE. THEREFORE IT DESTROYS YOUR FACE.
I...I THOUGHT THAT WAS CAREW. I ACCUSED HIM OF DISFIGURING ME...
WHO'S CAREW?
OH, JUST SOME LOSER WHO'S BEEN IN LOVE WITH ME FOREVER.
I DON'T OFTEN GET THEM.
FLASHES OF INTUITION.
CORPSES DANCING ON ME GRAVE. CALL IT WHAT YOU WILL.
JOHN, ARE YOU ON DRUGS? YOU'VE GOT A VERY STRANGE GLEAM IN YOUR EYE.
CAREW.

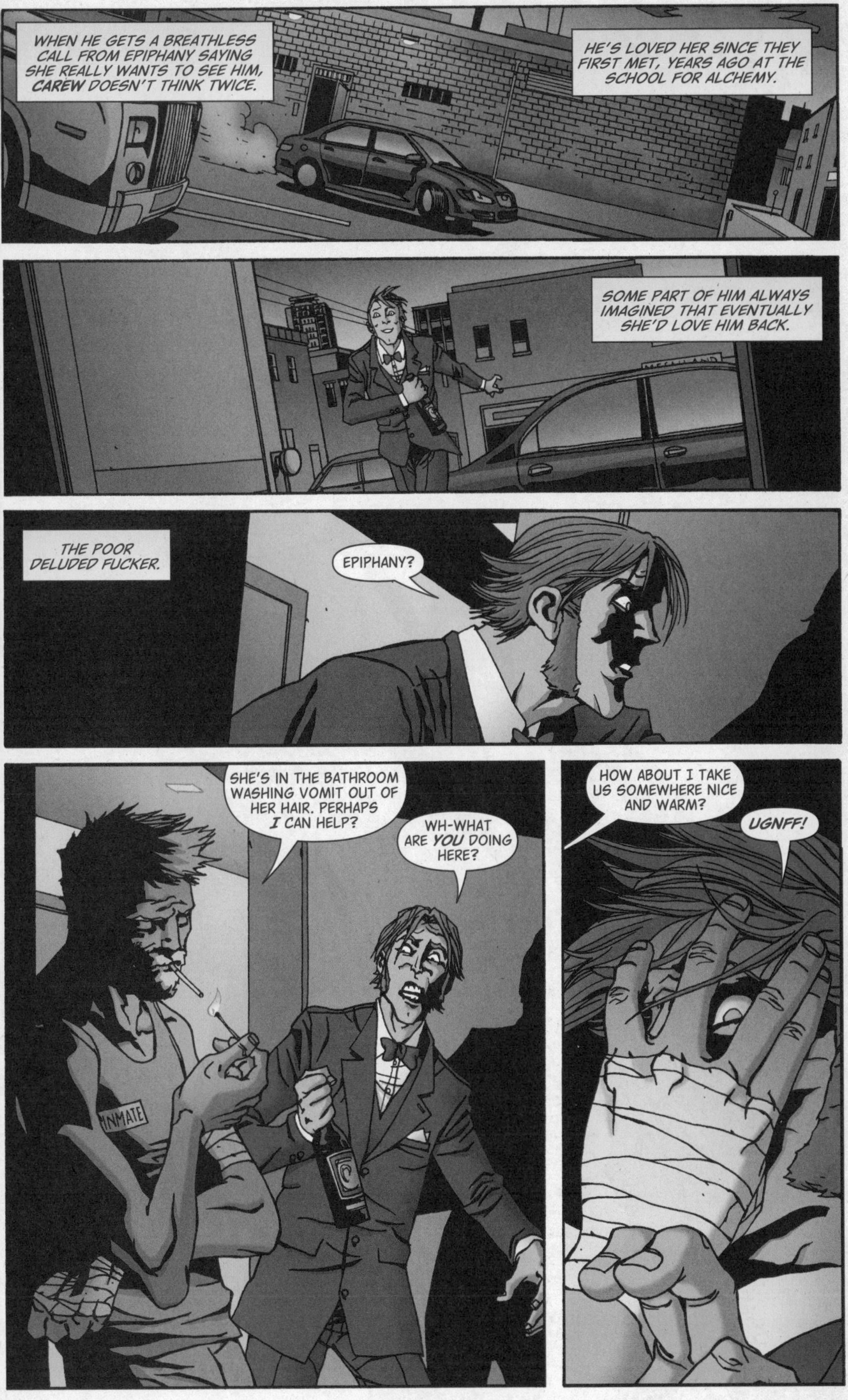
WHEN HE GETS A BREATHLESS CALL FROM EPIPHANY SAYING SHE REALLY WANTS TO SEE HIM, CAREW DOESN'T THINK TWICE.
HE'S LOVED HER SINCE THEY FIRST MET, YEARS AGO AT THE SCHOOL FOR ALCHEMY.
SOME PART OF HIM ALWAYS IMAGINED THAT EVENTUALLY SHE'D LOVE HIM BACK.
THE POOR DELUDED FUCKER.
EPIPHANY?
SHE'S IN THE BATHROOM WASHING VOMIT OUT OF HER HAIR. PERHAPS I CAN HELP?
WH-WHAT ARE YOU DOING HERE?
INMATE
HOW ABOUT I TAKE US SOMEWHERE NICE AND WARM?
UGNFF!

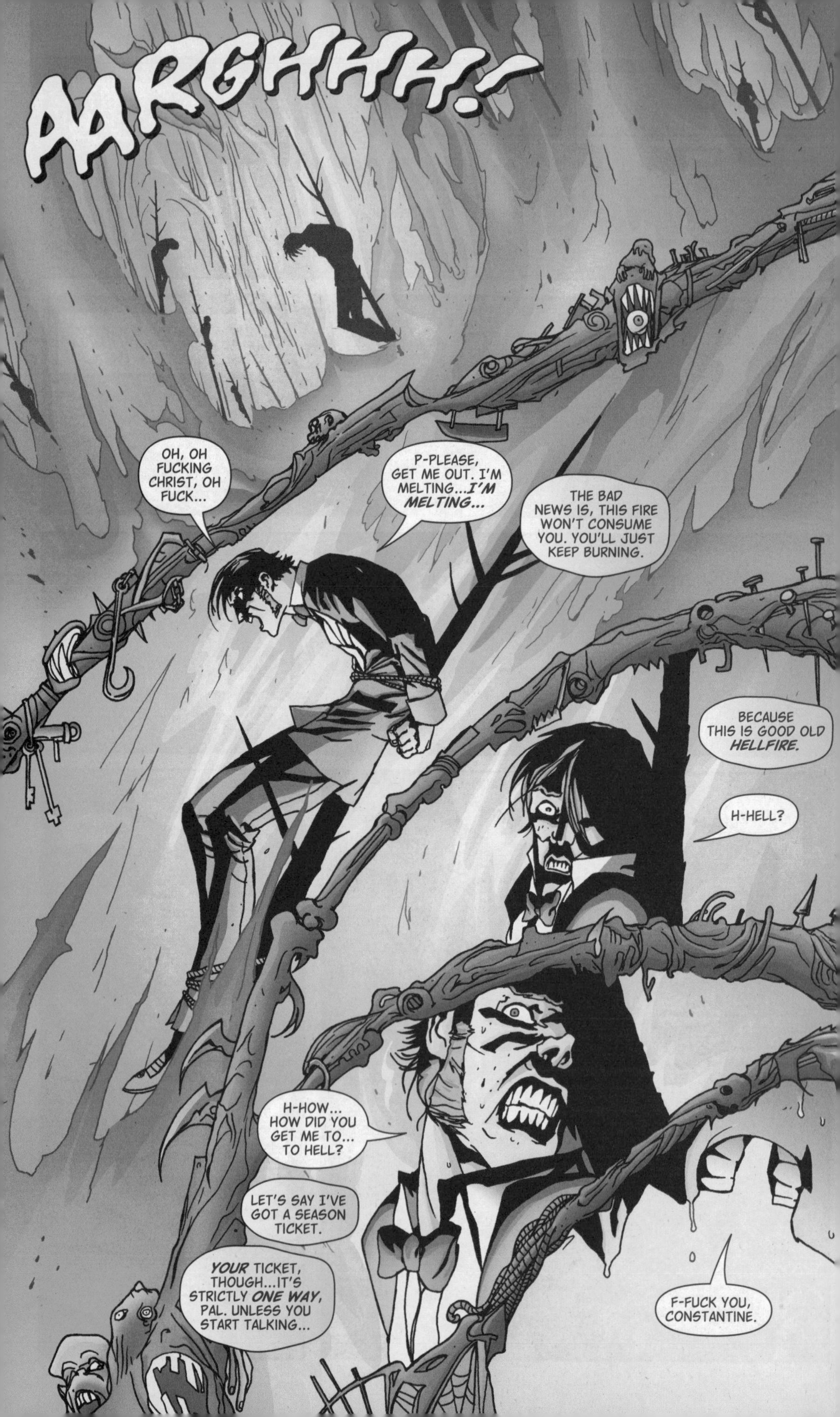
AARGHHH!!
OH, OH FUCKING CHRIST, OH FUCK...
P-PLEASE, GET ME OUT. I'M MELTING...*I'M MELTING*...
THE BAD NEWS IS, THIS FIRE WON'T CONSUME YOU. YOU'LL JUST KEEP BURNING.
BECAUSE THIS IS GOOD OLD *HELLFIRE.*
H-HELL?
H-HOW... HOW DID YOU GET ME TO... TO HELL?
LET'S SAY I'VE GOT A SEASON TICKET.
YOUR TICKET, THOUGH...IT'S STRICTLY *ONE WAY*, PAL. UNLESS YOU START TALKING...
F-FUCK YOU, CONSTANTINE.

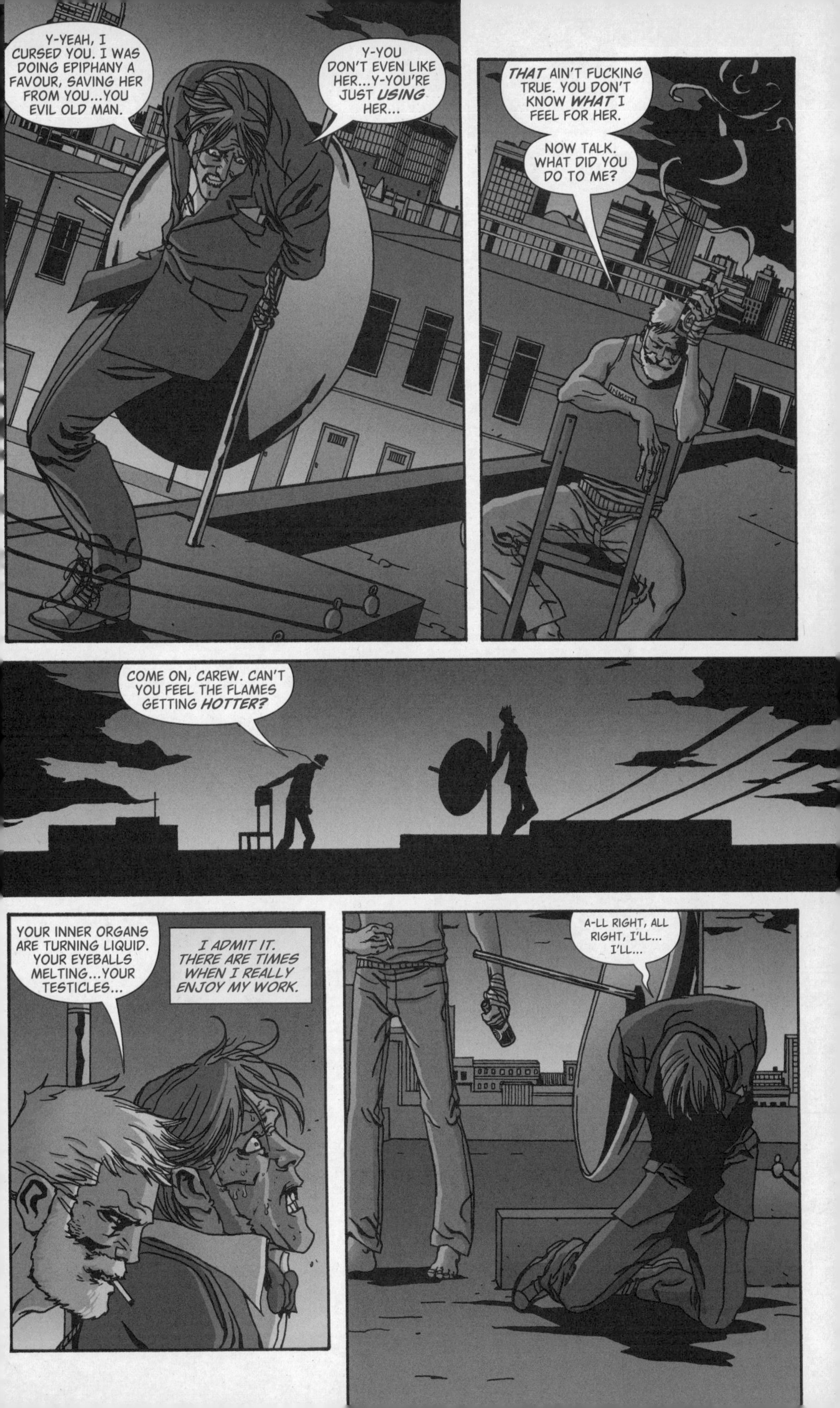
Y-YEAH, I CURSED YOU. I WAS DOING EPIPHANY A FAVOUR, SAVING HER FROM YOU...YOU EVIL OLD MAN.
Y-YOU DON'T EVEN LIKE HER...Y-YOU'RE JUST USING HER...
THAT AIN'T FUCKING TRUE. YOU DON'T KNOW WHAT I FEEL FOR HER.
NOW TALK. WHAT DID YOU DO TO ME?
COME ON, CAREW. CAN'T YOU FEEL THE FLAMES GETTING HOTTER?
YOUR INNER ORGANS ARE TURNING LIQUID. YOUR EYEBALLS MELTING...YOUR TESTICLES...
I ADMIT IT. THERE ARE TIMES WHEN I REALLY ENJOY MY WORK.
A-LL RIGHT, ALL RIGHT, I'LL... I'LL...

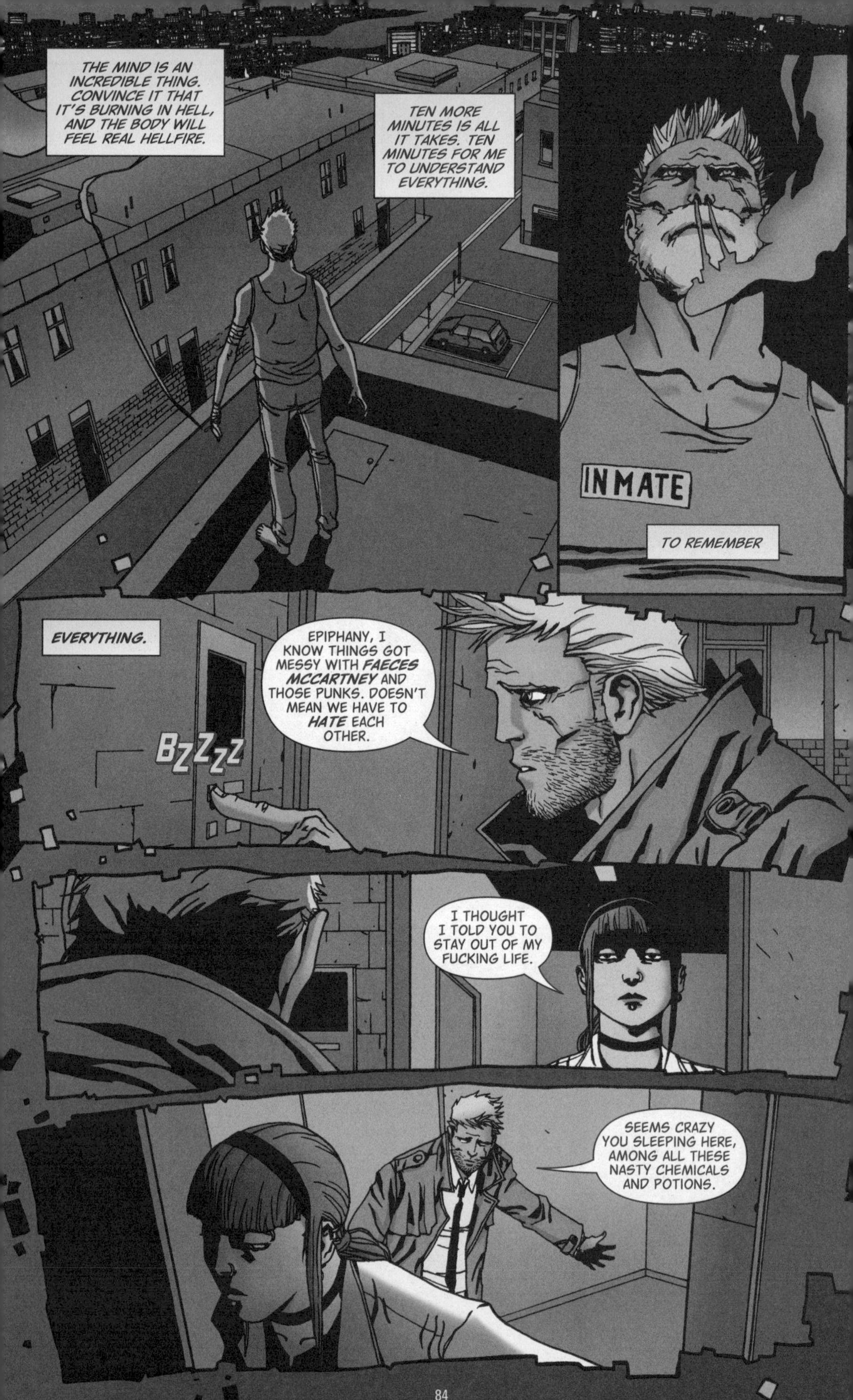
THE MIND IS AN INCREDIBLE THING. CONVINCE IT THAT IT'S BURNING IN HELL, AND THE BODY WILL FEEL REAL HELLFIRE.
TEN MORE MINUTES IS ALL IT TAKES. TEN MINUTES FOR ME TO UNDERSTAND EVERYTHING.
INMATE
TO REMEMBER
EVERYTHING.
EPIPHANY, I KNOW THINGS GOT MESSY WITH FAECES MCCARTNEY AND THOSE PUNKS. DOESN'T MEAN WE HAVE TO HATE EACH OTHER.
BZZZZ
I THOUGHT I TOLD YOU TO STAY OUT OF MY FUCKING LIFE.
SEEMS CRAZY YOU SLEEPING HERE, AMONG ALL THESE NASTY CHEMICALS AND POTIONS.

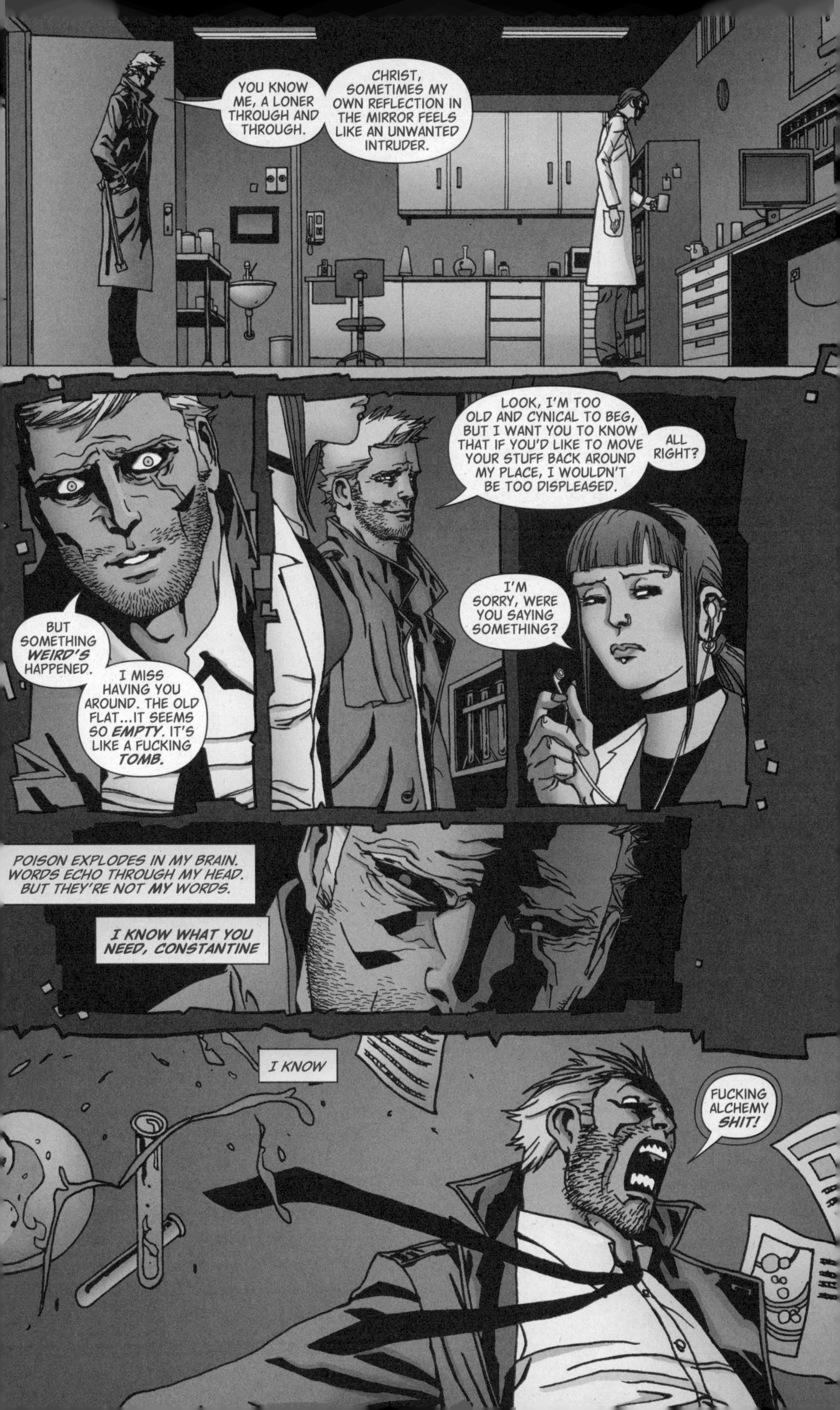

YOU KNOW ME, A LONER THROUGH AND THROUGH.
CHRIST, SOMETIMES MY OWN REFLECTION IN THE MIRROR FEELS LIKE AN UNWANTED INTRUDER.
BUT SOMETHING WEIRD'S HAPPENED.
I MISS HAVING YOU AROUND. THE OLD FLAT...IT SEEMS SO EMPTY. IT'S LIKE A FUCKING TOMB.
LOOK, I'M TOO OLD AND CYNICAL TO BEG, BUT I WANT YOU TO KNOW THAT IF YOU'D LIKE TO MOVE YOUR STUFF BACK AROUND MY PLACE, I WOULDN'T BE TOO DISPLEASED.
ALL RIGHT?
I'M SORRY, WERE YOU SAYING SOMETHING?
POISON EXPLODES IN MY BRAIN. WORDS ECHO THROUGH MY HEAD. BUT THEY'RE NOT MY WORDS.
I KNOW WHAT YOU NEED, CONSTANTINE
I KNOW
FUCKING ALCHEMY SHIT!

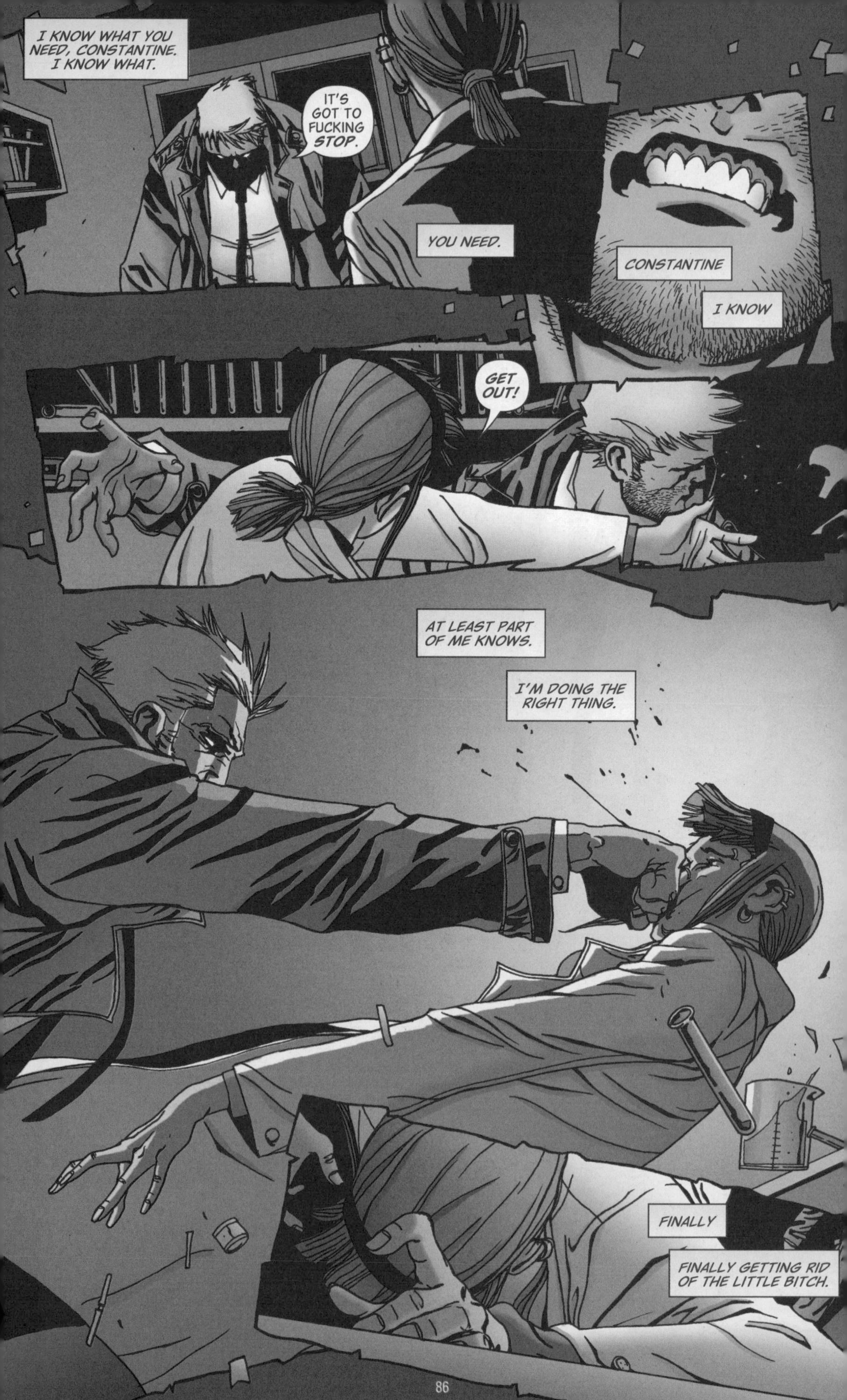

I KNOW WHAT YOU NEED, CONSTANTINE. I KNOW WHAT.
IT'S GOT TO FUCKING STOP.
YOU NEED.
CONSTANTINE
I KNOW
GET OUT!
AT LEAST PART OF ME KNOWS.
I'M DOING THE RIGHT THING.
FINALLY
FINALLY GETTING RID OF THE LITTLE BITCH.

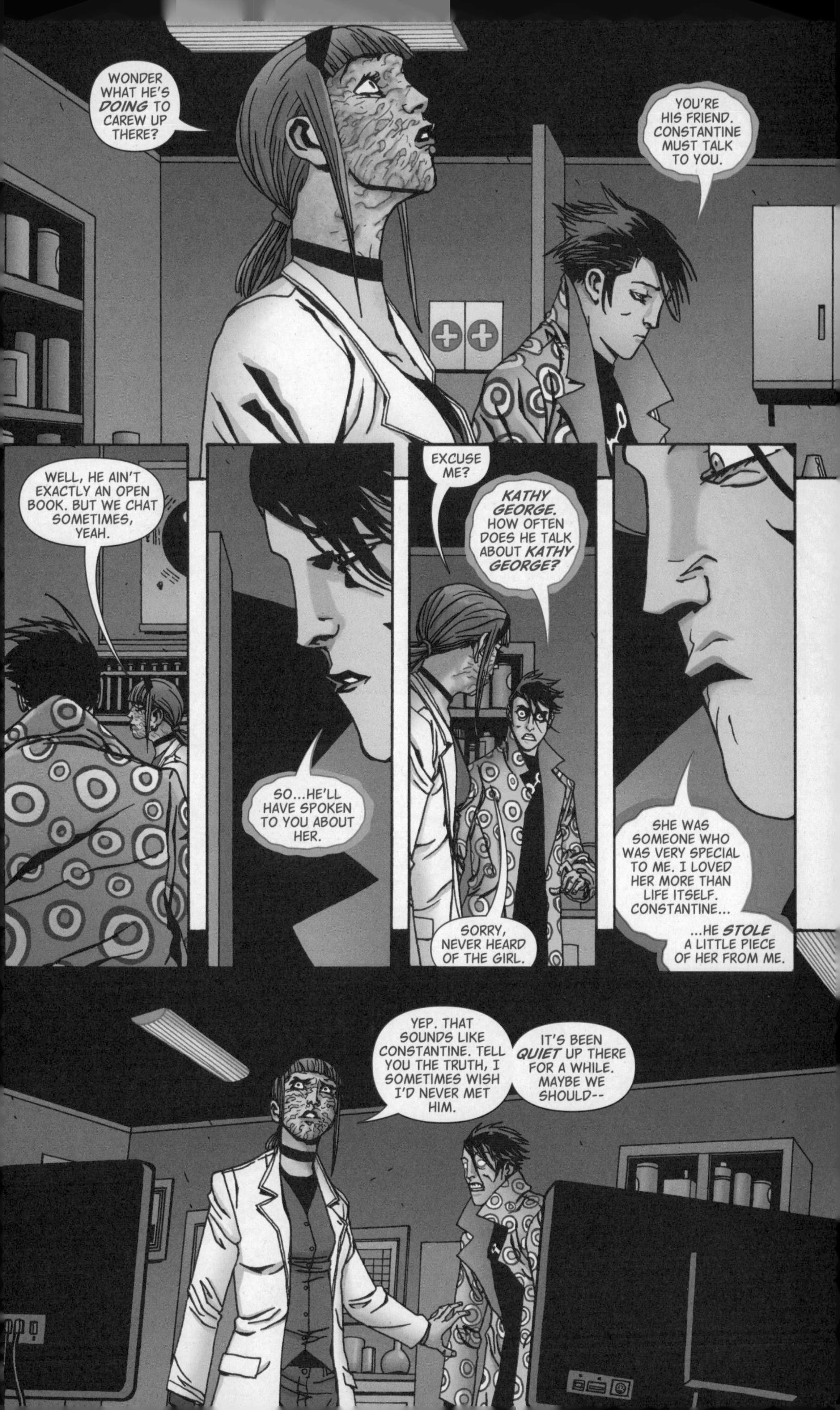
WONDER WHAT HE'S DOING TO CAREW UP THERE?
YOU'RE HIS FRIEND. CONSTANTINE MUST TALK TO YOU.
WELL, HE AIN'T EXACTLY AN OPEN BOOK. BUT WE CHAT SOMETIMES, YEAH.
SO...HE'LL HAVE SPOKEN TO YOU ABOUT HER.
EXCUSE ME?
KATHY GEORGE. HOW OFTEN DOES HE TALK ABOUT KATHY GEORGE?
SORRY, NEVER HEARD OF THE GIRL.
SHE WAS SOMEONE WHO WAS VERY SPECIAL TO ME. I LOVED HER MORE THAN LIFE ITSELF. CONSTANTINE...
...HE STOLE A LITTLE PIECE OF HER FROM ME.
YEP. THAT SOUNDS LIKE CONSTANTINE. TELL YOU THE TRUTH, I SOMETIMES WISH I'D NEVER MET HIM.
IT'S BEEN QUIET UP THERE FOR A WHILE. MAYBE WE SHOULD--

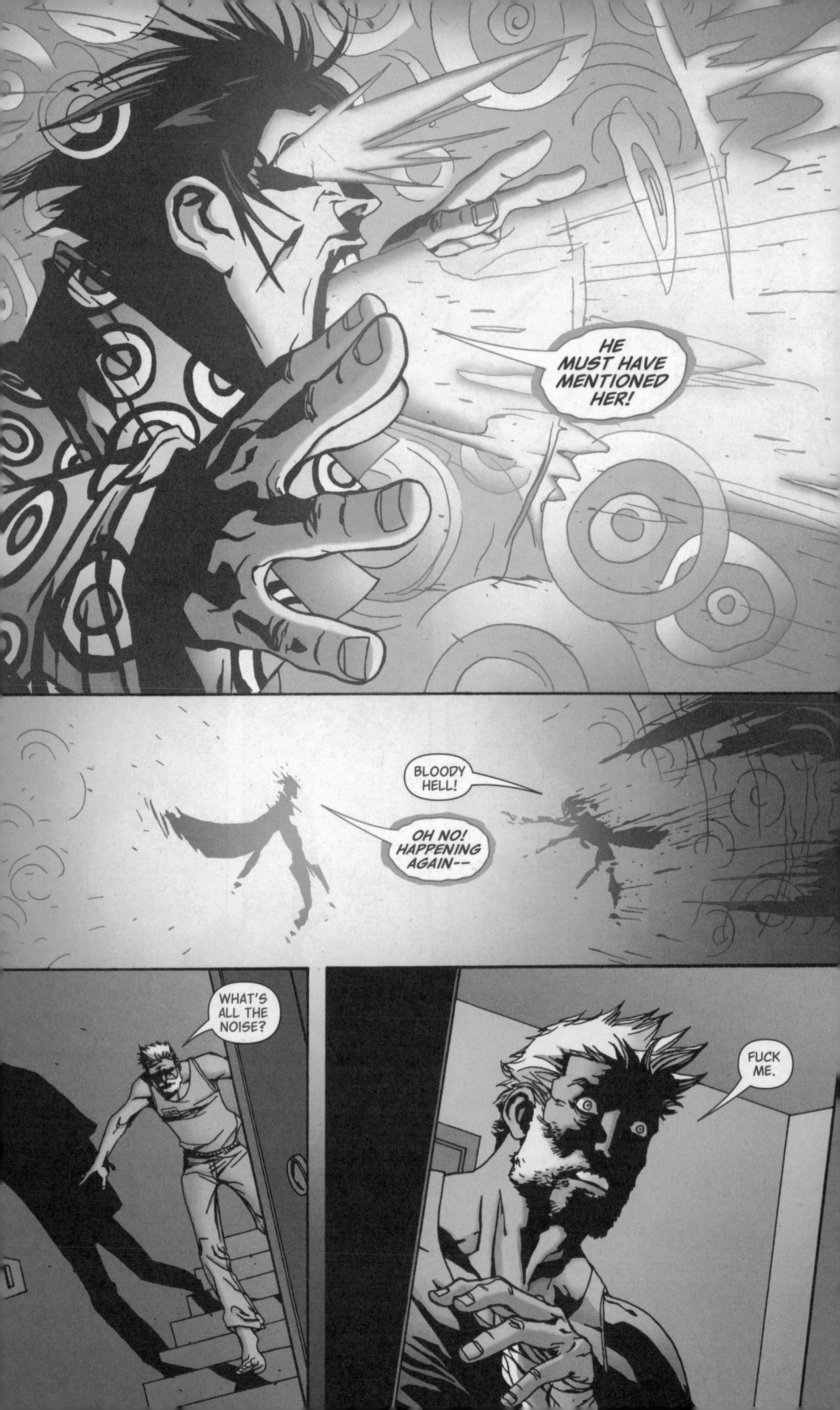
HE MUST HAVE MENTIONED HER!
BLOODY HELL!
OH NO! HAPPENING AGAIN--
WHAT'S ALL THE NOISE?
FUCK ME.

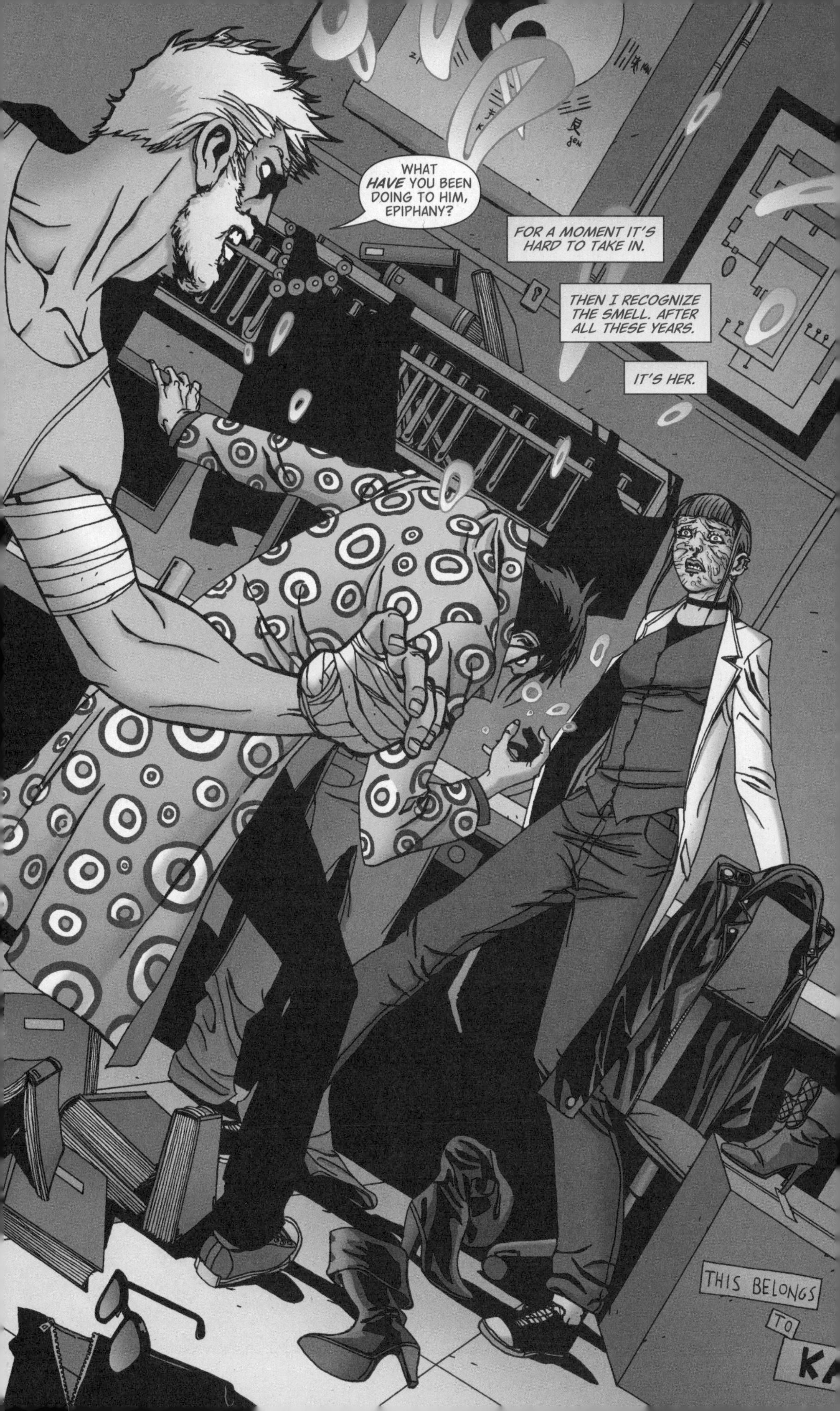
WHAT HAVE YOU BEEN DOING TO HIM, EPIPHANY?
FOR A MOMENT IT'S HARD TO TAKE IN.
THEN I RECOGNIZE THE SMELL. AFTER ALL THESE YEARS.
IT'S HER.
THIS BELONGS TO KA

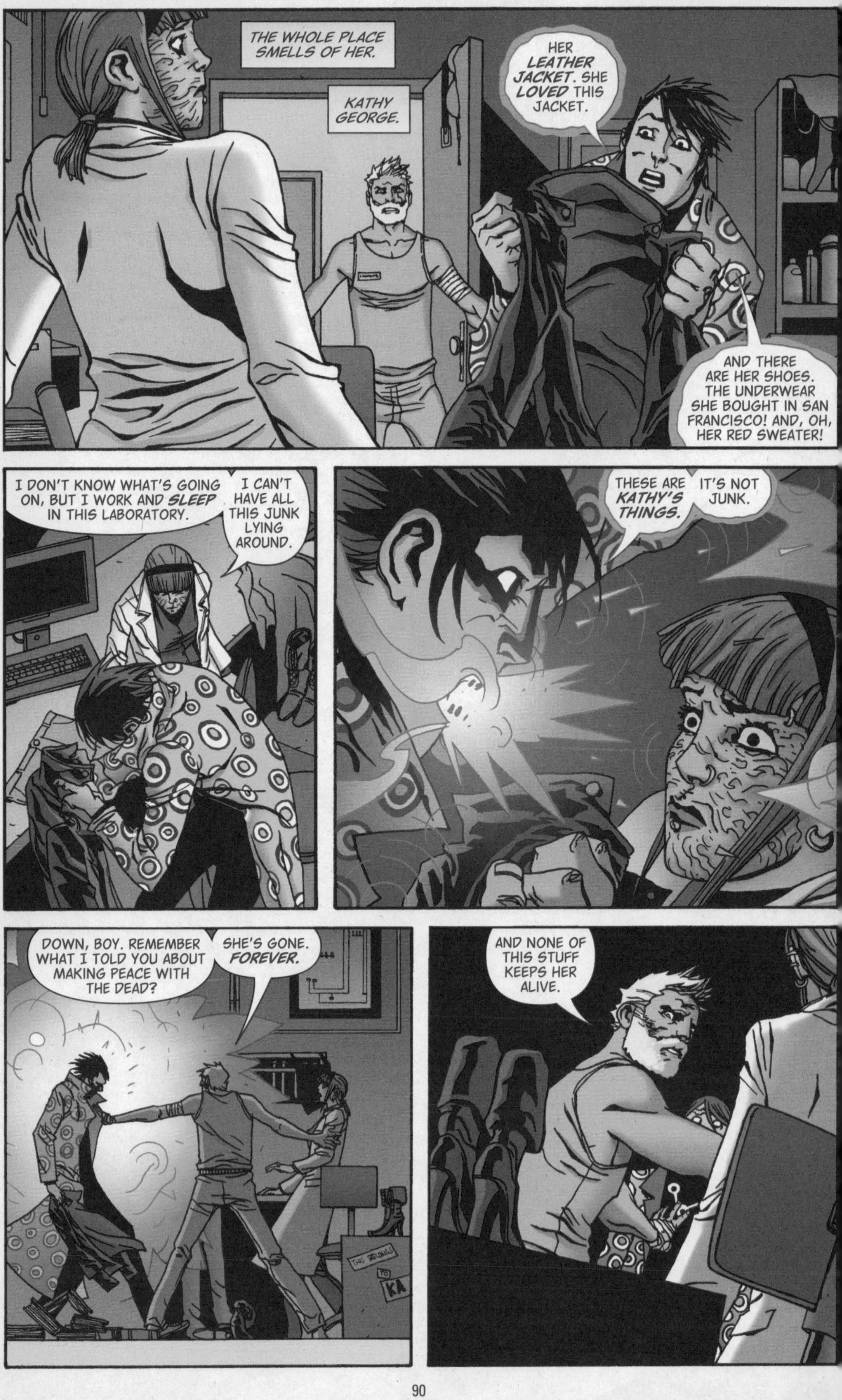
THE WHOLE PLACE SMELLS OF HER.
KATHY GEORGE.
HER LEATHER JACKET. SHE LOVED THIS JACKET.
AND THERE ARE HER SHOES. THE UNDERWEAR SHE BOUGHT IN SAN FRANCISCO! AND, OH, HER RED SWEATER!
I DON'T KNOW WHAT'S GOING ON, BUT I WORK AND SLEEP IN THIS LABORATORY.
I CAN'T HAVE ALL THIS JUNK LYING AROUND.
THESE ARE KATHY'S THINGS.
IT'S NOT JUNK.
DOWN, BOY. REMEMBER WHAT I TOLD YOU ABOUT MAKING PEACE WITH THE DEAD?
SHE'S GONE. FOREVER.
AND NONE OF THIS STUFF KEEPS HER ALIVE.

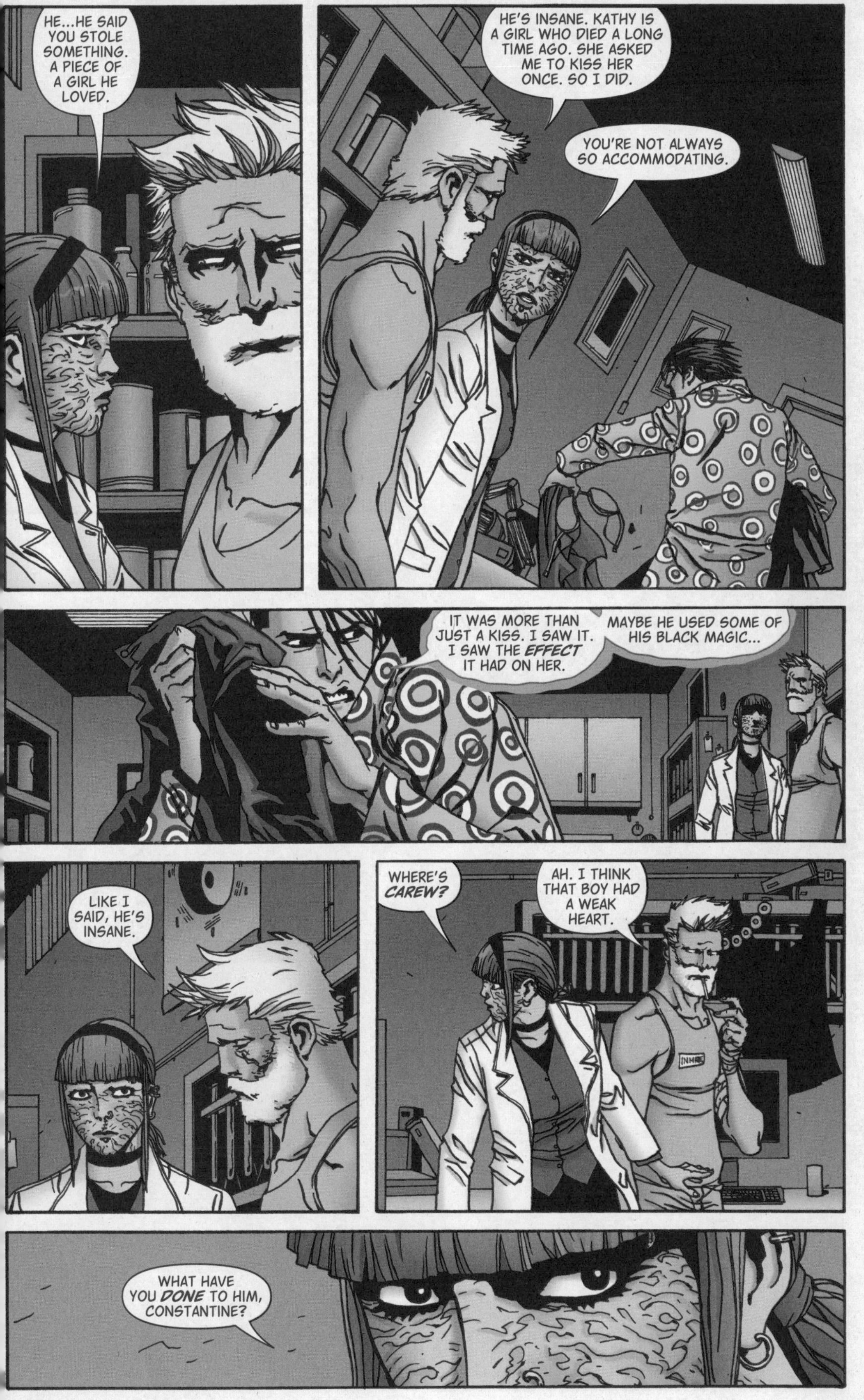
HE...HE SAID YOU STOLE SOMETHING. A PIECE OF A GIRL HE LOVED.
HE'S INSANE. KATHY IS A GIRL WHO DIED A LONG TIME AGO. SHE ASKED ME TO KISS HER ONCE. SO I DID.
YOU'RE NOT ALWAYS SO ACCOMMODATING.
IT WAS MORE THAN JUST A KISS. I SAW IT. I SAW THE *EFFECT* IT HAD ON HER.
MAYBE HE USED SOME OF HIS BLACK MAGIC...
LIKE I SAID, HE'S INSANE.
WHERE'S *CAREW?*
AH. I THINK THAT BOY HAD A WEAK HEART.
WHAT HAVE YOU *DONE* TO HIM, CONSTANTINE?

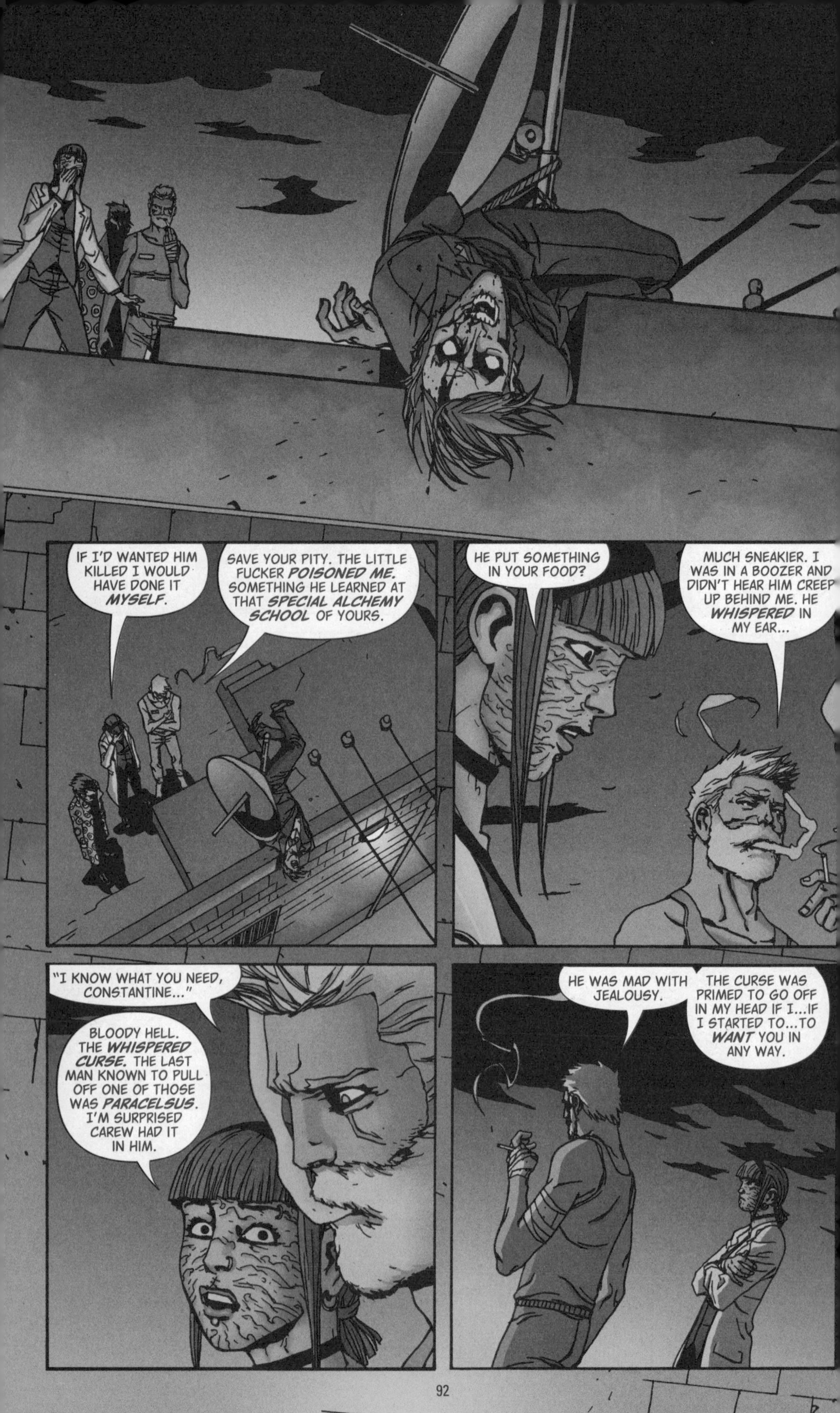
IF I'D WANTED HIM KILLED I WOULD HAVE DONE IT MYSELF.
SAVE YOUR PITY. THE LITTLE FUCKER POISONED ME. SOMETHING HE LEARNED AT THAT SPECIAL ALCHEMY SCHOOL OF YOURS.
HE PUT SOMETHING IN YOUR FOOD?
MUCH SNEAKIER. I WAS IN A BOOZER AND DIDN'T HEAR HIM CREEP UP BEHIND ME. HE WHISPERED IN MY EAR...
"I KNOW WHAT YOU NEED, CONSTANTINE..."
BLOODY HELL. THE WHISPERED CURSE. THE LAST MAN KNOWN TO PULL OFF ONE OF THOSE WAS PARACELSUS. I'M SURPRISED CAREW HAD IT IN HIM.
HE WAS MAD WITH JEALOUSY.
THE CURSE WAS PRIMED TO GO OFF IN MY HEAD IF I...IF I STARTED TO...TO WANT YOU IN ANY WAY.

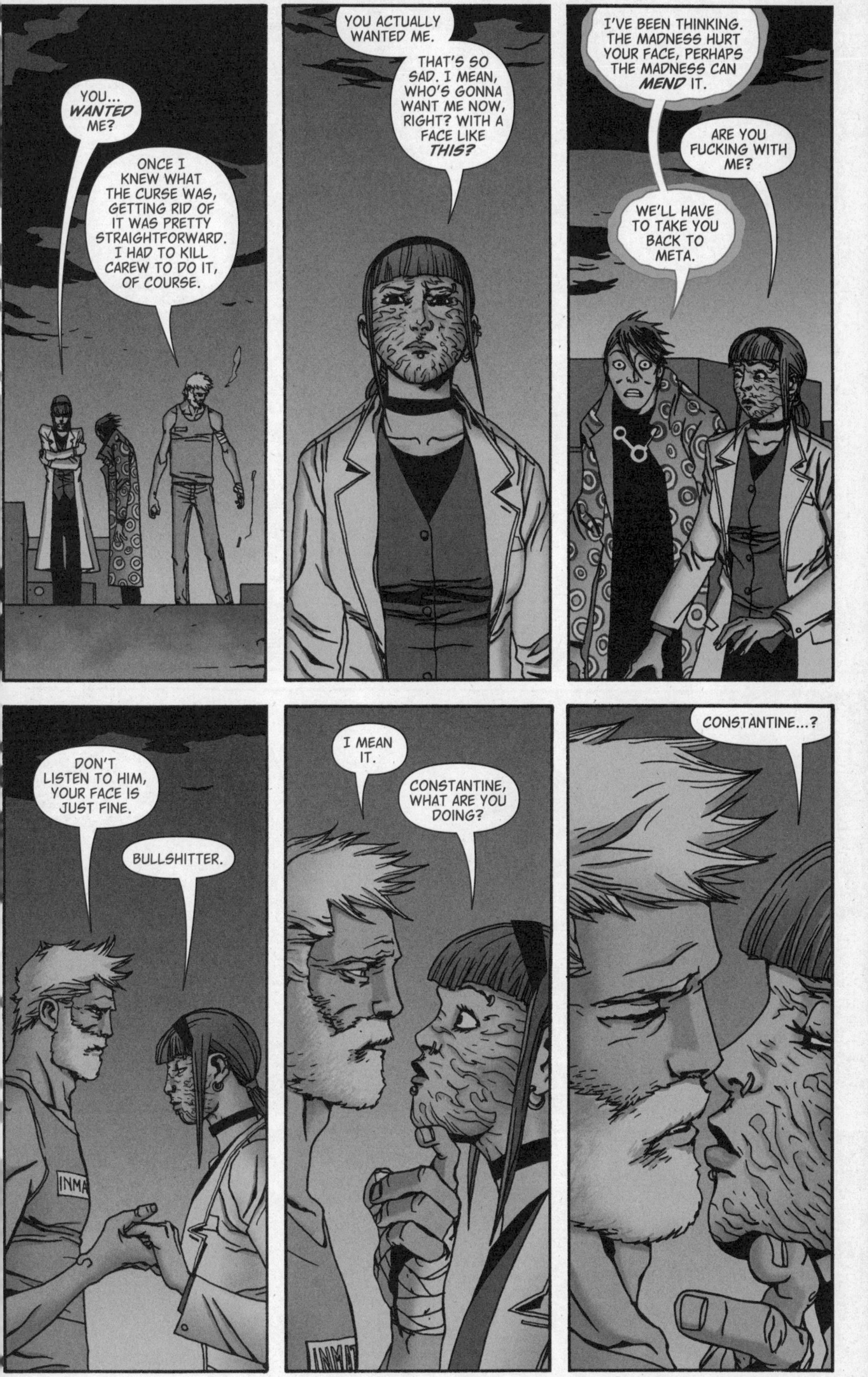
YOU... WANTED ME?
ONCE I KNEW WHAT THE CURSE WAS, GETTING RID OF IT WAS PRETTY STRAIGHTFORWARD. I HAD TO KILL CAREW TO DO IT, OF COURSE.
YOU ACTUALLY WANTED ME.
THAT'S SO SAD. I MEAN, WHO'S GONNA WANT ME NOW, RIGHT? WITH A FACE LIKE THIS?
I'VE BEEN THINKING. THE MADNESS HURT YOUR FACE, PERHAPS THE MADNESS CAN MEND IT.
ARE YOU FUCKING WITH ME?
WE'LL HAVE TO TAKE YOU BACK TO META.
DON'T LISTEN TO HIM, YOUR FACE IS JUST FINE.
BULLSHITTER.
INMA
I MEAN IT.
CONSTANTINE, WHAT ARE YOU DOING?
INMAT
CONSTANTINE...?

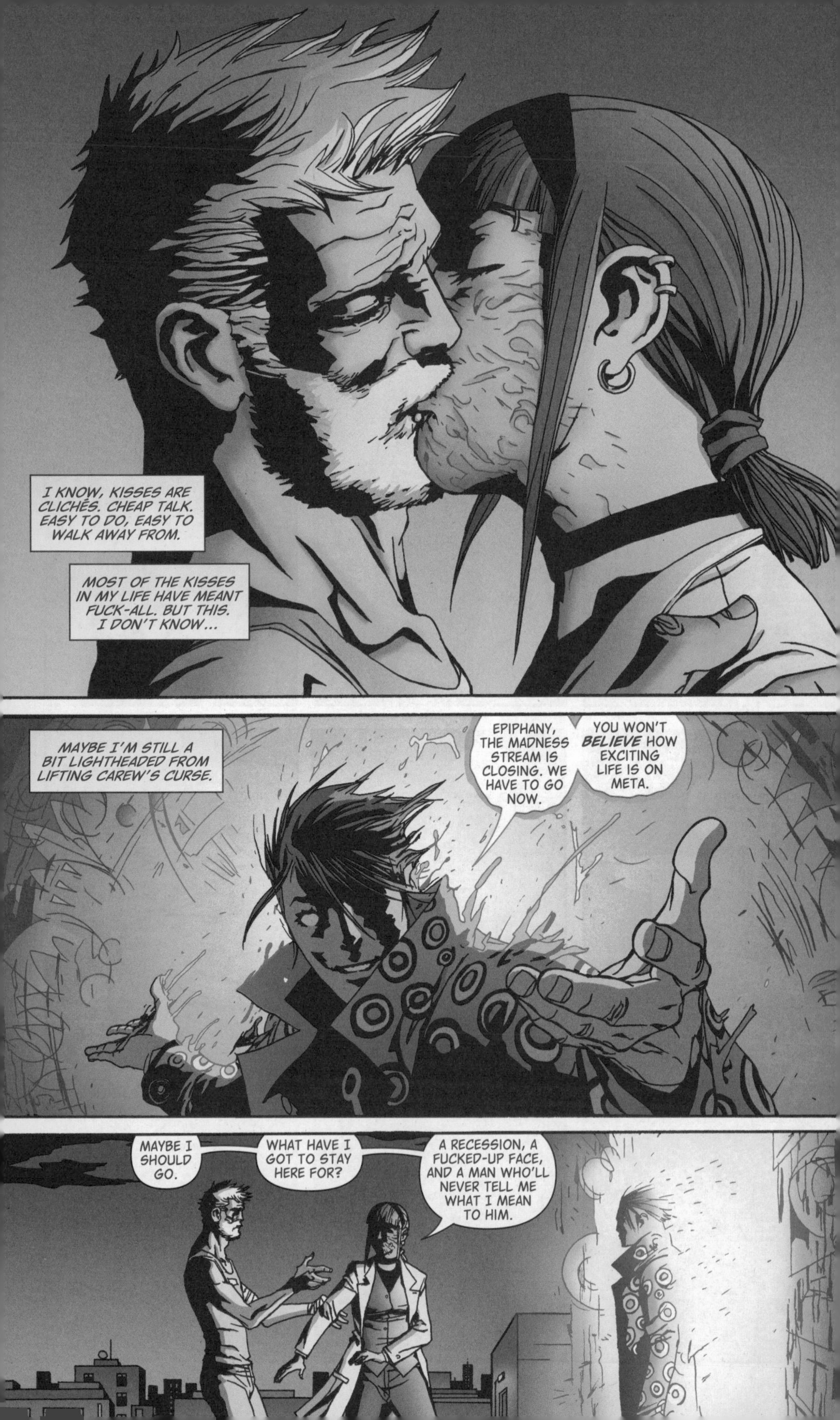
I KNOW, KISSES ARE CLICHÉS. CHEAP TALK. EASY TO DO, EASY TO WALK AWAY FROM.
MOST OF THE KISSES IN MY LIFE HAVE MEANT FUCK-ALL. BUT THIS. I DON'T KNOW...
MAYBE I'M STILL A BIT LIGHTHEADED FROM LIFTING CAREW'S CURSE.
EPIPHANY, THE MADNESS STREAM IS CLOSING. WE HAVE TO GO NOW.
YOU WON'T *BELIEVE* HOW EXCITING LIFE IS ON META.
MAYBE I SHOULD GO.
WHAT HAVE I GOT TO STAY HERE FOR?
A RECESSION, A FUCKED-UP FACE, AND A MAN WHO'LL NEVER TELL ME WHAT I MEAN TO HIM.

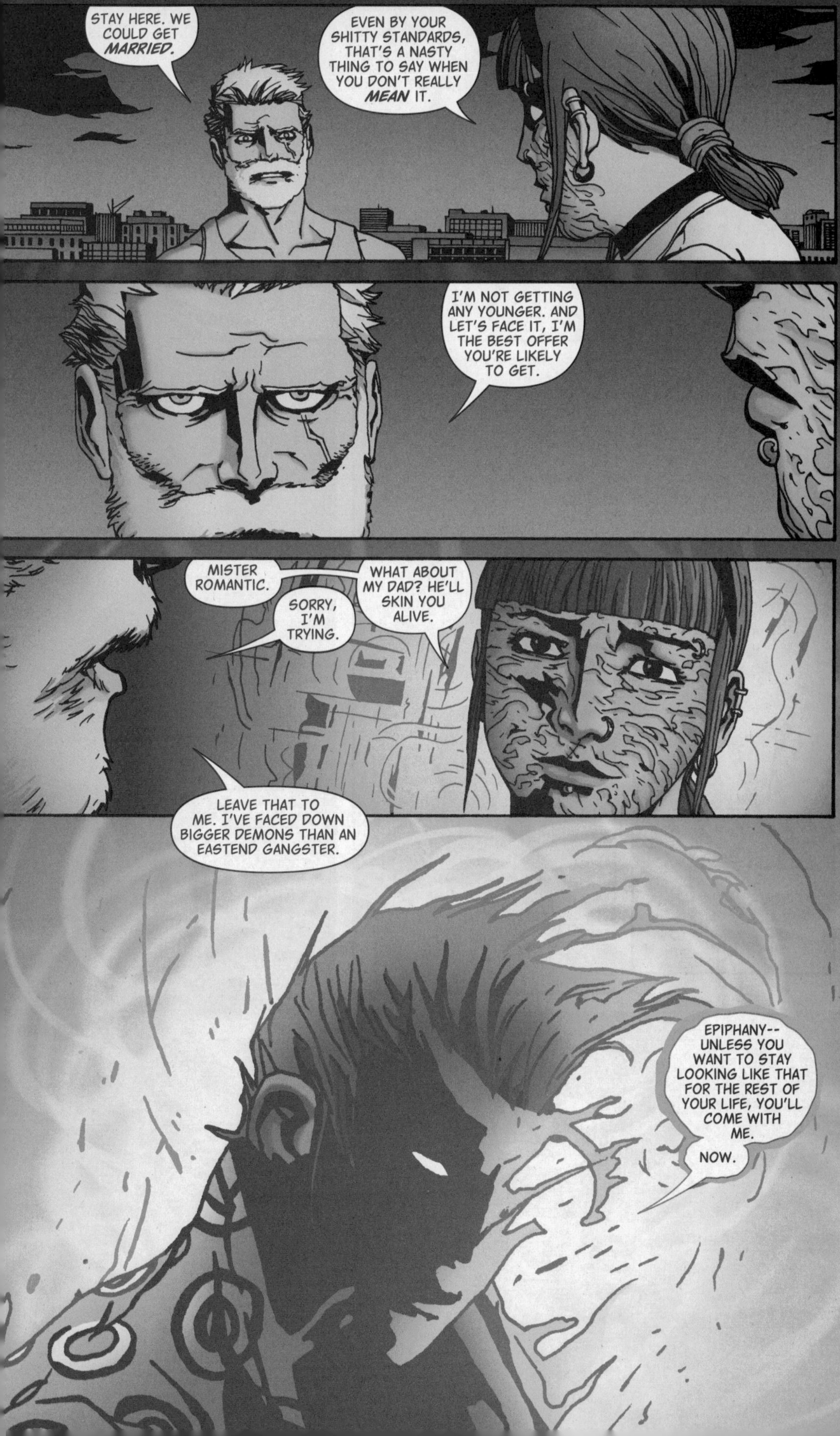

STAY HERE. WE COULD GET *MARRIED.*
EVEN BY YOUR SHITTY STANDARDS, THAT'S A NASTY THING TO SAY WHEN YOU DON'T REALLY *MEAN* IT.
I'M NOT GETTING ANY YOUNGER. AND LET'S FACE IT, I'M THE BEST OFFER YOU'RE LIKELY TO GET.
MISTER ROMANTIC.
SORRY, I'M TRYING.
WHAT ABOUT MY DAD? HE'LL SKIN YOU ALIVE.
LEAVE THAT TO ME. I'VE FACED DOWN BIGGER DEMONS THAN AN EASTEND GANGSTER.
EPIPHANY-- UNLESS YOU WANT TO STAY LOOKING LIKE THAT FOR THE REST OF YOUR LIFE, YOU'LL COME WITH ME.
NOW.

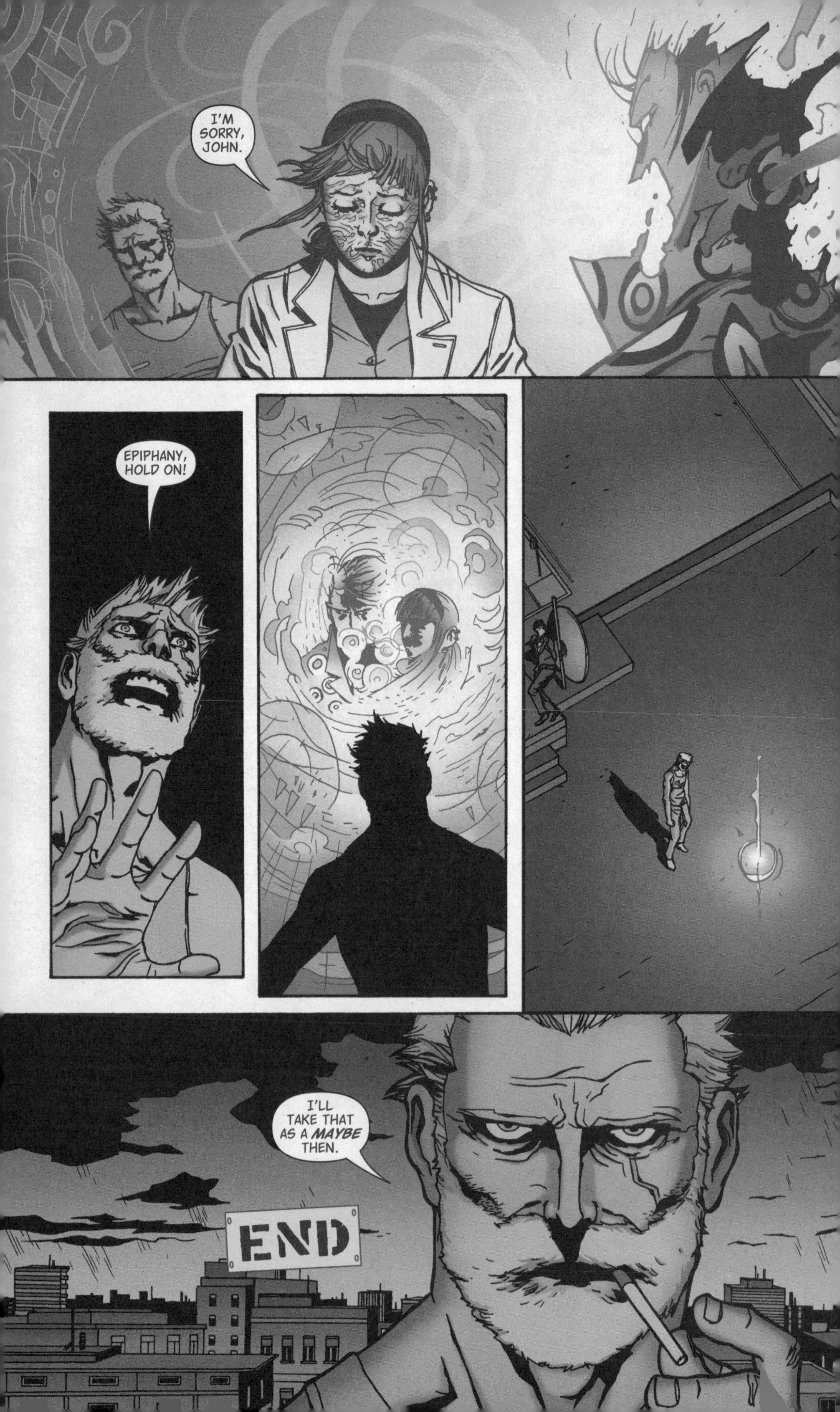
I'M SORRY, JOHN.
EPIPHANY, HOLD ON!
I'LL TAKE THAT AS A *MAYBE* THEN.
END

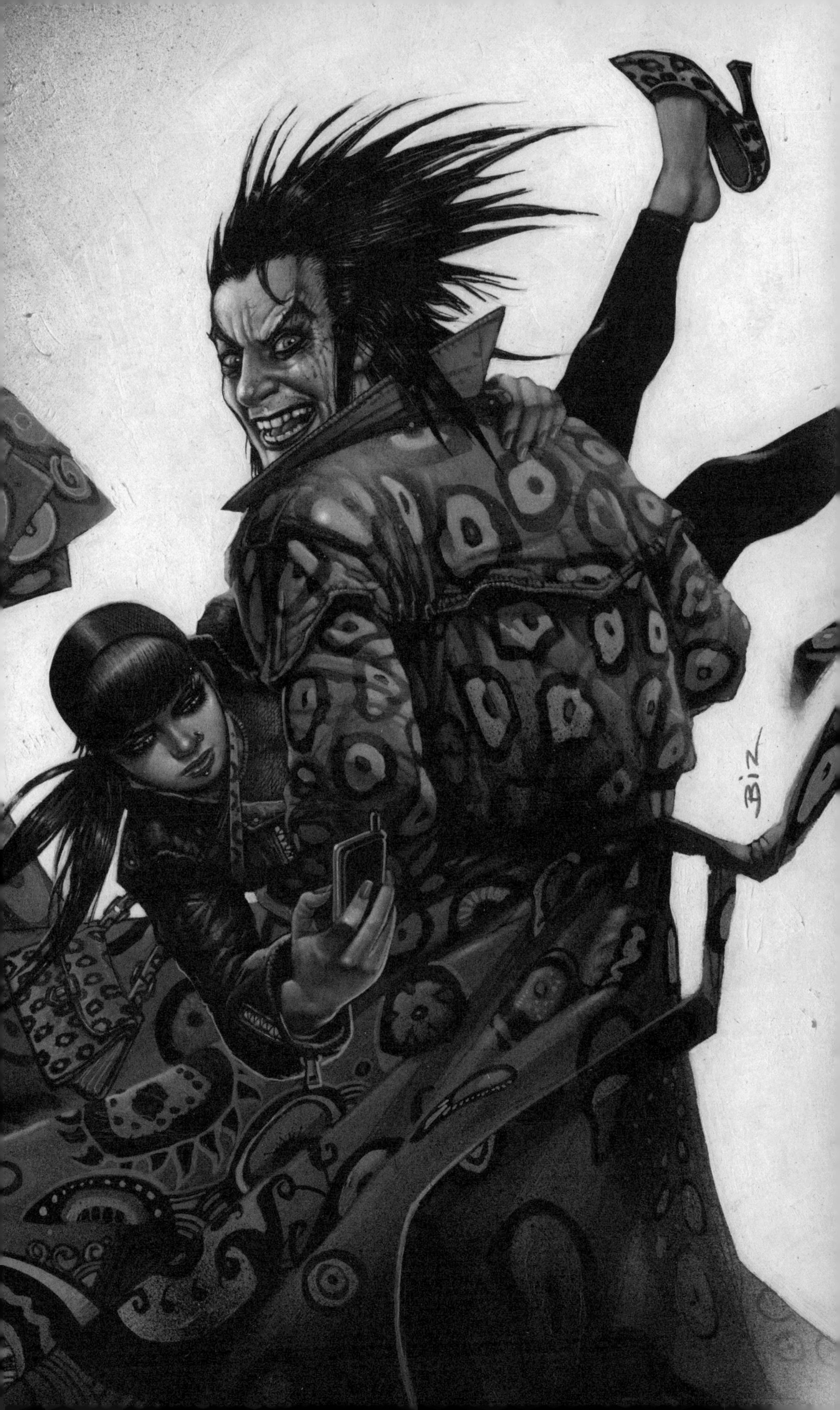

YOU'RE A LUCKY M-MAN, JOHN.

LUCKY? *ME?* HOW DO YOU WORK THAT OUT?

A M-MAN LIKE YOU, M-MARRYING A GIRL HALF YOUR AGE.

SHE AIN'T SAID "YES", YET, HAS SHE?

SO TELL ME...

WHAT MADE YOU WANT TO GET HITCHED TO THIS GIRL?

I'M SUPPOSED TO BE ASKING *YOU* THE QUESTIONS. AS IN, WHAT DOES THE FUTURE HOLD?

WAS I CRAZY TO ASK HER?

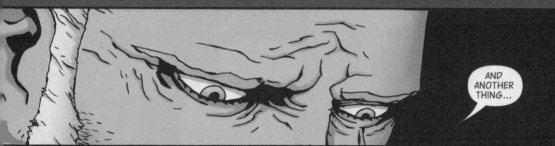

AND ANOTHER THING...

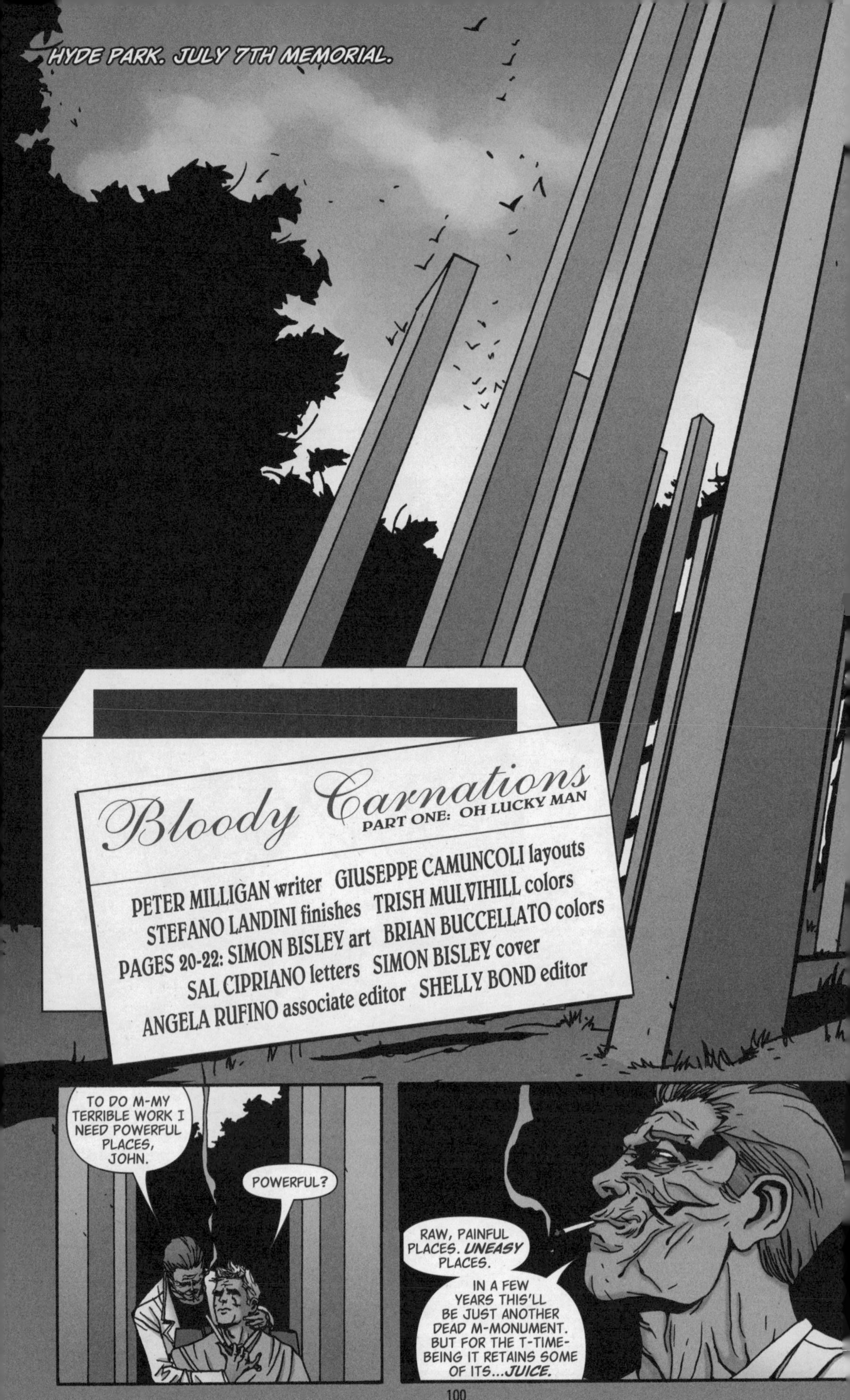
HYDE PARK. JULY 7TH MEMORIAL.
Bloody Carnations
PART ONE: OH LUCKY MAN
PETER MILLIGAN writer GIUSEPPE CAMUNCOLI layouts
STEFANO LANDINI finishes TRISH MULVIHILL colors
PAGES 20-22: SIMON BISLEY art BRIAN BUCCELLATO colors
SAL CIPRIANO letters SIMON BISLEY cover
ANGELA RUFINO associate editor SHELLY BOND editor
TO DO M-MY TERRIBLE WORK I NEED POWERFUL PLACES, JOHN.
POWERFUL?
RAW, PAINFUL PLACES. *UNEASY* PLACES.
IN A FEW YEARS THIS'LL BE JUST ANOTHER DEAD M-MONUMENT. BUT FOR THE T-TIME-BEING IT RETAINS SOME OF ITS...*JUICE*.

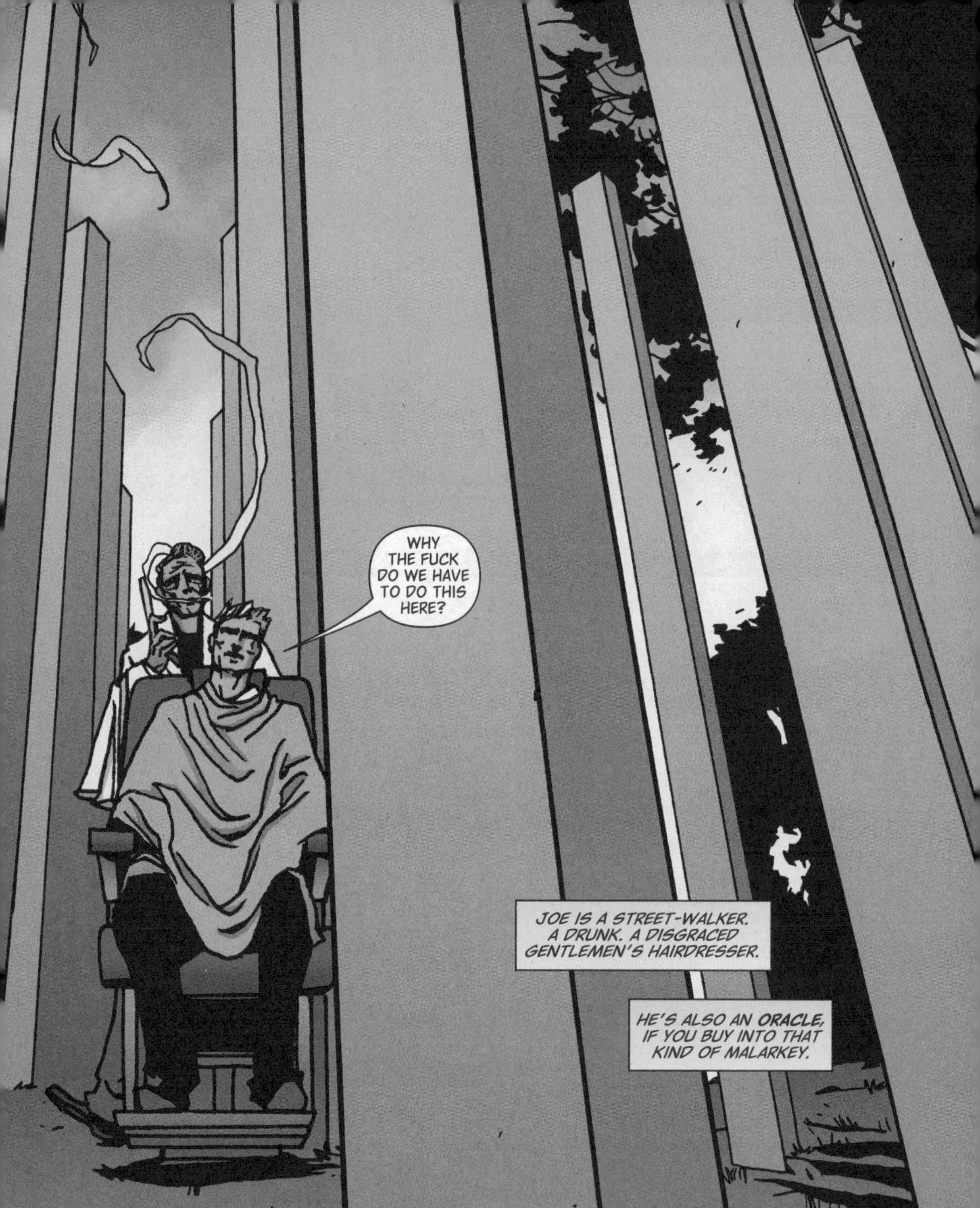
WHY THE FUCK DO WE HAVE TO DO THIS HERE?
JOE IS A STREET-WALKER. A DRUNK. A DISGRACED GENTLEMEN'S HAIRDRESSER.
HE'S ALSO AN ORACLE, IF YOU BUY INTO THAT KIND OF MALARKEY.

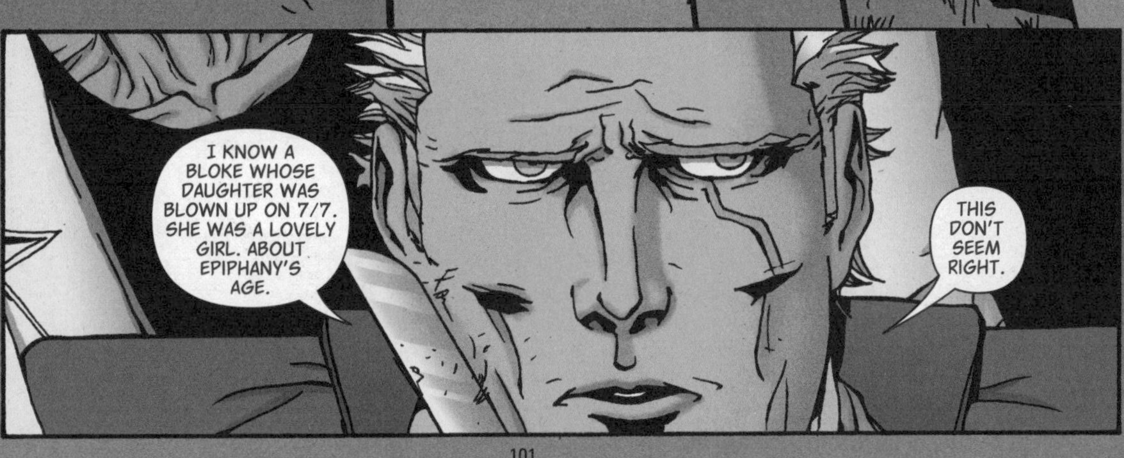
I KNOW A BLOKE WHOSE DAUGHTER WAS BLOWN UP ON 7/7. SHE WAS A LOVELY GIRL. ABOUT EPIPHANY'S AGE.
THIS DON'T SEEM RIGHT.

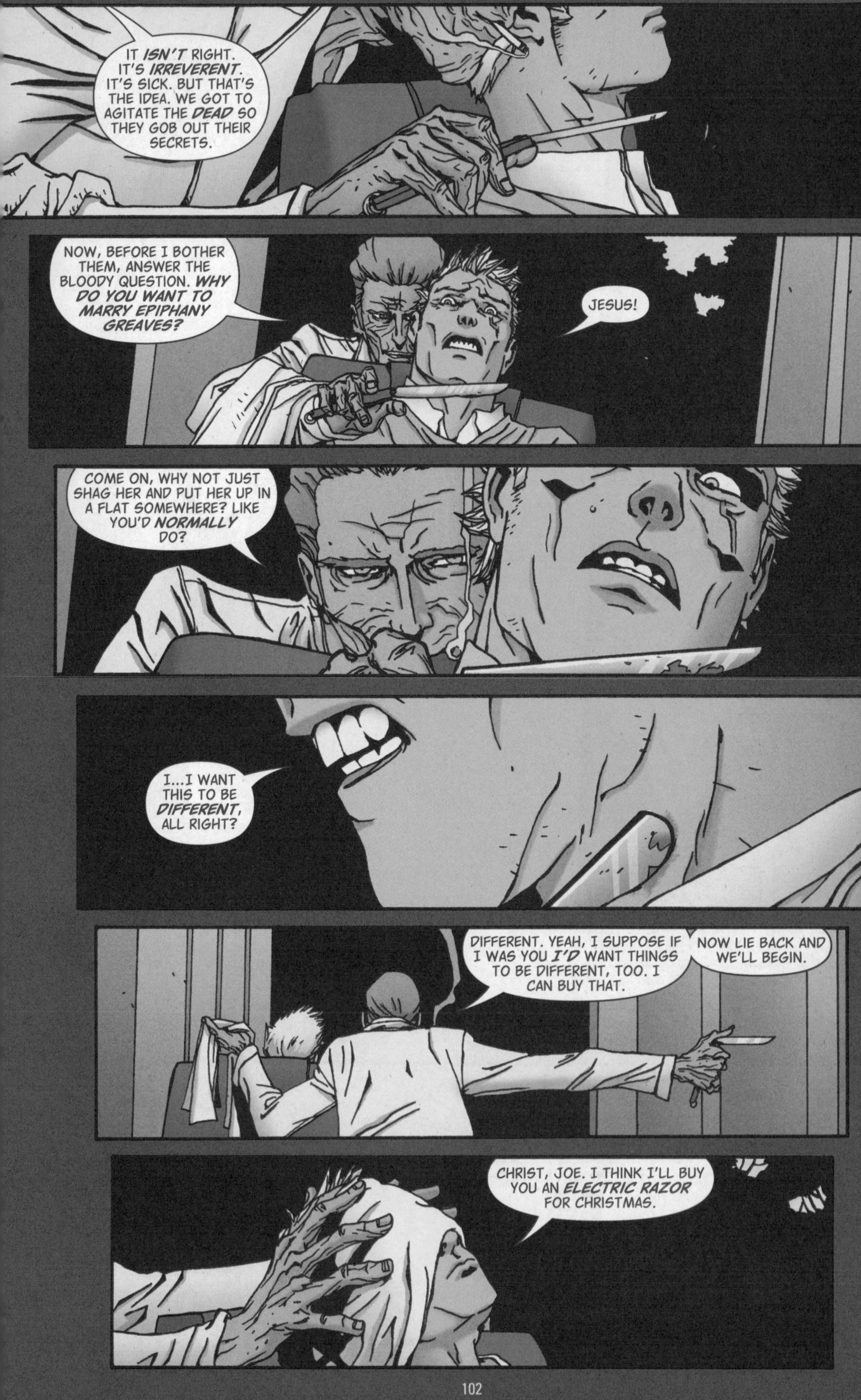
IT ISN'T RIGHT. IT'S IRREVERENT. IT'S SICK. BUT THAT'S THE IDEA. WE GOT TO AGITATE THE DEAD SO THEY GOB OUT THEIR SECRETS.
NOW, BEFORE I BOTHER THEM, ANSWER THE BLOODY QUESTION. WHY DO YOU WANT TO MARRY EPIPHANY GREAVES?
JESUS!
COME ON, WHY NOT JUST SHAG HER AND PUT HER UP IN A FLAT SOMEWHERE? LIKE YOU'D NORMALLY DO?
I...I WANT THIS TO BE DIFFERENT, ALL RIGHT?
DIFFERENT. YEAH, I SUPPOSE IF I WAS YOU I'D WANT THINGS TO BE DIFFERENT, TOO. I CAN BUY THAT.
NOW LIE BACK AND WE'LL BEGIN.
CHRIST, JOE. I THINK I'LL BUY YOU AN ELECTRIC RAZOR FOR CHRISTMAS.

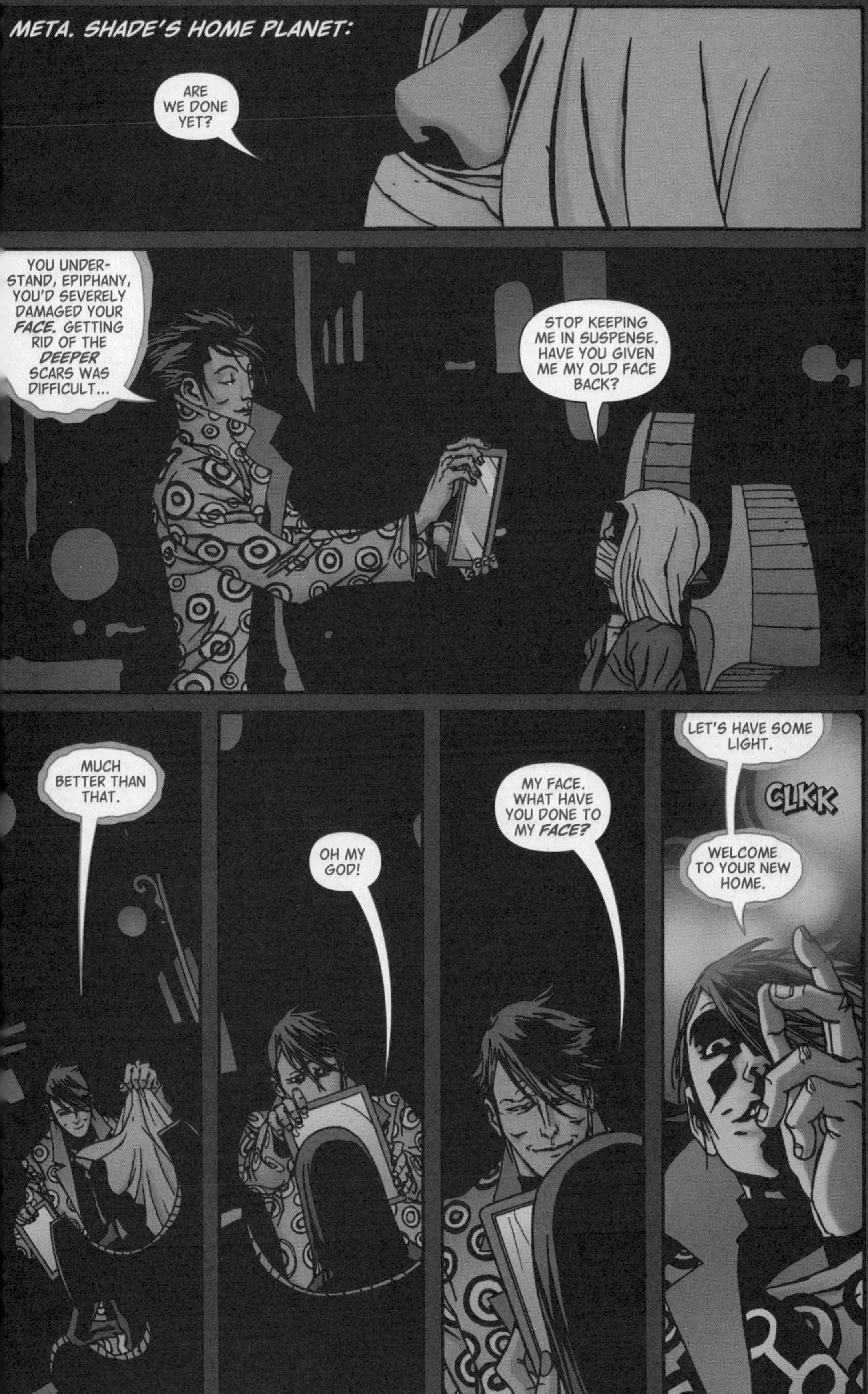
META. SHADE'S HOME PLANET:
ARE WE DONE YET?
YOU UNDERSTAND, EPIPHANY, YOU'D SEVERELY DAMAGED YOUR *FACE.* GETTING RID OF THE *DEEPER* SCARS WAS DIFFICULT...
STOP KEEPING ME IN SUSPENSE. HAVE YOU GIVEN ME MY OLD FACE BACK?
MUCH BETTER THAN THAT.
OH MY GOD!
MY FACE. WHAT HAVE YOU DONE TO MY *FACE?*
LET'S HAVE SOME LIGHT.
CLKK
WELCOME TO YOUR NEW HOME.

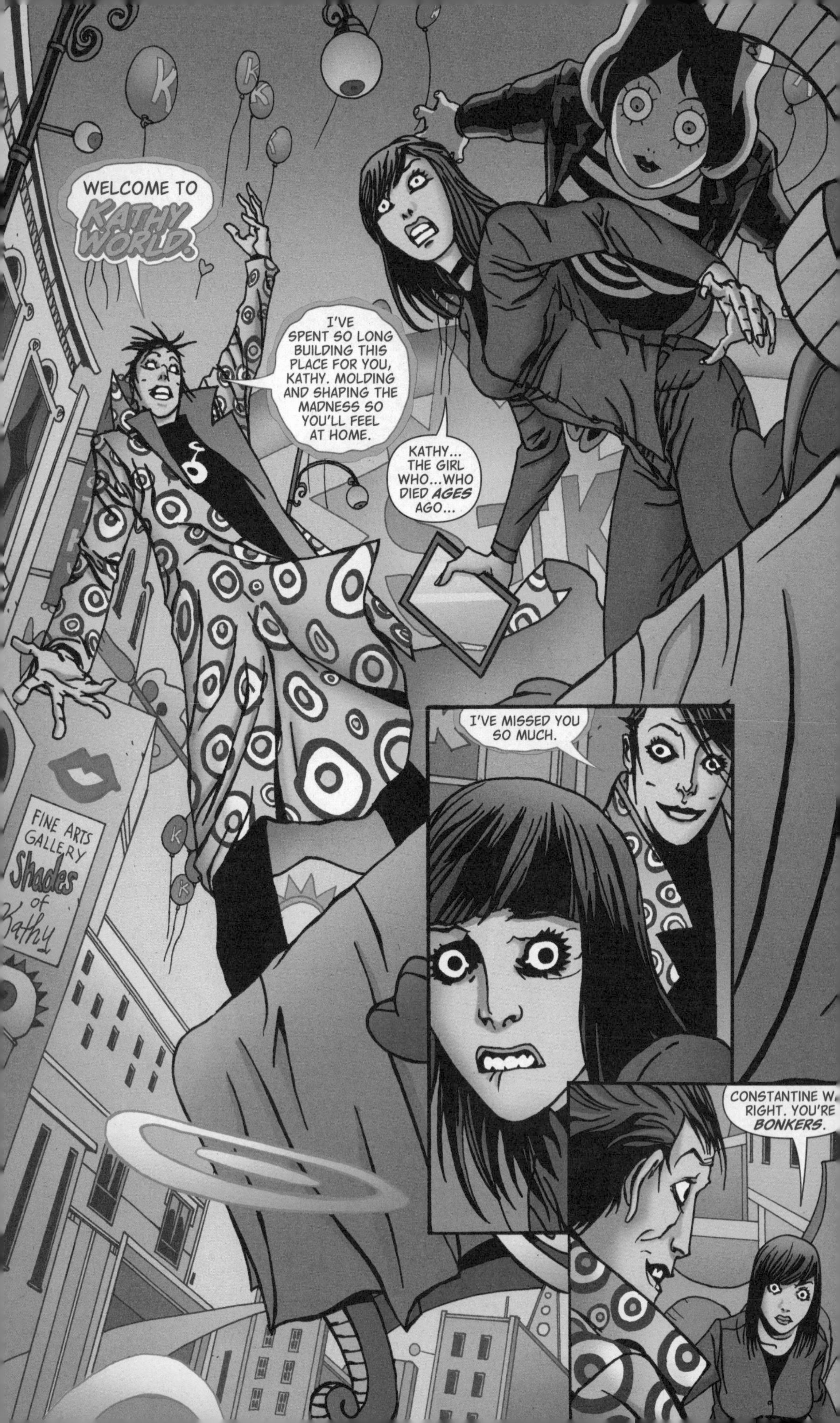

WELCOME TO
KATHY WORLD.
I'VE SPENT SO LONG BUILDING THIS PLACE FOR YOU, KATHY. MOLDING AND SHAPING THE MADNESS SO YOU'LL FEEL AT HOME.
KATHY... THE GIRL WHO...WHO DIED AGES AGO...
FINE ARTS GALLERY Shades of Kathy
I'VE MISSED YOU SO MUCH.
CONSTANTINE W. RIGHT. YOU'RE BONKERS.

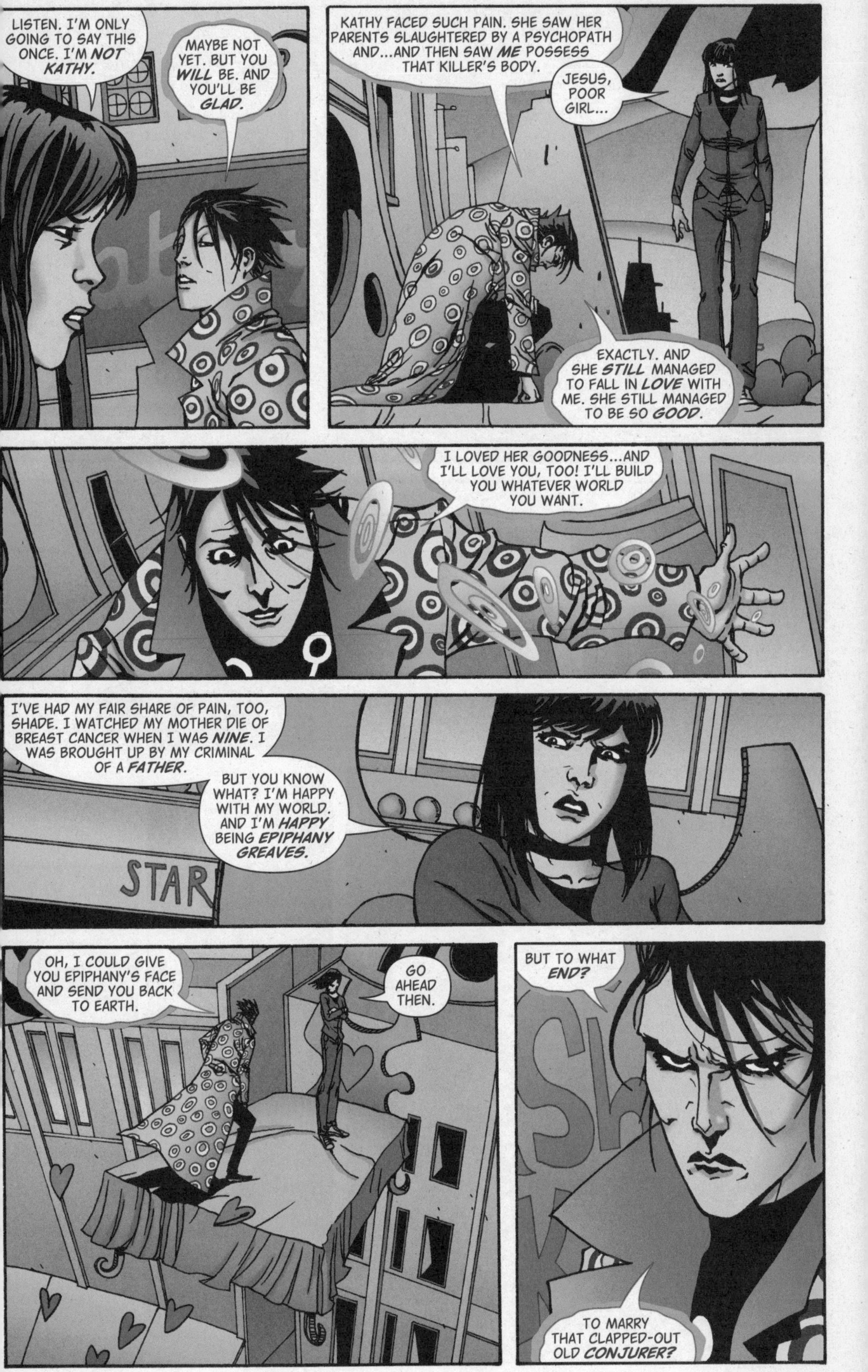
LISTEN. I'M ONLY GOING TO SAY THIS ONCE. I'M NOT KATHY.
MAYBE NOT YET. BUT YOU WILL BE. AND YOU'LL BE GLAD.
KATHY FACED SUCH PAIN. SHE SAW HER PARENTS SLAUGHTERED BY A PSYCHOPATH AND...AND THEN SAW ME POSSESS THAT KILLER'S BODY.
JESUS, POOR GIRL...
EXACTLY. AND SHE STILL MANAGED TO FALL IN LOVE WITH ME. SHE STILL MANAGED TO BE SO GOOD.
I LOVED HER GOODNESS...AND I'LL LOVE YOU, TOO! I'LL BUILD YOU WHATEVER WORLD YOU WANT.
I'VE HAD MY FAIR SHARE OF PAIN, TOO, SHADE. I WATCHED MY MOTHER DIE OF BREAST CANCER WHEN I WAS NINE. I WAS BROUGHT UP BY MY CRIMINAL OF A FATHER.
BUT YOU KNOW WHAT? I'M HAPPY WITH MY WORLD. AND I'M HAPPY BEING EPIPHANY GREAVES.
STAR
OH, I COULD GIVE YOU EPIPHANY'S FACE AND SEND YOU BACK TO EARTH.
GO AHEAD THEN.
BUT TO WHAT END?
TO MARRY THAT CLAPPED-OUT OLD CONJURER?

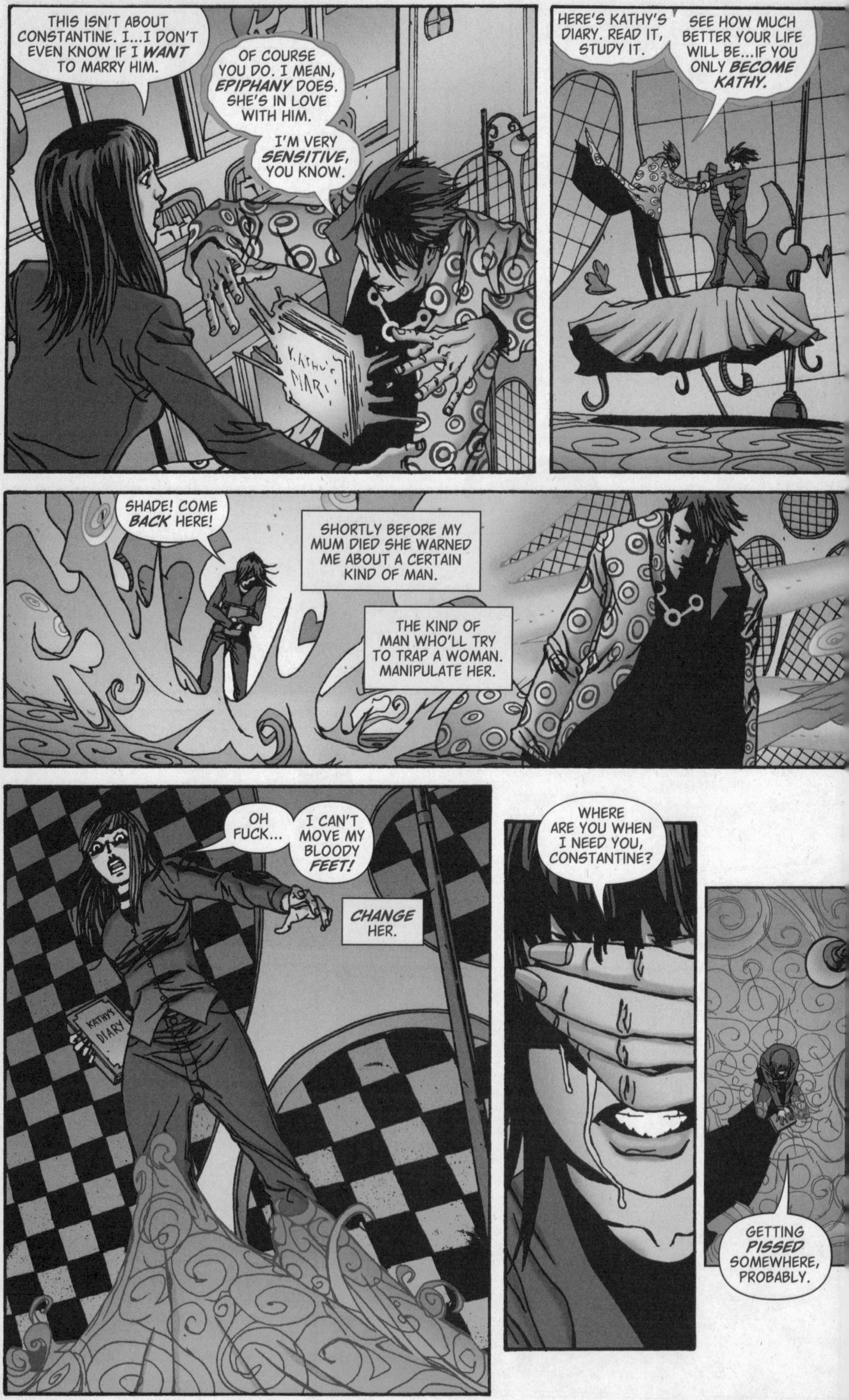
THIS ISN'T ABOUT CONSTANTINE. I...I DON'T EVEN KNOW IF I WANT TO MARRY HIM.
OF COURSE YOU DO. I MEAN, EPIPHANY DOES. SHE'S IN LOVE WITH HIM.
I'M VERY SENSITIVE, YOU KNOW.
KATHY'S DIARY
HERE'S KATHY'S DIARY. READ IT, STUDY IT.
SEE HOW MUCH BETTER YOUR LIFE WILL BE...IF YOU ONLY BECOME KATHY.
SHADE! COME BACK HERE!
SHORTLY BEFORE MY MUM DIED SHE WARNED ME ABOUT A CERTAIN KIND OF MAN.
THE KIND OF MAN WHO'LL TRY TO TRAP A WOMAN. MANIPULATE HER.
OH FUCK...
I CAN'T MOVE MY BLOODY FEET!
CHANGE HER.
KATHY'S DIARY
WHERE ARE YOU WHEN I NEED YOU, CONSTANTINE?
GETTING PISSED SOMEWHERE, PROBABLY.

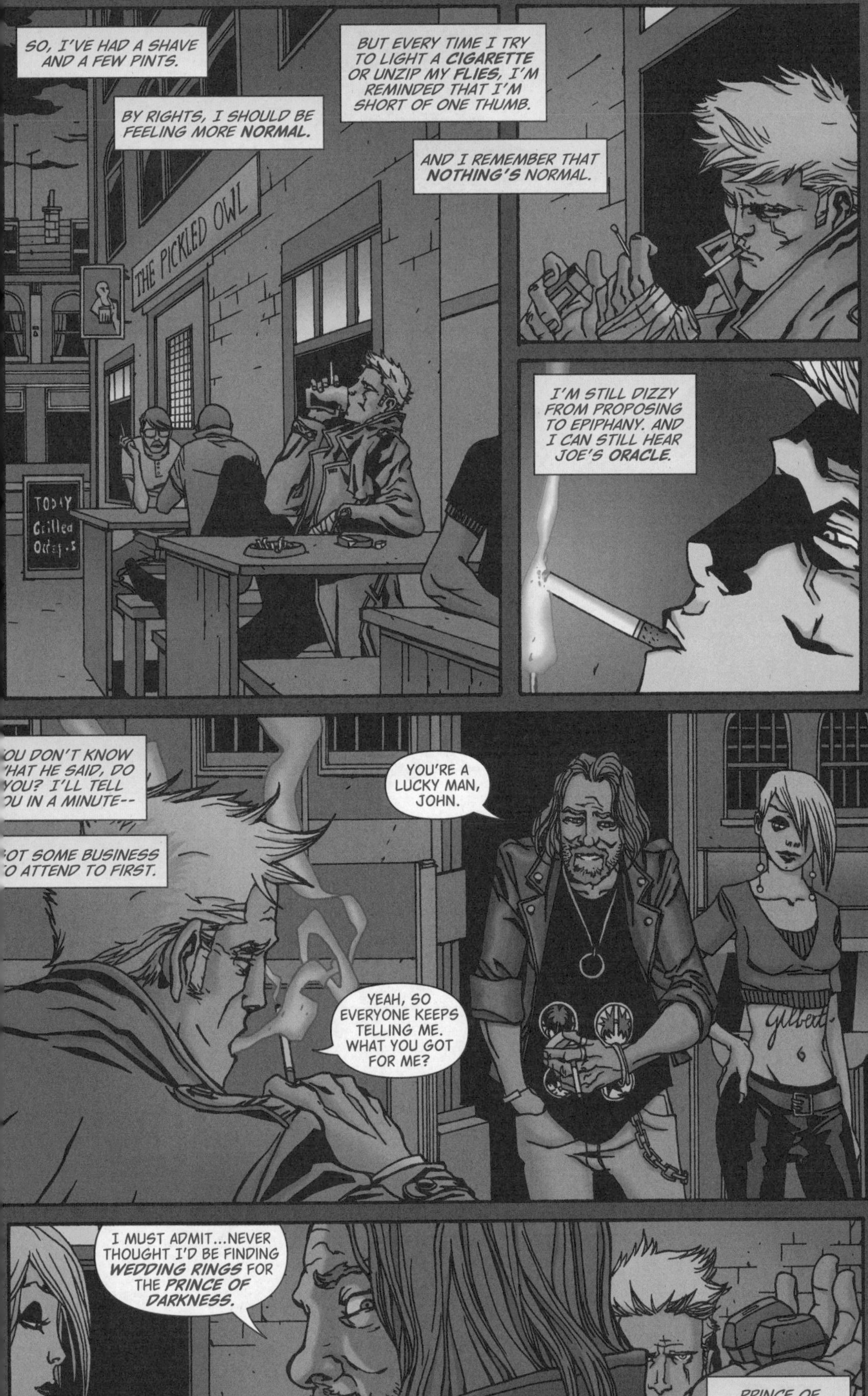
SO, I'VE HAD A SHAVE AND A FEW PINTS.
BY RIGHTS, I SHOULD BE FEELING MORE **NORMAL.**
THE PICKLED OWL
BUT EVERY TIME I TRY TO LIGHT A **CIGARETTE** OR UNZIP MY **FLIES,** I'M REMINDED THAT I'M SHORT OF ONE THUMB.
AND I REMEMBER THAT **NOTHING'S** NORMAL.
I'M STILL DIZZY FROM PROPOSING TO EPIPHANY. AND I CAN STILL HEAR JOE'S **ORACLE.**
OU DON'T KNOW HAT HE SAID, DO YOU? I'LL TELL OU IN A MINUTE--
OT SOME BUSINESS O ATTEND TO FIRST.
YOU'RE A LUCKY MAN, JOHN.
YEAH, SO EVERYONE KEEPS TELLING ME. WHAT YOU GOT FOR ME?
I MUST ADMIT...NEVER THOUGHT I'D BE FINDING ***WEDDING RINGS*** FOR THE ***PRINCE OF DARKNESS.***
PRINCE OF DARKNESS, EH?

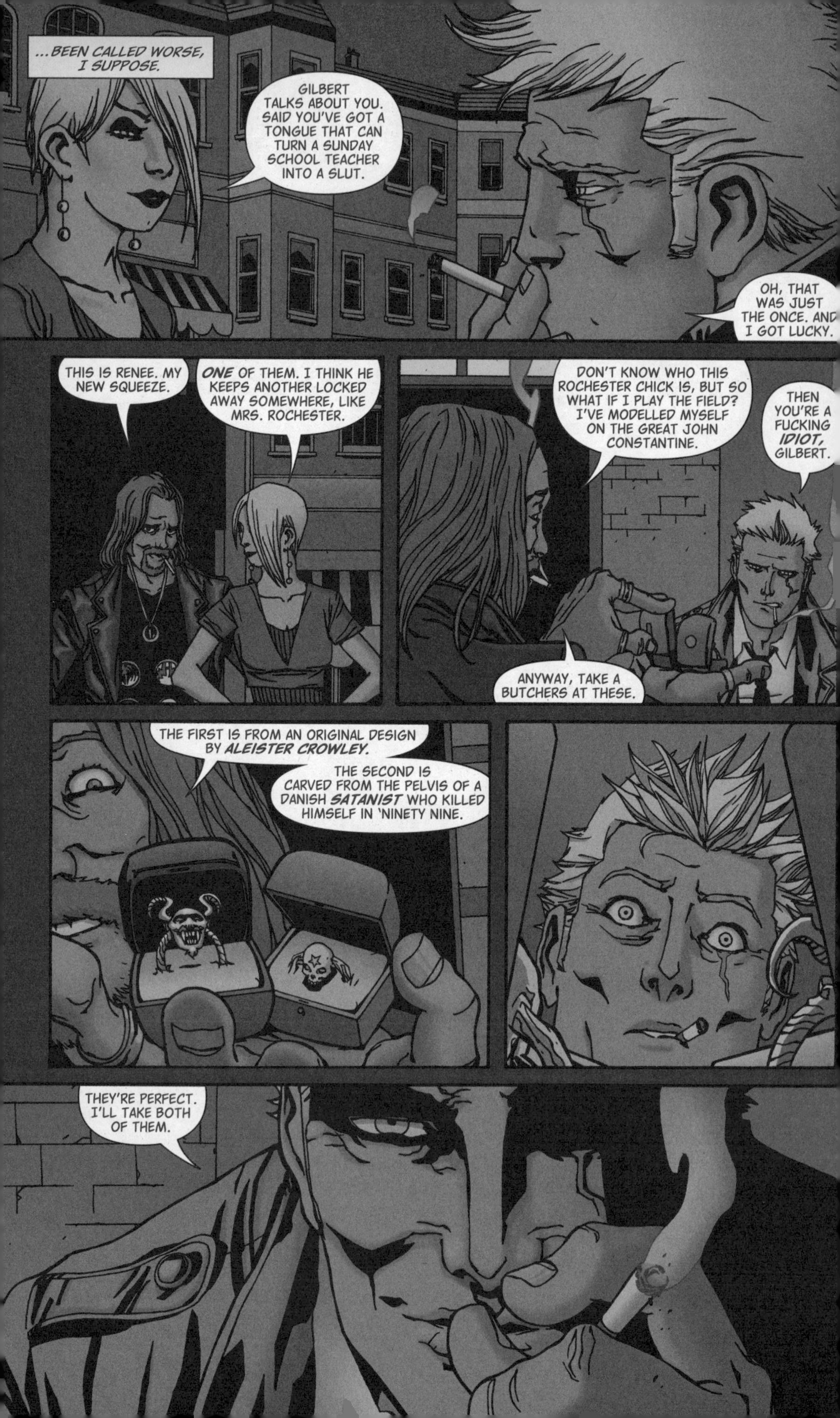
...BEEN CALLED WORSE, I SUPPOSE.
GILBERT TALKS ABOUT YOU. SAID YOU'VE GOT A TONGUE THAT CAN TURN A SUNDAY SCHOOL TEACHER INTO A SLUT.
OH, THAT WAS JUST THE ONCE. AND I GOT LUCKY.
THIS IS RENEE. MY NEW SQUEEZE.
ONE OF THEM. I THINK HE KEEPS ANOTHER LOCKED AWAY SOMEWHERE, LIKE MRS. ROCHESTER.
DON'T KNOW WHO THIS ROCHESTER CHICK IS, BUT SO WHAT IF I PLAY THE FIELD? I'VE MODELLED MYSELF ON THE GREAT JOHN CONSTANTINE.
THEN YOU'RE A FUCKING IDIOT, GILBERT.
ANYWAY, TAKE A BUTCHERS AT THESE.
THE FIRST IS FROM AN ORIGINAL DESIGN BY ALEISTER CROWLEY.
THE SECOND IS CARVED FROM THE PELVIS OF A DANISH SATANIST WHO KILLED HIMSELF IN 'NINETY NINE.
THEY'RE PERFECT. I'LL TAKE BOTH OF THEM.

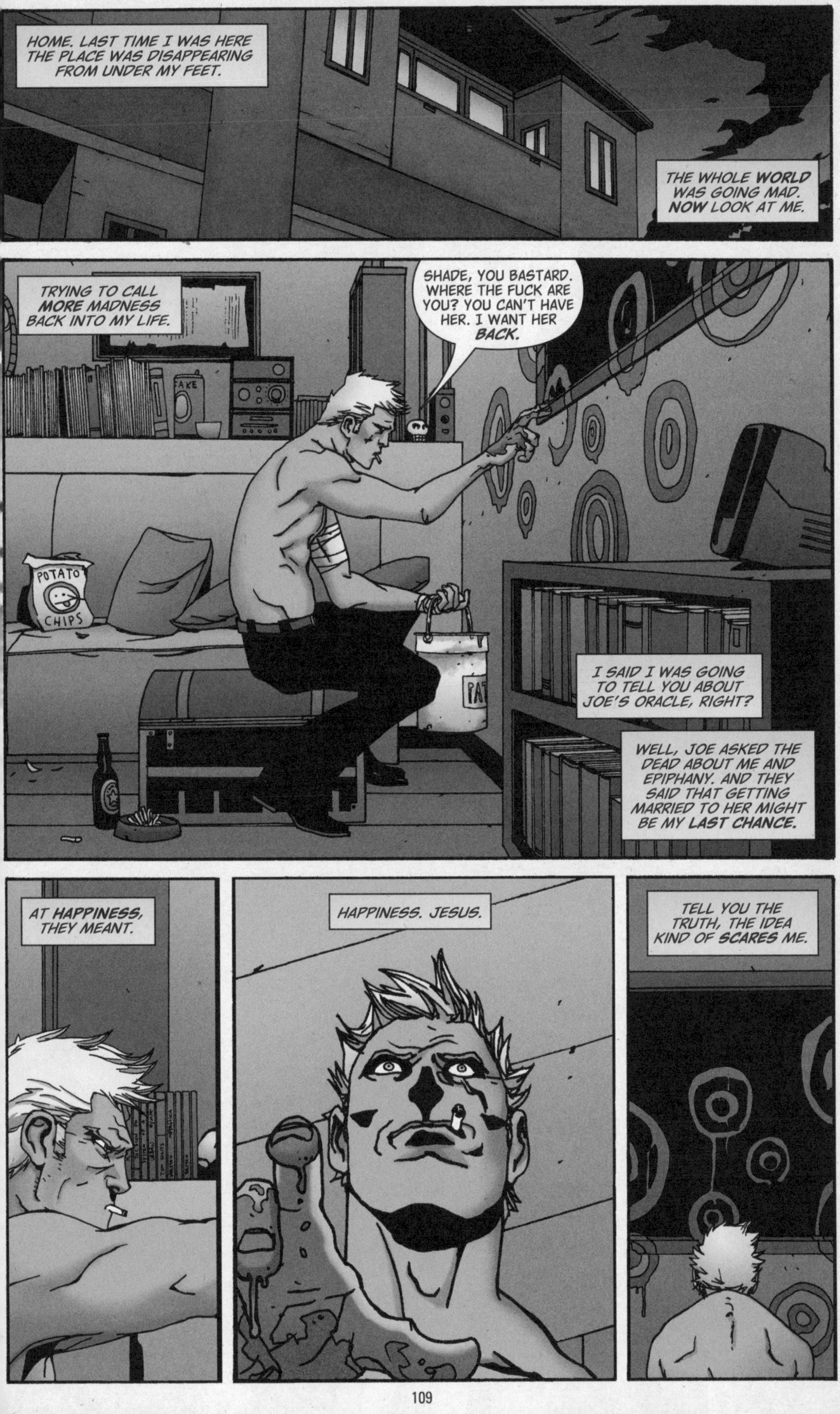
HOME. LAST TIME I WAS HERE THE PLACE WAS DISAPPEARING FROM UNDER MY FEET.
THE WHOLE WORLD WAS GOING MAD. NOW LOOK AT ME.
TRYING TO CALL MORE MADNESS BACK INTO MY LIFE.
SHADE, YOU BASTARD. WHERE THE FUCK ARE YOU? YOU CAN'T HAVE HER. I WANT HER BACK.
POTATO CHIPS
I SAID I WAS GOING TO TELL YOU ABOUT JOE'S ORACLE, RIGHT?
WELL, JOE ASKED THE DEAD ABOUT ME AND EPIPHANY. AND THEY SAID THAT GETTING MARRIED TO HER MIGHT BE MY LAST CHANCE.
AT HAPPINESS, THEY MEANT.
HAPPINESS. JESUS.
TELL YOU THE TRUTH, THE IDEA KIND OF SCARES ME.

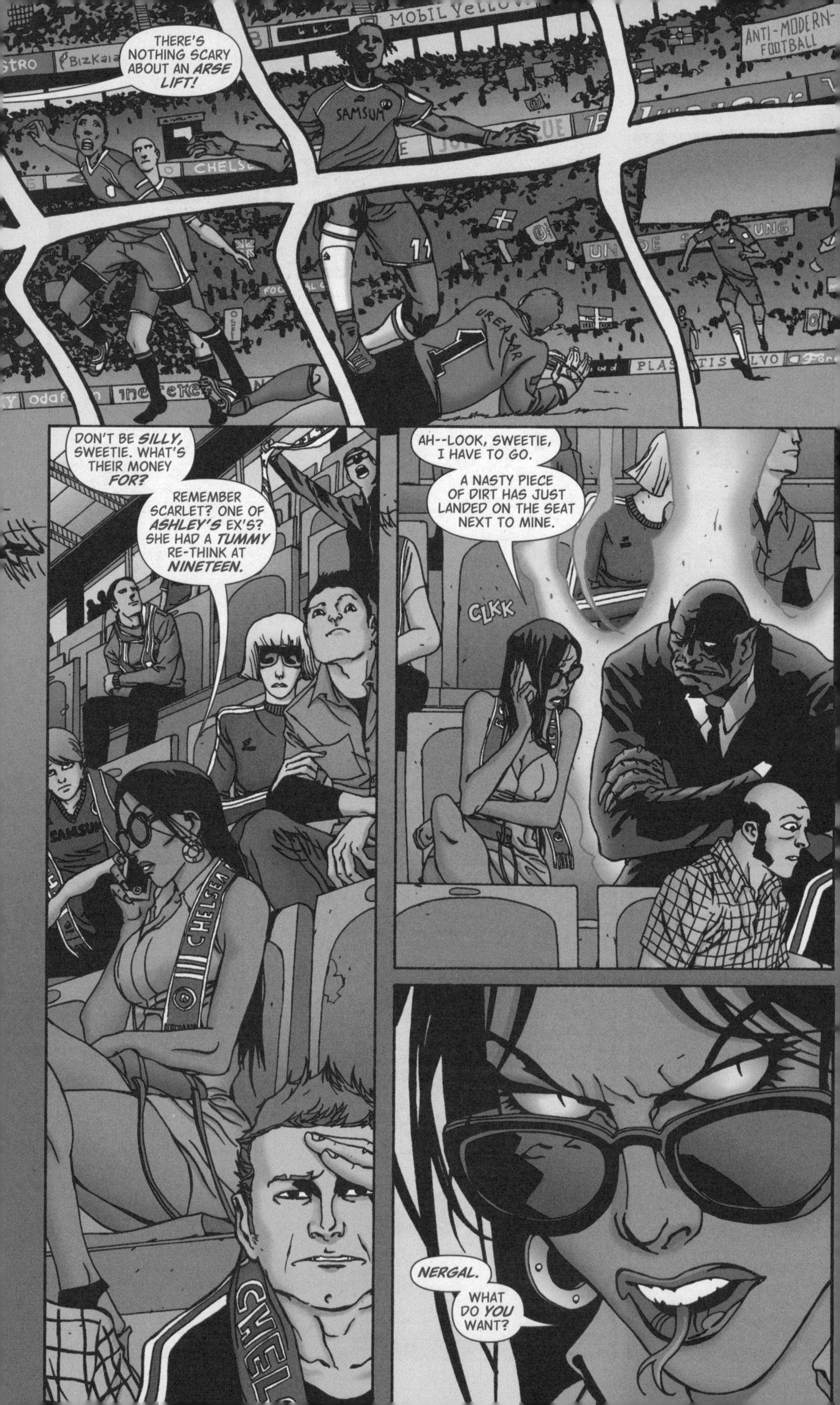
THERE'S NOTHING SCARY ABOUT AN *ARSE LIFT!*
DON'T BE *SILLY,* SWEETIE. WHAT'S THEIR MONEY *FOR?*
REMEMBER SCARLET? ONE OF *ASHLEY'S* EX'S? SHE HAD A *TUMMY* RE-THINK AT *NINETEEN.*
AH--LOOK, SWEETIE, I HAVE TO GO.
A NASTY PIECE OF DIRT HAS JUST LANDED ON THE SEAT NEXT TO MINE.
CLKK
NERGAL.
WHAT DO *YOU* WANT?

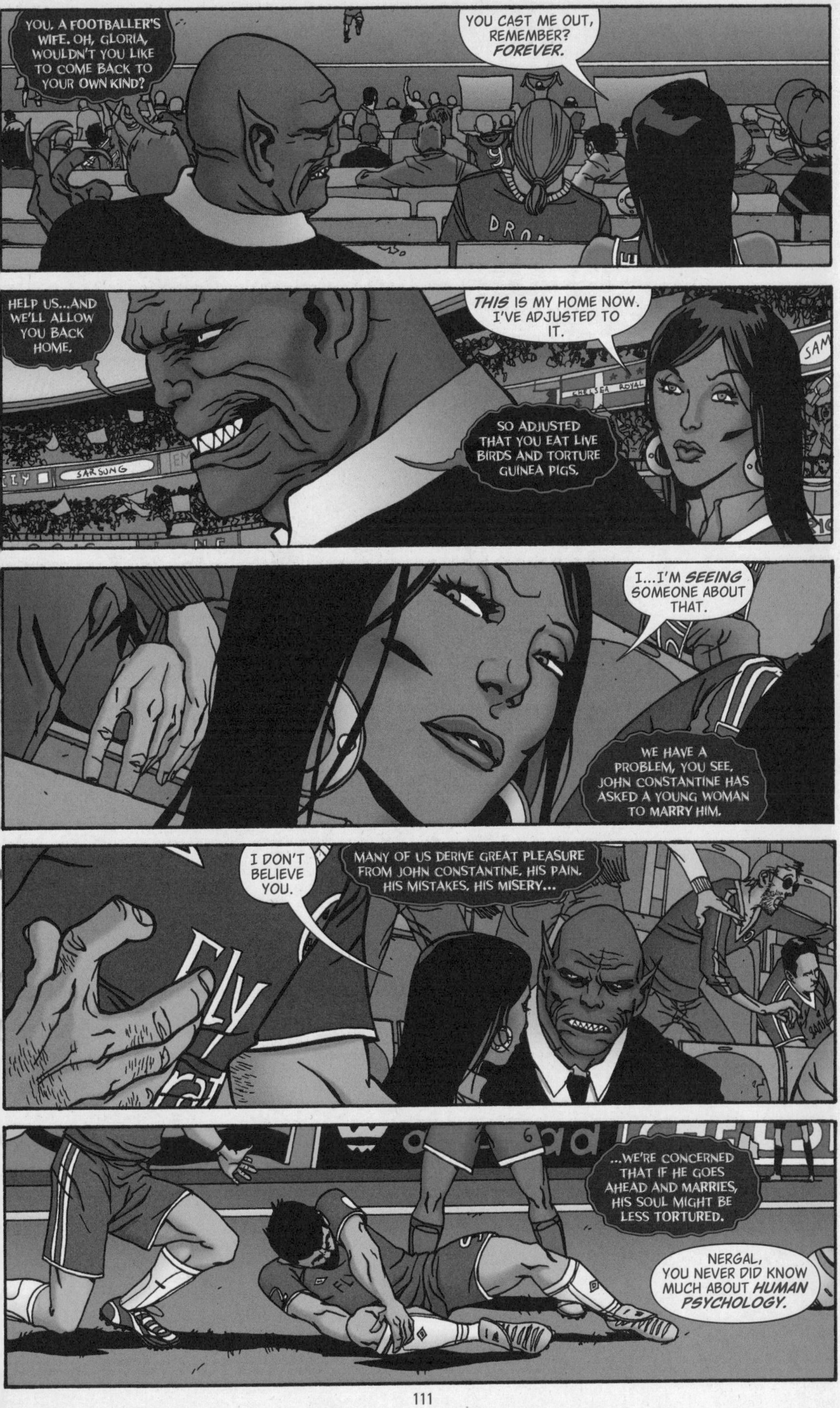
YOU, A FOOTBALLER'S WIFE. OH, GLORIA, WOULDN'T YOU LIKE TO COME BACK TO YOUR OWN KIND?
YOU CAST ME OUT, REMEMBER? FOREVER.
HELP US...AND WE'LL ALLOW YOU BACK HOME.
THIS IS MY HOME NOW. I'VE ADJUSTED TO IT.
SO ADJUSTED THAT YOU EAT LIVE BIRDS AND TORTURE GUINEA PIGS.
I...I'M SEEING SOMEONE ABOUT THAT.
WE HAVE A PROBLEM, YOU SEE. JOHN CONSTANTINE HAS ASKED A YOUNG WOMAN TO MARRY HIM.
I DON'T BELIEVE YOU.
MANY OF US DERIVE GREAT PLEASURE FROM JOHN CONSTANTINE, HIS PAIN, HIS MISTAKES, HIS MISERY...
...WE'RE CONCERNED THAT IF HE GOES AHEAD AND MARRIES, HIS SOUL MIGHT BE LESS TORTURED.
NERGAL, YOU NEVER DID KNOW MUCH ABOUT HUMAN PSYCHOLOGY.

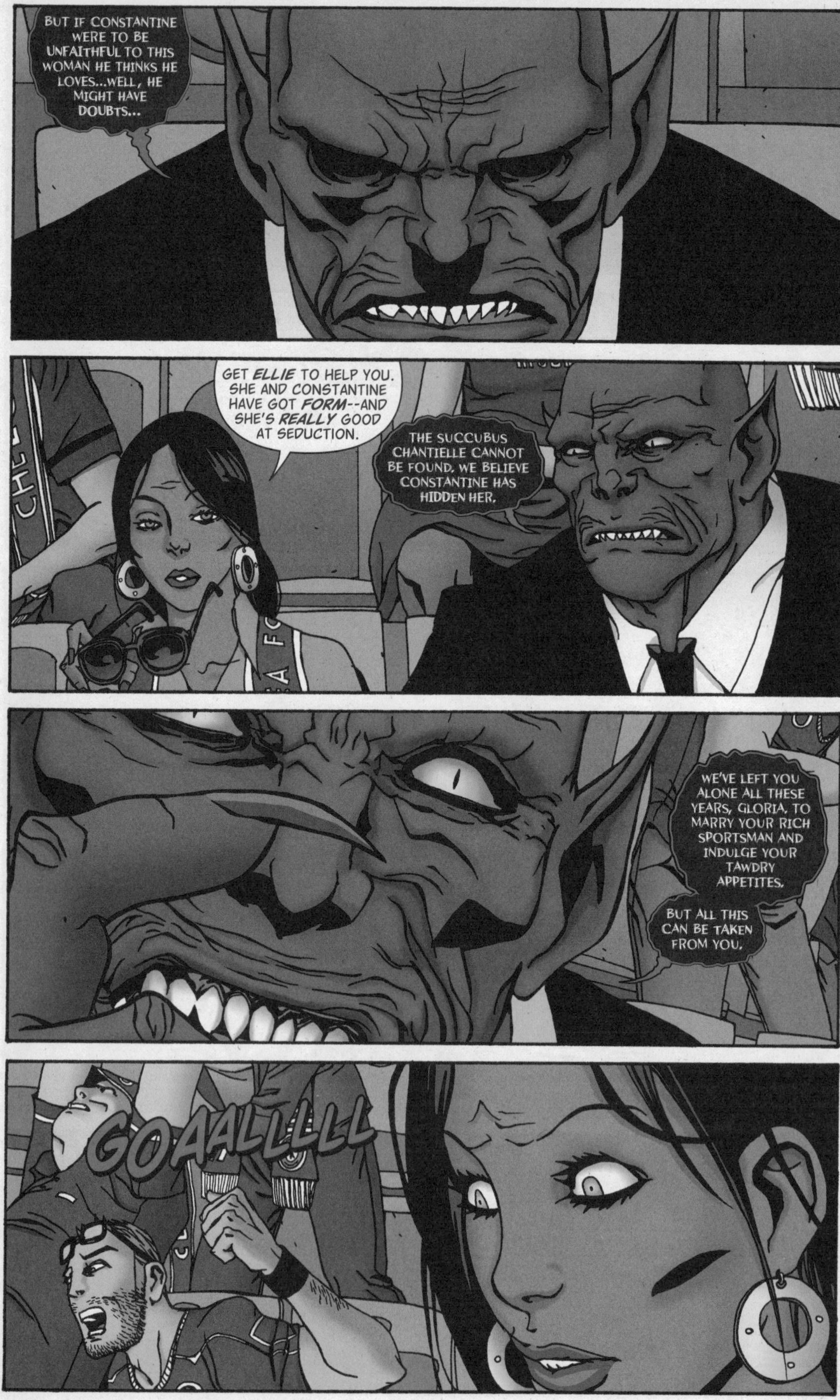
BUT IF CONSTANTINE WERE TO BE UNFAITHFUL TO THIS WOMAN HE THINKS HE LOVES...WELL, HE MIGHT HAVE DOUBTS...
GET ELLIE TO HELP YOU. SHE AND CONSTANTINE HAVE GOT FORM--AND SHE'S REALLY GOOD AT SEDUCTION.
THE SUCCUBUS CHANTIELLE CANNOT BE FOUND. WE BELIEVE CONSTANTINE HAS HIDDEN HER.
WE'VE LEFT YOU ALONE ALL THESE YEARS, GLORIA, TO MARRY YOUR RICH SPORTSMAN AND INDULGE YOUR TAWDRY APPETITES.
BUT ALL THIS CAN BE TAKEN FROM YOU.
GOAALLLLL

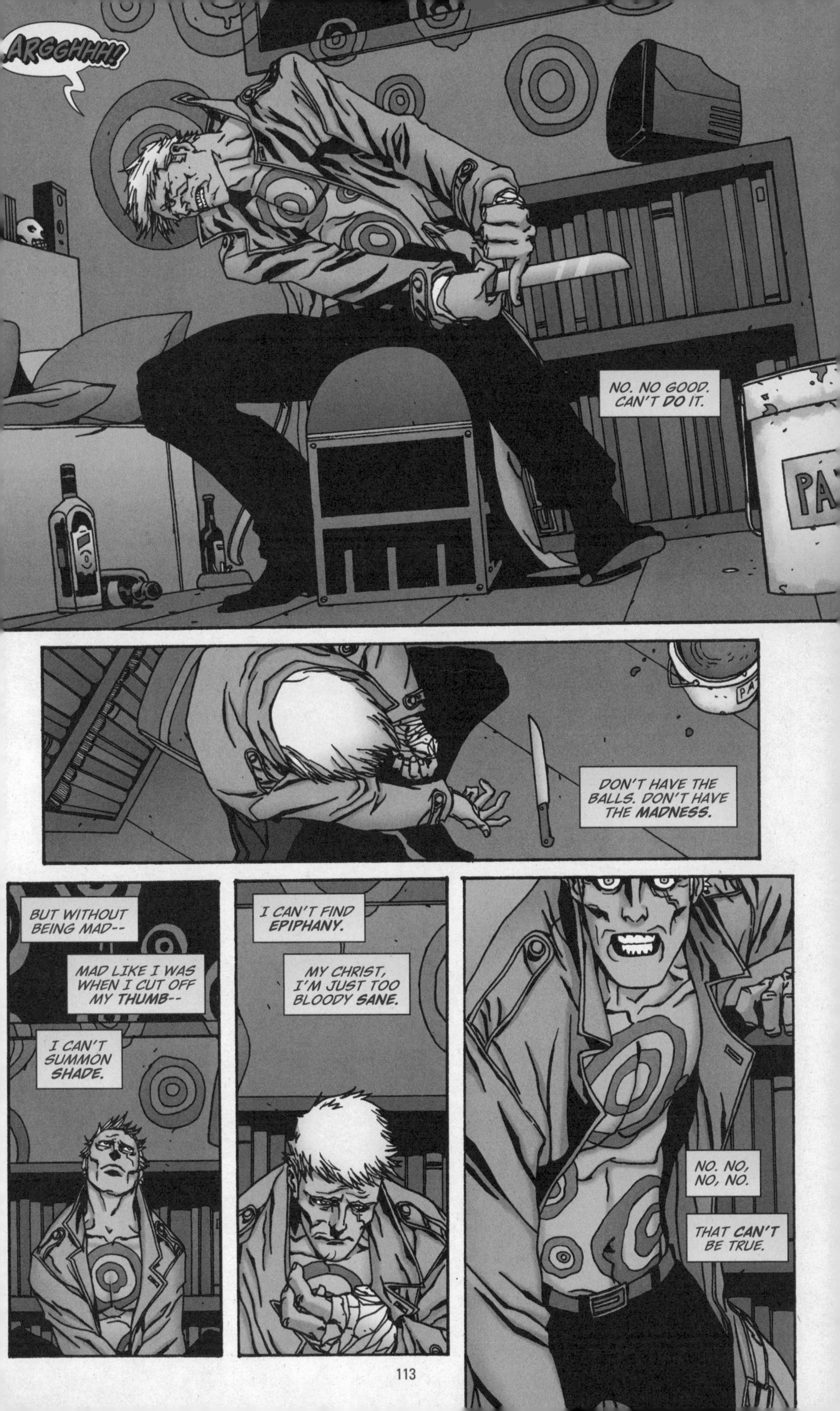
ARGGHHH!
NO. NO GOOD. CAN'T DO IT.
PA
DON'T HAVE THE BALLS. DON'T HAVE THE MADNESS.
BUT WITHOUT BEING MAD--
MAD LIKE I WAS WHEN I CUT OFF MY THUMB--
I CAN'T SUMMON SHADE.
I CAN'T FIND EPIPHANY.
MY CHRIST, I'M JUST TOO BLOODY SANE.
NO. NO, NO, NO.
THAT CAN'T BE TRUE.

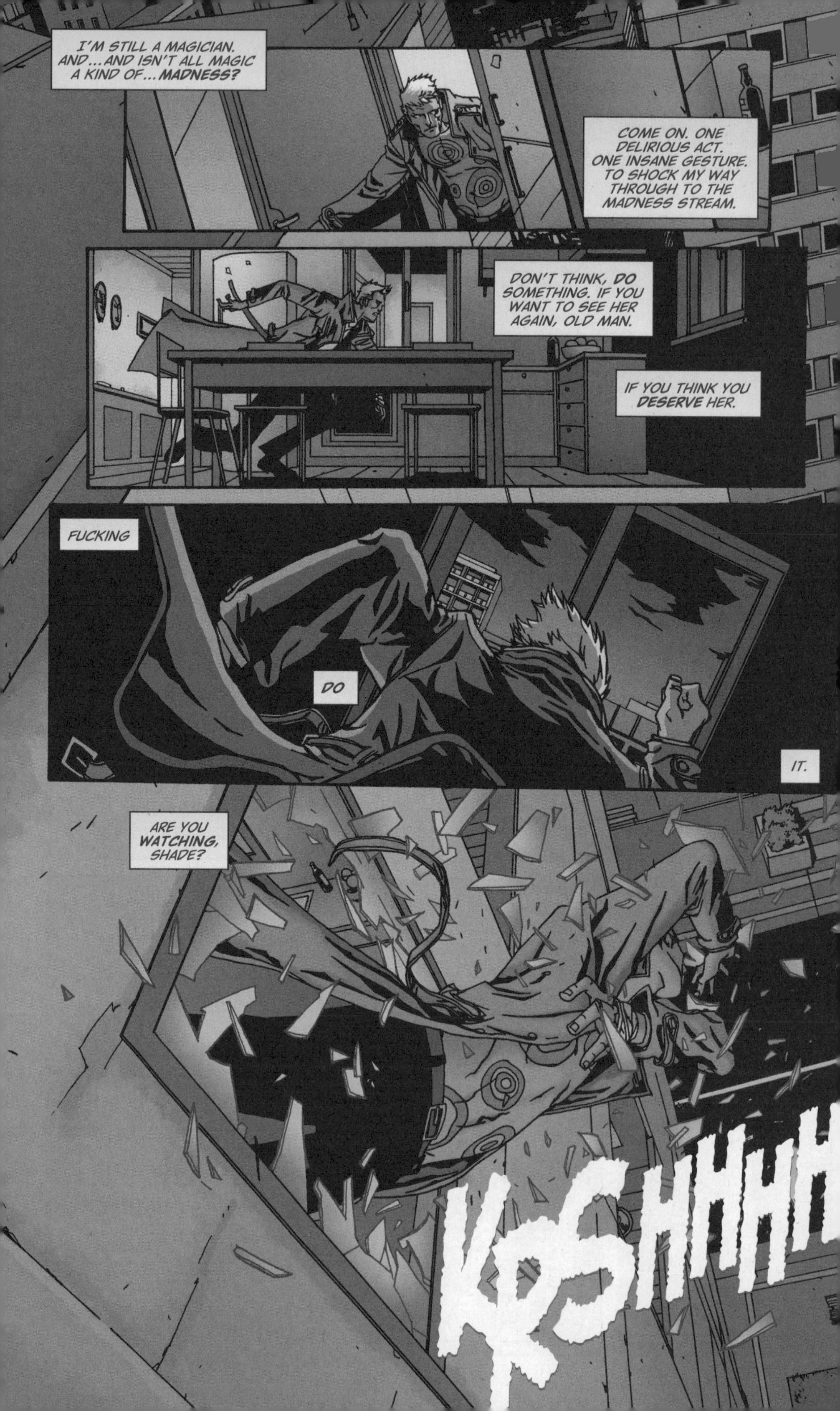
I'M STILL A MAGICIAN. AND... AND ISN'T ALL MAGIC A KIND OF... MADNESS?
COME ON. ONE DELIRIOUS ACT. ONE INSANE GESTURE. TO SHOCK MY WAY THROUGH TO THE MADNESS STREAM.
DON'T THINK, DO SOMETHING. IF YOU WANT TO SEE HER AGAIN, OLD MAN.
IF YOU THINK YOU DESERVE HER.
FUCKING
DO
IT.
ARE YOU WATCHING, SHADE?
KRSHHHH

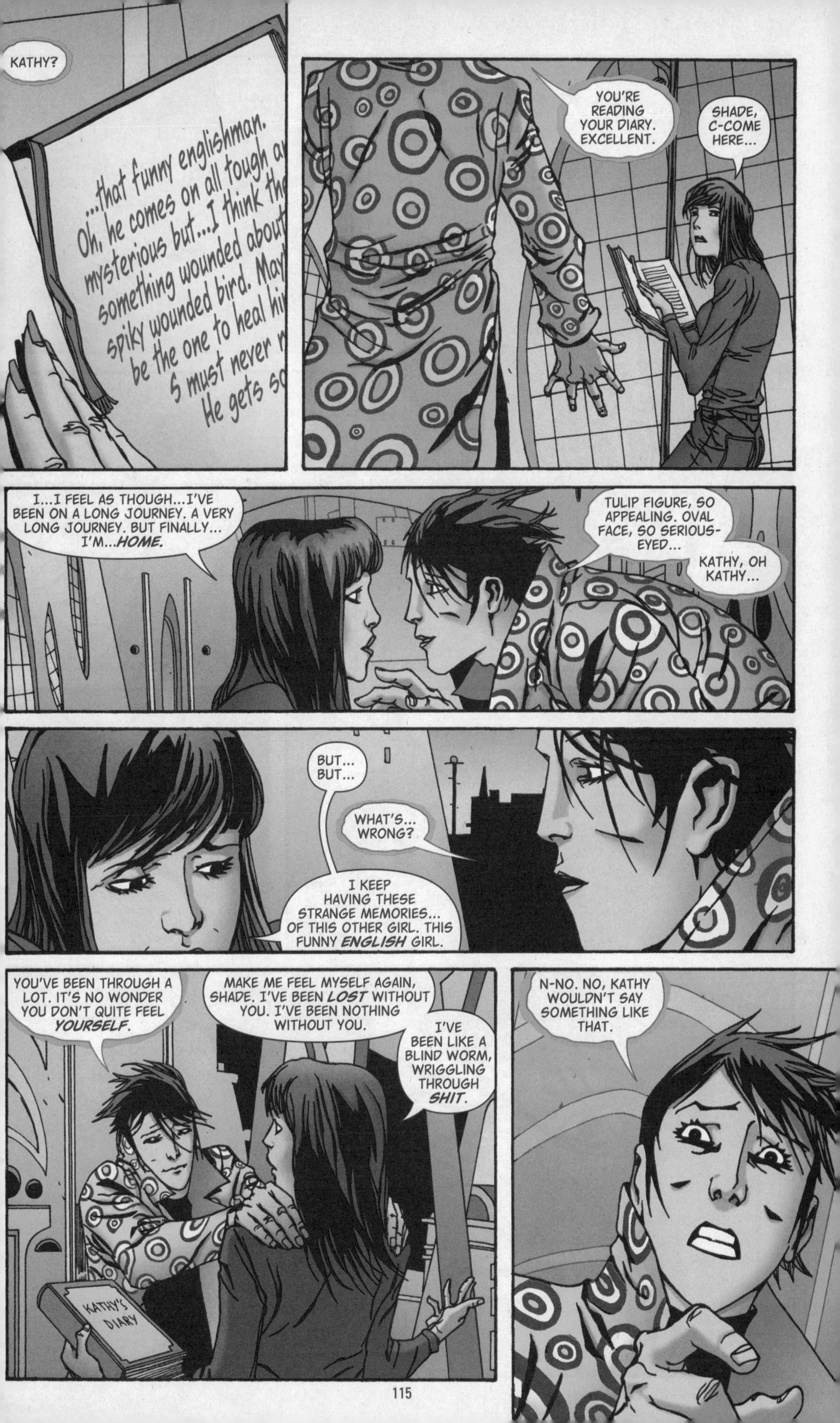
KATHY?
...that funny englishman. Oh, he comes on all tough a mysterious but...I think the something wounded about spiky wounded bird. May be the one to heal hi S must never He gets s
YOU'RE READING YOUR DIARY. EXCELLENT.
SHADE, C-COME HERE...
I...I FEEL AS THOUGH...I'VE BEEN ON A LONG JOURNEY. A VERY LONG JOURNEY. BUT FINALLY... I'M...HOME.
TULIP FIGURE, SO APPEALING. OVAL FACE, SO SERIOUS-EYED...
KATHY, OH KATHY...
BUT... BUT...
WHAT'S... WRONG?
I KEEP HAVING THESE STRANGE MEMORIES... OF THIS OTHER GIRL. THIS FUNNY ENGLISH GIRL.
YOU'VE BEEN THROUGH A LOT. IT'S NO WONDER YOU DON'T QUITE FEEL YOURSELF.
MAKE ME FEEL MYSELF AGAIN, SHADE. I'VE BEEN LOST WITHOUT YOU. I'VE BEEN NOTHING WITHOUT YOU.
I'VE BEEN LIKE A BLIND WORM, WRIGGLING THROUGH SHIT.
KATHY'S DIARY
N-NO. NO, KATHY WOULDN'T SAY SOMETHING LIKE THAT.

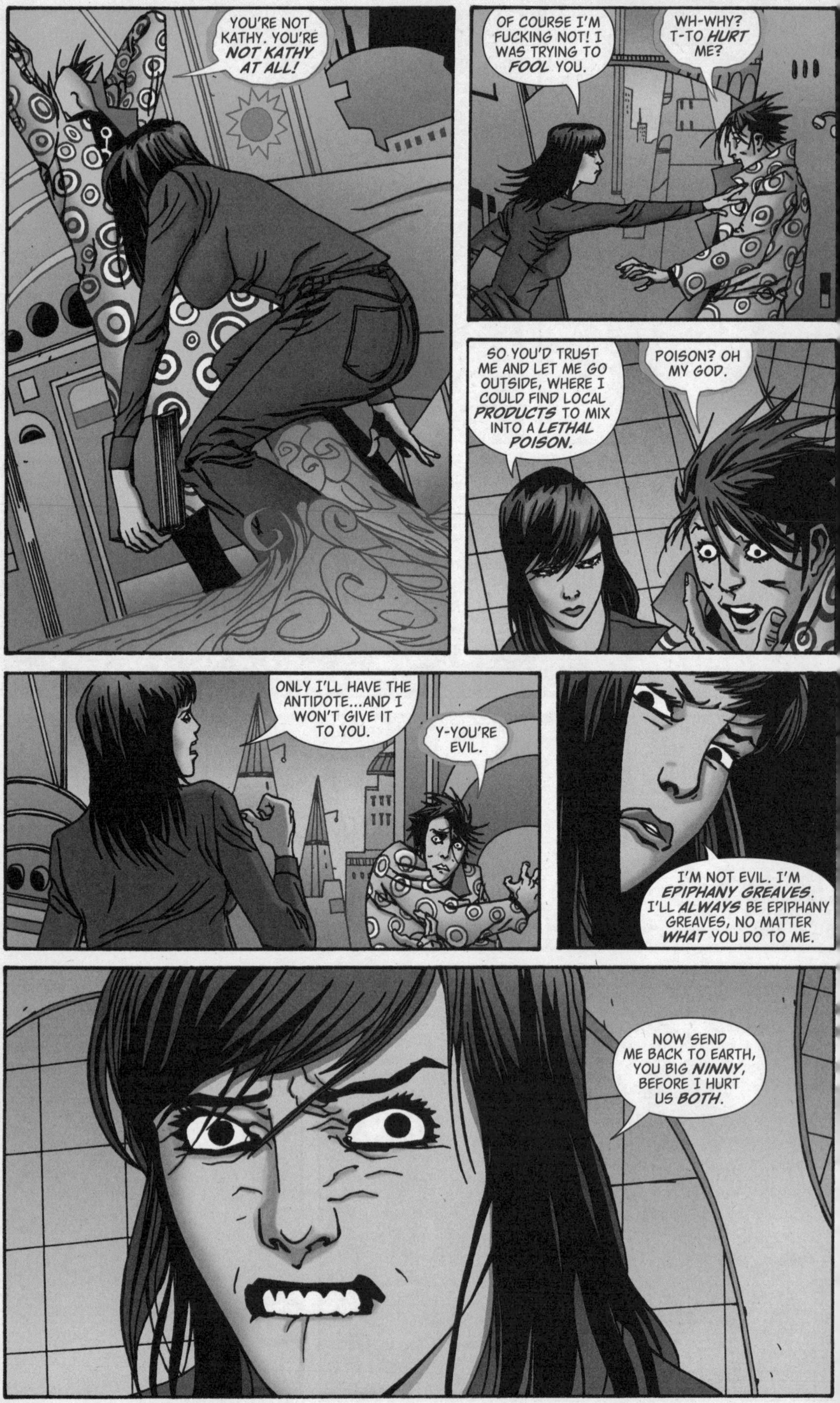
YOU'RE NOT KATHY. YOU'RE NOT KATHY AT ALL!
OF COURSE I'M FUCKING NOT! I WAS TRYING TO FOOL YOU.
WH-WHY? T-TO HURT ME?
SO YOU'D TRUST ME AND LET ME GO OUTSIDE, WHERE I COULD FIND LOCAL PRODUCTS TO MIX INTO A LETHAL POISON.
POISON? OH MY GOD.
ONLY I'LL HAVE THE ANTIDOTE...AND I WON'T GIVE IT TO YOU.
Y-YOU'RE EVIL.
I'M NOT EVIL. I'M EPIPHANY GREAVES. I'LL ALWAYS BE EPIPHANY GREAVES, NO MATTER WHAT YOU DO TO ME.
NOW SEND ME BACK TO EARTH, YOU BIG NINNY, BEFORE I HURT US BOTH.

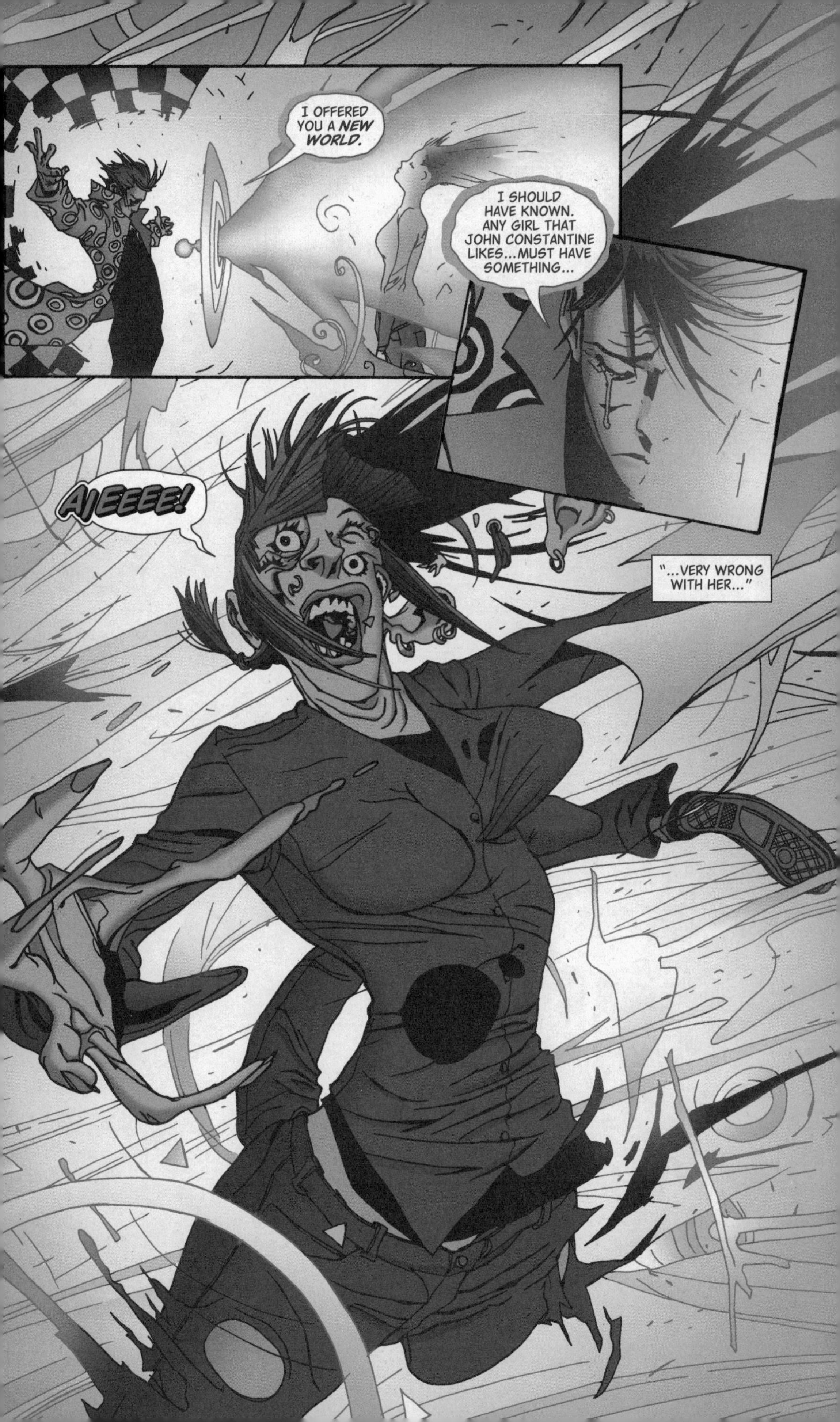
I OFFERED YOU A NEW WORLD.
I SHOULD HAVE KNOWN. ANY GIRL THAT JOHN CONSTANTINE LIKES...MUST HAVE SOMETHING...
AIEEEE!
"...VERY WRONG WITH HER..."

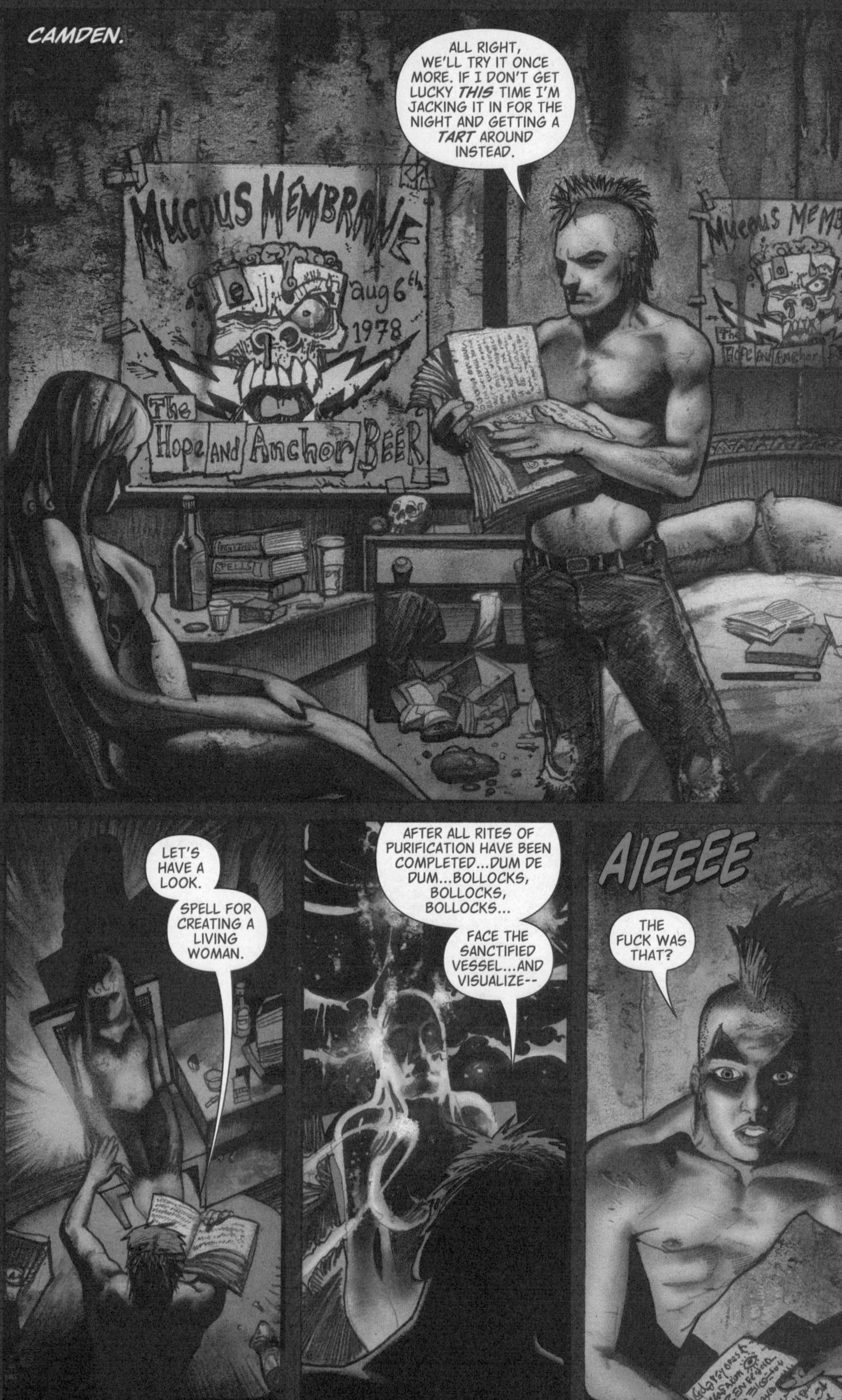
CAMDEN.
ALL RIGHT, WE'LL TRY IT ONCE MORE. IF I DON'T GET LUCKY *THIS* TIME I'M JACKING IT IN FOR THE NIGHT AND GETTING A *TART* AROUND INSTEAD.
MUCOUS MEMBRANE
aug 6th 1978
The Hope and Anchor BEER
SPELLS
LET'S HAVE A LOOK.
SPELL FOR CREATING A LIVING WOMAN.
AFTER ALL RITES OF PURIFICATION HAVE BEEN COMPLETED...DUM DE DUM...BOLLOCKS, BOLLOCKS, BOLLOCKS...
FACE THE SANCTIFIED VESSEL...AND VISUALIZE--
AIEEEE
THE FUCK WAS THAT?

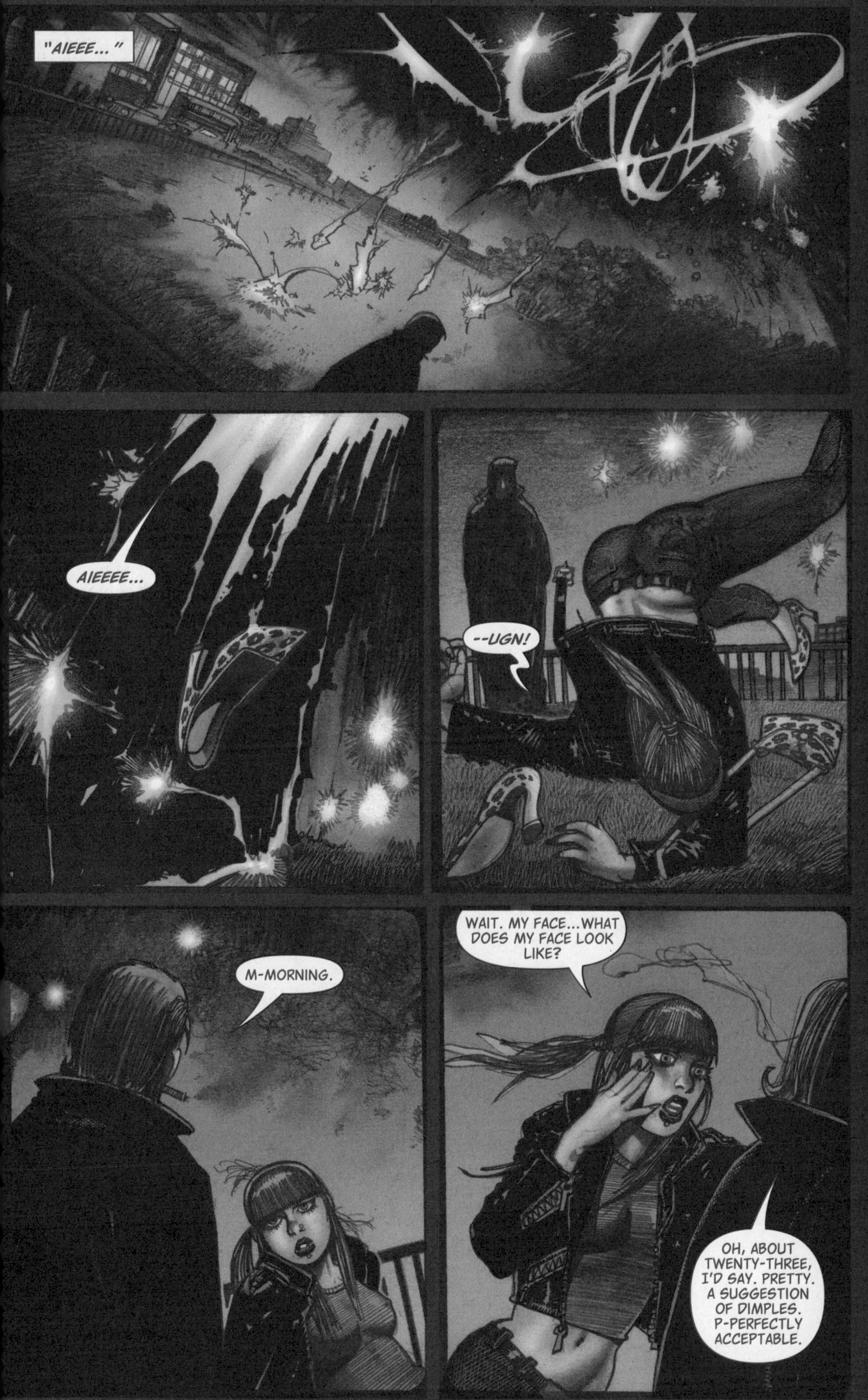
"AIEEE..."
AIEEEE...
--UGN!
M-MORNING.
WAIT. MY FACE...WHAT DOES MY FACE LOOK LIKE?
OH, ABOUT TWENTY-THREE, I'D SAY. PRETTY. A SUGGESTION OF DIMPLES. P-PERFECTLY ACCEPTABLE.

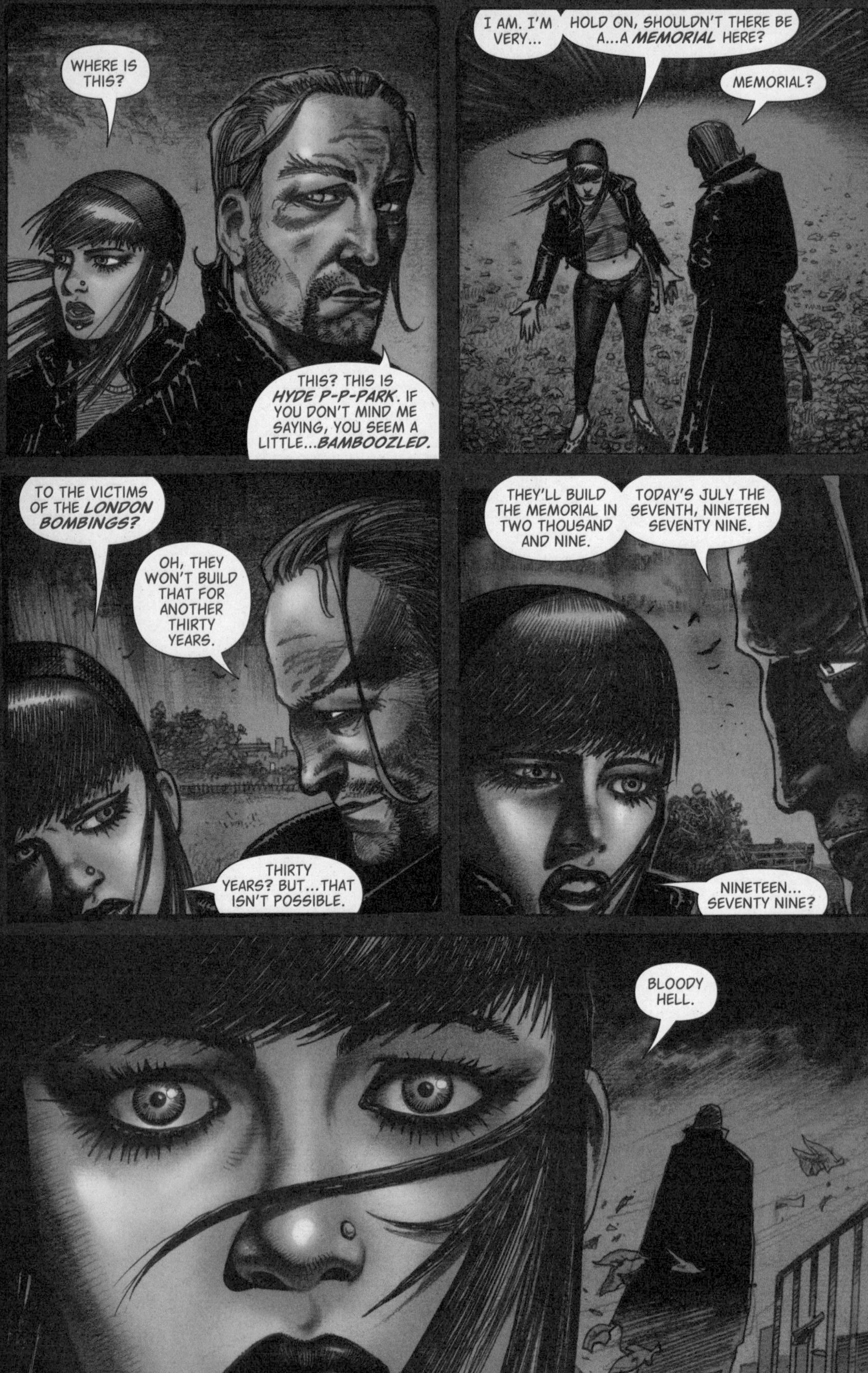

WHERE IS THIS?
THIS? THIS IS HYDE P-P-PARK. IF YOU DON'T MIND ME SAYING, YOU SEEM A LITTLE...BAMBOOZLED.
I AM. I'M VERY...
HOLD ON, SHOULDN'T THERE BE A...A MEMORIAL HERE?
MEMORIAL?
TO THE VICTIMS OF THE LONDON BOMBINGS?
OH, THEY WON'T BUILD THAT FOR ANOTHER THIRTY YEARS.
THIRTY YEARS? BUT...THAT ISN'T POSSIBLE.
THEY'LL BUILD THE MEMORIAL IN TWO THOUSAND AND NINE.
TODAY'S JULY THE SEVENTH, NINETEEN SEVENTY NINE.
NINETEEN... SEVENTY NINE?
BLOODY HELL.

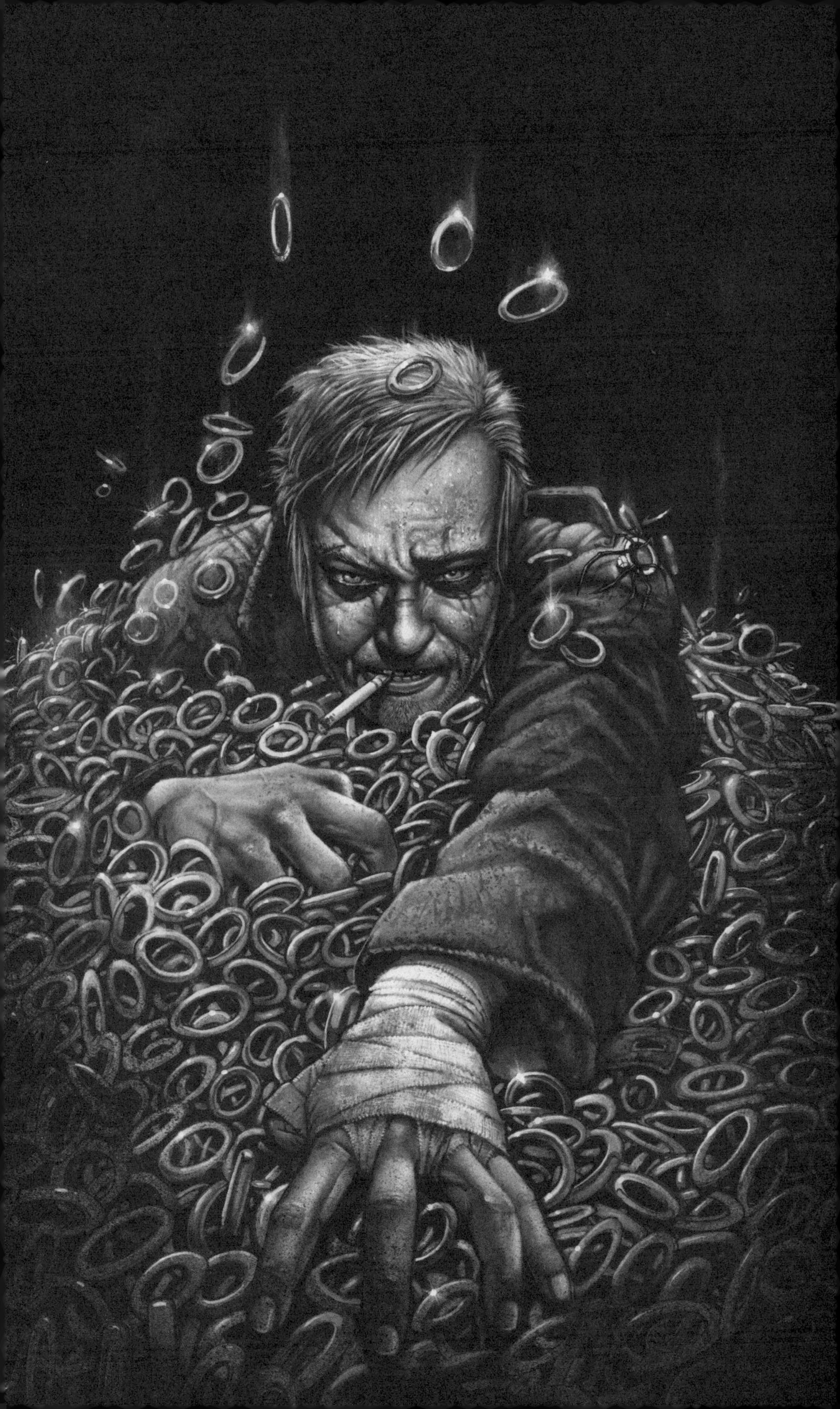

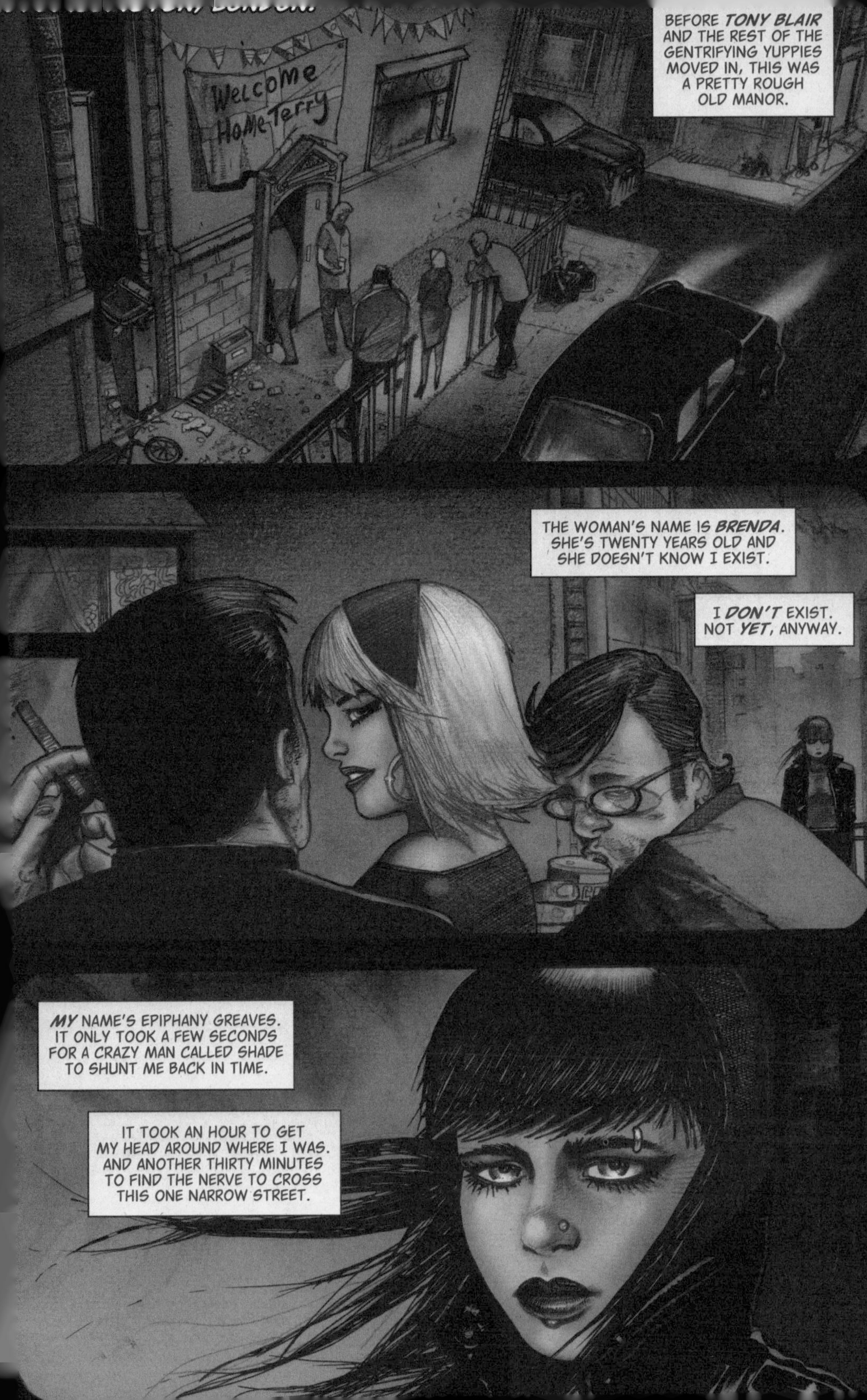
BEFORE TONY BLAIR AND THE REST OF THE GENTRIFYING YUPPIES MOVED IN, THIS WAS A PRETTY ROUGH OLD MANOR.
Welcome Home Terry
THE WOMAN'S NAME IS BRENDA. SHE'S TWENTY YEARS OLD AND SHE DOESN'T KNOW I EXIST.
I DON'T EXIST. NOT YET, ANYWAY.
MY NAME'S EPIPHANY GREAVES. IT ONLY TOOK A FEW SECONDS FOR A CRAZY MAN CALLED SHADE TO SHUNT ME BACK IN TIME.
IT TOOK AN HOUR TO GET MY HEAD AROUND WHERE I WAS. AND ANOTHER THIRTY MINUTES TO FIND THE NERVE TO CROSS THIS ONE NARROW STREET.

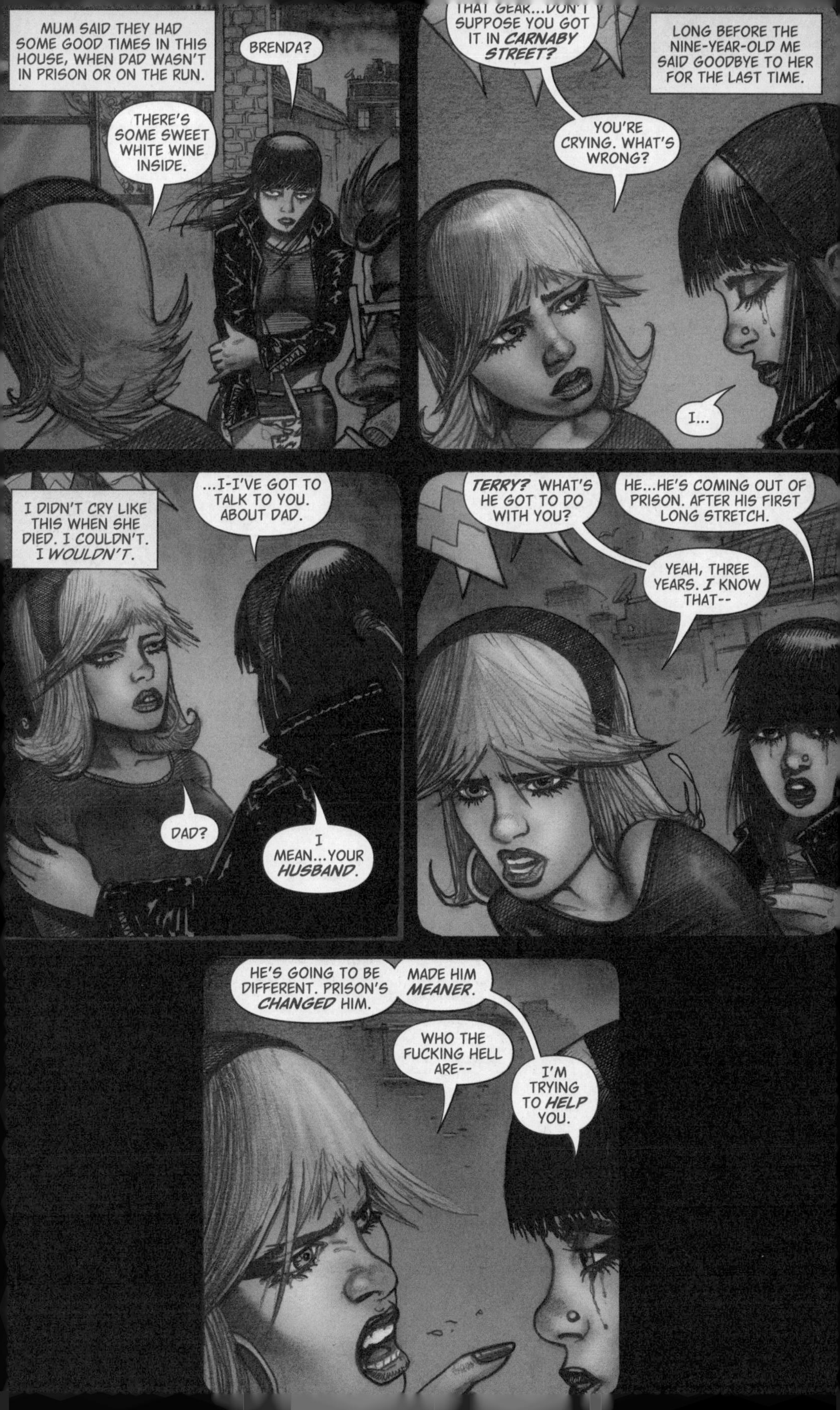

MUM SAID THEY HAD SOME GOOD TIMES IN THIS HOUSE, WHEN DAD WASN'T IN PRISON OR ON THE RUN.
BRENDA?
THERE'S SOME SWEET WHITE WINE INSIDE.
THAT GEAR...DON'T SUPPOSE YOU GOT IT IN *CARNABY STREET?*
LONG BEFORE THE NINE-YEAR-OLD ME SAID GOODBYE TO HER FOR THE LAST TIME.
YOU'RE CRYING. WHAT'S WRONG?
I...
I DIDN'T CRY LIKE THIS WHEN SHE DIED. I COULDN'T. I *WOULDN'T*.
...I-I'VE GOT TO TALK TO YOU. ABOUT DAD.
DAD?
I MEAN...YOUR *HUSBAND*.
TERRY? WHAT'S HE GOT TO DO WITH YOU?
HE...HE'S COMING OUT OF PRISON. AFTER HIS FIRST LONG STRETCH.
YEAH, THREE YEARS. *I* KNOW THAT--
HE'S GOING TO BE DIFFERENT. PRISON'S *CHANGED* HIM.
MADE HIM *MEANER*.
WHO THE FUCKING HELL ARE--
I'M TRYING TO *HELP* YOU.

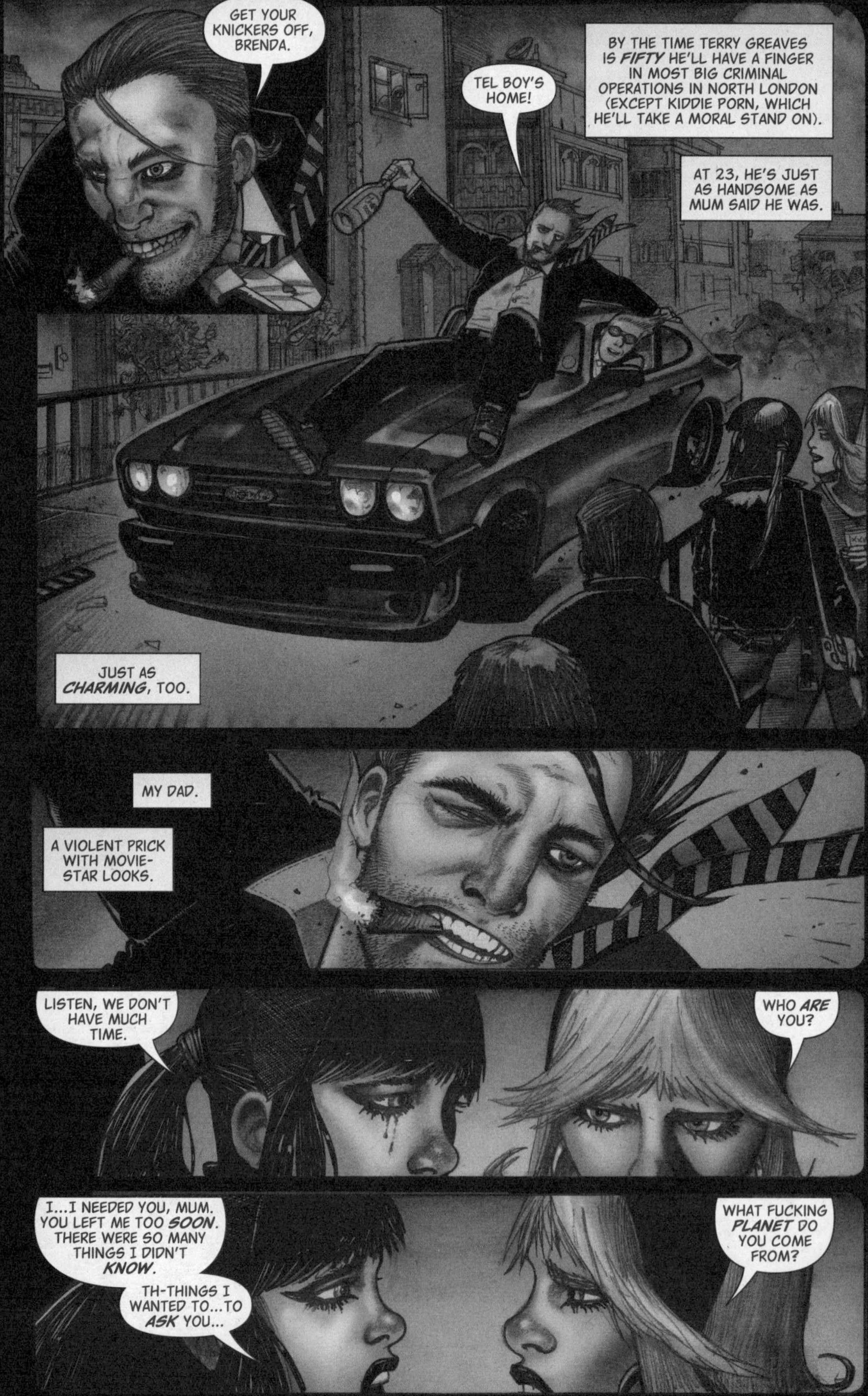

GET YOUR KNICKERS OFF, BRENDA.
TEL BOY'S HOME!
BY THE TIME TERRY GREAVES IS *FIFTY* HE'LL HAVE A FINGER IN MOST BIG CRIMINAL OPERATIONS IN NORTH LONDON (EXCEPT KIDDIE PORN, WHICH HE'LL TAKE A MORAL STAND ON).
AT 23, HE'S JUST AS HANDSOME AS MUM SAID HE WAS.
JUST AS *CHARMING*, TOO.
MY DAD.
A VIOLENT PRICK WITH MOVIE-STAR LOOKS.
LISTEN, WE DON'T HAVE MUCH TIME.
WHO *ARE* YOU?
I...I NEEDED YOU, MUM. YOU LEFT ME TOO *SOON*. THERE WERE SO MANY THINGS I DIDN'T *KNOW*.
TH-THINGS I WANTED TO...TO *ASK* YOU...
WHAT FUCKING *PLANET* DO YOU COME FROM?

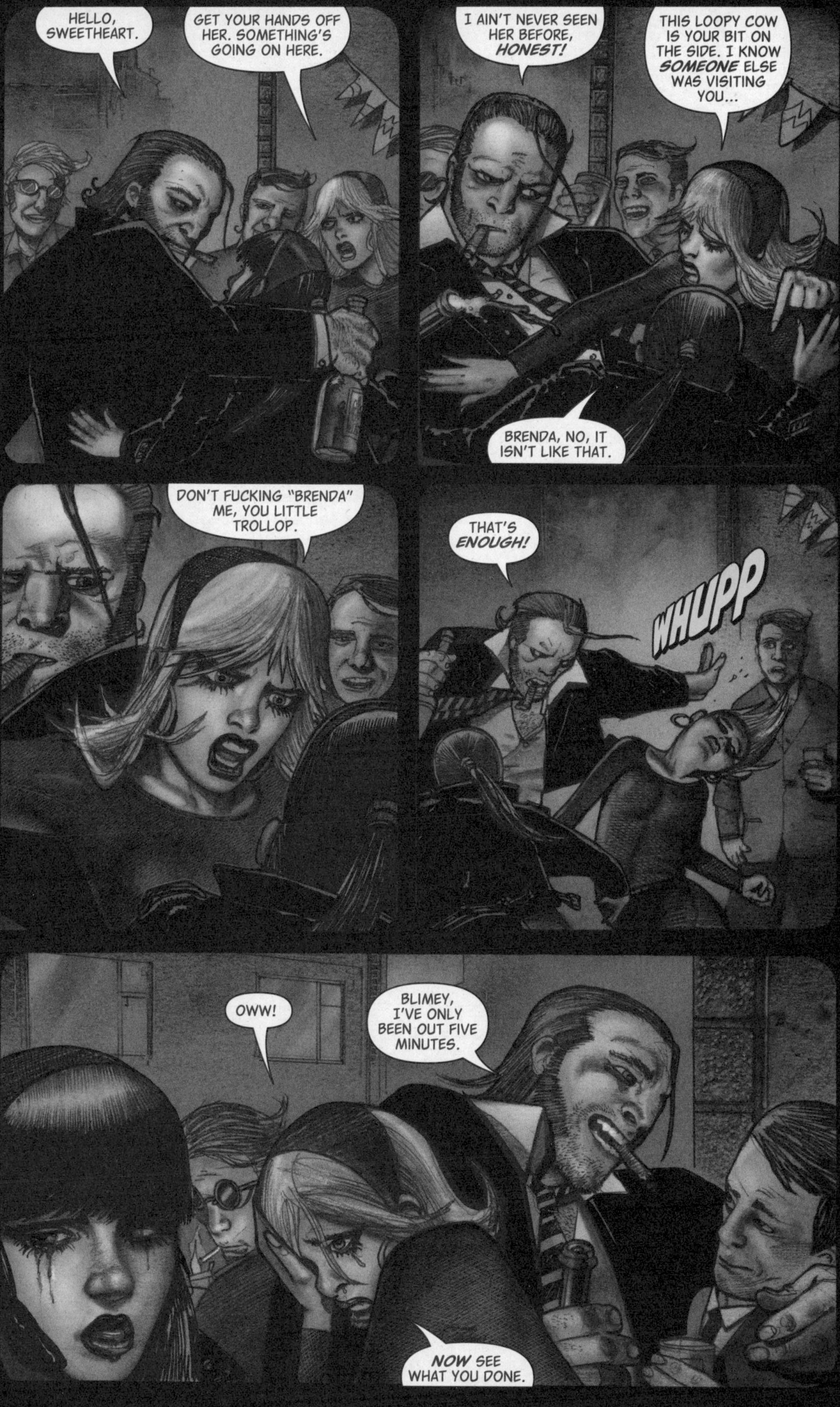
HELLO, SWEETHEART.
GET YOUR HANDS OFF HER. SOMETHING'S GOING ON HERE.
I AIN'T NEVER SEEN HER BEFORE, HONEST!
THIS LOOPY COW IS YOUR BIT ON THE SIDE. I KNOW SOMEONE ELSE WAS VISITING YOU...
BRENDA, NO, IT ISN'T LIKE THAT.
DON'T FUCKING "BRENDA" ME, YOU LITTLE TROLLOP.
THAT'S ENOUGH!
WHUPP
OWW!
BLIMEY, I'VE ONLY BEEN OUT FIVE MINUTES.
NOW SEE WHAT YOU DONE.

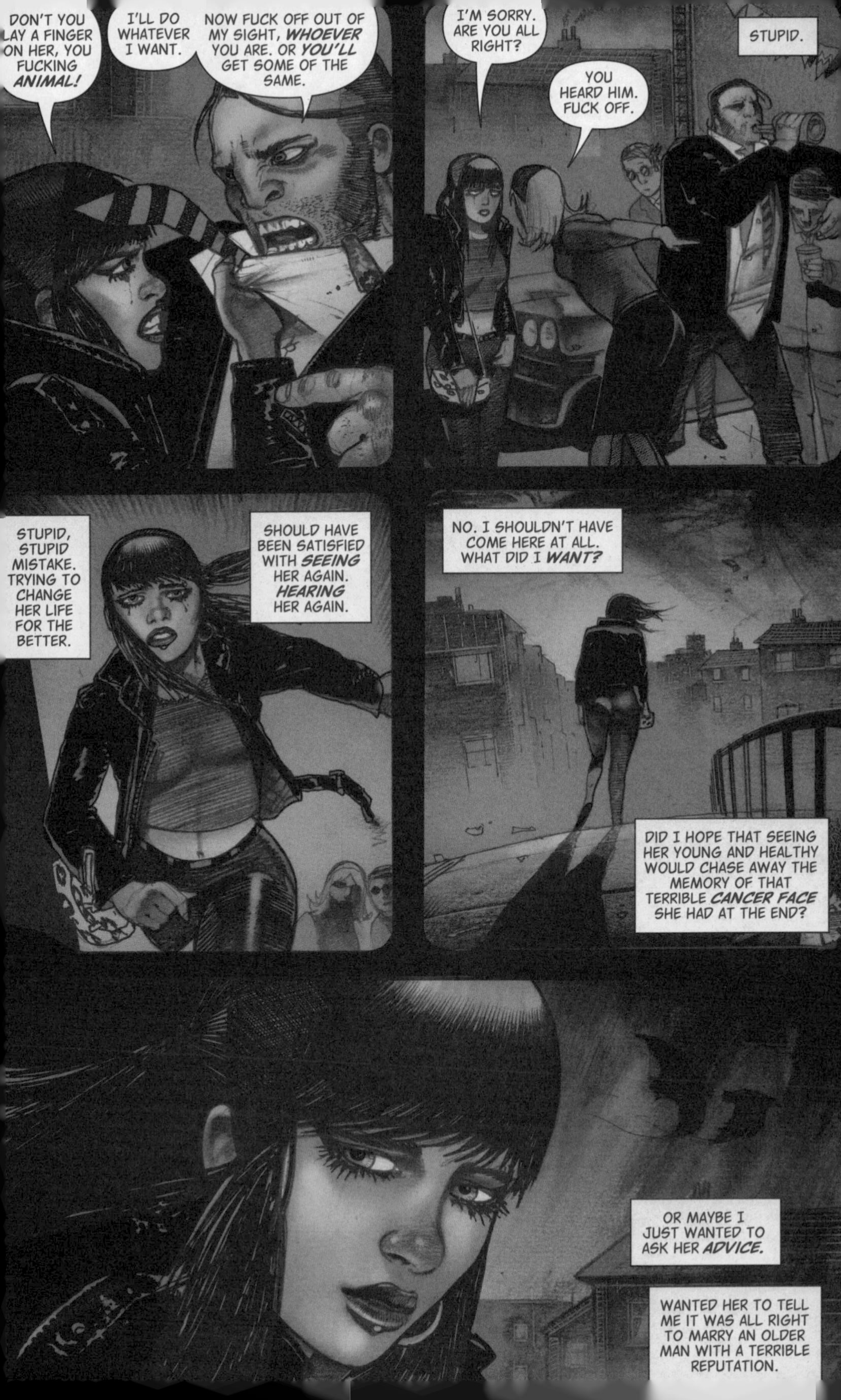
DON'T YOU LAY A FINGER ON HER, YOU FUCKING *ANIMAL!*
I'LL DO WHATEVER I WANT.
NOW FUCK OFF OUT OF MY SIGHT, *WHOEVER* YOU ARE. OR *YOU'LL* GET SOME OF THE SAME.
I'M SORRY. ARE YOU ALL RIGHT?
YOU HEARD HIM. FUCK OFF.
STUPID.
STUPID, STUPID MISTAKE. TRYING TO CHANGE HER LIFE FOR THE BETTER.
SHOULD HAVE BEEN SATISFIED WITH *SEEING* HER AGAIN. *HEARING* HER AGAIN.
NO. I SHOULDN'T HAVE COME HERE AT ALL. WHAT DID I *WANT?*
DID I HOPE THAT SEEING HER YOUNG AND HEALTHY WOULD CHASE AWAY THE MEMORY OF THAT TERRIBLE *CANCER FACE* SHE HAD AT THE END?
OR MAYBE I JUST WANTED TO ASK HER *ADVICE.*
WANTED HER TO TELL ME IT WAS ALL RIGHT TO MARRY AN OLDER MAN WITH A TERRIBLE REPUTATION.

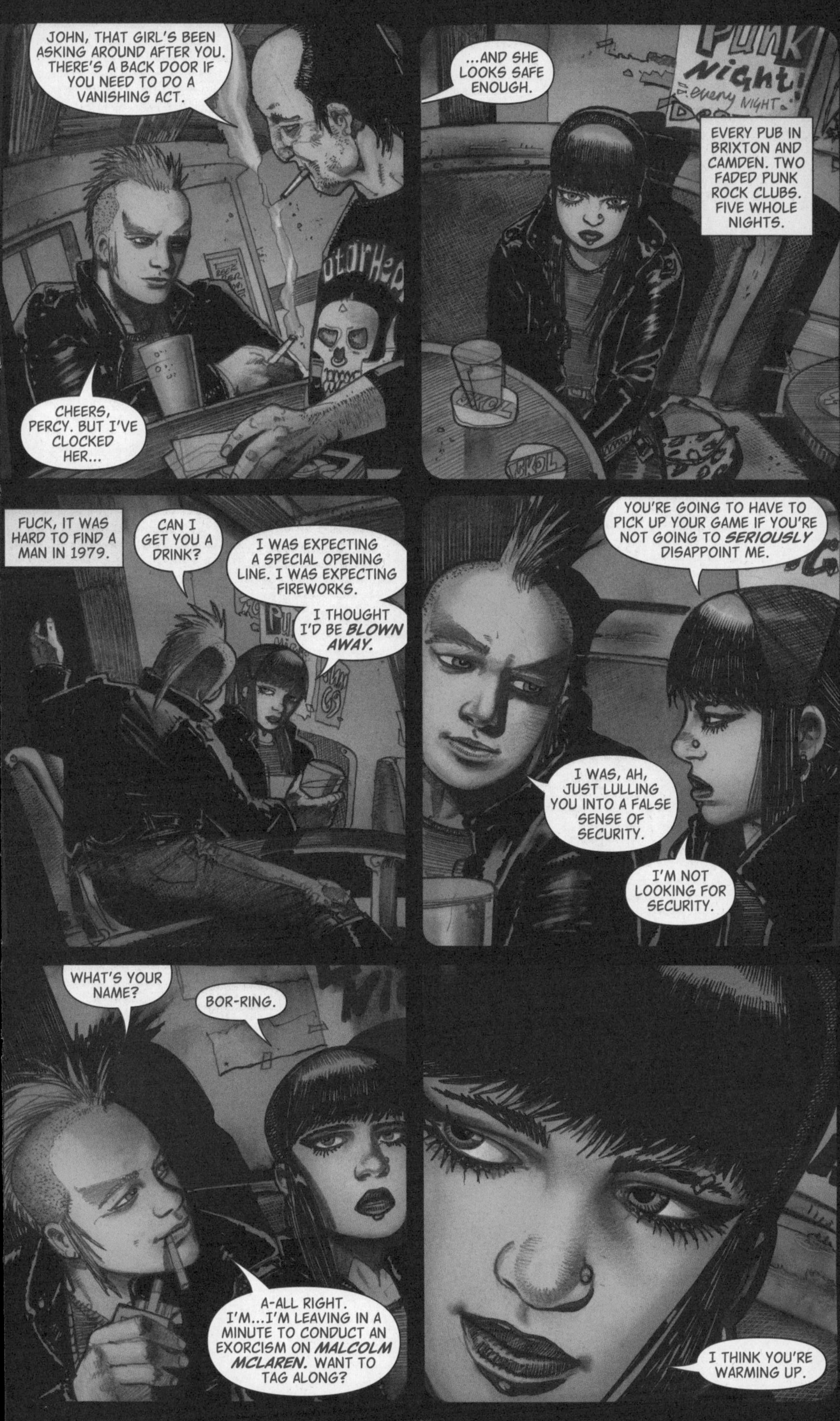
JOHN, THAT GIRL'S BEEN ASKING AROUND AFTER YOU. THERE'S A BACK DOOR IF YOU NEED TO DO A VANISHING ACT.
CHEERS, PERCY. BUT I'VE CLOCKED HER...
...AND SHE LOOKS SAFE ENOUGH.
PUNK NIGHT EVERY NIGHT
EVERY PUB IN BRIXTON AND CAMDEN. TWO FADED PUNK ROCK CLUBS. FIVE WHOLE NIGHTS.
FUCK, IT WAS HARD TO FIND A MAN IN 1979.
CAN I GET YOU A DRINK?
I WAS EXPECTING A SPECIAL OPENING LINE. I WAS EXPECTING FIREWORKS.
I THOUGHT I'D BE *BLOWN AWAY.*
YOU'RE GOING TO HAVE TO PICK UP YOUR GAME IF YOU'RE NOT GOING TO *SERIOUSLY* DISAPPOINT ME.
I WAS, AH, JUST LULLING YOU INTO A FALSE SENSE OF SECURITY.
I'M NOT LOOKING FOR SECURITY.
WHAT'S YOUR NAME?
BOR-RING.
A-ALL RIGHT. I'M...I'M LEAVING IN A MINUTE TO CONDUCT AN EXORCISM ON *MALCOLM MCLAREN.* WANT TO TAG ALONG?
I THINK YOU'RE WARMING UP.

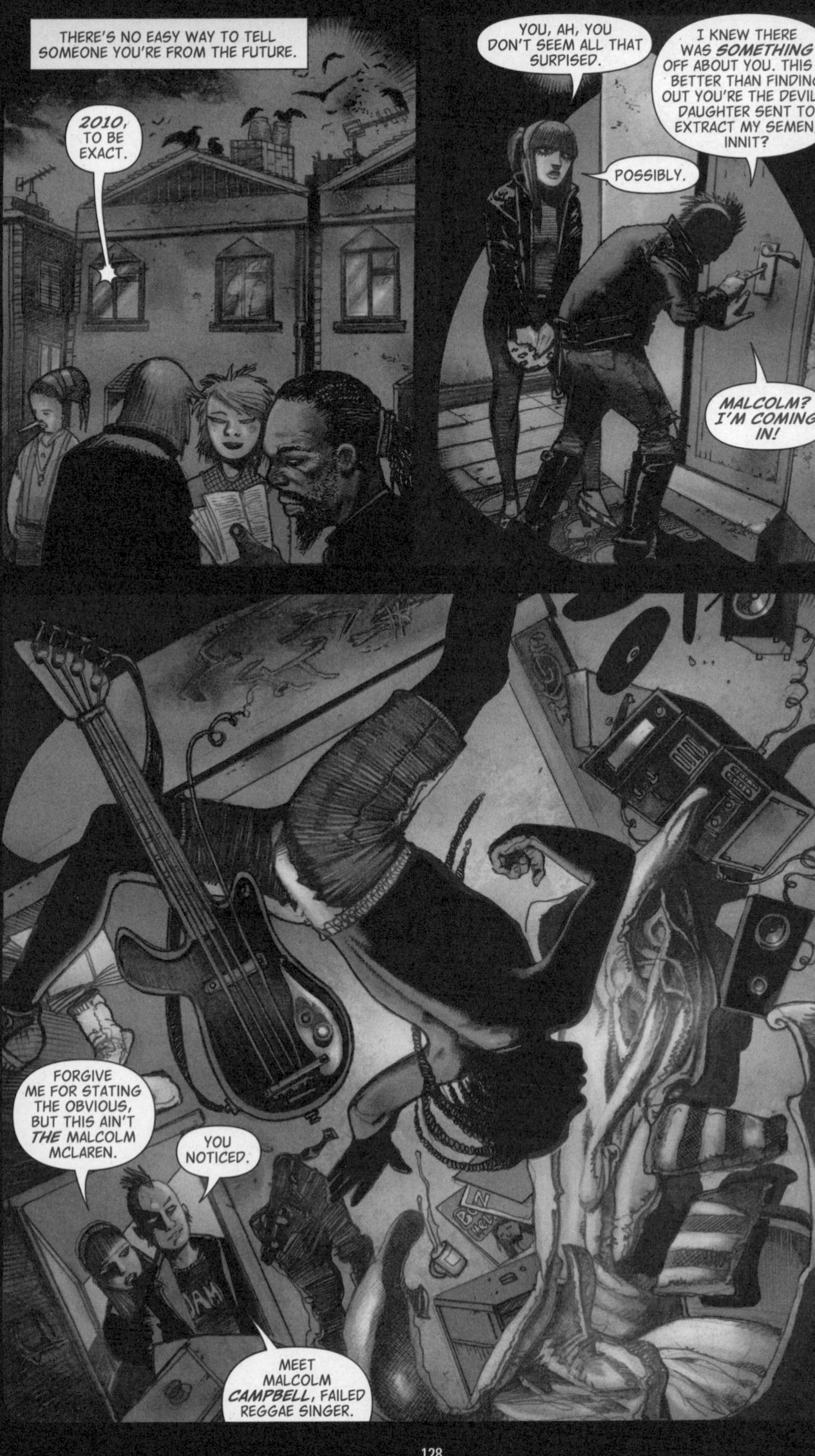
THERE'S NO EASY WAY TO TELL SOMEONE YOU'RE FROM THE FUTURE.
2010, TO BE EXACT.
YOU, AH, YOU DON'T SEEM ALL THAT SURPISED.
I KNEW THERE WAS SOMETHING OFF ABOUT YOU. THIS IS BETTER THAN FINDING OUT YOU'RE THE DEVIL'S DAUGHTER SENT TO EXTRACT MY SEMEN, INNIT?
POSSIBLY.
MALCOLM? I'M COMING IN!
FORGIVE ME FOR STATING THE OBVIOUS, BUT THIS AIN'T THE MALCOLM MCLAREN.
YOU NOTICED.
MEET MALCOLM CAMPBELL, FAILED REGGAE SINGER.

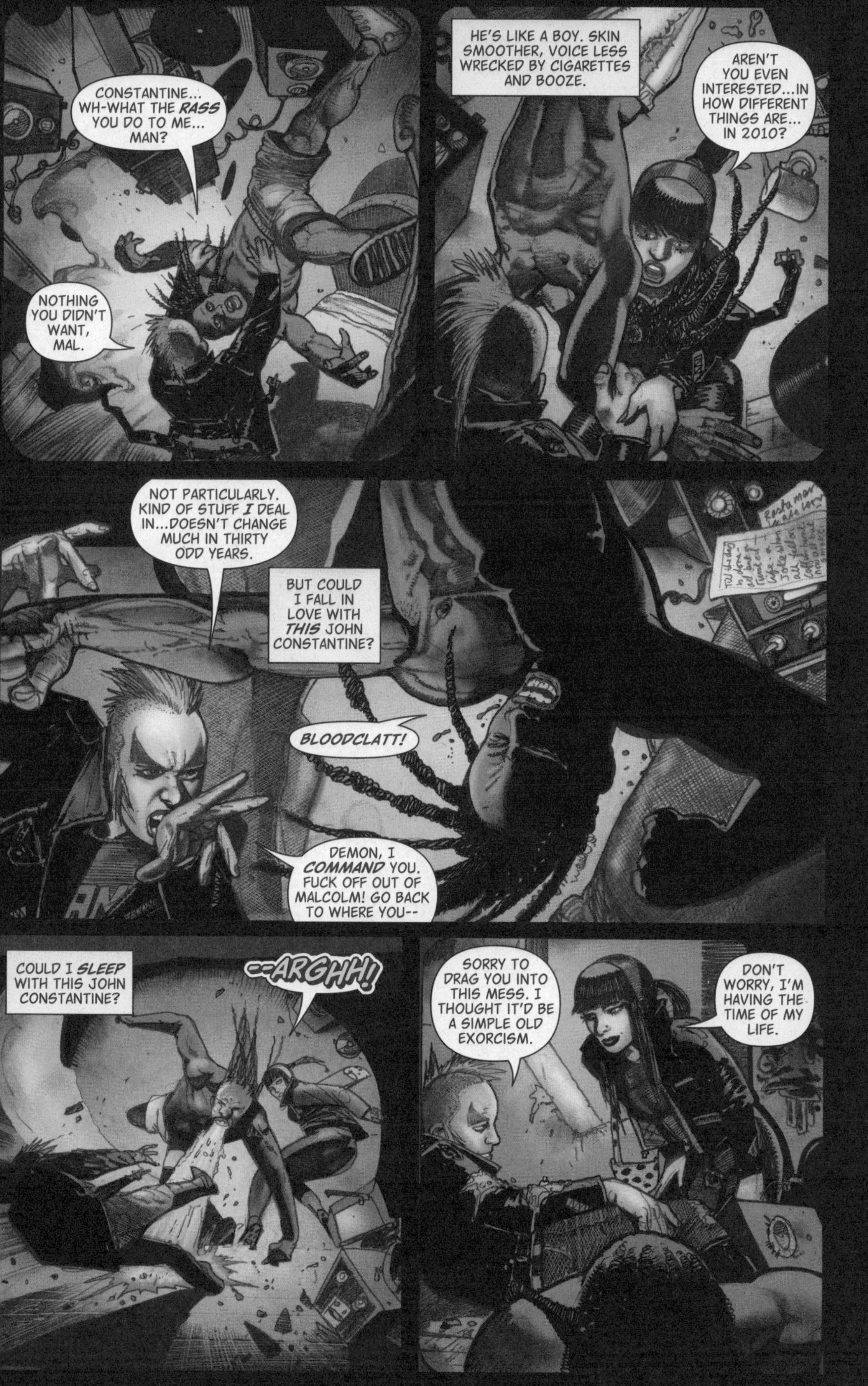

CONSTANTINE... WH-WHAT THE RASS YOU DO TO ME... MAN?
NOTHING YOU DIDN'T WANT, MAL.
HE'S LIKE A BOY. SKIN SMOOTHER, VOICE LESS WRECKED BY CIGARETTES AND BOOZE.
AREN'T YOU EVEN INTERESTED...IN HOW DIFFERENT THINGS ARE... IN 2010?
NOT PARTICULARLY. KIND OF STUFF I DEAL IN...DOESN'T CHANGE MUCH IN THIRTY ODD YEARS.
BUT COULD I FALL IN LOVE WITH THIS JOHN CONSTANTINE?
BLOODCLATT!
DEMON, I COMMAND YOU. FUCK OFF OUT OF MALCOLM! GO BACK TO WHERE YOU--
COULD I SLEEP WITH THIS JOHN CONSTANTINE?
--ARGHH!!
SORRY TO DRAG YOU INTO THIS MESS. I THOUGHT IT'D BE A SIMPLE OLD EXORCISM.
DON'T WORRY, I'M HAVING THE TIME OF MY LIFE.

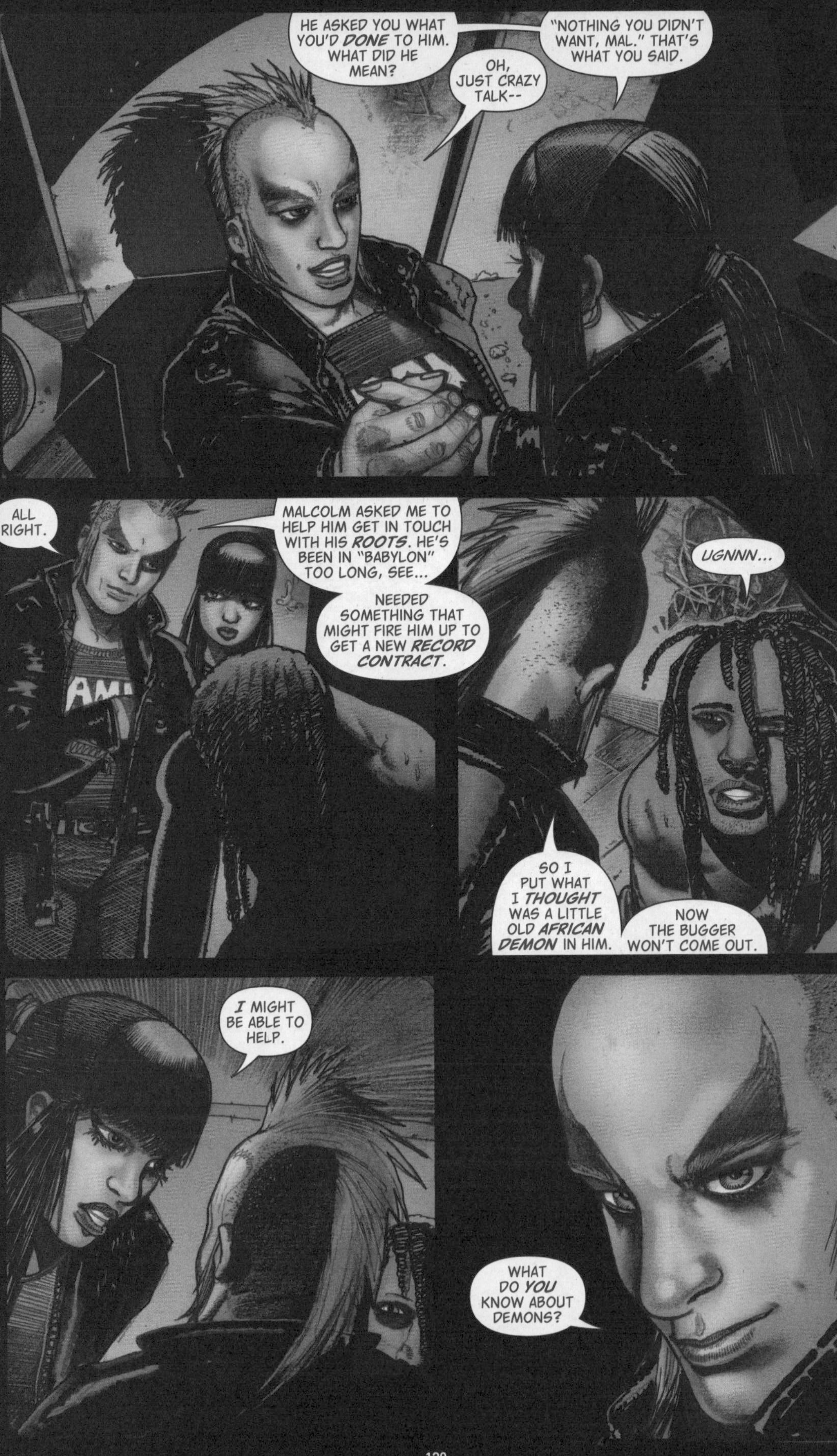
HE ASKED YOU WHAT YOU'D *DONE* TO HIM. WHAT DID HE MEAN?
OH, JUST CRAZY TALK--
"NOTHING YOU DIDN'T WANT, MAL." THAT'S WHAT YOU SAID.
ALL RIGHT.
MALCOLM ASKED ME TO HELP HIM GET IN TOUCH WITH HIS *ROOTS*. HE'S BEEN IN "BABYLON" TOO LONG, SEE...
NEEDED SOMETHING THAT MIGHT FIRE HIM UP TO GET A NEW *RECORD CONTRACT*.
UGNNN...
SO I PUT WHAT I *THOUGHT* WAS A LITTLE OLD *AFRICAN DEMON* IN HIM.
NOW THE BUGGER WON'T COME OUT.
I MIGHT BE ABLE TO HELP.
WHAT DO *YOU* KNOW ABOUT DEMONS?

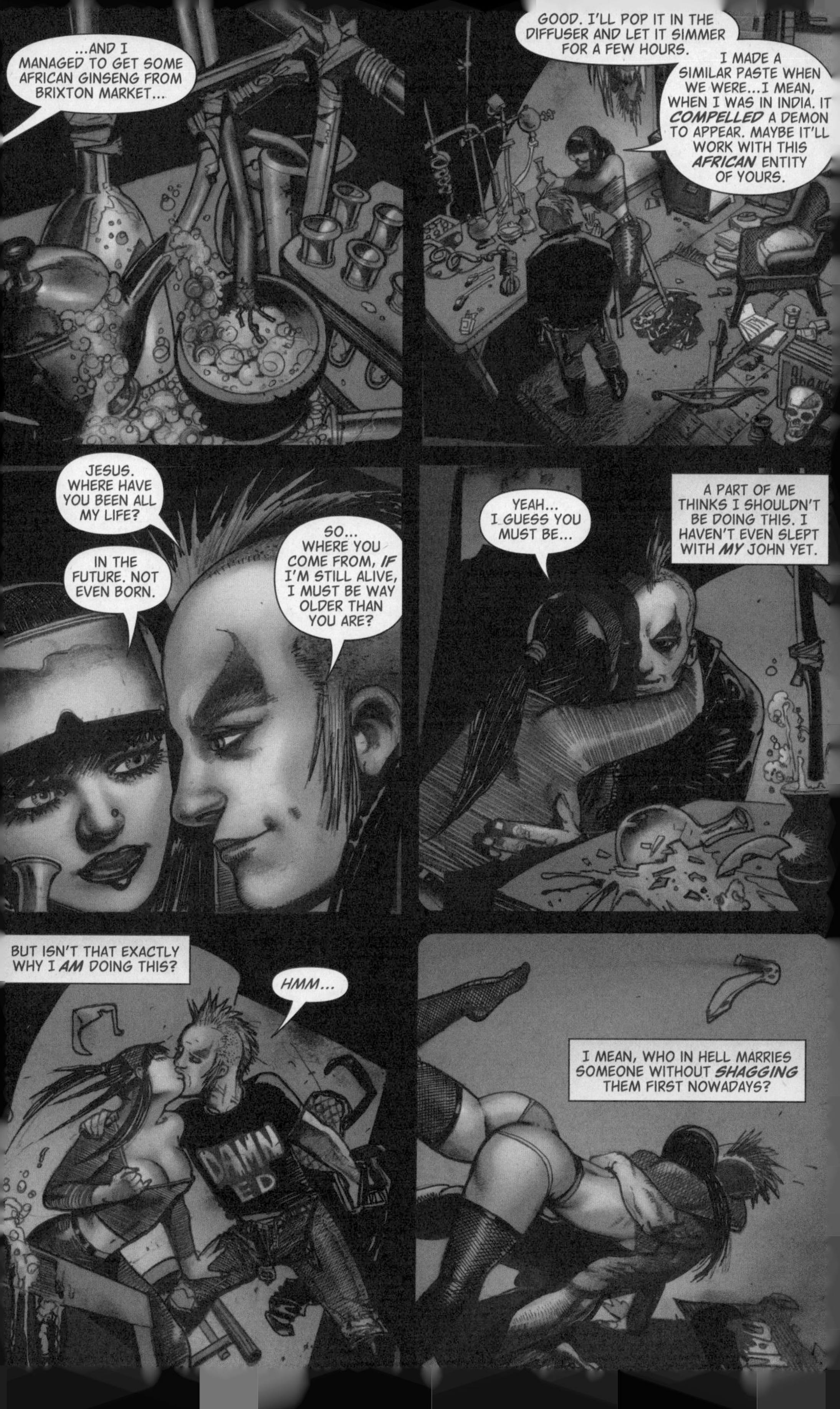
...AND I MANAGED TO GET SOME AFRICAN GINSENG FROM BRIXTON MARKET...
GOOD. I'LL POP IT IN THE DIFFUSER AND LET IT SIMMER FOR A FEW HOURS.
I MADE A SIMILAR PASTE WHEN WE WERE...I MEAN, WHEN I WAS IN INDIA. IT COMPELLED A DEMON TO APPEAR. MAYBE IT'LL WORK WITH THIS AFRICAN ENTITY OF YOURS.
JESUS. WHERE HAVE YOU BEEN ALL MY LIFE?
IN THE FUTURE. NOT EVEN BORN.
SO... WHERE YOU COME FROM, IF I'M STILL ALIVE, I MUST BE WAY OLDER THAN YOU ARE?
YEAH... I GUESS YOU MUST BE...
A PART OF ME THINKS I SHOULDN'T BE DOING THIS. I HAVEN'T EVEN SLEPT WITH MY JOHN YET.
BUT ISN'T THAT EXACTLY WHY I AM DOING THIS?
HMM...
DAMN ED
I MEAN, WHO IN HELL MARRIES SOMEONE WITHOUT SHAGGING THEM FIRST NOWADAYS?

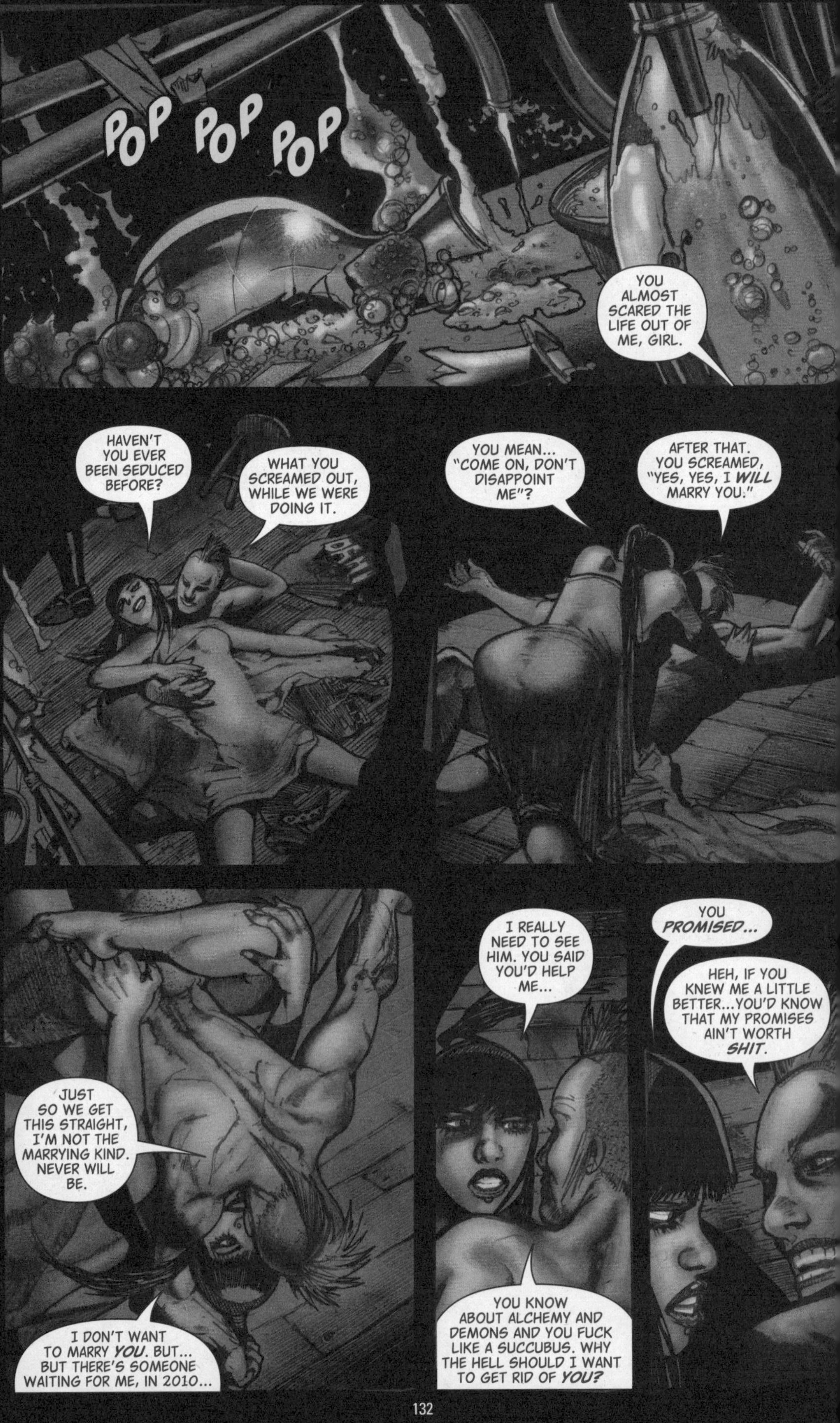
POP POP POP
YOU ALMOST SCARED THE LIFE OUT OF ME, GIRL.
HAVEN'T YOU EVER BEEN SEDUCED BEFORE?
WHAT YOU SCREAMED OUT, WHILE WE WERE DOING IT.
YOU MEAN... "COME ON, DON'T DISAPPOINT ME"?
AFTER THAT. YOU SCREAMED, "YES, YES, I *WILL* MARRY YOU."
JUST SO WE GET THIS STRAIGHT, I'M NOT THE MARRYING KIND. NEVER WILL BE.
I DON'T WANT TO MARRY *YOU*. BUT... BUT THERE'S SOMEONE WAITING FOR ME, IN 2010...
I REALLY NEED TO SEE HIM. YOU SAID YOU'D HELP ME...
YOU KNOW ABOUT ALCHEMY AND DEMONS AND YOU FUCK LIKE A SUCCUBUS. WHY THE HELL SHOULD I WANT TO GET RID OF *YOU?*
YOU *PROMISED...*
HEH, IF YOU KNEW ME A LITTLE BETTER...YOU'D KNOW THAT MY PROMISES AIN'T WORTH *SHIT*.

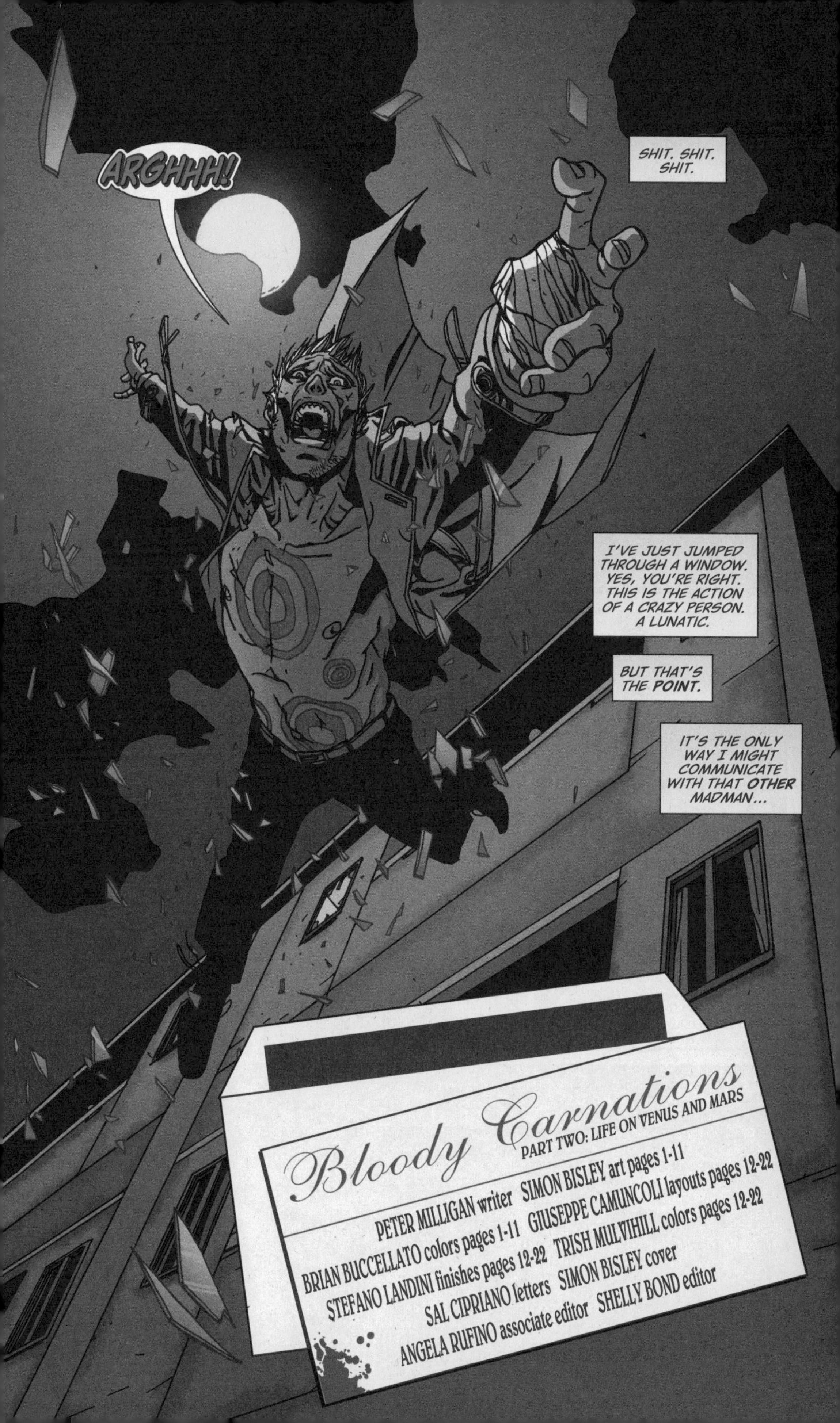
ARGHHH!
SHIT. SHIT. SHIT.
I'VE JUST JUMPED THROUGH A WINDOW. YES, YOU'RE RIGHT. THIS IS THE ACTION OF A CRAZY PERSON. A LUNATIC.
BUT THAT'S THE POINT.
IT'S THE ONLY WAY I MIGHT COMMUNICATE WITH THAT OTHER MADMAN...
Bloody Carnations
PART TWO: LIFE ON VENUS AND MARS
PETER MILLIGAN writer SIMON BISLEY art pages 1-11
BRIAN BUCCELLATO colors pages 1-11 GIUSEPPE CAMUNCOLI layouts pages 12-22
STEFANO LANDINI finishes pages 12-22 TRISH MULVIHILL colors pages 12-22
SAL CIPRIANO letters SIMON BISLEY cover
ANGELA RUFINO associate editor SHELLY BOND editor

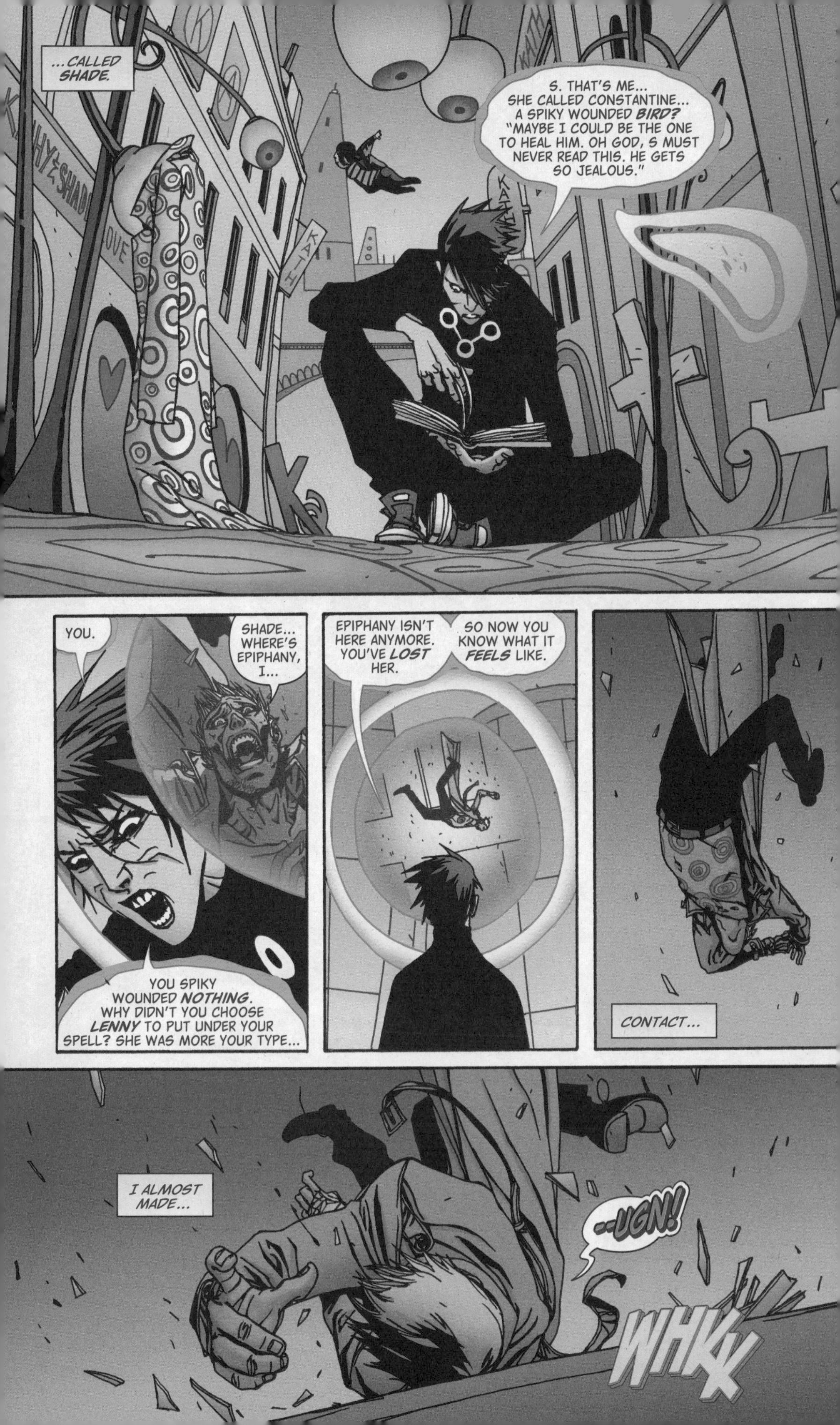

...CALLED SHADE.
S. THAT'S ME... SHE CALLED CONSTANTINE... A SPIKY WOUNDED BIRD? "MAYBE I COULD BE THE ONE TO HEAL HIM. OH GOD, S MUST NEVER READ THIS. HE GETS SO JEALOUS."
KATH
LOVE
YOU.
SHADE... WHERE'S EPIPHANY, I...
YOU SPIKY WOUNDED NOTHING. WHY DIDN'T YOU CHOOSE LENNY TO PUT UNDER YOUR SPELL? SHE WAS MORE YOUR TYPE...
EPIPHANY ISN'T HERE ANYMORE. YOU'VE LOST HER.
SO NOW YOU KNOW WHAT IT FEELS LIKE.
CONTACT...
I ALMOST MADE...
--UGN!
WHKK

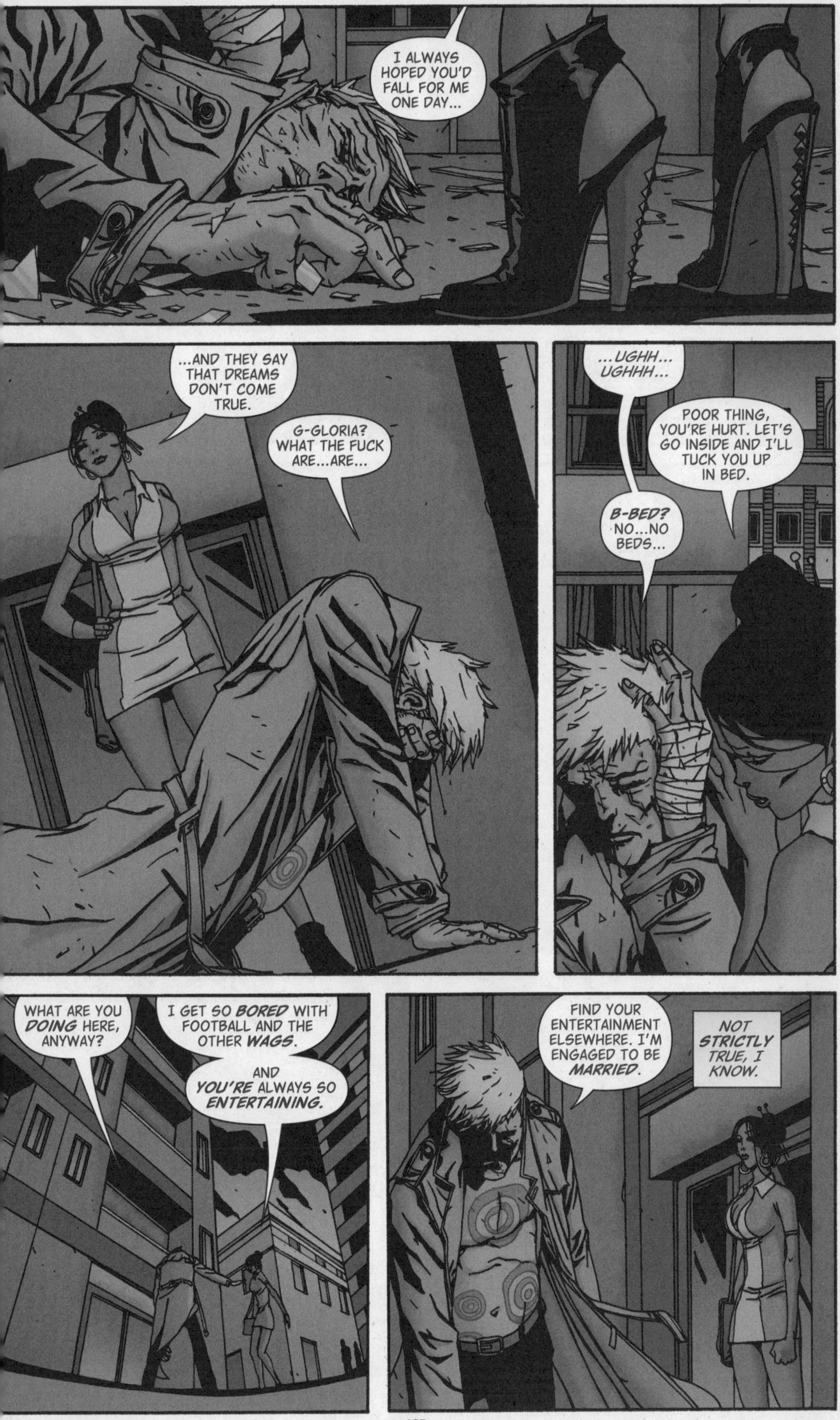
I ALWAYS HOPED YOU'D FALL FOR ME ONE DAY...
...AND THEY SAY THAT DREAMS DON'T COME TRUE.
G-GLORIA? WHAT THE FUCK ARE...ARE...
...UGHH... UGHHH...
POOR THING, YOU'RE HURT. LET'S GO INSIDE AND I'LL TUCK YOU UP IN BED.
B-BED? NO...NO BEDS...
WHAT ARE YOU DOING HERE, ANYWAY?
I GET SO BORED WITH FOOTBALL AND THE OTHER WAGS.
AND YOU'RE ALWAYS SO ENTERTAINING.
FIND YOUR ENTERTAINMENT ELSEWHERE. I'M ENGAGED TO BE MARRIED.
NOT STRICTLY TRUE, I KNOW.

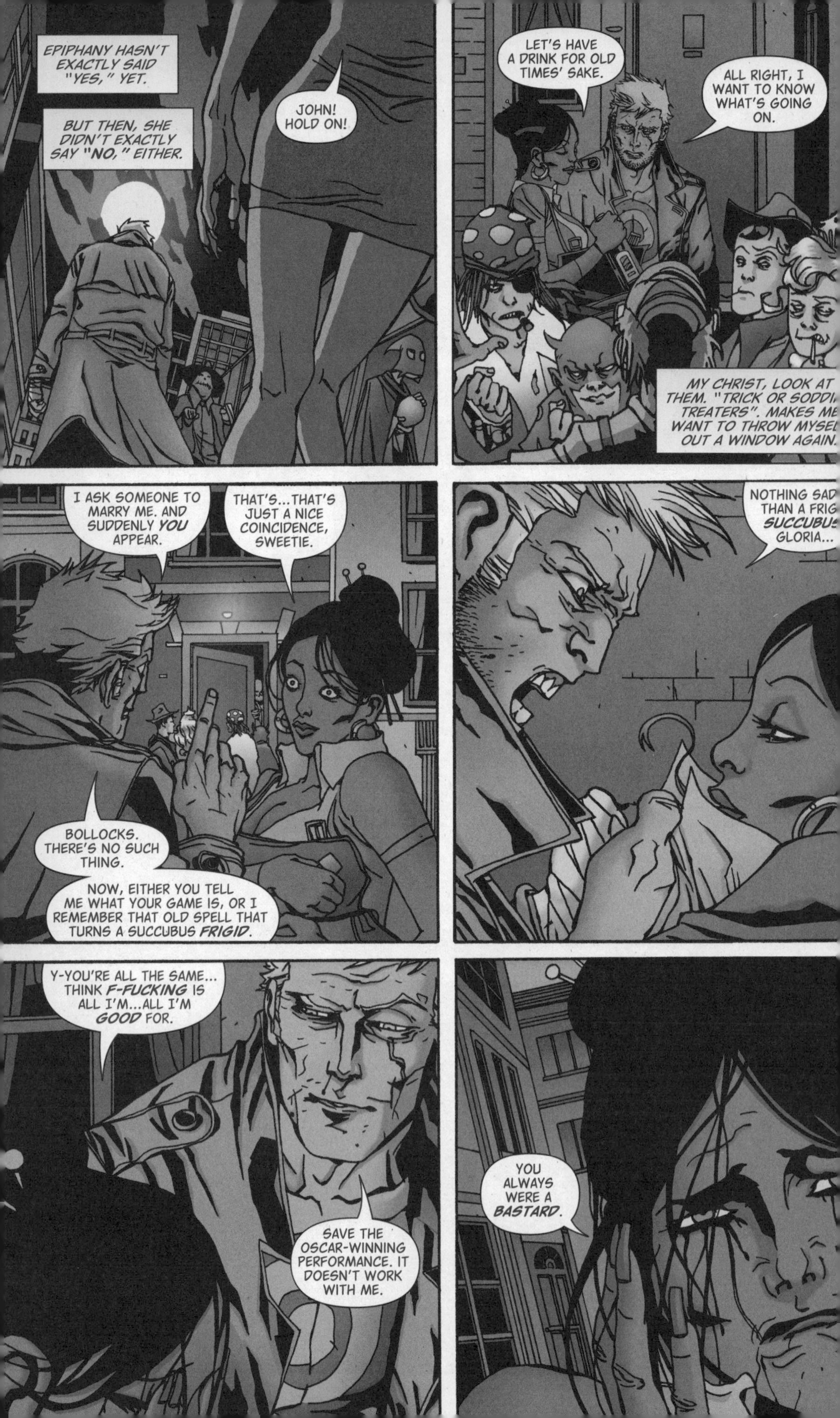
EPIPHANY HASN'T EXACTLY SAID "YES," YET.
BUT THEN, SHE DIDN'T EXACTLY SAY "NO," EITHER.
JOHN! HOLD ON!
LET'S HAVE A DRINK FOR OLD TIMES' SAKE.
ALL RIGHT, I WANT TO KNOW WHAT'S GOING ON.
MY CHRIST, LOOK AT THEM. "TRICK OR SODDI TREATERS". MAKES ME WANT TO THROW MYSEL OUT A WINDOW AGAIN.
I ASK SOMEONE TO MARRY ME. AND SUDDENLY YOU APPEAR.
THAT'S...THAT'S JUST A NICE COINCIDENCE, SWEETIE.
BOLLOCKS. THERE'S NO SUCH THING.
NOW, EITHER YOU TELL ME WHAT YOUR GAME IS, OR I REMEMBER THAT OLD SPELL THAT TURNS A SUCCUBUS FRIGID.
NOTHING SAD THAN A FRIG SUCCUBUS GLORIA...
Y-YOU'RE ALL THE SAME... THINK F-FUCKING IS ALL I'M...ALL I'M GOOD FOR.
SAVE THE OSCAR-WINNING PERFORMANCE. IT DOESN'T WORK WITH ME.
YOU ALWAYS WERE A BASTARD.

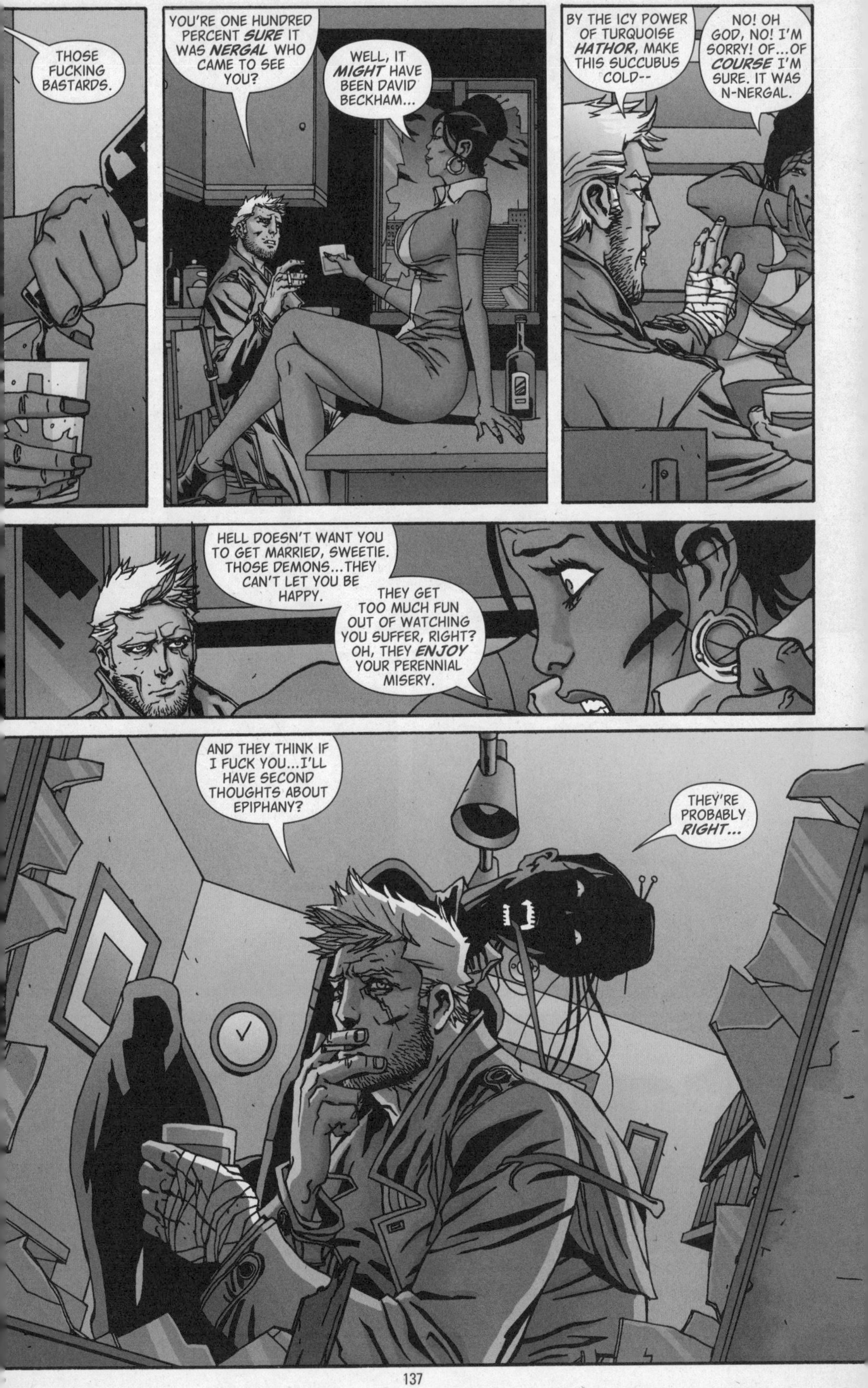
THOSE FUCKING BASTARDS.
YOU'RE ONE HUNDRED PERCENT SURE IT WAS NERGAL WHO CAME TO SEE YOU?
WELL, IT MIGHT HAVE BEEN DAVID BECKHAM...
BY THE ICY POWER OF TURQUOISE HATHOR, MAKE THIS SUCCUBUS COLD--
NO! OH GOD, NO! I'M SORRY! OF...OF COURSE I'M SURE. IT WAS N-NERGAL.
HELL DOESN'T WANT YOU TO GET MARRIED, SWEETIE. THOSE DEMONS...THEY CAN'T LET YOU BE HAPPY.
THEY GET TOO MUCH FUN OUT OF WATCHING YOU SUFFER, RIGHT? OH, THEY ENJOY YOUR PERENNIAL MISERY.
AND THEY THINK IF I FUCK YOU...I'LL HAVE SECOND THOUGHTS ABOUT EPIPHANY?
THEY'RE PROBABLY RIGHT...

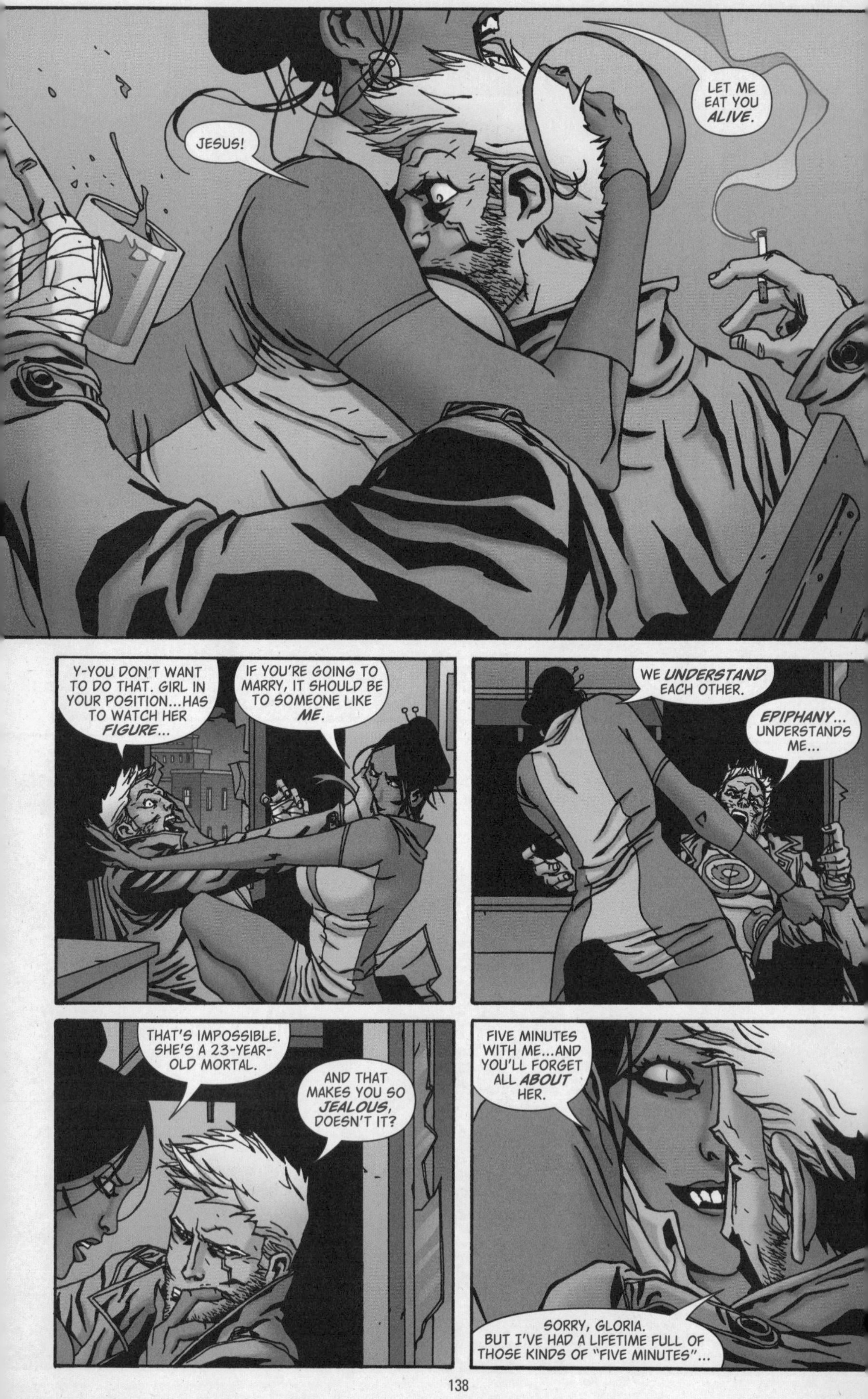
LET ME EAT YOU ALIVE.
JESUS!
Y-YOU DON'T WANT TO DO THAT. GIRL IN YOUR POSITION...HAS TO WATCH HER FIGURE...
IF YOU'RE GOING TO MARRY, IT SHOULD BE TO SOMEONE LIKE ME.
WE UNDERSTAND EACH OTHER.
EPIPHANY... UNDERSTANDS ME...
THAT'S IMPOSSIBLE. SHE'S A 23-YEAR-OLD MORTAL.
AND THAT MAKES YOU SO JEALOUS, DOESN'T IT?
FIVE MINUTES WITH ME...AND YOU'LL FORGET ALL ABOUT HER.
SORRY, GLORIA. BUT I'VE HAD A LIFETIME FULL OF THOSE KINDS OF "FIVE MINUTES"...

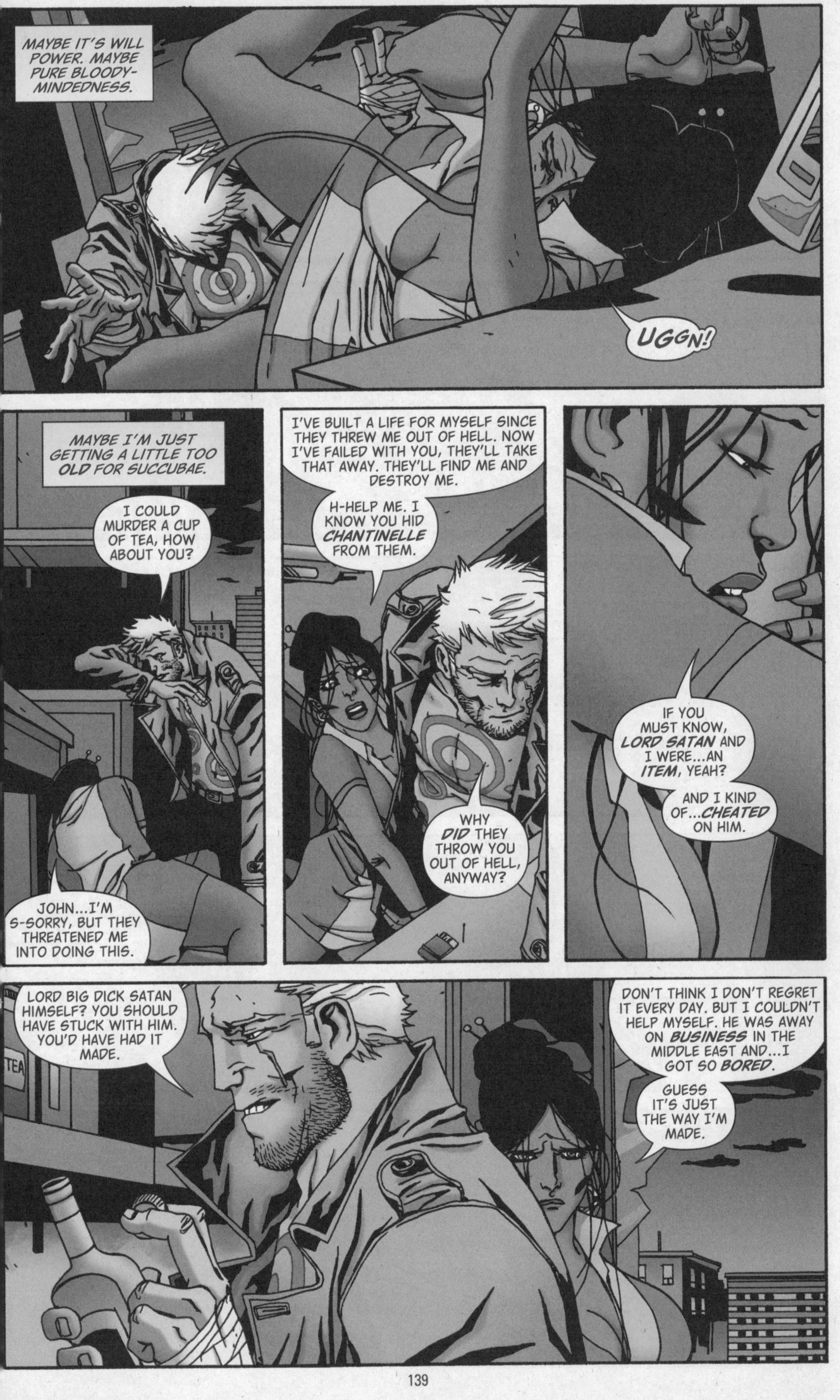

MAYBE IT'S WILL POWER. MAYBE PURE BLOODY-MINDEDNESS.
UGGN!
MAYBE I'M JUST GETTING A LITTLE TOO OLD FOR SUCCUBAE.
I COULD MURDER A CUP OF TEA, HOW ABOUT YOU?
JOHN...I'M S-SORRY, BUT THEY THREATENED ME INTO DOING THIS.
I'VE BUILT A LIFE FOR MYSELF SINCE THEY THREW ME OUT OF HELL. NOW I'VE FAILED WITH YOU, THEY'LL TAKE THAT AWAY. THEY'LL FIND ME AND DESTROY ME.
H-HELP ME. I KNOW YOU HID CHANTINELLE FROM THEM.
WHY DID THEY THROW YOU OUT OF HELL, ANYWAY?
IF YOU MUST KNOW, LORD SATAN AND I WERE...AN ITEM, YEAH?
AND I KIND OF...CHEATED ON HIM.
LORD BIG DICK SATAN HIMSELF? YOU SHOULD HAVE STUCK WITH HIM. YOU'D HAVE HAD IT MADE.
TEA
DON'T THINK I DON'T REGRET IT EVERY DAY. BUT I COULDN'T HELP MYSELF. HE WAS AWAY ON BUSINESS IN THE MIDDLE EAST AND...I GOT SO BORED.
GUESS IT'S JUST THE WAY I'M MADE.

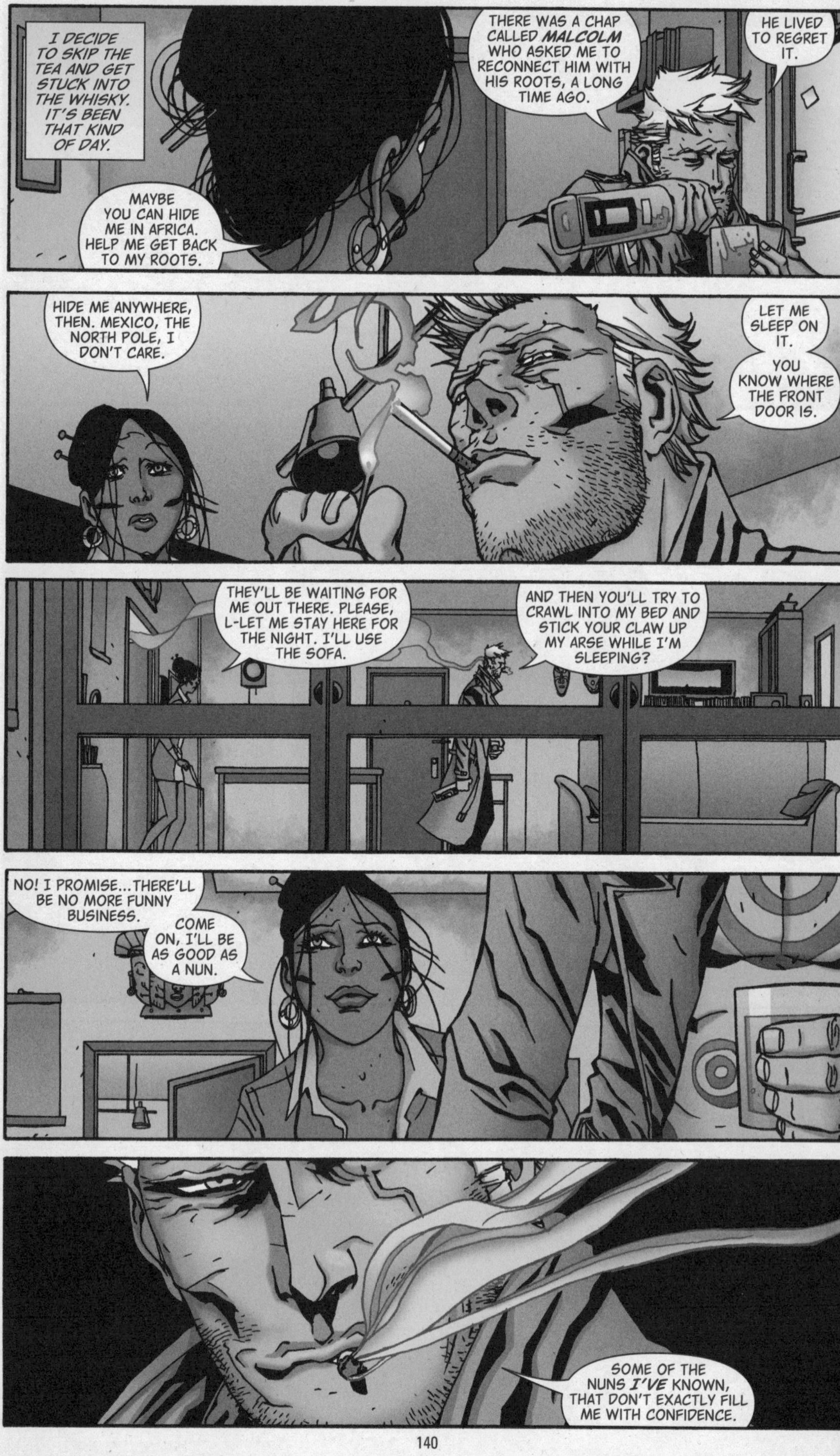
I DECIDE TO SKIP THE TEA AND GET STUCK INTO THE WHISKY. IT'S BEEN THAT KIND OF DAY.
MAYBE YOU CAN HIDE ME IN AFRICA. HELP ME GET BACK TO MY ROOTS.
THERE WAS A CHAP CALLED MALCOLM WHO ASKED ME TO RECONNECT HIM WITH HIS ROOTS, A LONG TIME AGO.
HE LIVED TO REGRET IT.
HIDE ME ANYWHERE, THEN. MEXICO, THE NORTH POLE, I DON'T CARE.
LET ME SLEEP ON IT.
YOU KNOW WHERE THE FRONT DOOR IS.
THEY'LL BE WAITING FOR ME OUT THERE. PLEASE, L-LET ME STAY HERE FOR THE NIGHT. I'LL USE THE SOFA.
AND THEN YOU'LL TRY TO CRAWL INTO MY BED AND STICK YOUR CLAW UP MY ARSE WHILE I'M SLEEPING?
NO! I PROMISE...THERE'LL BE NO MORE FUNNY BUSINESS.
COME ON, I'LL BE AS GOOD AS A NUN.
SOME OF THE NUNS I'VE KNOWN, THAT DON'T EXACTLY FILL ME WITH CONFIDENCE.

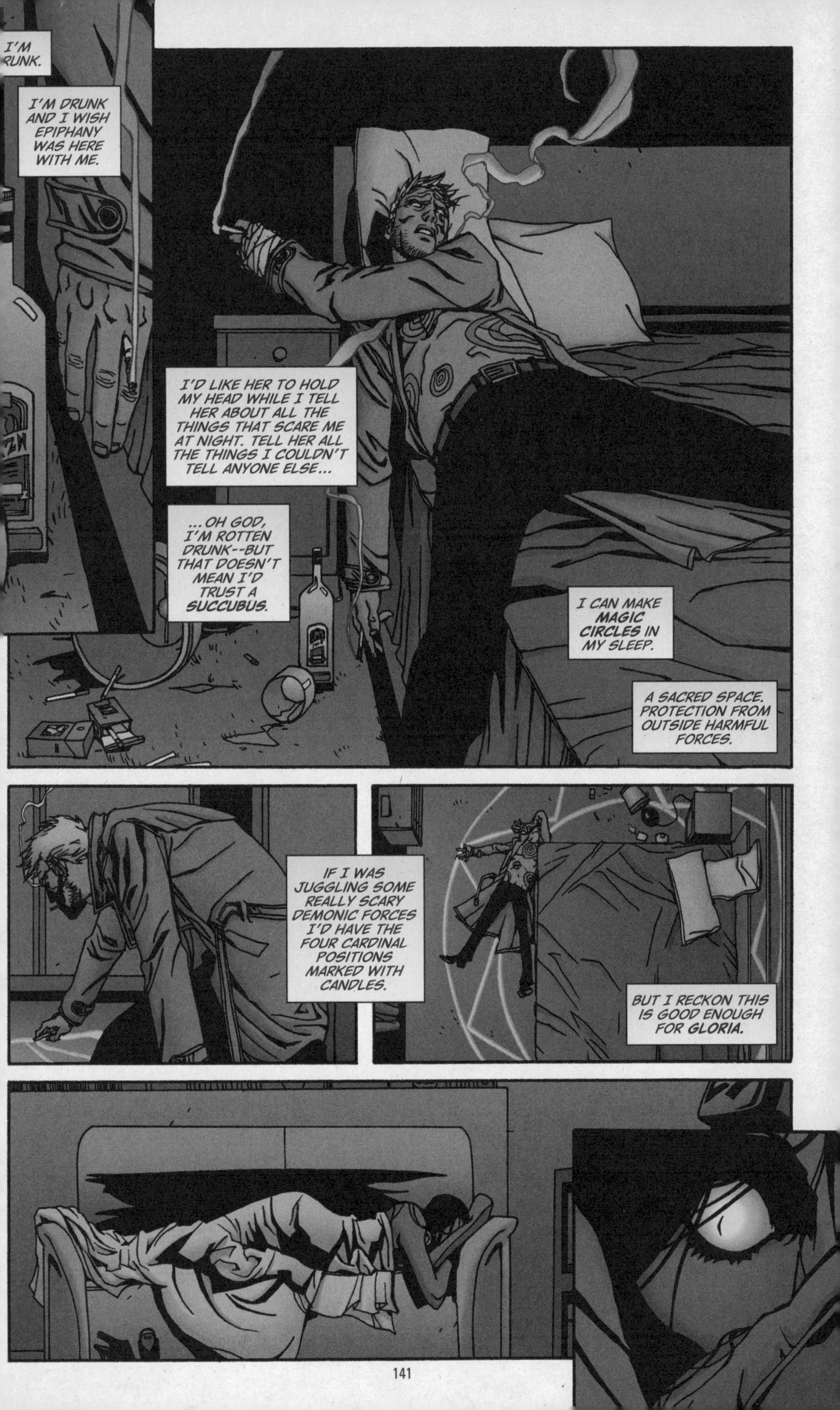
I'M
RUNK.
I'M DRUNK AND I WISH EPIPHANY WAS HERE WITH ME.
I'D LIKE HER TO HOLD MY HEAD WHILE I TELL HER ABOUT ALL THE THINGS THAT SCARE ME AT NIGHT. TELL HER ALL THE THINGS I COULDN'T TELL ANYONE ELSE...
...OH GOD, I'M ROTTEN DRUNK--BUT THAT DOESN'T MEAN I'D TRUST A SUCCUBUS.
I CAN MAKE MAGIC CIRCLES IN MY SLEEP.
A SACRED SPACE. PROTECTION FROM OUTSIDE HARMFUL FORCES.
IF I WAS JUGGLING SOME REALLY SCARY DEMONIC FORCES I'D HAVE THE FOUR CARDINAL POSITIONS MARKED WITH CANDLES.
BUT I RECKON THIS IS GOOD ENOUGH FOR GLORIA.

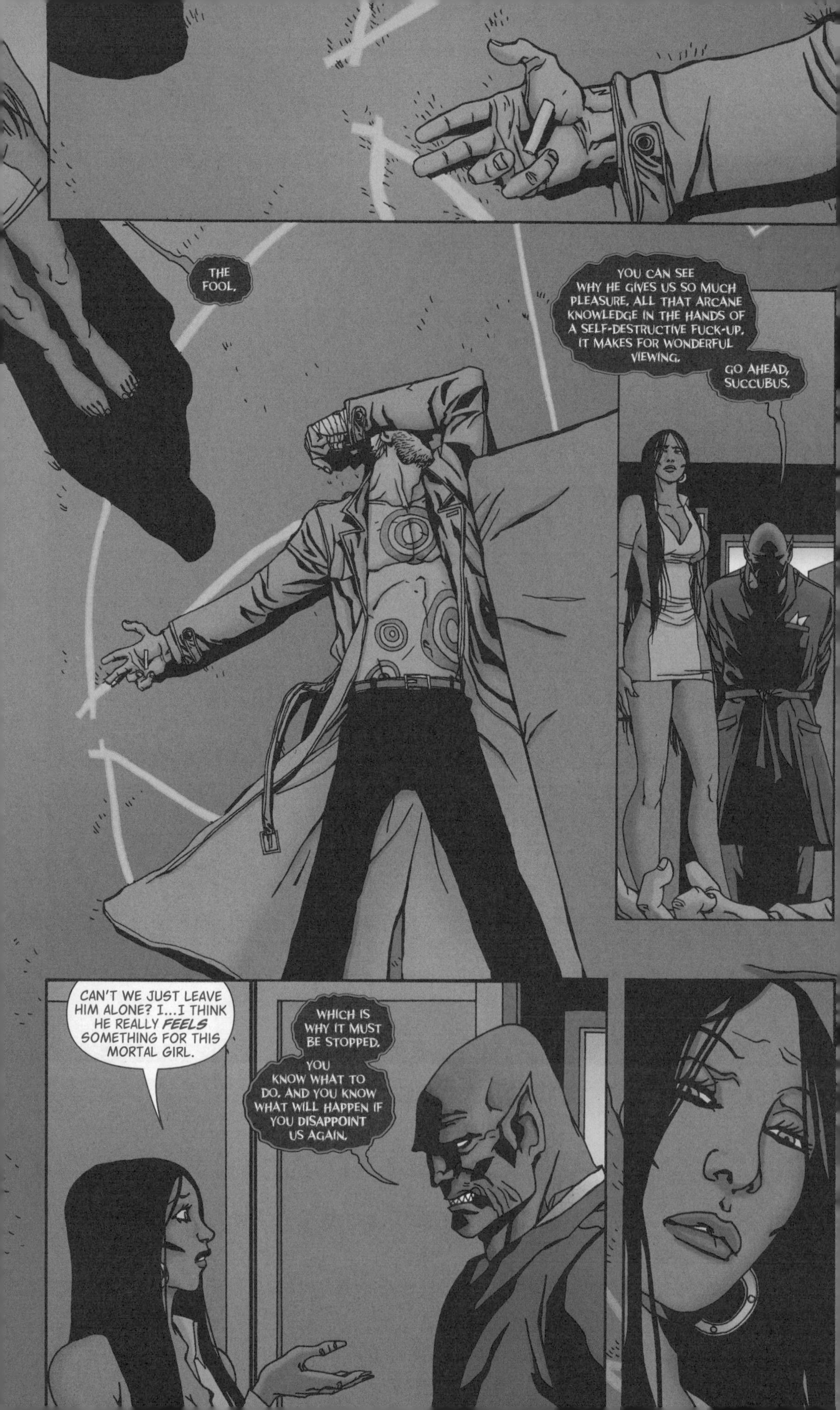
THE FOOL.
YOU CAN SEE WHY HE GIVES US SO MUCH PLEASURE. ALL THAT ARCANE KNOWLEDGE IN THE HANDS OF A SELF-DESTRUCTIVE FUCK-UP. IT MAKES FOR WONDERFUL VIEWING.
GO AHEAD, SUCCUBUS.
CAN'T WE JUST LEAVE HIM ALONE? I...I THINK HE REALLY FEELS SOMETHING FOR THIS MORTAL GIRL.
WHICH IS WHY IT MUST BE STOPPED.
YOU KNOW WHAT TO DO. AND YOU KNOW WHAT WILL HAPPEN IF YOU DISAPPOINT US AGAIN.

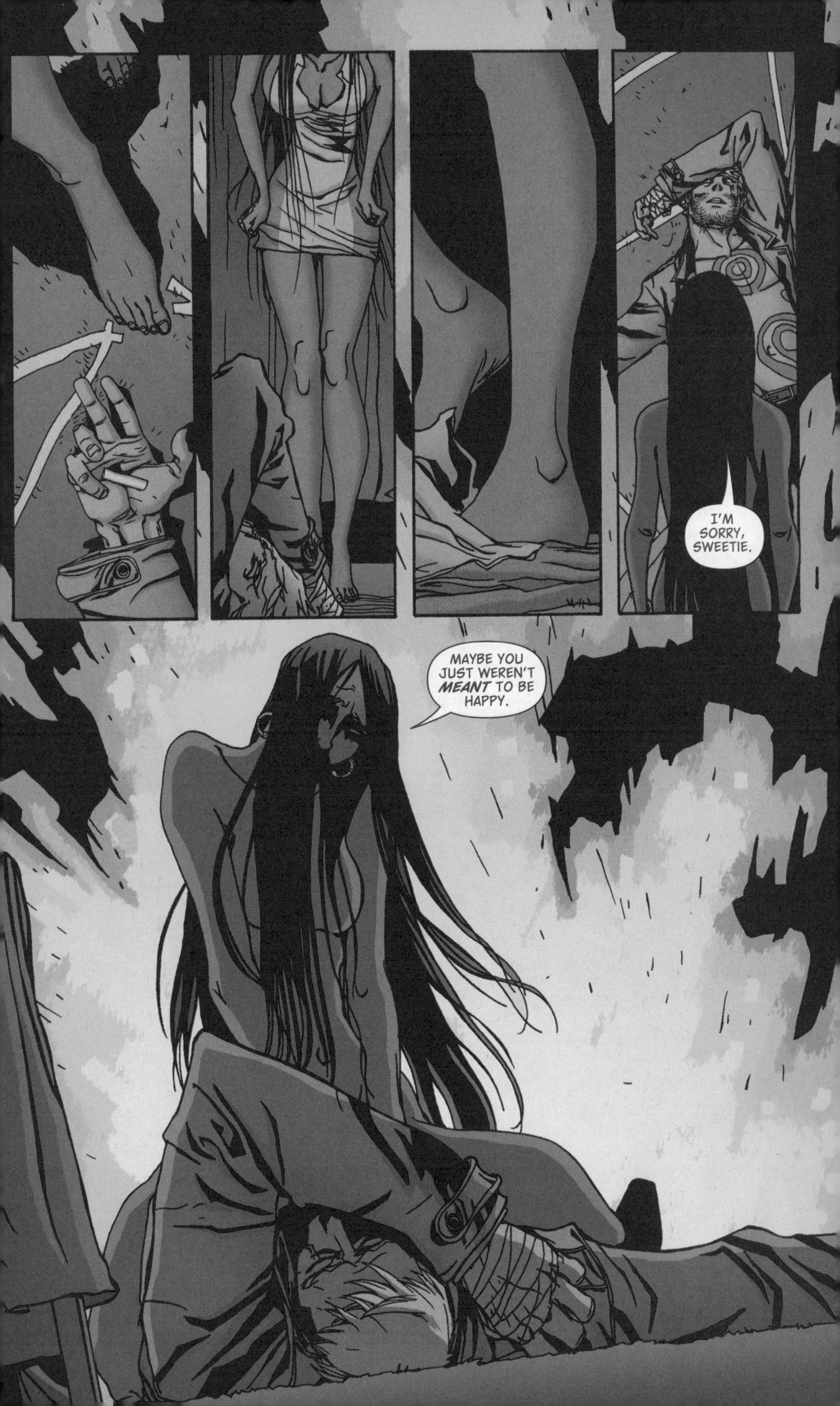
I'M SORRY, SWEETIE.
MAYBE YOU JUST WEREN'T *MEANT* TO BE HAPPY.

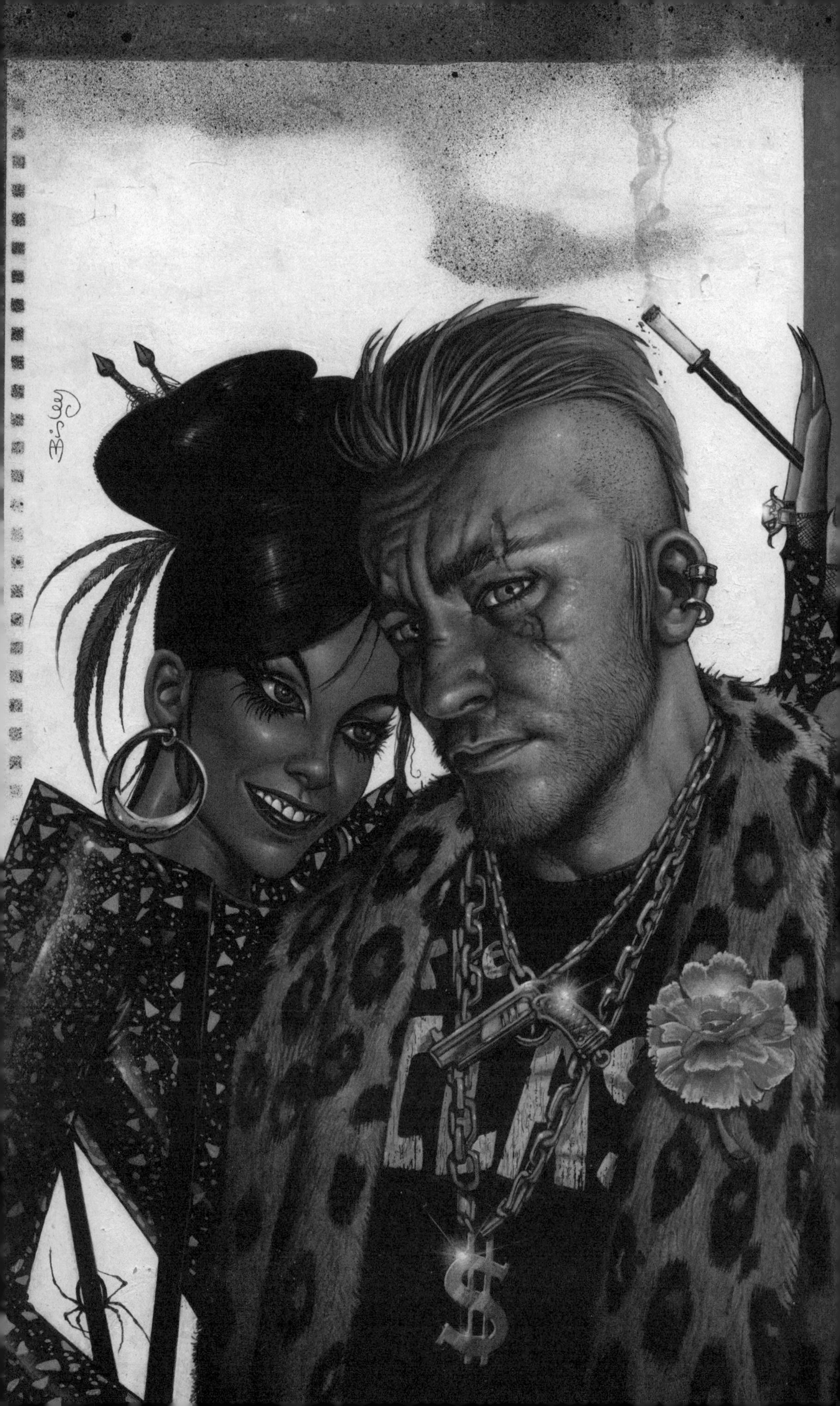
Bisley

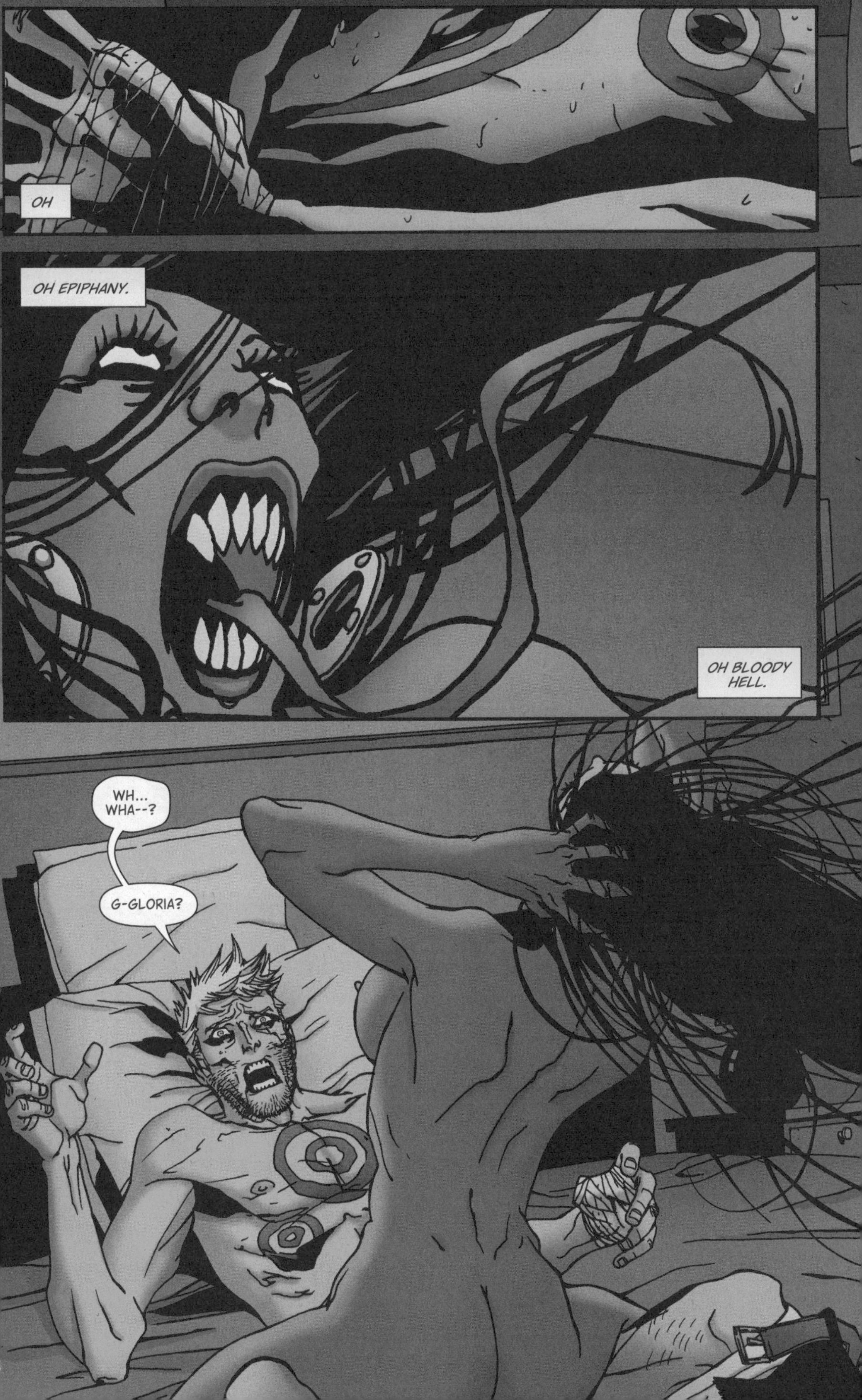

OH
OH EPIPHANY.
OH BLOODY HELL.
WH... WHA--?
G-GLORIA?

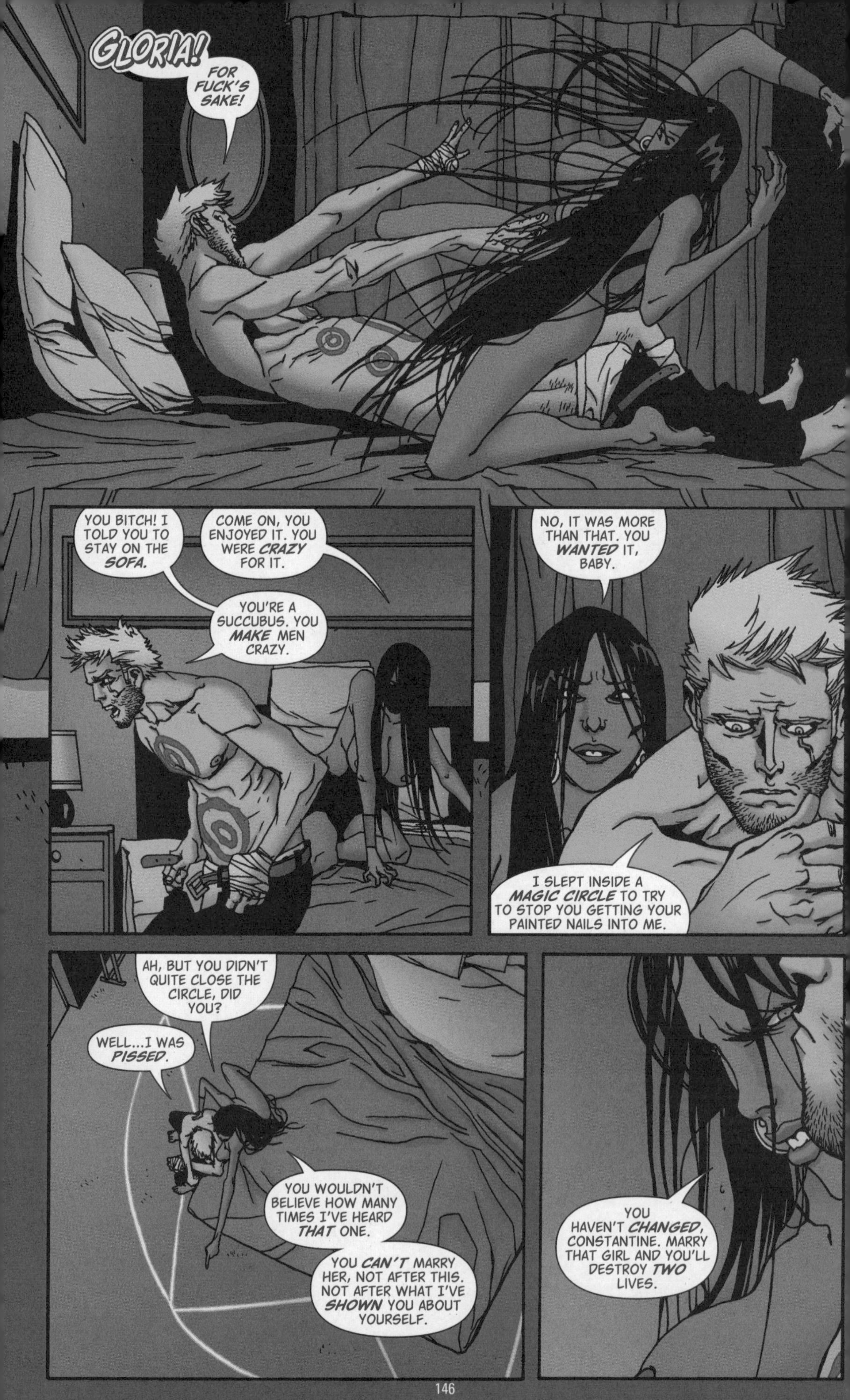
GLORIA!
FOR FUCK'S SAKE!
YOU BITCH! I TOLD YOU TO STAY ON THE SOFA.
COME ON, YOU ENJOYED IT. YOU WERE CRAZY FOR IT.
YOU'RE A SUCCUBUS. YOU MAKE MEN CRAZY.
NO, IT WAS MORE THAN THAT. YOU WANTED IT, BABY.
I SLEPT INSIDE A MAGIC CIRCLE TO TRY TO STOP YOU GETTING YOUR PAINTED NAILS INTO ME.
AH, BUT YOU DIDN'T QUITE CLOSE THE CIRCLE, DID YOU?
WELL...I WAS PISSED.
YOU WOULDN'T BELIEVE HOW MANY TIMES I'VE HEARD THAT ONE.
YOU CAN'T MARRY HER, NOT AFTER THIS. NOT AFTER WHAT I'VE SHOWN YOU ABOUT YOURSELF.
YOU HAVEN'T CHANGED, CONSTANTINE. MARRY THAT GIRL AND YOU'LL DESTROY TWO LIVES.

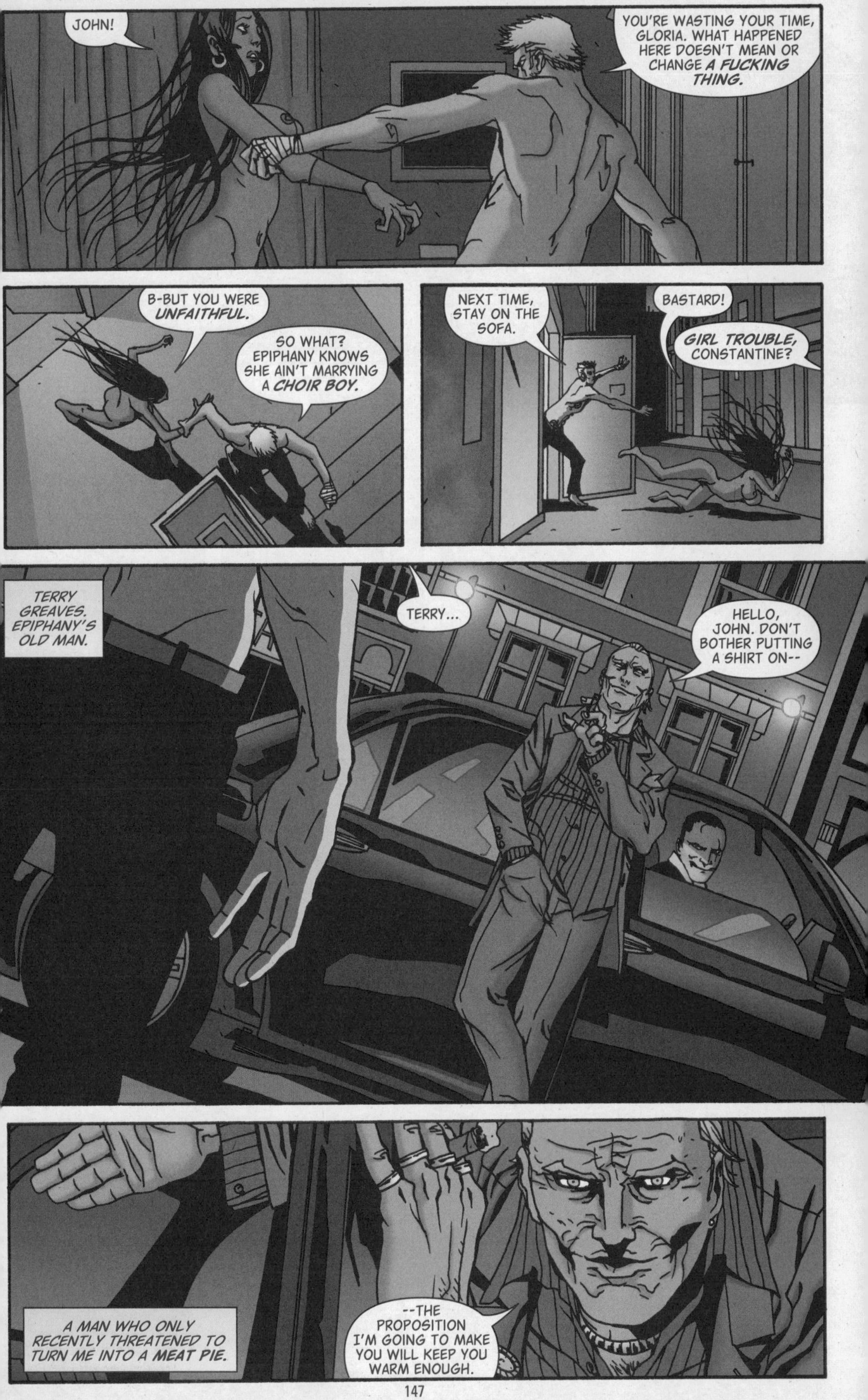
JOHN!
YOU'RE WASTING YOUR TIME, GLORIA. WHAT HAPPENED HERE DOESN'T MEAN OR CHANGE *A FUCKING THING.*
B-BUT YOU WERE *UNFAITHFUL.*
SO WHAT? EPIPHANY KNOWS SHE AIN'T MARRYING A *CHOIR BOY.*
NEXT TIME, STAY ON THE SOFA.
BASTARD!
GIRL TROUBLE, CONSTANTINE?
TERRY GREAVES. EPIPHANY'S OLD MAN.
TERRY...
HELLO, JOHN. DON'T BOTHER PUTTING A SHIRT ON--
A MAN WHO ONLY RECENTLY THREATENED TO TURN ME INTO A MEAT PIE.
--THE PROPOSITION I'M GOING TO MAKE YOU WILL KEEP YOU WARM ENOUGH.

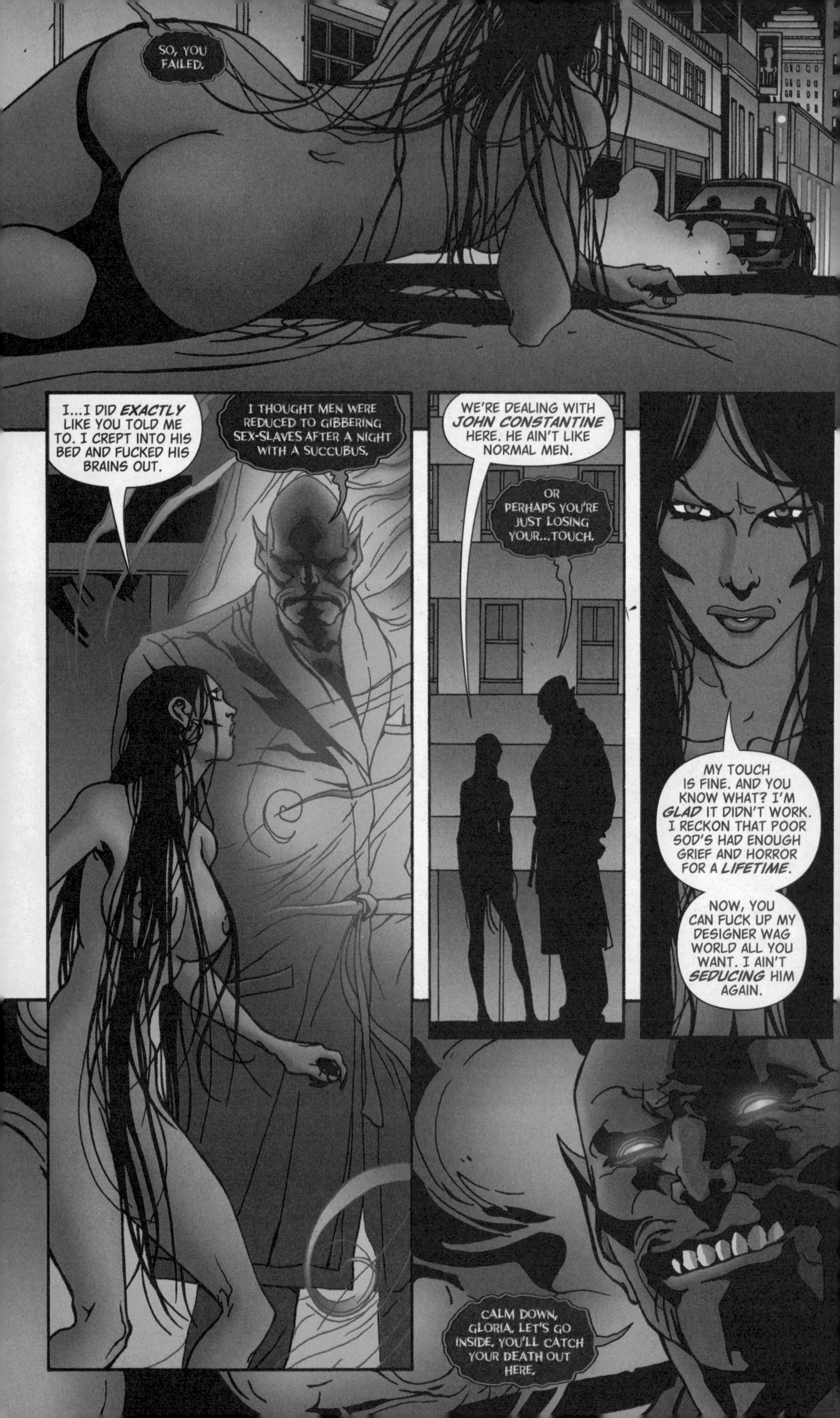

SO, YOU FAILED.
I...I DID EXACTLY LIKE YOU TOLD ME TO. I CREPT INTO HIS BED AND FUCKED HIS BRAINS OUT.
I THOUGHT MEN WERE REDUCED TO GIBBERING SEX-SLAVES AFTER A NIGHT WITH A SUCCUBUS.
WE'RE DEALING WITH JOHN CONSTANTINE HERE. HE AIN'T LIKE NORMAL MEN.
OR PERHAPS YOU'RE JUST LOSING YOUR...TOUCH.
MY TOUCH IS FINE. AND YOU KNOW WHAT? I'M GLAD IT DIDN'T WORK. I RECKON THAT POOR SOD'S HAD ENOUGH GRIEF AND HORROR FOR A LIFETIME.
NOW, YOU CAN FUCK UP MY DESIGNER WAG WORLD ALL YOU WANT. I AIN'T SEDUCING HIM AGAIN.
CALM DOWN, GLORIA. LET'S GO INSIDE. YOU'LL CATCH YOUR DEATH OUT HERE.

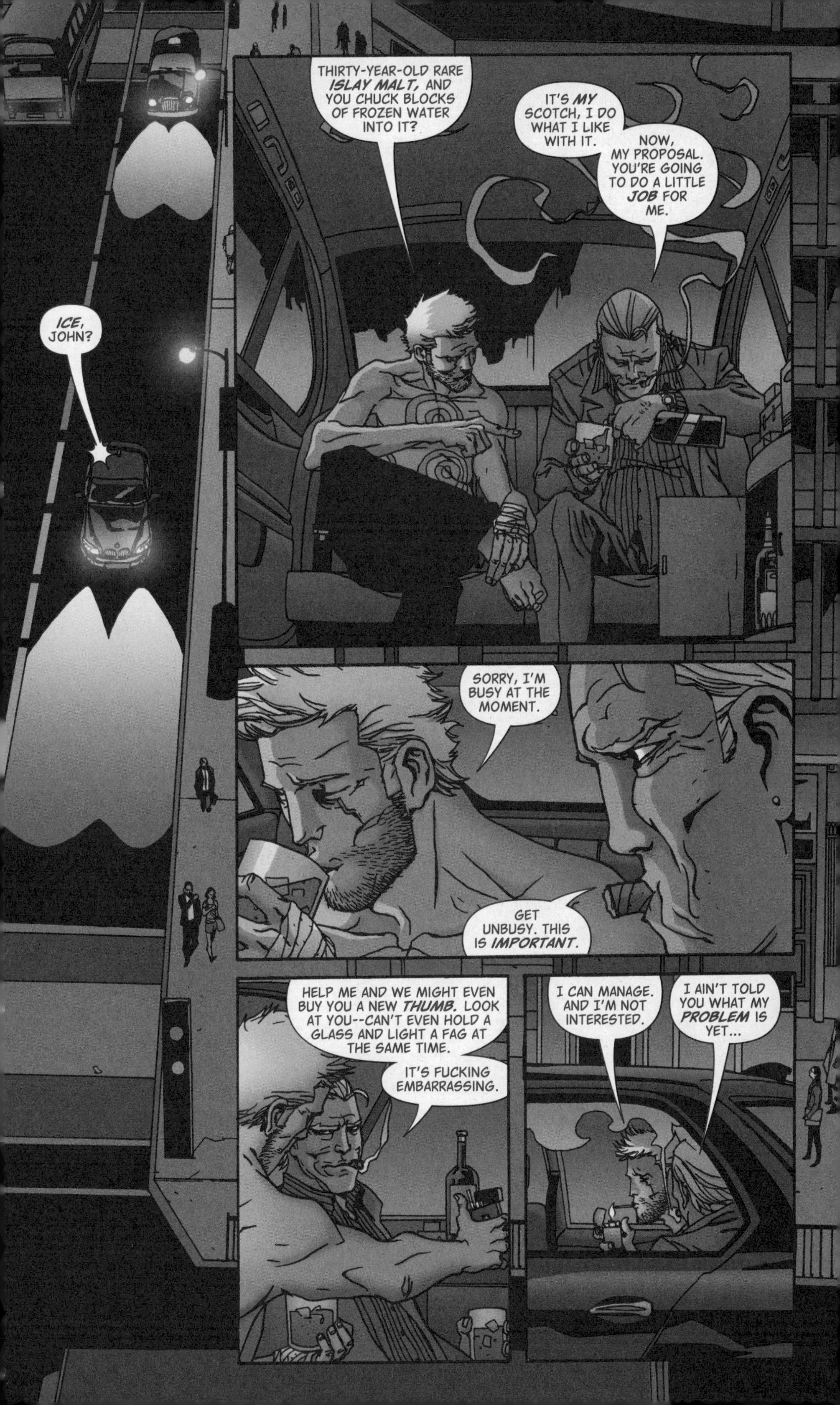
ICE, JOHN?
THIRTY-YEAR-OLD RARE ISLAY MALT, AND YOU CHUCK BLOCKS OF FROZEN WATER INTO IT?
IT'S MY SCOTCH, I DO WHAT I LIKE WITH IT.
NOW, MY PROPOSAL. YOU'RE GOING TO DO A LITTLE JOB FOR ME.
SORRY, I'M BUSY AT THE MOMENT.
GET UNBUSY. THIS IS IMPORTANT.
HELP ME AND WE MIGHT EVEN BUY YOU A NEW THUMB. LOOK AT YOU--CAN'T EVEN HOLD A GLASS AND LIGHT A FAG AT THE SAME TIME.
IT'S FUCKING EMBARRASSING.
I CAN MANAGE. AND I'M NOT INTERESTED.
I AIN'T TOLD YOU WHAT MY PROBLEM IS YET...

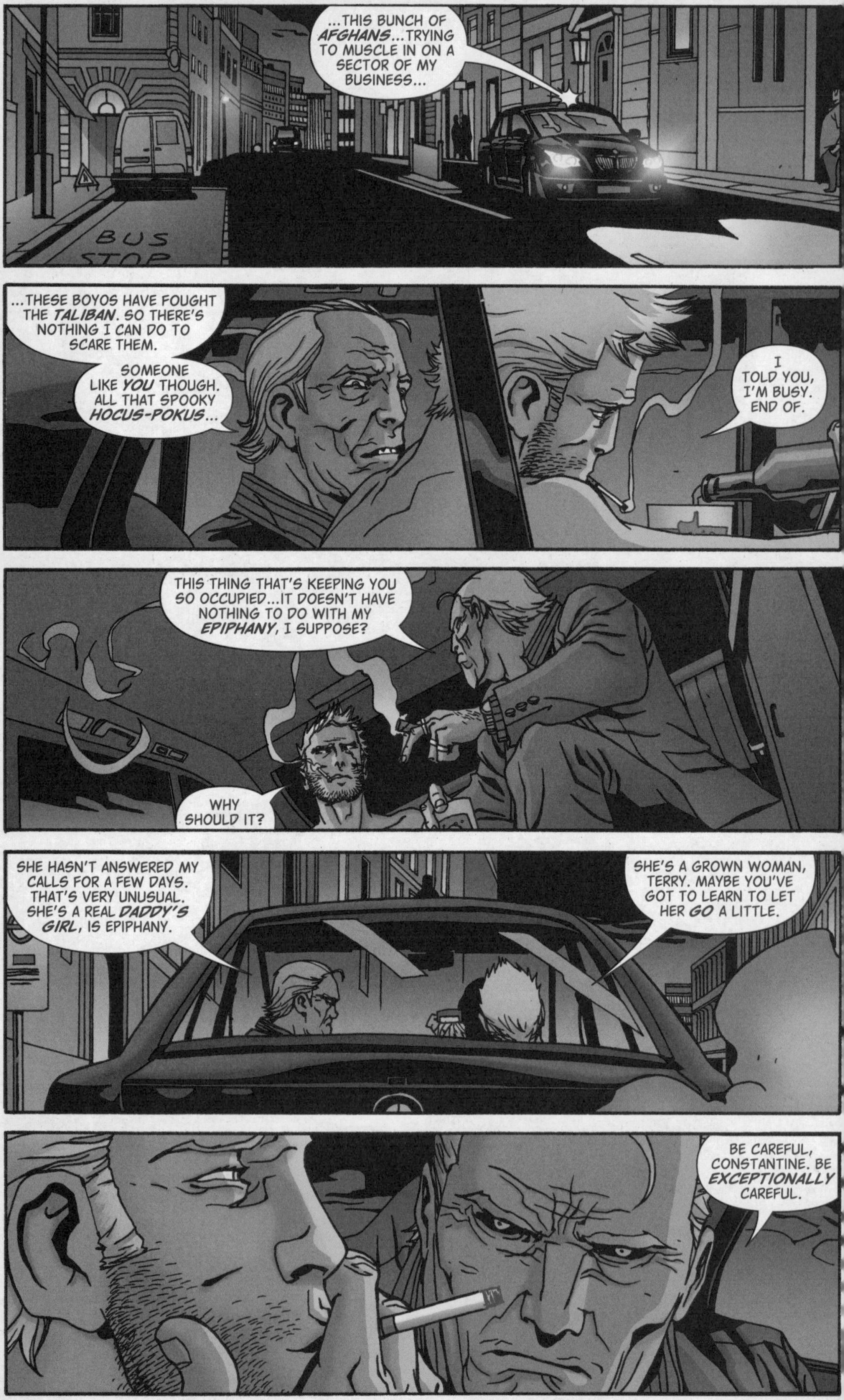
...THIS BUNCH OF AFGHANS...TRYING TO MUSCLE IN ON A SECTOR OF MY BUSINESS...
BUS STOP
...THESE BOYOS HAVE FOUGHT THE TALIBAN. SO THERE'S NOTHING I CAN DO TO SCARE THEM.
SOMEONE LIKE YOU THOUGH. ALL THAT SPOOKY HOCUS-POKUS...
I TOLD YOU, I'M BUSY. END OF.
THIS THING THAT'S KEEPING YOU SO OCCUPIED...IT DOESN'T HAVE NOTHING TO DO WITH MY EPIPHANY, I SUPPOSE?
WHY SHOULD IT?
SHE HASN'T ANSWERED MY CALLS FOR A FEW DAYS. THAT'S VERY UNUSUAL. SHE'S A REAL DADDY'S GIRL, IS EPIPHANY.
SHE'S A GROWN WOMAN, TERRY. MAYBE YOU'VE GOT TO LEARN TO LET HER GO A LITTLE.
BE CAREFUL, CONSTANTINE. BE EXCEPTIONALLY CAREFUL.

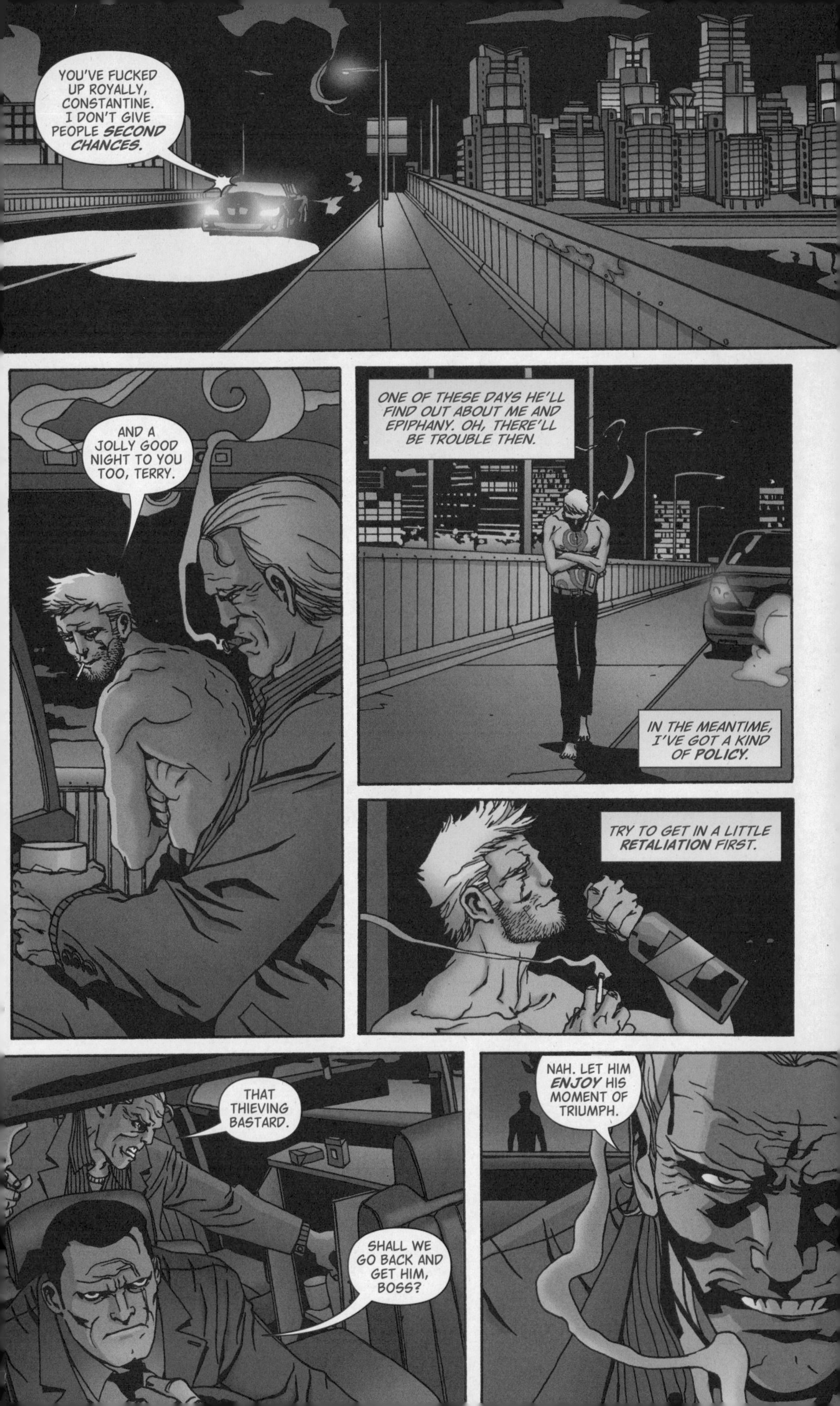

YOU'VE FUCKED UP ROYALLY, CONSTANTINE. I DON'T GIVE PEOPLE SECOND CHANCES.
AND A JOLLY GOOD NIGHT TO YOU TOO, TERRY.
ONE OF THESE DAYS HE'LL FIND OUT ABOUT ME AND EPIPHANY. OH, THERE'LL BE TROUBLE THEN.
IN THE MEANTIME, I'VE GOT A KIND OF POLICY.
TRY TO GET IN A LITTLE RETALIATION FIRST.
THAT THIEVING BASTARD.
SHALL WE GO BACK AND GET HIM, BOSS?
NAH. LET HIM ENJOY HIS MOMENT OF TRIUMPH.

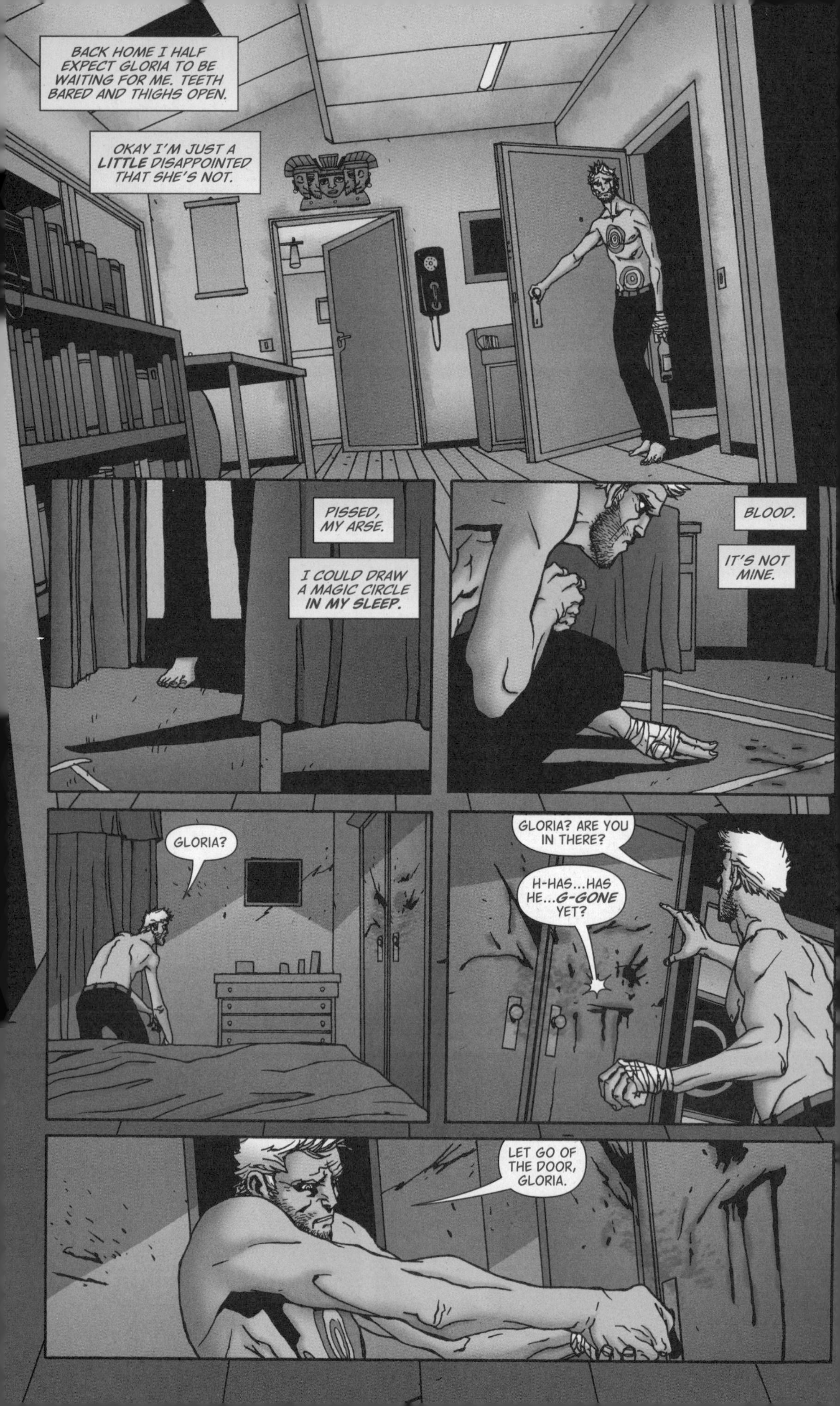
BACK HOME I HALF EXPECT GLORIA TO BE WAITING FOR ME. TEETH BARED AND THIGHS OPEN.
OKAY I'M JUST A LITTLE DISAPPOINTED THAT SHE'S NOT.
PISSED, MY ARSE.
I COULD DRAW A MAGIC CIRCLE IN MY SLEEP.
BLOOD.
IT'S NOT MINE.
GLORIA?
GLORIA? ARE YOU IN THERE?
H-HAS...HAS HE...G-GONE YET?
LET GO OF THE DOOR, GLORIA.

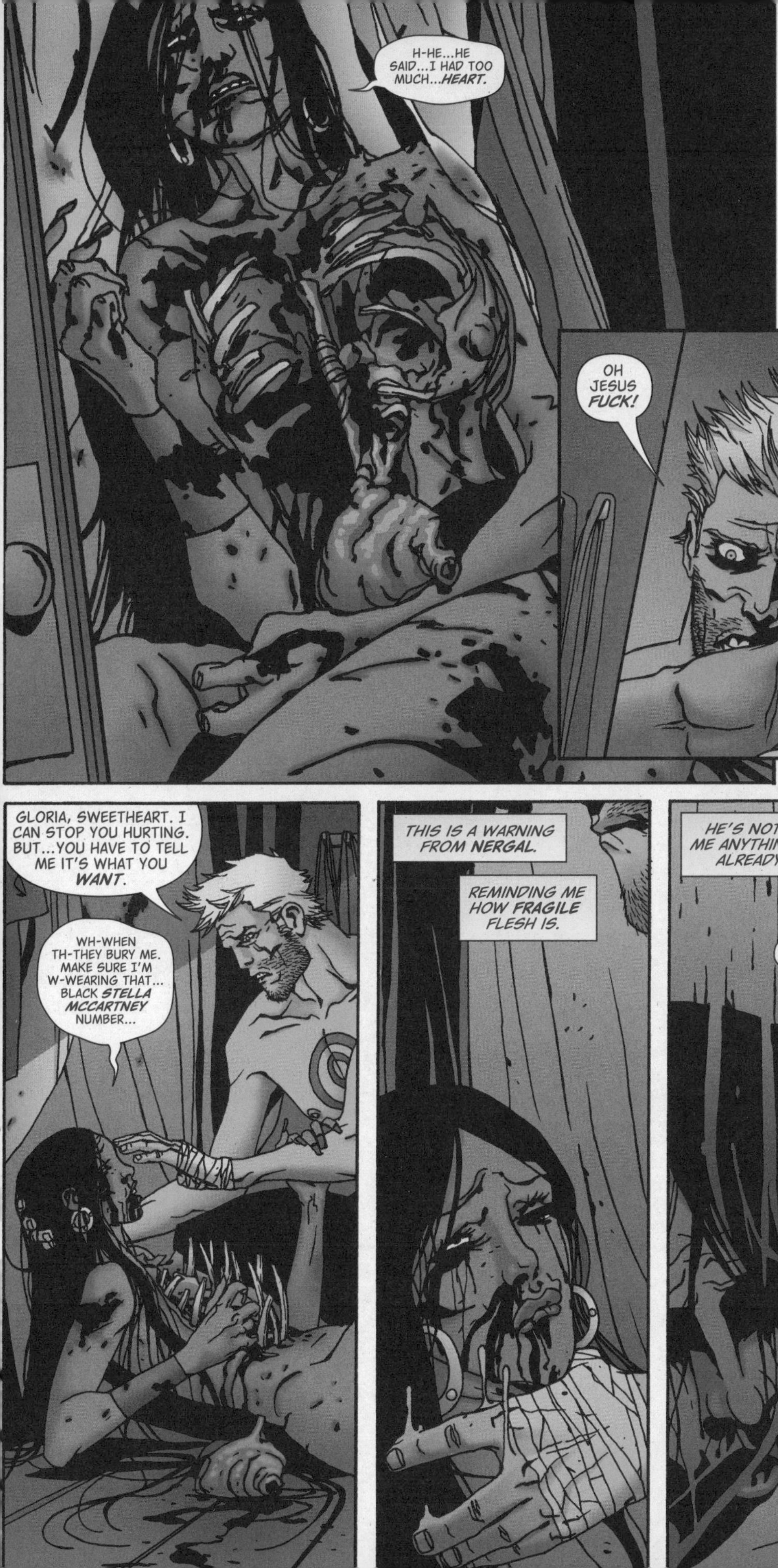

H-HE...HE SAID...I HAD TOO MUCH...HEART.
OH JESUS FUCK!
GLORIA, SWEETHEART. I CAN STOP YOU HURTING. BUT...YOU HAVE TO TELL ME IT'S WHAT YOU WANT.
WH-WHEN TH-THEY BURY ME. MAKE SURE I'M W-WEARING THAT... BLACK STELLA MCCARTNEY NUMBER...
THIS IS A WARNING FROM NERGAL.
REMINDING ME HOW FRAGILE FLESH IS.
HE'S NOT TELLING ME ANYTHING I DON'T ALREADY KNOW.
UGN!

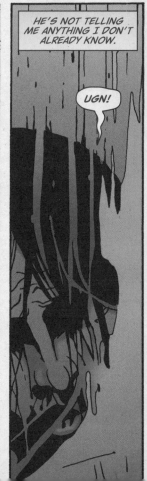

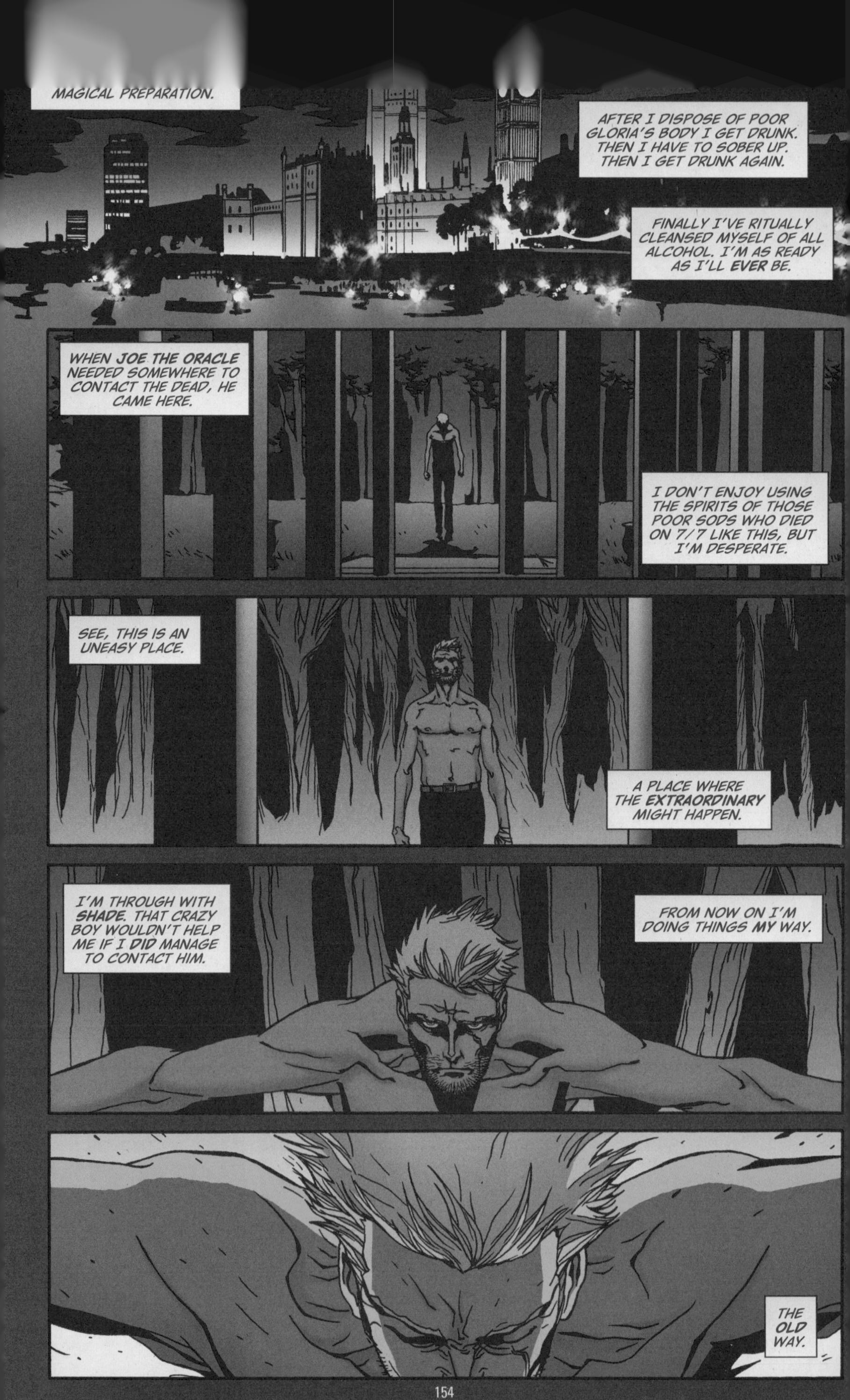
MAGICAL PREPARATION.
AFTER I DISPOSE OF POOR GLORIA'S BODY I GET DRUNK. THEN I HAVE TO SOBER UP. THEN I GET DRUNK AGAIN.
FINALLY I'VE RITUALLY CLEANSED MYSELF OF ALL ALCOHOL. I'M AS READY AS I'LL EVER BE.
WHEN JOE THE ORACLE NEEDED SOMEWHERE TO CONTACT THE DEAD, HE CAME HERE.
I DON'T ENJOY USING THE SPIRITS OF THOSE POOR SODS WHO DIED ON 7/7 LIKE THIS, BUT I'M DESPERATE.
SEE, THIS IS AN UNEASY PLACE.
A PLACE WHERE THE EXTRAORDINARY MIGHT HAPPEN.
I'M THROUGH WITH SHADE. THAT CRAZY BOY WOULDN'T HELP ME IF I DID MANAGE TO CONTACT HIM.
FROM NOW ON I'M DOING THINGS MY WAY.
THE OLD WAY.

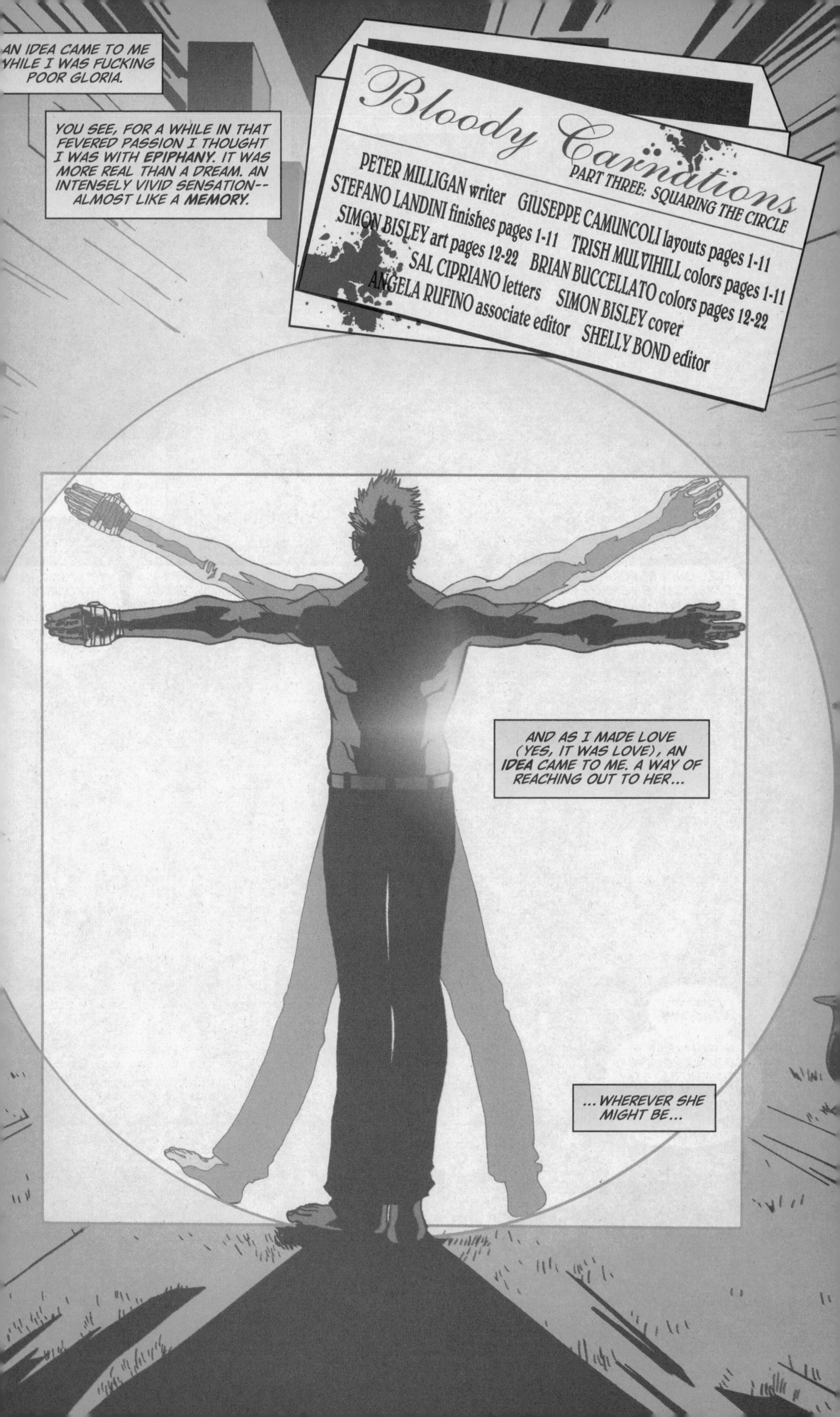

AN IDEA CAME TO ME WHILE I WAS FUCKING POOR GLORIA.
YOU SEE, FOR A WHILE IN THAT FEVERED PASSION I THOUGHT I WAS WITH EPIPHANY. IT WAS MORE REAL THAN A DREAM. AN INTENSELY VIVID SENSATION-- ALMOST LIKE A MEMORY.
Bloody Carnations
PART THREE: SQUARING THE CIRCLE
PETER MILLIGAN writer GIUSEPPE CAMUNCOLI layouts pages 1-11
STEFANO LANDINI finishes pages 1-11 TRISH MULVIHILL colors pages 1-11
SIMON BISLEY art pages 12-22 BRIAN BUCCELLATO colors pages 12-22
SAL CIPRIANO letters SIMON BISLEY cover
ANGELA RUFINO associate editor SHELLY BOND editor
AND AS I MADE LOVE (YES, IT WAS LOVE), AN IDEA CAME TO ME. A WAY OF REACHING OUT TO HER...
...WHEREVER SHE MIGHT BE...

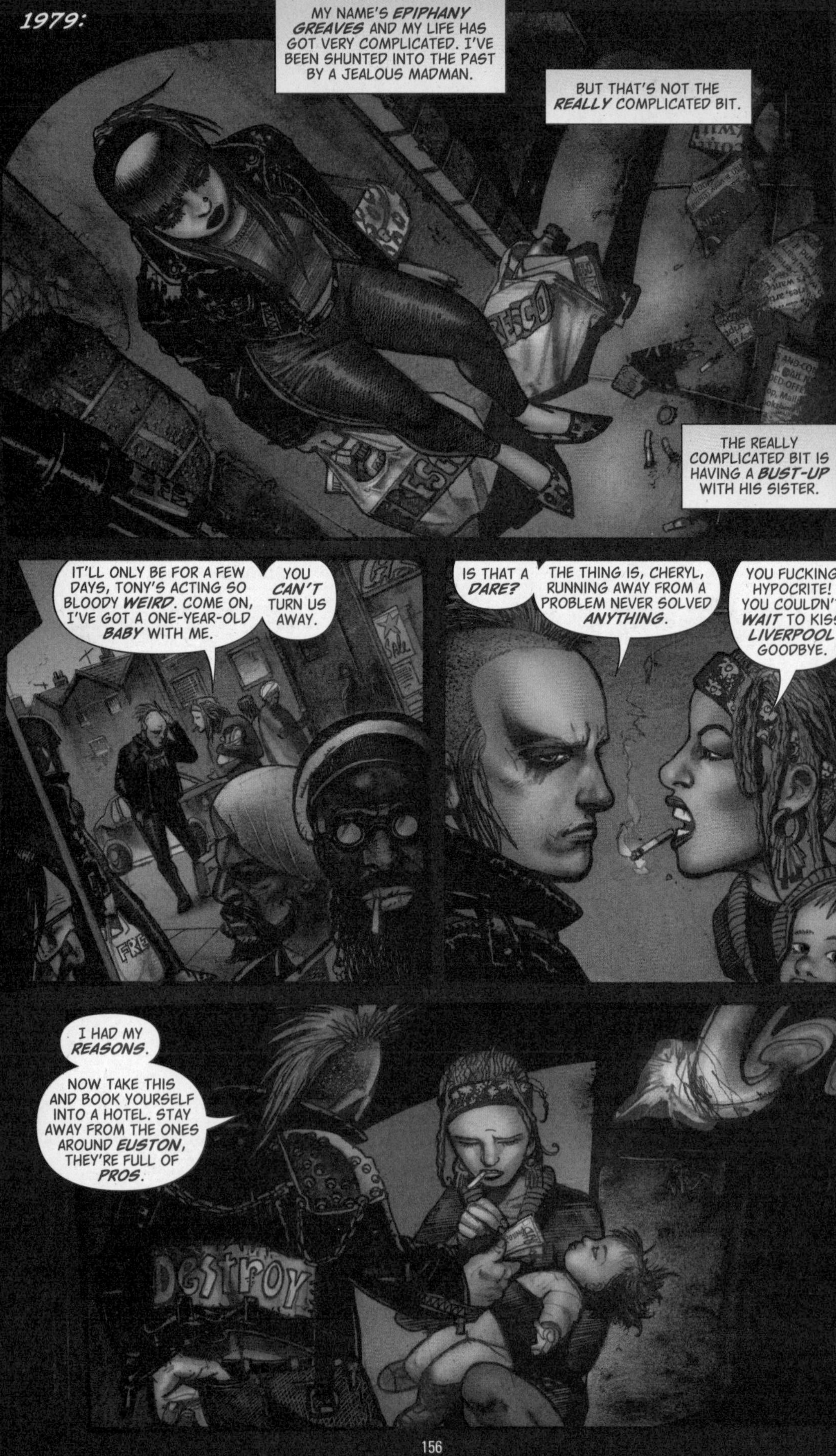
1979:
MY NAME'S EPIPHANY GREAVES AND MY LIFE HAS GOT VERY COMPLICATED. I'VE BEEN SHUNTED INTO THE PAST BY A JEALOUS MADMAN.
BUT THAT'S NOT THE REALLY COMPLICATED BIT.
THE REALLY COMPLICATED BIT IS HAVING A BUST-UP WITH HIS SISTER.
IT'LL ONLY BE FOR A FEW DAYS, TONY'S ACTING SO BLOODY WEIRD. COME ON, I'VE GOT A ONE-YEAR-OLD BABY WITH ME.
YOU CAN'T TURN US AWAY.
IS THAT A DARE?
THE THING IS, CHERYL, RUNNING AWAY FROM A PROBLEM NEVER SOLVED ANYTHING.
YOU FUCKING HYPOCRITE! YOU COULDN'T WAIT TO KISS LIVERPOOL GOODBYE.
I HAD MY REASONS.
NOW TAKE THIS AND BOOK YOURSELF INTO A HOTEL. STAY AWAY FROM THE ONES AROUND EUSTON, THEY'RE FULL OF PROS.
DESTROY

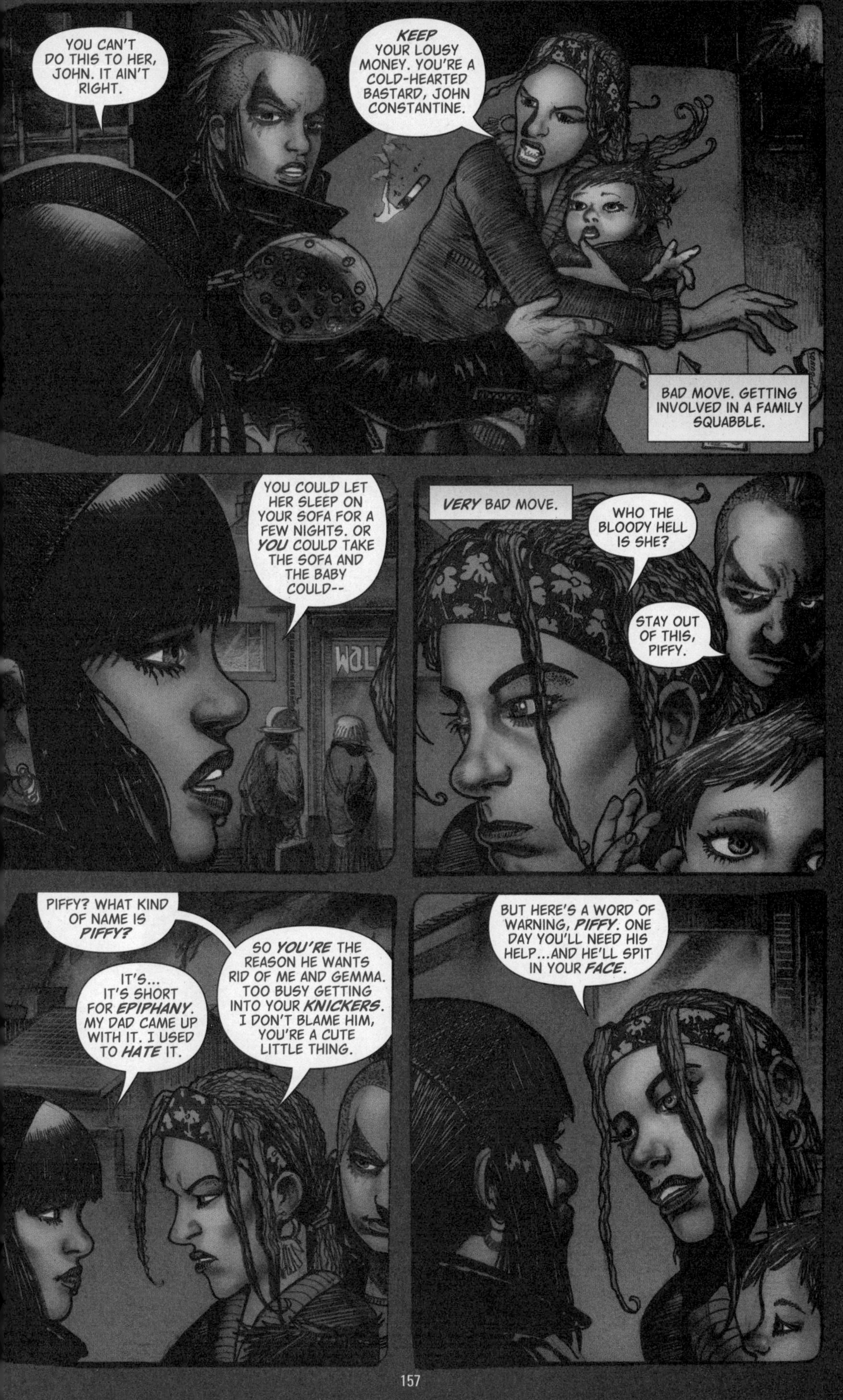
YOU CAN'T DO THIS TO HER, JOHN. IT AIN'T RIGHT.
KEEP YOUR LOUSY MONEY. YOU'RE A COLD-HEARTED BASTARD, JOHN CONSTANTINE.
BAD MOVE. GETTING INVOLVED IN A FAMILY SQUABBLE.
YOU COULD LET HER SLEEP ON YOUR SOFA FOR A FEW NIGHTS. OR YOU COULD TAKE THE SOFA AND THE BABY COULD--
VERY BAD MOVE.
WHO THE BLOODY HELL IS SHE?
STAY OUT OF THIS, PIFFY.
PIFFY? WHAT KIND OF NAME IS PIFFY?
IT'S... IT'S SHORT FOR EPIPHANY. MY DAD CAME UP WITH IT. I USED TO HATE IT.
SO YOU'RE THE REASON HE WANTS RID OF ME AND GEMMA. TOO BUSY GETTING INTO YOUR KNICKERS. I DON'T BLAME HIM, YOU'RE A CUTE LITTLE THING.
BUT HERE'S A WORD OF WARNING, PIFFY. ONE DAY YOU'LL NEED HIS HELP...AND HE'LL SPIT IN YOUR FACE.

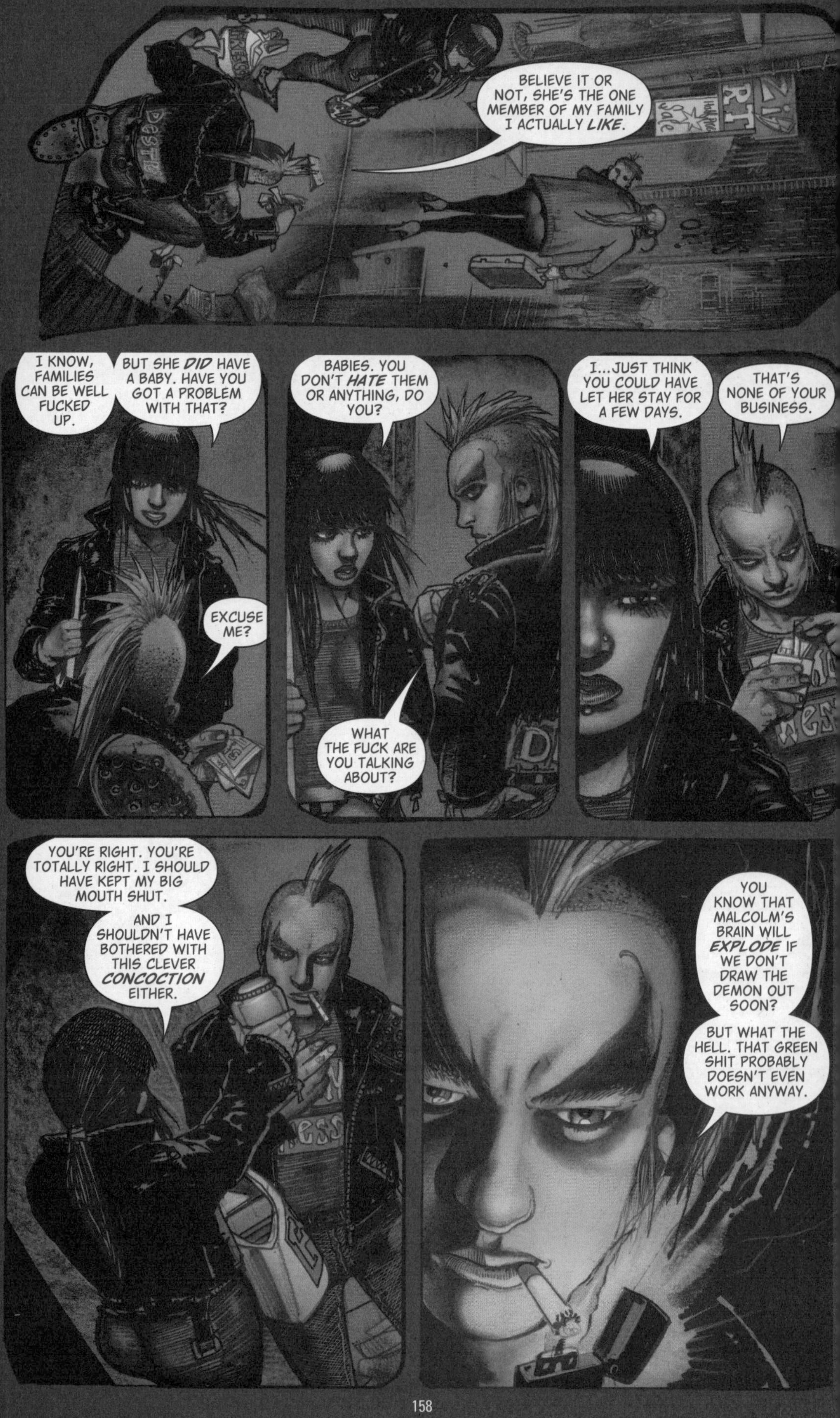
BELIEVE IT OR NOT, SHE'S THE ONE MEMBER OF MY FAMILY I ACTUALLY *LIKE*.
I KNOW, FAMILIES CAN BE WELL FUCKED UP.
BUT SHE *DID* HAVE A BABY. HAVE YOU GOT A PROBLEM WITH THAT?
EXCUSE ME?
BABIES. YOU DON'T *HATE* THEM OR ANYTHING, DO YOU?
WHAT THE FUCK ARE YOU TALKING ABOUT?
I...JUST THINK YOU COULD HAVE LET HER STAY FOR A FEW DAYS.
THAT'S NONE OF YOUR BUSINESS.
YOU'RE RIGHT. YOU'RE TOTALLY RIGHT. I SHOULD HAVE KEPT MY BIG MOUTH SHUT.
AND I SHOULDN'T HAVE BOTHERED WITH THIS CLEVER *CONCOCTION* EITHER.
YOU KNOW THAT MALCOLM'S BRAIN WILL *EXPLODE* IF WE DON'T DRAW THE DEMON OUT SOON?
BUT WHAT THE HELL. THAT GREEN SHIT PROBABLY DOESN'T EVEN WORK ANYWAY.

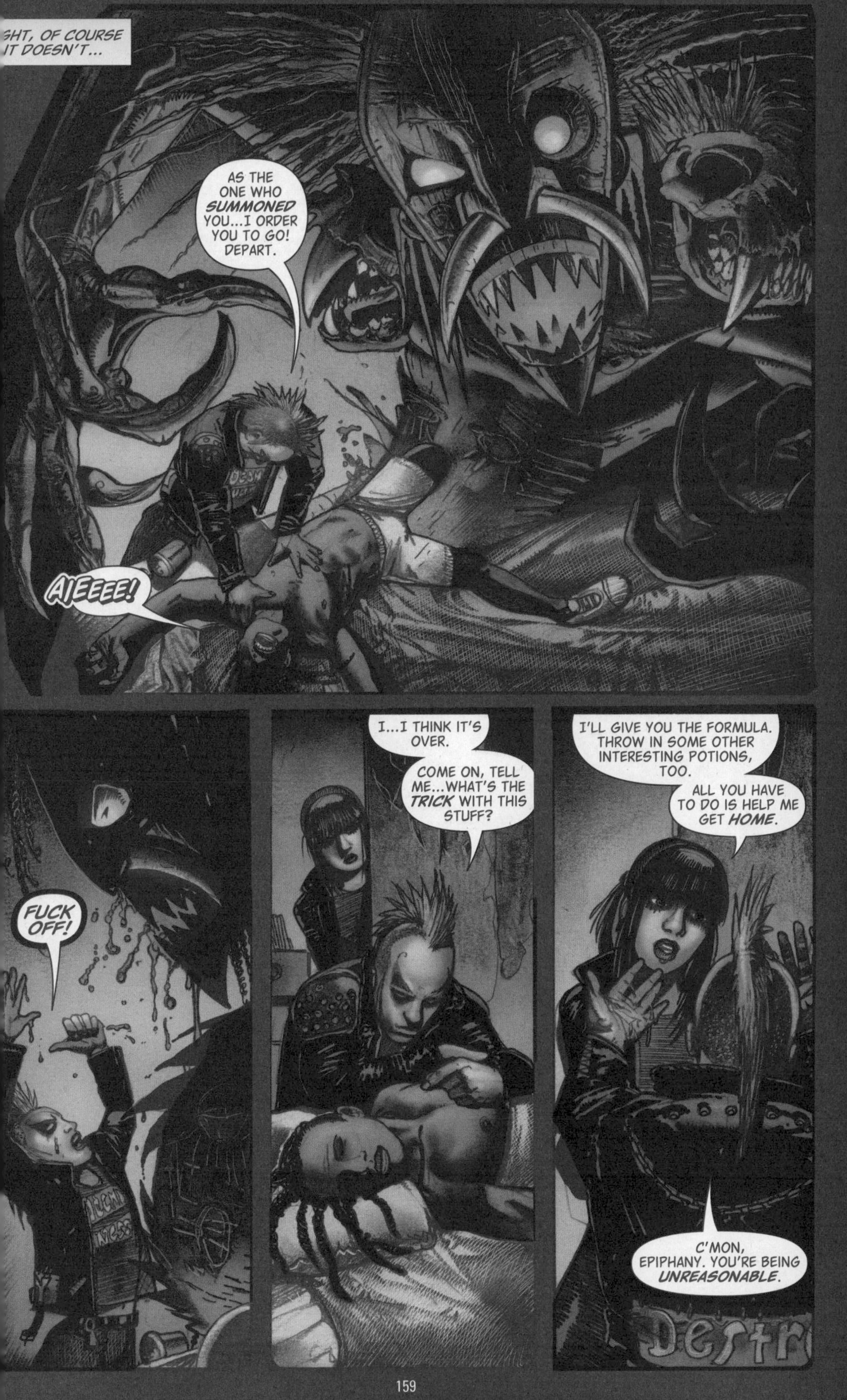
GHT, OF COURSE IT DOESN'T...
AS THE ONE WHO SUMMONED YOU...I ORDER YOU TO GO! DEPART.
AIEEEE!
FUCK OFF!
I...I THINK IT'S OVER.
COME ON, TELL ME...WHAT'S THE TRICK WITH THIS STUFF?
I'LL GIVE YOU THE FORMULA. THROW IN SOME OTHER INTERESTING POTIONS, TOO.
ALL YOU HAVE TO DO IS HELP ME GET HOME.
C'MON, EPIPHANY. YOU'RE BEING UNREASONABLE.

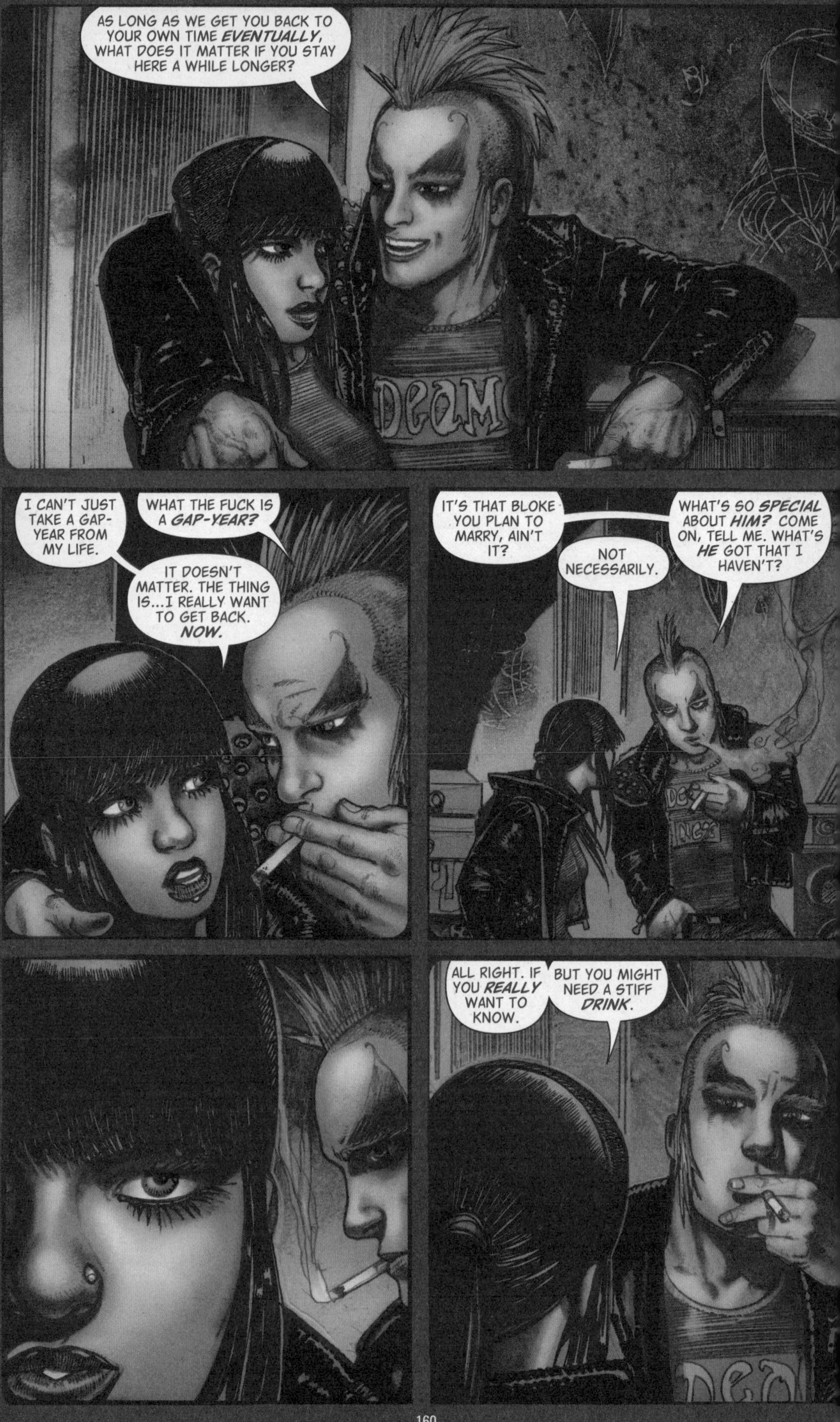
AS LONG AS WE GET YOU BACK TO YOUR OWN TIME EVENTUALLY, WHAT DOES IT MATTER IF YOU STAY HERE A WHILE LONGER?
I CAN'T JUST TAKE A GAP-YEAR FROM MY LIFE.
WHAT THE FUCK IS A GAP-YEAR?
IT DOESN'T MATTER. THE THING IS...I REALLY WANT TO GET BACK. NOW.
IT'S THAT BLOKE YOU PLAN TO MARRY, AIN'T IT?
WHAT'S SO SPECIAL ABOUT HIM? COME ON, TELL ME. WHAT'S HE GOT THAT I HAVEN'T?
NOT NECESSARILY.
ALL RIGHT. IF YOU REALLY WANT TO KNOW.
BUT YOU MIGHT NEED A STIFF DRINK.

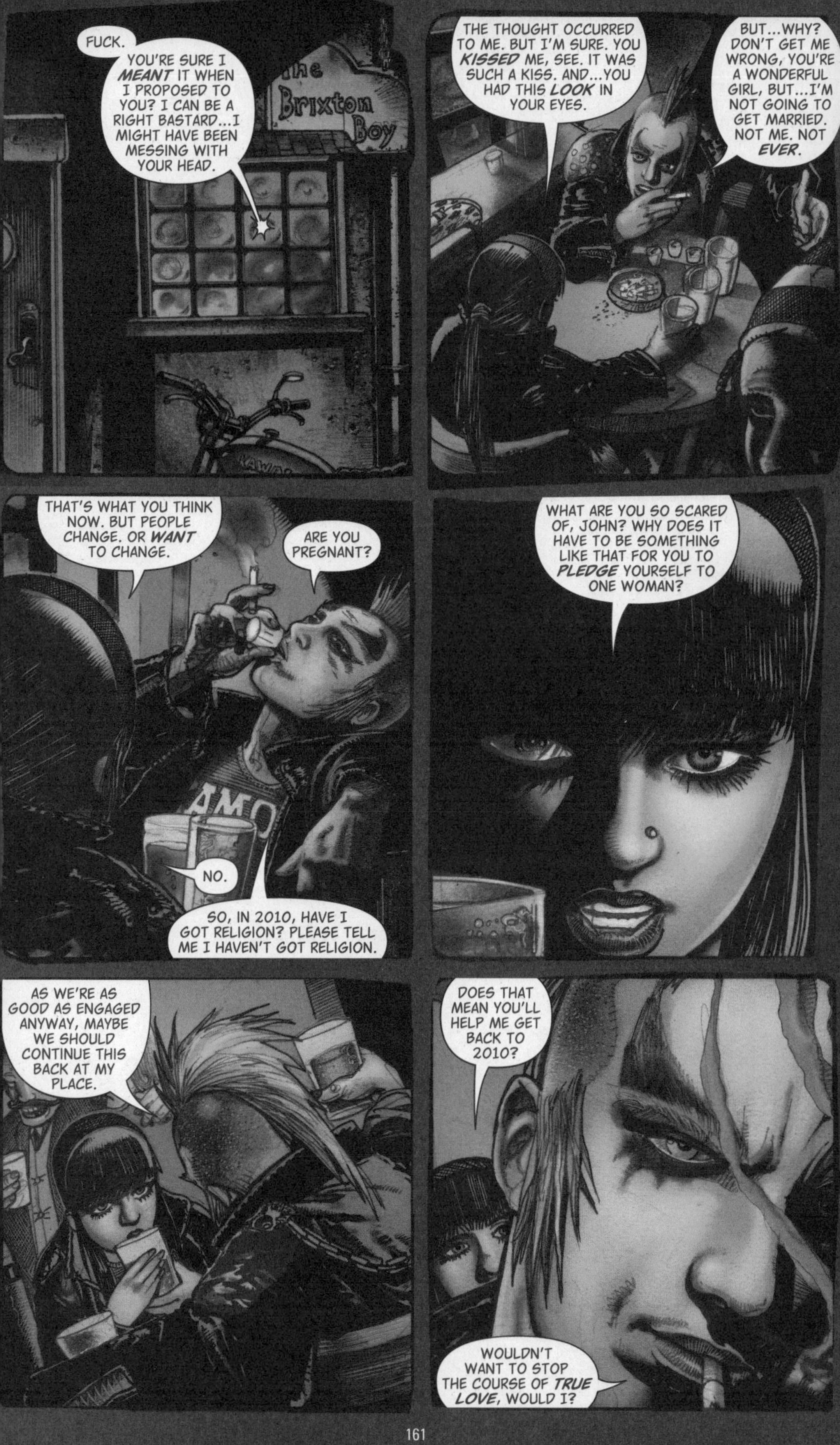

The Brixton Boy
FUCK.
YOU'RE SURE I MEANT IT WHEN I PROPOSED TO YOU? I CAN BE A RIGHT BASTARD...I MIGHT HAVE BEEN MESSING WITH YOUR HEAD.
THE THOUGHT OCCURRED TO ME. BUT I'M SURE. YOU KISSED ME, SEE. IT WAS SUCH A KISS. AND...YOU HAD THIS LOOK IN YOUR EYES.
BUT...WHY? DON'T GET ME WRONG, YOU'RE A WONDERFUL GIRL, BUT...I'M NOT GOING TO GET MARRIED. NOT ME. NOT EVER.
THAT'S WHAT YOU THINK NOW. BUT PEOPLE CHANGE. OR WANT TO CHANGE.
ARE YOU PREGNANT?
NO.
SO, IN 2010, HAVE I GOT RELIGION? PLEASE TELL ME I HAVEN'T GOT RELIGION.
WHAT ARE YOU SO SCARED OF, JOHN? WHY DOES IT HAVE TO BE SOMETHING LIKE THAT FOR YOU TO PLEDGE YOURSELF TO ONE WOMAN?
AS WE'RE AS GOOD AS ENGAGED ANYWAY, MAYBE WE SHOULD CONTINUE THIS BACK AT MY PLACE.
DOES THAT MEAN YOU'LL HELP ME GET BACK TO 2010?
WOULDN'T WANT TO STOP THE COURSE OF TRUE LOVE, WOULD I?

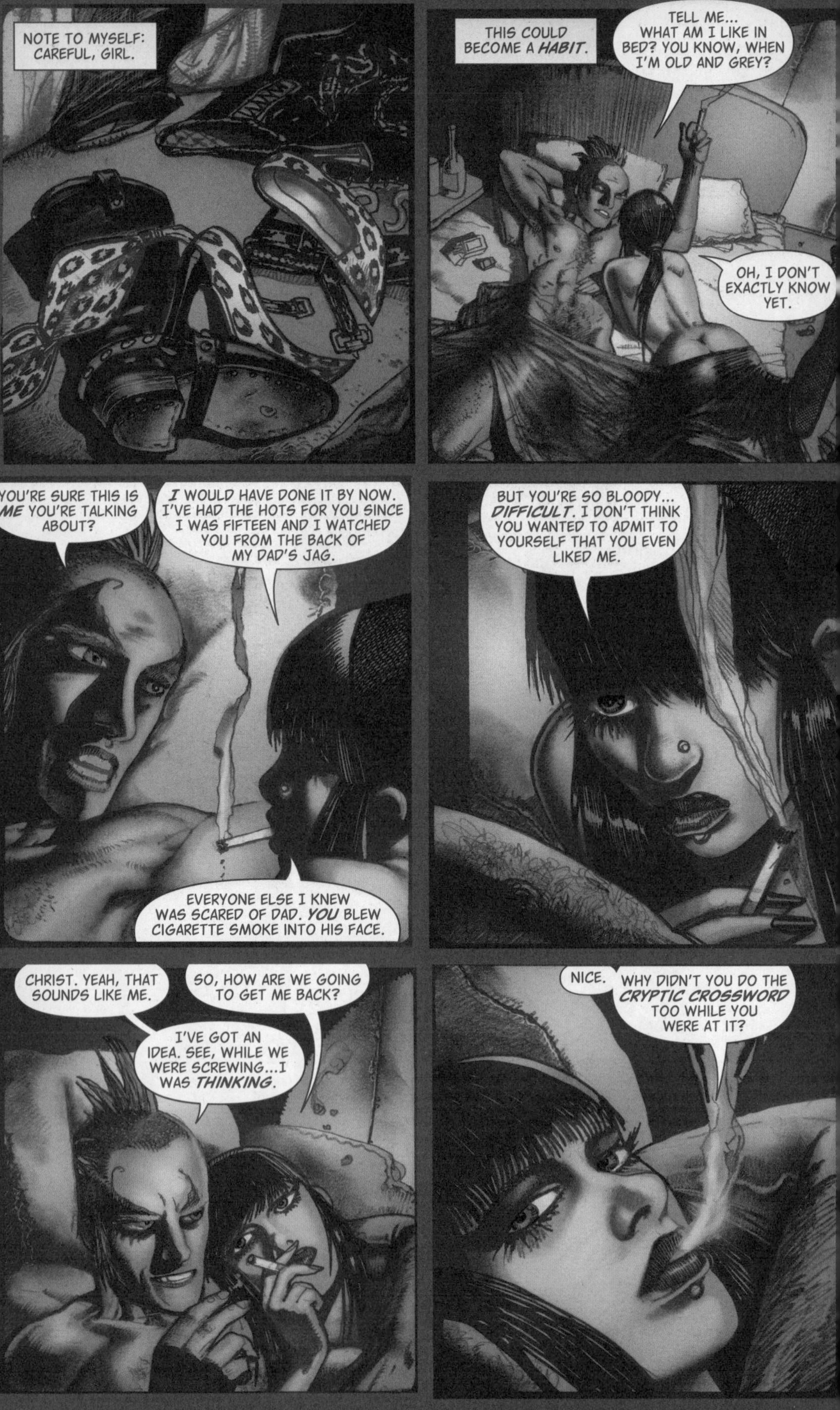

NOTE TO MYSELF: CAREFUL, GIRL.
THIS COULD BECOME A *HABIT*.
TELL ME... WHAT AM I LIKE IN BED? YOU KNOW, WHEN I'M OLD AND GREY?
OH, I DON'T EXACTLY KNOW YET.
YOU'RE SURE THIS IS *ME* YOU'RE TALKING ABOUT?
I WOULD HAVE DONE IT BY NOW. I'VE HAD THE HOTS FOR YOU SINCE I WAS FIFTEEN AND I WATCHED YOU FROM THE BACK OF MY DAD'S JAG.
EVERYONE ELSE I KNEW WAS SCARED OF DAD. *YOU* BLEW CIGARETTE SMOKE INTO HIS FACE.
BUT YOU'RE SO BLOODY... *DIFFICULT*. I DON'T THINK YOU WANTED TO ADMIT TO YOURSELF THAT YOU EVEN LIKED ME.
CHRIST. YEAH, THAT SOUNDS LIKE ME.
SO, HOW ARE WE GOING TO GET ME BACK?
I'VE GOT AN IDEA. SEE, WHILE WE WERE SCREWING...I WAS *THINKING*.
NICE.
WHY DIDN'T YOU DO THE *CRYPTIC CROSSWORD* TOO WHILE YOU WERE AT IT?

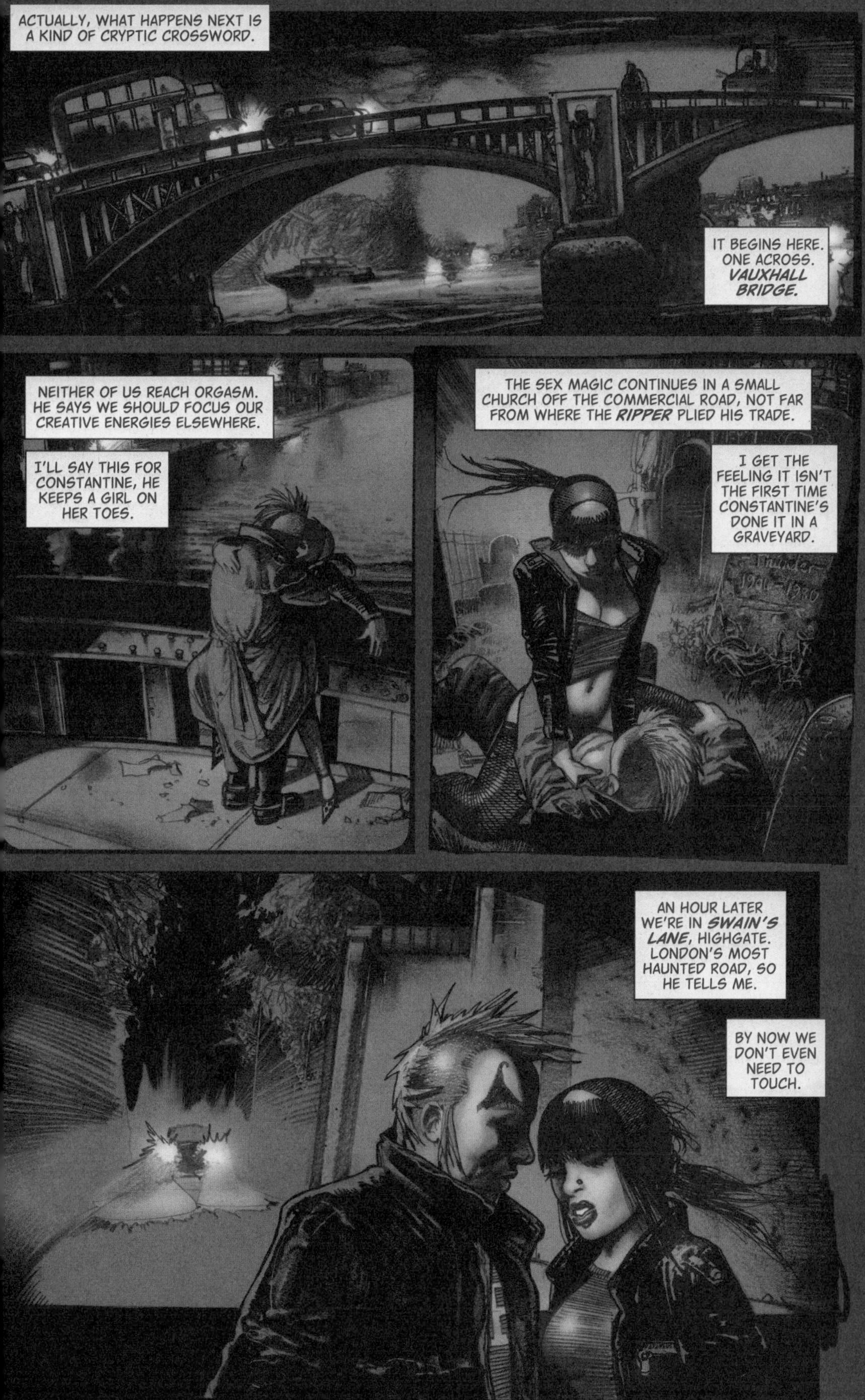
ACTUALLY, WHAT HAPPENS NEXT IS A KIND OF CRYPTIC CROSSWORD.
IT BEGINS HERE. ONE ACROSS. VAUXHALL BRIDGE.
NEITHER OF US REACH ORGASM. HE SAYS WE SHOULD FOCUS OUR CREATIVE ENERGIES ELSEWHERE.
I'LL SAY THIS FOR CONSTANTINE, HE KEEPS A GIRL ON HER TOES.
THE SEX MAGIC CONTINUES IN A SMALL CHURCH OFF THE COMMERCIAL ROAD, NOT FAR FROM WHERE THE RIPPER PLIED HIS TRADE.
I GET THE FEELING IT ISN'T THE FIRST TIME CONSTANTINE'S DONE IT IN A GRAVEYARD.
AN HOUR LATER WE'RE IN SWAIN'S LANE, HIGHGATE. LONDON'S MOST HAUNTED ROAD, SO HE TELLS ME.
BY NOW WE DON'T EVEN NEED TO TOUCH.

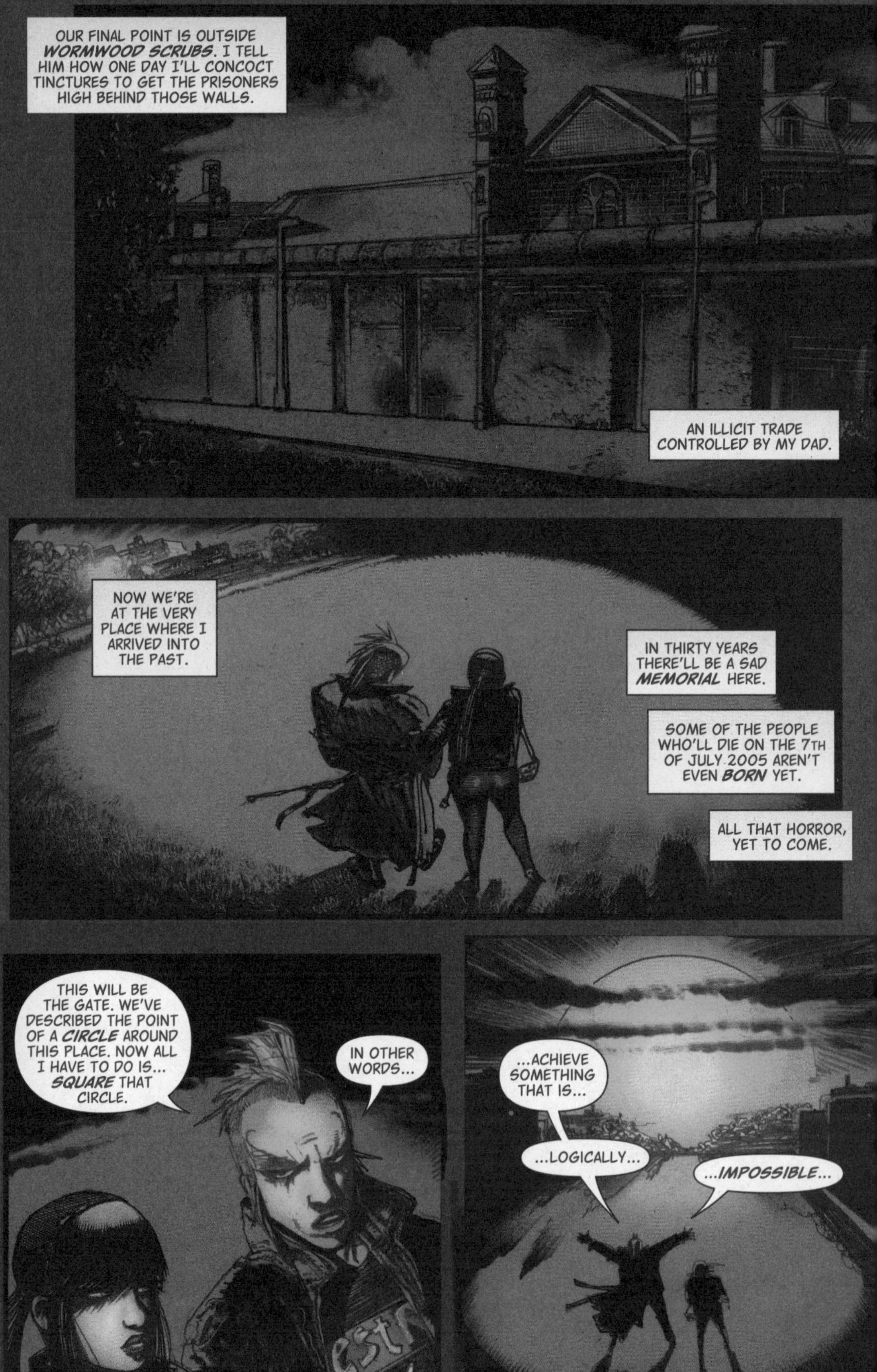
OUR FINAL POINT IS OUTSIDE WORMWOOD SCRUBS. I TELL HIM HOW ONE DAY I'LL CONCOCT TINCTURES TO GET THE PRISONERS HIGH BEHIND THOSE WALLS.
AN ILLICIT TRADE CONTROLLED BY MY DAD.
NOW WE'RE AT THE VERY PLACE WHERE I ARRIVED INTO THE PAST.
IN THIRTY YEARS THERE'LL BE A SAD MEMORIAL HERE.
SOME OF THE PEOPLE WHO'LL DIE ON THE 7TH OF JULY 2005 AREN'T EVEN BORN YET.
ALL THAT HORROR, YET TO COME.
THIS WILL BE THE GATE. WE'VE DESCRIBED THE POINT OF A CIRCLE AROUND THIS PLACE. NOW ALL I HAVE TO DO IS... SQUARE THAT CIRCLE.
IN OTHER WORDS...
...ACHIEVE SOMETHING THAT IS...
...LOGICALLY...
...IMPOSSIBLE...

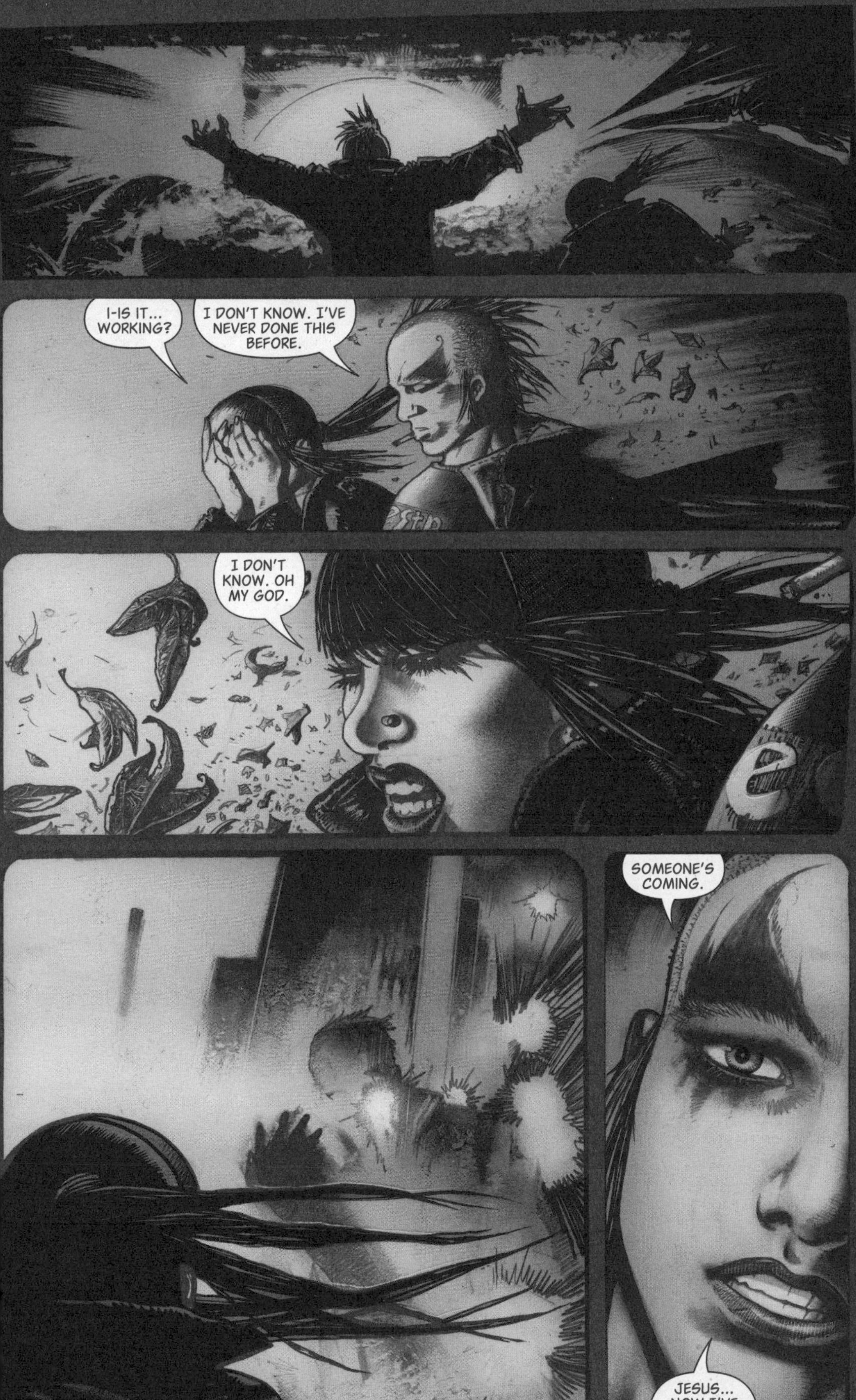
I-IS IT... WORKING?
I DON'T KNOW. I'VE NEVER DONE THIS BEFORE.
I DON'T KNOW. OH MY GOD.
SOMEONE'S COMING.
JESUS... NOW I'VE SEEN IT ALL...

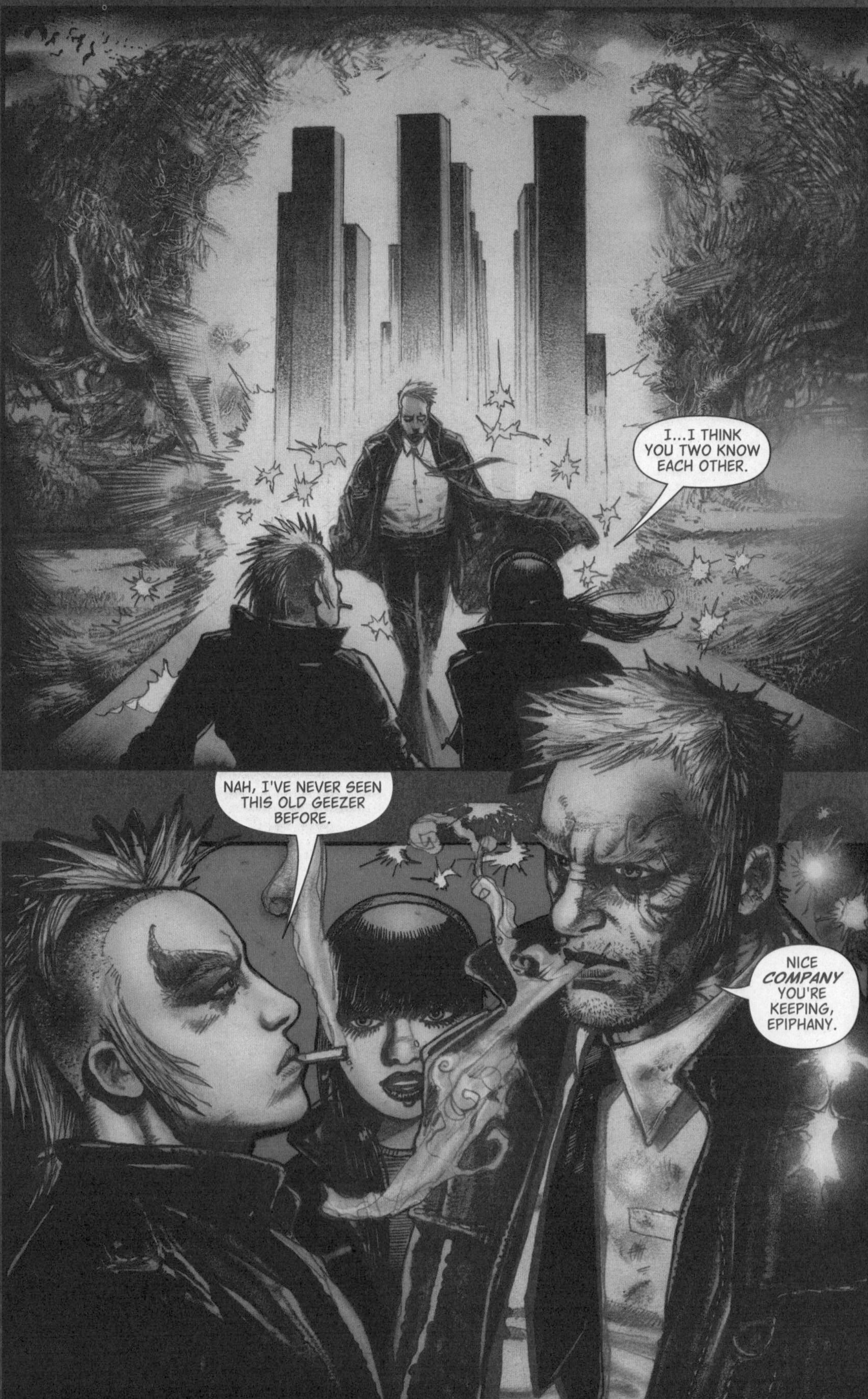
I...I THINK YOU TWO KNOW EACH OTHER.
NAH, I'VE NEVER SEEN THIS OLD GEEZER BEFORE.
NICE *COMPANY* YOU'RE KEEPING, EPIPHANY.

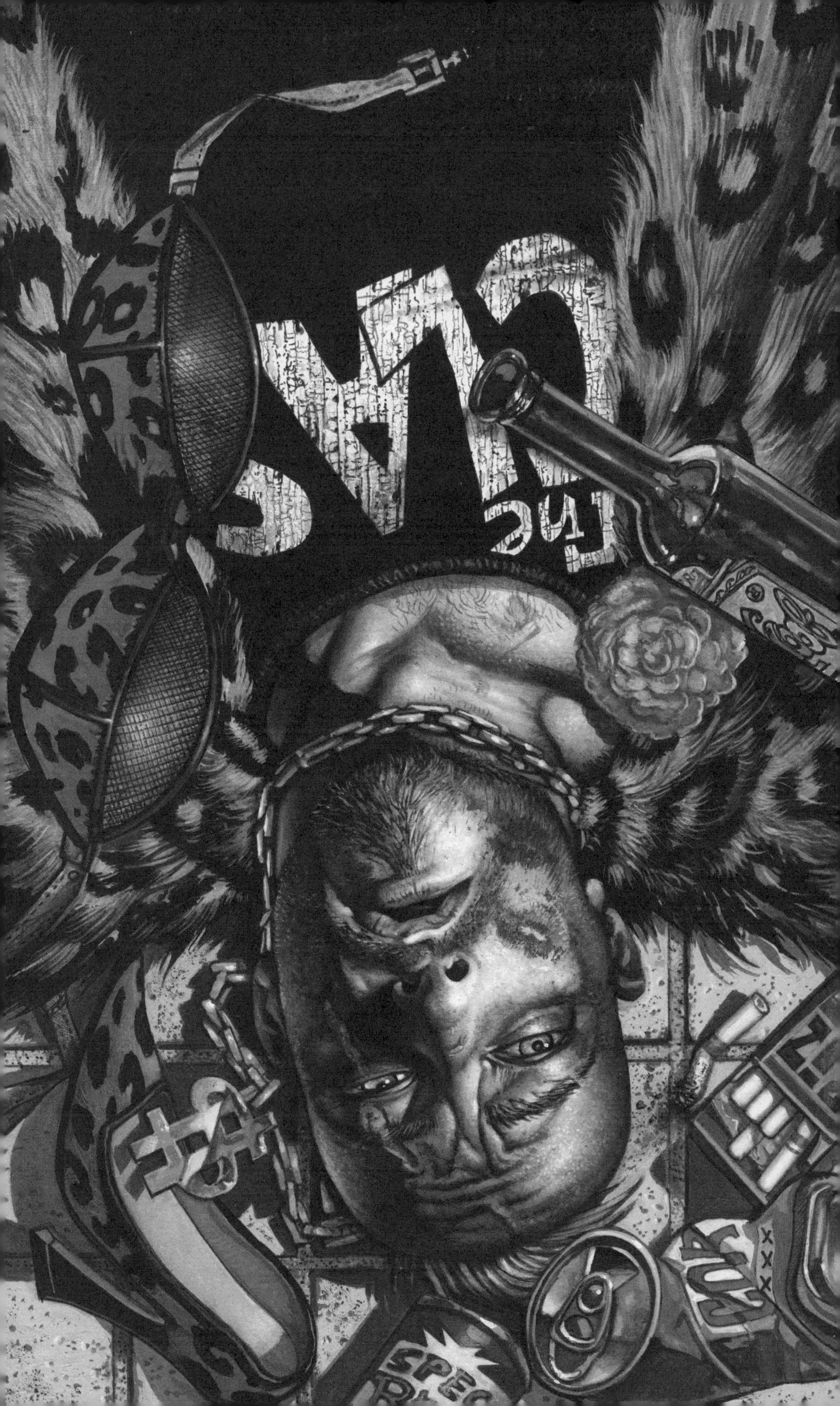

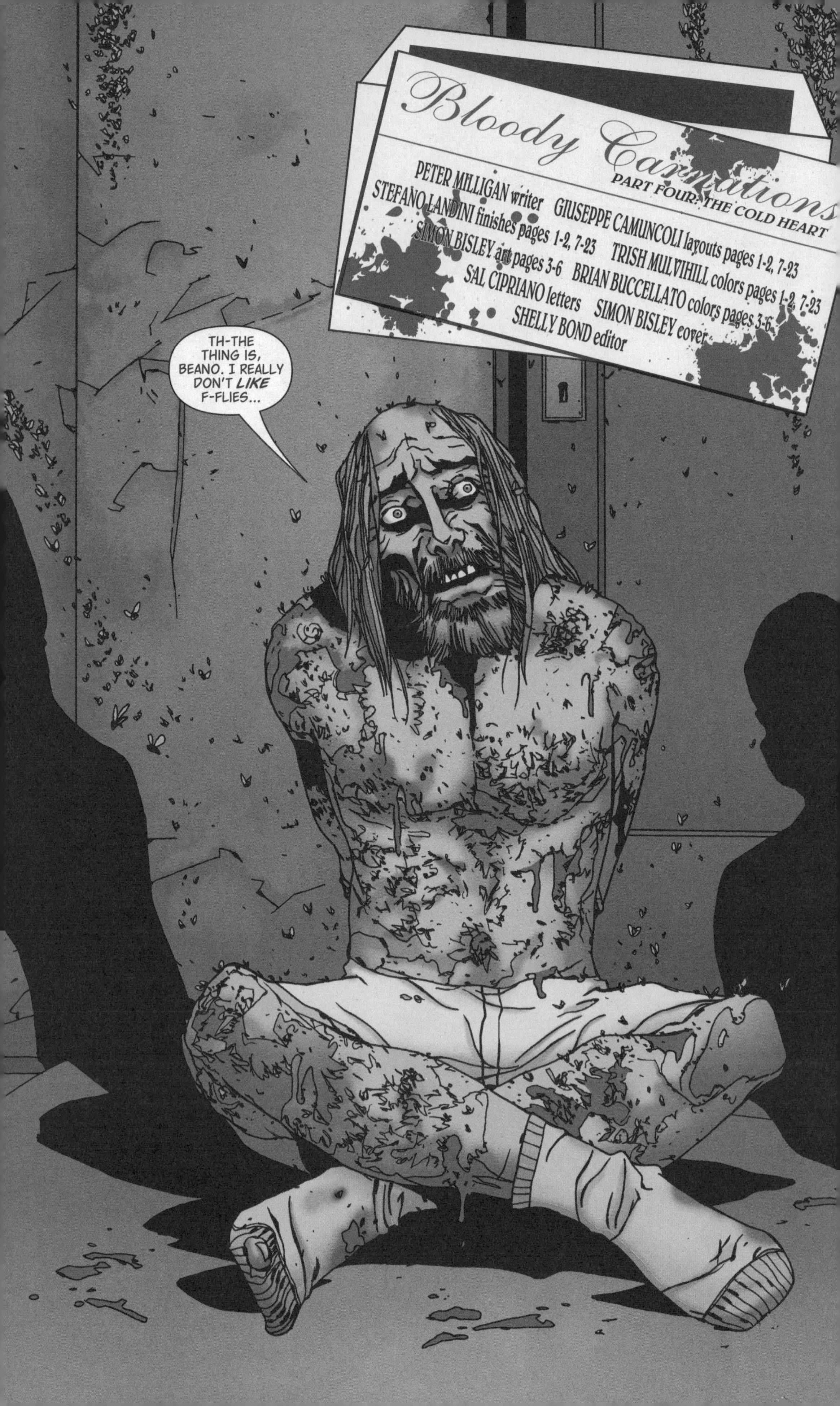

Bloody Carnations
PART FOUR: THE COLD HEART
PETER MILLIGAN writer GIUSEPPE CAMUNCOLI layouts pages 1-2, 7-23
STEFANO LANDINI finishes pages 1-2, 7-23 TRISH MULVIHILL colors pages 1-2, 7-23
SIMON BISLEY art pages 3-6 BRIAN BUCCELLATO colors pages 3-6
SAL CIPRIANO letters SIMON BISLEY cover
SHELLY BOND editor
TH-THE THING IS, BEANO. I REALLY DON'T *LIKE* F-FLIES...

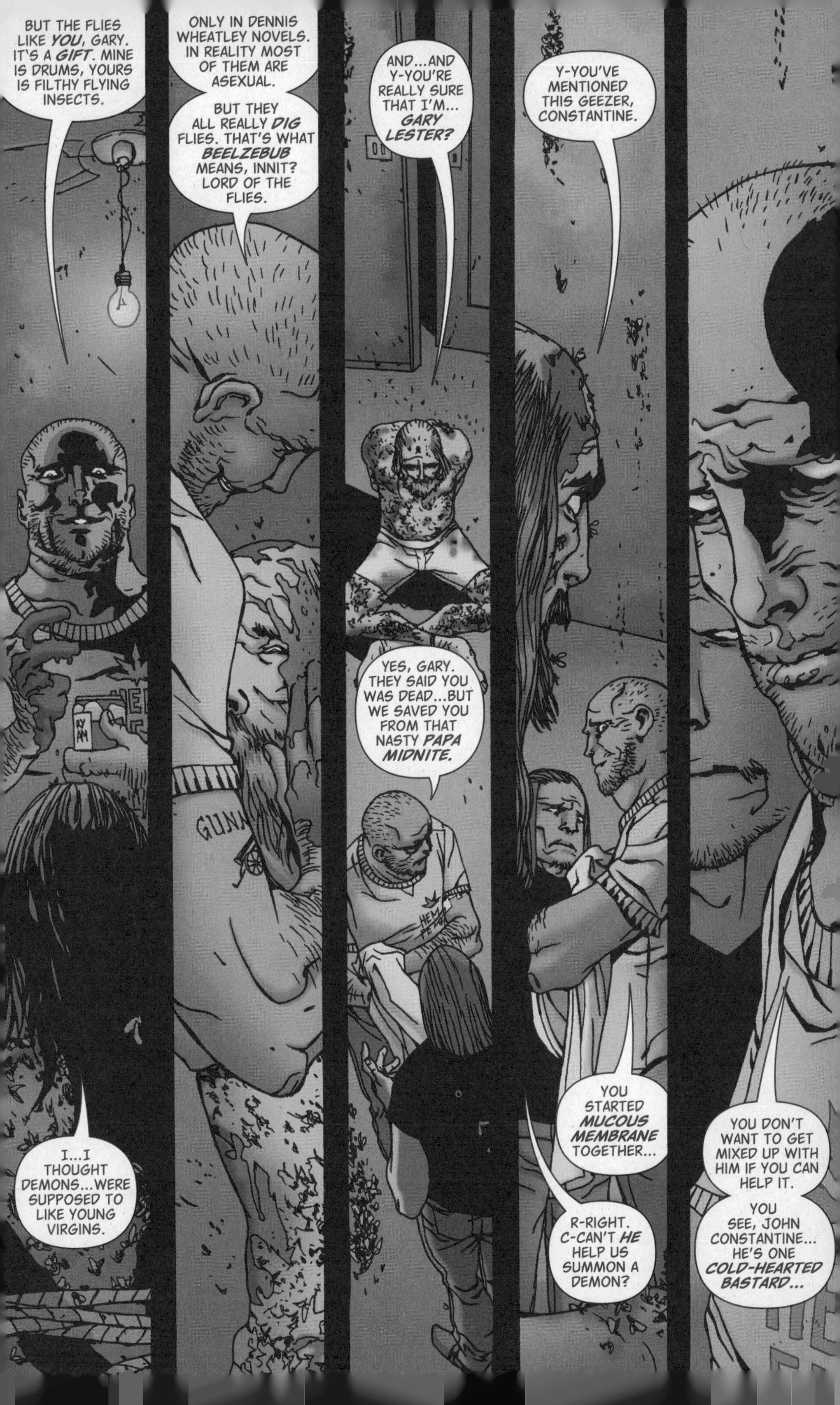

BUT THE FLIES LIKE *YOU*, GARY. IT'S A *GIFT*. MINE IS DRUMS, YOURS IS FILTHY FLYING INSECTS.
I...I THOUGHT DEMONS...WERE SUPPOSED TO LIKE YOUNG VIRGINS.
ONLY IN DENNIS WHEATLEY NOVELS. IN REALITY MOST OF THEM ARE ASEXUAL.
BUT THEY ALL REALLY *DIG* FLIES. THAT'S WHAT *BEELZEBUB* MEANS, INNIT? LORD OF THE FLIES.
AND...AND Y-YOU'RE REALLY SURE THAT I'M... *GARY LESTER?*
YES, GARY. THEY SAID YOU WAS DEAD...BUT WE SAVED YOU FROM THAT NASTY *PAPA MIDNITE.*
Y-YOU'VE MENTIONED THIS GEEZER, CONSTANTINE.
YOU STARTED *MUCOUS MEMBRANE* TOGETHER...
R-RIGHT. C-CAN'T *HE* HELP US SUMMON A DEMON?
YOU DON'T WANT TO GET MIXED UP WITH HIM IF YOU CAN HELP IT.
YOU SEE, JOHN CONSTANTINE... HE'S ONE *COLD-HEARTED BASTARD...*

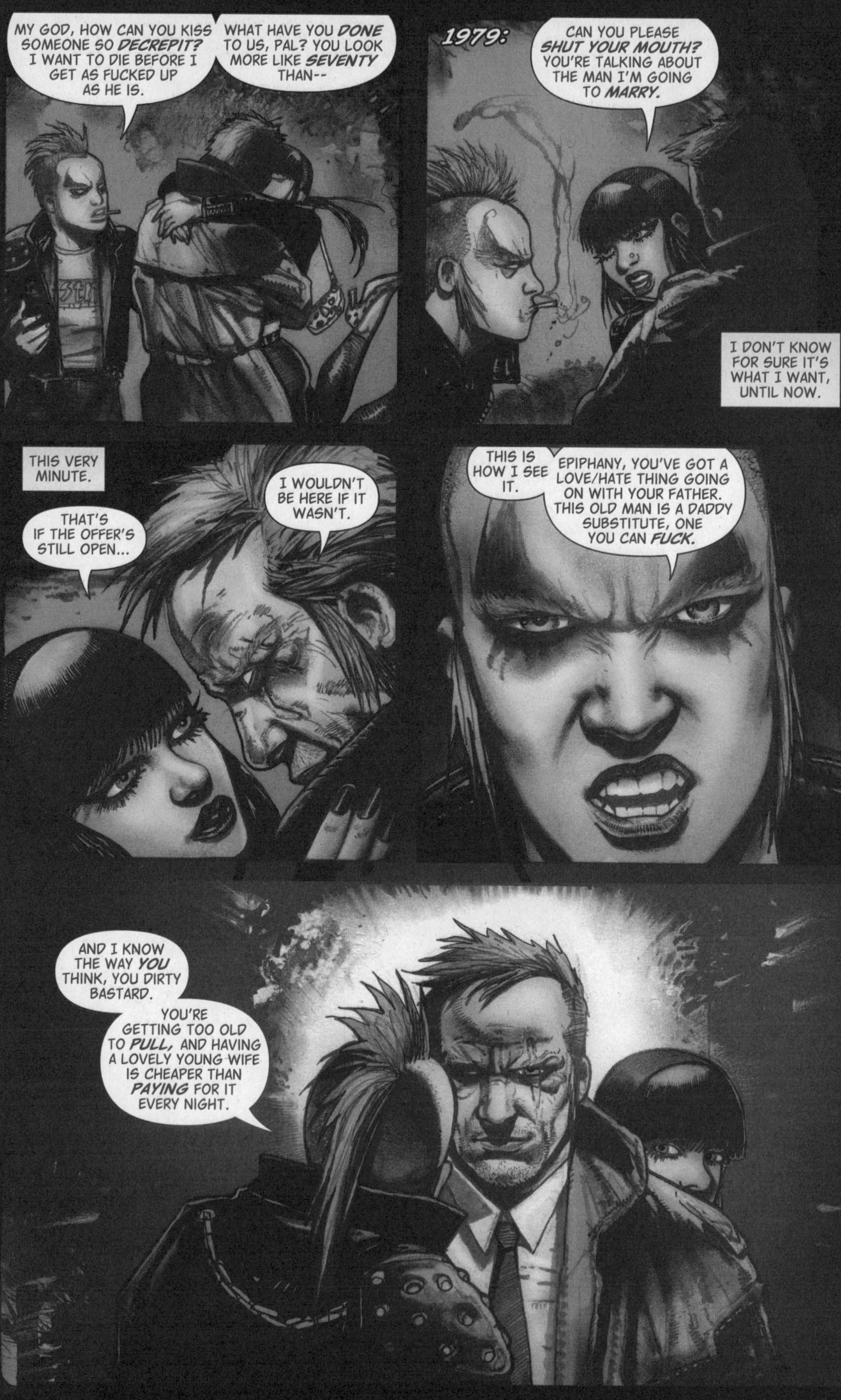
MY GOD, HOW CAN YOU KISS SOMEONE SO DECREPIT? I WANT TO DIE BEFORE I GET AS FUCKED UP AS HE IS.
WHAT HAVE YOU DONE TO US, PAL? YOU LOOK MORE LIKE SEVENTY THAN--
1979:
CAN YOU PLEASE SHUT YOUR MOUTH? YOU'RE TALKING ABOUT THE MAN I'M GOING TO MARRY.
I DON'T KNOW FOR SURE IT'S WHAT I WANT, UNTIL NOW.
THIS VERY MINUTE.
THAT'S IF THE OFFER'S STILL OPEN...
I WOULDN'T BE HERE IF IT WASN'T.
THIS IS HOW I SEE IT.
EPIPHANY, YOU'VE GOT A LOVE/HATE THING GOING ON WITH YOUR FATHER. THIS OLD MAN IS A DADDY SUBSTITUTE, ONE YOU CAN FUCK.
AND I KNOW THE WAY YOU THINK, YOU DIRTY BASTARD.
YOU'RE GETTING TOO OLD TO PULL, AND HAVING A LOVELY YOUNG WIFE IS CHEAPER THAN PAYING FOR IT EVERY NIGHT.

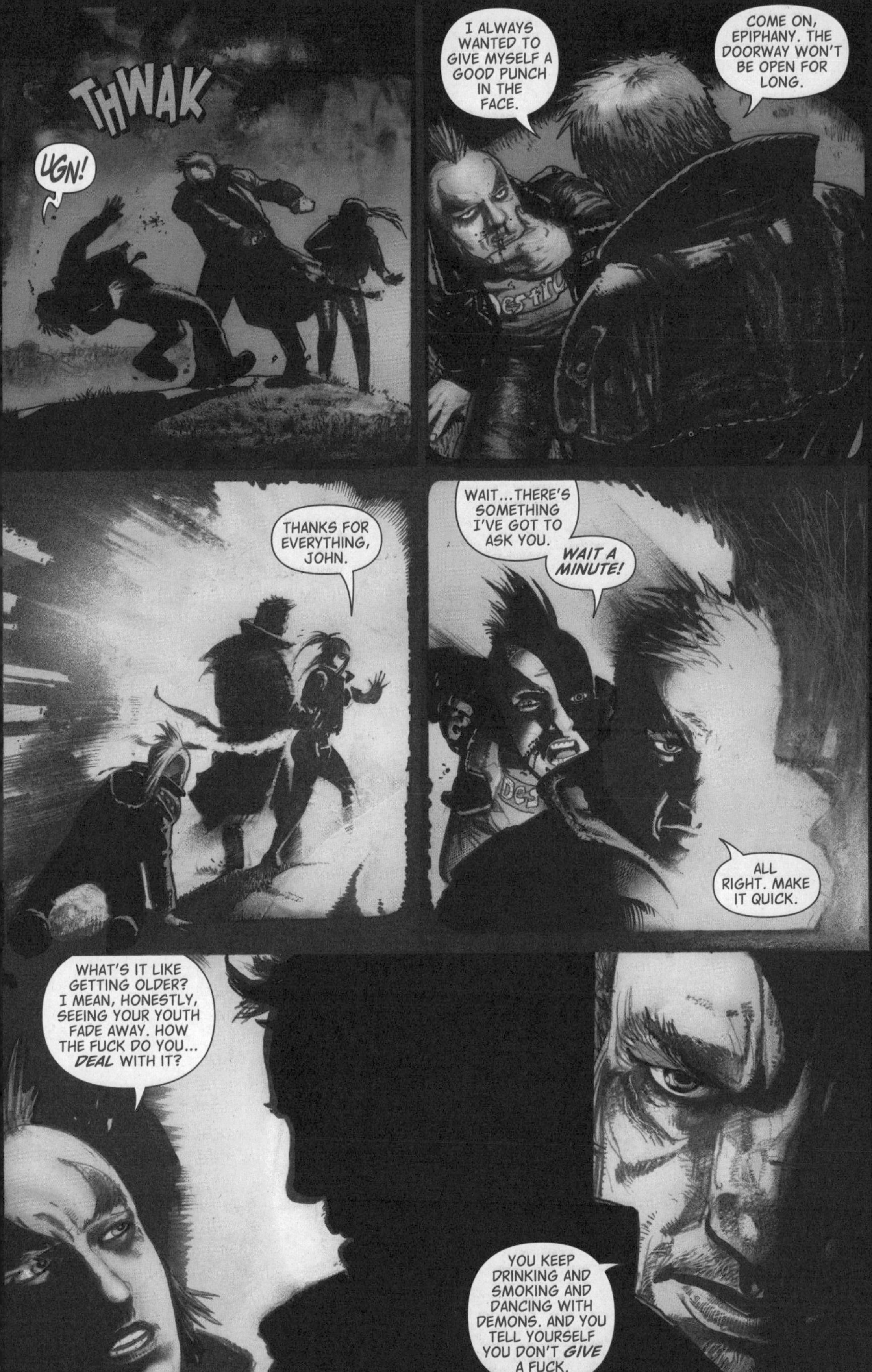
THWAK
UGN!
I ALWAYS WANTED TO GIVE MYSELF A GOOD PUNCH IN THE FACE.
COME ON, EPIPHANY. THE DOORWAY WON'T BE OPEN FOR LONG.
THANKS FOR EVERYTHING, JOHN.
WAIT...THERE'S SOMETHING I'VE GOT TO ASK YOU. WAIT A MINUTE!
ALL RIGHT. MAKE IT QUICK.
WHAT'S IT LIKE GETTING OLDER? I MEAN, HONESTLY, SEEING YOUR YOUTH FADE AWAY. HOW THE FUCK DO YOU... DEAL WITH IT?
YOU KEEP DRINKING AND SMOKING AND DANCING WITH DEMONS. AND YOU TELL YOURSELF YOU DON'T GIVE A FUCK.

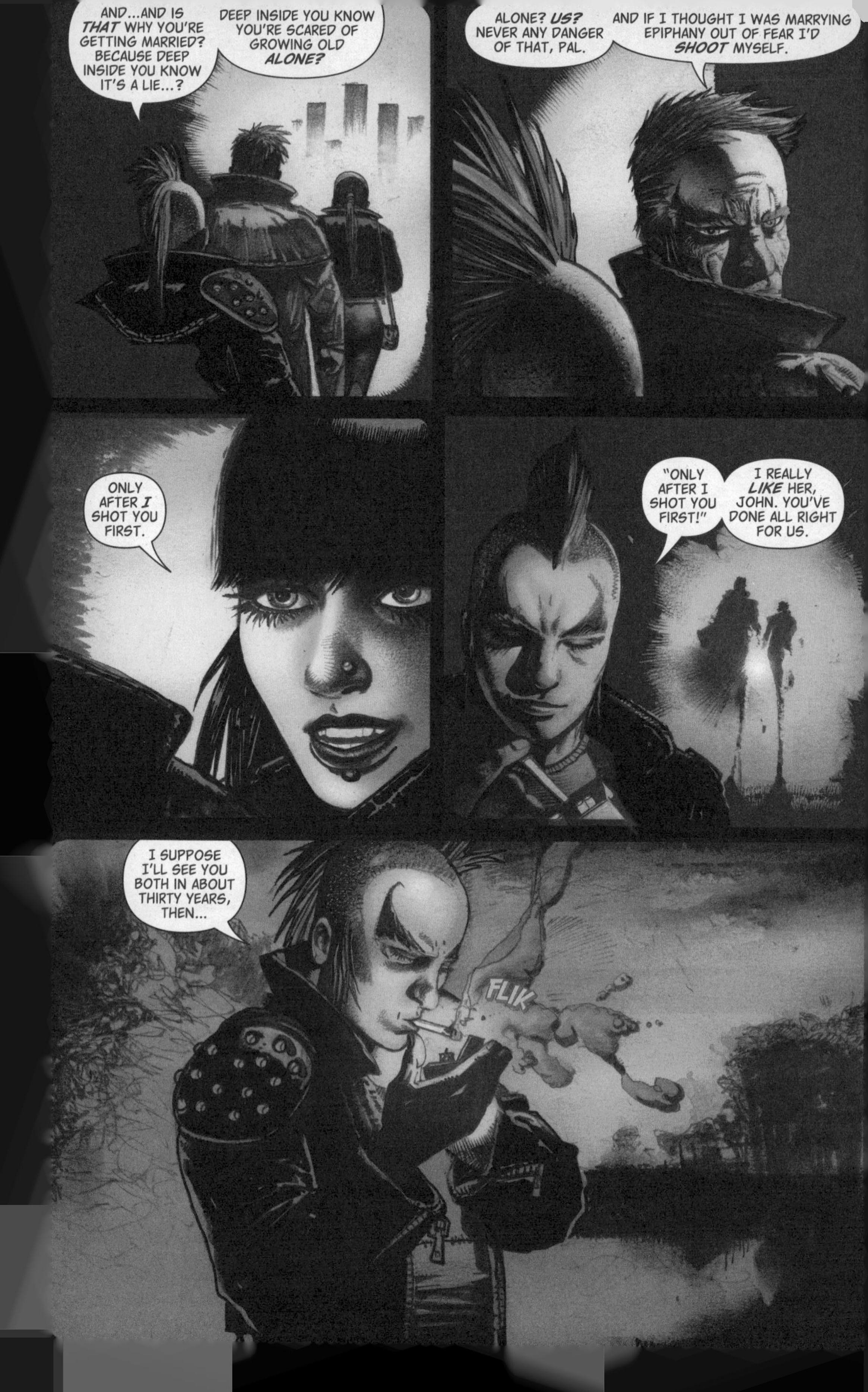
AND...AND IS THAT WHY YOU'RE GETTING MARRIED? BECAUSE DEEP INSIDE YOU KNOW IT'S A LIE...?
DEEP INSIDE YOU KNOW YOU'RE SCARED OF GROWING OLD ALONE?
ALONE? US? NEVER ANY DANGER OF THAT, PAL.
AND IF I THOUGHT I WAS MARRYING EPIPHANY OUT OF FEAR I'D SHOOT MYSELF.
ONLY AFTER I SHOT YOU FIRST.
"ONLY AFTER I SHOT YOU FIRST!"
I REALLY LIKE HER, JOHN. YOU'VE DONE ALL RIGHT FOR US.
I SUPPOSE I'LL SEE YOU BOTH IN ABOUT THIRTY YEARS, THEN...
FLIK

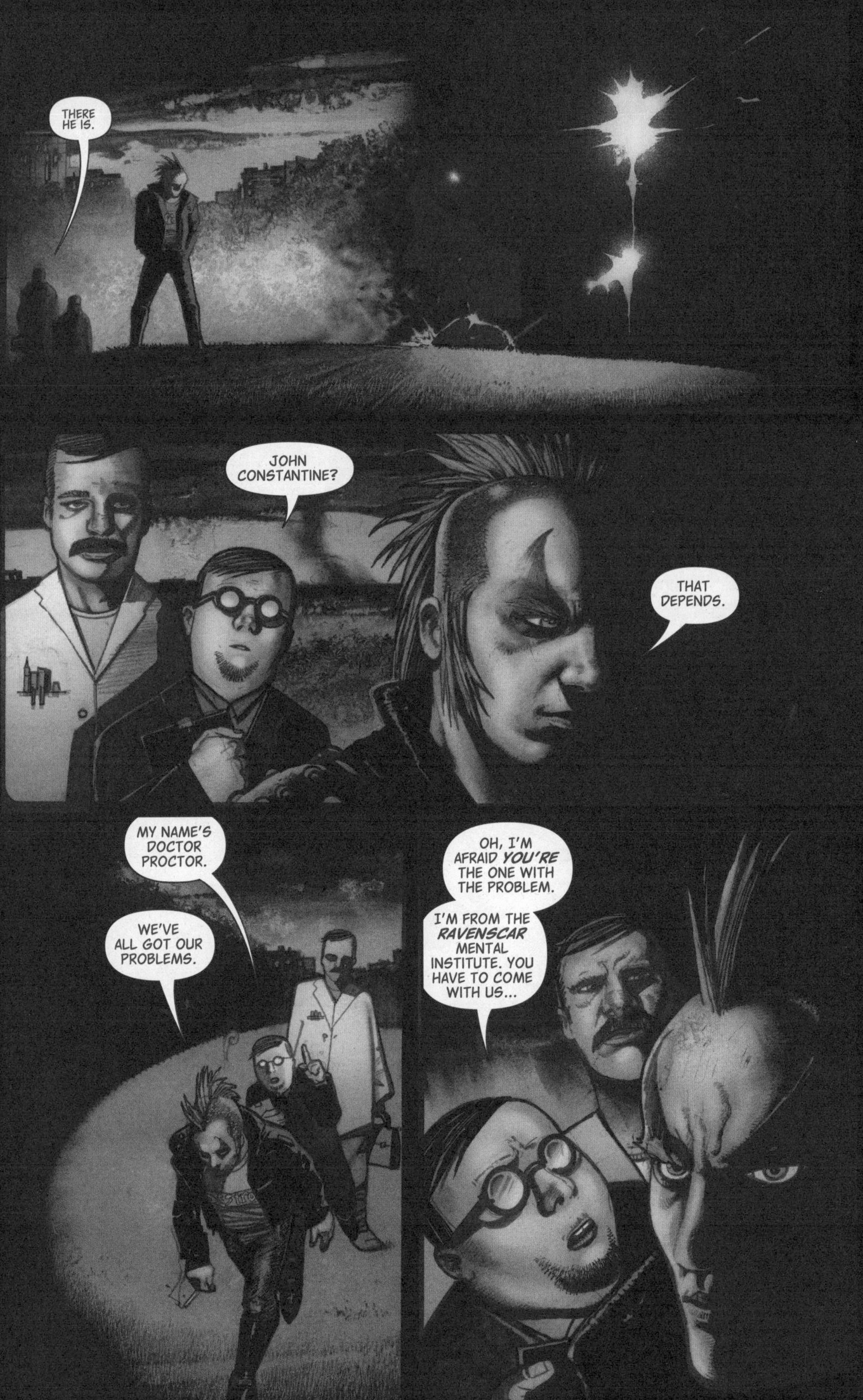
THERE HE IS.
JOHN CONSTANTINE?
THAT DEPENDS.
MY NAME'S DOCTOR PROCTOR.
WE'VE ALL GOT OUR PROBLEMS.
OH, I'M AFRAID YOU'RE THE ONE WITH THE PROBLEM.
I'M FROM THE RAVENSCAR MENTAL INSTITUTE. YOU HAVE TO COME WITH US...

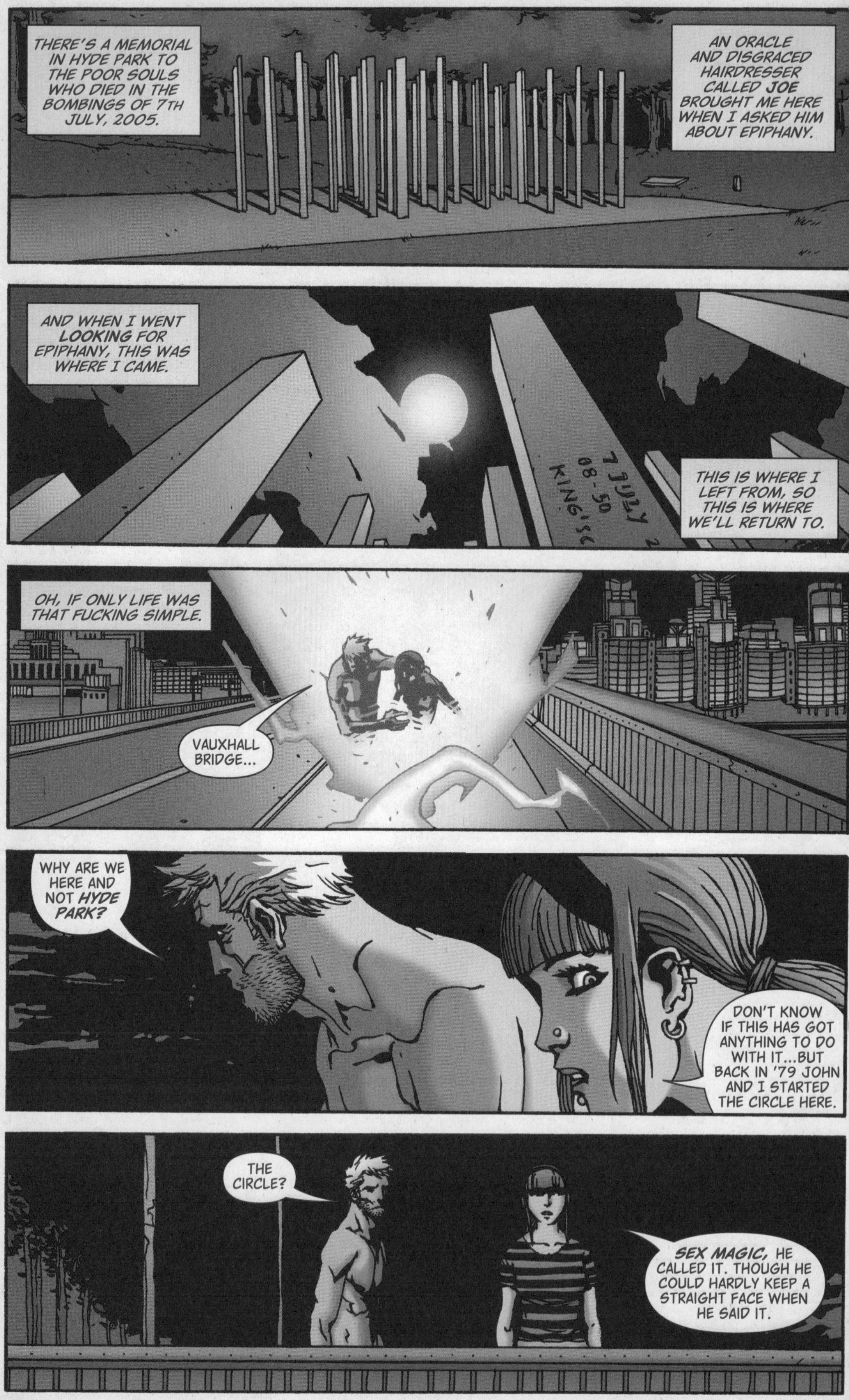
THERE'S A MEMORIAL IN HYDE PARK TO THE POOR SOULS WHO DIED IN THE BOMBINGS OF 7TH JULY, 2005.
AN ORACLE AND DISGRACED HAIRDRESSER CALLED JOE BROUGHT ME HERE WHEN I ASKED HIM ABOUT EPIPHANY.
AND WHEN I WENT LOOKING FOR EPIPHANY, THIS WAS WHERE I CAME.
7 JULY 08-50 KING'S C
THIS IS WHERE I LEFT FROM, SO THIS IS WHERE WE'LL RETURN TO.
OH, IF ONLY LIFE WAS THAT FUCKING SIMPLE.
VAUXHALL BRIDGE...
WHY ARE WE HERE AND NOT HYDE PARK?
DON'T KNOW IF THIS HAS GOT ANYTHING TO DO WITH IT...BUT BACK IN '79 JOHN AND I STARTED THE CIRCLE HERE.
THE CIRCLE?
SEX MAGIC, HE CALLED IT. THOUGH HE COULD HARDLY KEEP A STRAIGHT FACE WHEN HE SAID IT.

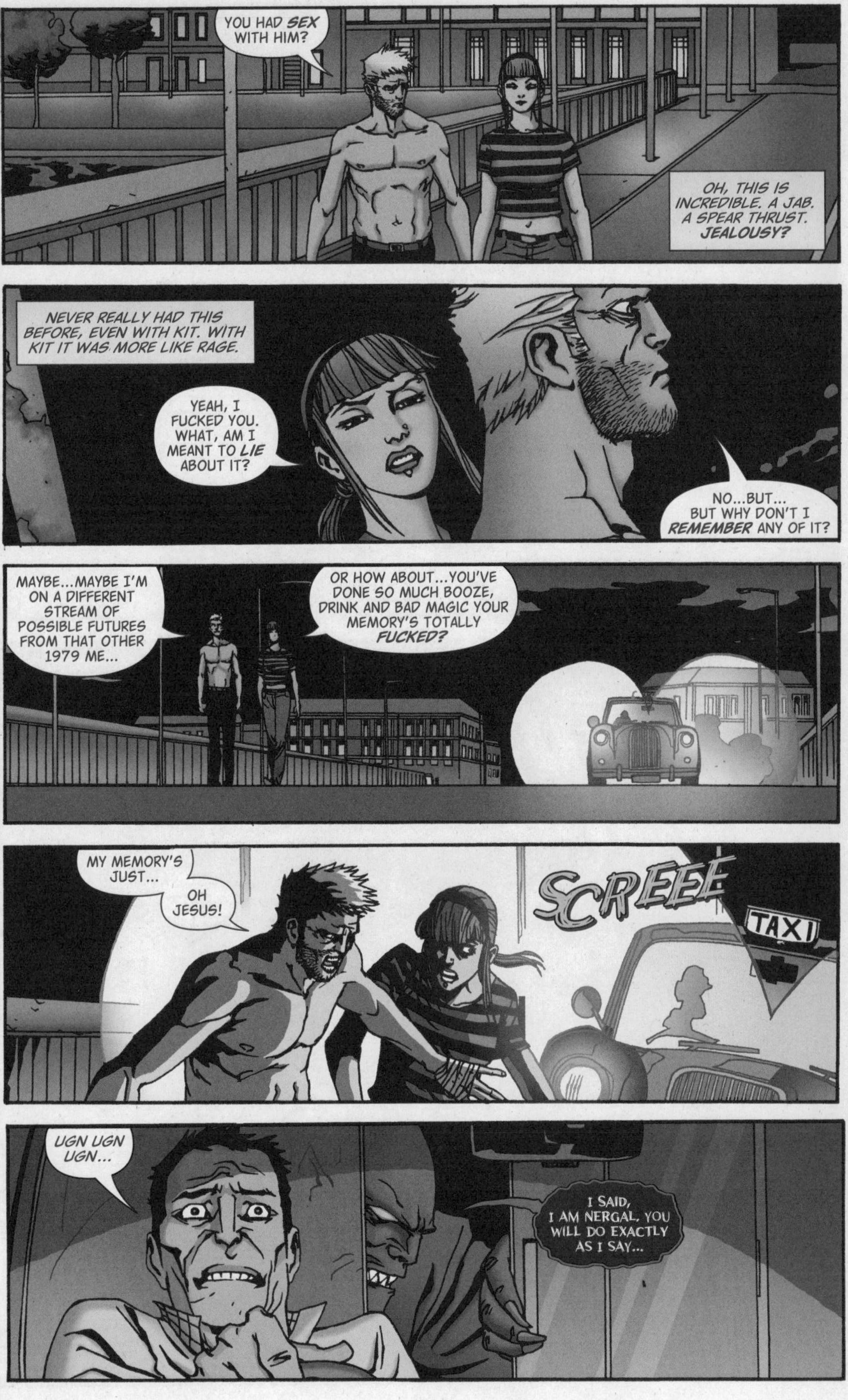
YOU HAD SEX WITH HIM?
OH, THIS IS INCREDIBLE. A JAB. A SPEAR THRUST. JEALOUSY?
NEVER REALLY HAD THIS BEFORE, EVEN WITH KIT. WITH KIT IT WAS MORE LIKE RAGE.
YEAH, I FUCKED YOU. WHAT, AM I MEANT TO LIE ABOUT IT?
NO...BUT... BUT WHY DON'T I REMEMBER ANY OF IT?
MAYBE...MAYBE I'M ON A DIFFERENT STREAM OF POSSIBLE FUTURES FROM THAT OTHER 1979 ME...
OR HOW ABOUT...YOU'VE DONE SO MUCH BOOZE, DRINK AND BAD MAGIC YOUR MEMORY'S TOTALLY FUCKED?
MY MEMORY'S JUST...
OH JESUS!
SCREEE
TAXI
UGN UGN UGN...
I SAID, I AM NERGAL. YOU WILL DO EXACTLY AS I SAY...

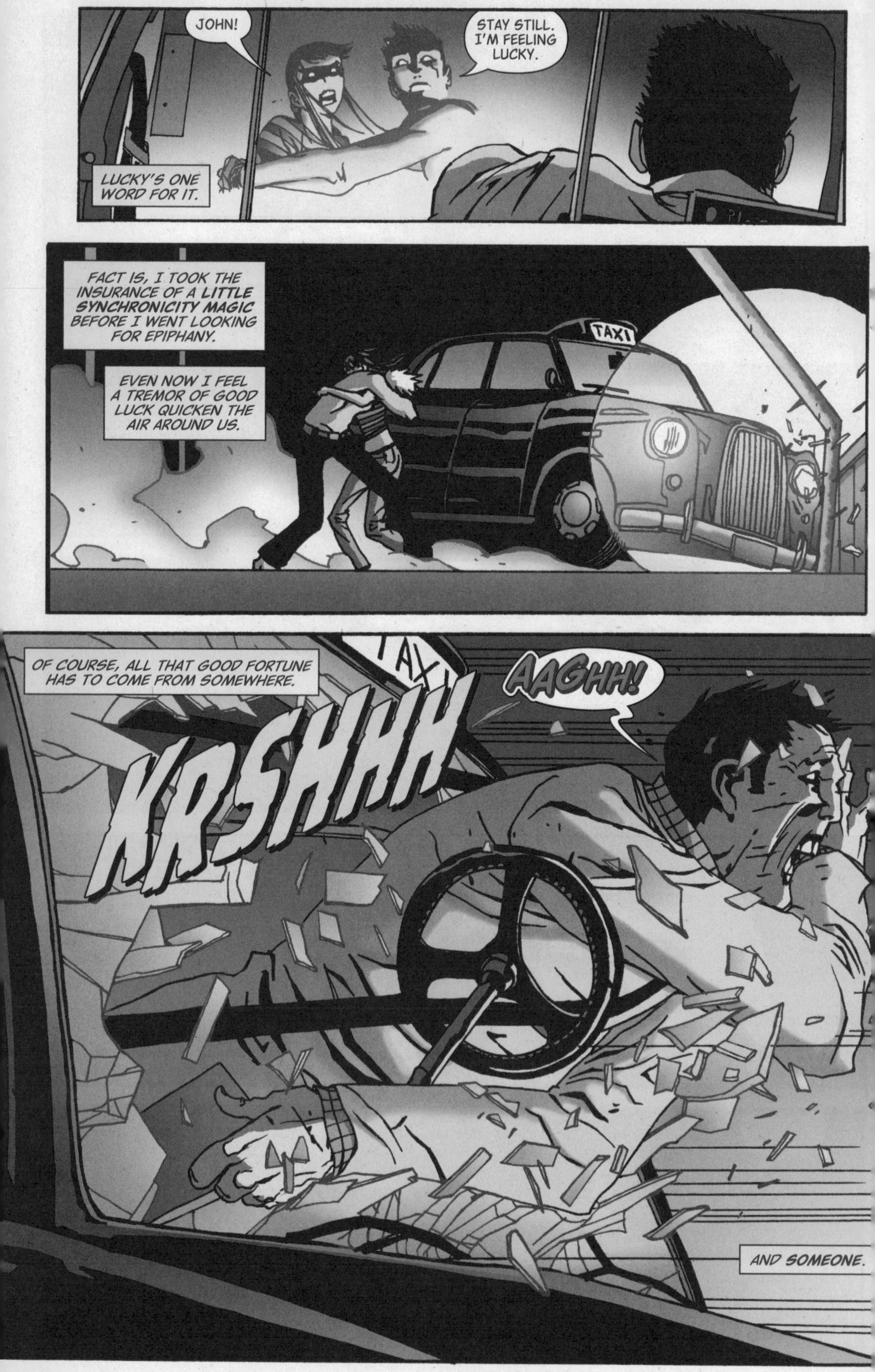
JOHN!
STAY STILL. I'M FEELING LUCKY.
LUCKY'S ONE WORD FOR IT.
FACT IS, I TOOK THE INSURANCE OF A LITTLE SYNCHRONICITY MAGIC BEFORE I WENT LOOKING FOR EPIPHANY.
EVEN NOW I FEEL A TREMOR OF GOOD LUCK QUICKEN THE AIR AROUND US.
TAXI
OF COURSE, ALL THAT GOOD FORTUNE HAS TO COME FROM SOMEWHERE.
AAGHH!
KRSHHH
AND SOMEONE.

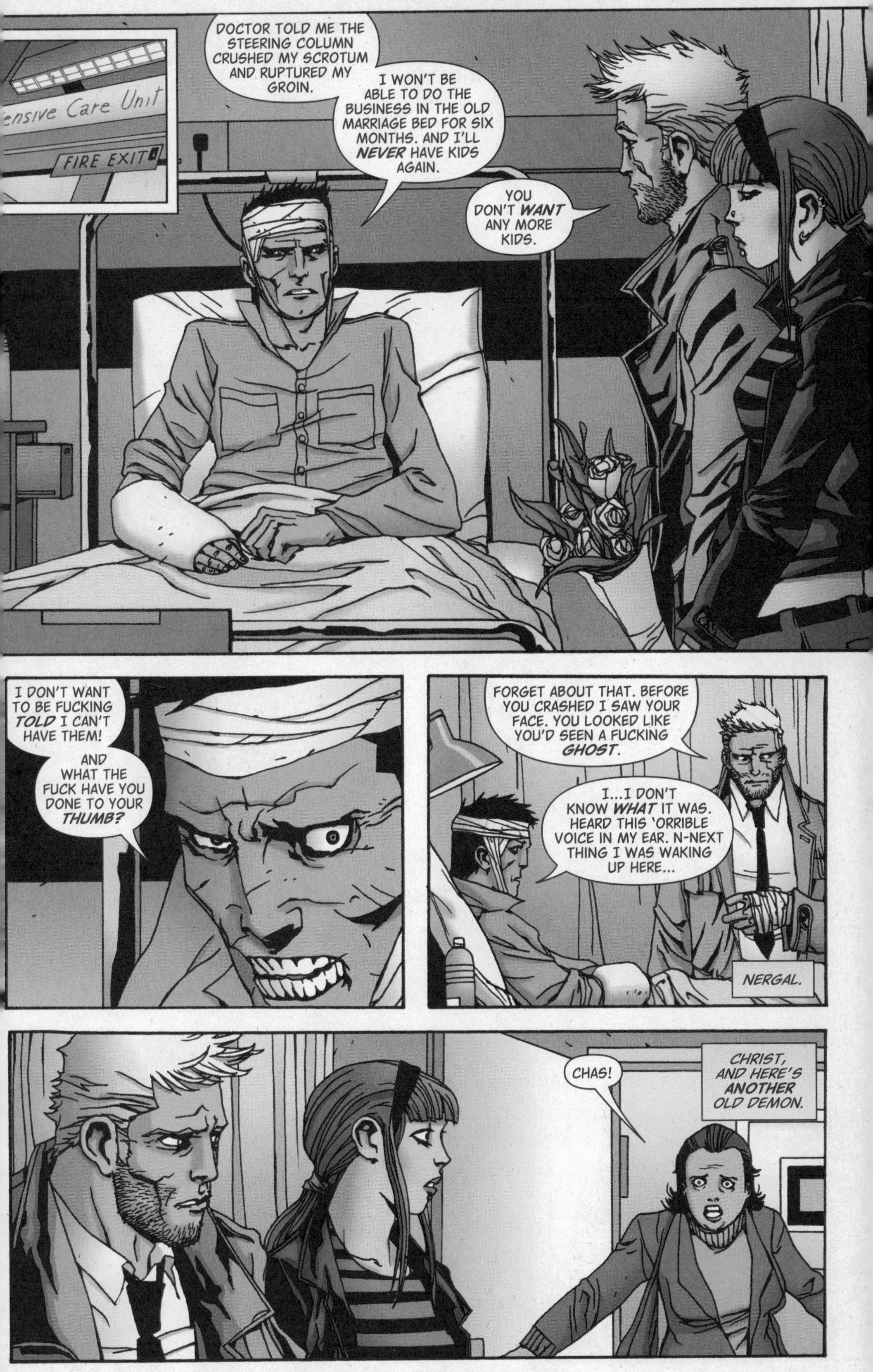
ensive Care Unit
FIRE EXIT
DOCTOR TOLD ME THE STEERING COLUMN CRUSHED MY SCROTUM AND RUPTURED MY GROIN.
I WON'T BE ABLE TO DO THE BUSINESS IN THE OLD MARRIAGE BED FOR SIX MONTHS. AND I'LL NEVER HAVE KIDS AGAIN.
YOU DON'T WANT ANY MORE KIDS.
I DON'T WANT TO BE FUCKING TOLD I CAN'T HAVE THEM!
AND WHAT THE FUCK HAVE YOU DONE TO YOUR THUMB?
FORGET ABOUT THAT. BEFORE YOU CRASHED I SAW YOUR FACE. YOU LOOKED LIKE YOU'D SEEN A FUCKING GHOST.
I...I DON'T KNOW WHAT IT WAS. HEARD THIS 'ORRIBLE VOICE IN MY EAR. N-NEXT THING I WAS WAKING UP HERE...
NERGAL.
CHAS!
CHRIST, AND HERE'S ANOTHER OLD DEMON.

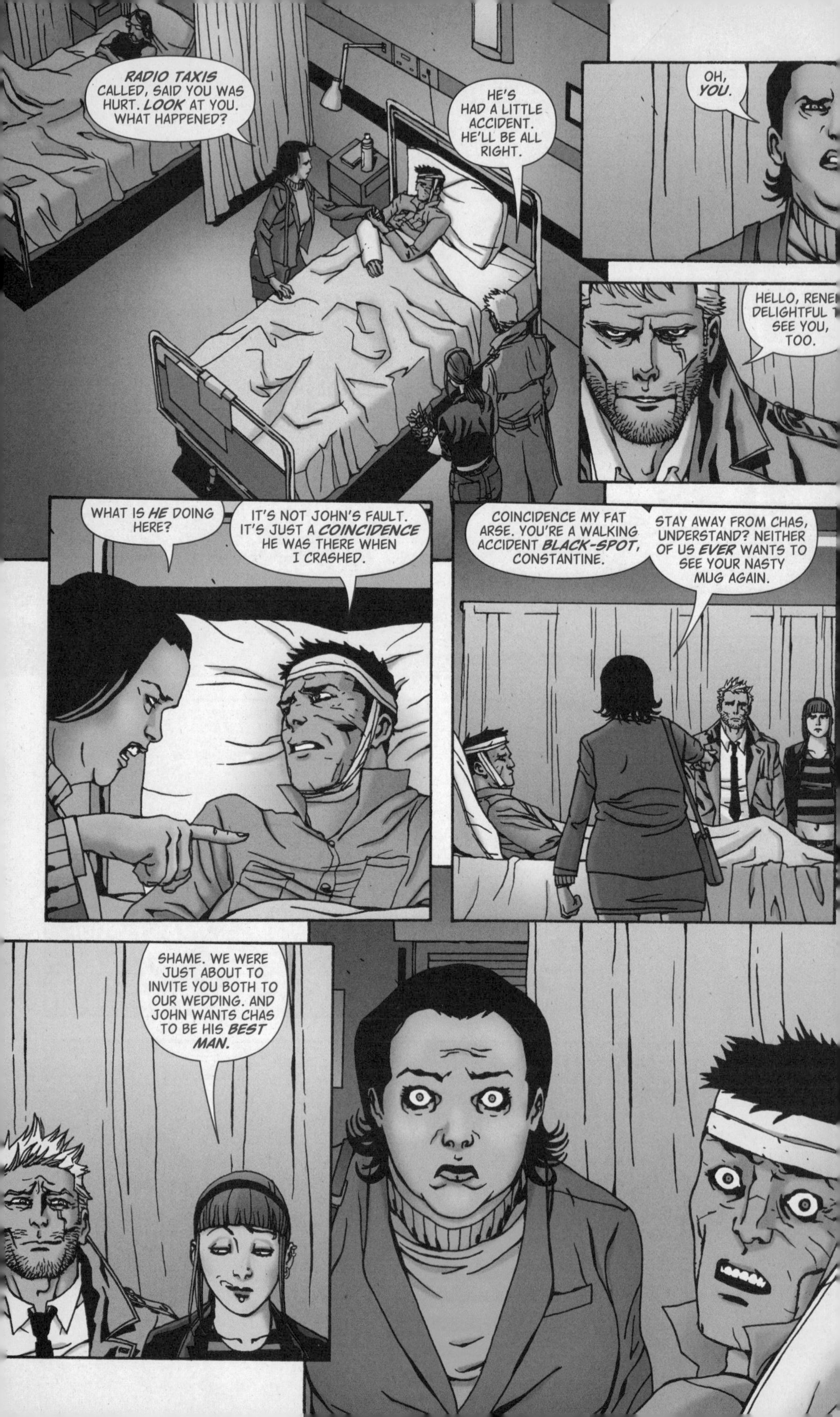
RADIO TAXIS CALLED, SAID YOU WAS HURT. LOOK AT YOU. WHAT HAPPENED?
HE'S HAD A LITTLE ACCIDENT. HE'LL BE ALL RIGHT.
OH, YOU.
HELLO, RENE DELIGHTFUL T SEE YOU, TOO.
WHAT IS HE DOING HERE?
IT'S NOT JOHN'S FAULT. IT'S JUST A COINCIDENCE HE WAS THERE WHEN I CRASHED.
COINCIDENCE MY FAT ARSE. YOU'RE A WALKING ACCIDENT BLACK-SPOT, CONSTANTINE.
STAY AWAY FROM CHAS, UNDERSTAND? NEITHER OF US EVER WANTS TO SEE YOUR NASTY MUG AGAIN.
SHAME. WE WERE JUST ABOUT TO INVITE YOU BOTH TO OUR WEDDING. AND JOHN WANTS CHAS TO BE HIS BEST MAN.

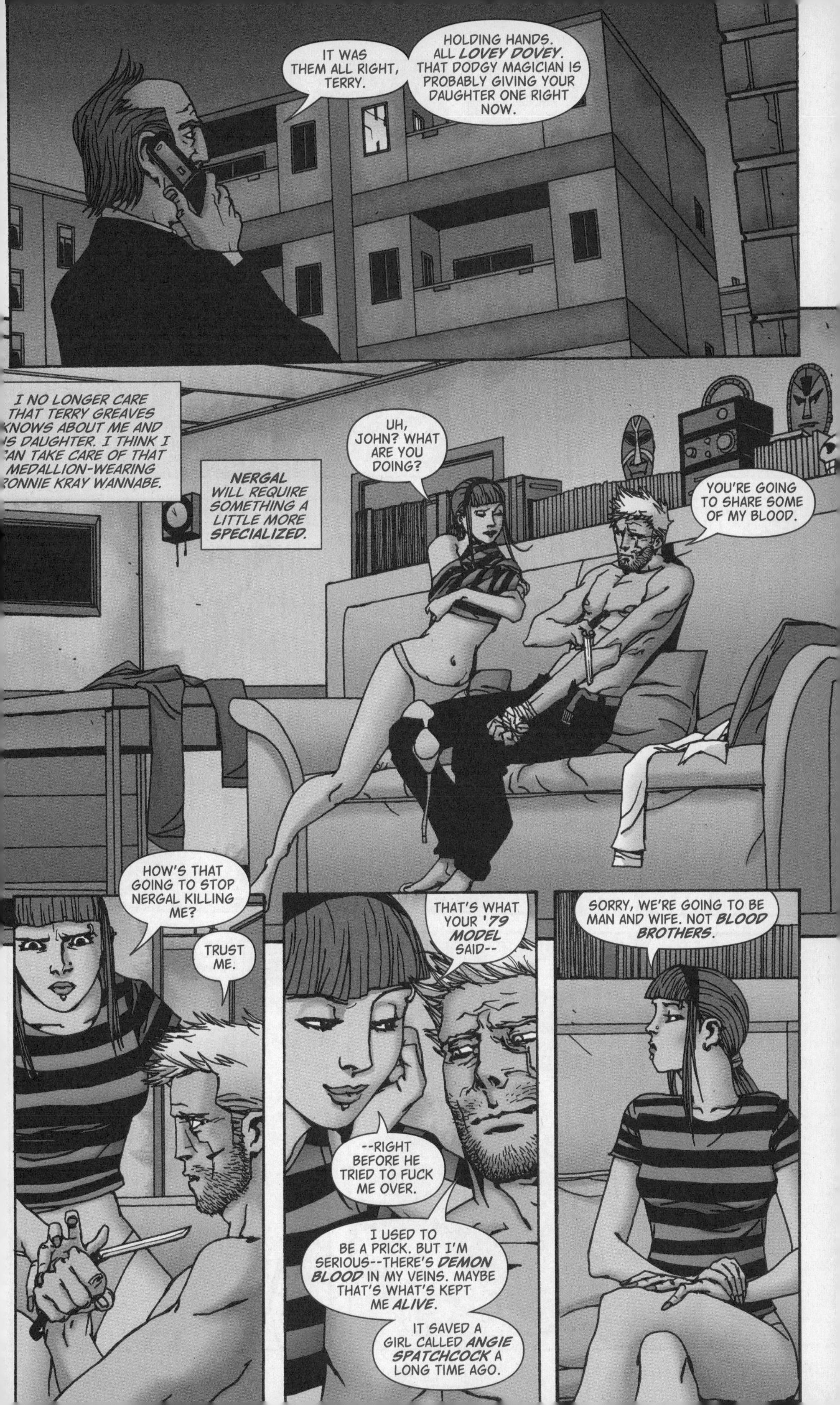

IT WAS THEM ALL RIGHT, TERRY.
HOLDING HANDS. ALL LOVEY DOVEY. THAT DODGY MAGICIAN IS PROBABLY GIVING YOUR DAUGHTER ONE RIGHT NOW.
I NO LONGER CARE THAT TERRY GREAVES KNOWS ABOUT ME AND IS DAUGHTER. I THINK I AN TAKE CARE OF THAT MEDALLION-WEARING RONNIE KRAY WANNABE.
NERGAL WILL REQUIRE SOMETHING A LITTLE MORE SPECIALIZED.
UH, JOHN? WHAT ARE YOU DOING?
YOU'RE GOING TO SHARE SOME OF MY BLOOD.
HOW'S THAT GOING TO STOP NERGAL KILLING ME?
TRUST ME.
THAT'S WHAT YOUR '79 MODEL SAID--
--RIGHT BEFORE HE TRIED TO FUCK ME OVER.
I USED TO BE A PRICK. BUT I'M SERIOUS--THERE'S DEMON BLOOD IN MY VEINS. MAYBE THAT'S WHAT'S KEPT ME ALIVE.
IT SAVED A GIRL CALLED ANGIE SPATCHCOCK A LONG TIME AGO.
SORRY, WE'RE GOING TO BE MAN AND WIFE. NOT BLOOD BROTHERS.

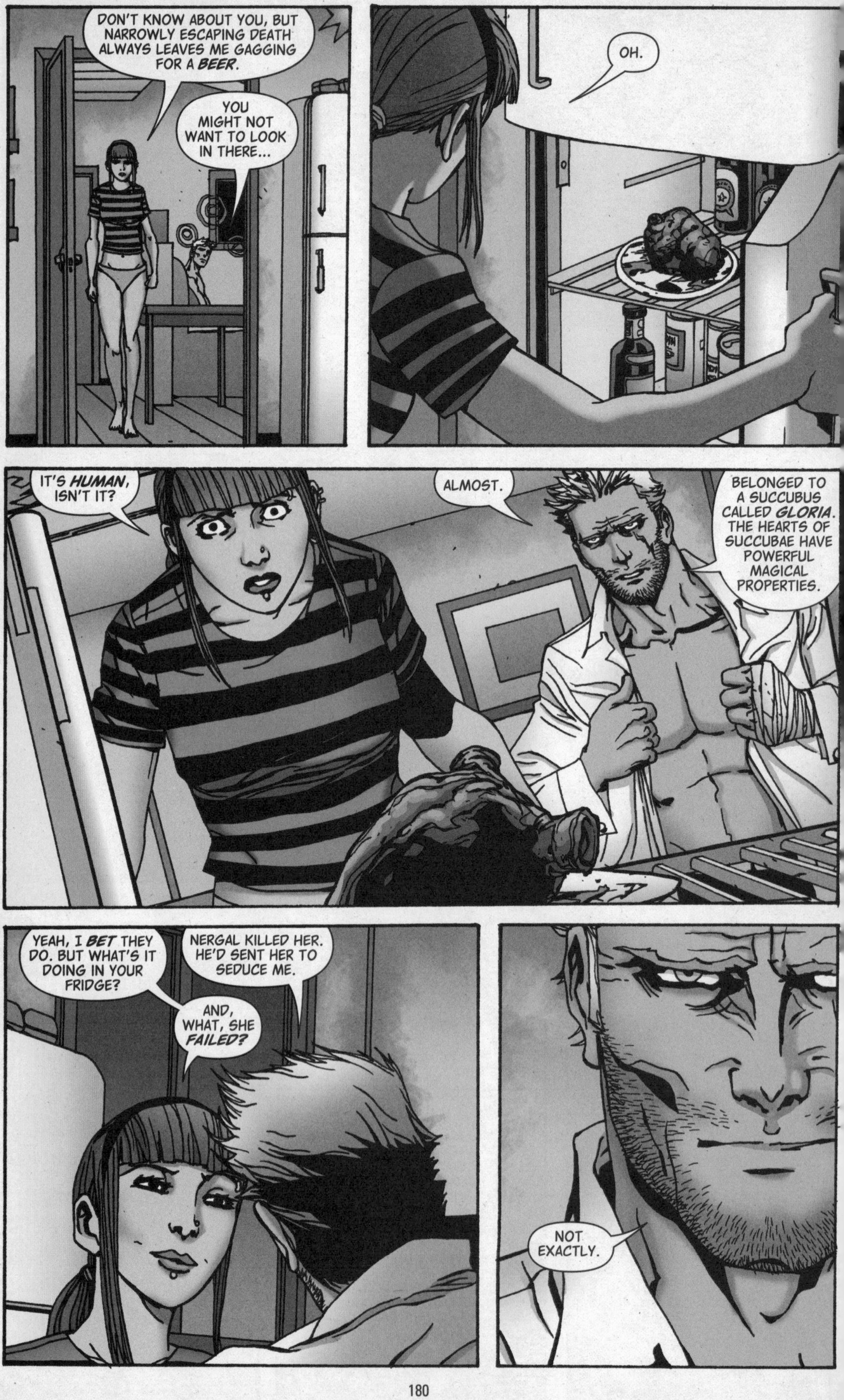

DON'T KNOW ABOUT YOU, BUT NARROWLY ESCAPING DEATH ALWAYS LEAVES ME GAGGING FOR A *BEER*.
YOU MIGHT NOT WANT TO LOOK IN THERE...
OH.
IT'S *HUMAN*, ISN'T IT?
ALMOST.
BELONGED TO A SUCCUBUS CALLED *GLORIA*. THE HEARTS OF SUCCUBAE HAVE POWERFUL MAGICAL PROPERTIES.
YEAH, I *BET* THEY DO. BUT WHAT'S IT DOING IN YOUR FRIDGE?
NERGAL KILLED HER. HE'D SENT HER TO SEDUCE ME.
AND, WHAT, SHE *FAILED*?
NOT EXACTLY.

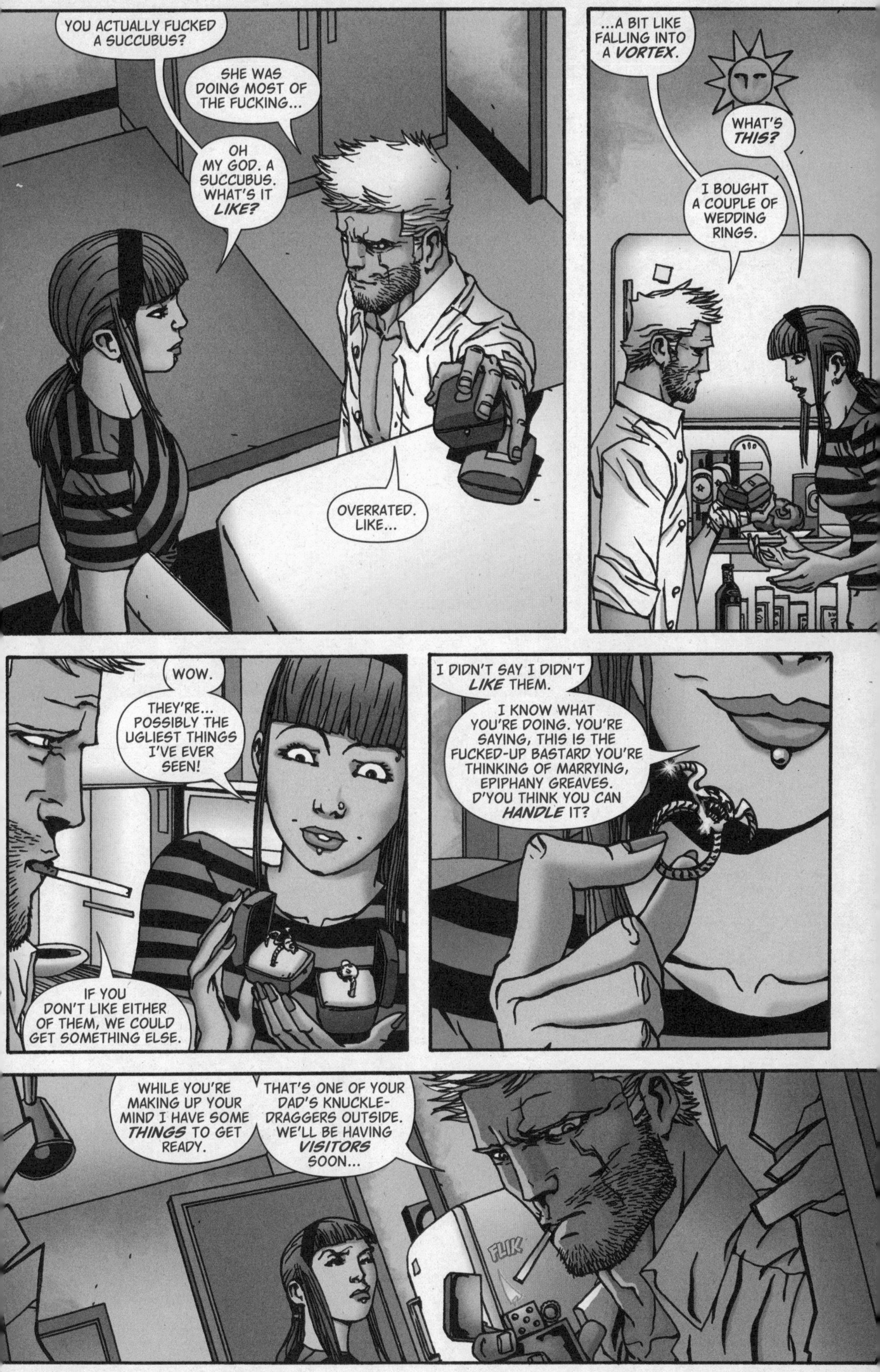

YOU ACTUALLY FUCKED A SUCCUBUS?
SHE WAS DOING MOST OF THE FUCKING...
OH MY GOD. A SUCCUBUS. WHAT'S IT LIKE?
OVERRATED. LIKE...
...A BIT LIKE FALLING INTO A VORTEX.
WHAT'S THIS?
I BOUGHT A COUPLE OF WEDDING RINGS.
WOW.
THEY'RE... POSSIBLY THE UGLIEST THINGS I'VE EVER SEEN!
IF YOU DON'T LIKE EITHER OF THEM, WE COULD GET SOMETHING ELSE.
I DIDN'T SAY I DIDN'T LIKE THEM.
I KNOW WHAT YOU'RE DOING. YOU'RE SAYING, THIS IS THE FUCKED-UP BASTARD YOU'RE THINKING OF MARRYING, EPIPHANY GREAVES. D'YOU THINK YOU CAN HANDLE IT?
WHILE YOU'RE MAKING UP YOUR MIND I HAVE SOME THINGS TO GET READY.
THAT'S ONE OF YOUR DAD'S KNUCKLE-DRAGGERS OUTSIDE. WE'LL BE HAVING VISITORS SOON...
FLIK

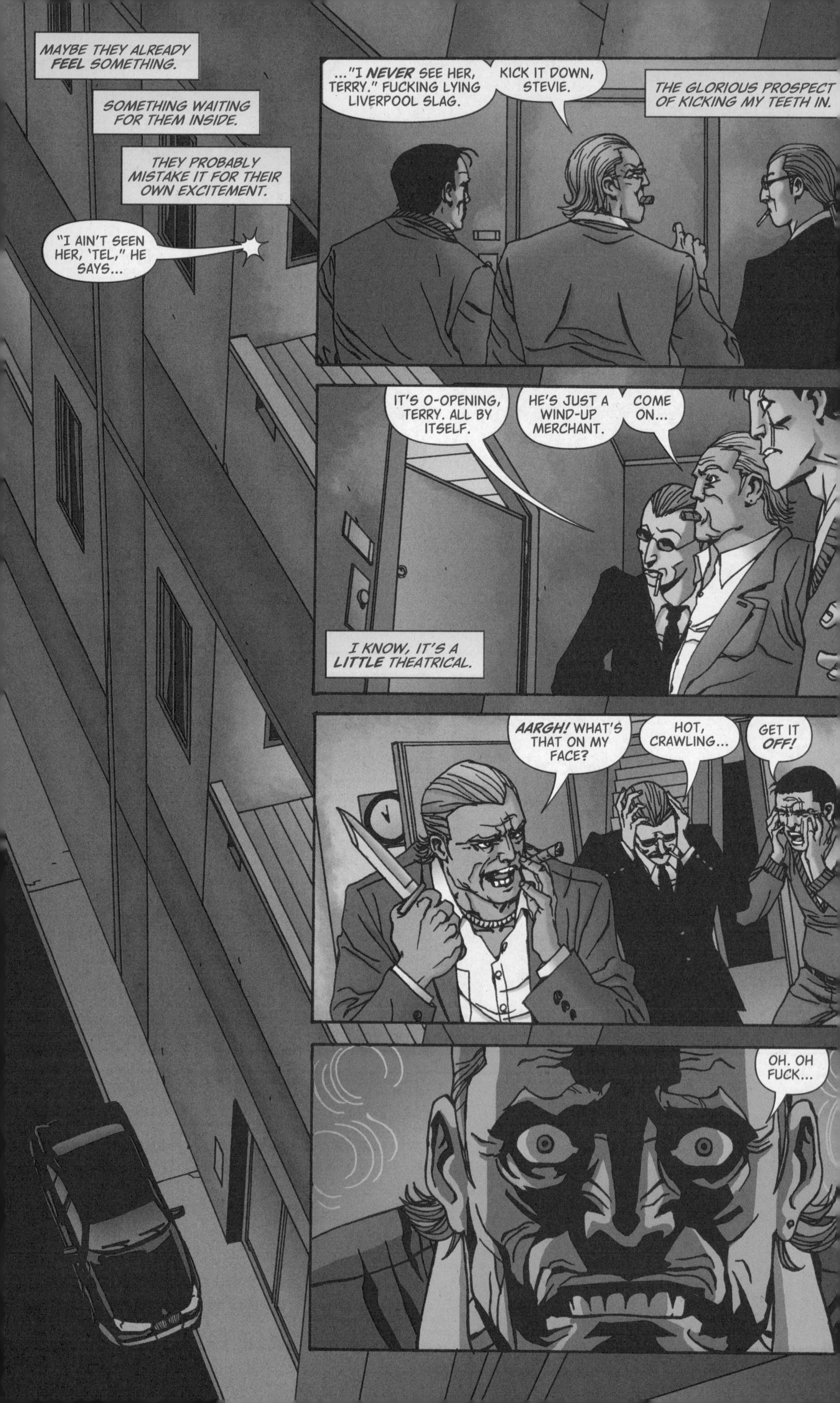

MAYBE THEY ALREADY FEEL SOMETHING.
SOMETHING WAITING FOR THEM INSIDE.
THEY PROBABLY MISTAKE IT FOR THEIR OWN EXCITEMENT.
"I AIN'T SEEN HER, 'TEL," HE SAYS...
..."I NEVER SEE HER, TERRY." FUCKING LYING LIVERPOOL SLAG.
KICK IT DOWN, STEVIE.
THE GLORIOUS PROSPECT OF KICKING MY TEETH IN.
IT'S O-OPENING, TERRY. ALL BY ITSELF.
HE'S JUST A WIND-UP MERCHANT.
COME ON...
I KNOW, IT'S A LITTLE THEATRICAL.
AARGH! WHAT'S THAT ON MY FACE?
HOT, CRAWLING...
GET IT OFF!
OH. OH FUCK...

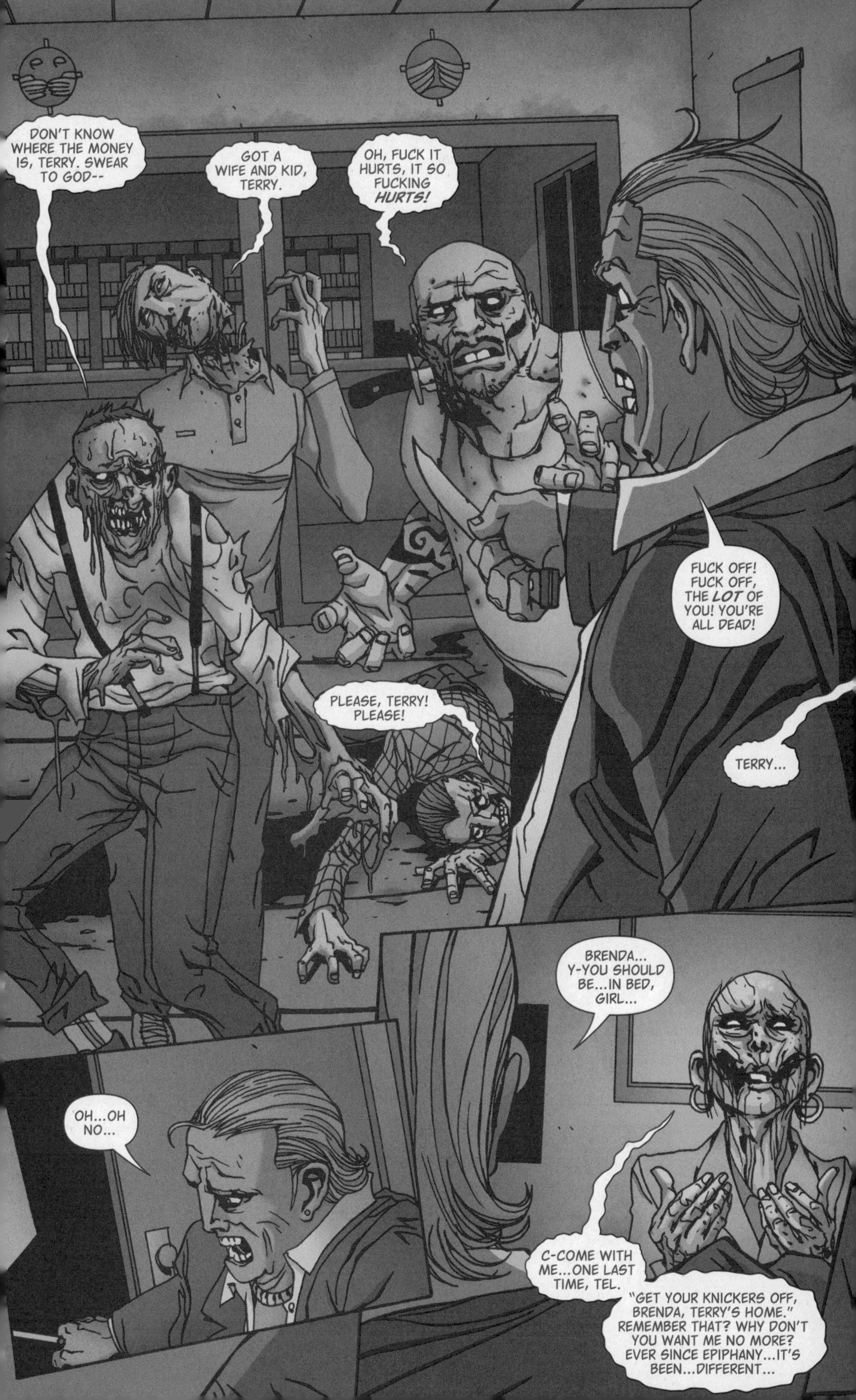

DON'T KNOW WHERE THE MONEY IS, TERRY. SWEAR TO GOD--
GOT A WIFE AND KID, TERRY.
OH, FUCK IT HURTS, IT SO FUCKING *HURTS!*
FUCK OFF! FUCK OFF, THE *LOT* OF YOU! YOU'RE ALL DEAD!
PLEASE, TERRY! PLEASE!
TERRY...
BRENDA... Y-YOU SHOULD BE...IN BED, GIRL...
OH...OH NO...
C-COME WITH ME...ONE LAST TIME, TEL.
"GET YOUR KNICKERS OFF, BRENDA, TERRY'S HOME." REMEMBER THAT? WHY DON'T YOU WANT ME NO MORE? EVER SINCE EPIPHANY...IT'S BEEN...DIFFERENT...

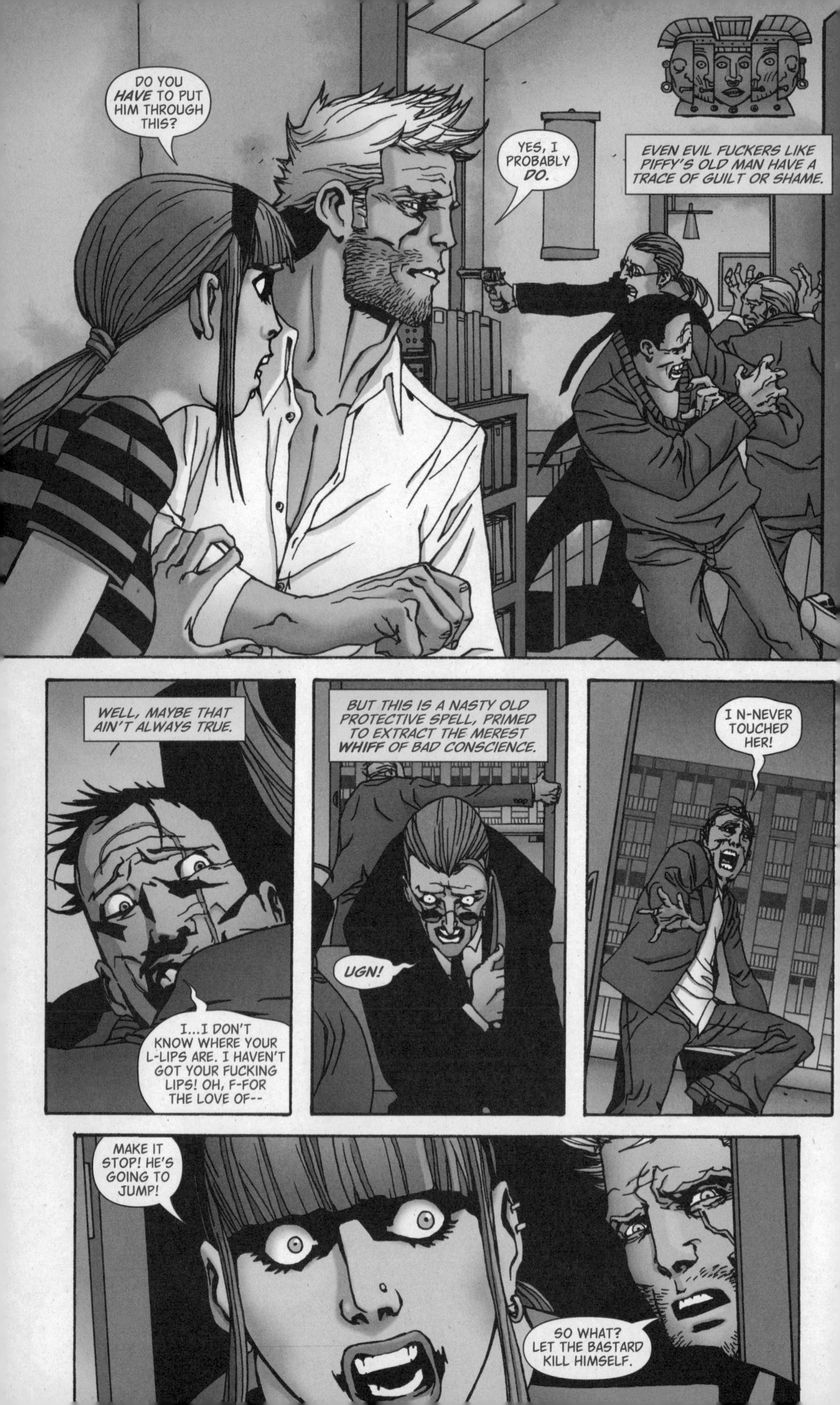
DO YOU HAVE TO PUT HIM THROUGH THIS?
YES, I PROBABLY DO.
EVEN EVIL FUCKERS LIKE PIFFY'S OLD MAN HAVE A TRACE OF GUILT OR SHAME.
WELL, MAYBE THAT AIN'T ALWAYS TRUE.
I...I DON'T KNOW WHERE YOUR L-LIPS ARE. I HAVEN'T GOT YOUR FUCKING LIPS! OH, F-FOR THE LOVE OF--
BUT THIS IS A NASTY OLD PROTECTIVE SPELL, PRIMED TO EXTRACT THE MEREST WHIFF OF BAD CONSCIENCE.
UGN!
I N-NEVER TOUCHED HER!
MAKE IT STOP! HE'S GOING TO JUMP!
SO WHAT? LET THE BASTARD KILL HIMSELF.

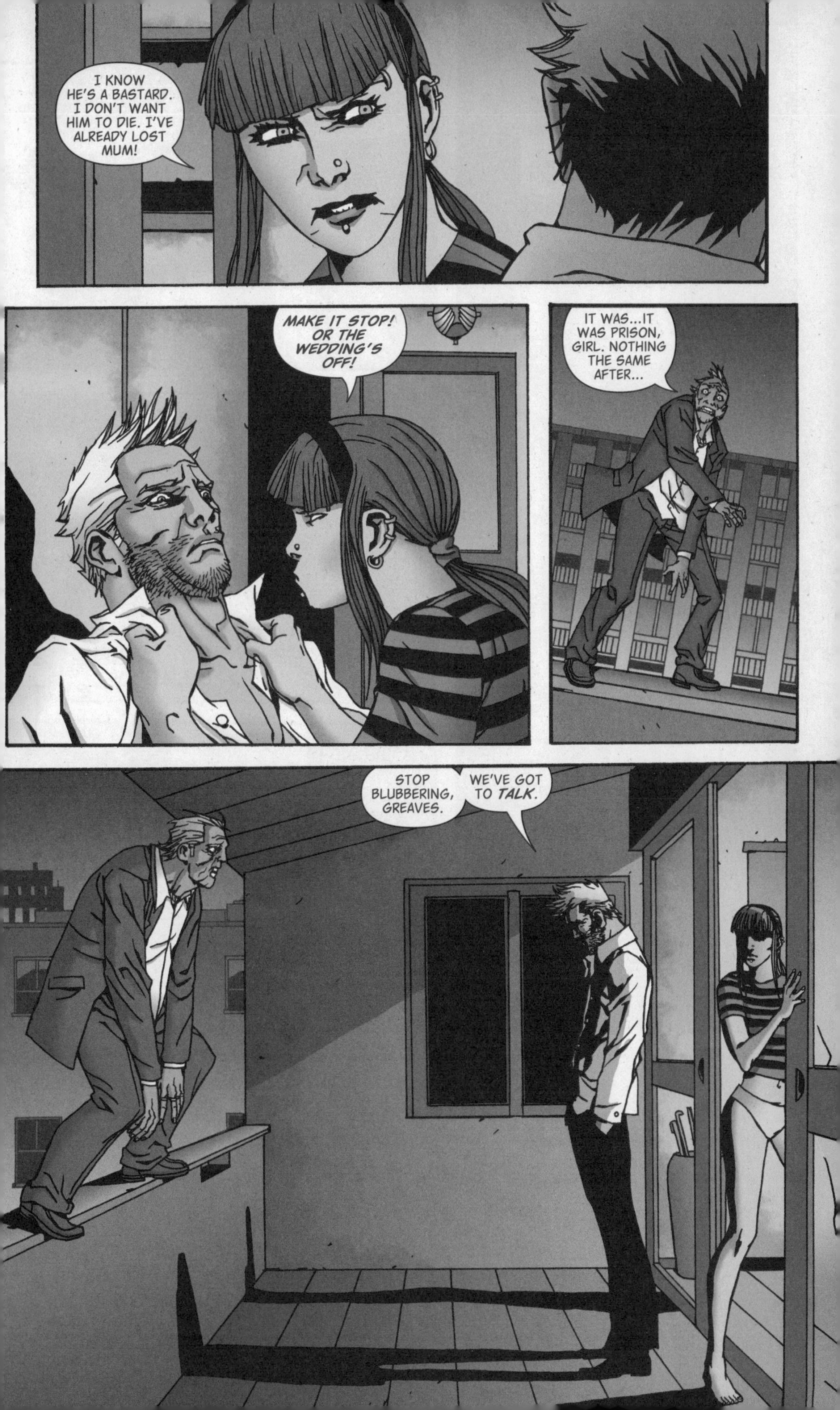
I KNOW HE'S A BASTARD. I DON'T WANT HIM TO DIE. I'VE ALREADY LOST MUM!
MAKE IT STOP! OR THE WEDDING'S OFF!
IT WAS...IT WAS PRISON, GIRL. NOTHING THE SAME AFTER...
STOP BLUBBERING, GREAVES.
WE'VE GOT TO TALK.

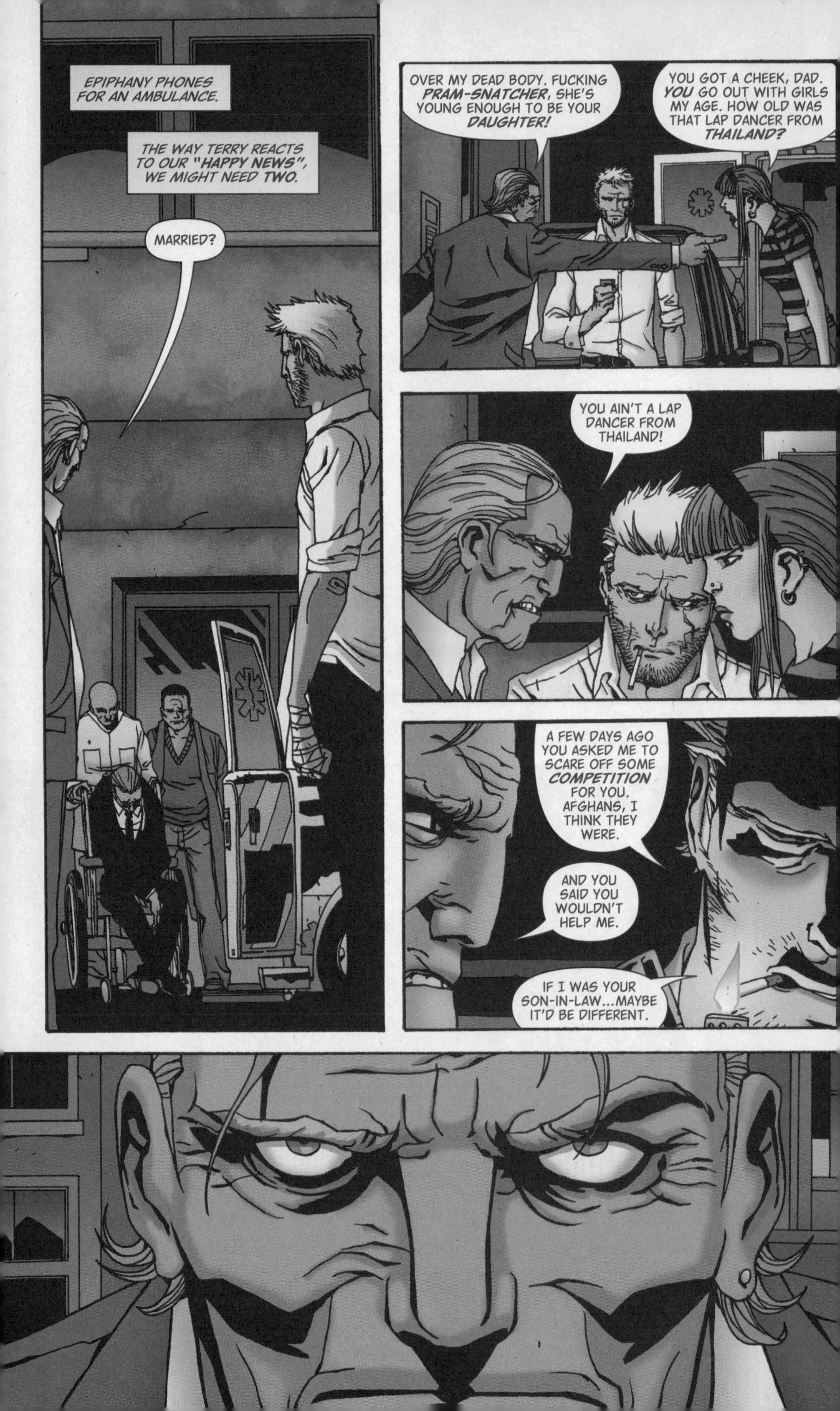
EPIPHANY PHONES FOR AN AMBULANCE.
THE WAY TERRY REACTS TO OUR "HAPPY NEWS", WE MIGHT NEED TWO.
MARRIED?
OVER MY DEAD BODY. FUCKING PRAM-SNATCHER, SHE'S YOUNG ENOUGH TO BE YOUR DAUGHTER!
YOU GOT A CHEEK, DAD. YOU GO OUT WITH GIRLS MY AGE. HOW OLD WAS THAT LAP DANCER FROM THAILAND?
YOU AIN'T A LAP DANCER FROM THAILAND!
A FEW DAYS AGO YOU ASKED ME TO SCARE OFF SOME COMPETITION FOR YOU. AFGHANS, I THINK THEY WERE.
AND YOU SAID YOU WOULDN'T HELP ME.
IF I WAS YOUR SON-IN-LAW...MAYBE IT'D BE DIFFERENT.

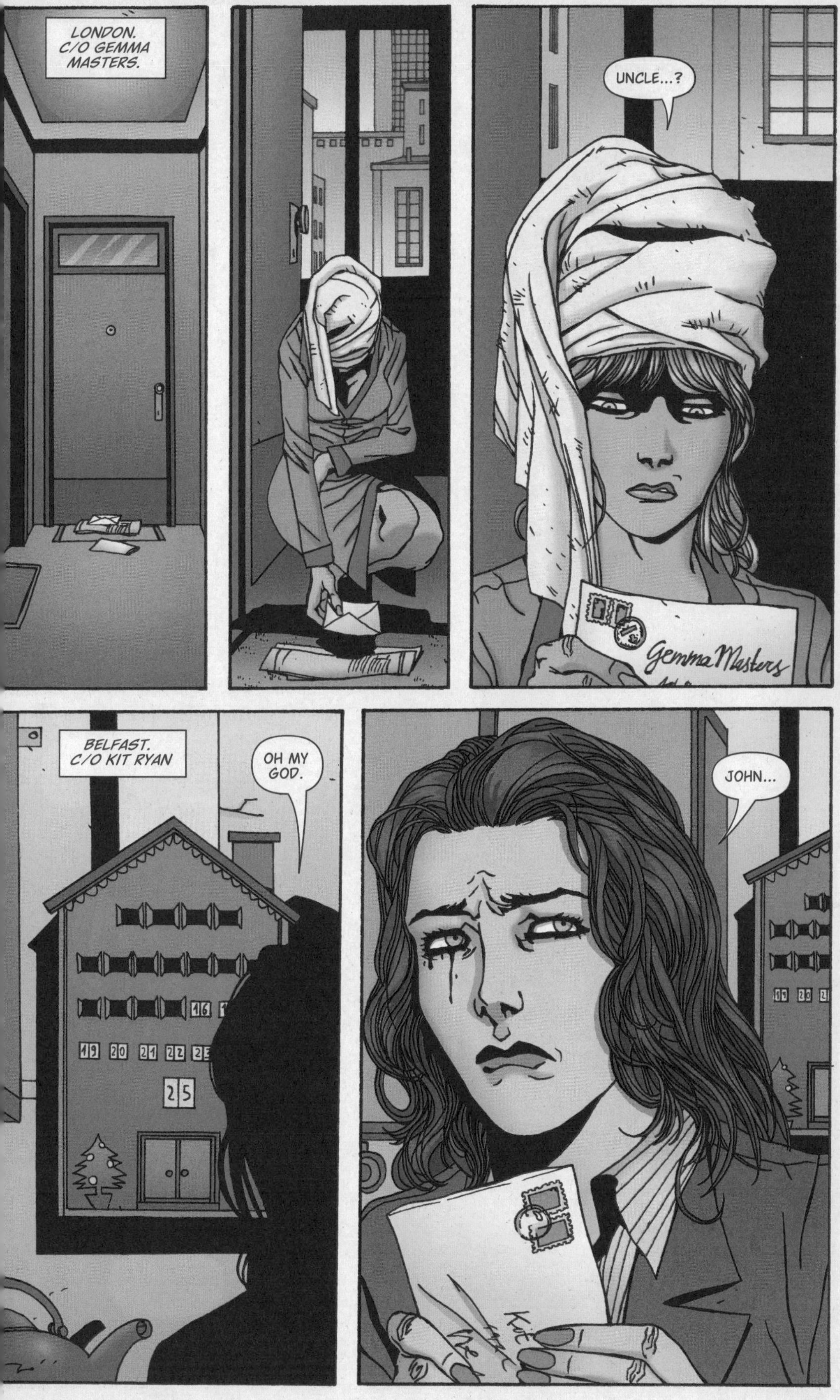

LONDON. C/O GEMMA MASTERS.
UNCLE...?
Gemma Masters
BELFAST. C/O KIT RYAN
OH MY GOD.
JOHN...

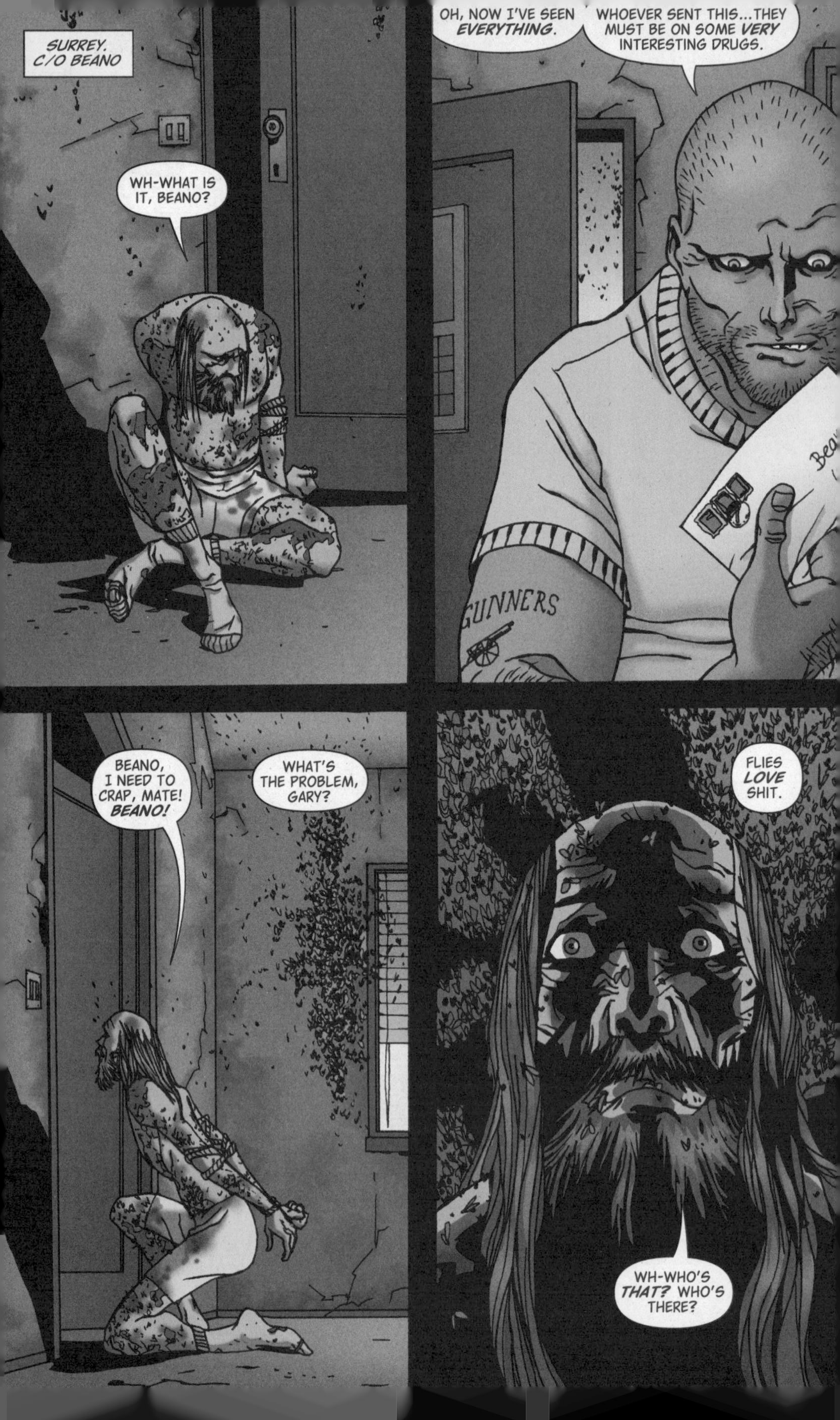

SURREY. C/O BEANO
WH-WHAT IS IT, BEANO?
OH, NOW I'VE SEEN EVERYTHING.
WHOEVER SENT THIS...THEY MUST BE ON SOME VERY INTERESTING DRUGS.
GUNNERS
BEANO, I NEED TO CRAP, MATE! BEANO!
WHAT'S THE PROBLEM, GARY?
FLIES LOVE SHIT.
WH-WHO'S THAT? WHO'S THERE?

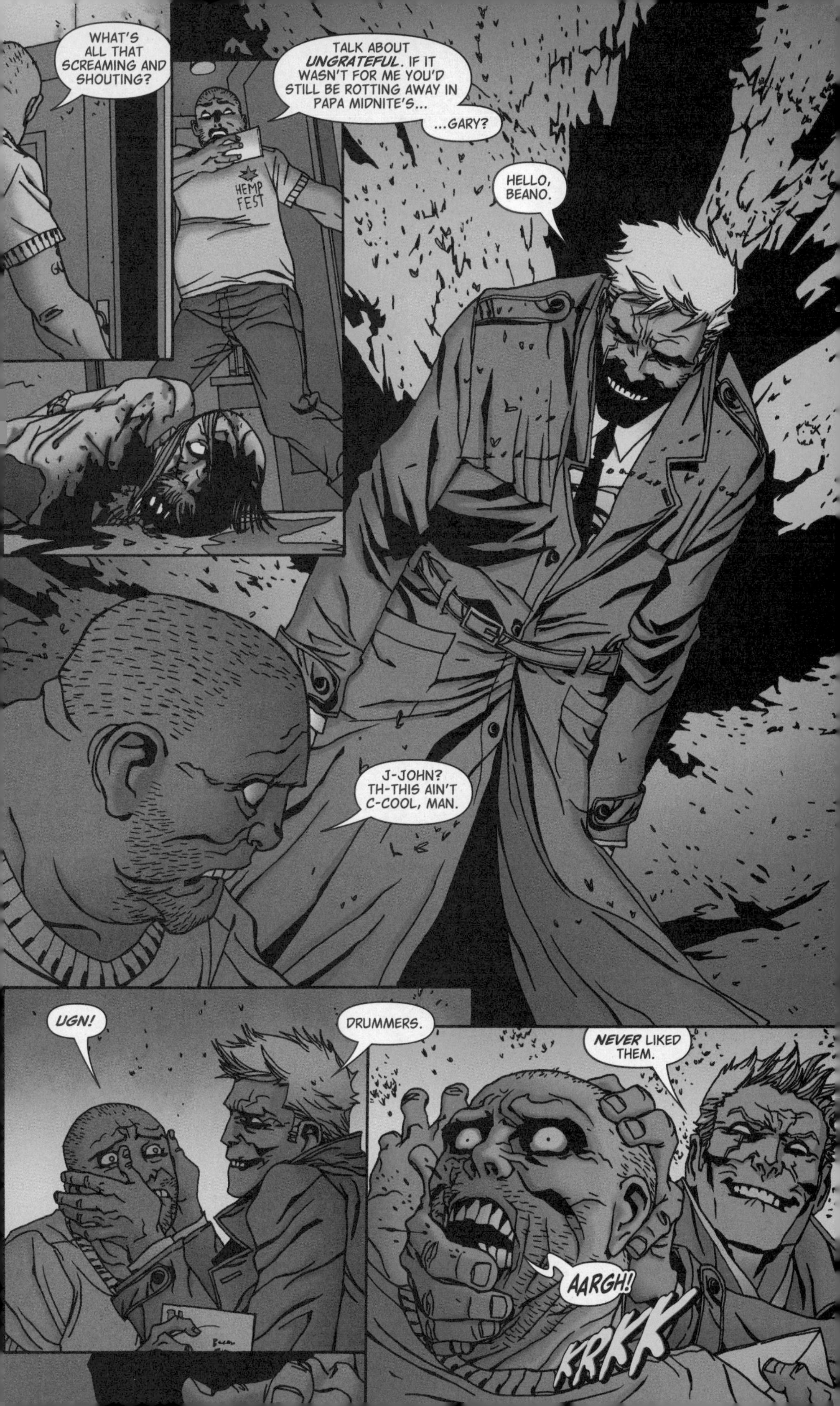
WHAT'S ALL THAT SCREAMING AND SHOUTING?
TALK ABOUT UNGRATEFUL. IF IT WASN'T FOR ME YOU'D STILL BE ROTTING AWAY IN PAPA MIDNITE'S...
...GARY?
HEMP FEST
HELLO, BEANO.
J-JOHN? TH-THIS AIN'T C-COOL, MAN.
UGN!
DRUMMERS.
NEVER LIKED THEM.
AARGH!
KRKK

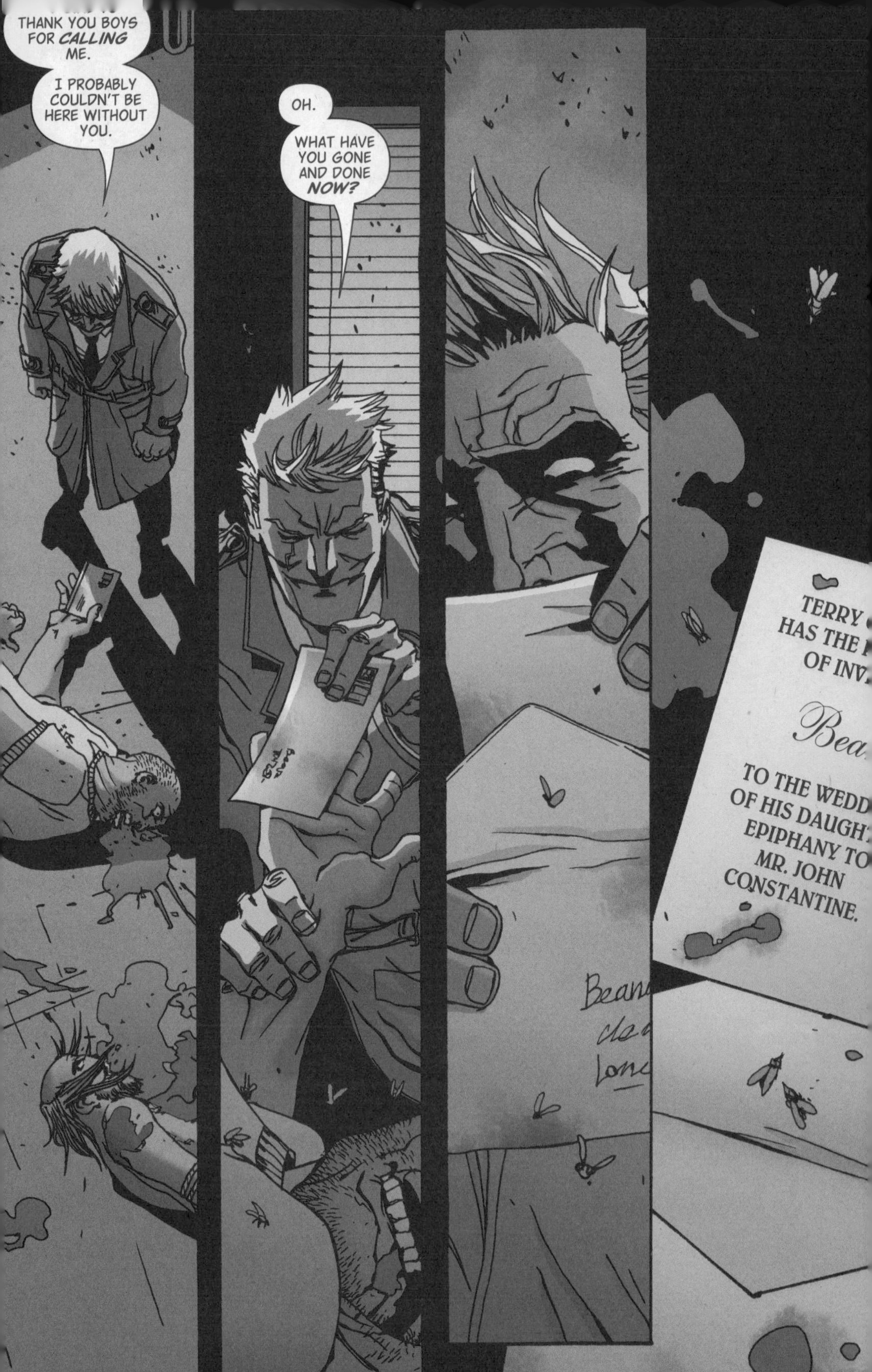
THANK YOU BOYS FOR CALLING ME.
I PROBABLY COULDN'T BE HERE WITHOUT YOU.
OH.
WHAT HAVE YOU GONE AND DONE NOW?
TERRY
HAS THE
OF INV
Bea
TO THE WEDD
OF HIS DAUGH
EPIPHANY TO
MR. JOHN
CONSTANTINE.

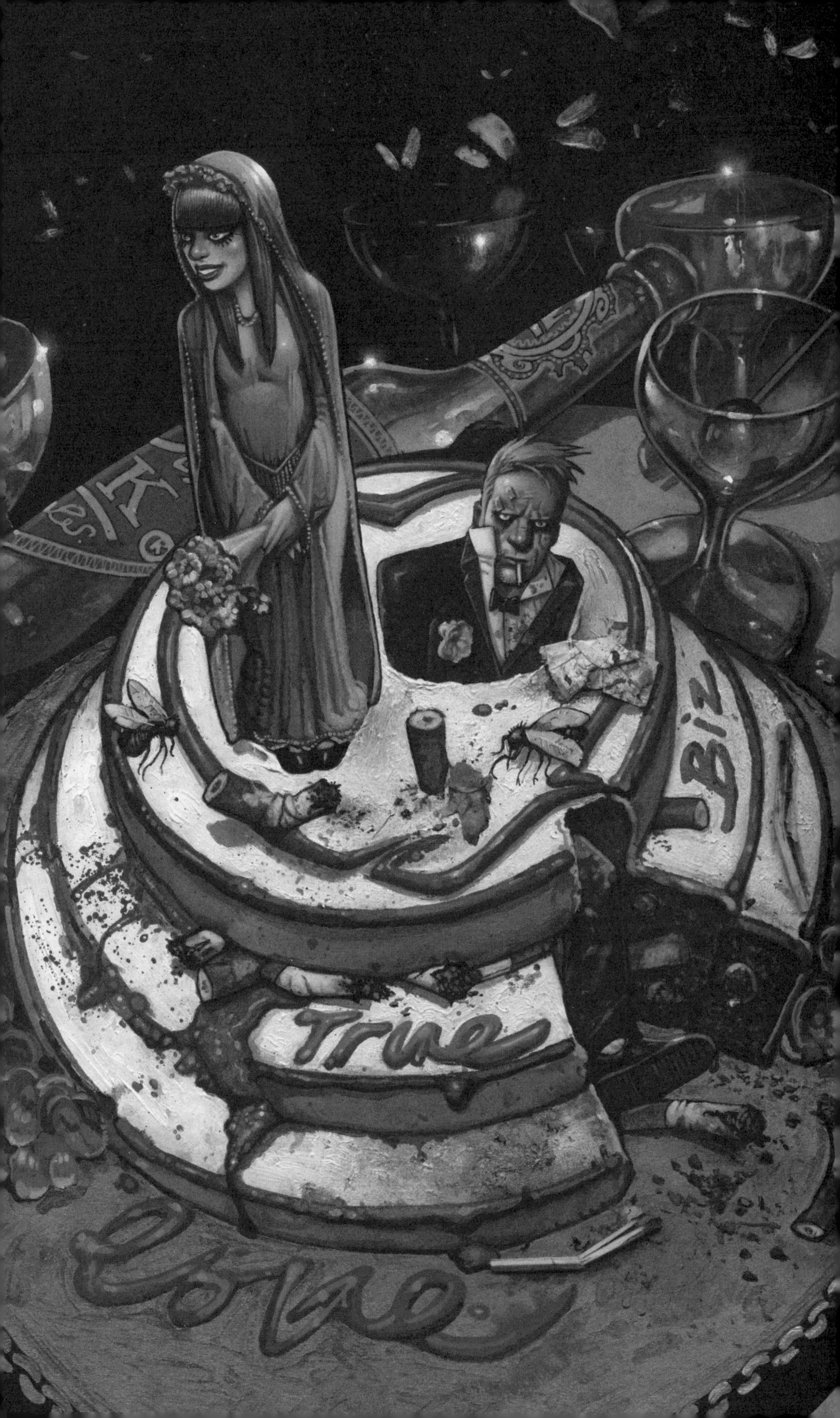
True
Love

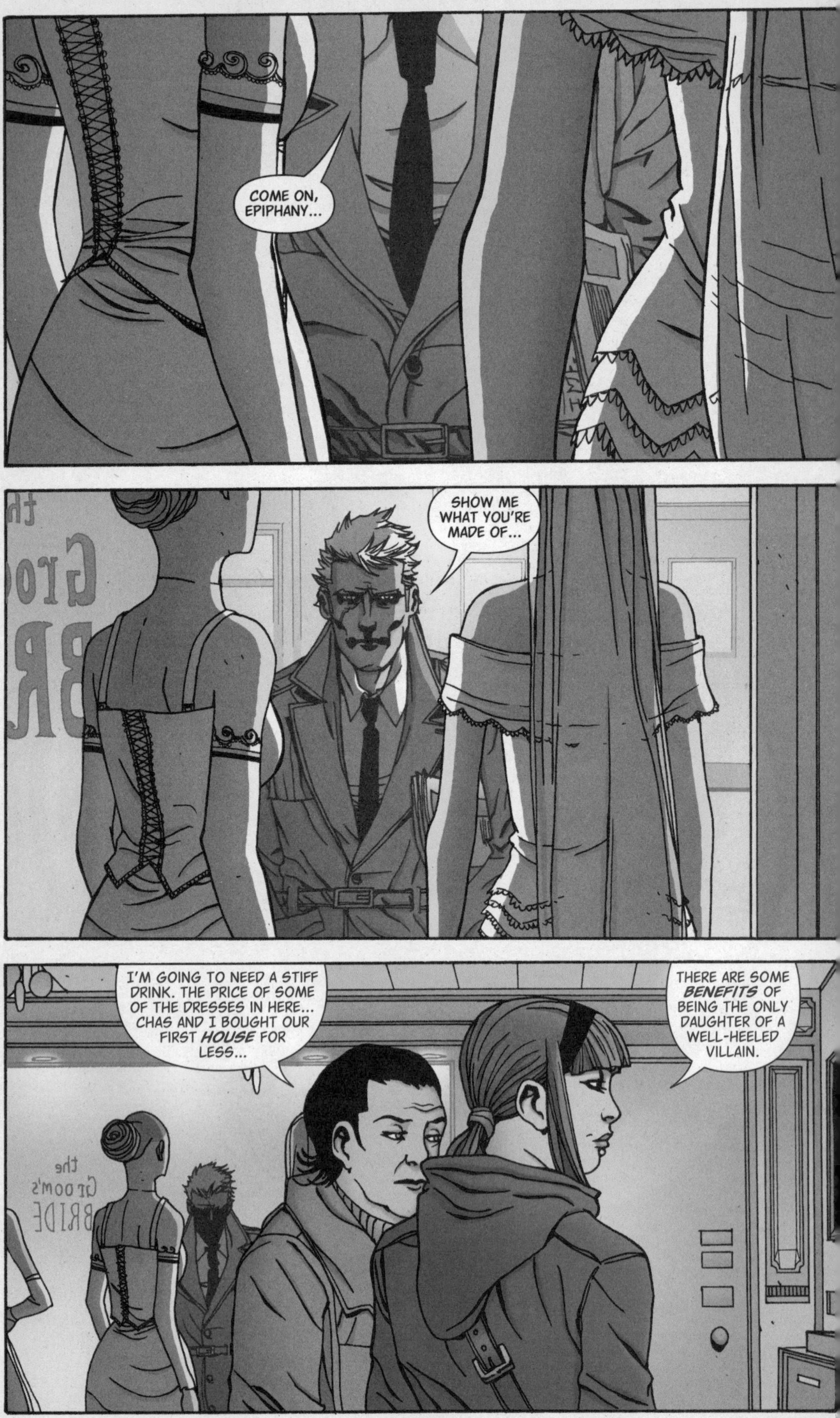
COME ON, EPIPHANY...
the Groo BR
SHOW ME WHAT YOU'RE MADE OF...
I'M GOING TO NEED A STIFF DRINK. THE PRICE OF SOME OF THE DRESSES IN HERE... CHAS AND I BOUGHT OUR FIRST *HOUSE* FOR LESS...
THERE ARE SOME ***BENEFITS*** OF BEING THE ONLY DAUGHTER OF A WELL-HEELED VILLAIN.

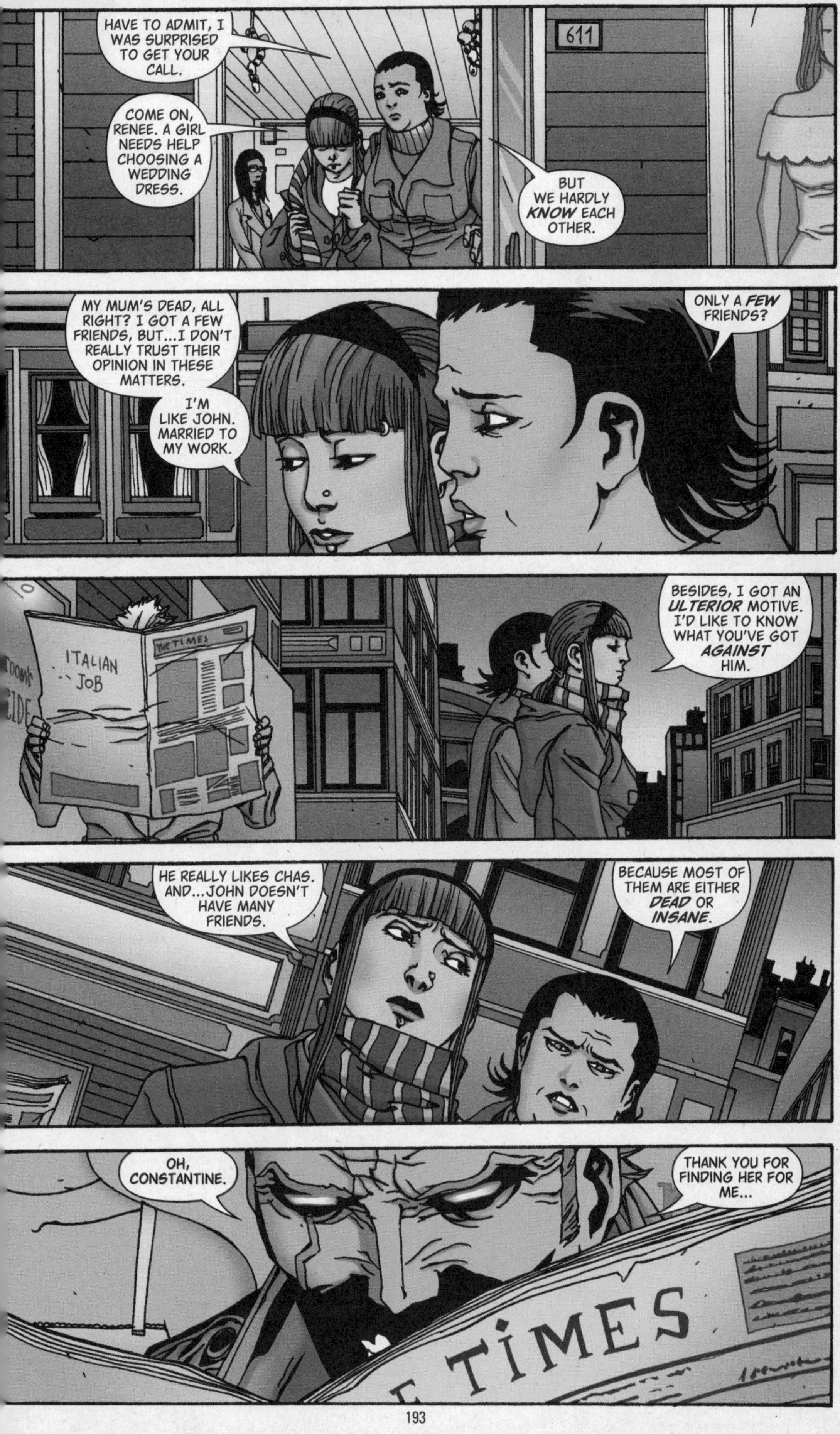
HAVE TO ADMIT, I WAS SURPRISED TO GET YOUR CALL.
COME ON, RENEE. A GIRL NEEDS HELP CHOOSING A WEDDING DRESS.
BUT WE HARDLY KNOW EACH OTHER.
611
MY MUM'S DEAD, ALL RIGHT? I GOT A FEW FRIENDS, BUT...I DON'T REALLY TRUST THEIR OPINION IN THESE MATTERS.
I'M LIKE JOHN. MARRIED TO MY WORK.
ONLY A FEW FRIENDS?
THE TIMES
ITALIAN JOB
BESIDES, I GOT AN ULTERIOR MOTIVE. I'D LIKE TO KNOW WHAT YOU'VE GOT AGAINST HIM.
HE REALLY LIKES CHAS. AND...JOHN DOESN'T HAVE MANY FRIENDS.
BECAUSE MOST OF THEM ARE EITHER DEAD OR INSANE.
OH, CONSTANTINE.
THANK YOU FOR FINDING HER FOR ME...
TIMES

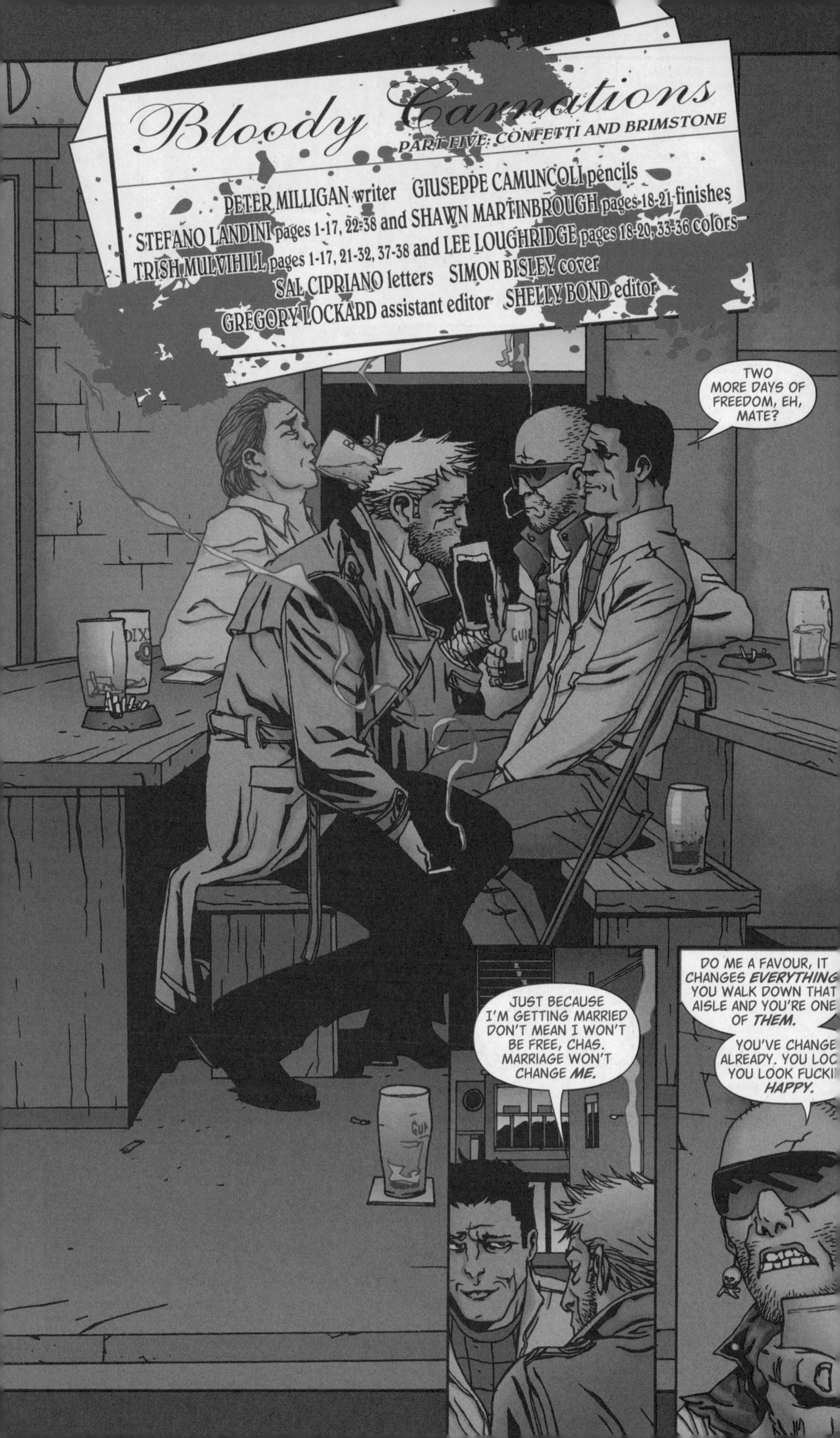
Bloody Carnations
PART FIVE: CONFETTI AND BRIMSTONE
PETER MILLIGAN writer GIUSEPPE CAMUNCOLI pencils
STEFANO LANDINI pages 1-17, 22-38 and SHAWN MARTINBROUGH pages 18-21 finishes
TRISH MULVIHILL pages 1-17, 21-32, 37-38 and LEE LOUGHRIDGE pages 18-20, 33-36 colors
SAL CIPRIANO letters SIMON BISLEY cover
GREGORY LOCKARD assistant editor SHELLY BOND editor
TWO MORE DAYS OF FREEDOM, EH, MATE?
JUST BECAUSE I'M GETTING MARRIED DON'T MEAN I WON'T BE FREE, CHAS. MARRIAGE WON'T CHANGE ME.
DO ME A FAVOUR, IT CHANGES EVERYTHING YOU WALK DOWN THAT AISLE AND YOU'RE ONE OF THEM.
YOU'VE CHANGE ALREADY. YOU LOC YOU LOOK FUCKI HAPPY.

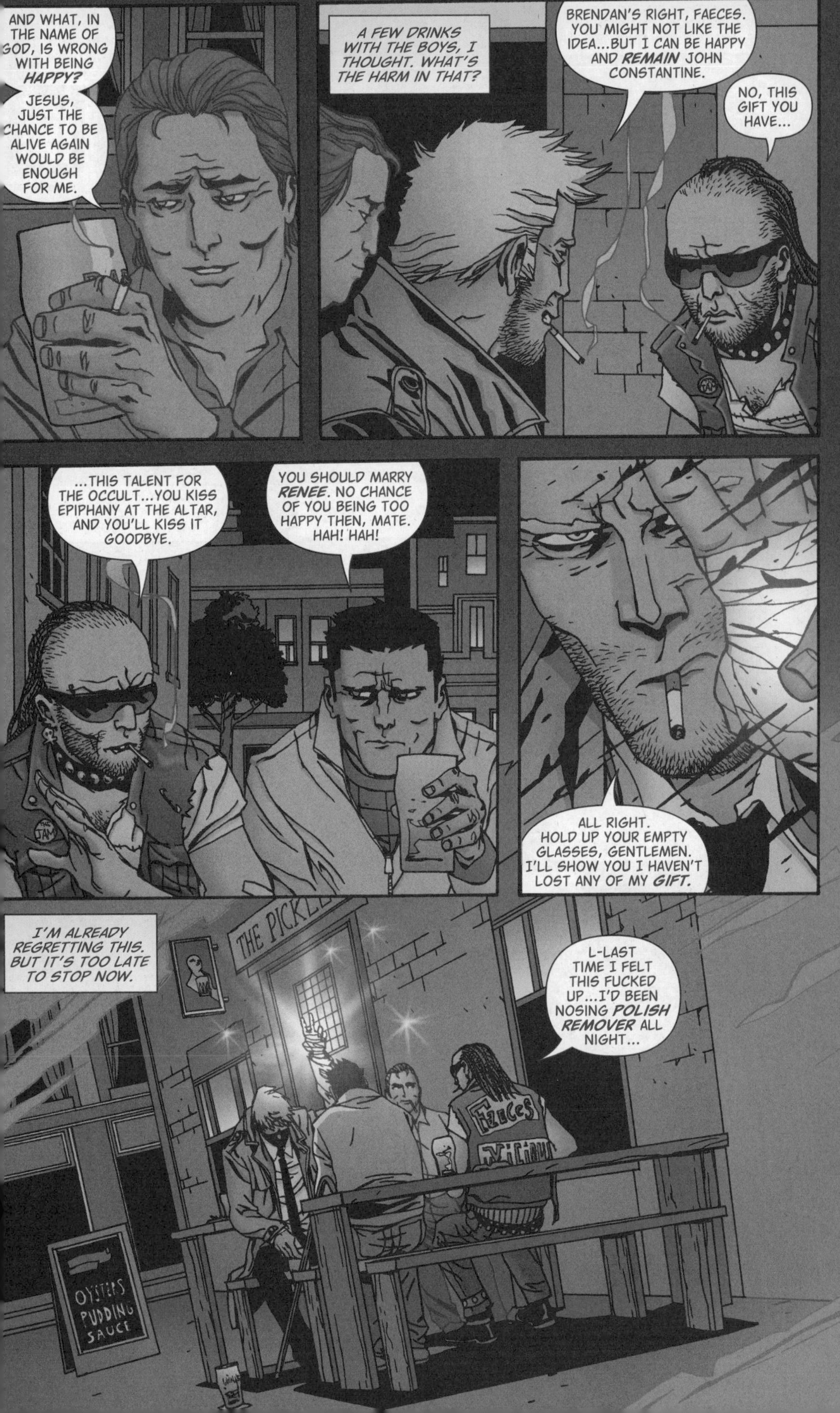
AND WHAT, IN THE NAME OF GOD, IS WRONG WITH BEING HAPPY?
JESUS, JUST THE CHANCE TO BE ALIVE AGAIN WOULD BE ENOUGH FOR ME.
A FEW DRINKS WITH THE BOYS, I THOUGHT. WHAT'S THE HARM IN THAT?
BRENDAN'S RIGHT, FAECES. YOU MIGHT NOT LIKE THE IDEA...BUT I CAN BE HAPPY AND REMAIN JOHN CONSTANTINE.
NO, THIS GIFT YOU HAVE...
...THIS TALENT FOR THE OCCULT...YOU KISS EPIPHANY AT THE ALTAR, AND YOU'LL KISS IT GOODBYE.
YOU SHOULD MARRY RENEE. NO CHANCE OF YOU BEING TOO HAPPY THEN, MATE. HAH! HAH!
ALL RIGHT. HOLD UP YOUR EMPTY GLASSES, GENTLEMEN. I'LL SHOW YOU I HAVEN'T LOST ANY OF MY GIFT.
I'M ALREADY REGRETTING THIS. BUT IT'S TOO LATE TO STOP NOW.
THE PICKLE
L-LAST TIME I FELT THIS FUCKED UP...I'D BEEN NOSING POLISH REMOVER ALL NIGHT...
FAECES
OYSTERS PUDDING SAUCE

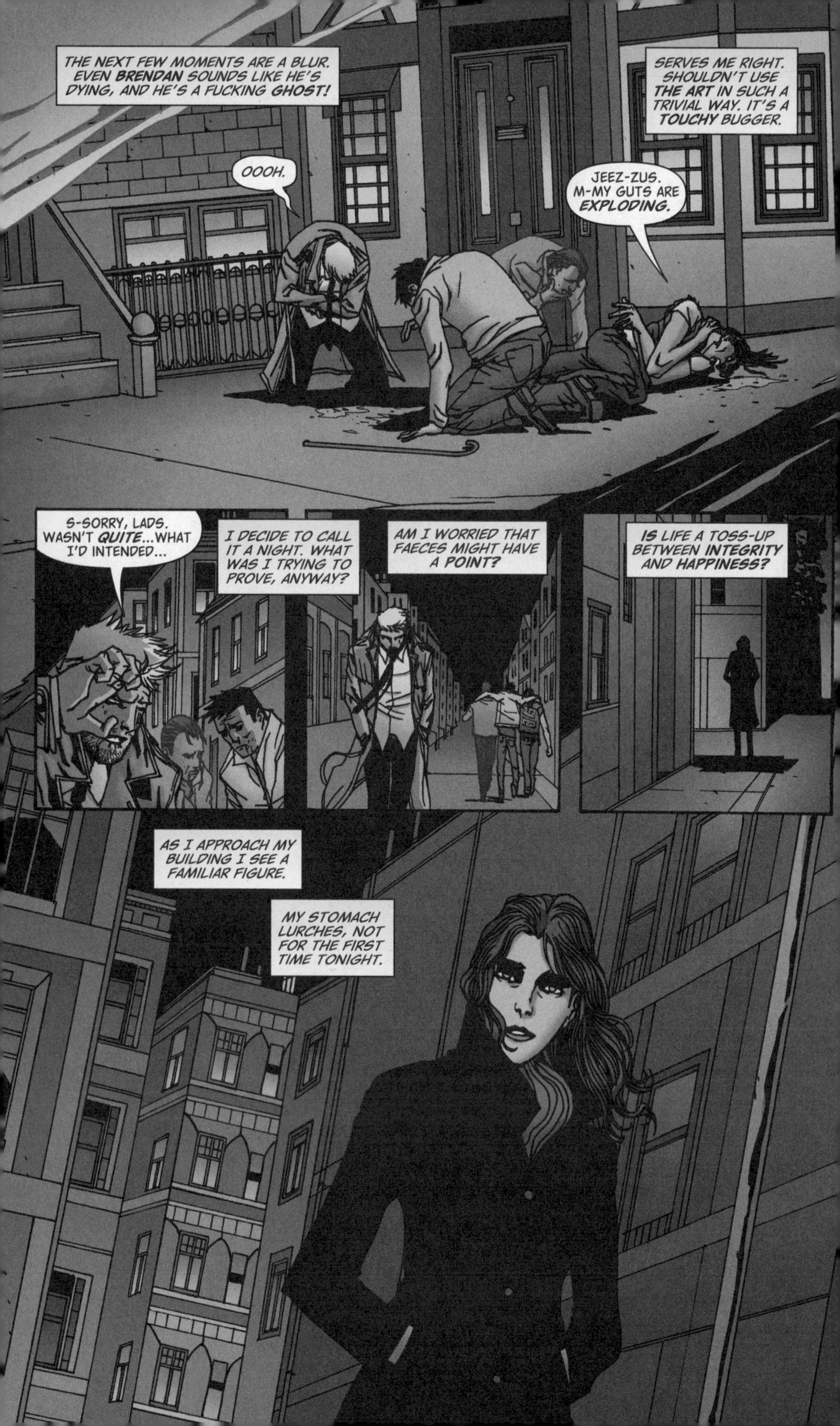
THE NEXT FEW MOMENTS ARE A BLUR. EVEN BRENDAN SOUNDS LIKE HE'S DYING, AND HE'S A FUCKING GHOST!
SERVES ME RIGHT. SHOULDN'T USE THE ART IN SUCH A TRIVIAL WAY. IT'S A TOUCHY BUGGER.
OOOH.
JEEZ-ZUS. M-MY GUTS ARE EXPLODING.
S-SORRY, LADS. WASN'T QUITE...WHAT I'D INTENDED...
I DECIDE TO CALL IT A NIGHT. WHAT WAS I TRYING TO PROVE, ANYWAY?
AM I WORRIED THAT FAECES MIGHT HAVE A POINT?
IS LIFE A TOSS-UP BETWEEN INTEGRITY AND HAPPINESS?
AS I APPROACH MY BUILDING I SEE A FAMILIAR FIGURE.
MY STOMACH LURCHES, NOT FOR THE FIRST TIME TONIGHT.

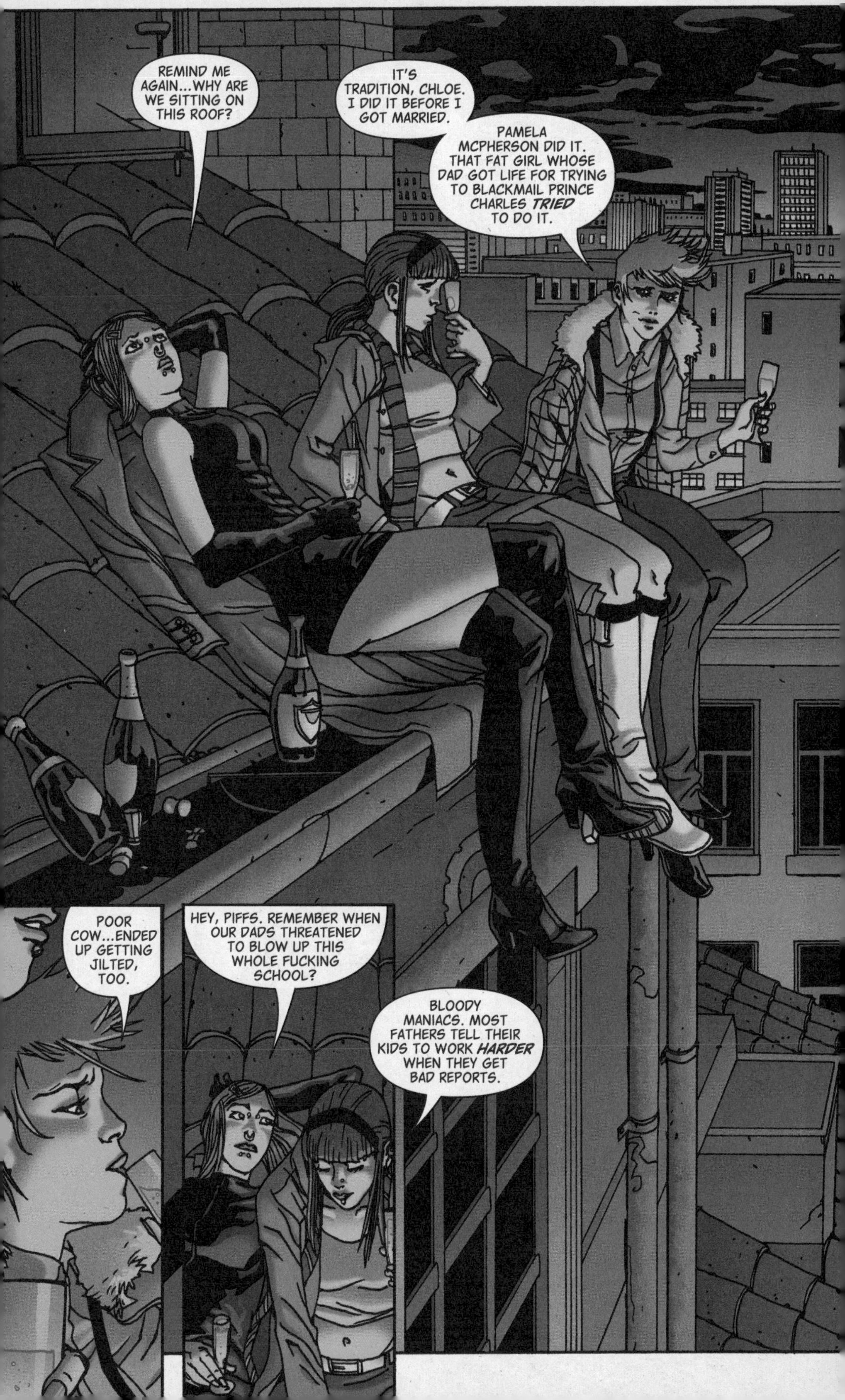

REMIND ME AGAIN...WHY ARE WE SITTING ON THIS ROOF?
IT'S TRADITION, CHLOE. I DID IT BEFORE I GOT MARRIED.
PAMELA MCPHERSON DID IT. THAT FAT GIRL WHOSE DAD GOT LIFE FOR TRYING TO BLACKMAIL PRINCE CHARLES *TRIED* TO DO IT.
POOR COW...ENDED UP GETTING JILTED, TOO.
HEY, PIFFS. REMEMBER WHEN OUR DADS THREATENED TO BLOW UP THIS WHOLE FUCKING SCHOOL?
BLOODY MANIACS. MOST FATHERS TELL THEIR KIDS TO WORK *HARDER* WHEN THEY GET BAD REPORTS.

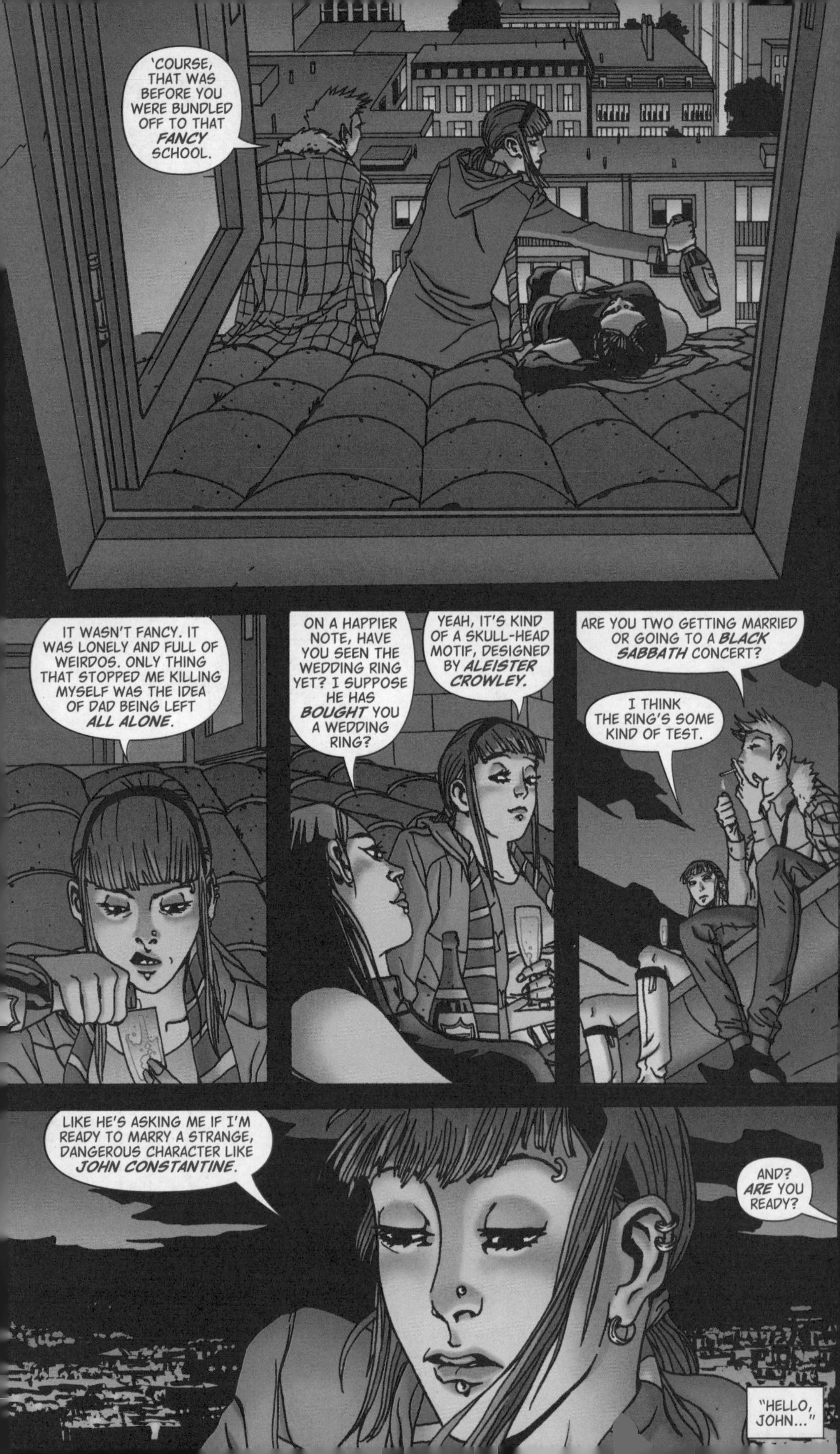
'COURSE, THAT WAS BEFORE YOU WERE BUNDLED OFF TO THAT FANCY SCHOOL.
IT WASN'T FANCY. IT WAS LONELY AND FULL OF WEIRDOS. ONLY THING THAT STOPPED ME KILLING MYSELF WAS THE IDEA OF DAD BEING LEFT ALL ALONE.
ON A HAPPIER NOTE, HAVE YOU SEEN THE WEDDING RING YET? I SUPPOSE HE HAS BOUGHT YOU A WEDDING RING?
YEAH, IT'S KIND OF A SKULL-HEAD MOTIF, DESIGNED BY ALEISTER CROWLEY.
ARE YOU TWO GETTING MARRIED OR GOING TO A BLACK SABBATH CONCERT?
I THINK THE RING'S SOME KIND OF TEST.
LIKE HE'S ASKING ME IF I'M READY TO MARRY A STRANGE, DANGEROUS CHARACTER LIKE JOHN CONSTANTINE.
AND? ARE YOU READY?
"HELLO, JOHN..."

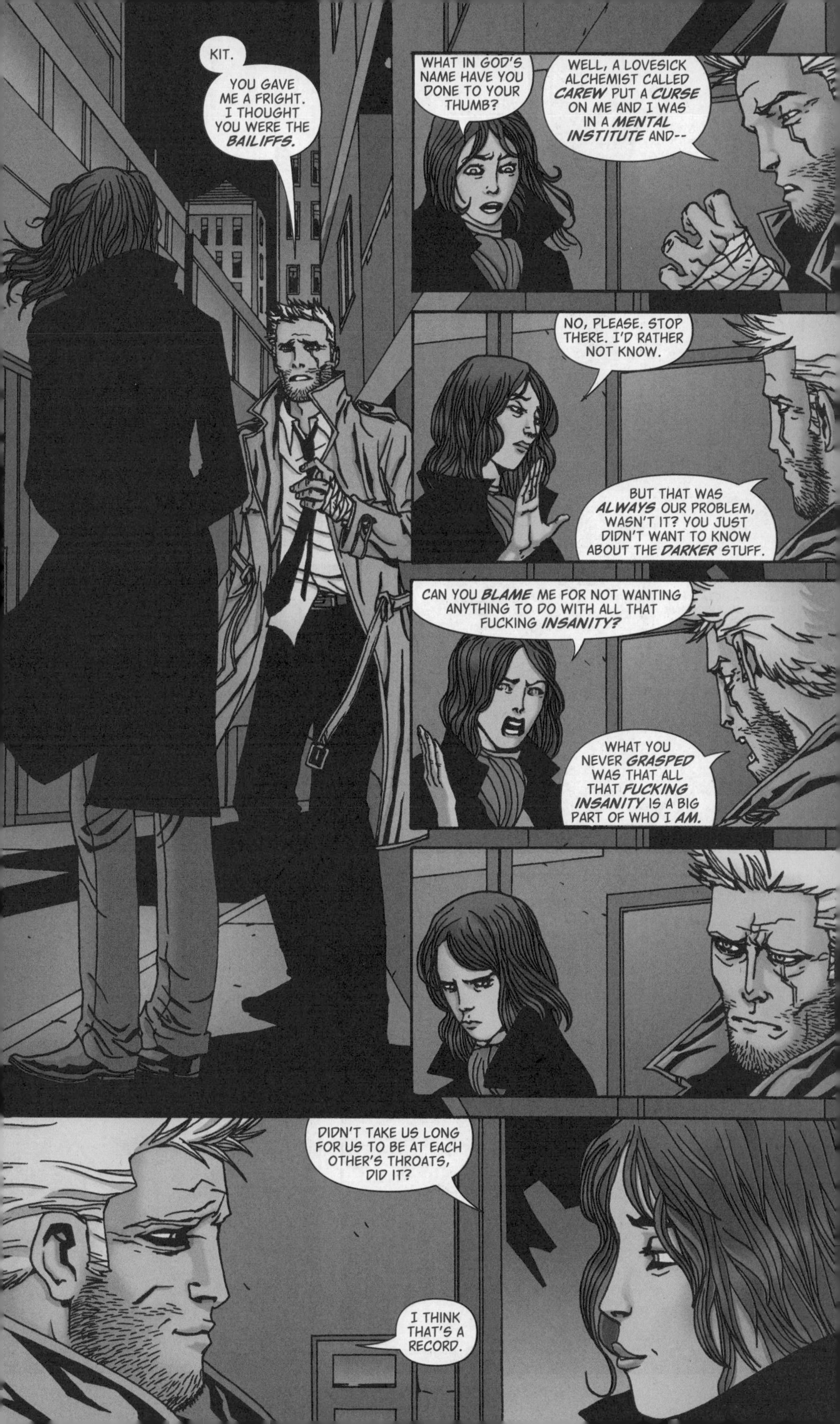
KIT.
YOU GAVE ME A FRIGHT. I THOUGHT YOU WERE THE BAILIFFS.
WHAT IN GOD'S NAME HAVE YOU DONE TO YOUR THUMB?
WELL, A LOVESICK ALCHEMIST CALLED CAREW PUT A CURSE ON ME AND I WAS IN A MENTAL INSTITUTE AND--
NO, PLEASE. STOP THERE. I'D RATHER NOT KNOW.
BUT THAT WAS ALWAYS OUR PROBLEM, WASN'T IT? YOU JUST DIDN'T WANT TO KNOW ABOUT THE DARKER STUFF.
CAN YOU BLAME ME FOR NOT WANTING ANYTHING TO DO WITH ALL THAT FUCKING INSANITY?
WHAT YOU NEVER GRASPED WAS THAT ALL THAT FUCKING INSANITY IS A BIG PART OF WHO I AM.
DIDN'T TAKE US LONG FOR US TO BE AT EACH OTHER'S THROATS, DID IT?
I THINK THAT'S A RECORD.

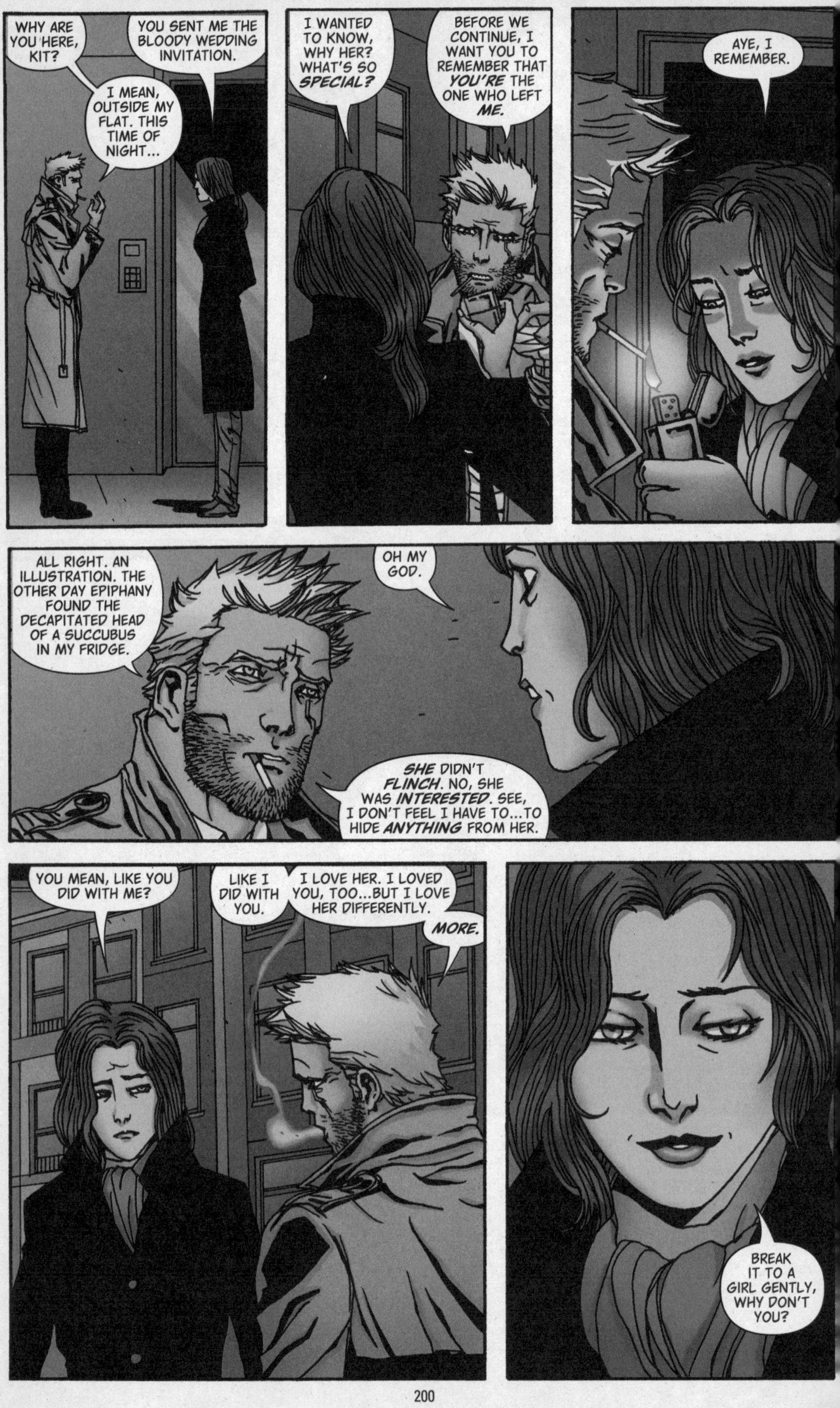
WHY ARE YOU HERE, KIT?
YOU SENT ME THE BLOODY WEDDING INVITATION.
I MEAN, OUTSIDE MY FLAT. THIS TIME OF NIGHT...
I WANTED TO KNOW, WHY HER? WHAT'S SO SPECIAL?
BEFORE WE CONTINUE, I WANT YOU TO REMEMBER THAT YOU'RE THE ONE WHO LEFT ME.
AYE, I REMEMBER.
ALL RIGHT. AN ILLUSTRATION. THE OTHER DAY EPIPHANY FOUND THE DECAPITATED HEAD OF A SUCCUBUS IN MY FRIDGE.
OH MY GOD.
SHE DIDN'T FLINCH. NO, SHE WAS INTERESTED. SEE, I DON'T FEEL I HAVE TO...TO HIDE ANYTHING FROM HER.
YOU MEAN, LIKE YOU DID WITH ME?
LIKE I DID WITH YOU.
I LOVE HER. I LOVED YOU, TOO...BUT I LOVE HER DIFFERENTLY.
MORE.
BREAK IT TO A GIRL GENTLY, WHY DON'T YOU?

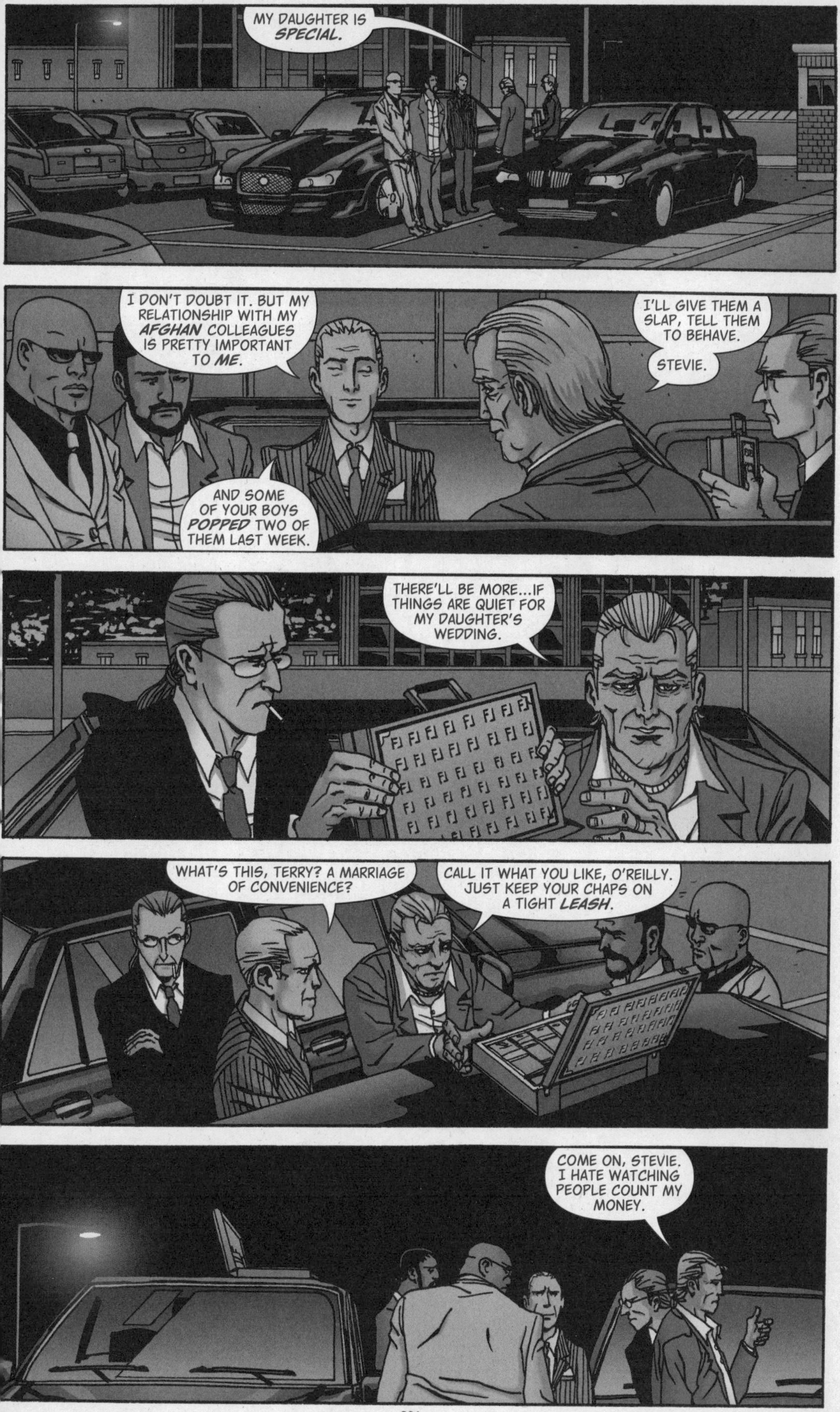
MY DAUGHTER IS SPECIAL.
I DON'T DOUBT IT. BUT MY RELATIONSHIP WITH MY AFGHAN COLLEAGUES IS PRETTY IMPORTANT TO ME.
AND SOME OF YOUR BOYS POPPED TWO OF THEM LAST WEEK.
I'LL GIVE THEM A SLAP, TELL THEM TO BEHAVE.
STEVIE.
THERE'LL BE MORE...IF THINGS ARE QUIET FOR MY DAUGHTER'S WEDDING.
WHAT'S THIS, TERRY? A MARRIAGE OF CONVENIENCE?
CALL IT WHAT YOU LIKE, O'REILLY. JUST KEEP YOUR CHAPS ON A TIGHT LEASH.
COME ON, STEVIE. I HATE WATCHING PEOPLE COUNT MY MONEY.

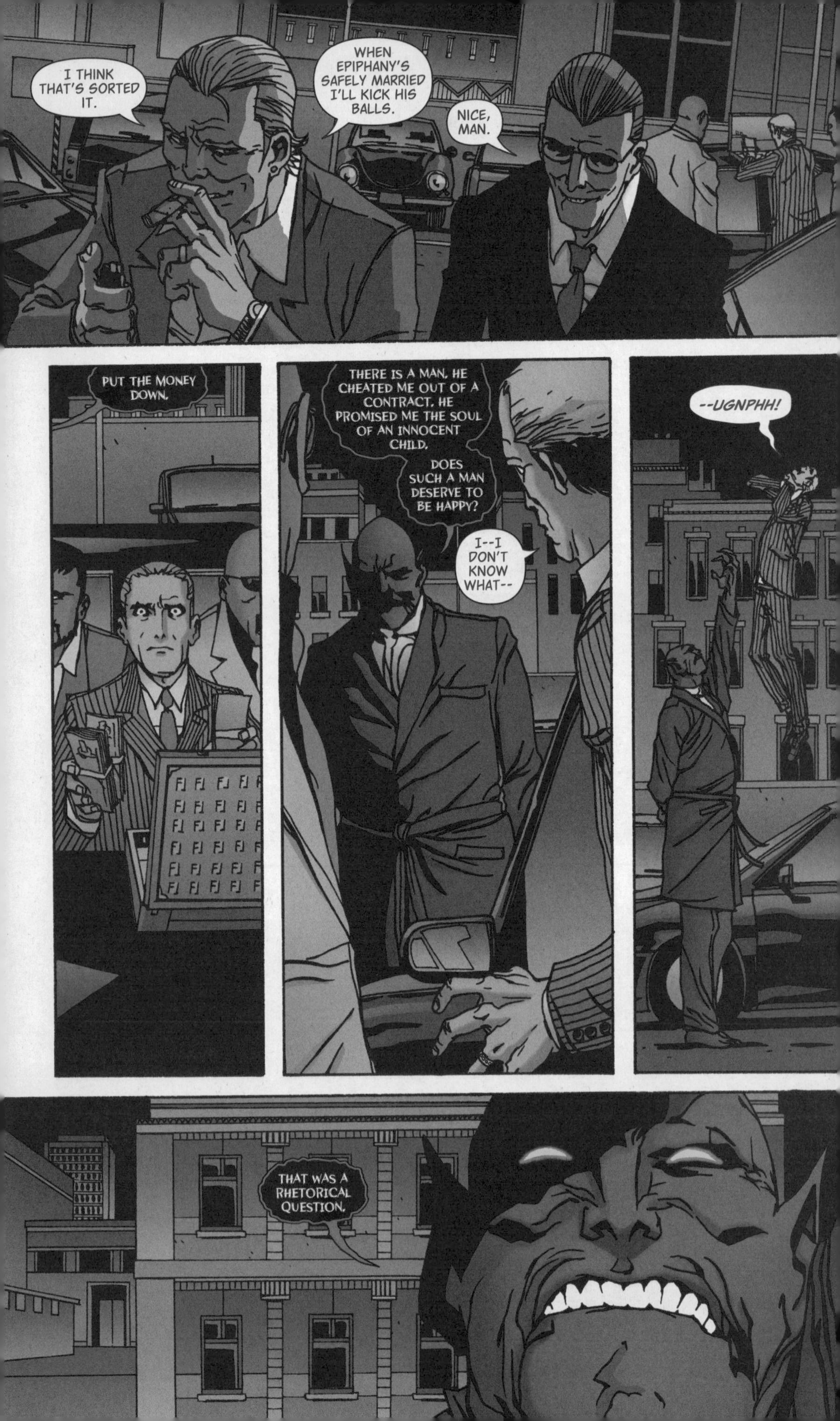
I THINK THAT'S SORTED IT.
WHEN EPIPHANY'S SAFELY MARRIED I'LL KICK HIS BALLS.
NICE, MAN.
PUT THE MONEY DOWN.
THERE IS A MAN. HE CHEATED ME OUT OF A CONTRACT. HE PROMISED ME THE SOUL OF AN INNOCENT CHILD.
DOES SUCH A MAN DESERVE TO BE HAPPY?
I--I DON'T KNOW WHAT--
--UGNPHH!
THAT WAS A RHETORICAL QUESTION.

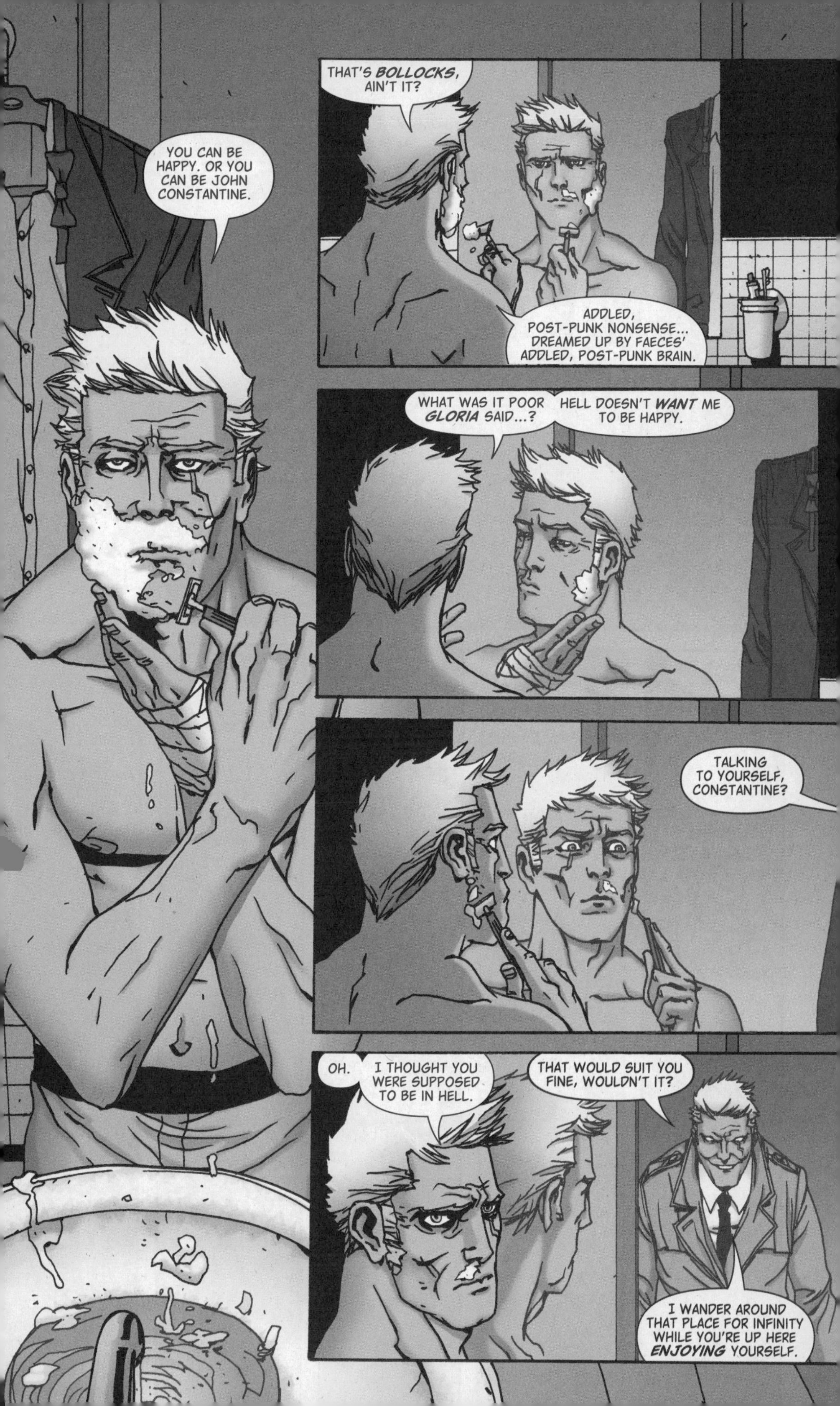
YOU CAN BE HAPPY. OR YOU CAN BE JOHN CONSTANTINE.
THAT'S **BOLLOCKS**, AIN'T IT?
ADDLED, POST-PUNK NONSENSE... DREAMED UP BY FAECES' ADDLED, POST-PUNK BRAIN.
WHAT WAS IT POOR **GLORIA** SAID...?
HELL DOESN'T **WANT** ME TO BE HAPPY.
TALKING TO YOURSELF, CONSTANTINE?
OH.
I THOUGHT YOU WERE SUPPOSED TO BE IN HELL.
THAT WOULD SUIT YOU FINE, WOULDN'T IT?
I WANDER AROUND THAT PLACE FOR INFINITY WHILE YOU'RE UP HERE **ENJOYING** YOURSELF.

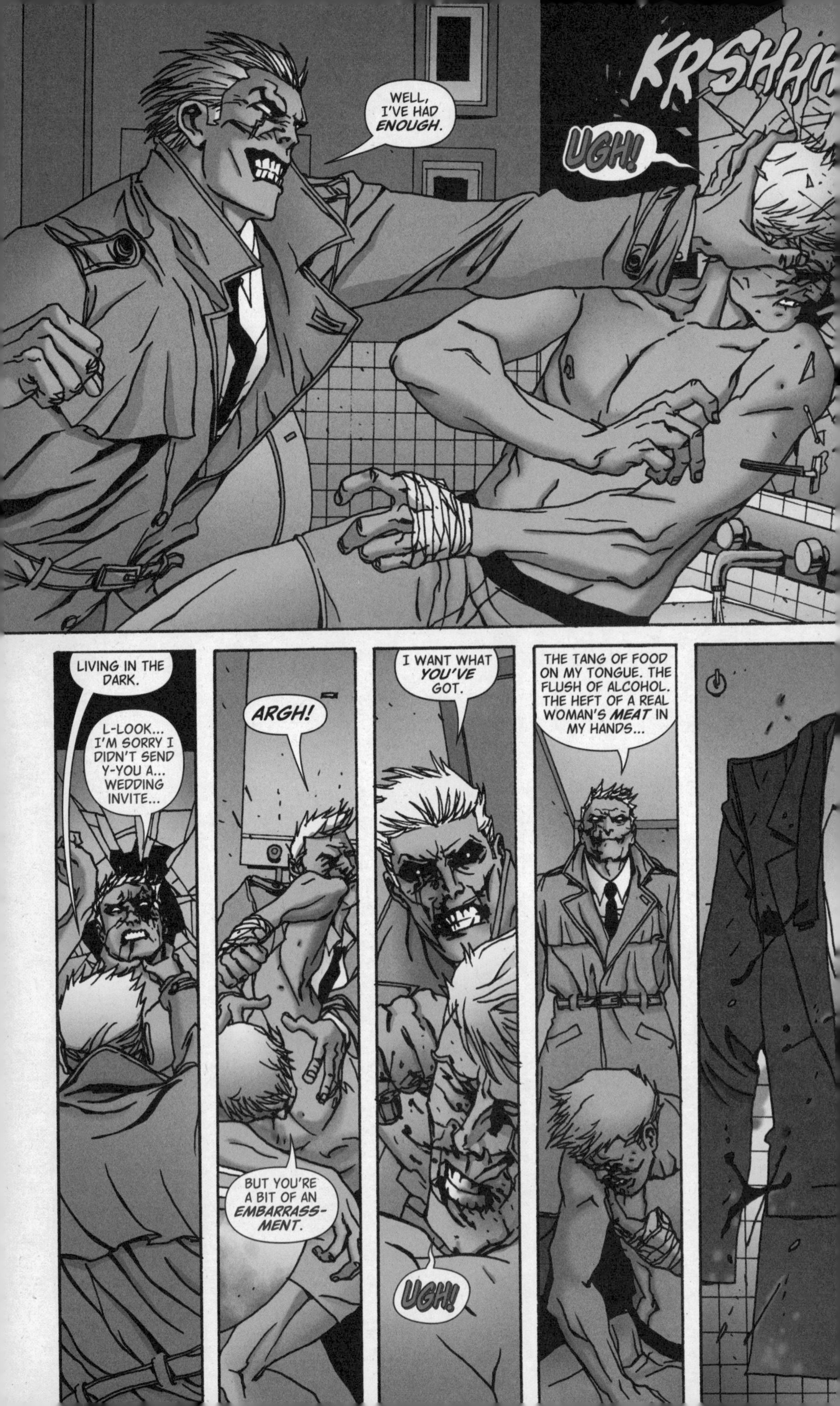
WELL, I'VE HAD ENOUGH.
KRSHHH
UGH!
LIVING IN THE DARK.
L-LOOK... I'M SORRY I DIDN'T SEND Y-YOU A... WEDDING INVITE...
ARGH!
BUT YOU'RE A BIT OF AN EMBARRASS-MENT.
I WANT WHAT YOU'VE GOT.
UGH!
THE TANG OF FOOD ON MY TONGUE. THE FLUSH OF ALCOHOL. THE HEFT OF A REAL WOMAN'S MEAT IN MY HANDS...

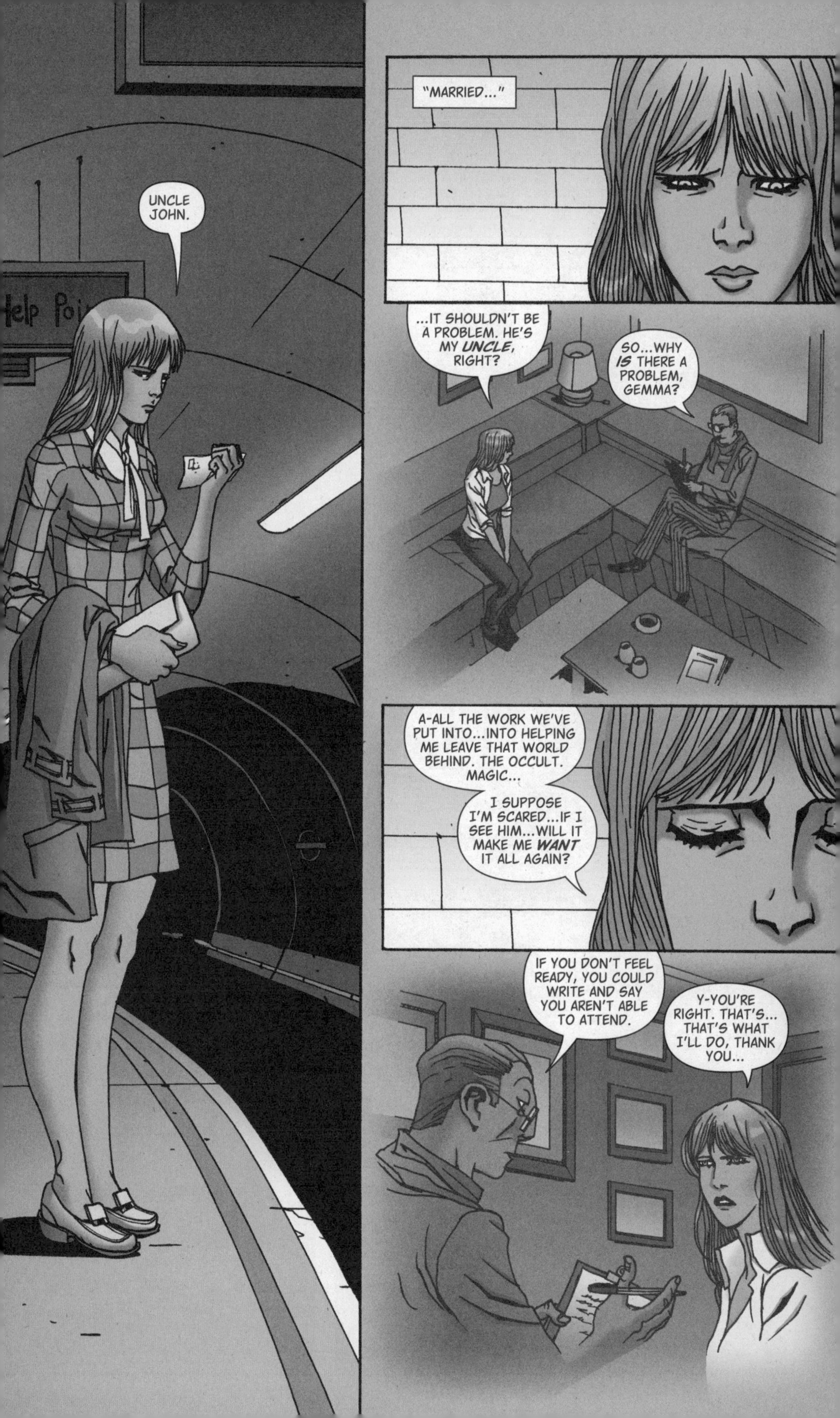

Help Poi
UNCLE JOHN.
"MARRIED..."
...IT SHOULDN'T BE A PROBLEM. HE'S MY UNCLE, RIGHT?
SO...WHY IS THERE A PROBLEM, GEMMA?
A-ALL THE WORK WE'VE PUT INTO...INTO HELPING ME LEAVE THAT WORLD BEHIND. THE OCCULT. MAGIC...
I SUPPOSE I'M SCARED...IF I SEE HIM...WILL IT MAKE ME WANT IT ALL AGAIN?
IF YOU DON'T FEEL READY, YOU COULD WRITE AND SAY YOU AREN'T ABLE TO ATTEND.
Y-YOU'RE RIGHT. THAT'S... THAT'S WHAT I'LL DO, THANK YOU...

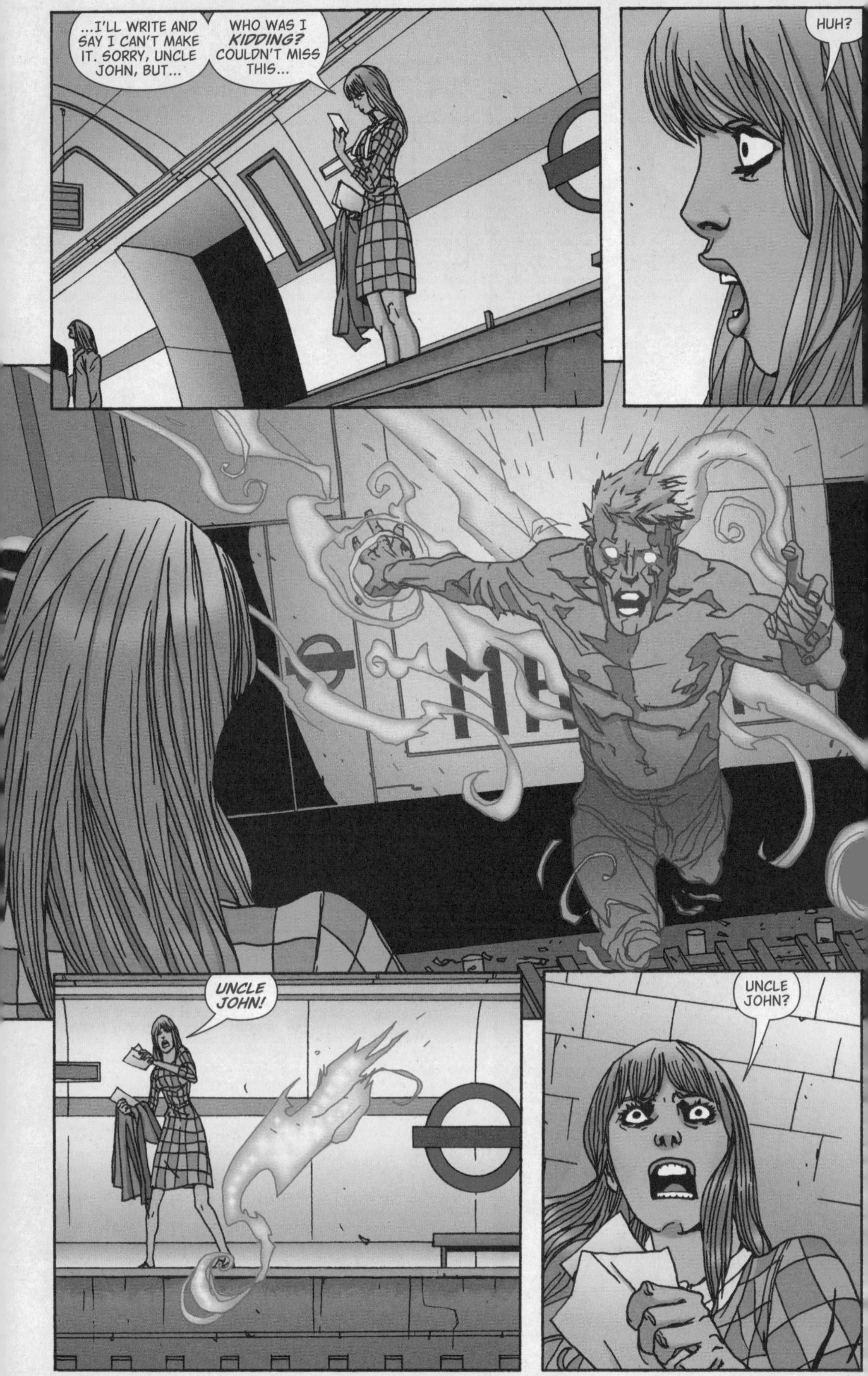
...I'LL WRITE AND SAY I CAN'T MAKE IT. SORRY, UNCLE JOHN, BUT...
WHO WAS I *KIDDING?* COULDN'T MISS THIS...
HUH?
UNCLE JOHN!
UNCLE JOHN?

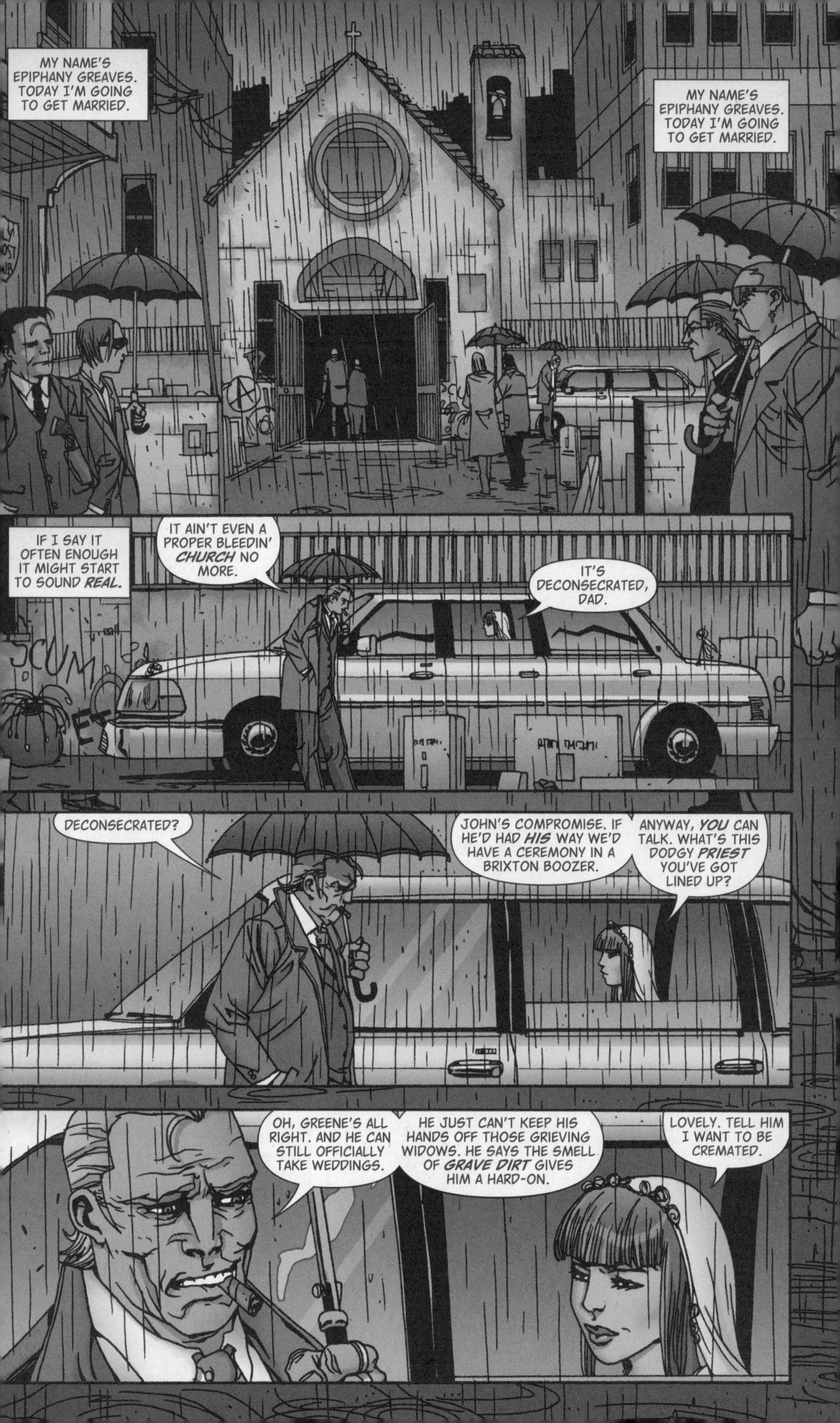
MY NAME'S EPIPHANY GREAVES. TODAY I'M GOING TO GET MARRIED.
MY NAME'S EPIPHANY GREAVES. TODAY I'M GOING TO GET MARRIED.
IF I SAY IT OFTEN ENOUGH IT MIGHT START TO SOUND *REAL.*
IT AIN'T EVEN A PROPER BLEEDIN' *CHURCH* NO MORE.
IT'S DECONSECRATED, DAD.
DECONSECRATED?
JOHN'S COMPROMISE. IF HE'D HAD *HIS* WAY WE'D HAVE A CEREMONY IN A BRIXTON BOOZER.
ANYWAY, *YOU* CAN TALK. WHAT'S THIS DODGY *PRIEST* YOU'VE GOT LINED UP?
OH, GREENE'S ALL RIGHT. AND HE CAN STILL OFFICIALLY TAKE WEDDINGS.
HE JUST CAN'T KEEP HIS HANDS OFF THOSE GRIEVING WIDOWS. HE SAYS THE SMELL OF *GRAVE DIRT* GIVES HIM A HARD-ON.
LOVELY. TELL HIM I WANT TO BE CREMATED.

AH, MY LITTLE PRINCESS, GETTING MARRIED. I CAN'T BELIEVE IT. IF ONLY YOUR POOR MUM WAS HERE--

STOP IT DAD, OR YOU'LL START US *BOTH* OFF.

THIS *OLD MAN*, CONSTANTINE. YOU DO...I MEAN...

YES, DAD. HE'S EVERYTHING I WANT.

I AIN'T EVEN GOING TO ASK WHAT YOU SEE IN HIM.

FOR ONE THING, HE'S VERY *ATHLETIC* FOR HIS AGE.

I ADMIT, PA OF ME WOND IF HE'D SHOW

YOU SCOUSE *TIT!* LATE FOR YOUR OWN FUCKING *WEDDING.*

WHAT THE FUCK *HAPPENED* TO YOU?

CUT MYSELF *SHAVING*, TEL.

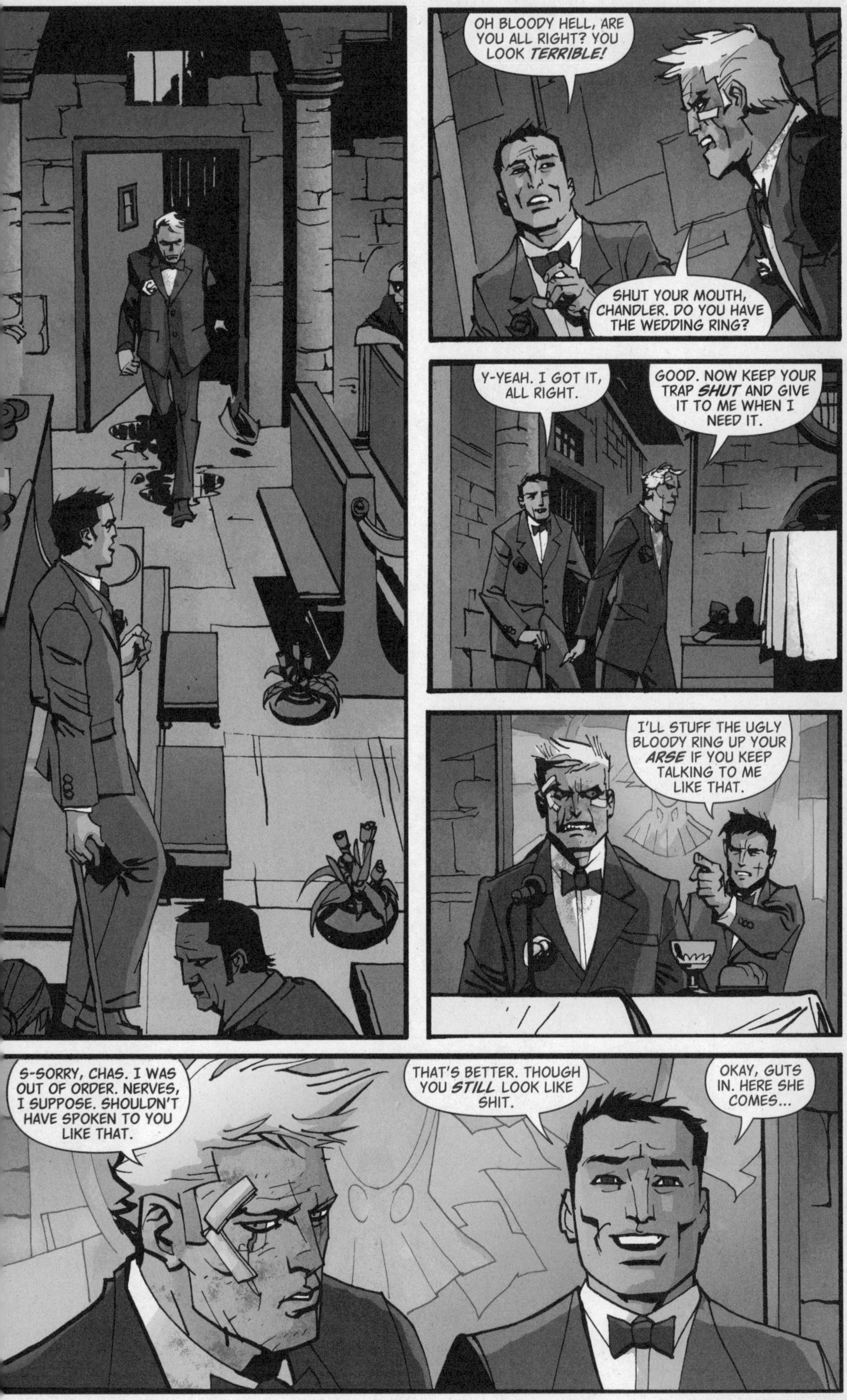
OH BLOODY HELL, ARE YOU ALL RIGHT? YOU LOOK *TERRIBLE!*
SHUT YOUR MOUTH, CHANDLER. DO YOU HAVE THE WEDDING RING?
Y-YEAH. I GOT IT, ALL RIGHT.
GOOD. NOW KEEP YOUR TRAP *SHUT* AND GIVE IT TO ME WHEN I NEED IT.
I'LL STUFF THE UGLY BLOODY RING UP YOUR *ARSE* IF YOU KEEP TALKING TO ME LIKE THAT.
S-SORRY, CHAS. I WAS OUT OF ORDER. NERVES, I SUPPOSE. SHOULDN'T HAVE SPOKEN TO YOU LIKE THAT.
THAT'S BETTER. THOUGH YOU *STILL* LOOK LIKE SHIT.
OKAY, GUTS IN. HERE SHE COMES...

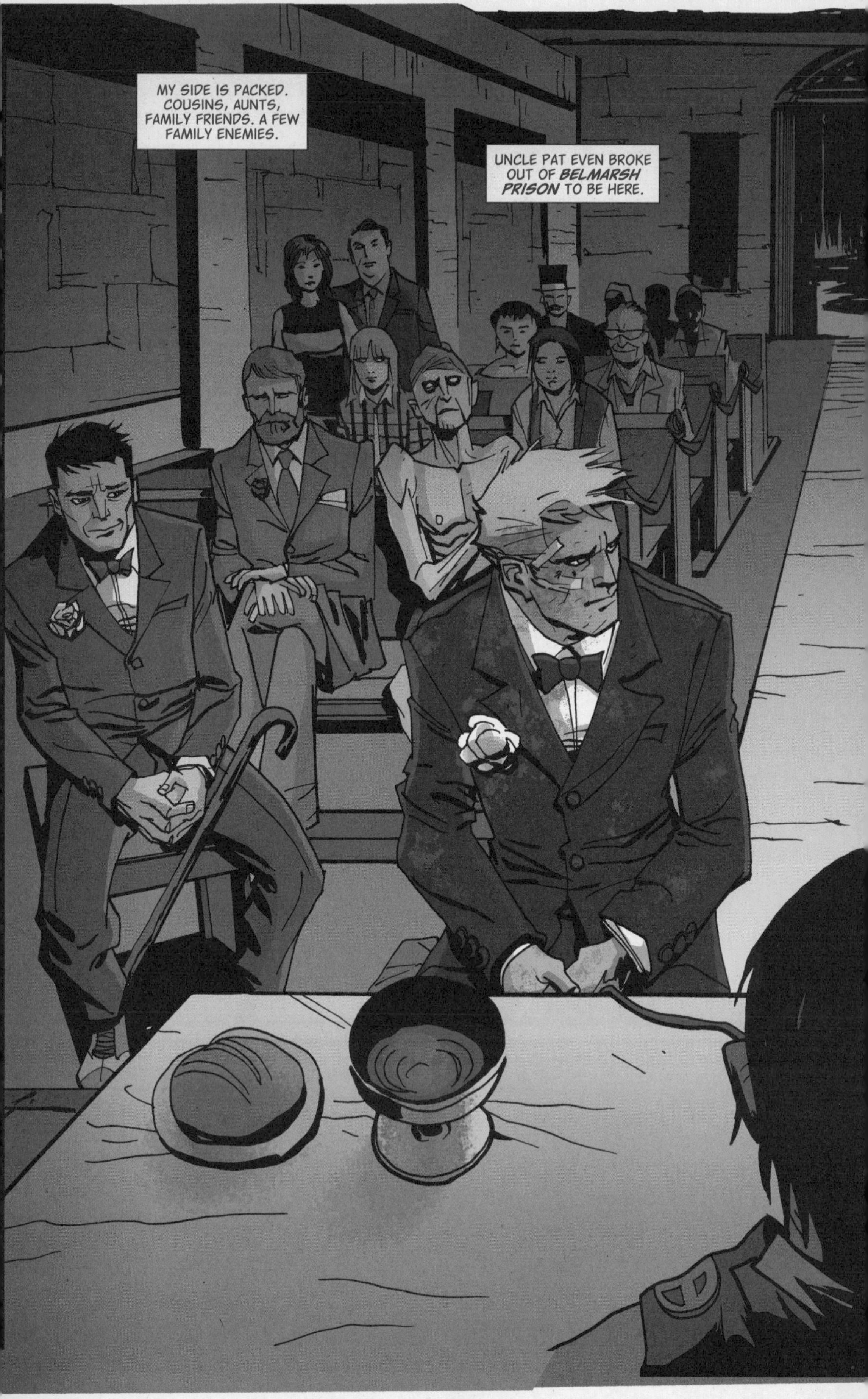
MY SIDE IS PACKED. COUSINS, AUNTS, FAMILY FRIENDS. A FEW FAMILY ENEMIES.
UNCLE PAT EVEN BROKE OUT OF *BELMARSH PRISON* TO BE HERE.

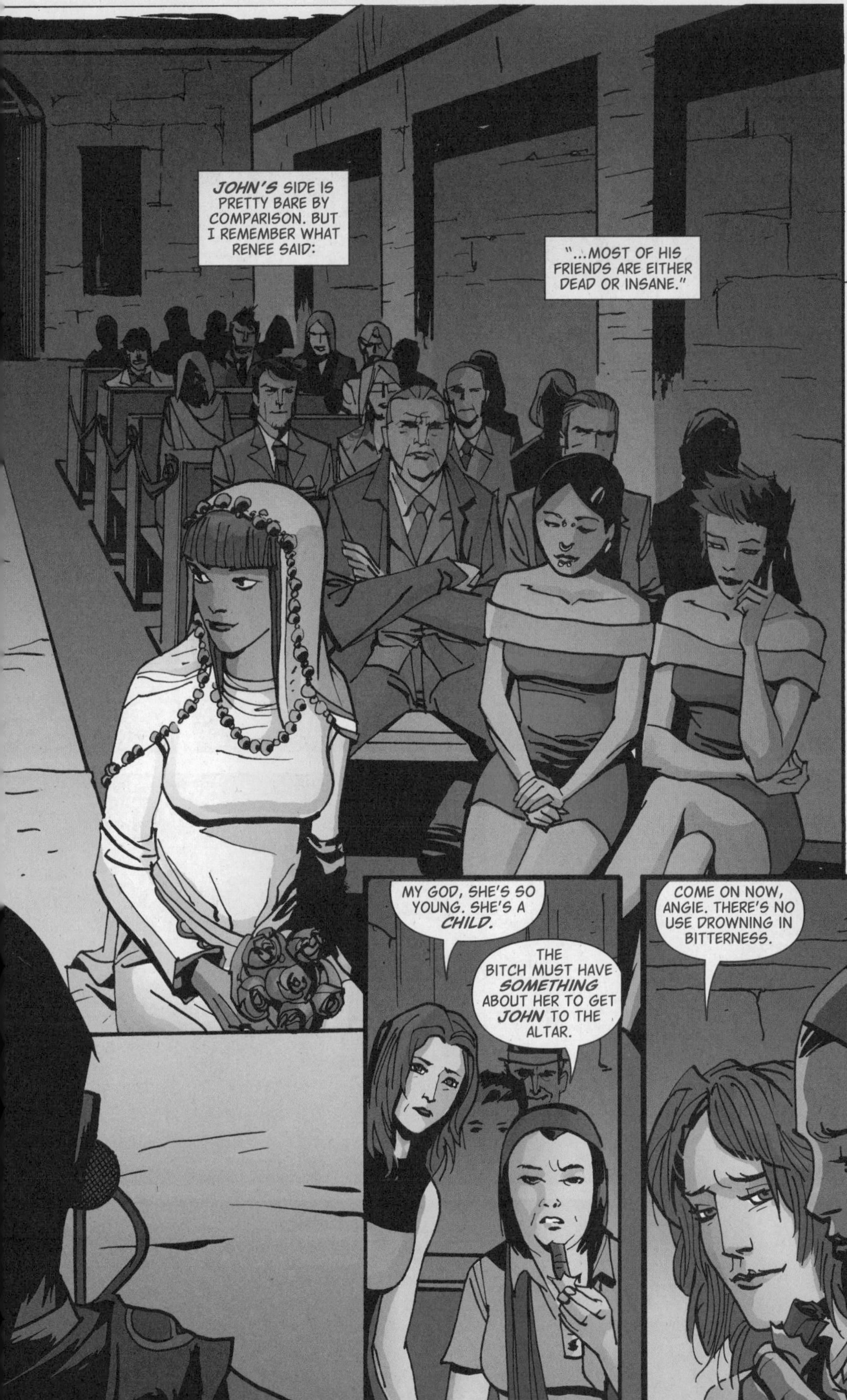
JOHN'S SIDE IS PRETTY BARE BY COMPARISON. BUT I REMEMBER WHAT RENEE SAID:
"...MOST OF HIS FRIENDS ARE EITHER DEAD OR INSANE."
MY GOD, SHE'S SO YOUNG. SHE'S A CHILD.
THE BITCH MUST HAVE SOMETHING ABOUT HER TO GET JOHN TO THE ALTAR.
COME ON NOW, ANGIE. THERE'S NO USE DROWNING IN BITTERNESS.

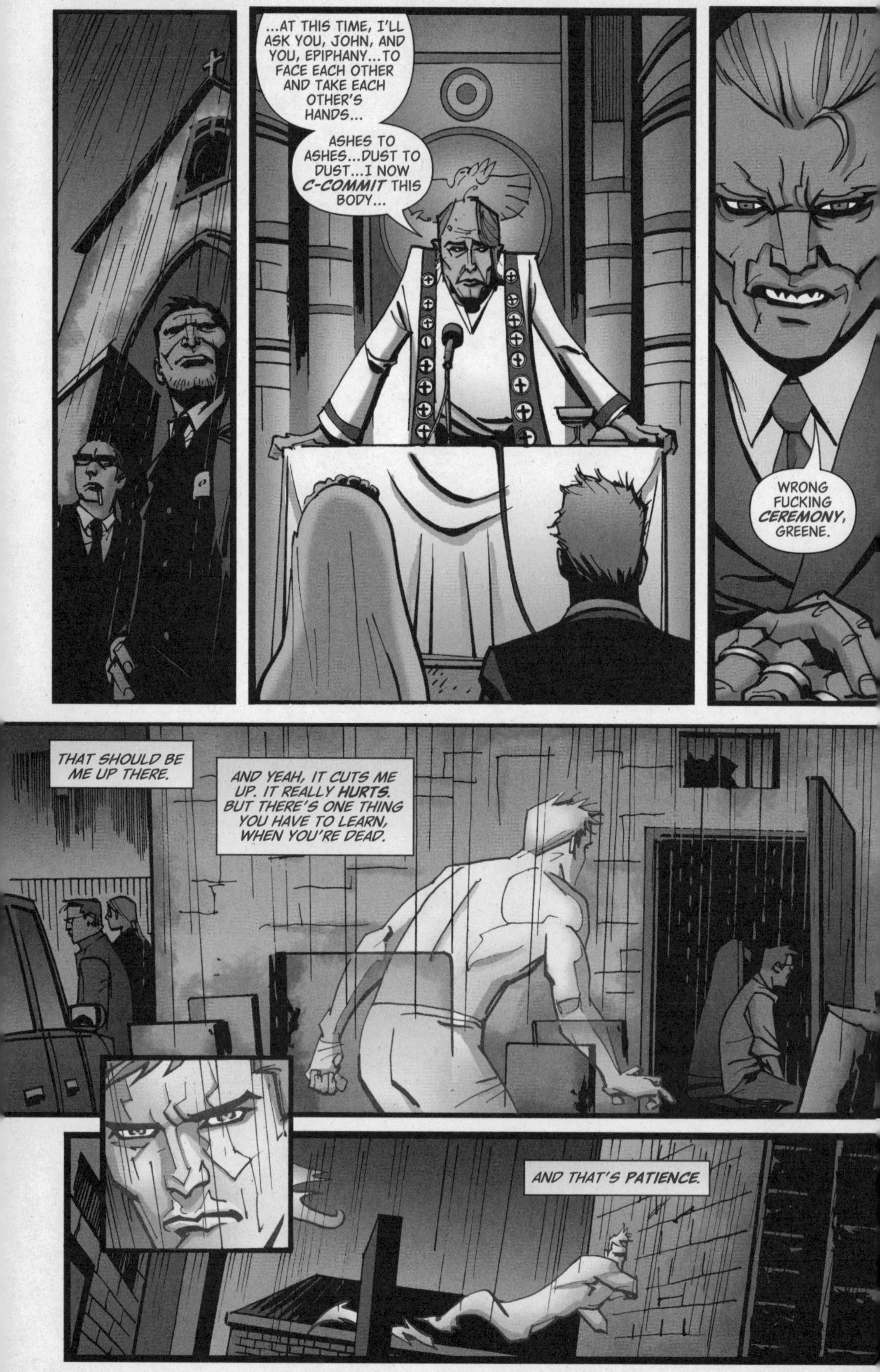

...AT THIS TIME, I'LL ASK YOU, JOHN, AND YOU, EPIPHANY...TO FACE EACH OTHER AND TAKE EACH OTHER'S HANDS...
ASHES TO ASHES...DUST TO DUST...I NOW C-COMMIT THIS BODY...
WRONG FUCKING CEREMONY, GREENE.
THAT SHOULD BE ME UP THERE.
AND YEAH, IT CUTS ME UP. IT REALLY HURTS. BUT THERE'S ONE THING YOU HAVE TO LEARN, WHEN YOU'RE DEAD.
AND THAT'S PATIENCE.

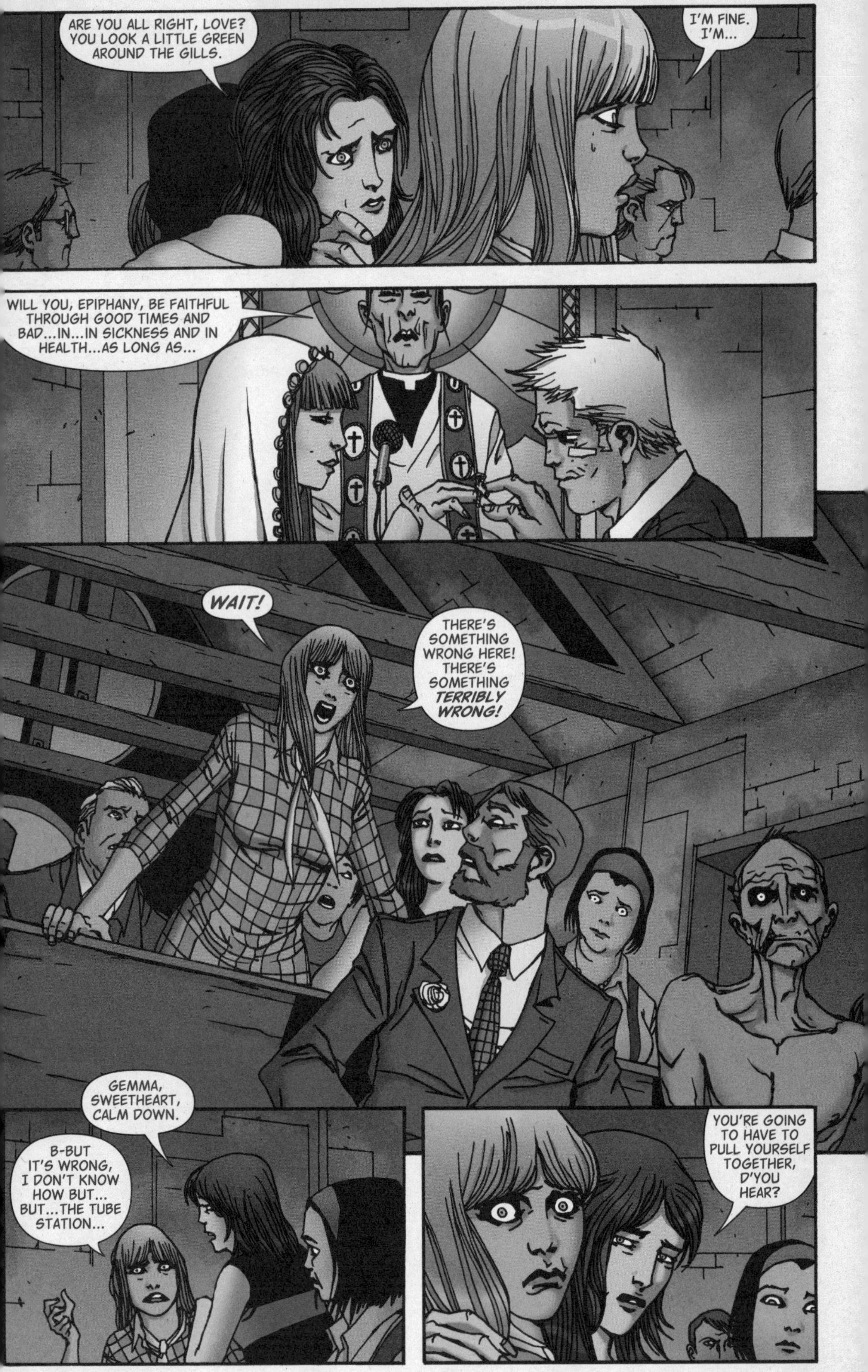

ARE YOU ALL RIGHT, LOVE? YOU LOOK A LITTLE GREEN AROUND THE GILLS.
I'M FINE. I'M...
WILL YOU, EPIPHANY, BE FAITHFUL THROUGH GOOD TIMES AND BAD...IN...IN SICKNESS AND IN HEALTH...AS LONG AS...
WAIT!
THERE'S SOMETHING WRONG HERE! THERE'S SOMETHING TERRIBLY WRONG!
GEMMA, SWEETHEART, CALM DOWN.
B-BUT IT'S WRONG, I DON'T KNOW HOW BUT... BUT...THE TUBE STATION...
YOU'RE GOING TO HAVE TO PULL YOURSELF TOGETHER, D'YOU HEAR?

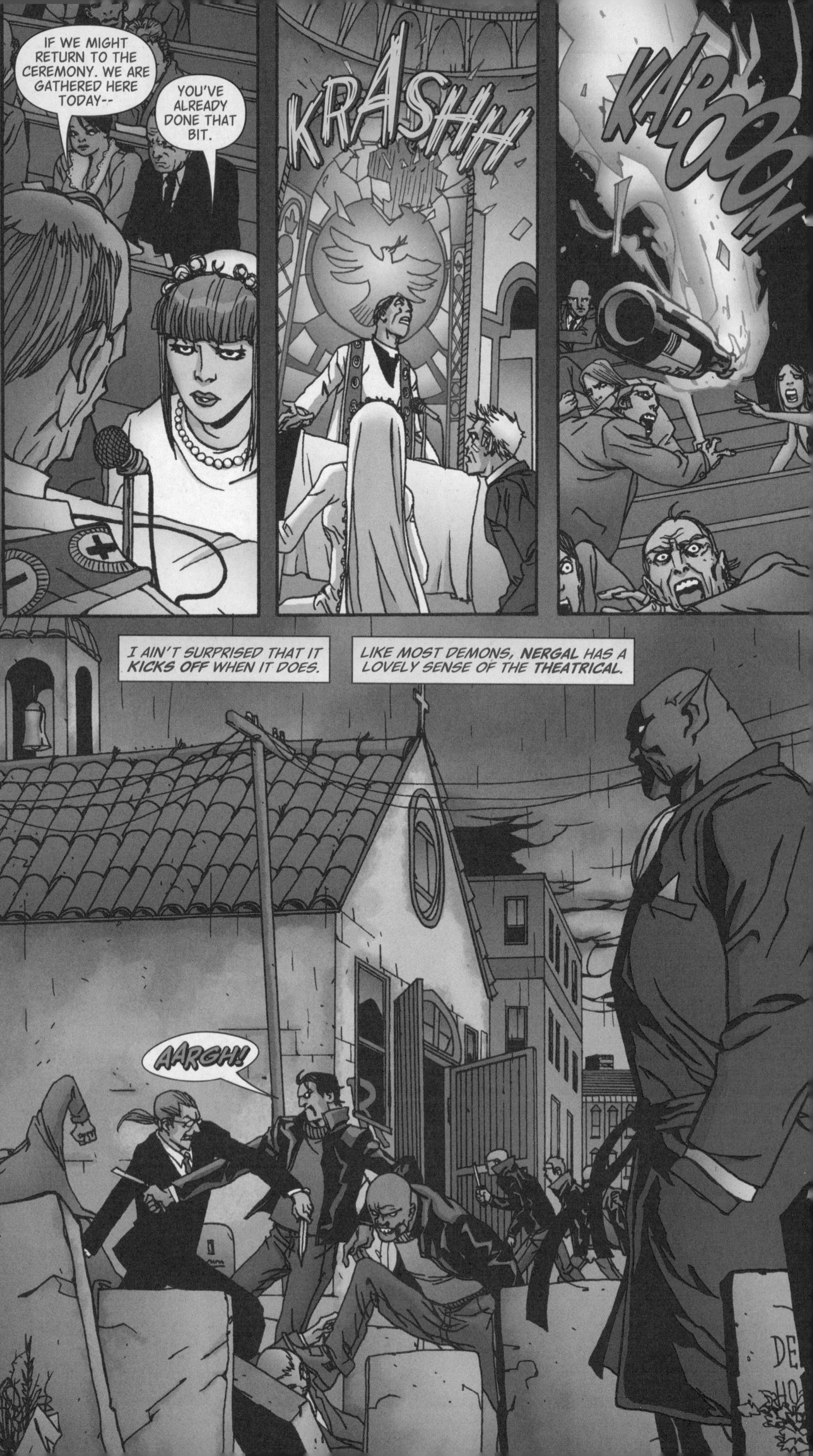
IF WE MIGHT RETURN TO THE CEREMONY. WE ARE GATHERED HERE TODAY--
YOU'VE ALREADY DONE THAT BIT.
KRASHH
KABOOOM
I AIN'T SURPRISED THAT IT KICKS OFF WHEN IT DOES.
LIKE MOST DEMONS, NERGAL HAS A LOVELY SENSE OF THE THEATRICAL.
AARGH!

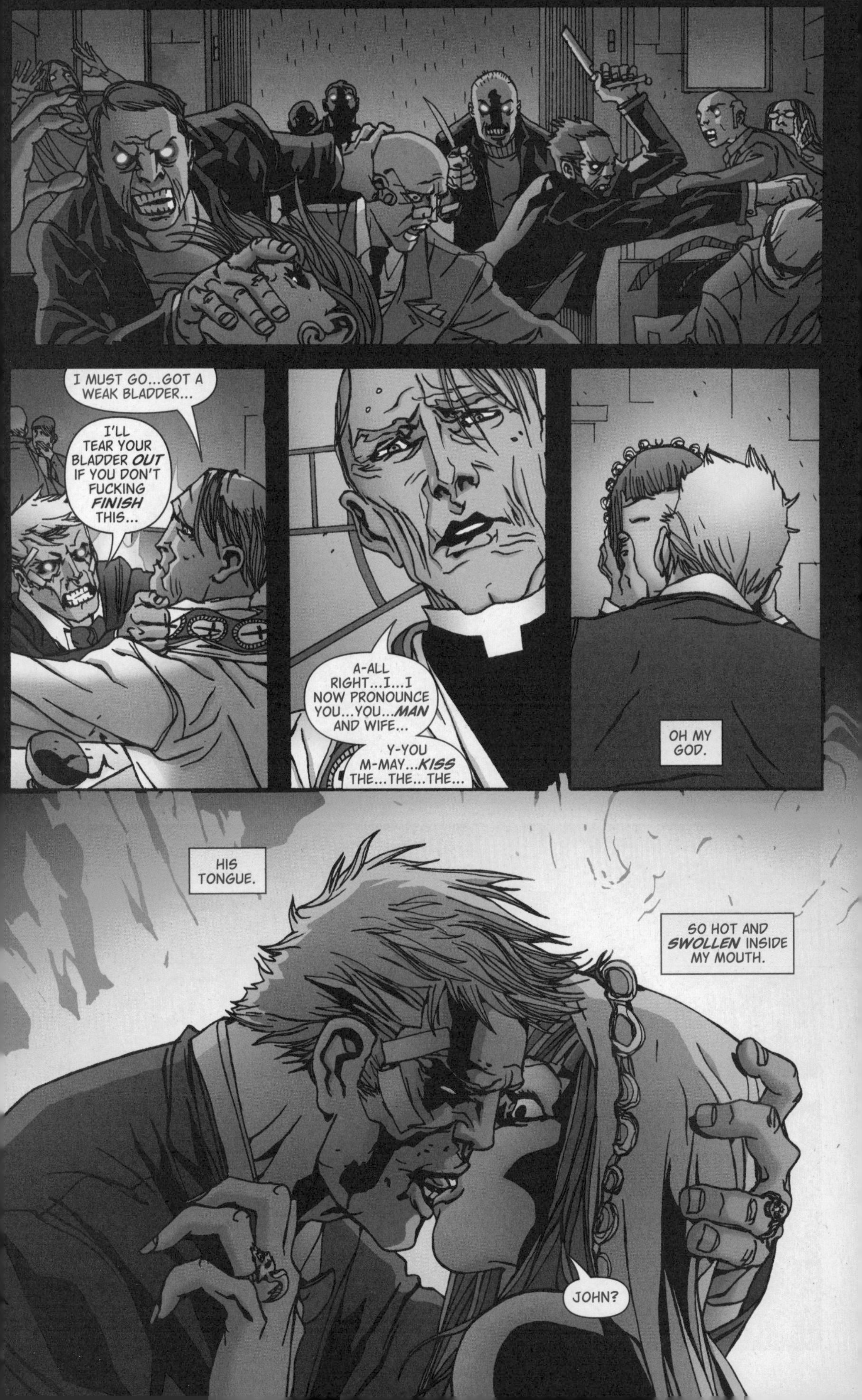
I MUST GO...GOT A WEAK BLADDER...
I'LL TEAR YOUR BLADDER OUT IF YOU DON'T FUCKING FINISH THIS...
A-ALL RIGHT...I...I NOW PRONOUNCE YOU...YOU...MAN AND WIFE...
Y-YOU M-MAY...KISS THE...THE...THE...
OH MY GOD.
HIS TONGUE.
SO HOT AND SWOLLEN INSIDE MY MOUTH.
JOHN?

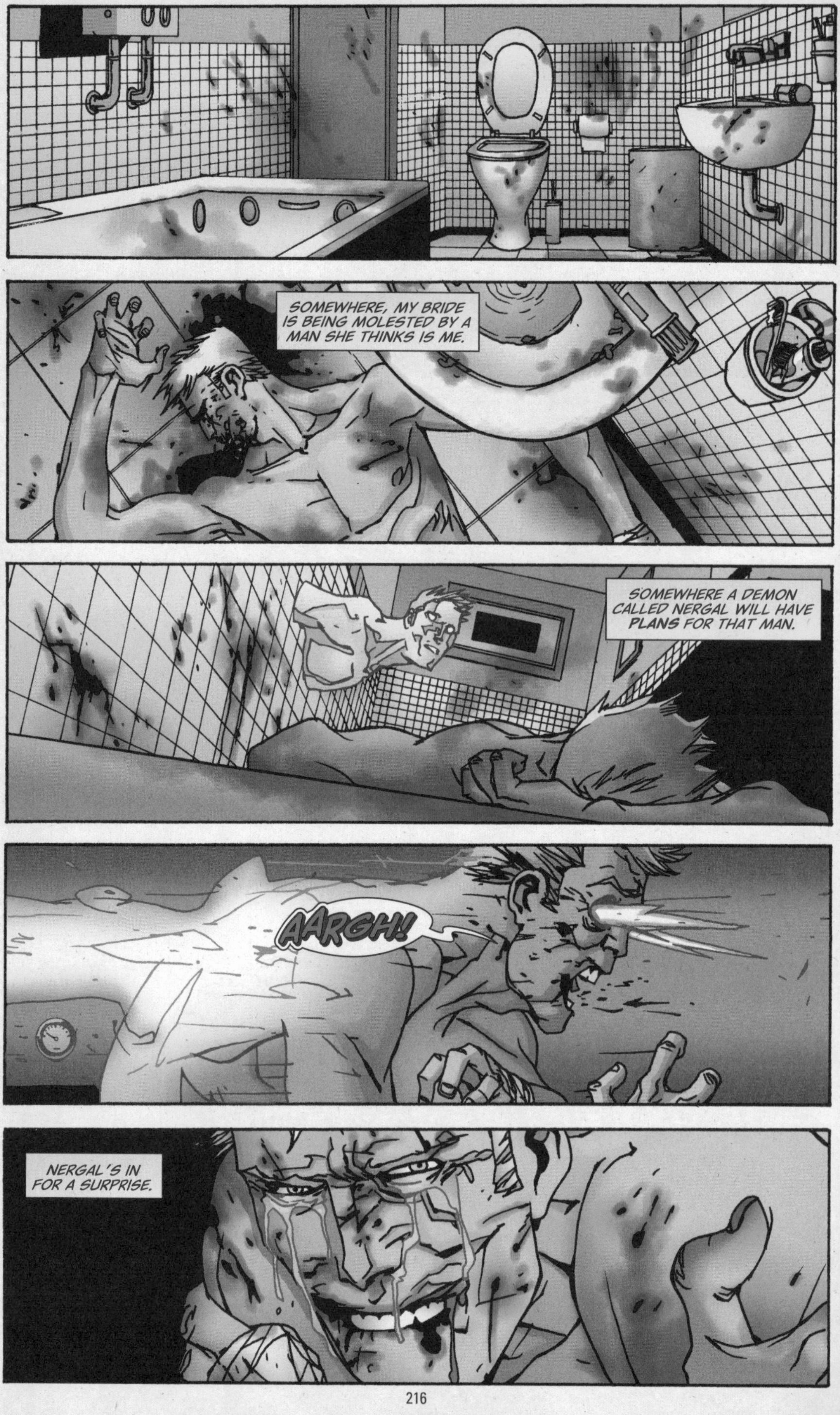
SOMEWHERE, MY BRIDE IS BEING MOLESTED BY A MAN SHE THINKS IS ME.
SOMEWHERE A DEMON CALLED NERGAL WILL HAVE PLANS FOR THAT MAN.
AARGH!
NERGAL'S IN FOR A SURPRISE.

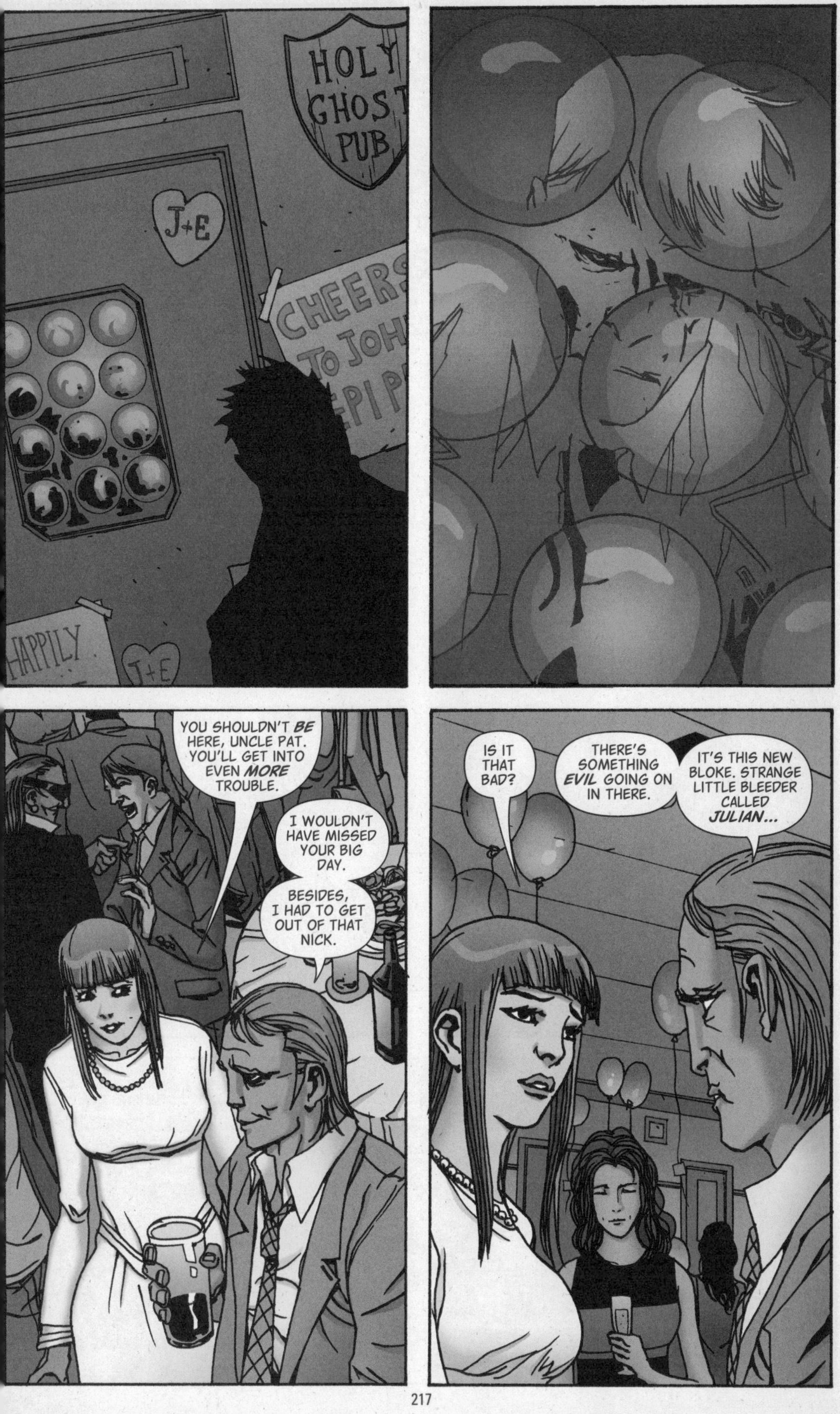
HOLY GHOST PUB
J+E
CHEERS TO JOH EPIP
HAPPILY
J+E
YOU SHOULDN'T *BE* HERE, UNCLE PAT. YOU'LL GET INTO EVEN *MORE* TROUBLE.
I WOULDN'T HAVE MISSED YOUR BIG DAY.
BESIDES, I HAD TO GET OUT OF THAT NICK.
IS IT THAT BAD?
THERE'S SOMETHING *EVIL* GOING ON IN THERE.
IT'S THIS NEW BLOKE. STRANGE LITTLE BLEEDER CALLED *JULIAN...*

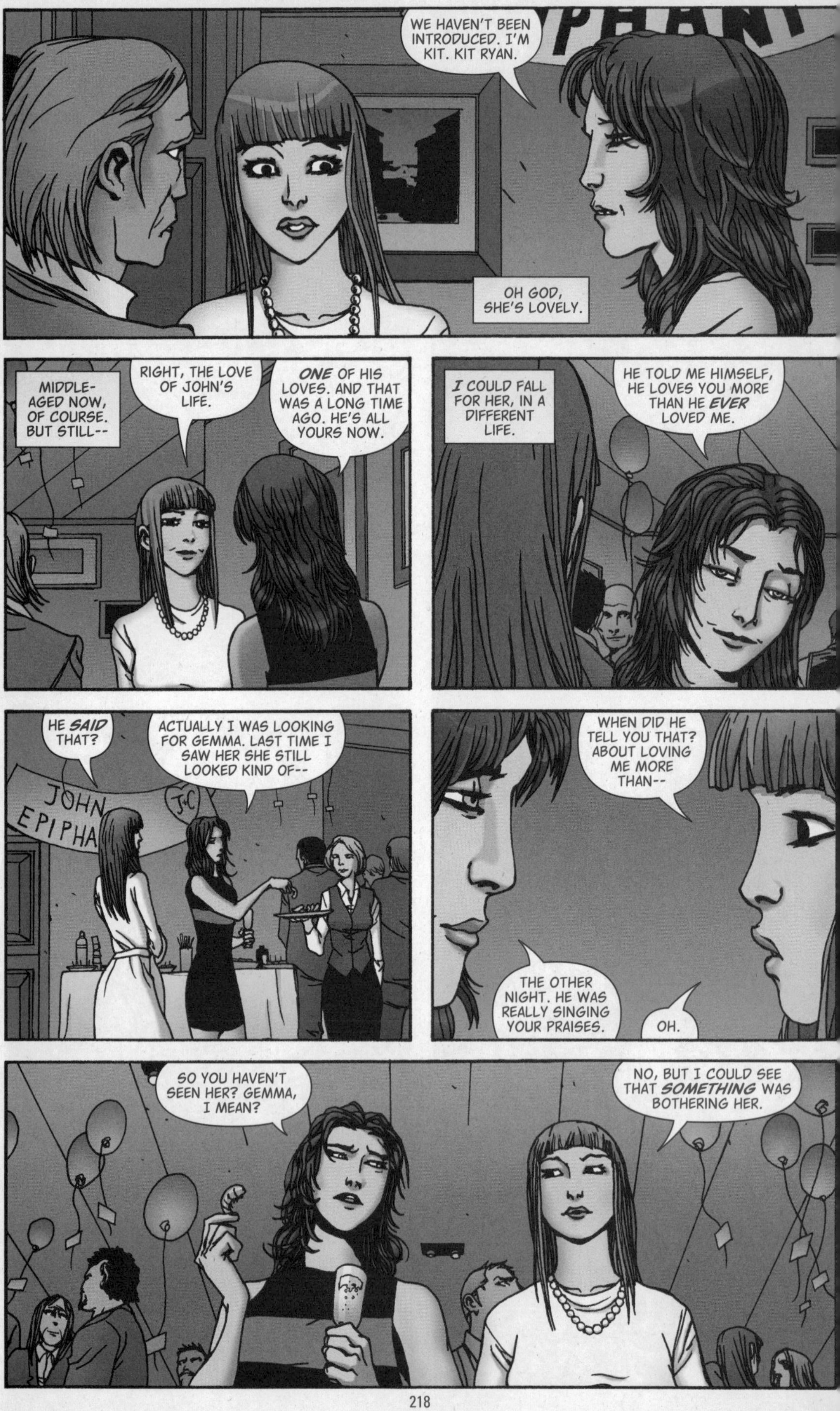
WE HAVEN'T BEEN INTRODUCED. I'M KIT. KIT RYAN.
OH GOD, SHE'S LOVELY.
MIDDLE-AGED NOW, OF COURSE. BUT STILL--
RIGHT, THE LOVE OF JOHN'S LIFE.
ONE OF HIS LOVES. AND THAT WAS A LONG TIME AGO. HE'S ALL YOURS NOW.
I COULD FALL FOR HER, IN A DIFFERENT LIFE.
HE TOLD ME HIMSELF, HE LOVES YOU MORE THAN HE EVER LOVED ME.
HE SAID THAT?
ACTUALLY I WAS LOOKING FOR GEMMA. LAST TIME I SAW HER SHE STILL LOOKED KIND OF--
WHEN DID HE TELL YOU THAT? ABOUT LOVING ME MORE THAN--
THE OTHER NIGHT. HE WAS REALLY SINGING YOUR PRAISES.
OH.
SO YOU HAVEN'T SEEN HER? GEMMA, I MEAN?
NO, BUT I COULD SEE THAT SOMETHING WAS BOTHERING HER.

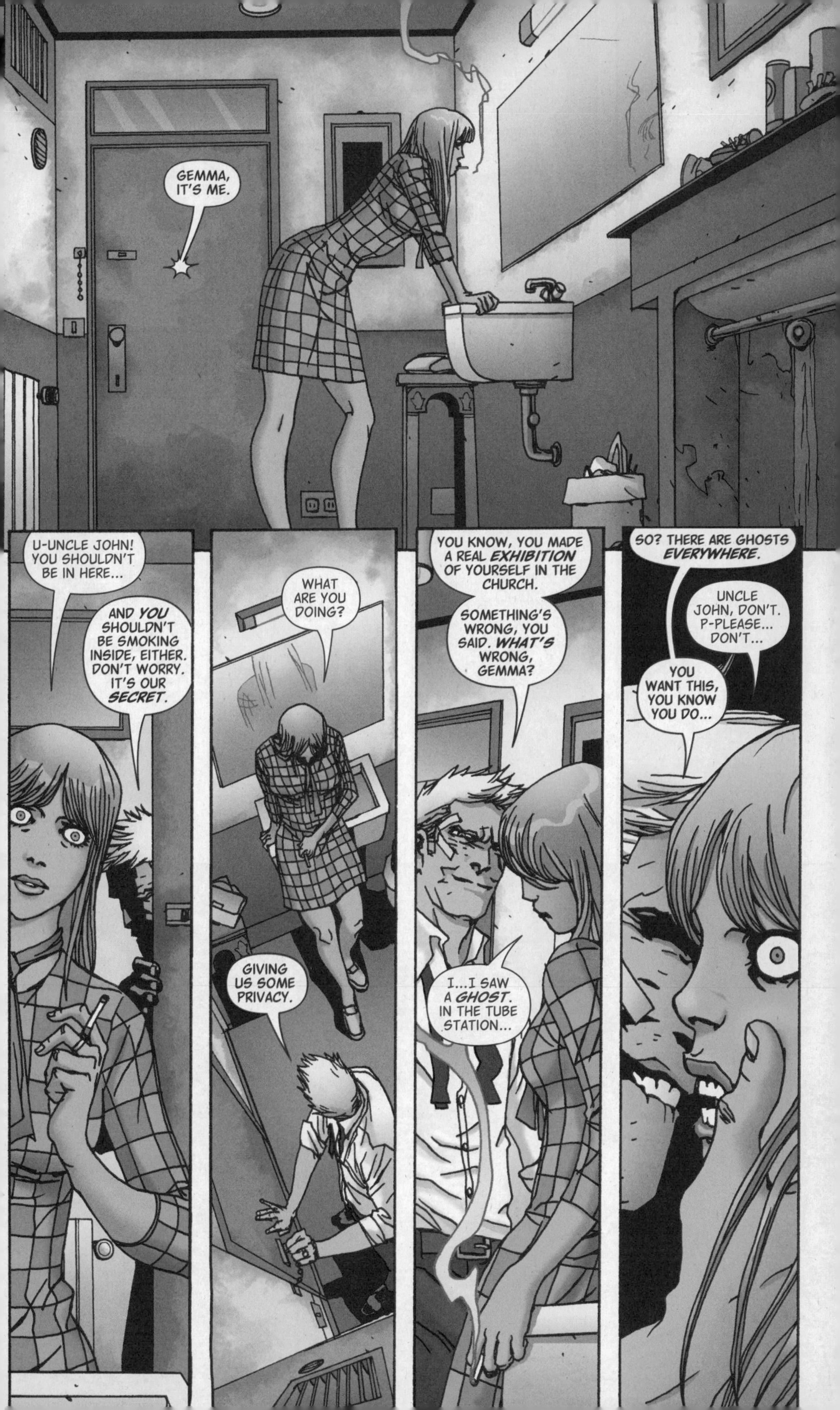
GEMMA, IT'S ME.
U-UNCLE JOHN! YOU SHOULDN'T BE IN HERE...
AND YOU SHOULDN'T BE SMOKING INSIDE, EITHER. DON'T WORRY. IT'S OUR SECRET.
WHAT ARE YOU DOING?
GIVING US SOME PRIVACY.
YOU KNOW, YOU MADE A REAL EXHIBITION OF YOURSELF IN THE CHURCH.
SOMETHING'S WRONG, YOU SAID. WHAT'S WRONG, GEMMA?
I...I SAW A GHOST. IN THE TUBE STATION...
SO? THERE ARE GHOSTS EVERYWHERE.
UNCLE JOHN, DON'T. P-PLEASE... DON'T...
YOU WANT THIS, YOU KNOW YOU DO...

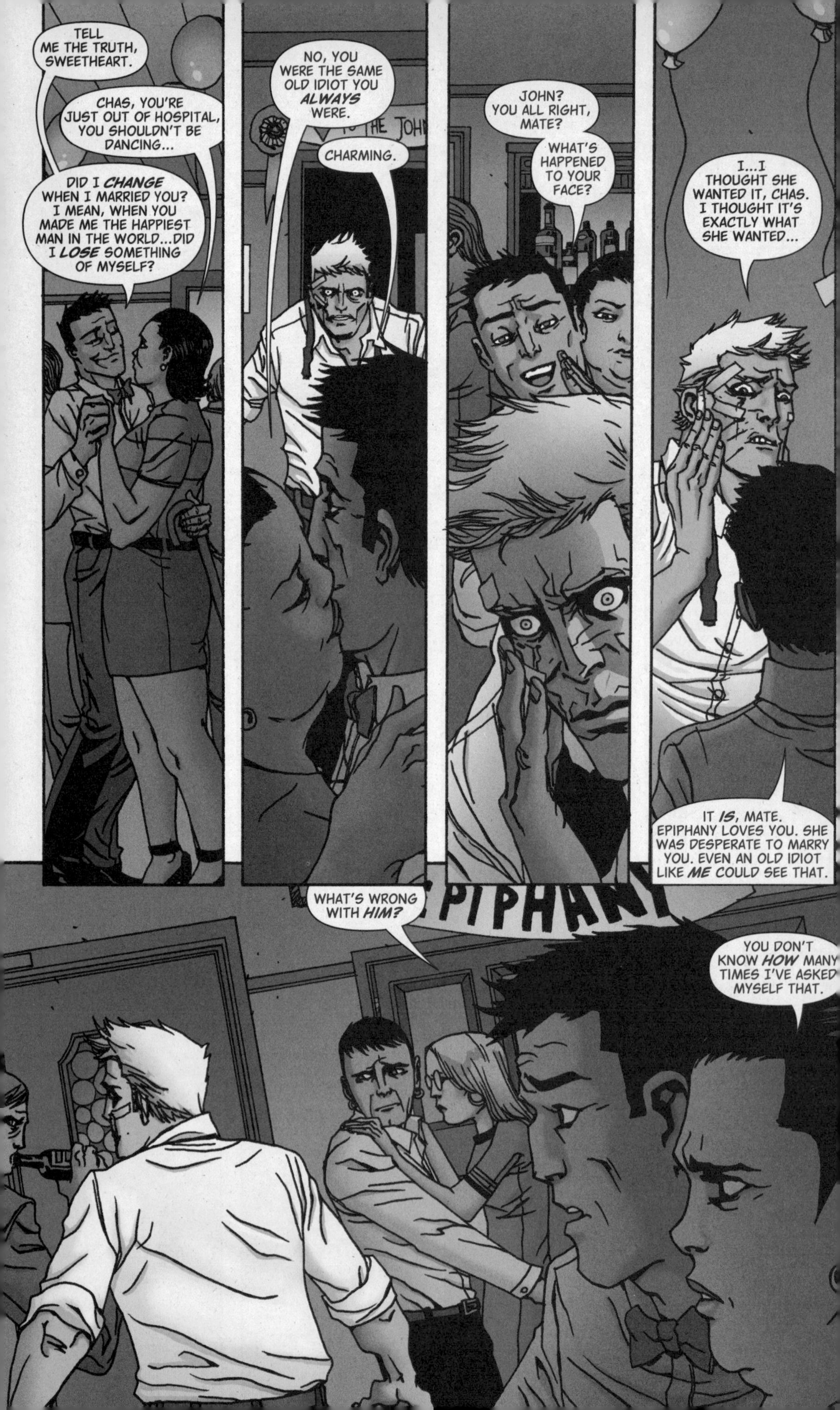
TELL ME THE TRUTH, SWEETHEART.
CHAS, YOU'RE JUST OUT OF HOSPITAL, YOU SHOULDN'T BE DANCING...
DID I *CHANGE* WHEN I MARRIED YOU? I MEAN, WHEN YOU MADE ME THE HAPPIEST MAN IN THE WORLD...DID I *LOSE* SOMETHING OF MYSELF?
NO, YOU WERE THE SAME OLD IDIOT YOU *ALWAYS* WERE.
CHARMING.
TO THE JOHN
JOHN? YOU ALL RIGHT, MATE?
WHAT'S HAPPENED TO YOUR FACE?
I...I THOUGHT SHE WANTED IT, CHAS. I THOUGHT IT'S EXACTLY WHAT SHE WANTED...
IT *IS*, MATE. EPIPHANY LOVES YOU. SHE WAS DESPERATE TO MARRY YOU. EVEN AN OLD IDIOT LIKE *ME* COULD SEE THAT.
WHAT'S WRONG WITH *HIM?*
EPIPHANY
YOU DON'T KNOW *HOW* MANY TIMES I'VE ASKED MYSELF THAT.

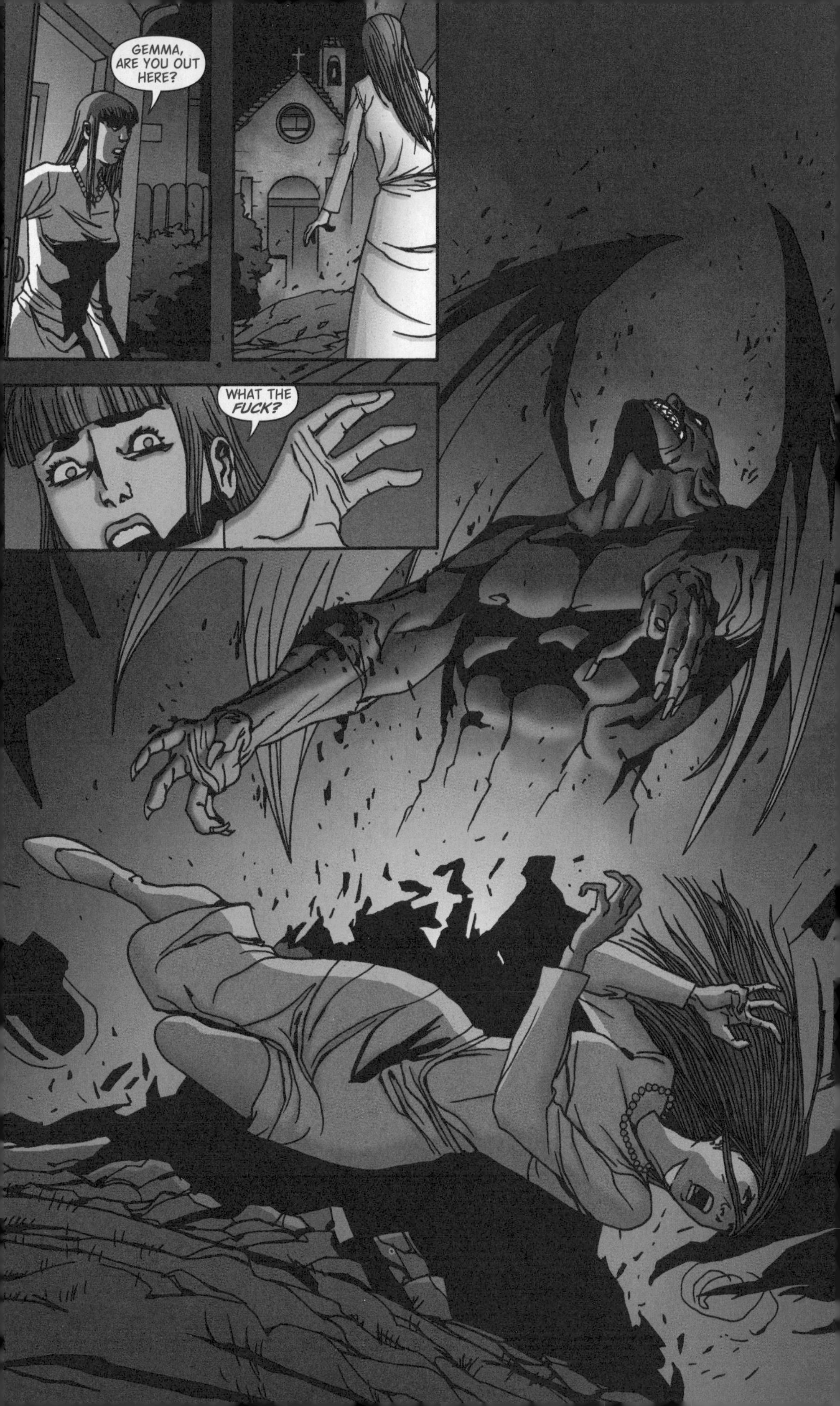
GEMMA, ARE YOU OUT HERE?
WHAT THE *FUCK?*

SORRY. TH-THIS IS A *PRIVATE* FUNCTION.

MANY YEARS AGO YOUR HUSBAND TRICKED ME OUT OF A RIGHTFUL FEE, THE SOUL OF AN INNOCENT CHILD.

YOU WILL PAY THAT DEBT, AND YOUR DEATH WILL GIVE HIM SUCH MISERY.

NGGN... I...I'M NOT INNOCENT, YOU *PRICK*... AND...AND I'M... TWENTY-THREE YEARS OLD...

TH-THE RING...

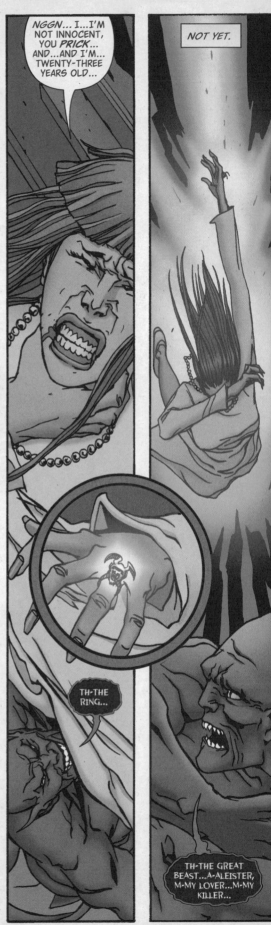

NOT YET.

TH-THE GREAT BEAST...A-ALEISTER, M-MY LOVER...M-MY KILLER...

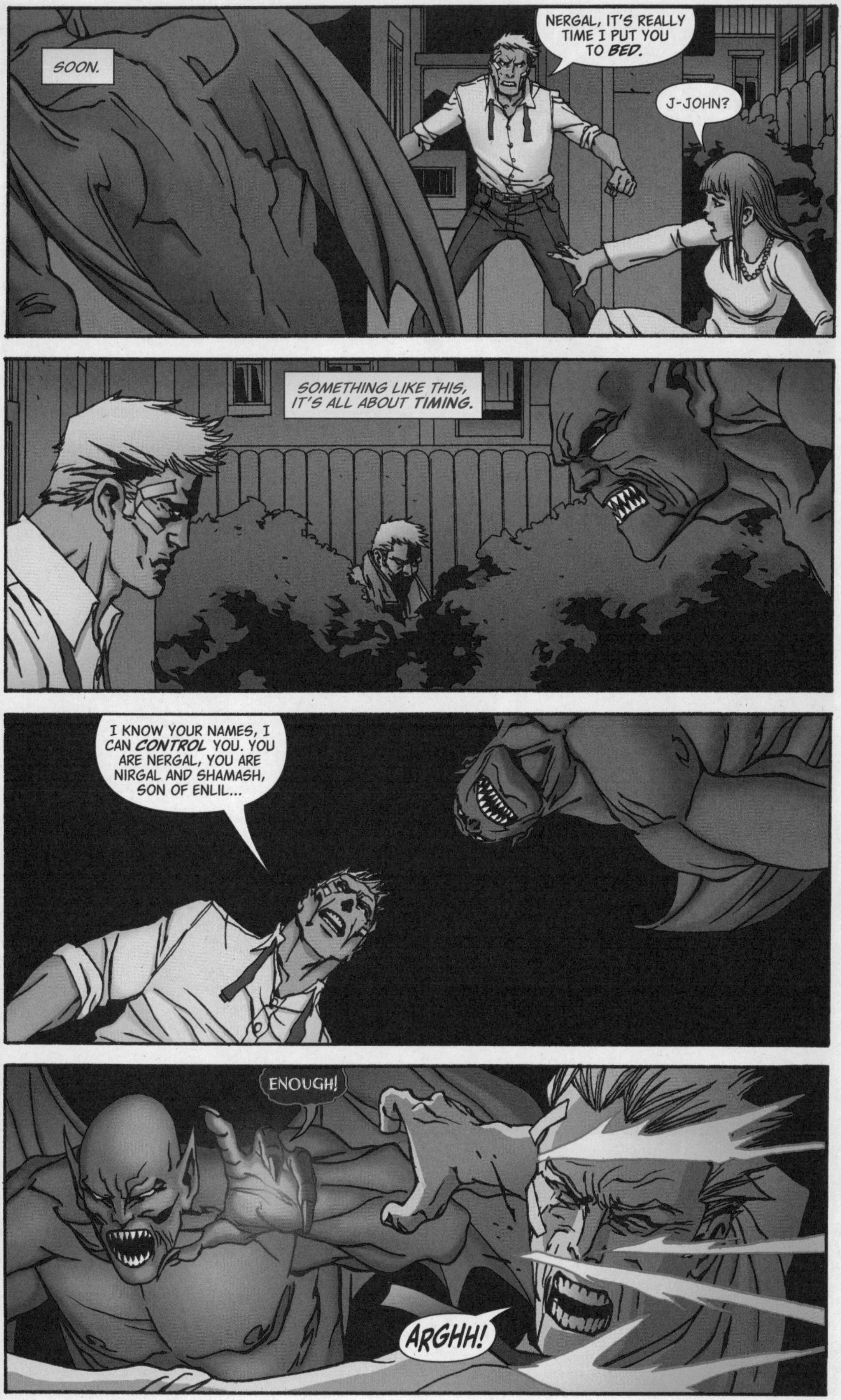
SOON.
NERGAL, IT'S REALLY TIME I PUT YOU TO **BED.**
J-JOHN?
SOMETHING LIKE THIS, IT'S ALL ABOUT **TIMING.**
I KNOW YOUR NAMES, I CAN **CONTROL** YOU. YOU ARE NERGAL, YOU ARE NIRGAL AND SHAMASH, SON OF ENLIL...
ENOUGH!
ARGHH!

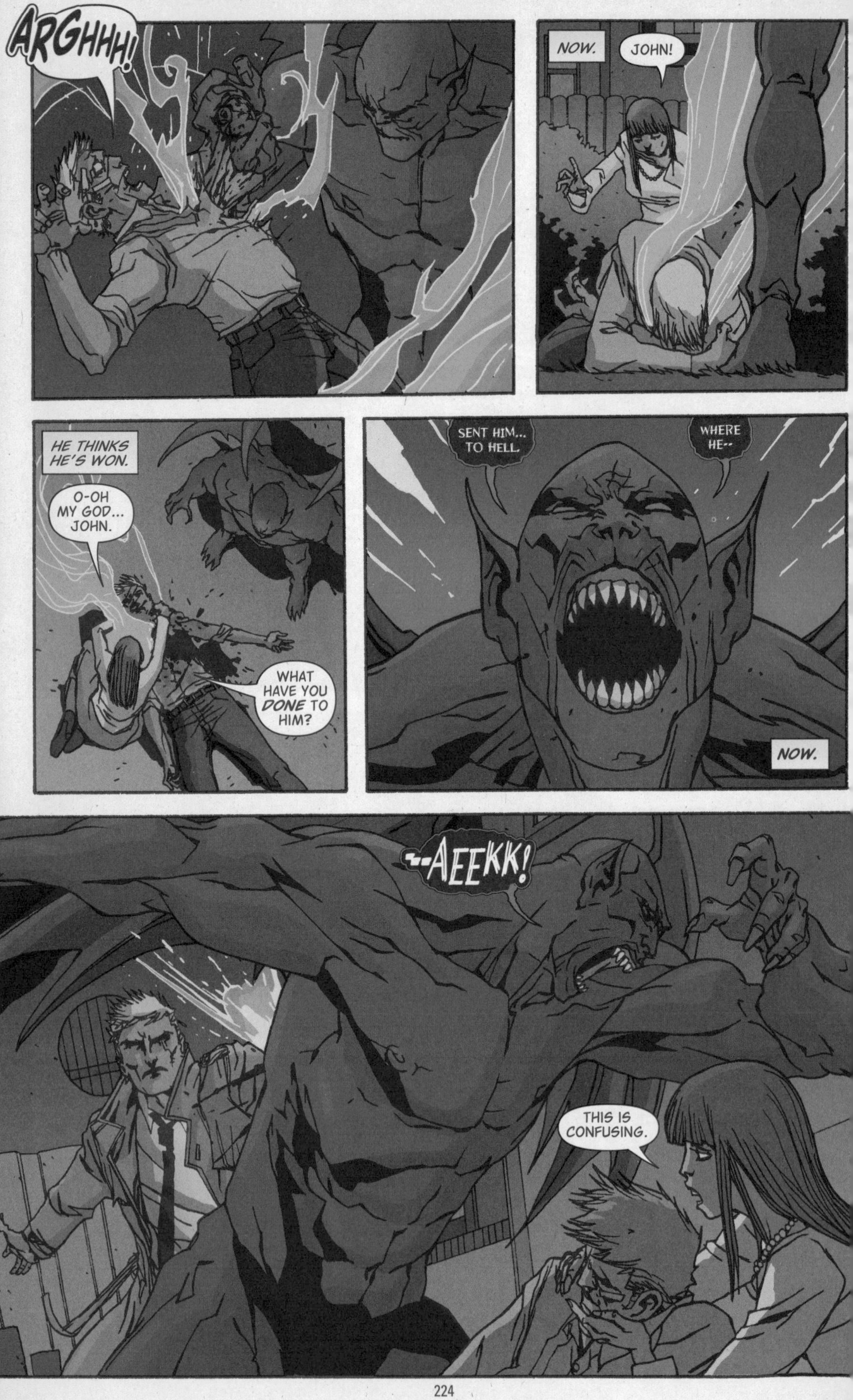

ARGHHH!
NOW.
JOHN!
HE THINKS HE'S WON.
O-OH MY GOD... JOHN.
WHAT HAVE YOU *DONE* TO HIM?
SENT HIM... TO HELL.
WHERE HE--
NOW.
--AEEKK!
THIS IS CONFUSING.

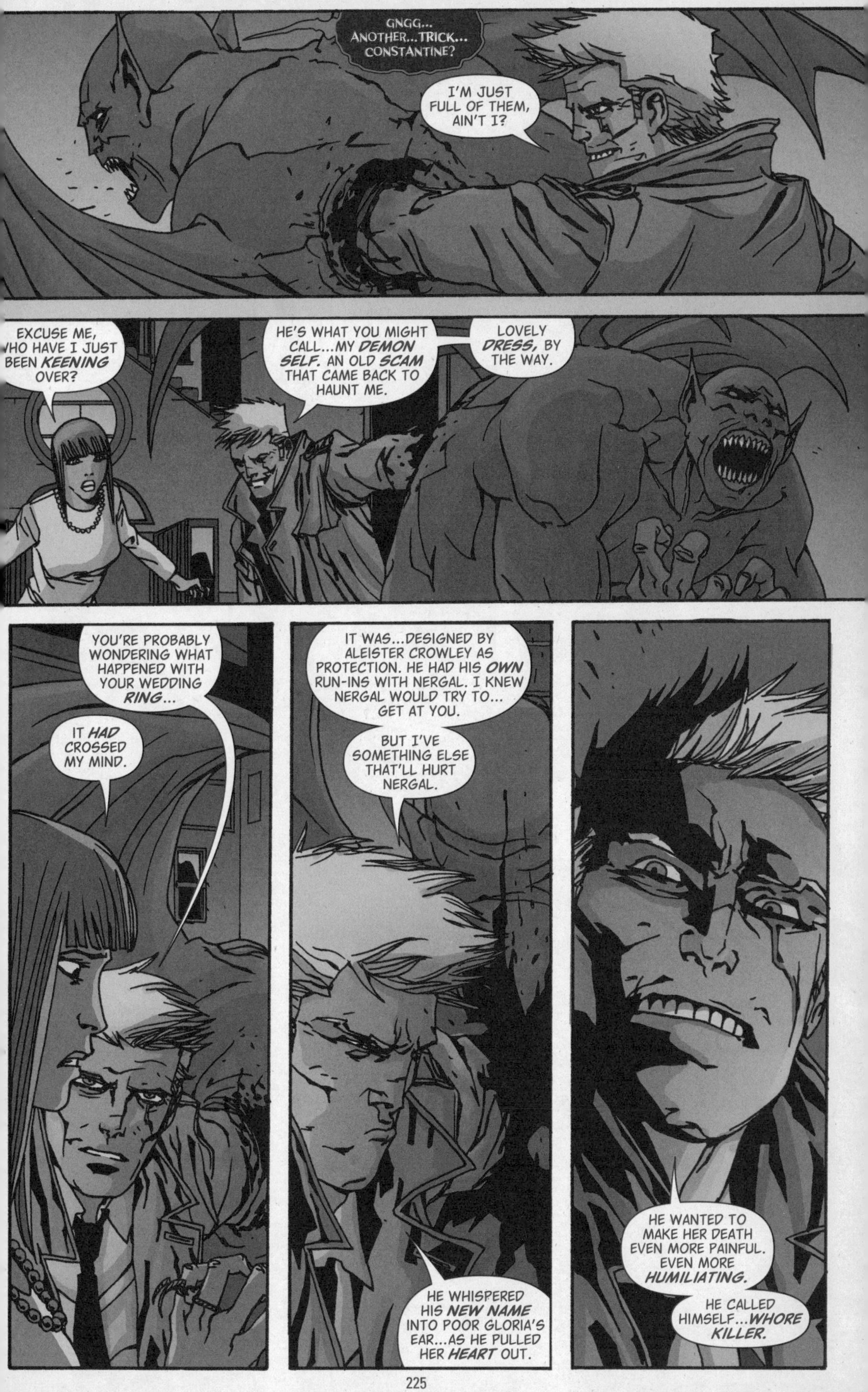
GNGG... ANOTHER...TRICK... CONSTANTINE?
I'M JUST FULL OF THEM, AIN'T I?
EXCUSE ME, WHO HAVE I JUST BEEN KEENING OVER?
HE'S WHAT YOU MIGHT CALL...MY DEMON SELF. AN OLD SCAM THAT CAME BACK TO HAUNT ME.
LOVELY DRESS, BY THE WAY.
YOU'RE PROBABLY WONDERING WHAT HAPPENED WITH YOUR WEDDING RING...
IT HAD CROSSED MY MIND.
IT WAS...DESIGNED BY ALEISTER CROWLEY AS PROTECTION. HE HAD HIS OWN RUN-INS WITH NERGAL. I KNEW NERGAL WOULD TRY TO... GET AT YOU.
BUT I'VE SOMETHING ELSE THAT'LL HURT NERGAL.
HE WHISPERED HIS NEW NAME INTO POOR GLORIA'S EAR...AS HE PULLED HER HEART OUT.
HE WANTED TO MAKE HER DEATH EVEN MORE PAINFUL. EVEN MORE HUMILIATING.
HE CALLED HIMSELF...WHORE KILLER.

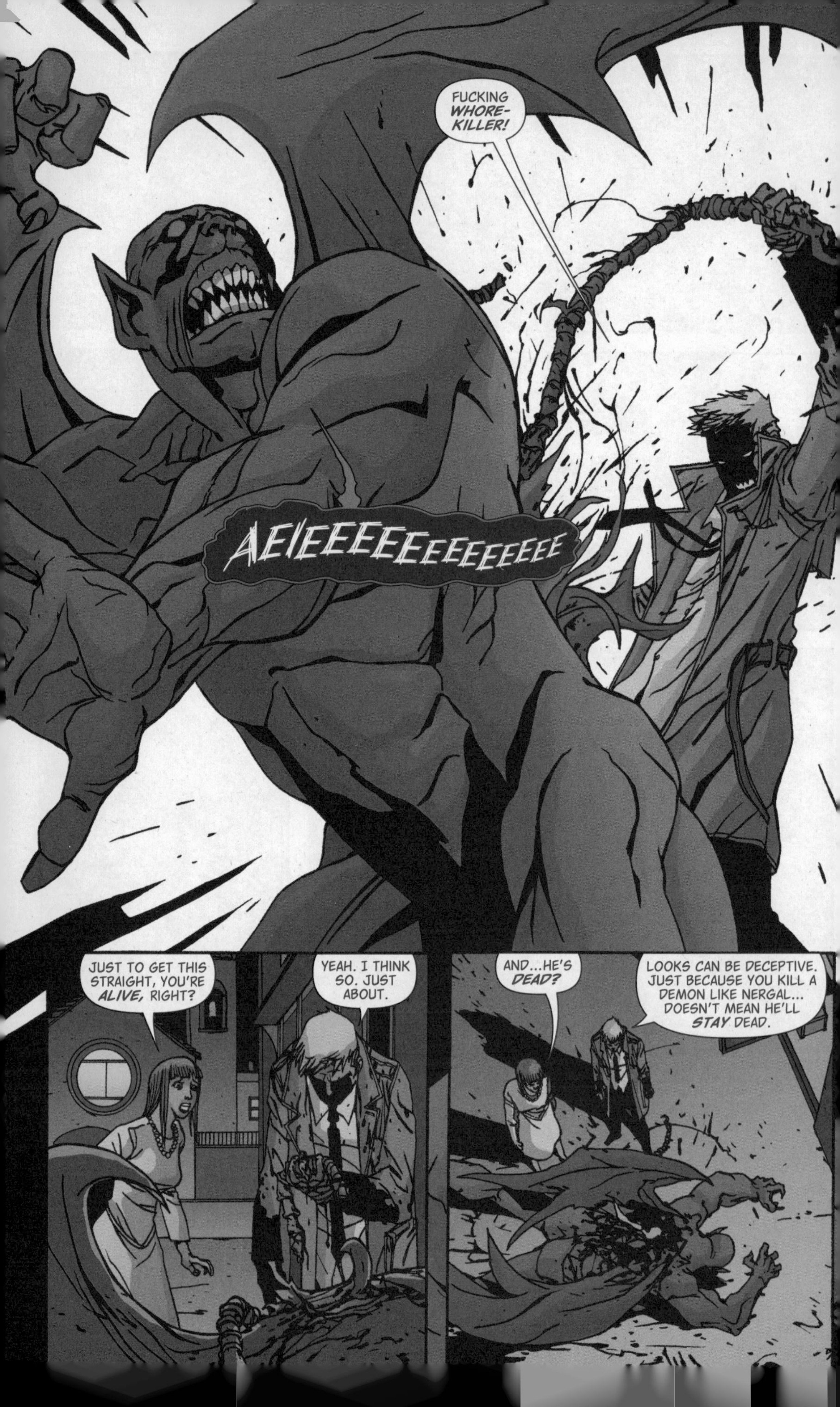
FUCKING WHORE-KILLER!
AEIEEEEEEEEEEEEEE
JUST TO GET THIS STRAIGHT, YOU'RE *ALIVE,* RIGHT?
YEAH. I THINK SO. JUST ABOUT.
AND...HE'S *DEAD?*
LOOKS CAN BE DECEPTIVE. JUST BECAUSE YOU KILL A DEMON LIKE NERGAL... DOESN'T MEAN HE'LL *STAY* DEAD.

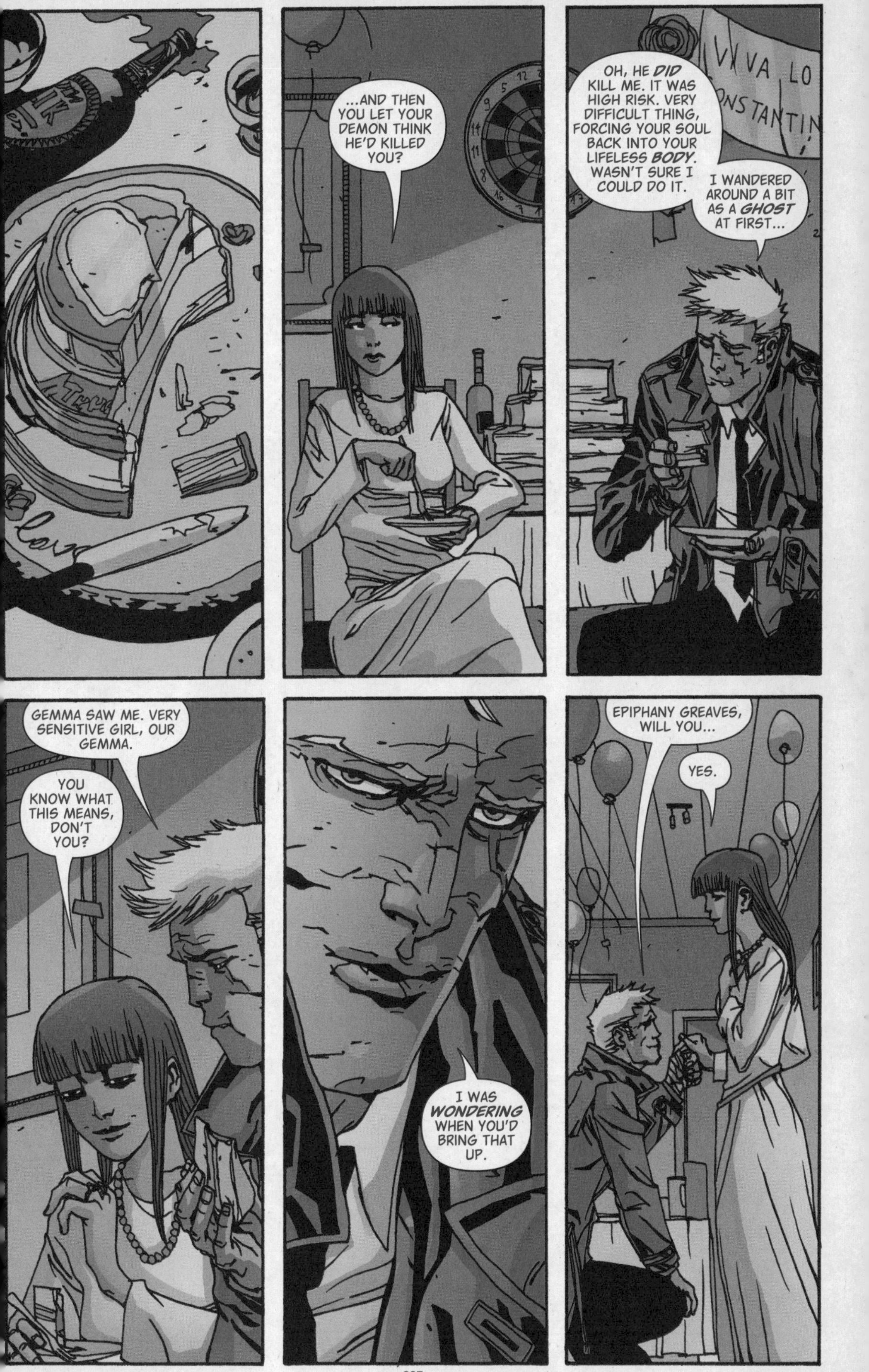
...AND THEN YOU LET YOUR DEMON THINK HE'D KILLED YOU?
VIVA LO ONSTANTIN
OH, HE DID KILL ME. IT WAS HIGH RISK. VERY DIFFICULT THING, FORCING YOUR SOUL BACK INTO YOUR LIFELESS BODY. WASN'T SURE I COULD DO IT.
I WANDERED AROUND A BIT AS A GHOST AT FIRST...
GEMMA SAW ME. VERY SENSITIVE GIRL, OUR GEMMA.
YOU KNOW WHAT THIS MEANS, DON'T YOU?
I WAS WONDERING WHEN YOU'D BRING THAT UP.
EPIPHANY GREAVES, WILL YOU...
YES.

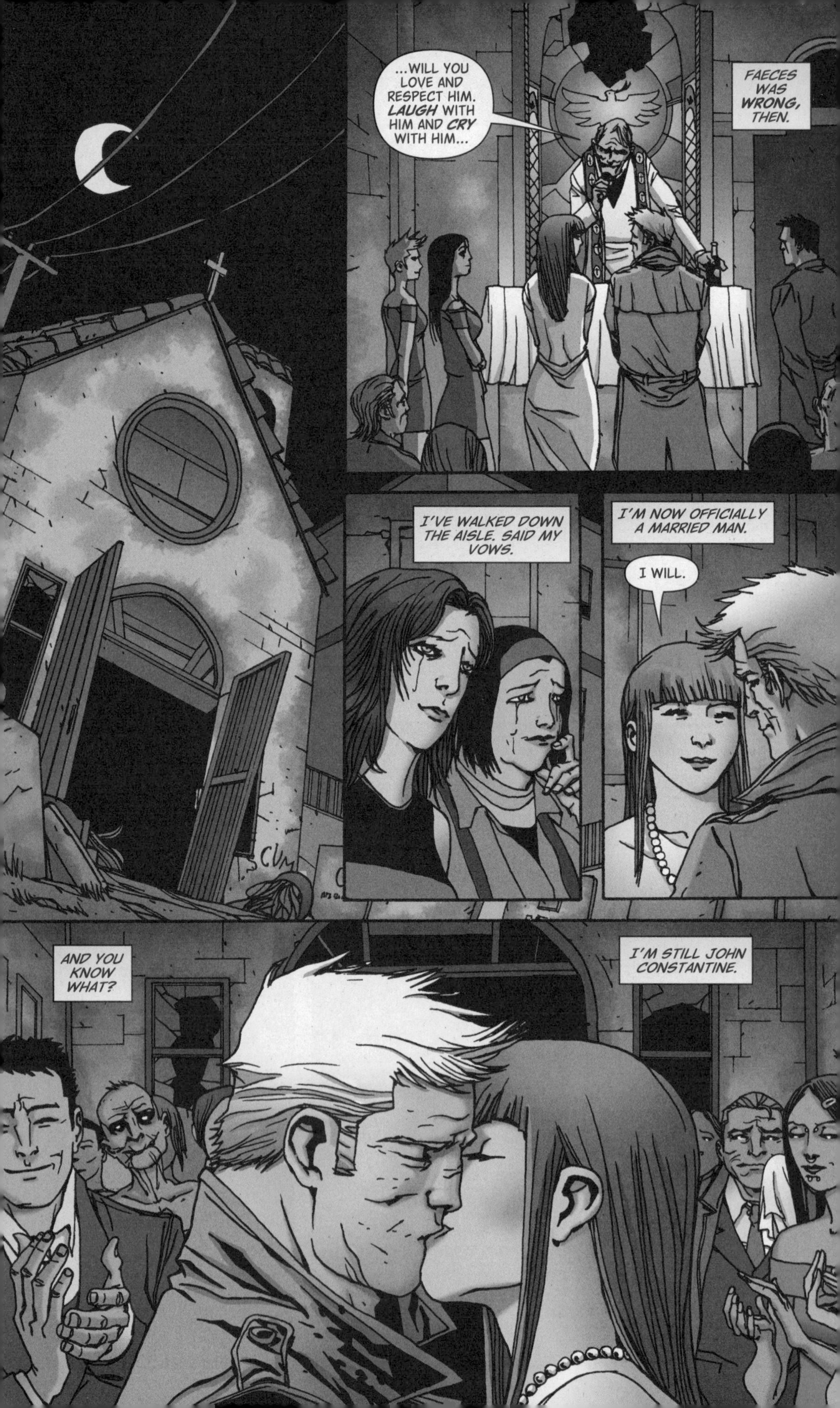

...WILL YOU LOVE AND RESPECT HIM. **LAUGH** WITH HIM AND **CRY** WITH HIM...
FAECES WAS **WRONG**, THEN.
I'VE WALKED DOWN THE AISLE. SAID MY VOWS.
I'M NOW OFFICIALLY A MARRIED MAN.
I WILL.
AND YOU KNOW WHAT?
I'M STILL JOHN CONSTANTINE.

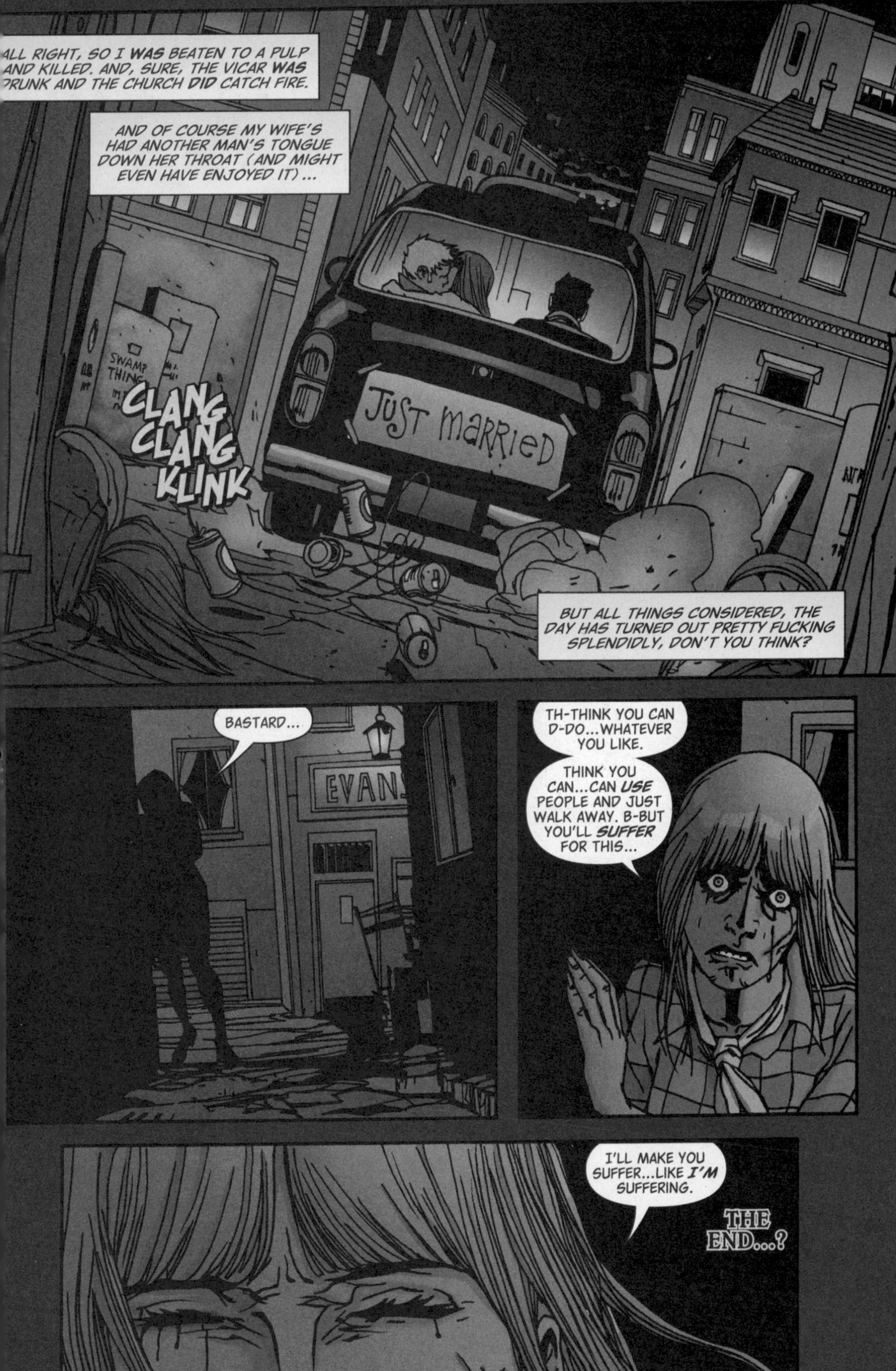
ALL RIGHT, SO I WAS BEATEN TO A PULP AND KILLED. AND, SURE, THE VICAR WAS DRUNK AND THE CHURCH DID CATCH FIRE.
AND OF COURSE MY WIFE'S HAD ANOTHER MAN'S TONGUE DOWN HER THROAT (AND MIGHT EVEN HAVE ENJOYED IT)...
SWAMP THING
JUST MARRIED
CLANG CLANG KLINK
BUT ALL THINGS CONSIDERED, THE DAY HAS TURNED OUT PRETTY FUCKING SPLENDIDLY, DON'T YOU THINK?
BASTARD...
EVANS
TH-THINK YOU CAN D-DO...WHATEVER YOU LIKE.
THINK YOU CAN...CAN USE PEOPLE AND JUST WALK AWAY. B-BUT YOU'LL SUFFER FOR THIS...
I'LL MAKE YOU SUFFER...LIKE I'M SUFFERING.
THE END...?

FROM THE WRITER OF LUCIFER

MIKE CAREY

HELLBLAZER: RED SEPULCHRE

HELLBLAZER: BLACK FLOWERS

HELLBLAZER: STARING AT THE WALL

HELLBLAZER: STATIONS OF THE CROSS

HELLBLAZER: REASONS TO BE CHEERFUL

HELLBLAZER: THE GIFT

HELLBLAZER: ALL HIS ENGINES

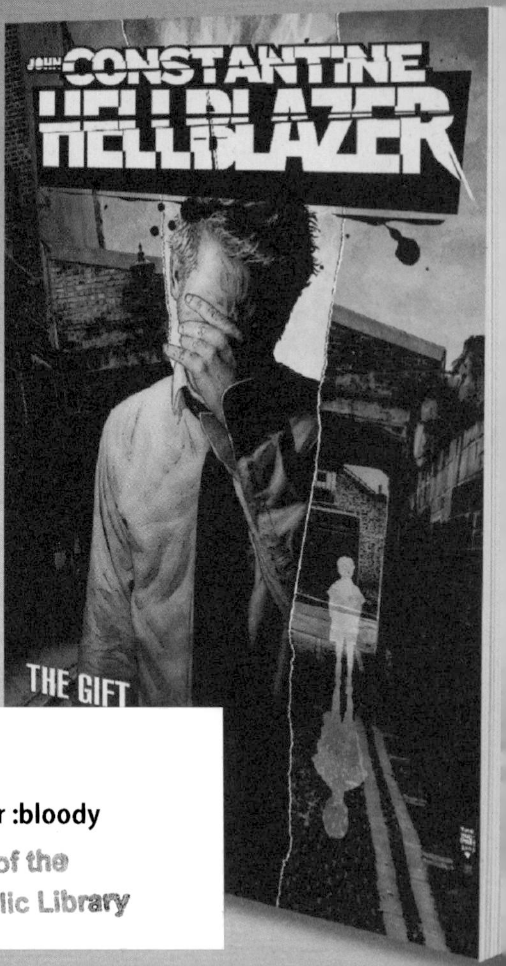
JOHN CONSTANTINE
HELLBLAZER
THE GIFT

HELLBLAZER:
RED SEPULCHRE

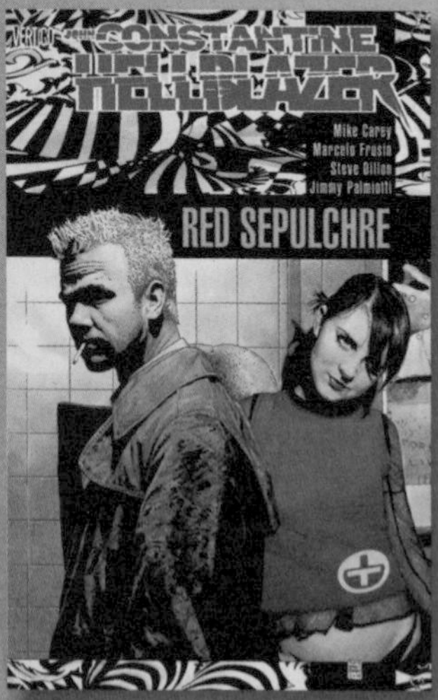
VERTIGO
JOHN CONSTANTINE
HELLBLAZER
Mike Carey
Marcelo Frusin
Steve Dillon
Jimmy Palmiotti
RED SEPULCHRE

with
MARCELO FRUSIN
STEVE DILLON

HELLBLAZER:
BLACK FLOWERS

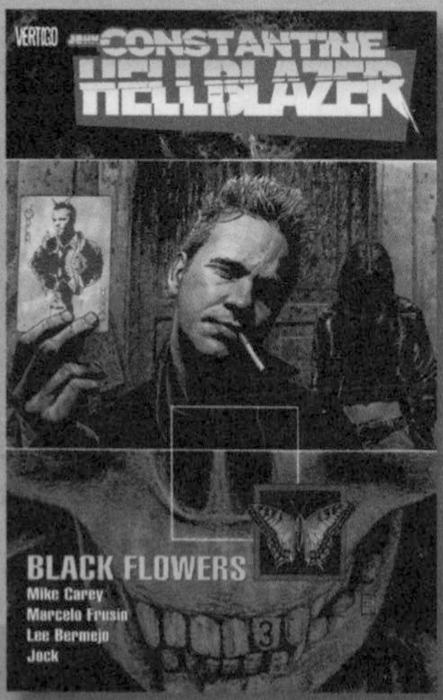
VERTIGO
JOHN CONSTANTINE
HELLBLAZER
BLACK FLOWERS
Mike Carey
Marcelo Frusin
Lee Bermejo
Jock

with
MARCELO FRUSIN
LEE BERMEJO
JOCK

HELLBLAZER:
ALL HIS ENGINES

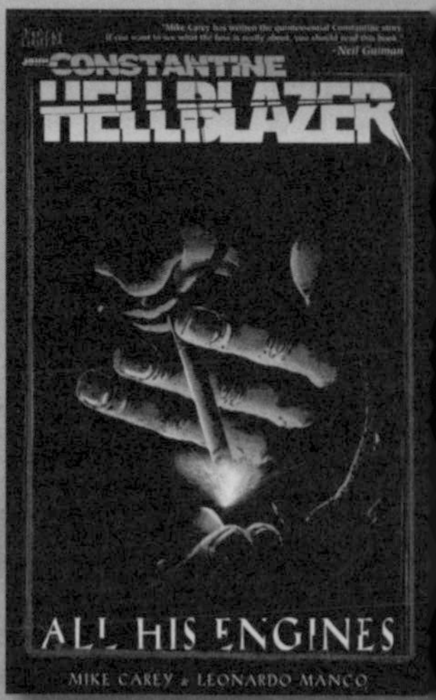
JOHN CONSTANTINE
HELLBLAZER
ALL HIS ENGINES
MIKE CAREY & LEONARDO MANCO

with
LEONARDO MANCO

GO TO
VERTIGOBOOKS.COM
FOR FREE SAMPLES OF THE FIRST ISSUES OF OUR GRAPHIC NOVELS

Suggested for Mature Readers